KU-656-964

THE CHILDREN'S WONDERFUL WORLD encyclopedia

THE CHILDREN'S WONDERFUL WORLD encyclopedia

HAMLYN

LONDON NEW YORK SYDNEY TORONTO

First published 1970
Second impression 1971
Third impression 1972
Published by
The Hamlyn Publishing Group Limited
London • New York • Sydney • Toronto
Hamlyn House, Feltham, Middlesex, England
by arrangement with Western Publishing Company, Inc.

ISBN 0 601 08907 3
Printed in Czechoslovakia by Svoboda, Prague
51009/3

CONTENTS

FOREWORD

Too often we take the world around us for granted. The hills seem to stay in the same place year after year, the rivers flow to the sea, and every year Dandelion seeds are carried by the wind to fall to earth and become new Dandelions. The world appears to remain much the same. But perhaps you have read in the newspapers that the ice caps of the North and South Poles are gradually melting and that eventually the sea will rise and may cover present land areas. Do you know why? Or have you ever wondered why the new leaves on a plant grow to become much like the older leaves? Somehow the simpler the questions the harder it is to answer them.

This encyclopedia describes our fascinating world, the rocks and minerals of which it is made, the climate, and the amazing variety of plant life found upon it. Man and the development of civilisations from the earliest times, his behaviour, his crafts and tools are all described. There are sections dealing with the moon to which we may travel some day, the other planets in our solar system, and the stars.

Except for Man, the animal kingdom is not included in this encyclopedia. Because of their great diversity and special interest, the animals have been grouped in a companion volume, *The Children's Animal World Encyclopedia in Colour*.

In this encyclopedia plants are listed under their common or everyday names, which vary from one country to another. Naturalists find it clearer to use scientific names, which are given here in italics. The modern system of scientific naming was established by the great Swedish naturalist Carolus Linnaeus, born in 1707. Latin was, in his time, the language in which all scientists wrote, and to this day scientific names are Latin words or words changed to look like Latin words.

A particular kind of plant or animal, such as the Dandelion, or Man, or the

House Sparrow, is called a *species*. A species is a member of a group of very similar plants or animals known as a *genus*. A genus may consist of just a few species, or hundreds of species. The scientific name of a particular plant or animal consists of its genus name followed by its 'trivial' or species name. Thus if you look up the Dandelion, you will see that its scientific name is *Taraxacum officinale*.

Each genus is a member of a *family*. Family names usually end in 'ae'. In a botany book, you will find that the Dandelion is a member of the family *Compositae*. Man's scientific name is *Homo sapiens,* and he is the only living member of the family *Hominidae*. The family in turn is a member of a larger group, and so on, but this is as far as we need to go for the purpose of this book.

Often we wish to describe the characteristics of all the plants in a genus, rather than describing each species separately. In this case we give the genus name followed by 'spp', which is just the plural abbreviation of species. For example, under PEA FAMILY you will find *Dalbergia* spp., which means all the species of the genus *Dalbergia*.

Frequently we encounter sub-species or varieties (abbreviated as 'var'.) of plants or animals. Some have developed naturally as an adaptation to local conditions, and others have been bred by man, such as the various vegetables that have been developed from the original Wild Cabbage. See for example, the entry on CABBAGE.

A book of this type cannot attempt to supply everything you might want to know about a particular subject. But you can use it to give you the outline of the facts before you refer to a more detailed book. Or you can open it at any page and in this way explore many different aspects of the wonderful world in which we live.

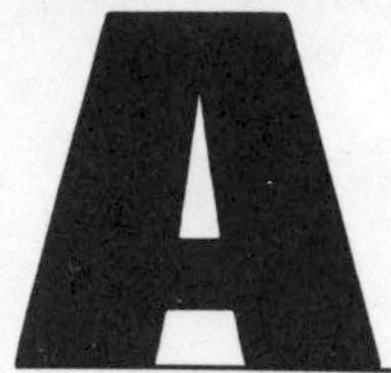

SILVER WATTLE — to 100 ft.
Acacia dealbata
Australia

ACACIAS (*Acacia* spp.), including more than 400 species of trees and shrubs, are found in northern Africa, southern Asia, the South Pacific Islands, Australia, South and Central America, Mexico, and south-western United States. Many tropical trees of this group are valuable for timber; others are planted as ornamentals. Many Australian acacias, usually called wattles, provide timber; those of arid inland areas are valued for forage, shade, and shelter. This variety also produces a mass of yellow flowers and though of no particular scent, it is an attractive plant, as the illustration shows. Boomerangs are carved from the wood of an acacia. The wood of many species of *Acacia* is valuable and much used in furniture making, etc. 'Gum arabic', collected from a North African species, (*Acacia senegal*), is used in glues, inks, medicines and confectionery.

Acacia is the wood used by the Australian aborigines for their boomerangs.

Camera Press

ACORNS are the nuts of the oak tree (*Quercus* spp.). American Indians used them as a staple diet after crushing and bleaching in water to remove the bitter taste. Today they are little used as human food, except by the poorest, or in an emergency, as in the making of synthetic coffee in Europe during the Second World War.

Many animals, especially pigs, relish them and, until recently, in southern England pigs were turned loose every autumn in the New Forest to feed on acorns.

AGAR or Agar-agar is a jelly-like substance obtained from several kinds of seaweeds, principally *Gelidium* and *Grairlaria*. Most of the world's supply comes from Japan, although durıng World War II, when the supply of agar from Japan was cut off, agar was produced in the British Isles, chiefly from species of *Chondrus* and *Gigartina* found in shallow bays. The seaweeds are collected at low tide or by diving. They are washed, dried, and bleached, then boiled to extract the gelatine. This is filtered from the pulp and allowed to cool to form a powder.

Agar's most important use is as a culture medium on which bacteria, fungi, orchid seeds, and animal tissues can be grown. The agar has little food value itself, but nutrients

Acorns of the White Oak group are good to eat, while those of the Black Oak group are quite bitter. Californian Indians made meal by cracking the acornsof the California Live Oak and extracting the kernels, then grinding them into a flour which was leached in water.

SOME WHITE OAKS

WHITE OAK

CHESTNUT OAK

OVERCUP OAK

CALIFORNIA LIVE OAK

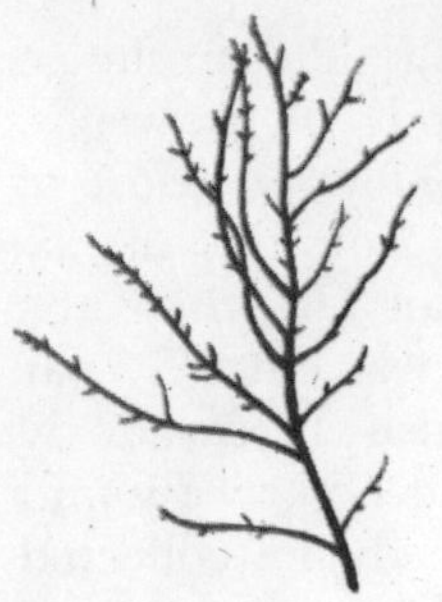

***Gelidium*, the main source of agar, is a red seaweed that grows abundantly in both the Atlantic and Pacific.**

such as sugars, proteins, and minerals are easily added to it. These food ingredients, plus the agar, are dissolved in water. It cools into a firm jelly with a high melting point. Thousands of pounds of agar are used each year in hospitals, laboratories and orchid establishments. Agar is used also as a smoothing agent for ice-cream, to blend cheeses, and in making photographic papers and films.

AGRICULTURE. One of the most important discoveries in human history was that planted seeds would grow. This happened early in the New Stone Age, eight to ten thousand years ago. Earlier, men hunted, fished, and gathered wild grains, berries, and roots. The first people to save seeds and then plant them lived in the temperate grasslands of North Africa and the Middle East. Domestication of animals soon followed. This provided meat, milk, eggs, and hides. For the first time men had a regular food supply and did not have to keep moving in search of game. About 5000 B.C. permanent farming villages appeared, and later, cities. Early civilisations grew where agriculture was practised. None developed elsewhere.

Earliest crops in the Middle East were cereals: wheat, rye, barley, and oats. These were really wild grasses, cultivated and

Today's farm machinery does the work of many hands more swiftly and more efficiently. Shown below, on the vast contour-planted slopes of the American wheat belt, is a combine harvester, which both harvests and threshes grain.

Courtesy of Massey-Ferguson, Inc

John Hardman

Even in the mechanised Western world there is still plenty of work for the farm horse.

improved to give larger grain. In India and China the growing of another cereal, rice, was developed, and its use spread widely. American Indians domesticated maize (Indian corn), and this, with beans and squash, formed the most important basis for much of their farming.

Early farmers used few tools. New Stone Age farmers in Palestine harvested their grain with stone-toothed sickles. Everywhere the digging stick, the ancestor of the plough, was an important implement, as it is even today among primitive peoples. Another important tool of early agriculture was the hoe. The hoe is a flat blade set at right angles to a handle. Early hoe blades were made of various materials: stone, large clam shells, bone, and wood. As metals were discovered, iron blades became general through most of the world. About 3000 B.C., the plough was invented in the Near East, or in Egypt. Its use usually depended upon domestic animals to pull it, often oxen or buffaloes. The plough is still an essential tool throughout the world. In Western countries it was greatly improved after the eighteenth century. Most farmers of Asia use a light wooden plough that pushes through the soil without lifting and turning it over.

Methods of farming in the world today vary immensely. How agriculture is practised depends upon many factors, but especially the climate and soil, the natural vegetation, the crops produced, and the kind of tools available.

Shifting cultivation is practised in the forested tropics of Asia, Africa, and America. The farmer chooses a place in the forest or

Primitive methods of irrigation: a buffalo-powered water wheel, and primitive ploughing by camel.

Palmer Pictures

Tom Hollyman — Photo Researchers

OOR 568G

Joe Barnell — Shostal

Oxen, though slower than horses, are used for farm work in many regions.

jungle for his crop. At the start of the dry season, he slashes down the undergrowth and allows it to dry in the sun. Then he burns off this brush, leaving the big trees. His planting is done at the time rains are expected. Little attempt is made to cultivate the field or to keep weeds out. He expects his seeds to outgrow the weeds. All the attention the field needs now is to keep wild animals away. In the tropics the natural store of fertility is soon depleted and every year or two the farmer may have to choose a different plot, allowing his former one to grow up in jungle again before he returns to it. People who practise this type of farming generally have a poor standard of living.

Many of the early civilisations developed in the flood plains of great rivers, using 'irrigation' farming methods. The natural flooding of rivers was utilised, streams were diverted from their beds, and seasonal rains were dammed up in artificial lakes and canals to provide water throughout the year. Often great artificial lakes were built to store the seasonal rains. Water was then carried by carefully engineered channels through

Primitive wooden rakes are used by many Chinese farmers.

John Strohm: FORD ALMANAC 1962

Picturepoint Ltd

Well over half of the world's 3,000 million people live in areas of food shortages and rapidly rising populations.

Ford Motor Co: FORD ALMANAC 1962

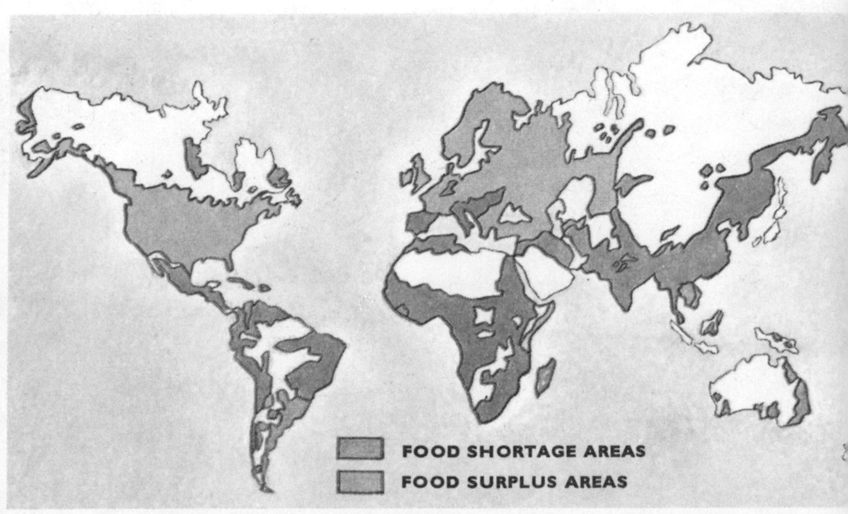

mile after mile of fields and also to great cities. When, owing to war or political decay, the irrigation system broke down, the cities and most of the farmland returned to jungle or desert.

Terrace agriculture is practised widely in mountainous areas. Much of the rice farming of Asia is done in this manner. By terracing, a hillside can be made into a series of level plots. This system permits the farmer to hold water for his crops and prevents the soil from being washed down into the valley.

The most striking aspect of modern agriculture is its great use of machinery and its scientific breeding of plants. Large farms are well adapted to the use of machines in cultivation and harvesting. New and more productive seeds have been developed, and a knowledge of soil chemistry has helped the farmer to protect the fertility of his land and choose the crops best suited to it. Potatoes in Britain and cotton in America are now planted with a tractor and cultivated by mechanical tools; pests are killed by spraying with insecticides and the harvesting is done

John Strohm: FORD ALMANAC 1962

These women are loading grain by hand in Russia.

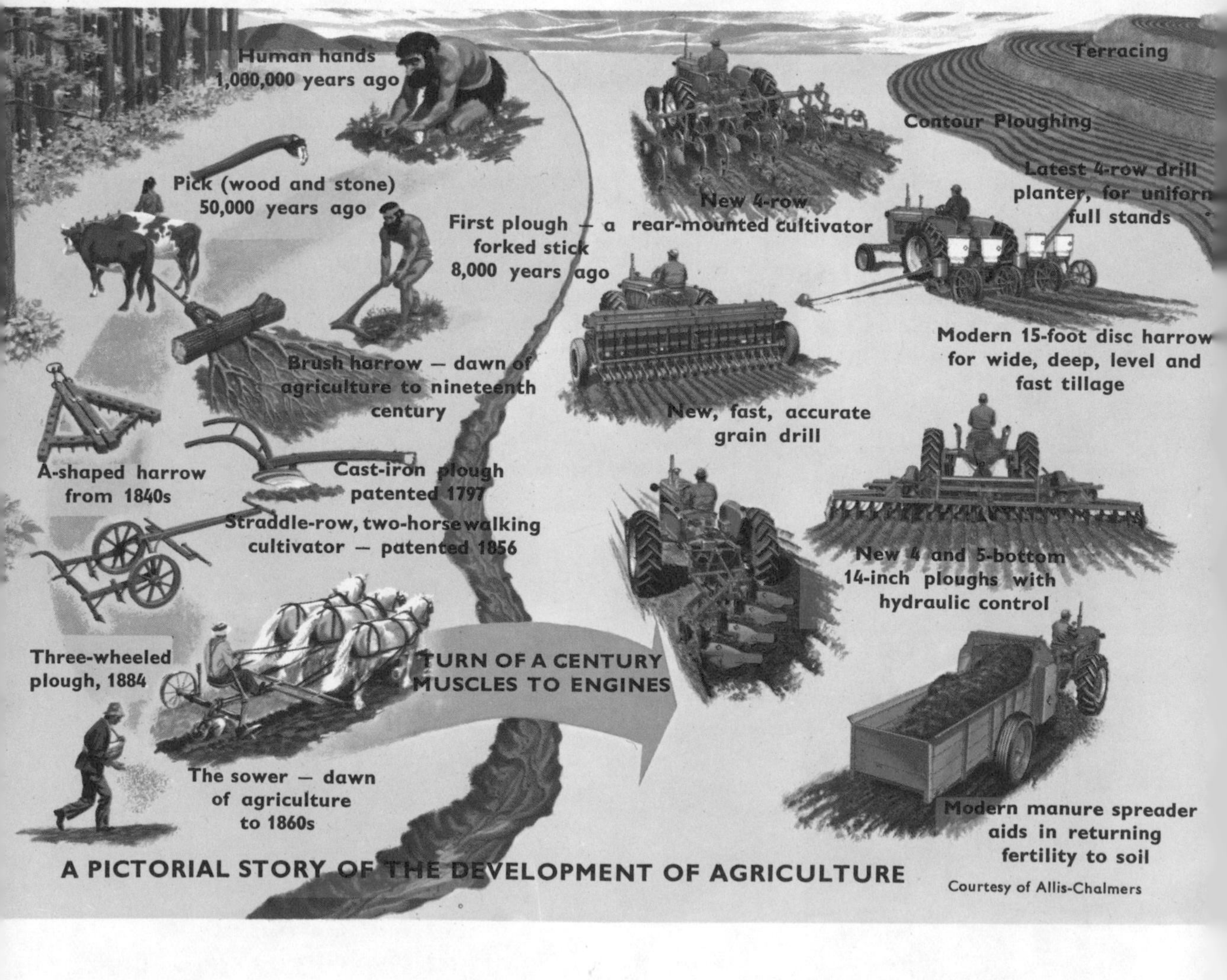

Human hands 1,000,000 years ago

Pick (wood and stone) 50,000 years ago

First plough — a forked stick 8,000 years ago

Brush harrow — dawn of agriculture to nineteenth century

A-shaped harrow from 1840s

Cast-iron plough patented 1797

Straddle-row, two-horse walking cultivator — patented 1856

Three-wheeled plough, 1884

The sower — dawn of agriculture to 1860s

TURN OF A CENTURY MUSCLES TO ENGINES

New 4-row rear-mounted cultivator

Terracing

Contour Ploughing

Latest 4-row drill planter, for uniform full stands

New, fast, accurate grain drill

Modern 15-foot disc harrow for wide, deep, level and fast tillage

New 4 and 5-bottom 14-inch ploughs with hydraulic control

Modern manure spreader aids in returning fertility to soil

A PICTORIAL STORY OF THE DEVELOPMENT OF AGRICULTURE

Courtesy of Allis-Chalmers

Grant Heilman

Aeroplanes are used to control insect pests by spraying large areas of vegetable crops. This plane is spraying a field of peas with parathion, a highly toxic insecticide with an unpleasant odour.

PAF International

This terraced hillside produces rice.

John Strohm: FORD ALMANAC 1962

Sowing wheat by hand on a farm in India.

by machine. Similar changes have occurred in the farming of many crops. A given area produces much more today than formerly. Fewer and fewer people are needed to produce more and more food for the world's rapidly expanding population.

ALCOHOL. Methyl alcohol (refined wood alcohol or wood spirits) is made by the distillation of hard woods such as beech, maple and oak. Methyl alcohol is also manufactured synthetically from carbon monoxide and hydrogen. Methyl alcohol is highly poisonous and, if drunk, may cause blindness or death. It is used as a solvent in paint and varnish and in the manufacture of such products as cellulose acetate, medicines, refrigerants, and perfumes. Ethyl alcohol (grain alcohol) is obtained by fermentation of sugars found in grains, vegetables, or fruits. Ethyl alcohol is colourless and has a characteristic odour and burning taste. The stimulative properties of all alcoholic drinks come from ethyl alcohol. Alcoholic drinks have a limited value as food, and excessive use is detrimental to health. Relatively small amounts of alcohol affect the nervous system. Large amounts have been the cause of death. It is also used as a solvent for waxes, dyes, drugs, chemicals, inks, gums, resins, and oils. Ethyl alcohol has been used in rocket fuels. Denatured alcohol is ethyl alcohol to which methyl alcohol or other chemicals are added — this makes it undrinkable. Denatured alcohol is the base of many antiseptics.

ALDERS (*Alnus* spp.), members of the birch family (see BIRCHES), are widely distributed in the Northern Hemisphere but some American species are found as far south as Peru. The genus consists of some 30 species of deciduous trees and shrubs. The Common Alder (*Alnus glutinosa*) is native to the British Isles and is also widely distributed in Europe, Asia Minor and North Africa.

Alder leaves are oval, coarsely toothed, and alternately arranged on the twigs. They have prominent, hairy veins. Yellowish-green catkins, similar to those of birches, appear in early spring. The seeds are contained in thick, woody cones, called strobiles. At first green, the strobiles change to black over the many months they hang on the tree.

In the early post-glacial period, Alder appears to have been the most widespread tree in the British Isles, largely due to its ability to grow in cold, wet situations. It is still commonly found on river banks and forming a narrow fringe around lakes and meres. It is frequently planted on river banks to prevent erosion.

The native alder was once widely used as a timber tree, particularly for piles and also for clog soles. It is once again becoming increasingly important commercially and is used in the manufacture of plywood and other laminated boards.

More important in this respect, than our native alder, is the American Red Alder (*A. Rubra*), which is the most common deciduous tree in a narrow coastal strip from central California northward to Alaska. It may grow to a height of 100 feet or more, and its trunk may be 2 or 3 feet in diameter.

The Green Alder (*Alnus crispa*) from North America and *A. viridis*, a similar form from Europe, are shrubs grown as ornamentals.

Black, Japanese, and golden-leaved forms, as well as weeping and fastigiate (pointed) forms, are also planted as ornamentals.

ALEXANDRITE, a dark green gem stone, is a variety of chrysoberyl which is one of the hardest of all minerals. In transmitted or in artificial light, it appears red. Alexandrite is found in the U.S.A., Brazil, and Russia.

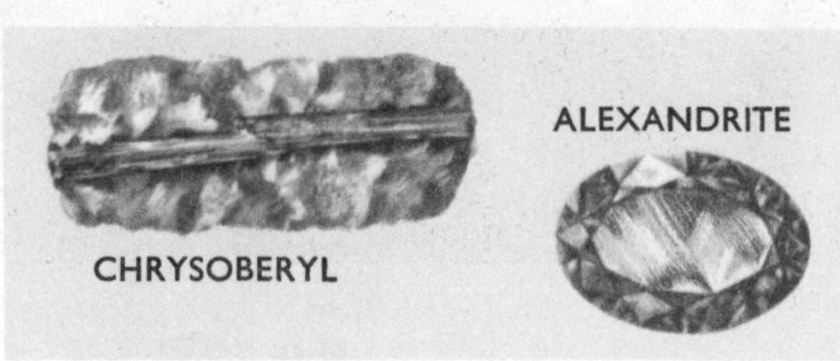

ALGAE. Some algae are simple, one-celled plants visible only under a microscope; others are large seaweeds up to 300 feet long. Most of nearly 18,000 species of algae live in water. Since light is necessary for manufacturing food, algae generally grow in fairly shallow water. A few kinds of seaweeds, however, grow at depths of more than 400 feet where the light is very dim.

Algae contain chlorophyll, the green pigment that enables plants to manufacture food. Algae may also have red, blue, brown, or yellow pigments which give some groups of algae their common names: blue-green, yellow-green, green, red, and brown. Other groups (classes) of algae include diatoms, dinoflagellates, stoneworts, and euglenoids.

Some kinds of algae, such as *Nostoc* and *Vaucheria*, grow on or in moist soil. A teaspoon of such soil may contain as many as a million of these tiny one-celled plants. Some algae live in hot springs; others grow on the surface of snow. *Protococcus* grows in symbiosis with lichen on trees, rocks, or tiled roofs, especially in shaded areas. A covering of gelatine over their cells filters out the harmful or drying rays of the sunlight. There are kinds of algae that grow in the roots of epiphytes. Some live inside the bodies of small animals. Some cling to the bodies of aquatic animals, such as crustaceans and turtles, and one kind grows on the hair of the sloth, giving the animal a greenish tinge.

Algae also vary greatly in form. Some live as independent single cells. The cells of others are loosely attached to make long filaments. Some algae grow as flat, leaf-like sheets; others are greatly branched. No algae have roots, stems, and leaves like the flowering plants. Some kinds float in the water, while others are attached to roots, sticks, or other plants. Some kinds have whip-like flagella which they use in swimming. They may also have sensitive eyespots. Some biologists put the kinds that have both plant and animal characteristics in a special group

MERMAID'S HAIR
Lyngbya majuscula
a common blue-green alga

Howard L. Garrett — Shostal

Algae, simple one-celled plants visible only under a microscope, can be found growing in many strange places. Some even grow on the surface of snow.

called Protista to distinguish them from living things that are definitely either plant or animal.

Algae reproduce in several ways. Some of the one-celled kind merely divide into two cells. Other kinds produce spores. Many also have sexual reproduction or may have an alternation of generations between asexual and sexual stages.

Floating and swimming algae (phytoplankton) are the basic food of animals in both fresh and salt water. Some large fishes and even whales eat only plankton. Ordinarily the plankton is eaten by small animals which in turn are eaten by larger animals. This is called a food chain, and algae are the basic link in many food chains.

People in various parts of the world also eat algae — the seaweeds. These are eaten raw in salads, cooked into soups or puddings, or brewed to make a tea-like drink. Algae are also processed to make a food for livestock. Piles of seaweeds are allowed to decay partially, then are spread over fields as fertiliser. Agar and algin are important products obtained from seaweeds. (See AGAR.)

The pollution of water by algae is also often a serious problem. The decay of tremendous growths or 'blooms' of algae in ponds or lakes may use up the oxygen and cause the fish to suffocate. (See BLUE-GREEN ALGAE.)

ALMOND

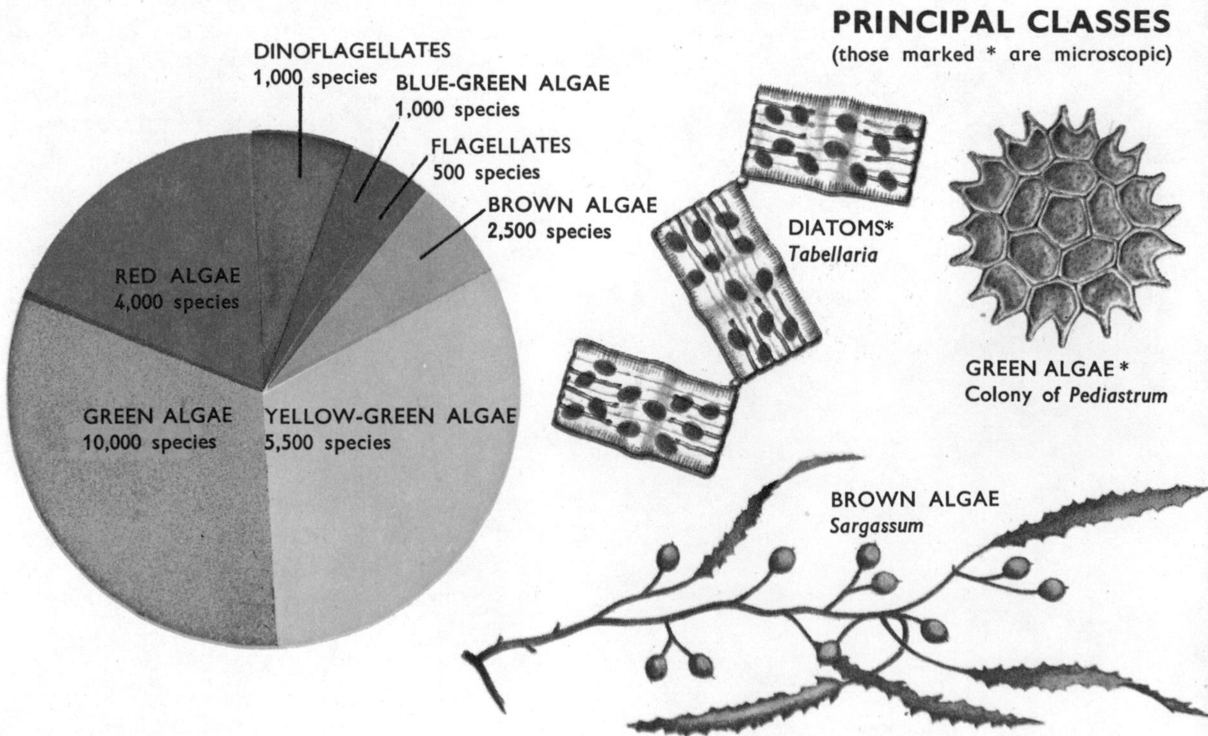

ALMONDS (*Prunus amygdalus*) are relatives of the peach. The so-called nut develops in a fibrous tough flesh that splits open when the fruit is ripe. Almonds are marketed shelled or whole and eaten raw or roasted. The pith or nut is often ground into almond paste, used in the baking industry. A flavouring, almond extract, is also obtained from the nut. Almonds are of two types: an edible sweet variety and a poisonous bitter type from which oil of bitter almonds is extracted. They are imported into the British Isles mainly from southern Europe. The almond tree planted in British gardens is grown because of its attractive blossom; the nut of the tree is not suitable for commercial use.

ALPINE ZONE. Immediately above the timber line on high mountains is an area of stunted shrubs and trees, often bent and twisted by the winds. Higher still are the meadows where only grasses and dwarf plants grow. Above these meadows is a rocky region with patches of soil, and capping them all is a zone of eternal snows which extends to the top of high mountains. These areas above the timber line are known as the alpine zone.

Alpine zones begin at different altitudes depending on the distance of the mountains from the equator. On the south slope of the Himalayas, the alpine zone starts at about 12,000 feet; in the Andes, at 8,500 feet; on Mt. Rainier in the state of Washington, North America, at 6,500 feet. In the arctic climate of Norway, the alpine zone starts at an altitude of only 800 feet. There is only a general similarity between plants in arctic lands and those high up on mountains at the equator. Light and other climatic factors are not the same. The actual flowers to be found are often quite different.

Both temperature and atmospheric pressure are low in alpine zones. Winds are strong, and the light is intense as there is little dust in the air to screen it. Summers are short and winters long.

Conditions of life in alpine zones are similar to those in polar regions, except that the atmospheric pressure is much lower. The ground temperature is generally higher than in polar regions because the light is so much more intense. Vegetation is naturally limited

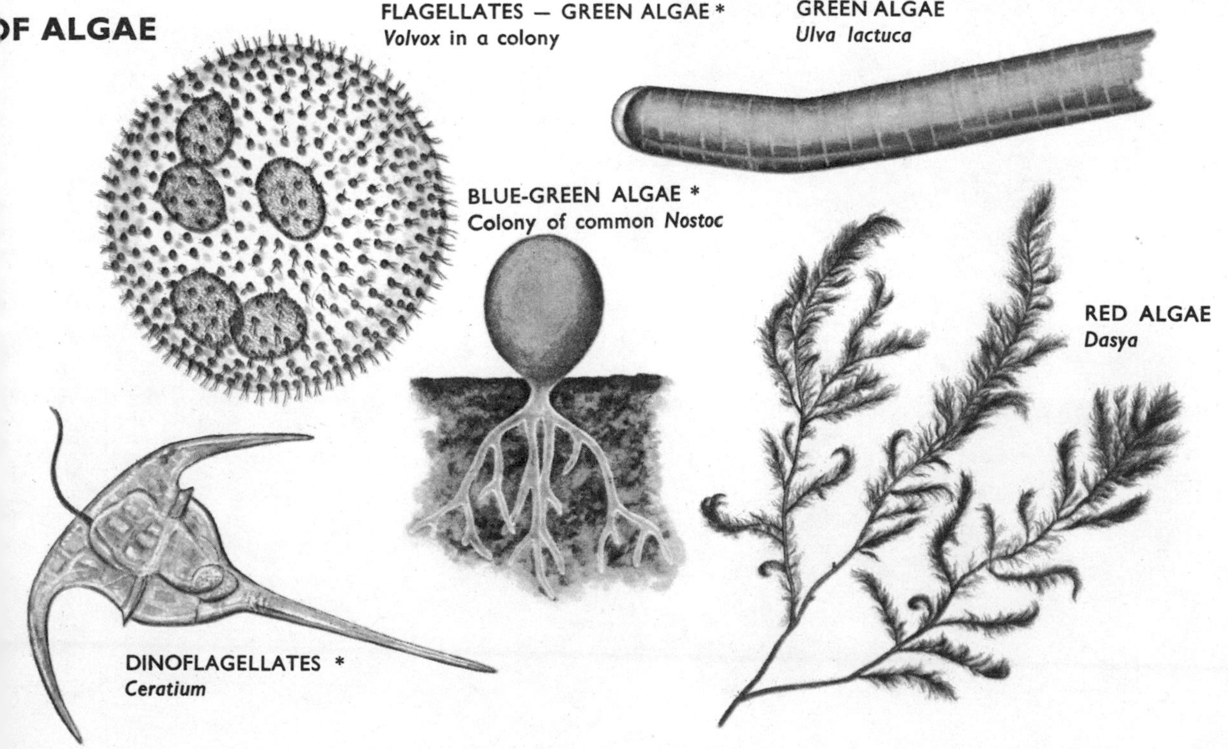

Josef Muench

The Matterhorn rears above the alpine meadows around Zermatt in Switzerland.

in polar regions. It can also show drastic variation within a comparatively small area. In one place there could be a plantless desert, in another, an area plentiful with hardy rosette plants such as saxifrages and arctic poppies *(Papaver radicatum)* while in more favourable conditions still, a continuous area of mosses and lichens could be found.

In the alpine zones near the equator a large proportion of the plants are small, very hairy or otherwise modified to conserve water loss. In west Nepal, in the Himalayas (19,500 feet) an unusually wide range of flowering plants is to be found. At high altitudes in tropical regions where the rainfall is low, such as in central Asia, the southern slopes of mountains would have an arid steppe-like vegetation while luxuriant alpine meadows would clothe the northern slopes. Above the tree limit in northern Norway dwarf birch and silky-leaved dwarf willows are to be found. In the severe drought and temperature conditions of the Punas of South America and the Pamirs of Tibet the vegetation consists of scattered tufts of grasses and hardy cushion plants. In the high Andes of Peru, the cushions formed by some plants may be so large as to resemble recumbent elephants.

A truly alpine vegetation is to be found in the high mountain ranges which separate central Europe from the Mediterranean; in

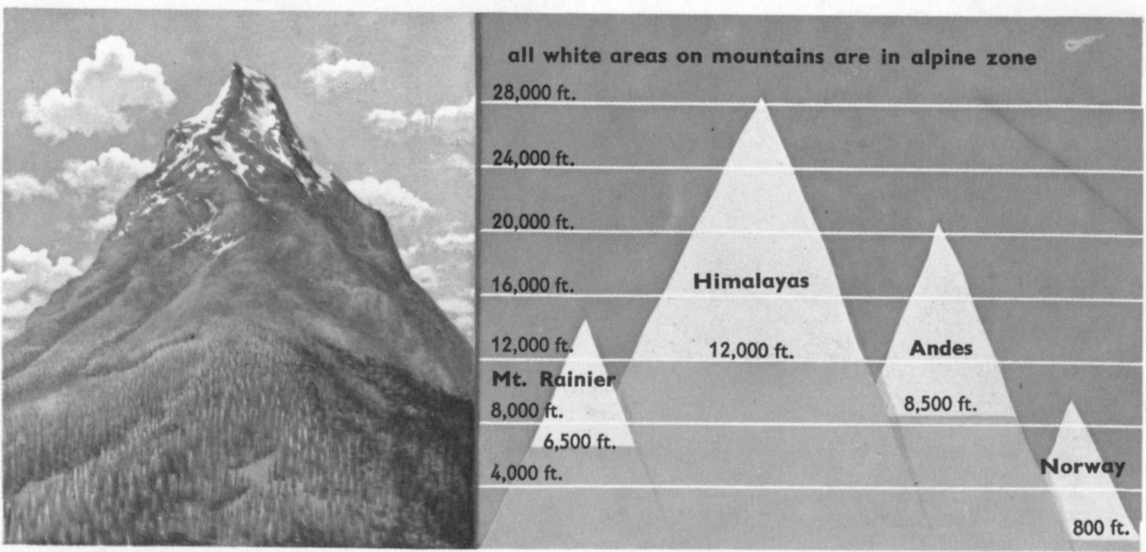

Close to the equator, the alpine zone begins at a high altitude. Nearer to the poles, it begins at low altitudes.

GROUP OF SCREE-BED FLOWERS ON LIMESTONE

1. Alpine Toadflax (*Linaria alpina*)
2. Broad-leaved Mouse-ear Chickweed (*Cerastium latifolium*)
3. Mount-Cenis Campanula (*Campanula cenisia*)
4. Whitlow Grass (*Draba dubia*)
5. Black Wormwood (*Artemisia genipi*)
6. Cobweb Houseleak (*Sempervivum arachnoideum*)
7. Species of Saxifrage (*Saxifraga exarata*)
8. Alpine Rock Jasmine (*Androsace alpina*)
9. Dwarf Fairy Borage (*Eritrichium nanum*)
10. Ice Crowfoot (*Ranunculus glacialis*)
11. Alpine Rock Rose (*Helianthemum alpestre*)
12. Alpine Hedysarum (*Hedysarum hedysaroides*)
13. Yellow Mountain Milk Vetch (*Oxytropis campestris*)
14. Blue Moor Grass (*Sesleria coerulea*)
15. Musk Milfoil (*Achillea moschata*)
16. Leopards Bane Ragwort (*Senecio doronicum*)
17. Centaurea (*Centaurea nervosa*)
18. Shrubby Speedwell (*Veronica fruticans*)

ALPINE MEADOW-PLANTS ON SILICA

GROUP OF ROCK PLANTS ON SILICA

ALPINE MEADOW-PLANTS ON LIMESTONE

GROUP OF SCREE-BED PLANTS ON SILICA

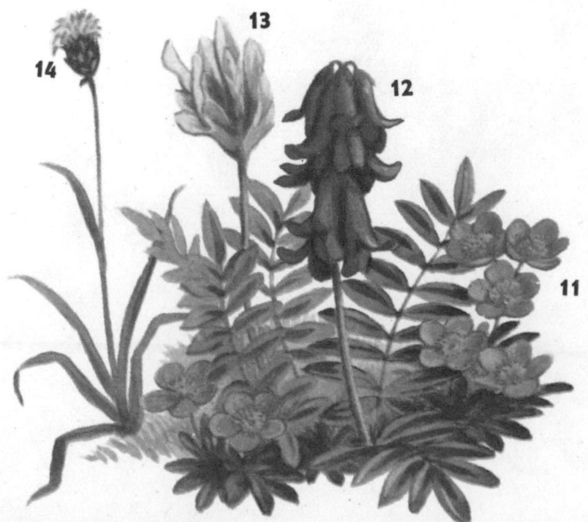

The European Alps have always presented a challenge to climbers. Pictured below is a mountaineer on the face of the famous Eiger in Switzerland.

Syndication International

the Alps, Pyrenees and the Carpathians. Many plants are peculiar to these regions and many others are also to be found in the arctic.

Plants, especially in summer, are the most striking feature of the alpine zone. Dwarf pines, junipers, and creeping azaleas can be found growing just above the timber line. Flowers grow among the rocks, blooming briefly in a world of frosts and snows, avalanches and winds. Sub-alpine meadows come to life with solid beds of beautiful flowers which almost conceal the low-growing grass. Meadow flowers often include great masses of yellow pansies, forget-me-nots, some orchids, clovers, lotuses, daisies, buttercups, and deep blue gentians. Wood anemones, marsh marigolds, and lilies of the valley can be seen in the woods. At high elevations, such flowers as gentians, alpine roses, and the beautiful edelweiss are common, as well as such rock plants as lichens, mosses, small ferns, saxifrages, and little alpine poppies. Lower plants include species especially resistant to cold and drying. Some lichens can survive and grow on bare, exposed rocks well above the timber line.

ALUMINIUM, the most abundant metal in the Earth's crust, is fast becoming the world's most important metal. In places where corrosion or weight is a problem, aluminium has replaced steel. It is used in aircraft, trains, window frames, cameras, toothpaste tubes — in literally thousands of ways. The manufacture of pottery and ceramics utilises great quantities of aluminium minerals.

Bauxite, the most common aluminium ore, contains aluminium, oxygen, and water. Iron impurities, which give bauxite a reddish colour, are abundant in the ore, and chemicals are added to remove them. Processing plants are located in places where electricity is generated by water power, as at Niagara Falls. Other processing plants are located in Oregon, Washington, and British Columbia in North America, and in the Alps in Europe.

Bauxite, a soft grey or red rock, is a mixture of several similar aluminium minerals. When magnified, the aluminium minerals are seen in glossy or scaly masses. Bauxite was formed

Phot. Péchiney

In this open-cast bauxite mine at Delarieux-l'Arboussas in France, the ore is loaded by mechanical means.

millions of years ago in tropical swamps from such aluminium-rich rocks as granite or syenite. Rain and the chemical action of the atmosphere broke down the rock and carried away everything except the clay-like bauxite. Sometimes the bauxite was carried by streams into nearby seas, for some bauxite deposits are found in thick beds between layers of marine sands and clays.

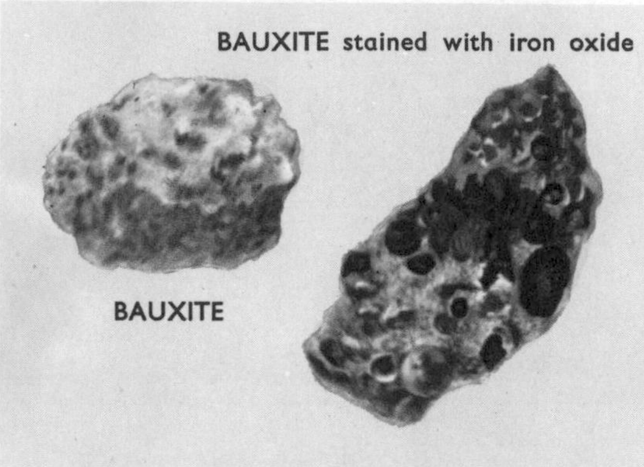

About half of the world's bauxite is mined in southern Europe. North-eastern South America is another important source of bauxite and provides most of the ore used in the United States. A small amount of bauxite is found in Ayrshire and Co. Antrim. Countries that process the largest amount of bauxite generally do not have much ore but do have an abundance of cheap electricity necessary in reducing the ore to metal. Other aluminium minerals are: corundum, one of the hardest minerals; spinel, often used as a gem stone, particularly the varieties found in Ceylon, Thailand and Burma; other localities are Sweden, Brazil, and the U.S.A.; alum, often occurring in shales as at Whitby in Yorkshire.

Aluminium occurs in many other minerals, such as the feldspars, amphiboles, pyroxenes, micas, garnets, and clays. In these minerals the aluminium is bound in such tight chemical combinations that, without more research, it is of no commercial importance.

AMARANTHS (*Amaranthus* spp.) are tall, coarse-leaved plants of tropical and temperate zones. Their small flowers occur in dense, showy spikes. Amaranths grow best in the sun and produce their most colourful leaves where the soil is not too rich. Several species are grown in gardens and are used as cut flowers. They hold their colours even after drying. Love-Lies-Bleeding or Tassel Flower, one of the common cultivated species, has red flowers on droopy spikes. There are also white and yellow varieties of this species. Prince's Feather has stiff, erect spikes and

Seabrooks

greenish-red leaves. Joseph's Coat has greenish-purple leaves. Several amaranths known as pigweeds grow wild on wastelands.

AMBER is the fossil of resin of extinct conifers. Insects, leaves, flowers, and fruits are found embedded and preserved in amber. Amber is found chiefly in northern Europe,

Fossil ant in amber.

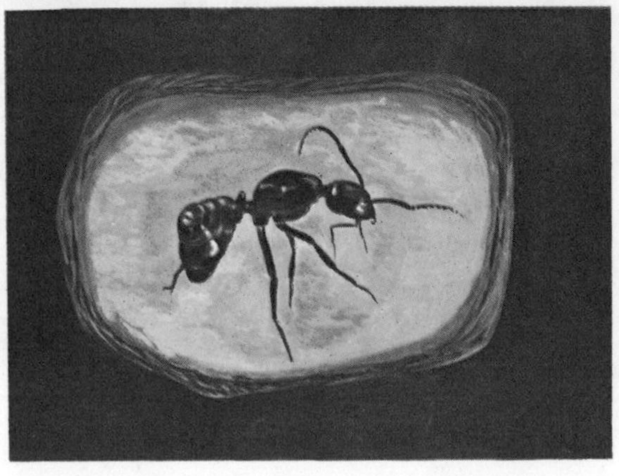

where it is mined. Nets are used in shallow waters to dislodge pieces of amber entangled in seaweed, and divers and dredges seek submerged deposits in deeper waters. In some areas, small pieces of amber may be found on the beach.

The Greeks and Romans admired amber for its yellow to brown colour, translucency, and hardness. They used it for jewellery and ornaments. Rubbing a piece of amber with a cloth produces a strong negative charge and causes the amber to attract small light objects. This property was known by the Greeks, whose word for amber was *elecktron* from which our word *electricity* is derived.

AMPHIBOLES are a group of rock-forming minerals in which the simple, six-sided crystals are needle-like or sometimes fibrous. Like pyroxenes, with which they are often confused, amphiboles are formed of silicon and oxygen combined with such elements as calcium, sodium, magnesium, aluminium, and iron. Their similarities and differences are shown in the chart below.

Amphiboles

simple, needle-like, six-sided crystals
silky lustre; black to green
most abundant in light-coloured
metamorphic rocks;
with quartz and orthoclase
contain water
low specific gravity
alter to chlorites

Pyroxenes

complex, stubby, eight-sided crystals
dull or sub-metallic lustre; black to brown
most abundant in dark-coloured
igneous rocks; with
plagioclase and olivine
no water
high specific gravity
alter to amphiboles

The following are six members of the amphibole group. Actinolite is a green amphibole which occurs as elongated crystals or aggregates in talc and chlorite. It is found in Switzerland, Norway and the U.S.A. Anthophyllite, another amphibole, is brown or green and fibrous. It is formed from olivine. Anthophyllite is found in Norway, South Africa, and several states of the U.S.A. Hornblende is the most common amphibole. Usually dark green or black, it is found in both igneous and metamorphic rocks. Widespread in occurrence, good crystals have been obtained in Italy, Romania and the U.S.A.

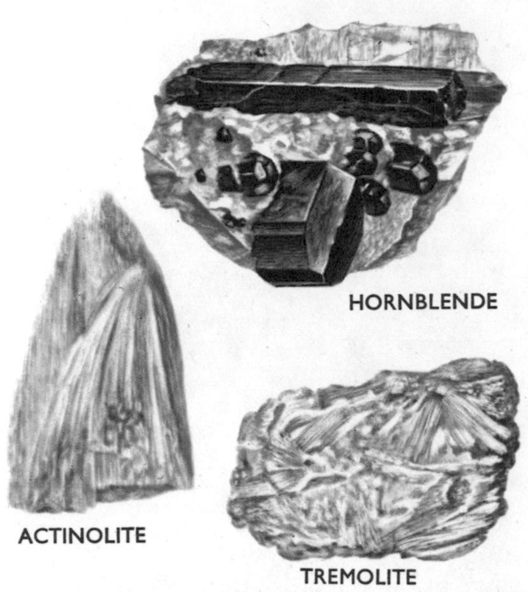
HORNBLENDE
ACTINOLITE
TREMOLITE

Nephrite is a variety of jade and is found as dark green or white nodules in serpentine in Turkestan, and the U.S.A. Crocidolite or Blue Asbestos is found in Austria, Africa, France, and the U.S.A. Tremolite occurs as white tangles of sharp needles in marble and talc schist from Switzerland, Elba, Canada and the U.S.A.

ANEMONES (*Anemone* spp.) are a group of about 150 dainty flowers related to buttercups. They grow in Europe, Siberia, North America, Japan, and other fairly cool regions. Many anemones (a-NEM-o-neez) are so large and attractive (up to 3 inches across) that they are used in flower gardens. Most kinds grow best in loamy well-drained soils.

The stately Japanese Anemone, over 3 feet tall with white, pink, or purple upright flowers, grows best in shady gardens. The Pasque-flower, in contrast, is a stubby anemone with large bluish-purple flowers on stalks 4 to 6 inches tall. It grows on the sunny slopes in south-east England. Still another well-known anemone is the delicate white or pinkish Wind Flower, which blooms in early

spring in woodlands throughout Britain. Wind Flower is what the Greek word *anemone* means.

All anemones have similar flowers. The parts that look like petals are really coloured sepals, and they vary in number from five to nine or more. All anemones have many stamens. They produce numerous flattened dry seeds, often tufted, with a point or tail at the top end. Their leaves are usually divided. Anemones are believed to be the flowers referred to as lilies in the Bible. Common names of flowers vary geographically, so the same name may be used for several plants.

ANTIBIOTICS are substances produced by fungi that prevent the growth of some kinds of bacteria. Their use in the treatment of human diseases is a recent development. In 1929, Sir Alexander Fleming, an English doctor, noticed that bacteria did not grow in his agar cultures on which grew a blue-green mould, a kind of *Penicillium*. The mould produced a substance that prevented the growth of the bacteria. He called this substance penicillin.

During World War II, scientists studied the effect of penicillin on diseases. It became the world's first 'wonder drug', produced commercially by growing the mould in a liquid culture in large tanks. Aureomycin, streptomycin, terramycin, and other antibiotics obtained from fungi are now used to treat various human diseases. Antibiotics vary in the type of bacteria they prevent from growing. Penicillin, for example, has no effect on tuberculosis bacteria, but streptomycin is very effective in treating this disease.

Antibiotics are added also to cattle, pig and chicken feed. Terramycin is added to pig feed to prevent or to treat digestive and

Courtesy of and © 1957 Parke, Davis & Company

Antibiotics are mass-produced in vats under controlled laboratory conditions and are tested for effectiveness.

respiratory ailments and also secondary infections. The result is healthier, heavier pigs and a correspondingly higher market value. Aureomycin is added to cattle feed to protect cows from respiratory diseases, foot rot, and other diseases. Terramycin added to drinking water checks many diseases of chickens.

Recently the value of adding antibiotics to animal feeding stuffs has been questioned. The quality of the meat has unquestionably been improved, but the consumer may ultimately suffer rather than benefit because our bodies will be receiving constant small quantities of a variety of antibiotics. Bacteria are known to become modified to withstand such small dosage. This could mean that when a human has a severe infection the strain of bacteria causing it will no longer be killed by the normal dosage of a specific antibiotic.

APATITE, usually found in blue-green, six-sided crystals, is a mineral that occurs in all igneous rocks. It is calcium phosphate and commonly contains some chlorine or fluorine. Crystals up to 500 pounds are found in pegmatites. Apatite weathered out of igneous

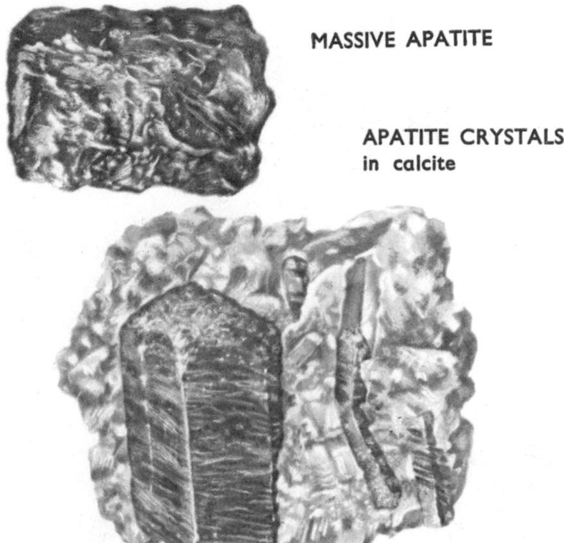

MASSIVE APATITE

APATITE CRYSTALS in calcite

rocks is deposited as nodules in the seas. Marine deposits from Canada, United States, and U.S.S.R. supply the world with phosphate fertiliser. The largest deposits are on the Kola Peninsula in Russia and in Norway. Flawless yellow or green apatite is cut as gem stones.

APPLES (*Malus* spp.) are natives of temperate regions in Europe, North America, and Asia. There are about 25 species. The species from which the many varieties of commercial fruit were developed is a native of south-western Europe and central Asia. Apples were eaten by the Lake Dwellers of northern Italy and Switzerland in Stone Age times. Several varieties existed as early as 325 B.C. They have been cultivated in Great Britain

John Topham Limited

Much of the apple picking in English orchards is still done by hand.

since ancient times. As apples do not grow 'true to seed', new varieties developed naturally. Hardy ones and those that bore good fruit were propagated.

Commercially they are propagated by budding or grafting a desired variety to a hardy seedling stock. Pink and white flowers are borne in clusters. Because many varieties are self-sterile — that is, the flowers must be pollinated by some other variety in order

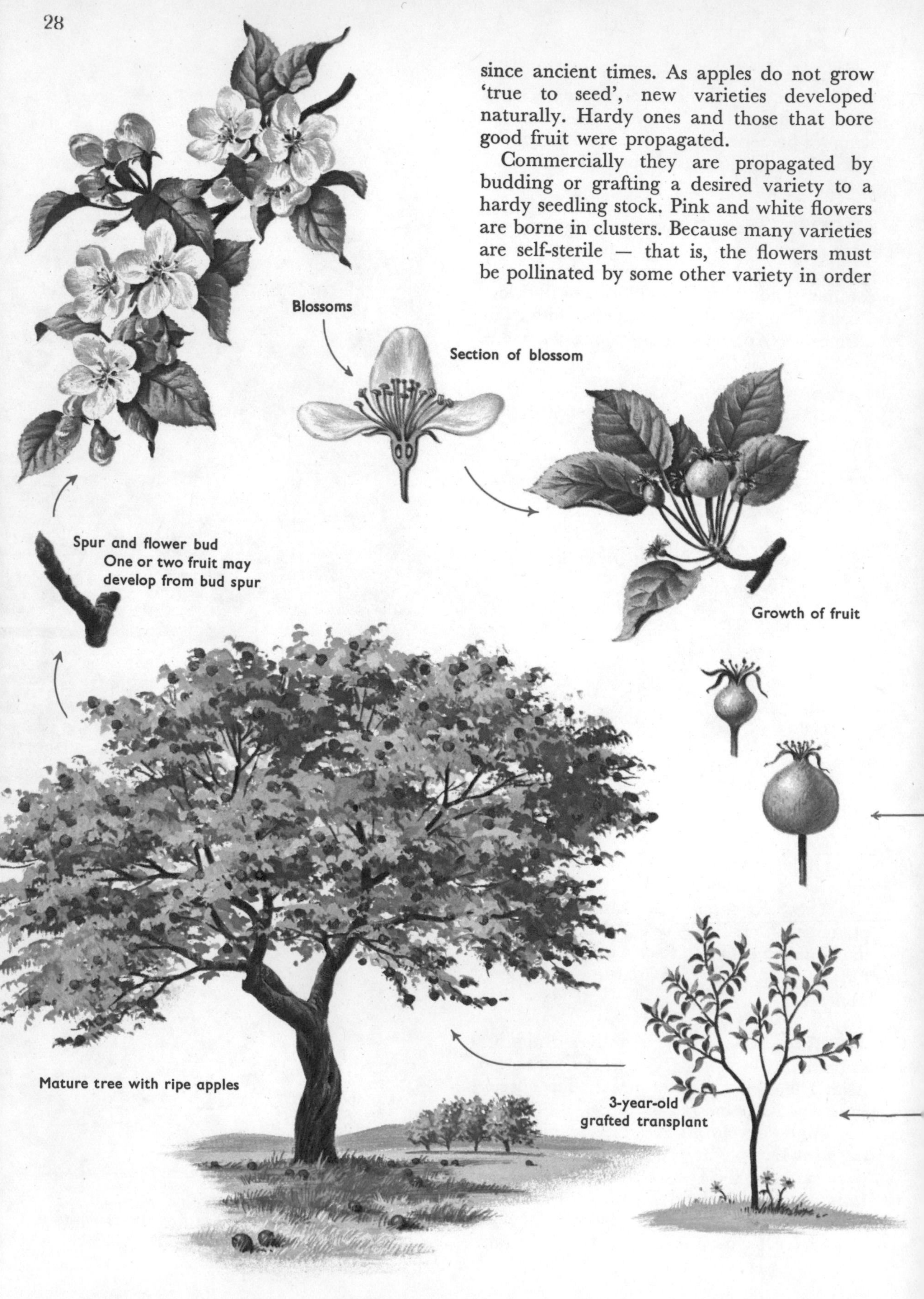

to bear fruit — a mixture of trees must be planted in an orchard, or branches of pollinating varieties must be grafted on the trees. Insects carry the pollen from flower to flower. Some apple trees bear a very heavy crop one year but fail to produce much fruit the following year. This is called alternate bearing. If a heavy crop is thinned, the tree will usually bear the following season. Some varieties shed their fruit soon after it matures. Chemical sprays recently developed retard the shedding in many varieties so that the apples stay on the trees long enough to develop full flavour. New varieties sometimes develop as sports or mutants, and so a branch from a new variety must be grafted to a

Apples are grown from seed from varieties resistant to root disease. The seeds germinate and grow into a 'whip' on to which a good fruit stock is grafted. The grafted seedling is transplanted and may begin to bear in five years. Small spurs bear the spring blossoms which are pollinated by bees. The fruit develops slowly at first but reaches full size and flavour before autumn frosts.

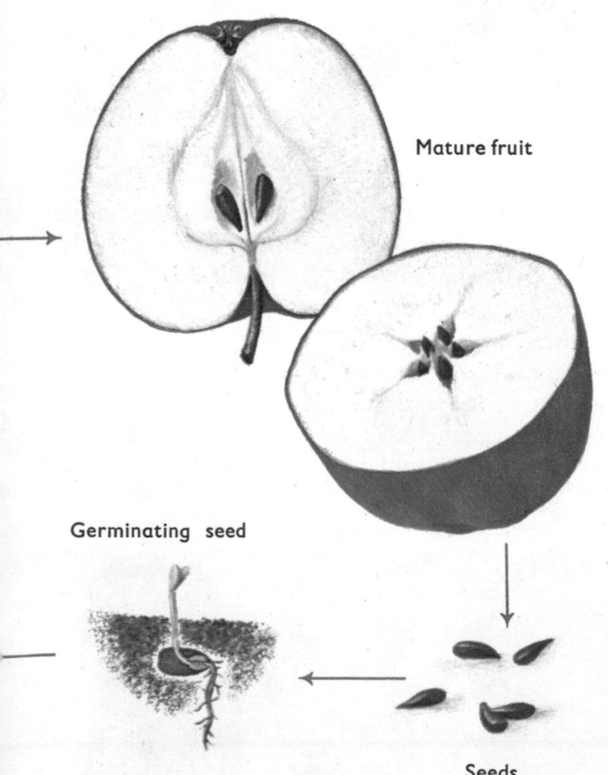

seedling rootstock to propagate the fruit. The fruit of a seedling is a small wild-type apple. New apple varieties are developed and selected regularly, based on such qualities as flavour, resistance to cold or disease, and size of crop. About 2,000 have been named. British varieties widely cultivated today are — eating apples, James Grieve, Worcester, Permain and Cox's Orange; cooking apples, Bramley.

The ovary of an apple flower is enclosed in a tube that consists of the base of the sepals, petals, and stamens. Much of the flesh of the apple is believed to be the tissues of this floral tube that enlarge as the ovary does. The characteristic colour of an apple depends on sunlight, proper nutrition, and adequate water.

Apples were originally consumed largely as cider in Great Britain and the United States. This is still true in some other countries, such as France. Cider apples in Great Britain are grown widely in Herefordshire. As better varieties were selected and propagated, their popularity as a fresh fruit increased. Apples are also canned, frozen, dried and made into apple jelly. Apple vinegar is manufactured from fermented apple juice or cider. Commercial apple pectin (used in making jam) is a by-product of the production of cider and vinegar.

Apples grow in temperate regions throughout the world, especially in Europe, North America, New Zealand, South Africa and Australia. Around 6,500 tons of apples are produced annually in Great Britain.

Malus sylvestris (Crab Apple) and its subspecies *sylvestris* and *mitis* are common in Great Britain. Included among ornamental apple trees are the Siberian Crab, which bears white flowers and red or yellowish fruit, and the Japanese Flowering Crab, which bears masses of pink flowers that later turn white. Crab apples make excellent apple jelly.

APRICOTS *(Prunus armeniaca)* were once believed to be native to Armenia, but later research indicated they originated in China.

Apricot trees resemble peach trees, and the fruits are similar in size and colour. Young apricots have a velvety skin like peaches, but they are smooth-skinned when ripe. The

APRICOTS

fruit contains a single, hard woody seed or stone, like peaches, plums, and cherries. Because they ripen so rapidly, most apricots are sold dried, tinned, or frozen. Apricot trees flower so early in spring that they can be grown only in warm regions.

ARAGONITE is a type of calcium carbonate that forms under conditions of low temperature and pressure. It is a white or light-coloured mineral, often fibrous in appearance. It differs from calcite by its greater hardness and specific gravity and by its lack of rhombohedral cleavage. Also, it becomes a powder when heated in a blowpipe flame, while calcite simply whitens.

Pearls, sea shells (bivalves and snails), and corals are formed of aragonite. Oolites — small spherical concretions — and hot spring deposits are also aragonite. Aragonite is much less common than calcite, possibly because it alters so readily to calcite. Fossil shells, old hot spring deposits, and many stalactites and stalagmites were originally aragonite but over the years have changed to calcite.

PRECIOUS CORAL

ARAGONITE CRYSTALS ARAGONITE CRYSTALS

Aragonite is found in England, France, Switzerland, Austria, Spain, Czechoslovakia, and in Greenland and several states of the U.S.A.

ARBORVITAES are evergreen trees with scale-like foliage. Arborvitae means 'tree of life' and refers to a preparation once made from the Northern White-Cedar or Eastern Arborvitae (*Thuja occidentalis*) for treating scurvy. The Western Red-Cedar or Giant Arborvitae (*Thuja plicata*) is an important timber tree of the American West Coast. *Thuja* are often planted as ornamentals.

WESTERN RED-CEDAR

NORTHERN WHITE-CEDAR

ARSENIC is an abundant element extracted from minerals as a by-product in the smelting of such metals as copper, zinc, lead, gold, and silver. Arsenic compounds are poisonous and are used widely in insecticides and weed killers. Arsenic is used also in fusing glass, in preservatives, and in medicines. It is used in the tanning industry to remove hair from hides and as an alloy of lead to make more perfect shot for firearms.

Pure arsenic is a metallic tin-white. It powders easily and tarnishes quickly to dark

ORPIMENT ARSENOPYRITE REALGAR

grey. Arsenic burns with a light blue flame and gives off a garlic odour.

Orpiment and realgar are mineral combinations of arsenic and sulphur. Orpiment generally occurs in sheet-like masses, and its crystals have perfect cleavage. Realgar is found in granular or earthy masses, often with orpiment. Arsenopyrite is a combination of iron, arsenic, and sulphur; it sparks and gives off a garlic odour when struck with a hammer.

ARTICHOKES. Globe artichoke *(Cynara scolymus)* is grown for its edible flower-head or bud. If allowed to develop fully, the bud produces a purple flower much like the Common Thistle. Artichoke plants are perennials and are propagated from sprouts that arise from the root crowns in early spring. They reach a height of 4 to 5 feet.

Globe artichokes are highly prized by the French. They are generally eaten cooked but are also good raw. Green Globe and Purple Globe Artichokes are the common varieties in Great Britain where it is a luxury vegetable.

GLOBE ARTICHOKE
Cynara scolymus

Jerusalem Artichoke (*Helianthus tuberosus)* is neither a native of Jerusalem nor an artichoke. It is a North American sunflower with tuber-like roots that are eaten cooked, pickled, or raw. It is widely used in Europe and Asia. It reached Great Britain sometime in the seventeenth century.

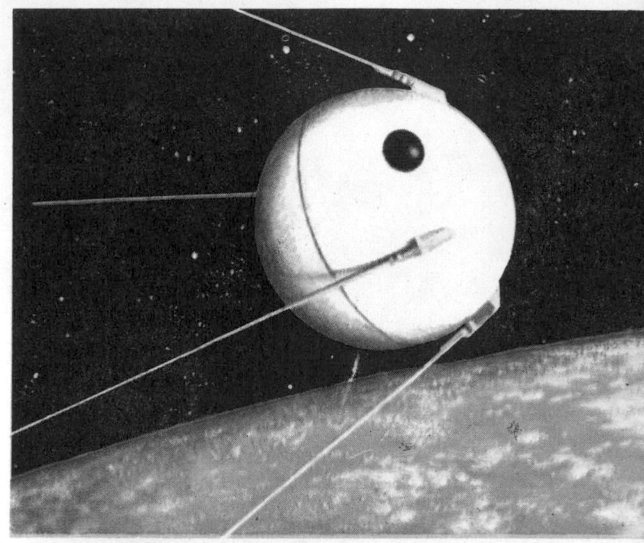

Sputnik I was the first man-made satellite.

ARTIFICIAL SATELLITES. The space age began on October 4, 1957, with the launching of the first artificial satellite. Since then hundreds of other satellites have been launched, carrying all sorts of scientific and military equipment.

Launching a satellite requires a powerful rocket, along with delicate controls. First the rocket must raise the satellite at least 100 miles above the Earth's surface to avoid serious air resistance. Then it must point the satellite horizontally and give it a speed of at least 5 miles per second. At that speed the satellite will keep moving around and around the Earth without any further attention. The satellite's speed is enough to keep it from falling down on to the Earth's surface, and the Earth's gravitational force is enough to keep the satellite from flying off into space. (See ORBIT.)

A satellite's orbit (the path of the satellite) goes completely around the Earth in the shape of an ellipse, which looks like a circle stretched at one side. The satellite's low point is called its perigee and its high point the apogee. The length of time that a satellite takes to go around, or its period, depends on the size of its orbit. The period of a low satellite is about an hour and a half, but a high satellite has a longer period. Satellites would remain up forever if it were not for air

National Aeronautics and Space Administration

The blast-off is always an awe-inspiring sight, whether the rocket is carrying an artificial satellite or a manned space vehicle as in the picture, left, of Apollo 6.

drag. Even hundreds of miles above the Earth's surface there is some air, and its drag on the satellite gradually brings it down. Since the lower layers of the atmosphere are denser, the lifetime of a satellite depends mainly on its height at perigee. If the perigee is lower than 100 miles, the satellite will quickly plunge deeper into the atmosphere and will burn up. On the other hand, a satellite with a perigee higher than 300 miles will continue in its orbit for centuries.

Satellites can be detected by visible light or by radio signals. To see a satellite, however, requires a special set of circumstances. We must be in darkness while the satellite above us is in sunlight, so that we see the satellite bright against a dark sky. Low satellites can be seen only just after sundown or just before sunrise, but higher satellites may be visible all night. For more continuous observation, most satellites have carried radio transmitters so that their positions can be determined by marking the direction of the radio signals from them.

Satellites can be used for many different scientific purposes. First of all, valuable information comes from simply observing the satellite's motion. The shape of the Earth can be determined, because the attraction of the bulge around the Earth's equator makes the whole orbit of a satellite slowly turn. And the rate at which air drag brings a satellite down tells us the density of the upper atmosphere and how hot it is. Besides, satellites can carry measuring instruments. Some study details of the upper atmosphere; others measure things that do not reach the Earth's surface, such as various types of cosmic rays and short wave length radiation from the sun. Finally, astronomers hope that satellites will one day carry telescopes to observe the stars from outside the Earth's atmosphere.

ASBESTOS is a unique mineral that can be spun into thread and woven into cloth. Its fibres are fireproof. There are two common sources: chrysotile (commonly known as a fibrous variety of serpentine) and amphibole asbestos. Chrysotile, from which most commercial asbestos is obtained, has fibres that run across the veins in which it occurs. Amphibole asbestos comes from such fibrous amphiboles as anthophyllite and tremolite. They are hard and brittle but may have long fibres. Amosite, an amphibole asbestos from Africa, may have fibres as much as 11 inches long. Amosite usually contains some iron.

Long-fibred asbestos is used for fabrics, insulating cloth, for brake linings, fire safety clothing, packing material, plastics, and gasmask filters. Short fibres are used for

Vanguard, which is the smallest satellite, is still in orbit.

Ziff-Davis Publishing

Project Mercury Capsule, first American space vehicle.

Courtesy of McDonnell Aircraft Corporation

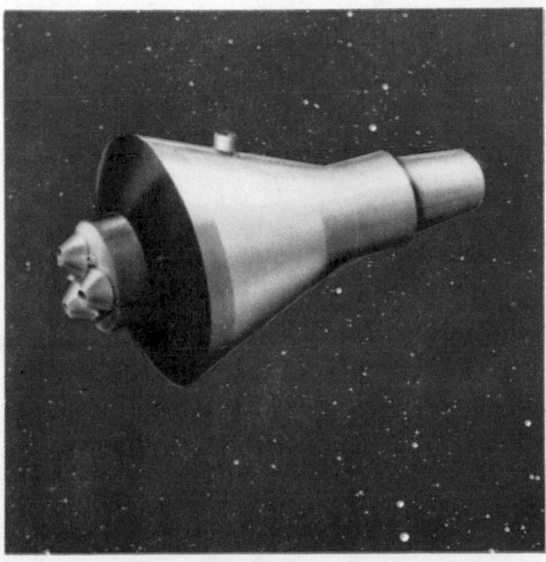

asbestos paper and millboard or are combined with 80 per cent Portland cement to make roofing shingles, siding, and pipes. Asbestos is combined with magnesia for bricks and for pipe covering. Shorter fibres are used for making boiler and roofing cements, their fire-proof qualities making them an invaluable contribution to modern life. More frequently, perhaps, they are used as a filler in floor tiles, and in plastic as well as paint.

Asbestos is widely distributed, but sources for commercial supplies are limited to such countries as the U.S.S.R., Finland, Italy, Cyprus, Japan, Rhodesia, South Africa, Swaziland, Bolivia, British Columbia, Quebec, and the U.S.A.

CROCIDOLITE ASBESTOS

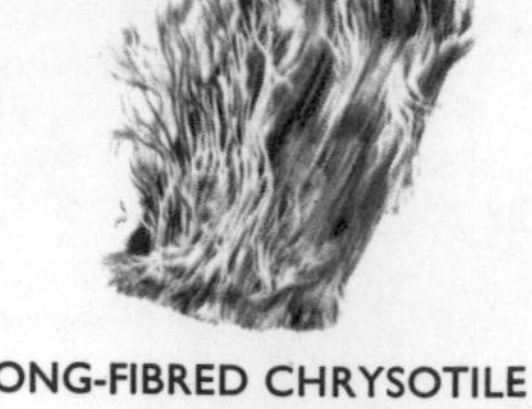

LONG-FIBRED CHRYSOTILE

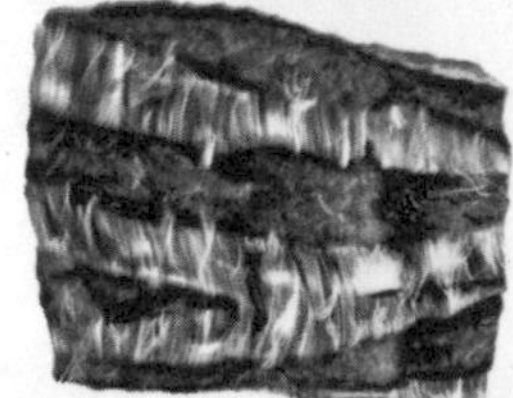

CHRYSOTILE ASBESTOS

Fibres of chrysotile are silky, strong, and very fine. Those of crocidolite and amphibole asbestos are heavier, and much more brittle.

Aluminised asbestos cloth is used in the manufacture of these protective suits. It has revolutionised fire-fighting techniques.

Turner Bros. Asbestos Co. Ltd

ASHES (*Fraxinus* spp.) are a group of about 60 species of deciduous trees and shrubs of the olive family. They are found mainly in Europe, Asia, and North America. A few kinds grow in the tropics of Cuba and Java. Such well-known shrubs as lilacs, privets, jasmines, and forsythias are also members of this family. *(Oleaceae.)*

Ashes have opposite, pinnately compound leaves about 12 inches long, usually composed of three to nine leaflets with toothed margins. Clusters of small flowers, like loose catkins, appear early in spring about the same time as the leaves. Later, dense, drooping clusters of single-winged, paddle-like seeds, to 2 inches long, hang from the branches. Naked ash twigs can be identified in winter by their opposite, half-round leaf scars containing smaller scars in a C-shaped line.

The tall English ash *(Fraxinus excelsior)* is commonly found on moist, rich, well-drained soil and particularly on alkaline soils. Many become stately trees, more than 100 feet high and several feet in diameter, with broadly rounded crowns. They are planted as shade trees, and their tough, straight-grained, elastic wood is valuable for tool handles and for such sports equipment as billiard cues, hockey sticks, tennis rackets, skis, and oars. The timber was widely used in the construction of farm implements, carts and coaches. The American Ash *(Fraxinus americanci)* is still widely used in coach-work as it is flexible, strong and has an attractive appearence when polished. A number of ornamental species are commonly found in parks and gardens in Britain, including the 'Weeping ash. *(Fraxinus pendula wentworthii)*. Tamo, a beautiful veneer, is made from an Oriental ash. Manna, used in laxatives, is obtained from sap in the stems of the Flowering Ash *(Fraxinus ornus)* of southern Europe and Asia. The inner bark of the European Ash was used to write on before the invention of paper.

Robin Hall-Ski-plan

Ash wood is used for much sports equipment, like these skis.

COMMON ASH
Fraxinus excelsior

Trees of several other families are also called 'ash'. Mountain Ash is a member of the rose family, and a species of eucalyptus is also known as Mountain Ash in Australia.

ASPENS are trees of the willow family. They grow fast and often sprout in dense thickets on burned-over land. They are short-lived. Some grow 60 feet tall and are 2 feet in

diameter. Their flowers are drooping catkins.

The Quaking Aspen *(Populus tremuloides)*, also called 'The Aspen', grows from north-eastern United States to Alaska and at high elevations in the mountains southwards into Mexico. Its broad leaves are simple and alternate, dark green above and light green below. In autumn they turn gold or yellow. The Quaking Aspen's leaves quiver in the slightest breeze, giving the tree its common name. The tree's bark is smooth and cream-coloured to chalky white, with black, warty patches. The bark becomes darker and rougher as the tree ages.

Aspens are planted as ornamental trees in the British Isles, for screens and wind breaks and occasionally planted as timber trees although *Populus robusta* and *Populus x. eugenii* are more widely used for this purpose.

Both these species differ from the Aspens in that they have larger, heart-shaped leaves with more coarsely toothed margins. Both species have soft white wood, used for matches, packaging and paper pulp.

ASTEROIDS. The planets are not the only cold, solid bodies that travel in orbits around the Sun. There are also many smaller bodies called asteroids. The orbits of asteroids are not as round as those of the planets, and not as close to the same plane. Most of them lie completely between the orbits of Mars and Jupiter, where there would otherwise be a gap in the solar system. A few range farther. One asteroid, Hidalgo, goes out as far as Saturn; Icarus comes closer to the Sun than Mercury. Astronomers keep track of about 1,500 asteroids, but there are probably tens of thousands bright enough to be photographed.

Asteroids are much smaller than planets.

THE ASTEROIDS

Average distance from Sun	135,000,000 miles to 400,000,000 miles
Diameters	a few feet to 480 miles
Periods of revolution (year)	2 to 9 years
Orbital speeds	9 to 14 miles per second
Total mass	1/500 of Earth

FOUR LARGEST ASTEROIDS

Name	Diameter	Discovered
Ceres	480 miles	1801
Pallas	300 miles	1802
Vesta	250 miles	1807
Juno	120 miles	1804

The asteroid belt, which includes the orbits of most but not all asteroids, lies between Mars and Jupiter.

The largest of them, Ceres, Pallas, Vesta, and Juno, are from 100 to 440 miles in diameter, but the fainter asteroids are much smaller. All are bare rock, with no atmospheres. The large asteroids are round, but many of the smaller ones are irregular in shape and sail through space, turning end over end.

Astronomers have always wondered why the region between Mars and Jupiter is filled with this swarm of small bodies instead of a single planet. Some believe that a planet once existed there but that it was smashed in a collision with another large body. But other astronomers think asteroids are material that never gathered to form a planet.

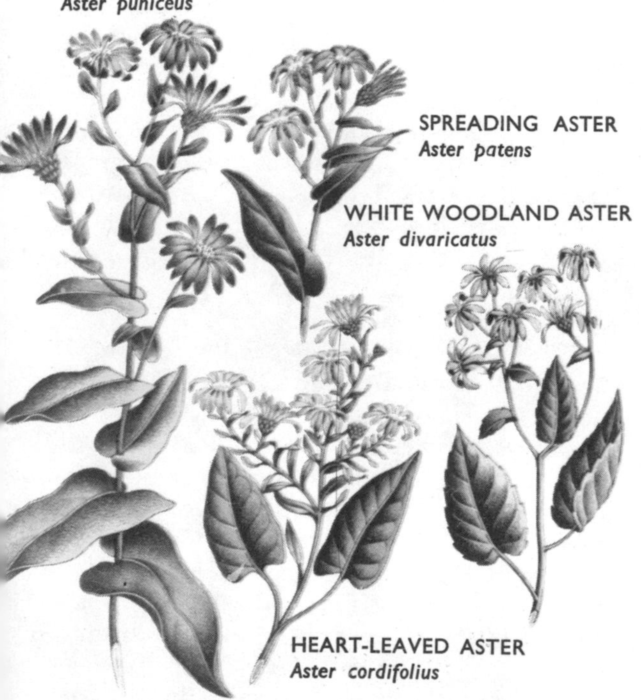

ASTERS (MICHAELMAS DAISIES) (*Aster* spp.) *Aster* means 'star' in Greek. Many of the 500 asters are native to eastern North America.

They begin growth in late spring, and during the summer produce their roots, stems, and leaves. When the days shorten in late summer, the lessened sunlight causes them to blossom. The flowers — in flower-heads — are varying shades of blue, pink and white.

Though asters are especially common in eastern North America, they can also be found elsewhere in Europe, Asia and South America — in fields, forests, and swamps, on mountains, or even along beaches. In these varied habitats, asters may show particular adaptations for survival. Alpine asters grow close to the ground. Plants that grow on beaches have thickened leaves to conserve water. The Seaside Aster *(Aster tripolium)* is the only British native species.

From the two American species *Aster novae belgii* and *Aster novae-angliae* and the European species *Aster amellus* have been bred our familiar garden Michaelmas Daisies. Most Michaelmas Daisies are swamp plants and are consequently moisture lovers. Heavy loam or clay is the best of all soils for these plants.

Another well-known aster is the Chinese or Summer Aster *(Callistepnus)*. Its fluffy, chrysanthemum-like blooms of pink, light blue, or white are seen commonly in homes, florist shops, and gardens. Chinese Asters are annuals and must be started from seed each year.

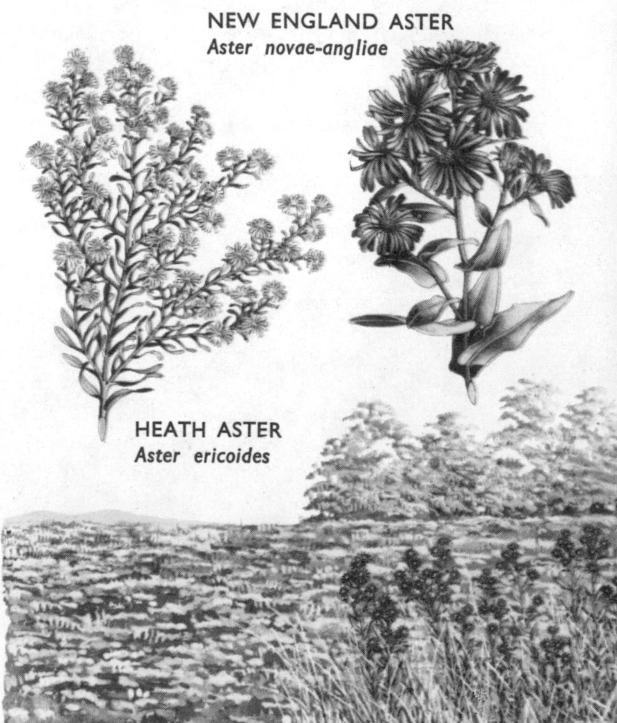

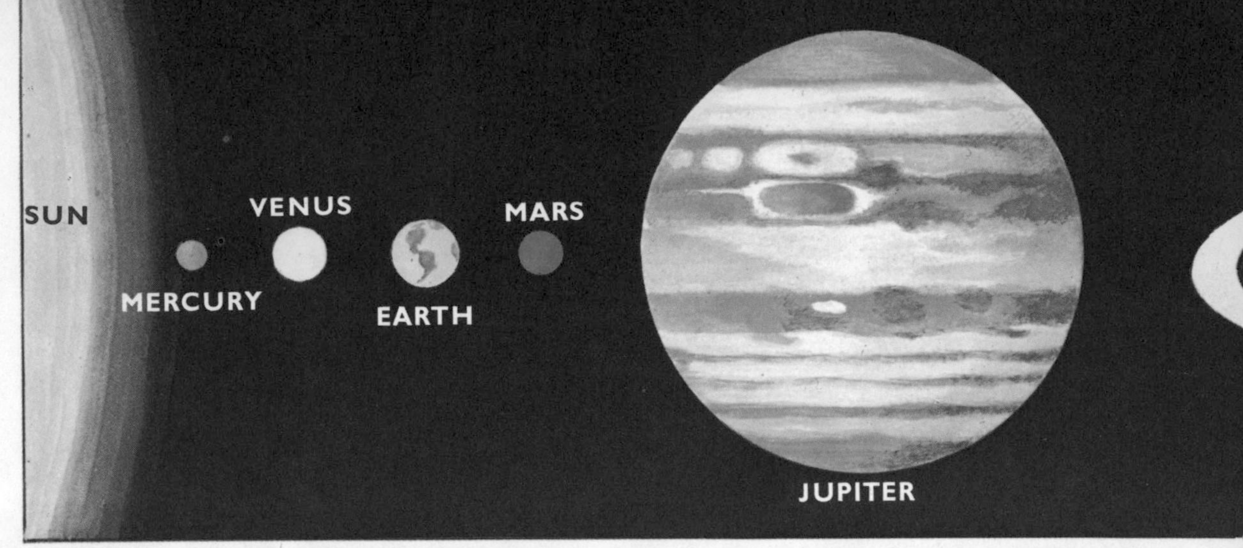

This diagram shows the succession and relative sizes of the nine planets of the solar system. Their distances from the Sun are not drawn to scale.

ASTRONOMY is the oldest of the sciences. Four thousand years ago the ancient Egyptians set their calendar by observing the position of the stars. Nearly three thousand years ago the Babylonians knew how to predict when eclipses would occur. The first astronomers whose names we know are among the Greek philosophers. Around 600 B.C. Thales learned how to predict eclipses. At about the same time Pythagoras argued that the Earth was a round body floating in space, and about 200 B.C. Eratosthenes measured the size of the Earth. Aristarchus measured the distances of the Sun and Moon about 250 B.C., and he believed, as we do today, that the Earth goes around the Sun.

Tycho Brahe measured the orbits of planets but believed that the heavens moved around the Earth.

Most Greek astronomers believed that the Earth was stationary, with the Sun, Moon, planets, and stars all going around it. Hipparchus believed this and worked out possible shapes for the orbits. He also made a great catalogue of stars. The last great Greek astronomer was Ptolemy. About A.D. 100 he wrote a book describing how everything went around the Earth. His ideas became known as the Ptolemaic System.

Nicolaus Copernicus, Tycho Brahe, Johannes Kepler, and Galileo Galilei established modern astronomy and overthrew the Ptolemaic System. Galileo used the telescope to discover the moons of Jupiter and to establish the modern picture of the solar system. Isaac Newton, in 1687, explained the law of gravity and established the science of celestial mechanics. Astronomy, first centred on the solar system, later explored the stars and distant galaxies. A few years before 1900, astronomers began taking photographs instead of making slow visual observations. Measurements of positions, distances, and motions of stars were made in great numbers. At about this time physicists discovered the structure of the atom, and astronomers were soon able to study the nature of the stars by analysing starlight.

Today's astronomer is half physicist, since so much of astronomy depends on applying the laws of physics to the distant bodies of the universe. Research in astronomy is of two

sorts. Theoretical studies predict and interpret the behaviour of astronomical bodies, while observational work produces the facts on which theories must be based. In the whole world only a few hundred people do research in astronomy. They are highly trained specialists who work at observatories or universities. But one does not have to be a professional astronomer to enjoy astronomy. Countless thousands enjoy studying the stars, and amateur astronomy clubs meet in most cities.

Young amateurs are sometimes faced with deciding whether to take up astronomy as a

A view of the Royal Greenwich Observatory, Hurstmonceaux, Sussex (left) which houses the giant Isaac Newton telescope (right). The telescope's mirror will 'collect' light from stars and galaxies millions of miles out in space and focus it on to photographic plates.

Keystone Press

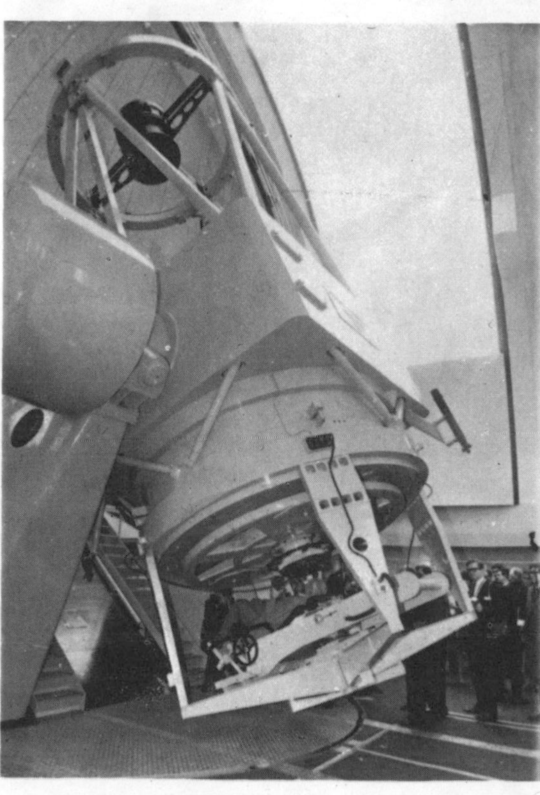

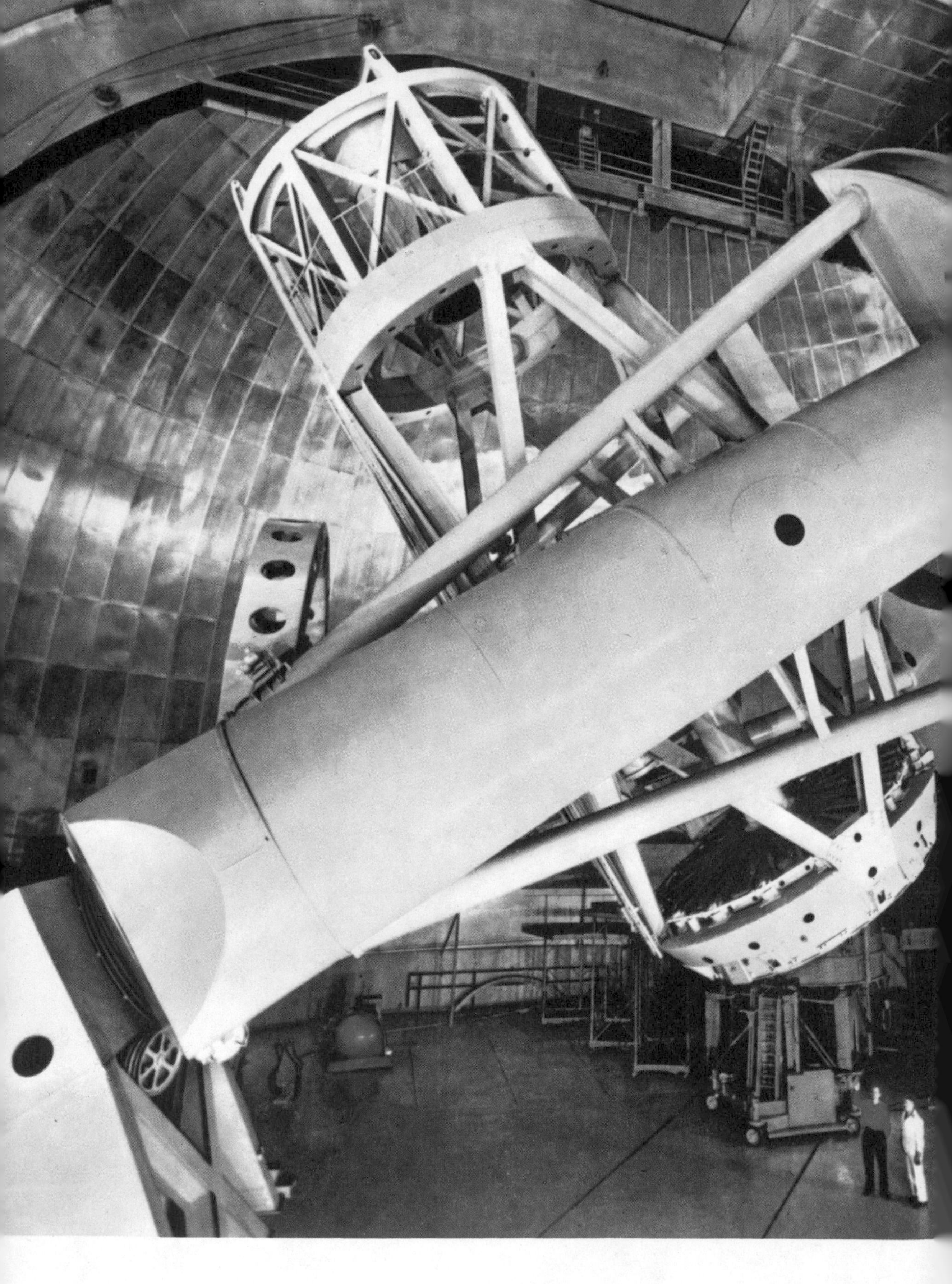

The 200-inch Hale reflector on Mt. Palomar in California is the world's largest optical telescope. Astronomers ride on a platform lift that follows a track across the dome of the observatory to the observer's cage at upper left. Movement of the telescope to keep the same objects in view is controlled by associates at a control panel on the floor, 75 feet below.

life-time career. There are no fixed rules, but in general the prospective astronomer should have high marks in school and should do especially well in science and mathematics. Even so, it is a hard decision because a man with the talent to be an astronomer has many other opportunities, and most of them offer a higher salary. For the astronomer the rewards are in the work itself and the pride of knowing that he has helped a little to unravel the workings of the universe.

A professional astronomer adjusts a photographic plate in the eyepiece of the 200-inch Hale reflector. Modern studies reveal how stars are born and die and how chemical elements are created or changed inside stars.

Mt. Wilson and Palomar Observatories

Mt. Wilson and Palomar Observatories

The 18th-century astronomer Johannes Kepler, celebrated for his 'Astronomy'.

THE SCOPE OF ASTRONOMY. Astronomy's realm begins at the top of the Earth's atmosphere and includes all the rest of the universe — the Sun, Moon, and the planets, the stars and the galaxies, out to the farthest limits of observation.

The two concerns of astronomy are the solar system and the other stars. The Sun is a star, and the solar system is its family of smaller bodies, from planets like the Earth down to grains of dust. Much farther away, surrounding us in all directions, are the stars. They are great hot, shining globes of gas, like the Sun. Stars look faint only because they are so far away.

The globular star cluster (M13) is found in the constellation Hercules.

Mt. Wilson and Palomar Observatories

Distances in astronomy are so large that it is difficult to express them so they can be understood. One large number looks like another when all are 'astronomical' in size. But astronomical distances actually fall into several distinct scales that differ tremendously from each other. It is important to understand them, for the main features of the universe then become clear.

A good starting point is the size of the Earth, for we all know what our globe looks like. The Earth is 7,927 miles in diameter. Some other planets are larger, and some are smaller, but the size of the Earth gives us an idea of the size of the eight other planets in our solar system.

The planets are separated by large distances. We can easily see this by looking at the planets at night. The other planets are so far from us that they look like mere points of light, and only a telescope shows their sizes. The Earth is 93 million miles from the Sun, which is the centre of our solar system. It would take over 10,000 Earths, side by side, to span this distance. Some planets are closer to the Sun, and some are farther from the Sun. Pluto, the most distant planet, averages 40 times the Earth's distance from the Sun.

But the whole solar system shrinks to nothing compared with the distances that separate the stars. The nearest other star is 250,000 times as far from us as is the Sun. Similar large distances separate other neighbouring stars. A typical star is about the size of the Sun. This is large by our standards on Earth, but the stars are tiny compared with the distances that separate them from their neighbours. The universe is really an empty place!

The other stars are scattered at various distances, but about 200 times the distance of the nearest star takes in nearly all the stars that we can see without a telescope. The more distant stars are too faint to see easily, but the stars go on and on, through the great disc of stars that we call the Milky Way. Our Sun is just one of the 100,000 million stars that make up the Milky Way Galaxy.

Even the Milky Way is insignificant when we consider the total universe, for the Milky Way is just one of countless millions of galaxies, each containing millions or thousands of millions of stars. Again, the space of the universe is mostly empty, with the galaxies scattered through it here and there. There is no end to our view of the universe, only a gradual fading out.

The universe is overwhelmingly diverse, yet the universe also has a unity that extends from here to the farthest galaxies that we can see. Everything everywhere is made up of the same chemical elements, and the material of the most distant star behaves in the same way as material here on Earth. One star may have more hydrogen, while another has an excess of carbon, but atoms of hydrogen and carbon in those stars follow the same rules of behaviour as the hydrogen and carbon atoms that we study in laboratories here on Earth. These rules are called the laws of physics, and they are the key to astronomy.

Astronomy gives us a new view of the world. We are small animals on a minor planet circling an ordinary star lost in the outer fringes of one galaxy among millions. Yet we can range as far as we like by studying the science that carries us as high as the stars.

Composition of air at altitudes up to about 45 miles

nitrogen 78%

oxygen 21%

argon 0.93%

carbon dioxide 0.03%

all other gases 0.04%

Composition of air at altitudes above 500 miles

helium 50%

hydrogen 50%

Clarence P. Custer, M.D.

Today's amateurs with excellent telescopes have made important discoveries of comets and variable stars.

ATMOSPHERE. Here on the Earth's surface we live at the bottom of a sea of air. When the wind blows we notice the air, but more often we forget that it is there. Yet without this blanket of air that we call the atmosphere, we could not live. It contains the oxygen that we breathe, the carbon dioxide that plants require, and the water that all living things need. The atmosphere acts as a protective blanket for the whole Earth. It filters out most of the Sun's ultra-violet light, which produces sunburns. It blocks nearly all of the damaging cosmic rays and protects us from meteors that travel many times faster than a rifle bullet. The atmosphere also makes our world a prettier place. Without it we would have no blue sky, no clouds, and no rainbow.

The atmosphere extends hundreds of miles up, but most of the air is close to the Earth's surface. Half of the atmosphere lies within $3\frac{1}{2}$ miles of the surface. At high altitudes the air thins rapidly. On top of high mountains, 2 miles or more above sea level, climbers have difficulty breathing. Above 15 or 20 miles aircraft cannot fly and balloons can hardly rise. Very high altitudes can be explored only by rockets, which do not need air to support them. The atmosphere has no real end. The air simply becomes much thinner. The aurora or northern lights sometimes

The Mount Everest Foundation.

Sherpa Tenzing breathing bottled oxygen on the summit of Everest.

glows as high up as 600 miles. This proves there is some air even at that altitude.

Different levels of the atmosphere have different properties. The lowest level is called the troposphere. It contains the clouds and all the phenomena that make up our weather. Above 6 or 8 miles is the stratosphere where the air is always clear and pure. The lower stratosphere is very cold, but higher up the air gets warm again and then hot. Beyond 50 miles is the ionosphere. It contains layers of charged particles that reflect radio waves. Without the ionosphere we would not have long-distance radio communication. Highest of all is the exosphere, which begins about 300 miles above the Earth's surface. In the exosphere atoms move about almost without contact with each other.

Most of the other planets also have atmospheres. The large planets — Jupiter, Saturn, Uranus, and Neptune — have deep, dense atmospheres of hydrogen and helium gases. They also have large amounts of the poisonous gases methane and ammonia. The atmosphere on Venus is probably nitrogen with much larger amounts of carbon dioxide and water vapour than in the Earth's atmosphere. On Mars, the atmosphere is much thinner than the Earth's. Its air is made up substantially of carbon dioxide plus some small amounts of oxygen and water vapour. The smallest planets, Mercury and Pluto, have no atmosphere. Our Moon has little atmosphere, either. It is bare rock and dust, with no sounds and no winds.

There is a reason why some planets have dense atmospheres and some have none at all. In order to hold an atmosphere a planet must have enough gravitational force or else the atmosphere will escape into space. A large planet like Jupiter has a large force of gravity and holds a dense atmosphere. The Earth is smaller, and its gravity is weaker, so its atmosphere is not as dense. And a small body like the Moon has too weak a force of gravity to hold much air at all. Until recently the Moon was thought to have no atmosphere, but new apparatus and techniques have detected traces of gases. (See AURORA; EARTH.)

ATOMS are the building blocks of all things in the universe — living and non-living. Though too small to be seen, when joined together by the billions atoms give everything their form and structure. Atoms are the

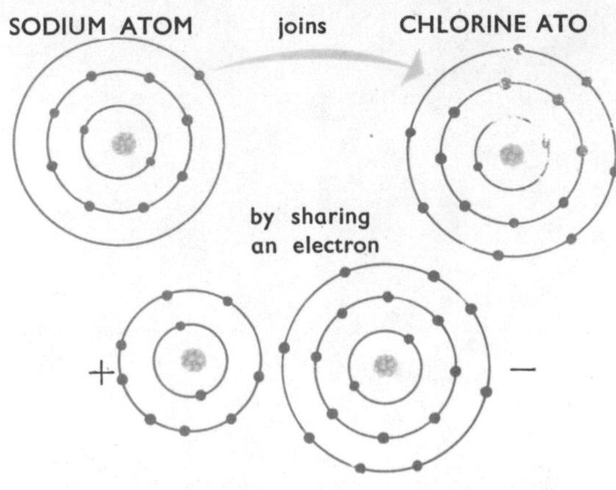

to form a molecule of sodium chloride or salt

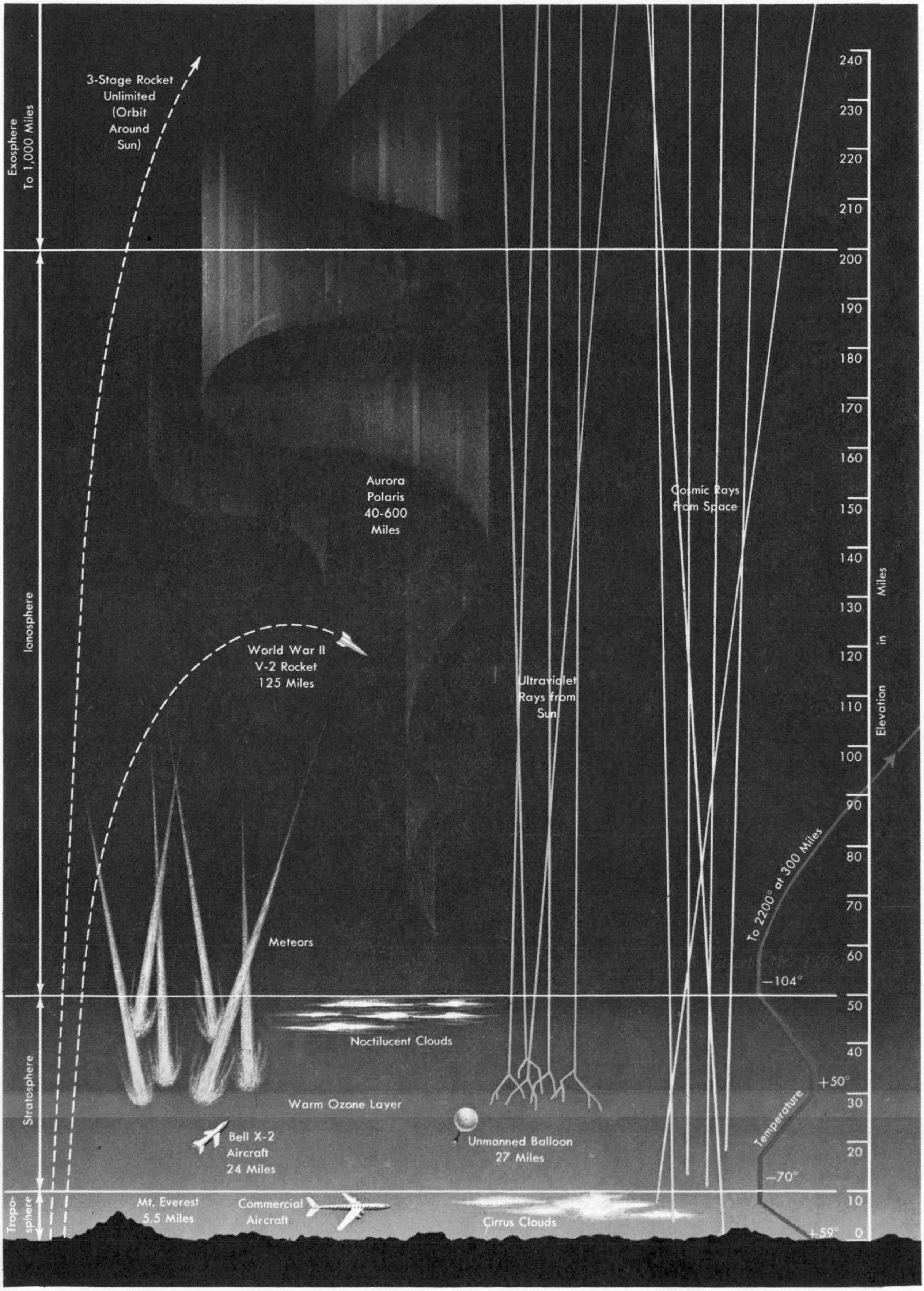

Exosphere
To 1,000 Miles

Ionosphere

Stratosphere

Tropo-
sphere

3-Stage Rocket
Unlimited
(Orbit
Around
Sun)

Aurora
Polaris
40-600
Miles

Cosmic Rays
from Space

World War II
V-2 Rocket
125 Miles

Ultraviolet
Rays from
Sun

Meteors

Noctilucent Clouds

Warm Ozone Layer

Bell X-2
Aircraft
24 Miles

Unmanned Balloon
27 Miles

Mt. Everest
5.5 Miles

Commercial
Aircraft

Cirrus Clouds

To 2200° at 300 Miles

−104°

+50°

Temperature

−70°

+59°

Elevation in Miles

240
230
220
210
200
190
180
170
160
150
140
130
120
110
100
90
80
70
60
50
40
30
20
10
0

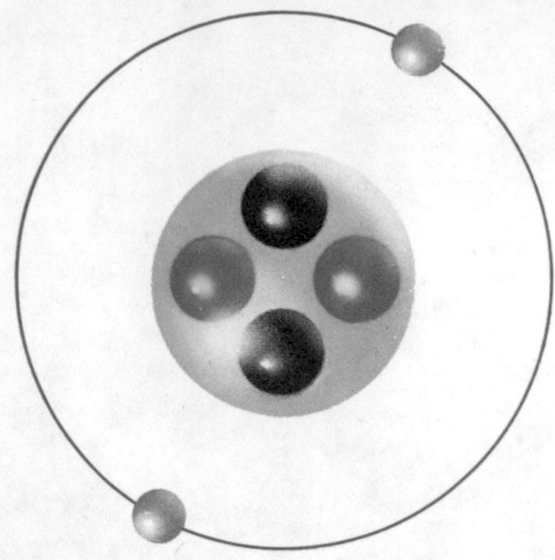

Model of a helium atom shows protons (black) and neutrons (red) in nucleus and two electrons (blue).

smallest units of the hundred or so elements of which everything is made. Each element and hence each kind of atom has its own distinct characteristics and its own behaviour determined by those characteristics. Two or more atoms of the same or different kinds unite to form molecules. A molecule of oxygen consists of two atoms of oxygen. A molecule of salt consists of one atom of sodium combined with two atoms of chlorine. The most common form of things you see are either molecules or combinations and mixtures of molecules. Occasionally, atoms of the same element may differ very much in form and in structure. Pure carbon, for example, may exist in three very different forms — diamonds, graphite, and ordinary carbon such as soot or charcoal.

AURORA. The aurora borealis or northern lights is a glow in the sky. It takes many different forms. Sometimes it is a pale arch low in the north, sometimes rays point up from the northern horizon, and sometimes the lights hang from overhead like curtains. The patterns change, and pulses of light often flash across them. The colour is usually pale green or deep red.

The aurora is a glowing of the Earth's atmosphere, more than 50 miles up. It is caused by particles that stream out of the Sun. When these particles strike our atmosphere, the atoms of air glow, like the gas in a neon tube. The particles from the Sun are charged, and the Earth's magnetic field makes them

The colourful aurora is visible evidence of the Earth's strong magnetic fields in both polar regions.

curve in towards the North and South Poles. So auroras occur most frequently in high latitudes. In Britain, auroras are rare but farther north in Scandinavia they are commonly seen. Auroras are also seen in the Southern Hemisphere but only very far south. In the Southern Hemisphere they are called the aurora australis or southern lights.

Because auroras are caused by disturbances on the Sun, they are more frequent in the periods of sun-spot maximum. Such a maximum period occurred in 1958, another in 1969, and the next is predicted for 1980. The rate of occurrence diminishes between times, and is lowest at the halfway point in the cycle. Delicate optical instruments have disclosed that auroras are present day and night. Their great concentration near the poles makes them visible there. (See ATMOSPHERE; SUN.)

AVOCADOS *(Persea americana)* are tropical or sub-tropical evergreen fruit trees of the laurel family. Originally native to Central America, avocados are now grown in Florida, California, Hawaii, Cuba, the West Indies, and to a lesser extent in other subtropical areas. Avocado is probably a sound substitute for the original Aztec name — ahuacatl.

Avocado trees vary in shape from tall and slender to low and spreading. Most varieties bear clusters of small flowers in profusion from autumn to spring. The flowers open twice instead of only once. On the first opening, only the female part (pistil) is functional. The following day, when the flowers reopen, the male parts (stamens) are functional. This may prevent the flowers of a tree from fertilising themselves.

Avocados vary greatly in size, shape, colour, and skin texture. Some weigh only a few ounces; others as much as three pounds. Some kinds are round; others oval or pear-shaped. Some varieties have thin, smooth skins, others have rough, thick woody skins. Most avocados are green when ripe, but a few become crimson or maroon. When fully ripened, the flesh is oily and as soft as butter. In most areas avocados are eaten as a salad fruit, but Indians of Central America have for centuries used avocados as a substitute for meat. Most avocados are bland in flavour, but some varieties have a nutty flavour. Avocados are rich in vitamin A and B and in fat content, which may be as much as 20 per cent. Their caloric rating is about three times as much as an equal serving of bananas or apples, making them unusually nutritious.

Because of their exotic nature, they are considered a great luxury in Britain.

Avocados are usually propagated by budding or grafting small seedling trees to the variety desired.

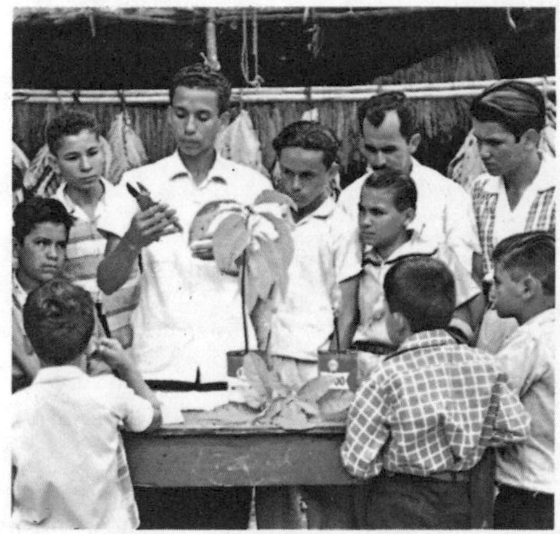

Ford Motor Co: FORD ALMANAC 1962

An instructor gives hints on the art of avocado grafting.

Avocados vary greatly in size, shape, colour and skin texture.

B

BACTERIA are the smallest of all plants. All are one-celled, but sometimes the cells are held together in pairs, in long chains, or in irregular masses. About 250,000 of the smallest bacteria laid end to end would measure only an inch in length. The largest are about 1/250 of an inch long – about 1,000 times larger. Even these largest of the bacteria cannot be seen without a microscope.

Courtesy of and © 1959 Parke, Davis & Company

Leeuwenhoek, using a simple microscope, was the first man to observe and study bacteria, about 300 years ago.

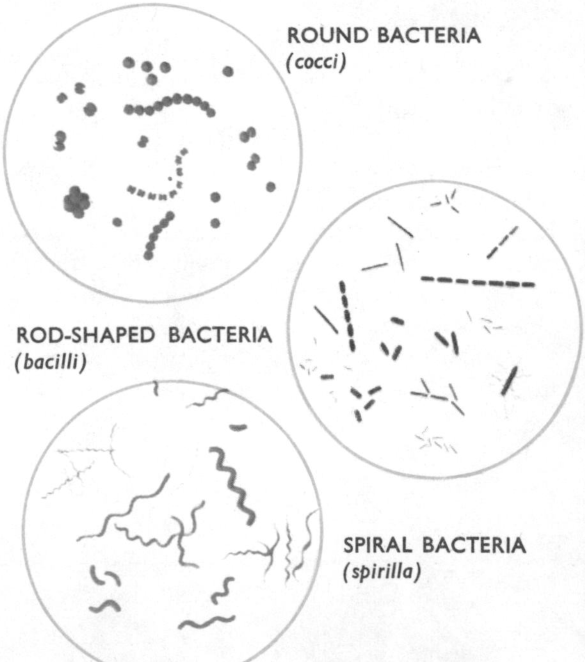

Some bacteria are round, others rod-like, and some spiral. All bacteria have cell walls, but these are not made of cellulose as in higher plants. The cell wall of bacteria is made of chitin, a substance found also in the skeletons of insects and crustaceans. In some species the wall is surrounded by a gelatinous sheath or capsule. The living part inside the cell wall seems primitive compared to other cells. There is no definite nucleus surrounded by a membrane, although granules of nuclear material can be seen with an electron microscope. Round bacteria and most others are not able to move, but certain of the rod-shaped bacteria and all of the spiral forms move by means of threads, called flagella.

ROUND BACTERIA
(cocci)

ROD-SHAPED BACTERIA
(bacilli)

SPIRAL BACTERIA
(spirilla)

Bacteria reproduce by dividing into two cells, a process called fission. This may happen every 20 or 30 minutes. Starting with a single bacterium there would be 281 million bacteria at the end of 24 hours if the process were not stopped. Such rapid divisions could not continue for that length of time, however, as the supply of food, water, and oxygen surrounding the cells would soon be exhausted. Nevertheless, bacteria are capable of multiplying rapidly, and they are found almost everywhere. They are absent only on surfaces fatal to their existence. Generally, for example, bacteria cannot live long if exposed to direct sunlight. They can withstand a wide range of temperatures — from slightly above freezing to over 36 degrees centigrade (100 degrees Fahrenheit). Bacteria do not die at lower temperatures, but they do not grow. Typhoic bacteria have been known to live in ice-cream for five months. Certain bacteria have lived for several days exposed to the temperature of liquid air — minus 190 degrees centigrade (about 310 degrees below zero Fahrenheit). Bacteria abound in water and milk, in animal and vegetable substances and in soil.

Louis Pasteur (1822–1895), French chemist and biologist, was the founder of modern bacteriology.

Most bacteria need the oxygen of the air in order to respire. These bacteria are called aerobes. Others, called anaerobes, can live without free oxygen. The bacterium that causes tetanus or lockjaw is one of this type, and this is one reason why wounds are not closed as the lockjaw organism cannot grow if air reaches it.

Under certain conditions some bacteria form spores. Usually only one spore is formed in each bacterial cell. These spores are very resistant to unfavourable conditions, such as high or low temperatures, lack of water, or even the presence of chemicals. Boiling does not kill some spores. When conditions become favourable, the spores start to grow. Not all bacteria form spores, but those that do include many that live in soil or cause decay. Spores of bacteria that cause tetanus may occur in the soil, especially in warm regions.

Bacteria play an essential role in the balance of nature by destroying the remains of dead animals and plants. They are mainly responsible for decay, thus returning to the soil and air the chemicals of which plants and animals are made.

All living cells are composed in part of nitrogen, and this element is essential to plant and animal growth. Yet all animals and nearly all plants cannot use the nitrogen that makes up 80 per cent of the air. Plants can use nitrogen only if it is in a suitable form, as in nitrates. Certain bacteria take free nitrogen of the air and change it into nitrites. Other bacteria convert nitrites into nitrates that higher plants can use.

Both plants and animals may become infected with disease-causing bacteria. Diphtheria, tonsillitis, some types of pneumonia, typhoid, cholera, tuberculosis, and other diseases are caused by bacteria. Fire blight of apples and pears, crown gall of many plants, soft rot, and many other plant diseases are caused by bacteria.

Bacteria are useful to mankind in the preparation of several kinds of foodstuffs. Some kinds aid in cheese-making, others add flavour to butter, and still others are important in the making of vinegar.

Bacteria may be destroyed by different means, depending upon the species. Most of them are killed by boiling water or steam. Others are susceptible to certain chemicals that break down their cell walls. (See FUNGI.)

BALSA *(Ochroma lagopus)* trees grow in the tropical forests of Central and South America. Balsa wood is the lightest commercial timber. It is commonly used for life-belts for refrigerator linings, for packing delicate items and for model-making.

In 1947 the Norwegian Thor Heyerdahl and his companions sailed from South America to Polynesia in this balsa wood raft named the Kon-Tiki.

Balsa trees may grow up to 70 feet in height and 2 feet in diameter within six years. They commonly sprout thickly in areas burned-over by fire or cleared for cultivation. Their large, deciduous, three-lobed leaves resemble those of maples. A balsa's long, slim flowers develop into unusual seed pods that burst when mature and scatter grape-sized seeds, which are embedded in a floss.

The Kon-Tiki Expedition. In 1947 a Norwegian, Thor Heyerdahl, and five companions constructed a raft (which they named Kon-Tiki) of Balsa trunks cut from the jungles of Peru and set sail from Callao across the Pacific to Polynesia. Heyerdahl believed that the natives of Polynesia were direct descendants of the ancient South American civilisation and that they had sailed from Peru about A.D. 500 on rafts similar to his own.

The voyage, which took 101 days and covered a distance of some 5,000 miles, was successful although many had doubted whether the raft would survive. It was widely believed that the raft would become waterlogged and sink, but Heyerdahl used unseasoned logs and the sap in the timbers prevented sea water from entering.

BAMBOOS are large woody-stemmed perennial grasses, forming the sub-family Bambusoideae. Most of the more than 700 species are tropical, but a few can withstand temperatures of about minus 20 degrees centigrade (a few degrees below zero Fahrenheit). Tropical bamboos are evergreen, but northern species shed their leaves in the autumn.

Bamboos are similar in structure to other grasses. Their stems have prominent joints, or nodes, and they often grow in clumps from a single rootstock. Short leaf blades may project from the numerous branches, and the fruit of many kinds looks like grain.

Some bamboos grow to a height of more than 100 feet and measure as much as 3 feet in circumference. Fresh shoots are soft and edible, like asparagus, but the stems quickly become so firm that cutting tools can be made from them. Many types produce flowers every year, others may bloom infrequently. One kind blooms only every 32 years.

Most people are familiar with hollow, round types of bamboo, but there are also solid bamboos and some that are square or

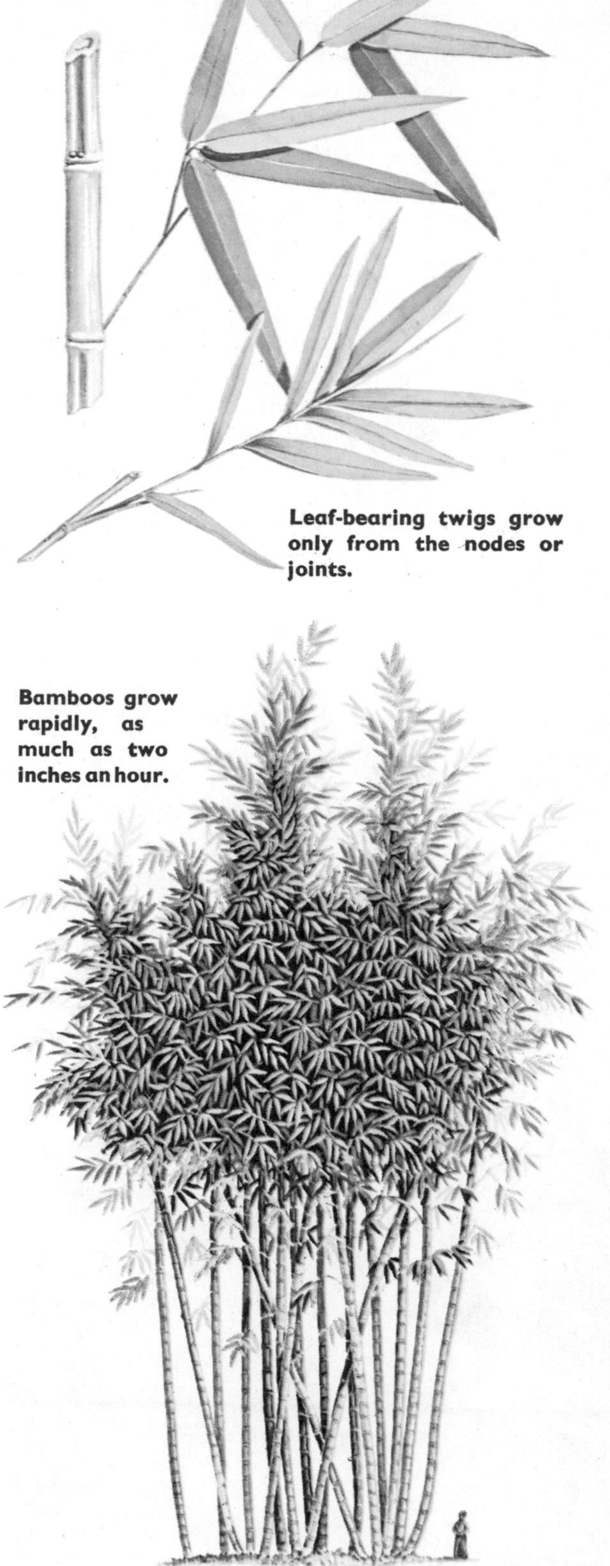

Leaf-bearing twigs grow only from the nodes or joints.

Bamboos grow rapidly, as much as two inches an hour.

triangular in cross section. There are also dwarf and giant types. Some kinds grow only in tropical climates while others are found at the snow line in the Himalayas. Bamboos grow in tropical zones throughout the world but are most abundant in south-eastern Asia.

A few species are grown as ornamental plants in Great Britain. These largely belong to the genus *Arundinaria.*

Many thousands of bamboo canes are imported into this country each year for use in gardens and in the manufacture of furniture, fishing rods and household furnishings. The limited use of bamboo in the American tropics is due in part to the weakness of the native bamboos and their susceptibility to attack by powder-post beetles.

Bamboo is most important in the Orient. Food, clothes, bridges, boats, paper, and utensils are among the countless items made from bamboo in the Far East. Complete homes, from the flooring of flattened stems to roofing tiles, are constructed of bamboo. Fields are watered with bamboo irrigation pipes; baskets are made from woven strips of bamboo, and hollow joints of bamboo are used as bottles and buckets. Everything from fans to fences and flutes to furniture can be made of some variety of bamboo.

Courtesy of the Puerto Rico News Service

As bananas bruise easily, they are wrapped in blankets before a mule trip to train or ship.

BANANAS (*Musa* spp.) are among the most widely known of tropical fruits. The Common Banana is closely related to the Cooking Banana or Plantain but has a higher sugar content. Bananas are a good source of vitamin A. They are believed to be native to southern Asia, where they have been cultivated since prehistoric times. There are about a hundred varieties.

The banana plant may reach a height of 10 to 30 feet. It is not really a tree but a giant herb. Its trunk is composed of compressed,

Bananas are loaded into the refrigerated hold of a freighter for shipment to northern markets.

Courtesy of the United Fruit Company

On some large plantations, the bunches of green bananas are moved to loading docks by conveyors.

Courtesy of the United Fruit Company

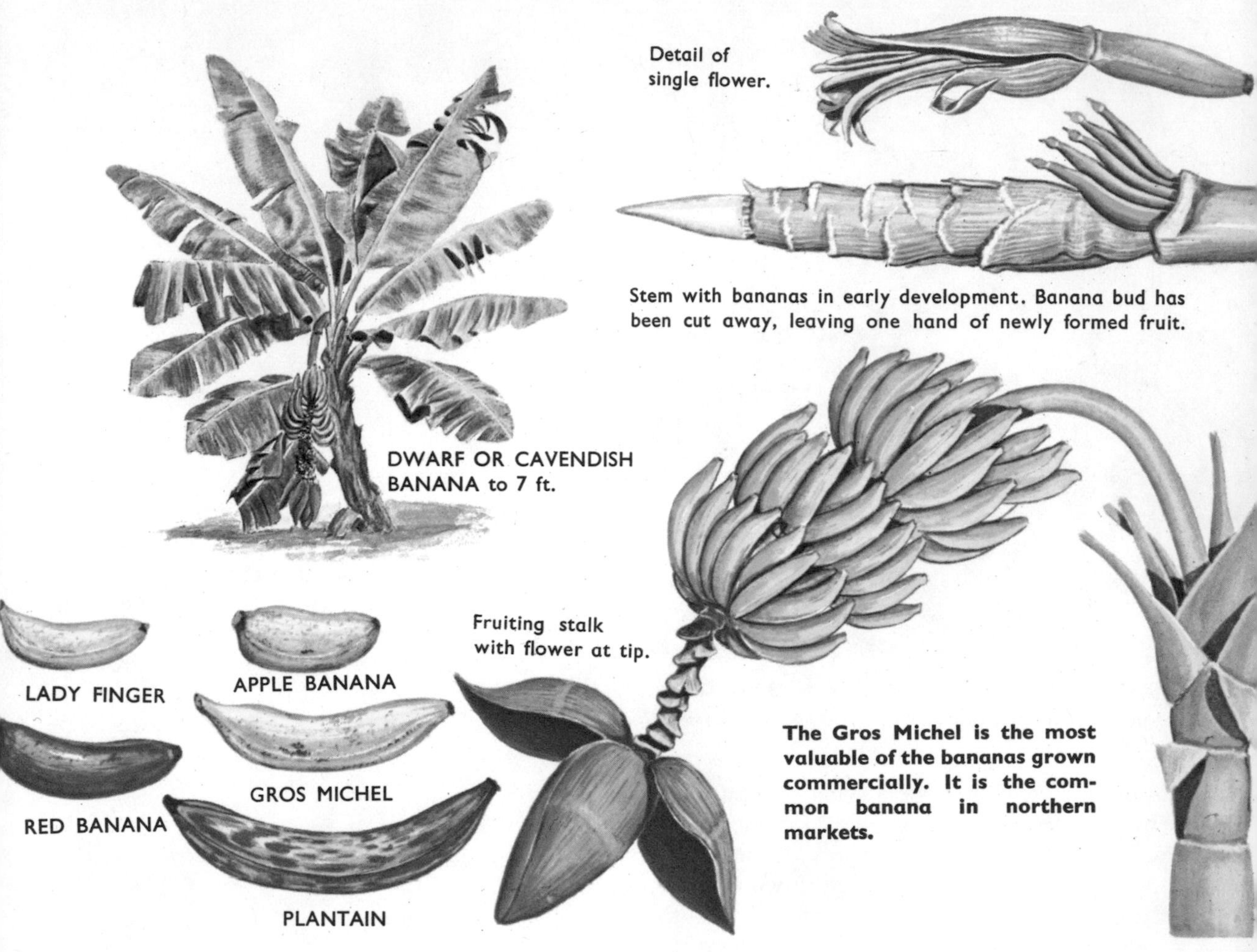

overlapping, spirally arranged leaf stalks. Thus the leaf and leaf stalk extend from the tip of the leaf down to ground level, and there each is attached to an underground stem or rhizome. New leaves and leaf stalks grow through the surrounding cylinder of older stalks. After the last leaf is produced, a flower cluster forms at the base of the plant in the cylinder of leaf stalks. It grows upwards and emerges at the top of the plant. When it has grown free of the stalk, it droops down. Each flower cluster is protected by a modified leaf, or bract. The female flowers appear at the base of the stalk and are the first to open. Male flowers are produced last — at the tip of the flower cluster — and are covered with overlapping bracts. Each cluster eventually develops into a 'hand' of bananas. The number of such 'hands' per bunch varies as does the number of fruit or 'fingers'. In most cultivated varieties the fruit is usually seedless and develops without pollination. A single stalk of the Common Banana may produce from 100 to 400 individual bananas with as many as two dozen fingers on each hand. The plant bears fruit only once and is usually destroyed when the crop is harvested. It sprouts again from the roots.

Bananas are usually propagated by planting pieces of the underground stem or rhizome. The buds located on such pieces grow into new plants. Suckers that develop at the base of the old plant are also capable of growing into new plants.

Commercial plantings of bananas were first made in Central America between 1870 and 1880. Since that time the production of bananas has become a major industry in Central America, Colombia, and the West Indies.

Courtesy of the United Fruit Company

Bananas are sprayed to prevent spread of disease.

BANYAN FRUIT

Bananas are harvested by cutting part-way through the leaf stalks a few feet below the point where the stalk of fruit is attached. The top of the plant is then pulled down until the fruit rests on a man's shoulder. Then the fruit stalk is cut off completely. Pieces of the leaf stalks are used as cushions to protect the fruit during shipment. Bananas are harvested green to avoid spoilage and are shipped to distant markets in refrigerated ships.

BANYANS *(Ficus benghalensis)* are tropical trees which have many trunks supporting a single huge crown. A single tree may develop thousands of trunks and spread in a tangled wilderness over several acres. Alexander the Great is said to have camped his entire army under a particularly large Banyan in north-western India. The extra trunks are formed by aerial roots which drop down from the branches and take root. Banyan seeds that become lodged in other trees soon sprout and send several roots towards the ground. More roots grow and become wound tightly around the 'host' tree's trunk. When the 'host' dies, the Banyan is able to support itself.

Sacred to the Hindus, the Banyan is a native of India and nearby lands of southern Asia. Indian merchants, who were called *banians*, used the trees for their market places — hence the name. A member of the mulberry family, the Banyan's small, red fruits, or figs are eaten by many kinds of animals and birds which spread the seeds. The tree's large, leathery, evergreen leaves are forage for elephants.

The Banyan tree of India has been introduced into sub-tropical regions of the world as an ornamental.

BAOBABS *(Adansonia digitata)* are odd trees that grow in the dry regions of central Africa. Although the trees are only 50 to 60 feet tall, their bulbous trunks are often 30 feet in diameter at the base, tapering rapidly to whorls of thick, horizontal branches. Cavities in their soft, spongy wood may be filled with water absorbed by their deep taproots. This water is used by the trees during the dry season, which usually starts in early March and lasts on into October.

The inner fibres of a Baobab's grey-brown wrinkled bark are used for rope and cloth. Its deciduous leaves resemble those of horse-chestnuts (see HORSECHESTNUTS), and its showy, creamy-white flowers, which smell like cantaloupes, develop into gourd-like fruits up to a foot in length. Each fruit contains about 30 kidney-shaped seeds embedded in a sticky pulp.

Baobabs belong to the cotton-tree family

BAOBABS

which includes the balsa (see BALSA) and other tropical trees with peculiar trunks, large showy flowers, or unusual fruits. The Silk Cotton-tree *(C. casearia)* of South America, the West Indies, and southern Asia, grows 100 feet tall and bears cucumber-like seed pods, 3 to 8 inches long. These contain kapok, the silky floss used as a stuffing for mattresses and sleeping bags. The massive trunk of the Silk Cotton-tree is studded with woody spines and has numerous plank-like roots that radiate from its swollen base. The thorny floss silktrees (*Chorisia* spp.), of Central and South America, are famed for large white, pink, or purple, lily-like flowers. A Brazilian species is commonly called Bottletree because its thick trunk often has a flask-like bulge. The Bongo *(Cavanillesia platanifolia)*, a large tree of Panama and Colombia, has wood lighter in weight even than the balsa's, although it is not used commercially in very large quantities. The Red Cotton-tree *(Bombax malibaricum)*, from the American and Asian tropics, resembles the Silk Cotton-tree in general appearance but bears showy crimson flowers about 4 inches across. The Guinea Chestnut *(Pachira aquatica)* of the American tropics has large pumpkin-like pods which contain edible seeds that look like chestnuts. Unlike other trees of this family, its seeds are not embedded in floss. Some members of the cotton-tree family are known as 'shaving brush trees' because their showy, colourful flowers look like brushes.

Buttresses supporting the Silk Cotton-tree or Ceiba may spread as far as 30 feet from the trunk.

BARLEY *(Hordeum vulgare)* is one of the oldest of cultivated plants. It was grown in ancient Egypt. Once barley was widely used for making bread, and it is still used in soups, breakfast foods, and infants' foods. Malt, prepared from partially sprouted barley that has been dried, is used in brewing and in other drinks, including malted milk. Its other use in Britain is as feed for livestock. A hardy grain, barley can be grown in the northern

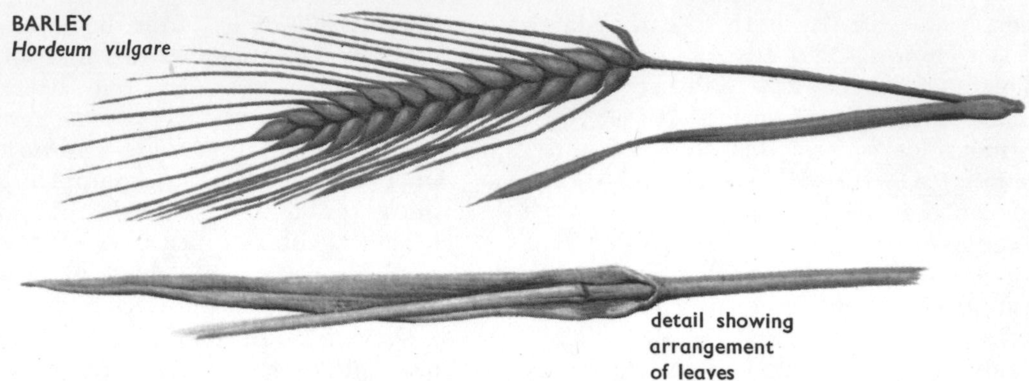

areas of Europe and Asia and also in the sub-tropical parts of Africa. (See CEREALS.)

BARYTES is a mineral that may occur as alternating red and grey layers of clay-like replacements; as coarsely crystalline veins and masses with lead, zinc, and silver ores; or as rosebud-like crystal clusters called 'desert or baryte roses'. Its crystals, which may be white, blue, brown, yellow, or other colours, have perfect cleavage in three directions.

'Desert Rose', a cluster of barytes crystals.

Barytes is added to drilling mud in oil wells to prevent blow-outs.

Shell Photographic Service

Barytes produces a yellow-green flame. Its streak is white, and its lustre, glassy or pearly.

Barytes is added to drilling mud in oil wells to prevent blow-outs from excess gas pressure. The Barytes also coats the sides of the well and helps to prevent cave-ins. Barytes is used also in making rubber, paper, oilcloth, leather, ceramics, magnesium, and a large amount is used as a white pigment (lithopone) in paint. Barytes increases the brilliance of glass.

Barytes is produced in northern England, Germany, Greece, the U.S.S.R., Japan, China, South Africa, Mexico and Nova Scotia. In the United States, it comes from Arkansas, Missouri, Nevada, Georgia, and Tennessee.

BASALT is a dark, fine-grained igneous rock. It is the commonest rock formed by hardened lava. Basalts are easily recognised by their high density, close texture, and dark green, grey or black colour. They are rich in iron, and weathering may change their colour to red or brown. The chief minerals in basalt are pyroxenes and feldspars. When large crystals (phenocrysts) of these minerals occur, the rocks are called basalt porphyry. Many

Northern Ireland Tourist Board

The Giant's Causeway, Co. Antrim, Northern Ireland is a striking example of six-sided basalt columns.

basalts are porous because gas bubbles were present when they hardened. If the openings were later filled with other minerals, such as calcite, quartz, and zeolites, they are called amygdaloidal basalts. Cinder-like basalt is known as basalt scoria. Basalt has a tendency to form six-sided columns on cooling. Such a phenomenon is well displayed at the Giant's Causeway in Antrim and at the famous Fingal's Cave on the Isle of Staffa. These columns can also be seen along the Columbia River in Oregon and in the Devil's Postpile National Monument in California.

Basalt appears in the dykes, sills, volcanic plugs, and old lava flows of western Scotland. Crushed basalt, called trap rock, is often used for surfacing road metal.

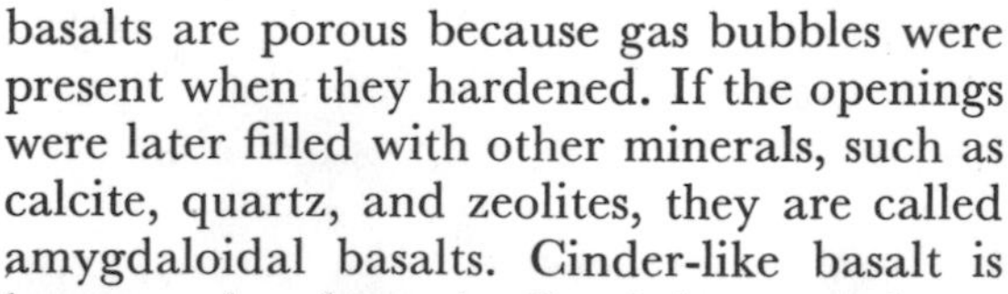

arid weathering

humid weathering

Basalt weathers to dark grey in dry climates and to brown in moist climates.

BEECHES (*Fagus* spp.) are stately, round-topped, deciduous trees found in cooler parts of Europe, Asia, and North America. Their distinctive grey bark is thin and smooth, even on large trunks. Their short-stemmed, oval, pointed leaves are 2-$3\frac{1}{2}$ inches long (up to 6 inches in some species), prominently veined and have toothed or wavy margins. In winter, spindle-shaped scaly buds over one inch long extend at a sharp angle from the twigs.

Beeches have hard, heavy, close-grained, reddish wood with qualities of strength and durability, but except for a limited use as underwater piles for small piers and jetties, it is unsuitable for outdoor use.

Beech wood is widely used for kitchen ware, butchers' blocks, tool handles, and in the past was used for the cogs of mill wheels. Today it is principally used in the manufacture of furniture and, in particular, chair legs, and other turned work. Beeches are also planted as ornamentals, and their nuts are eaten by man as well as by wild and domestic animals. Oil from the nuts is sometimes used in European countries for cooking.

The Common Beech *(Fagus sylvatica)* is found principally on well-drained soil overlying chalk, when it grows to a height of 100 feet or more. When it is found growing in a forest, it is invariably a tall and slender tree with a long central trunk and particularly narrow crown. In more open areas, the trunk grows short and thick; the crown broad and spreading. Beech trees are shallow rooting and cast dense shade, so that the forest floor is often devoid of undergrowth. In addition to its value for timber a number of species of beech are grown as ornamental trees, notably the purple-leaved or copper Beech.

Beeches belong to the same family as the chestnuts and oaks. (See OAKS). Also in the beech family are more than a dozen species known as Antarctic Beeches (*Nothofagus* spp.). These grow in parts of South America, Australia, and New Zealand. They resemble beeches of the Northern Hemisphere except for their smaller leaves, which are evergreen in some species.

Hornbeams, which are members of the birch family, are also known as Blue Beeches.

These are a smallish catkin-bearing tree.

Beech trees are best known for the glorious russet-colour of their leaves in autumn.

Picturepoint — London

BERRIES are fleshy fruits, the hard bodies enclosed being seeds. The fruits of cucumber, gooseberry, grape and tomato are berries with numerous seeds. The fruit of the date palm is a one-seeded berry, the familiar date 'stone' being a hard-coated seed. The 'stones' of cherries, plums and peaches are hard woody cases enclosing a seed (kernel).

The fruits of raspberries, loganberries, and blackberries are not true berries as the enclosed 'pips' are 'stones' encasing seeds. These 'stone' fruits are termed drupes. The fruits of the blackberry and strawberry are aggregates of drupes.

Raspberries and blackberries are native to Asia, Europe, and North America. Red Raspberries are grown chiefly in cool climates. Black Raspberries, an American development, grow in warmer climates. Harvested raspberries are hollow and thimble-like, as the central portion of the fruit remains attached to the plant. Blackberry bushes are quite thorny and grow either as upright bushes or as trailing vines. Blackberries are solid rather than hollow as the central core comes off when the fruit is picked.

The love apple or tomato *(Lycopersicum esculenteum)*, a native of western South America was introduced into Europe around 1596.

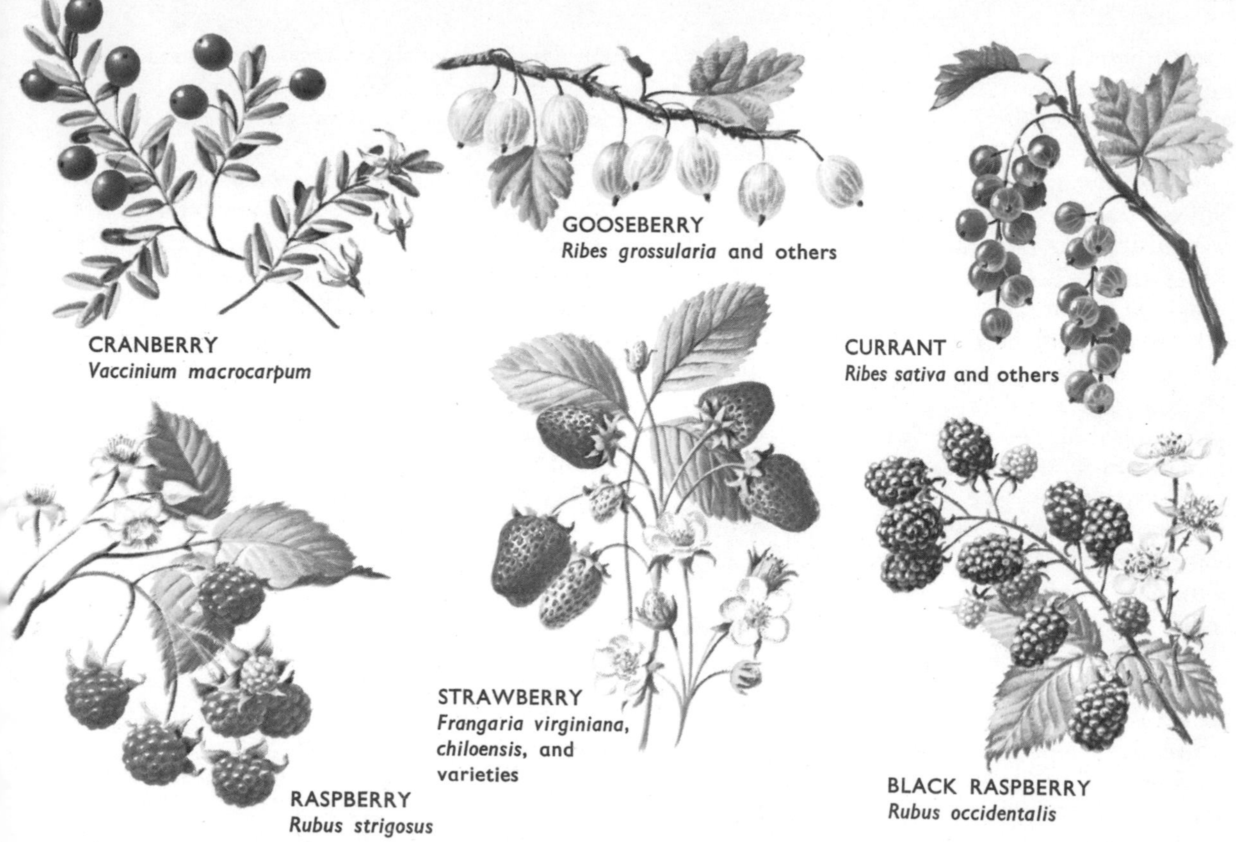

CRANBERRY
Vaccinium macrocarpum

GOOSEBERRY
Ribes grossularia and others

CURRANT
Ribes sativa and others

RASPBERRY
Rubus strigosus

STRAWBERRY
Frangaria virginiana, chiloensis, and varieties

BLACK RASPBERRY
Rubus occidentalis

Blueberry blossoms are pink and white. The fruit changes from white through red to blue when fully ripe.

Arnold M. Davis

COMMERCIAL CULTIVATION OF 'BERRIES'. Commercial strawberries *(Fragaria* spp.) developed from a chance cross-pollination of flowers of two species — the small Wild Strawberry *(Fragaria virginiana)* that grows in eastern North America and the Chilean Strawberry *(Fragaria chilbensis)*, also native to the Americas. English gardeners planted the two side by side, and the plants cross-pollinated. Many of the hybrids produced fruit of larger size, and these became the ancestors of the strawberries now produced by the strawberry industry. Many varieties have been produced for growing in various regions. These are the result of crossbreeding the two varieties of the same species. Strawberries are marketed both fresh and frozen and are used in jams, jellies, ice-cream pastries, and confectionery.

Cranberries *(Vaccinium macrocarpum)* were used by American Indians both as food and medicine. The vine-like shrubs grow in cool, swampy areas, and the berries are harvested by pulling a rake through the vines. Massachusetts, New Jersey, Wisconsin, Washington, and Oregon are the principal growing areas in the U.S.A. and growers have developed a number of varieties.

Blueberries (several species of *Vaccinium*) grow on low shrubs. Recently several large-fruited varieties have been developed and are cultivated. They are marketed fresh and frozen or are canned for use in pies, pastries, and jams or on ice-cream.

Currants and Gooseberries, related fruits of the genus *Ribes*, are popular in Europe. The tart fruits make fine flavoured pies, jams and jellies. Dried 'currants' are not true currants but are the dried fruit of a small type of grape.

Huckleberries *(Gaylussacia baccata)*, which contain several large bony seeds, are of minor commercial importance and are seldom marketed. They are used in the same manner as blueberries.

BERYL is a mineral consisting of beryllium, aluminium, silicon, and oxygen. It is found in six-sided crystals, some no longer than small needles and others as long as 18 feet. It also occurs in compact granular masses. Beryl has poor cleavage and a shell-like fracture. It is usually pale green or blue but may be almost any colour. Beryl is common

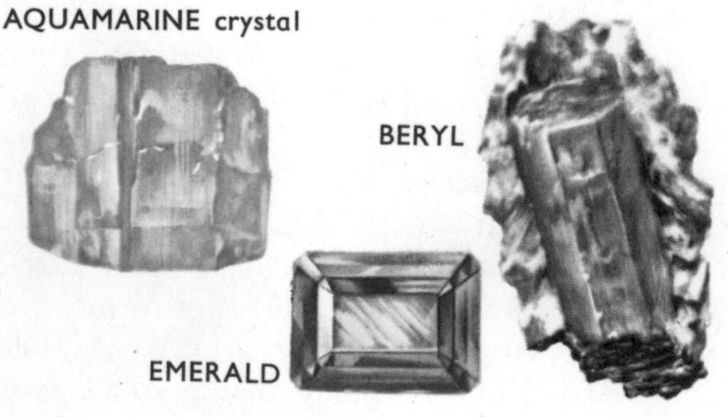

in such rocks as pegmatites, granites, schists, gneisses, marble, and slate. As one of the most important transparent gem stones, beryl is known by a variety of names depending on colour. Aquamarine is blue-green or blue; morganite, pale pink to rose-red; golden beryl, golden-yellow. Emerald, probably the most highly prized gem stone, is bright green. Unlike diamonds, emeralds are seldom found without flaws, cracks or bubbles. Emeralds come from Colombia, Brazil, the Ural Mountains of the U.S.S.R., and Ceylon. Other beryl gems come from Brazil, India, Ceylon, Ireland, and Germany.

Beryl is the only commercial source of beryllium, an increasingly important industrial metal. Small amounts of beryllium alloyed with copper, aluminium, iron, and other metals greatly increase their strength. These alloys also have more fatigue resistance, are harder, and resist corrosion. Beryllium alloys are used for springs and diaphragms in aircraft instruments, pressure gauges, moulds for precision casting of plastics, and contact points in electrical apparatus. Beryllium oxide will withstand very high temperature and may be used for lining rocket chambers or as a coating for rocket nose cones. Because they absorb neutrons slowly, beryllium and its alloys are used in nuclear power plants. Because of beryllium's non-sparking quality it is used in places where there may be danger of concentrations of explosive gases.

Leading producers of beryl for the metal are Brazil, Argentina, Rhodesia, and South-West Africa. Beryl is also produced in the United States in a number of states, such as South Dakota, Colorado, New Mexico, North Carolina, and Georgia.

BIRCHES (*Betula* spp.) grow in the cooler parts of the Northern Hemisphere. Most of the 40 species are small to medium-sized trees; some are shrubs. A few dwarf forms grow near the Arctic Circle or high on mountains. The Ground Birch is an important food for reindeer in Alaska. Oil of wintergreen is obtained from the bark and twigs of Sweet and Yellow birches of North America.

Birches have distinctive bark, attractive foliage, and hard, fine-grained wood used for furniture, cabinet work, veneer, and various wooden-ware products. It is also used to produce the smooth, white-wood finish on many forms of plywood and other laminated boards. Birch Bark varies in colour with different species from silver, greyish-white, orange, yellow and reddish brown and is usually marked with numerous horizontal slits or lenticels. Leaves of birches are deciduous, alternate, and long-stemmed. They may be round, oval, or roughly triangular, but they always have coarsely-toothed and

National Museum of Canada, Ottawa

Paper Bark Birch has been used to make this canoe.

occasionally deeply-cut margins. Birches are conspicuous in early spring because of their slender, tassel-like, pollen-bearing catkins. Small winged seeds are produced in compact 'cones'. These fall apart when the seeds are ripe. The Native Birch *(Betula pendula)* is a small, graceful, fast-growing tree with slender and often pendulous branches. While young trees have bronze bark, the bark of older trees is chalky-white and peels off in narrow, horizontal strips. The highly inflammable bark is ideal for starting camp-fires. Mature trees often grow to a height of 50—60 feet and a few species will reach 100 feet.

Birches will grow on a wide range of soils but show a marked preference for light sandy loams that are slightly acid. They are among the hardiest of trees and can be found at higher altitudes than any other tree.

The White Birch *(Betula pubesceus)* is the first tree to colonise areas on the edge of the Northern Ice Cap. Other birches include the Yellow Birch of north-eastern United States and south-eastern Canada; the River or Red Birch, found throughout the eastern United States, but most commonly in wet or swampy soils in the south; and the Canoe or Paper Bark Birch *(Betula papyrifera)*, so named because of the paper-white appearance of the bark which was used by the American Indians to build canoes. Three species native to Britain comprise two trees, the Silver Birch

PAPER BIRCH
Betula papyrifera
60—70 ft.

GREY BIRCH
Betula populifolia
20—40 ft.

SILVER BIRCH
Betula pendula
40—60 ft.

(B. pendula) noted for its white bark, and the Downy Birch *(B. pubescens)*, as well as one small shrub, the Dwarf Birch *(B. nana)*, confined almost entirely to the Highlands. (See ALDERS.)

BISMUTH. Bismuthinite is the most important mineral containing bismuth. It occurs in leafy masses associated with chalcopyrite and pyrite. It has one perfect cleavage and is white with a yellow tarnish. Bismuth, the native metal, occurs in layers or granular masses and has one perfect cleavage. It is red-white or silver-white and makes a shiny, lead-grey streak. Both are found in veins and are mined as by-products of silver, cobalt, tin, and other ores.

Bismuth is used in drugs, the manufacture of glass, and printing on cloth. Alloys of bismuth with tin, copper, and other metals have such a low melting point that some of them will melt in hot water. For this reason they are used in automatic sprinkler systems for fire protection and safety plugs in boilers. A small amount of bismuth added to molten iron makes the liquid more fluid; therefore, sharper, cleaner castings can be made. Bismuth is used in the manufacture of aluminium and stainless steel. It is also used in medicines, cosmetics, paints, fabric dyes, and in the manufacture of glass and ceramics.

Bismuth is obtained chiefly from South America, Australia and Mexico. In England, it occurs in Cornwall and Cumberland.

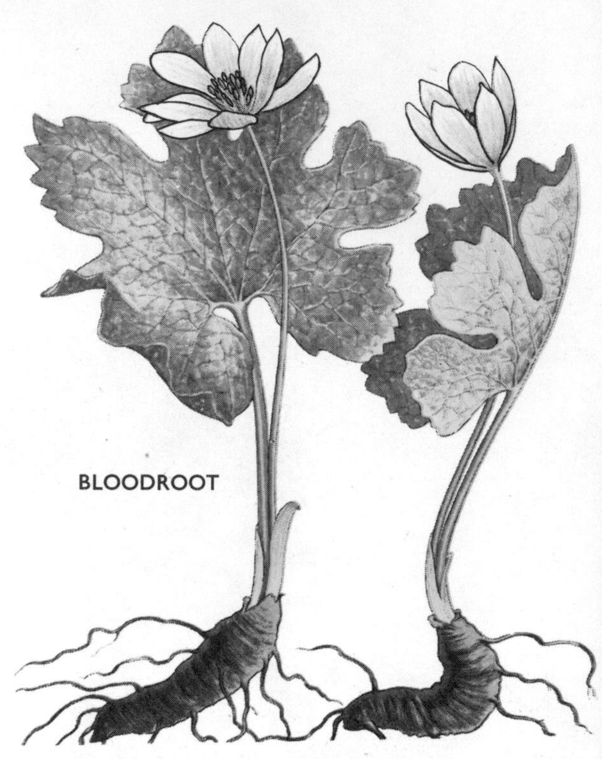

One of the favourite wild flowers of eastern North America.

BLOODROOT *(Potentilla tormentilla)*, a member of the rose family, is found in Britain in two forms. The small-flowered one is common on heaths and dry pastures; the larger flowered form is found in woods and hedges. The flowers of the bloodroot are yellow; its leaves which spring from the root

Bismuth has been used in the manufacture of the glass sides of this terrarium and the glass specimen jars shown here.

Roy Pinney

stock have either 3 or 5 oval leaflets. The name *tormentil* signifies this herb's power to relieve stomach gripes and toothache. It is also a safe and powerful aromatic astringent and because of its tonic properties has been called English Sarsaparilla. In the Western Isles of Scotland and in the Orkneys the roots were used for tanning leather. Laplanders also employed the thickened red juice of the root for staining leather red.

The common name of *Potentilla tormentilla* dates back to the medieval Doctrine of Signatures, which was an ingenious system for discovering from certain marks on the various portions of a plant's structure the supposed medicinal virtue attached to it. Bloodroot was derived from the red colour of its roots.

The American bloodroot, *Sanguinaria canadensis*, which is one of the favourite wild flowers of eastern North America is actually a member of the poppy family.

BLUE-GREEN ALGAE are the simplest of the algae and the most ancient of the chlorophyll-bearing plants. All are single-celled, although the cells often hang together in threads or form regular or irregular masses. Like bacteria, blue-green algae cells have no well-defined nuclei. In addition to green chlorophyll, they contain a blue pigment which gives them their name. Red and yellow pigments may be present also but are usually hidden by the green and blue. The Red Sea gets its red colour from a blue-green alga in which the red pigment is dominant.

Most blue-green algae are enclosed in a gelatinous sheath, and for this reason they are sometimes called 'slime algae'. They reproduce by fission — each cell simply splitting into two. Instead of storing their reserve food as starch as higher plants do, they store it as glycogen, sometimes called animal starch.

Blue-green algae are found in both fresh and salt waters. Some kinds grow in hot springs. They take lime from the water to form a porous, pastel-coloured rock called travertine. Other blue-green algae live in cold regions and can survive freezing for long periods. Some kinds grow in or on moist soil, and rich growths or 'blooms' sometimes form a film over the surface of pools or tanks of standing water and give colour to the water. In salt waters, especially in sheltered inlets, blue-green algae are often so abundant that they give the water a sulphur odour as they die and decay. In tropical and sub-tropical regions, they grow on roofs and walls, giving them a blackish, mildewed look. Other Kinds of algae give drinking water an unpleasant

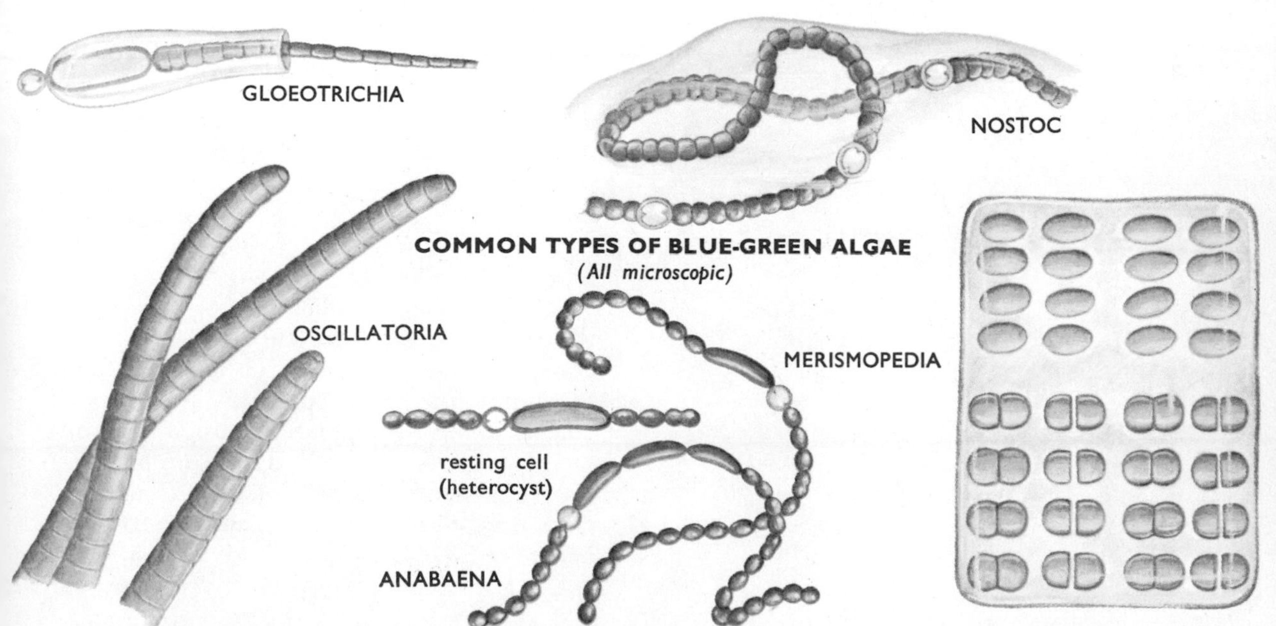

COMMON TYPES OF BLUE-GREEN ALGAE
(All microscopic)

odour or fishy taste. Livestock that drink from pools in which these algae are abundant may be poisoned.

Under the microscope, both *Nostoc* and *Anabaena*, two of the most common blue-green algae, look like strings of beads. Thousands of these filaments may be bound together in a gelatinous mass as big as a golf ball. In 1937 *Oscillatoria* and *Anabaena* 'blooms' directly contributed to the death of large numbers of trout in two Scottish lochs.

Gloeotrichia has a long tapering filament with a specialised dead cell (heterocyst) at the basal end. It also forms large thick-walled resting cells which permit it to survive conditions which are unfavourable for growth. *Merismopedia* grows as a flat colony of cells held together by a gelatinous mass. In *Gloeothece* the cells occur singly or are held in groups.

BLUEBELLS. Although there are several species of flower that may have the local name of bluebell given to them, we usually mean *Endymion non-scripta* — the wild bluebell of the woodlands on light acid soils in England where it is often the dominant spring flower.

The bluebell of Scotland is the wild harebell *(Campanula rotundifolia)* and is the national flower of the Scots.

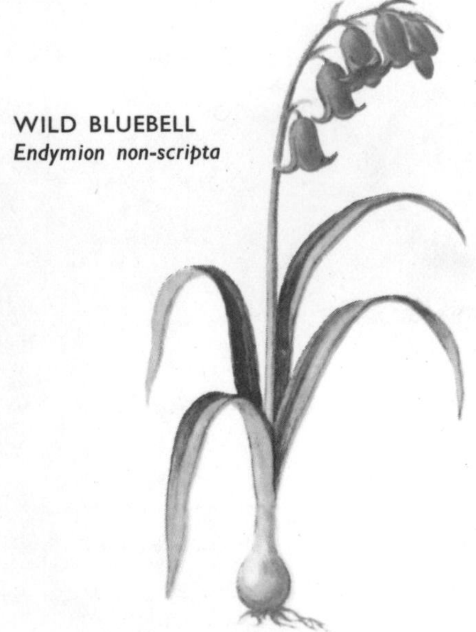

WILD BLUEBELL
Endymion non-scripta

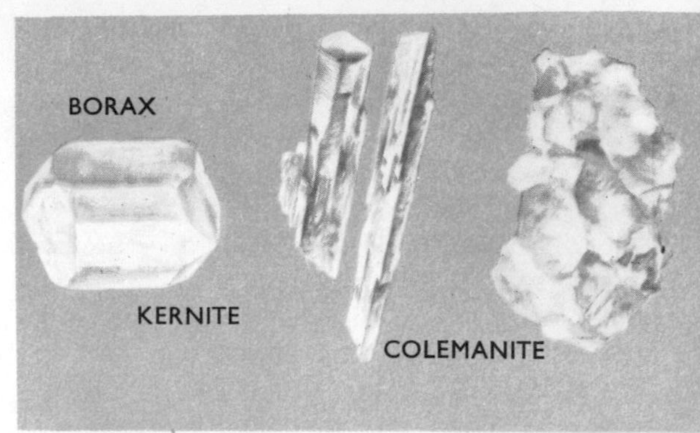

BORAX

KERNITE

COLEMANITE

BORAX. The white minerals from which boron is obtained originated from the evaporation of inland lakes. Borax, the most common, is powdery or occurs in prisms. It has a sweetish alkaline taste. *Ulexite*, also called cotton-ball borax, is found in round silky masses. Colemanite is found as crystals or in masses that resemble porcelain. Kernite, the principal source of commercial borax, occurs in fibrous masses.

Boron compounds are used in making glass and ceramics more durable, to absorb gases in electronic tubes, and in soaps, detergents, fungicides, fireproofing cloth, and fertilisers. Borax is also used as a water softener. Small amounts of boron increase the hardness, strength, elasticity, and workability of steel. Boron carbide is used as an abrasive. Boron absorbs neutrons, and so boron compounds are now used as shields in atomic reactors. Boron compounds are used in solid fuels for rockets and are added to petrol. Ninety per cent of the world's borax comes from the desert areas of western United States. Boron minerals also come from Argentina and Chile.

BOTANY is the scientific study of plants. Agriculture, forestry, and horticulture are aspects of applied botany that are concerned with the useful application of knowledge about plants and how they grow. Also included in the science of botany are plant taxonomy (the naming of plants), and ecology (the relationship of plants to their environment). Other specialised aspects are morphology (structure), physiology (function), embryology (development), and genetics (inheritance). Botanists may study only a particular group of plants. A mycologist, for example, is a specialist in the study of fungi, and a dendrologist specialises in the study of woody plants. Botany and zoology together comprise the science of biology, which treats all aspects of living things.

BOTTLE-TREES (*Sterculia represtre,* also known as *Brachychiton),* are members of the tropical cocoa or chocolate family. About 60 feet tall, they have bottle-shaped trunks. Often 6 feet in diameter at the base, the trunks taper rapidly to narrow 'necks'. Their heavy, wide-spreading branches bear narrow, willow-like leaves that are sometimes used as fodder for cattle. The leaves on 'sucker' branches are lobed. Loose flower clusters develop into oval, beaked pods. The light spongy wood, though little used, is much like balsa wood (see BALSA). Bottle-trees grow in the grassy plains of Queensland, Australia. The Kurrajong (*Starculia diversifolia,* syn. *B. populnea*) grows in dry regions of Australia and its foliage is used as fodder for cattle. The Flame-tree *(Sterculia acerifolium)* is planted as an ornamental and is only fully hardy in the Scilly Isles. Clusters of scarlet, bell-shaped flowers massed on naked branches, appearing after the leaves fall, give the tree its name.

In the dry season, Bottle-trees use the water stored in the spongy wood of their flask-shaped trunks.

Baobabs and other floss silk trees are also called 'bottle-trees' (see BAOBABS).

BOUGAINVILLEA (*Bougainvillea* spp.) is a brilliantly coloured semi-tropical vine. Its name commemorates Louis Antoine de Bougainville (1729—1811), the first Frenchman to cross the Pacific Ocean.

Originally a South American tropical vine, Bougainvillea is sometimes cultivated for porch coverings and trellises or for decorating the sides of buildings in warm climes, and can be trained as a shrub or grown as a hedge. It is a woody plant with occasional thorns. The leaves are simple and oval. They alternate on the stems.

In warm climates, bougainvilleas bloom the year-round.

Arnold M. Davis

The true flowers of Bougainvillea (boo-gin-VIL-ee-uh) are small and white. They are hidden in brightly coloured, purplish-red modified leaves, or bracts, which are often mistaken for parts of the flower. They like full sunshine and cannot tolerate much cold or freezing weather.

BREADFRUIT *(Artocarpus communis),* a melon-sized tropical fruit, has been cultivated in the South Pacific since ancient times. The starchy cream-coloured pulp is eaten raw or is cooked — fried, boiled, or baked. Dried pulp is made into flour. One kind of breadfruit

Barnaby's Picture Library

Breadfruit is part of the staple diet in the South Pacific tropics.

has seeds that resemble chestnuts, but the most commonly eaten breadfruit is seedless. Round or oval in shape, it is 4 to 10 inches in diameter and has a rough skin that becomes greenish-brown or yellow when the fruit is ripe.

Captain William Bligh's ill-fated voyage on the *Bounty* began because of the glowing reports about the food value of breadfruit. Sir Joseph Banks first saw the breadfruit in Tahiti when he accompanied Captain Cook on his first voyage round the world. Later he suggested that the breadfruit be introduced to the West Indies, where it could become a cheap food for Negro slaves. The *Bounty* sailed to Tahiti where the length of time needed to raise seedlings led to the demoralisation of the *Bounty's* crew, the famous mutiny and consequent abandonment of the prized seedlings. Bligh managed to return to England and later, in 1793, commanded a more successful expedition. The Breadfruit tree was established in Jamaica and spread throughout the West Indies, Mexico, and Brazil. It has never become as popular as Plantain and Common Bananas in those areas, however, but continues to be an important food where it grows naturally in the East Indies. It often becomes a dense-leafed, spreading tree 60 feet tall.

BROWN ALGAE have a brown pigment in addition to green chlorophyll. They vary in colour from dark green to light or dark brown. Brown algae are all marine and are commonly called seaweeds. All are big enough to be seen without a lens, and some grow several hundred feet in length. The largest are the kelps (see KELPS). Most of the nearly 900 species are found in cool, fairly shallow seas.

Some are exposed at low tides; others are always submerged. Many grow attached to rocks, and some of the larger kinds have air bladders that serve as floats.

Brown algae are found in tropic, temperate, and arctic seas. *Fucus* or Bladder Wrack is a common seaweed with Y-shaped branches. It grows attached to rocks by a root-like holdfast. Small air bladders keep it afloat at high tide. *Fucus* grows in cool seas all over the world. *Fucus* reproduces sexually; the sperms and eggs are produced on different plants.

Sargassum, which takes its name from the Spanish *sargazo* meaning 'floating seaweed', is found in warm seas. An abundance of this seaweed in the North Atlantic forms the Sargasso Sea (see SARGASSUM). *Sargassum* has branched leaf-like blades on which there are smaller branches with air bladders that keep the seaweed floating. There are a number of species of *Dictyota*. Each is a narrow flat ribbon that also has Y-shaped branches but lacks air bladders such as found in *Fucus*. *Padina*, sometimes called the Potatochip Seaweed, is a thin, rounded plant with concentric zones of light and dark areas.

Bladder Wrack, or Rockweed, a widely distributed brown alga found along the shores of cool seas, has swollen air bladders along the main stem.

BUTTERCUPS (*Ranunculus* spp.) are best known as cheerful golden flowers that grow in wet meadows, pastures, and along streams in temperate parts of Europe, Asia, and North America. Even in cities the yellow blooms turn up on lawns.

Buttercups have alternate leaves often divided into leaflets. The flowers have five parts with many yellow stamens at the centre. The little white flowers seen floating on the surface of some ponds are the lacy-leafed Water Buttercup or Water Crowfoot. Their hard seeds are eaten by many water birds. The beautiful cut flowers which florists sell as Ranunculus are also buttercups. These large, showy flowers, available in winter or early spring, may be blue, purple, red, or white. Creeping Buttercup, a native of Europe and Asia, is a pernicious weed in our gardens. A number of buttercups contain a chemical which is poisonous to cattle. Fortunately this substance is destroyed when the plant is dried in haymaking.

Another common yellow buttercup that grows in lawns and meadows is called the Bulbous Buttercup because of its swollen bulb-like base.

CABBAGE and its relatives are excellent examples of how different varieties of plants can be developed from one species. Broccoli, Cauliflower, Cabbage, Brussels Sprouts, Collards, Kale, and Kohl Rabi were all derived from the Wild Cabbage *(Brassica oleracea)*, which is native to the Mediterranean region.

Cauliflower and Broccoli *(Brassica oleracea* var. *botrytis cauliflora)* are the only common vegetables that produce edible flowers. Cauliflower, sometimes called the aristocrat of the cabbage family, has been cultivated in the

Members of the cabbage family have edible buds (Broccoli), blossoms (Cauliflower), stems (Chinese Cabbage), roots (Kohl Rabi), and leaves (Kale, Cabbage, and Collards).

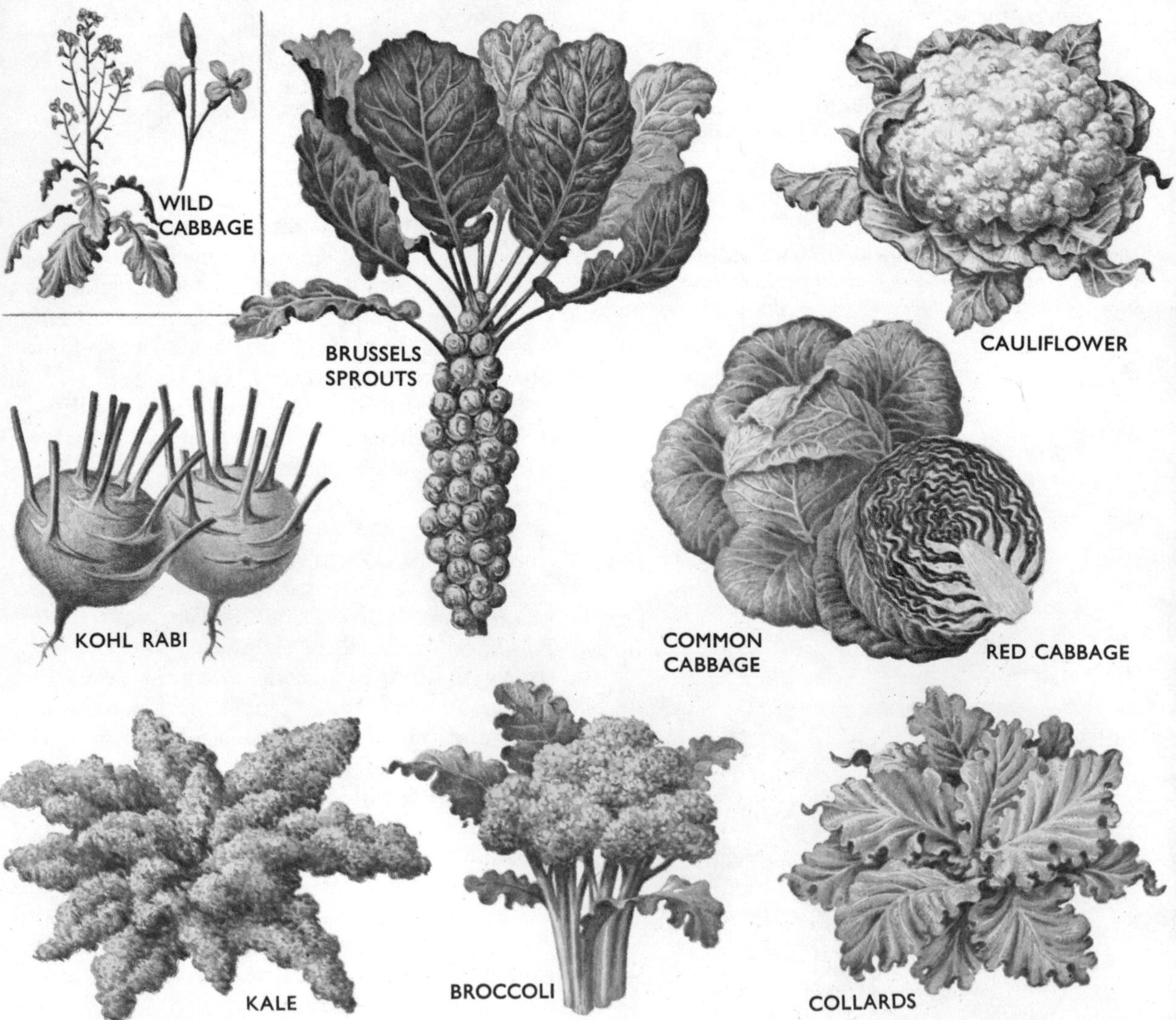

Near East since before the time of Christ. Its under-developed fleshy white flowers are a very popular vegetable, both fresh and to a lesser degree as a pickled product.

Broccoli, *(Brassica oleracea* var. *cymosa)* grown for its under-developed thick green flowers, was known to the Romans.

Kohl Rabi *(Brassica oleracea* var. *gongyloides)* is grown for its large round stems which may be white or purple. Kohl Rabi is a German name that means 'cabbage turnip', for the flavour of the vegetable is much like turnips. This vegetable originated recently in northern Europe and is not popular yet in Great Britain.

Kale *(Brassica oleracea* var. *acephala)* is served as a boiled vegetable and is recommended highly by experts on nutrition as a good source of minerals and vitamins.

Brussels Sprouts *(Brassica oleracea* var. *gemmifera)* is a tall-stemmed cabbage that develops small, cabbage-like heads (buds) called 'sprouts' along the stems at the base of the leaves. This vegetable, developed within the last few centuries in northern Europe, became popular early in the Brussels, Belgium, area — hence its name.

Cabbages *(Brassica oleracea* var. *capitata)* have a short stem with overlapping leaves that form a head resembling a gigantic bud. The leaves may be relatively smooth and form a solid head as in Common Cabbage or may be curled and form a loose head as in Savoy Cabbage. Leaves of Common Cabbage may be green or purple. This vegetable was introduced to Europe by the Romans or Celts.

CACAO *(Theobroma cacao)* is a tropical American tree that produces the seeds from which cocoa and other chocolate products are made. The Aztec and Mayan Indians of Mexico and Central America drank chocolate long before the discovery of the New World. Montezuma, the great Aztec emperor, is said to have consumed many jugs of chocolate drink every day. Cacao seeds or 'beans' were valued so highly they were used as currency. Spanish explorers introduced a sweetened version of the beverage to Europe.

Cacao trees are cultivated in many tropical regions. Most of the world's supply is grown in Ghana and Nigeria in western Africa.

Nestles

A workman cuts the cacao pod from the tree.

Some of the finest cacao is raised in Costa Rica, Nicaragua and Brazil.

Cacao trees range from 15 to 30 feet in height. Those grown on plantations are protected from the wind and sun by taller trees. The flowers and fruit appear in areas known as flowering pads or cushions on the trunk and limbs. The fruit is a pod-like capsule 6 to 9 inches long and half as thick. When ripe it is yellow, red, or maroon. Each fruit contains as many as 25 to 35 seeds embedded in a sticky pulp. The seeds are either sun-dried or artificially dried and then shipped to processing plants.

In processing plants, the initial steps are the same for making both chocolate and cocoa. The beans are first cleaned and roasted. Roasting helps develop their flavour and aroma and also makes them easier to grind. After they are roasted, the beans are run

Cacao pods grow directly from the trunk of the tree. Seeds are separated from the fleshy pulp and dried for processing.

through a machine which cracks them. The hulls or shells are blown away, leaving only the kernels, called 'nibs'. These are ground, and the heat of the grinding melts the cocoa fat they contain. The fat combined with the solid is known as chocolate liquor or cacao-mass.

To make cocoa, the cacao-mass is put in a hydraulic press to squeeze out most of the fat. The fat is called cocoa butter. The compressed cake is broken into small pieces, pulverised, sifted, and packaged for sale as cocoa.

To make chocolate, the cacao-mass is combined with sugar and cocoa butter. Milk chocolate is made by adding condensed or powdered milk. Salt, vanilla, and other flavourings may also be added. Chocolate is a valuable quick-energy food. When mixed with milk, its food value is increased. During World War II chocolate was included in the emergency rations of soldiers. Chocolate contains a mild stimulant (theobromine), similar to the caffeine in coffee.

CACTI *(Cactaceae)* have unusual beauty of form as well as lovely, fragrant flowers. This well-known family includes 2,000 or more species. All are natives of North America except a few that are found in West Africa. Many fleshy plants with thorns are not cacti.

SENITA CACTUS
Cereus schottii
4—8 ft.

SAGUARO
Carnegiea gigantea
to 40 ft.

PURPLE TINGE PEAR
Opuntia gosseliniana
1½—4 ft.

ENGLEMANN'S PEAR
Opuntia engelmannii
1½—5 ft.

HEDGEHOG CACTUS
Echinocereus fendleri
1—1½ ft.

BARREL CACTUS
Echinocactus wislizenii
1—6 ft.

Cacti grow in arid places where few other plants can survive. They store precious water in their thick, leafless, green stems, and their sharp spines ward off the hungry or thirsty desert animals. Most kinds bear fruits which can be eaten by animals and by man. Cacti have very small leaves that often fall soon after they form. The usual work of the leaves is done by the fleshy green stems.

Prickly pears are an especially widespread group of cacti. Their flattish, spiny branches — called 'slabs' — bear pink or yellow flowers which are followed by edible fruits known as 'tunas'. The slabs are sometimes chopped up for cattle food. Other common kinds of cacti include the barrel, pincushion, organ-pipe, and cholla types.

Outstanding among these remarkable desert plants is the Giant Cactus or Saguaro (sa-WAH-ro), said to live as long as 250 years. Its stately, fluted trunks, with candelabra-like branches, stand like giant sentinels in the arid south-west of the United States. Desert woodpeckers and owls nest in holes bored into the stems.

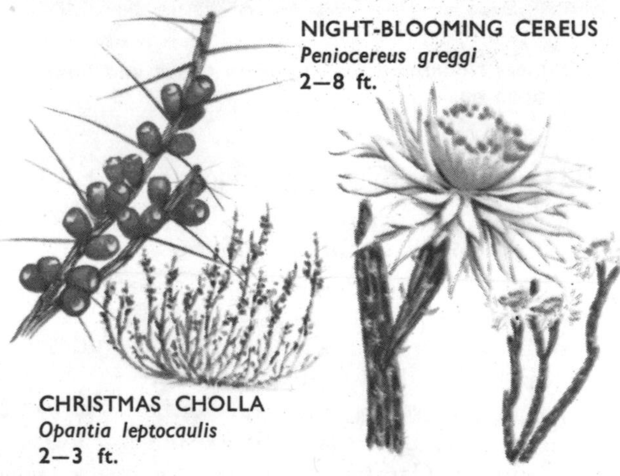

NIGHT-BLOOMING CEREUS
Peniocereus greggi
2–8 ft.

CHRISTMAS CHOLLA
Opantia leptocaulis
2–3 ft.

CALCITE, one of the most common and useful of all minerals, is easily recognised by its excellent crystals, glassy lustre, and vigorous effervescence (bubbling) in acids. Even vinegar is a strong enough acid to make calcite bubble. In Iceland spar, a transparent colourless calcite, double refraction can be seen without a microscope; that is, a line or a dot appears as two lines or dots when looked at through the calcite. It is used in the manufacture of optical instruments.

Josef Muench

Stalactites (from roof of cave) and stalagmites (from floor) consist of calcite. Water percolating down through the strata above picks up calcium carbonate in solution. The calcite is deposited in icicle form as the water evaporates in the cave.

Calcite occurs everywhere but is not common in igneous rocks. It dissolves in water containing carbon dioxide (rain water) and remains in solution as calcium bicarbonate as long as there is an excess of carbon dioxide. Waters containing large amounts of calcium bicarbonate are called hard. Plants growing in water use carbon dioxide and cause calcite to be deposited. Soap does not lather well and forms curds in hard water. Lime deposits form in hot-water pipes and in kettles, because calcite is precipitated by an increase in temperature. In water-treatment plants calcite is added to hard water to remove the dissolved calcite. The added calcite attracts the excess carbon dioxide that holds the bicarbonate in solution and causes calcite to be precipitated. Evaporation also causes calcite to precipitate. Stalactites and stalagmites are a form of travertine that occur in caves as a result of evaporation. Limestone, a widely distributed rock, consists mainly of dull-lustred varieties of calcite. Calcite in the form of limestone is used as building stone, in road

ICELAND SPAR
transparent calcite

DOGTOOTH SPAR

CALCITE TWINNED CRYSTALS

CALCITE SAND CRYSTALS
quartz sand cemented with calcite

construction, and in the manufacture of cement. In smelting iron, calcite makes the slag more fluid. As marble, calcite occurs in a wide variation of pleasing colours and takes a fine polish. Calcite is made into lime for use in agriculture to neutralise acid soils.

Tufa is a porous deposit of calcite that accumulates where spring water highly charged with calcium bicarbonate comes to the surface. Objects are often left at such springs, for a small sum, to become so encrusted; an example is found at Knaresborough in Yorkshire. (See LIMESTONE.)

Calcite is used in the manufacture of cement, so necessary for modern construction work like this dam.

Ray Atkeson

Ward's Natural Science Establishment

Trilobites flourished in Cambrian times and have long been extinct.

CAMBRIAN PERIOD. This period of Earth's history began about 510 million years ago and ended about 500 million years ago. It was named after Cambria, the old Roman name for Wales, where rocks of this age were first described. Cambrian rocks are the oldest in which abundant fossils are found.

All major groups of animals without backbones (invertebrates) were in existence before the end of Cambrian times, but life was apparently confined to the seas. Most abundant were small brachiopods or lamp shells and trilobites. Trilobites were enormously varied. Most were about 2 inches in length. Some were only an eighth of an inch long, however, and the largest grew to 18 inches. Many had long spines, giving them a rather shaggy appearance; others were oval and nearly smooth. Among other Cambrian animals were primitive sponges, snails, worms, jellyfish, and echinoderms. There were also various kinds of seaweeds.

All creatures of the Cambrian were simple compared to their present-day descendants, yet they were far from being as primitive as might be expected for the oldest fossils. One of the riddles of geology is the lack of fossil ancestors in the Pre-Cambrian rocks. Most geologists now believe that Pre-Cambrian animals were soft-bodied creatures largely unknown as fossils because they lacked the hard parts usually essential to form fossils.

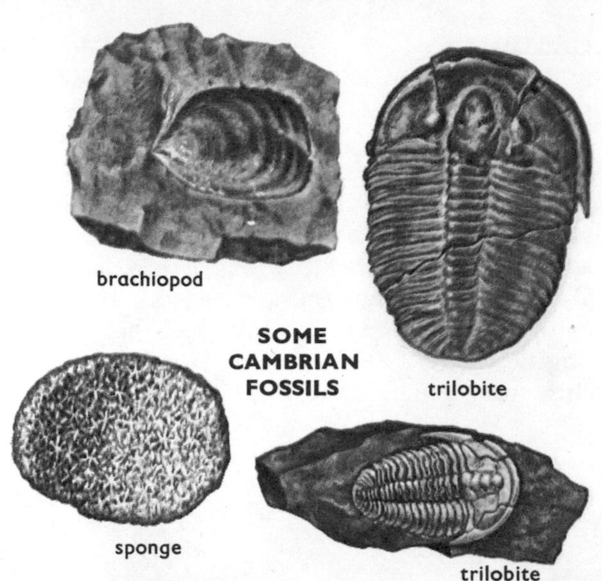

SOME CAMBRIAN FOSSILS

All life in Cambrian times was confined to the sea. Seaweeds or algae grew in profusion, and there were representatives of all major animal groups (phyla) without backbones. Most common were the brachiopods (1) and the now-extinct trilobites (2), jellyfish (3) and various kinds of sponges (4 & 6), some of which are still in existence. Snails or gastropods (5) appeared, too, in Cambrian times.

CAMPHOR, a white crystalline substance, is extracted from the Camphor tree *(Cinnamomum camphora)*, a close relative of the tree from which cinnamon is obtained. Camphor trees are natives of Formosa, Japan, and China, but have been introduced into many other tropical and sub-tropical regions, such as Italy, India, Africa, Ceylon, Florida, and California. A common and very wasteful method of obtaining camphor consists of cutting down the tree. The wood is reduced to chips and ground up with the leaves and

then distilled. A better method is to harvest and extract the camphor from the leaves twice a year. Camphor is used mainly in the manufacture of plastics, photographic film, medicines, perfumes, and insecticides. Camphor is now produced in quantity from turpentine.

CANDYTUFTS (*Iberis* spp.) are a group of wild and cultivated plants that are familiar in Europe and America. The 'tuft' part of the name comes from the plants' rather tufted growth. The 'candy' comes from Candia, which is the ancient name for the Mediterranean island of Crete. More than 40 kinds of candytufts grow wild on Crete and on nearby islands. Nearly 400 years ago seeds of these wild candytufts were sent to England. Now these beautiful low-growing plants with flat-topped flowers are popular ornamentals in many parts of the world. Some are annuals; others are perennials. Often they are used in rock gardens. Their blossoms are white and various shades of red and purple. The larger individual blossoms are always at the outside edge of the flower clusters.

Candytufts are closely related to Sweet

CANDYTUFTS

Alyssum, which they resemble. Both belong to the mustard family. All members of this family have flowers with only four petals and their seeds are in pods.

CARBON CYCLE. Carbon is one of the chemical elements essential to life. It is a part of all basic foods (proteins, fats, and carbohydrates) and all other organic compounds. Because of the carbon cycle, the carbon in the bodies of plants and animals today is the same carbon that was used by plants and animals millions of years ago.

About 6 tons of carbon in the form of carbon dioxide (CO_2) are in the air over each acre of the Earth's surface. Each year the plants on an acre of land withdraw as much as 20 tons of carbon from the air in the manufacture of food as they grow. Animals eat the plants and return much carbon to the air as carbon dioxide, which they exhale in breathing. Decay bacteria and fungi convert

CARBON CYCLE

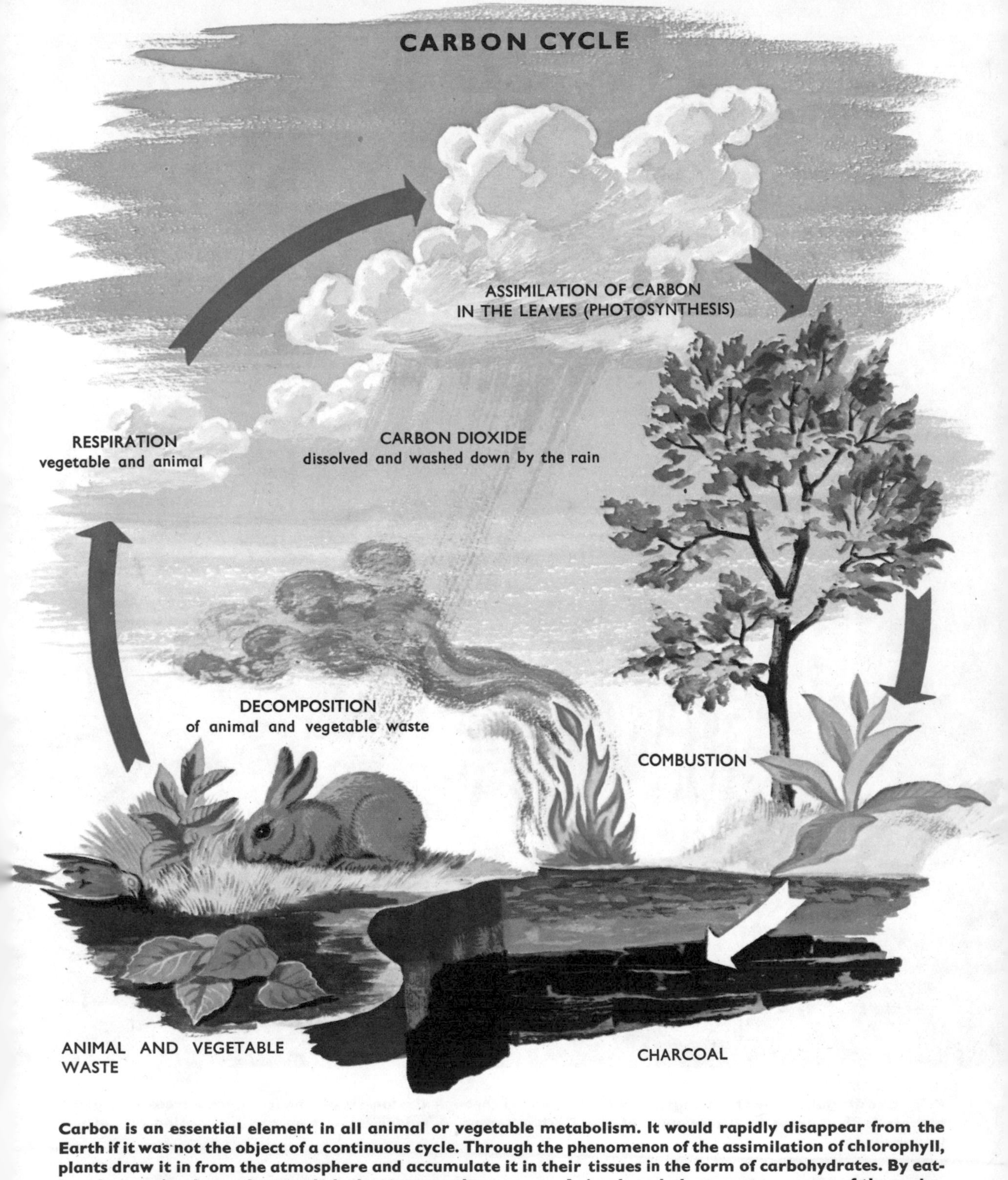

ASSIMILATION OF CARBON
IN THE LEAVES (PHOTOSYNTHESIS)

RESPIRATION
vegetable and animal

CARBON DIOXIDE
dissolved and washed down by the rain

DECOMPOSITION
of animal and vegetable waste

COMBUSTION

ANIMAL AND VEGETABLE
WASTE

CHARCOAL

Carbon is an essential element in all animal or vegetable metabolism. It would rapidly disappear from the Earth if it was not the object of a continuous cycle. Through the phenomenon of the assimilation of chlorophyll, plants draw it in from the atmosphere and accumulate it in their tissues in the form of carbohydrates. By eating plants animals use these carbohydrates to produce energy. Animals and plants restore some of the carbohydrates to the atmosphere by respiration: the remainder return to the soil in the form of dead vegetable matter and excrement or animal carcases. The decomposition of these produces carbon gas which returns to the atmosphere. Sometimes vegetable debris accumulates in the subsoil and is transformed into peat or charcoal, and when this is burnt it gives off more oxides of carbon. Finally, it should be noted that numerous other elements may be introduced into the cycle.

Primitive dragonflies with a wingspan of 2½ feet soared through the forests of tree ferns, scale trees, and giant horsetails that grew in the swamps of the Carboniferous. A spider in its web and a scorpion are in the foreground.

the carbon in the bodies of dead plants and animals into carbon dioxide, also returning it to the air. This cycle of borrowing carbon from the air and returning it for use again and again is endless.

CARBONIFEROUS. This period, named after the great coal deposits which its upper part contains in many areas, began about 345 million years ago and lasted about 65 million years. In North America it is divided into two periods: Mississippian (from the limestone bluffs along the Mississippi River) and Pennsylvanian (from Pennsylvania). In many parts of North America and Europe, Mississippian times were marked by warm, shallow limestone seas in which brachiopods or lamp shells, corals, sea lilies, blastoids, bryozoans, foraminifera (protozoans), and algae lived. There were reefs in places. In some other areas sandstonea and shale were deposited.

On the land amphibians increased in numbers and diversity. Some of the labyrinthodonts were 10 feet long. Land plants included scale trees up to 150 feet tall, ferns, and seed ferns. These were the forerunners of the great coal-forming forests of later Pennsylvanian times. The oldest known reptiles are of Pennsylvanian age. Clams and fishes abounded in streams and bays, and on the land there were cockroaches, spiders, scorpions, and dragonfly-like insects with wing-spreads of 30 inches.

Pennsylvanian forests grew on low-lying swamps and deltas that were periodically flooded by the sea. When the sea invaded, sediments were laid over the decayed vegetation. Eventually the sea retreated and the process was repeated. The Ganges delta is an example of a modern 'coal forest', although the trees are not the same as in Carboniferous times. (See COAL; FERNS.)

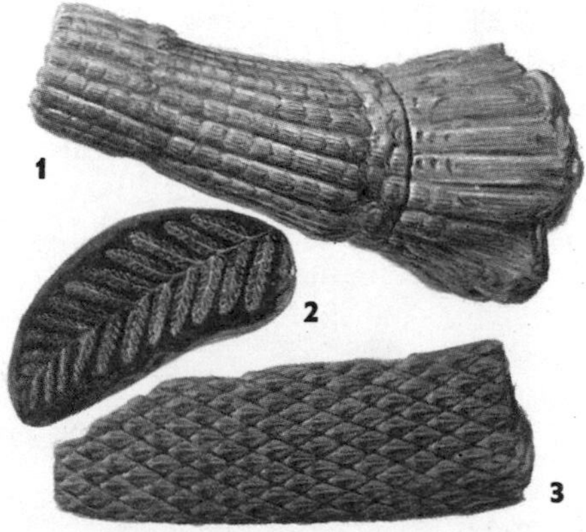

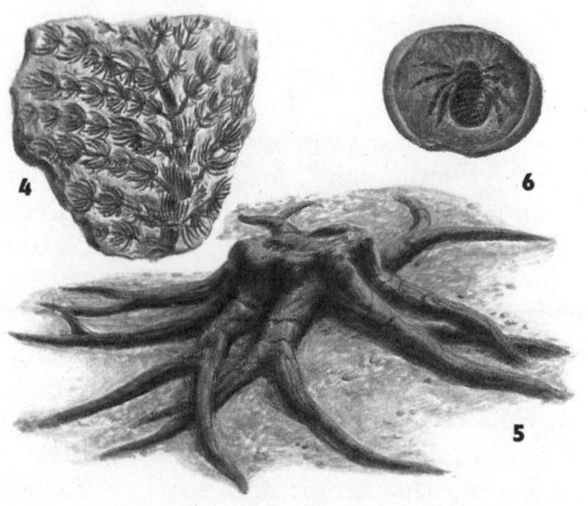

Dense forests of giant non-flowering plants grew in the swampy lowlands of the Carboniferous. Fossil remains include: (1) part of a trunk of a giant scouring rush, (2) the frond of a fern, (3) bark from a scale tree, (4) the whorls of leaves from a rush, and (5) the spreading roots of a scale tree. Among the land-dwelling animals were (6) primitive spiders as well as insects, scorpions, and centipedes.

CARNATIONS (*Dianthus* spp.) are popular flowers grown extensively in commercial greenhouses. They can be found in florist shops at any season of the year. They have long stems, beautiful colour and form and they keep well. Most carnations have a spicy, clove-like fragrance, so another name for them is Clove Pink. There are many varieties.

Carnations have been cultivated for about 20 centuries. They came from a rather plain

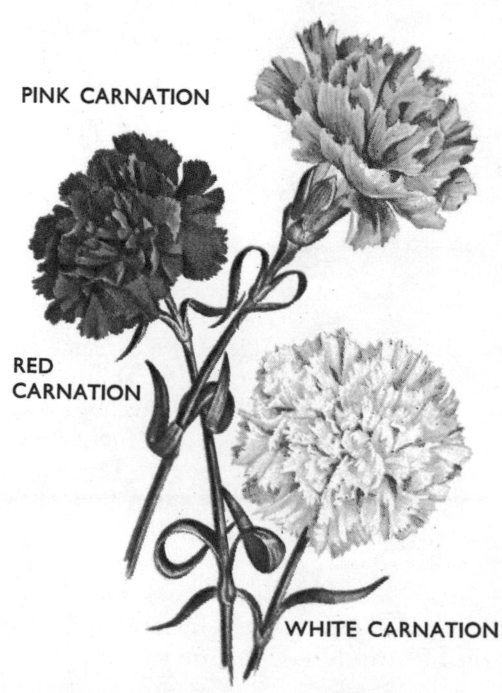

looking species that grows wild in the Mediterranean region. Some 200 kinds of wild carnations are known. The flesh-coloured flowers of the European wild plant were the basis of the name carnation, for *carnis* means flesh in Latin. Besides red, pink, and white or combinations of these colours, carnation blossoms can now be seen in yellow, orange, and purple. A good blue carnation may be developed some time in the future.

Many smaller members of the carnation group are called pinks. Some of these dainty, free-flowering pinks are pleasantly scented and are popular in gardens. Most pinks are natives of Asia or Europe. The old-fashioned garden favourite, Sweet William or Bunch Pink, belongs to this group. Its small, variously coloured flowers are borne in flattish clusters.

CAROB TREES *(Ceratonia siliqua)* are natives of the eastern Mediterranean and members of the pea family (see PEA FAMILY). This tree has been of interest and value since ancient times. It has evergreen, pinnately compound leaves with shiny, oval leaflets. Clusters of small red flowers develop into pulpy, bean-like pods (4 to 12 inches long) that are rich in sugar and protein. These pods are a valuable food and are eaten by man as well as by many lower animals. They are often referred to as Locust Beans. It is said that these pods sustained the Prodigal Son and served as food for John the Baptist during his wanderings in the desert.

The Carob tree thrives only in warm climates. It is planted in sheltered sites in parts of Cornwall and the west country but elsewhere requires greenhouse protection. The Carob tree is able to survive long periods of drought. For this reason it is a valuable tree for planting in arid regions where soil erosion is a problem.

Each Carob tree develops either male or female flowers, never both. In regions where the fruit is an important crop, female branches are grafted on to male trees. Some trees bear fruit for 100 years. Most of the Carobs for commercial use are grown on the Island of Cyprus, in the Mediterranean Sea.

CARROTS *(Daucus carota)*. The carrot is a hardy biennial native of Europe including Britain, and long cultivated in lands bordering the eastern Mediterranean. Like beets, carrots produce flowers and seeds only in their second year. They are usually harvested a few months after planting. The most familiar varieties in this country have deep orange or orange-red roots. The colour is due to the pigment carotene, an excellent source of vitamin A. Carrots are also rich in sugar. The best carrots are grown on sandy loam such as that found in parts of Norfolk, Worcestershire, Kent, Surrey and Shropshire.

Carrots are members of the parsley family.

CASHEWS are trees native to tropical America but of greater commercial importance in India and other tropical areas. The Cashew

CASHEW NUT

(Anacardium occidentale) is a straggling evergreen tree that may grow 30 feet tall. Its pink flowers, like those of the related mango (see MANGO), occur in short clusters.

Cashew fruits are very unusual. The true fruit — or so-called cashew nut — projects from the end of the cashew 'apple' and contains a single seed. The apple itself is bright red or yellow and can be eaten fresh or made into jams or wines and other beverages. An oil extracted from the shell is used in manufacturing such items as varnishes and floor tiles. The oil is irritating to the skin.

CATMINT *(Nepeta cataria)* is grown in many parts of the world for its aromatic leaves and stems used in tonics. The odour of Catmint attracts cats — hence the name — and a preparation from the dried plants is used by trappers to lure animals. It stands about 2—3 feet tall and bears clusters of purple or white flowers. A member of the mint family, it has square stems, and its flowers and soft leaves are often covered with whitish hairs. Catmint is a native of Britain occurring as a wayside plant in calcareous districts. More than 150 species are included in the genus. Several species are cultivated as edging plants.

CEDAR is the name used most commonly for several species of trees.

Although no true cedars, trees which are members of the large pine family, are actually native to the British Isles, there do exist various kinds which have been planted as ornamentals.

True cedars (*Cedrus* spp.) are large, handsome trees with dense tufts of evergreen, needle-like foliage. Their barrel-shaped cones (3 to 4 inches) stand upright on the branches and fall apart when mature (in about two years). The Deodar Cedar, a valuable timber tree of the Himalayas, has a thick crown of long, downswept branches and a slender, nodding tip. The Lebanon Cedar of Asia Minor was an important source of wood in Biblical times. We know, for example, that Solomon's temple was built mainly from wood of the Lebanon Cedar. Only remnants of the once-large forests of Lebanon Cedars

CATMINT

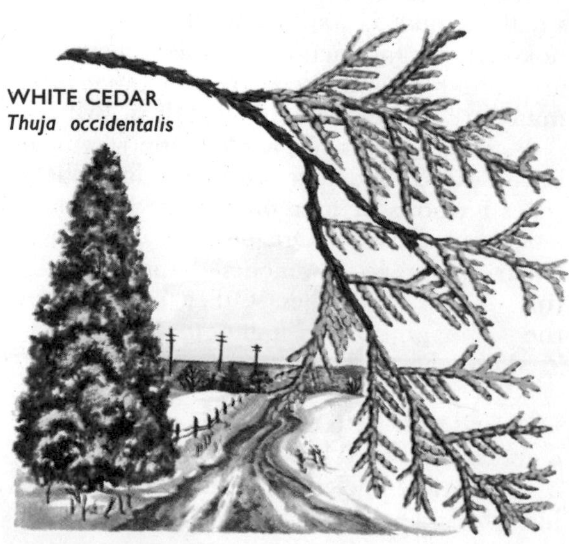

WHITE CEDAR
Thuja occidentalis

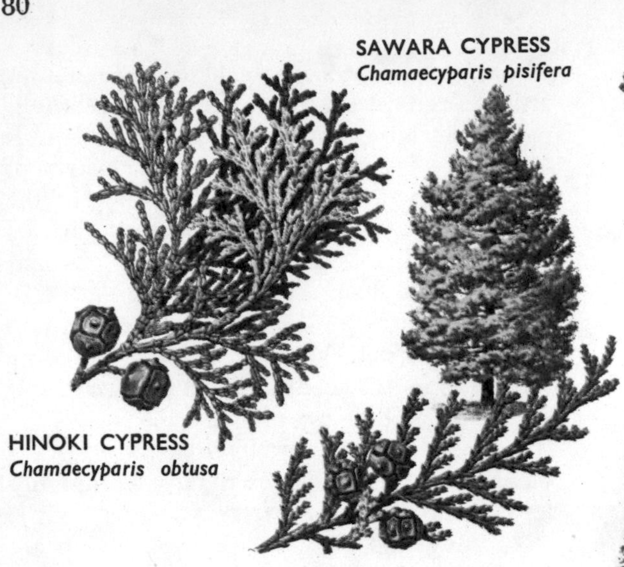

PORT ORFORD CEDAR
Chamaecyparis lawsoniana

ALASKA CEDAR
Chamaecyparis nootkatensis

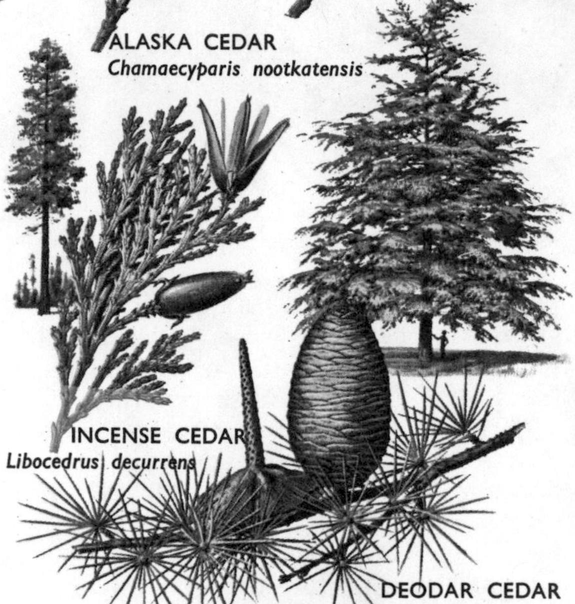

INCENSE CEDAR
Libocedrus decurrens

DEODAR CEDAR
Cedrus deodara

LEBANON CEDAR
Cedrus libani

exist today. Like the Atlas Cedar, a native of North Africa, the Lebanon Cedar's branches are uplifted rather than down-swept, and its needles are shorter and the crown not as dense as the Deodar Cedar. Its tip stands more erect.

The Lawson Cypress *(Chamaecyparis lawsoniana)* and Atlantic White-Cedar are members of still another group (*Chamaecyparis* spp.), native to Asia and North America. They have flat, scale-like foliage and small round cones. Lawson's Cypress and Alaska cedars grow along the west coast of the United States. The Atlantic Cedar *(Cham. thyoides)*, which grows in moist or boggy coastal lands from Maine to Louisiana, has small, wrinkled, and raisin-like cones. Hinoki-cypress and members of the same genus, are valuable commercial trees of Japan and many are planted as ornamentals in Britain.

Incense Cedars (*Libocedrus* spp.), which have scale-like foliage arranged in widely spaced whorls of four on flattened branchlets, are native to Oregon and California. Their cones ($\frac{3}{4}$ — $2\frac{1}{2}$ inches) hang from the tips of their branches. Other members of the same group are found in Chile, New Zealand, Formosa, and southern China.

CELESTIAL SPHERE. The sky looks like a great overturned bowl all around us — and, in fact, many ancient peoples thought it was just that. They thought that the Sun and

Moon and the stars and planets were all attached to the inside of the bowl. We know today that this is not so. All the heavenly bodies are at different distances from the Earth. The Sun, Moon, and planets are fairly close to us, but the stars are very far away.

Even though we know it is not really so, it is convenient to think of the heavenly bodies as being attached to a very large sphere all around us. This imaginary sphere, called the celestial sphere, makes the study of positions in the sky much easier.

Several circles and particular points on the celestial sphere have names. All around, exactly level with us, runs the horizon. Directly above us, straight up, is the zenith, while straight down is the nadir. The position of any object in the sky is given by two angles: its altitude is measured up from the horizon, while its azimuth is measured around the horizon starting from the north point.

Another important circle is the celestial meridian. It runs through the zenith directly from north to south. The heavenly bodies

P & O

Ship's Officers are seen here 'shooting the Sun' with their sextants.

Navigators of ships and aircraft use the positions of heavenly bodies, such as the Sun, Moon, and stars, to determine their own position. With a sextant, the navigator measures a celestial body's angle of altitude above the horizon. Then he compares this measurement with the data in an astronomical table that gives the location of the celestial body at the exact time of the observation. The difference between the two gives the navigator his line of position.

Celestial North Pole

Celestial Equator

For charting the stars, astronomers use a system based on the poles and equator of the Earth. Declination in the sky corresponds to latitude on the Earth. Corresponding to longitude on Earth, astronomers chart star positions in right ascension, while the hour angle locates a star in relation to the observer's celestial meridian.

ZENITH

Observer's Celestial Meridian

Altitude

North

Azimuth

Horizon

reach their highest point in the sky as they cross the meridian.

The celestial North Pole is directly above the North Pole of the Earth. As the Earth rotates about its axis every day, the sky seems to rotate about the celestial North Pole. The North Star, or Polaris, is very close to the celestial North Pole. It remains nearly stationary, and so it always marks the north. People in the Southern Hemisphere of the Earth cannot see the North Star. They see the south celestial pole, but there is no bright star to mark the spot.

Halfway between the two celestial poles (90 degrees from each) is the celestial equator. It can also be used to give the positions of objects in the sky. In this case the angle measured up or down from the equator is called the declination, while the angle measured westward around the equator, starting at the meridian, is called the hour angle.

CELESTITE, the only important strontium mineral, occurs in tabular crystals or in granular, cleavable masses. It has three perfect cleavages. Celestite is pale blue-white. It looks like barite but gives a carmine-red flame test instead of yellow-green. It occurs in sedimentary rocks or is found as a lining in cavities and in veins.

Celestite is found in the Bristol area in England, in Germany, Italy, Sicily and several states of the U.S.A.

CENOZOIC, which means 'recent life', is the era of about 70 million years from the end of the Mesozoic Era to the present. It is divided into the Tertiary Period, which includes the Palaeocene, Eocene, Oligocene, Miocene and Pliocene epochs, and the more recent and much shorter (about 3 million years) Quaternary Period, which includes the Pleistocene and Recent epochs.

Animals and plants of the Cenozoic resembled those of today much more than did those of earlier eras. Even the general geography of the Earth had a modern look during Cenozoic times. The Earth was not static however. Many mountain ranges, including the Alps and the Himalayas were formed during the Cenozoic. Others, among them the Rockies, were eroded and later uplifted again to give them their present form. During the Cenozoic, too, the Earth's crust was deformed and volcanic outbursts occurred in many areas. The great lava flows of western Scotland and Ireland are of Tertiary age. The famous Fingal's Cave and Giant's Causeway

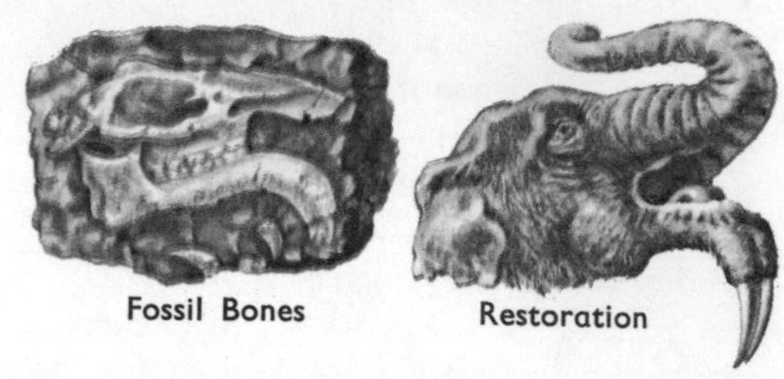

Dinotherium, **which stood 12 feet high at the shoulders, is believed to have used its unusual tusks for digging roots and tubers.**

Many grazing mammals developed on the grassy prairies that became widespread during the dry Miocene epoch of the Cenozoic era. Among them were (1) *Dinohyus*, **a six-foot primitive pig; (2)** *Syndyoceras*, **a deer-like animal that had an extra set of horns on its nose; (3)** *Diceratherium*, **a small rhinoceros; (4)** *Merychippus*, **a nearly modern horse that had a hoofed middle toe and a small useless toe on each side; (5)** *Moropus*, **an ungainly chalicothere; and (6)** *Alticamelus*, **a long-necked primitive camel without a hump.**

are made of basalts of this age. These and other Cenozoic strata are important petroleum reservoir rocks. Great canyons of major rivers were carved in Cenozoic times, and the era ended with glaciers spread widely over the continents as the beginning of the Ice Ages.

Flowering plants and mammals dominated in the Cenozoic, which is often called the 'Age of Mammals'. Mammals, which had existed as a small, rather insignificant group for at least 100 million years of the Mesozoic, replaced the extinct dinosaurs and spread to almost every environment. Early in the Cenozoic, mammals were divided into two groups: plant eaters (condylarths) and flesh eaters (creodonts). The history of many groups of mammals can be traced in detail, for Cenozoic fossils are common in many areas. Many Cenozoic mammals are now extinct, but others still exist today, relatively unchanged. (See EOCENE; ICE AGES; LIFE'S ORIGIN AND DEVELOPMENT; MIOCENE; OLIGOCENE; PALAEOCENE; PLIOCENE; QUATERNARY PERIOD.)

CEPHEIDS. Most stars shine with the same brightness night after night, but a few are noticeably brighter some nights than others. Among these are the cepheid variables. They take their name from Delta Cephei, a fourth-magnitude star in the constellation of Cepheus. A cepheid changes in brightness

because it pulsates. The star actually grows larger and smaller, in a period of a few days; and as the star's size changes, its brightness changes, too. We cannot see the size change directly because even in the most powerful telescope a star is only a point of light. But from the changes of brightness and the spectrum of the star, astronomers are able to calculate the size of the star and to follow the pulsation. The brightness changes continuously, and its variation can be shown in a graph called a light curve.

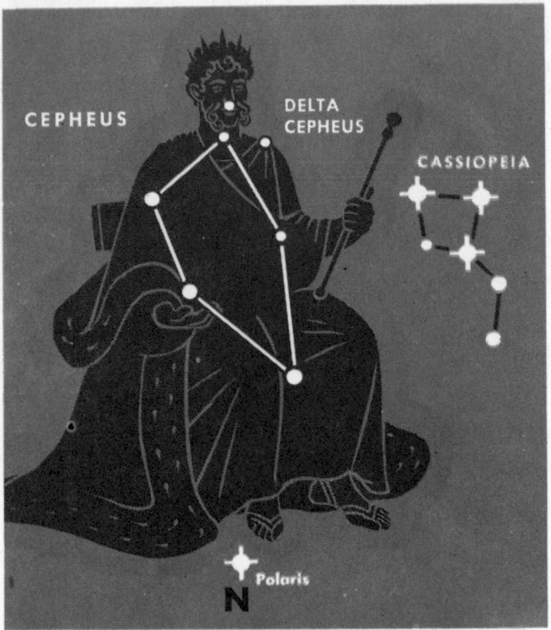

No one knows just why cepheids pulsate. It is known that the gas that makes up a star is very 'bouncy', like the air in a pumped-up tyre. But the star's pulsation would die out very quickly, like the waves that come from a splash in a pond, unless there were something to keep it going. That something must be inside the star. Some cepheids are old stars that are running short of fuel, and the cause of the pulsation may have something to do with this stage of development.

Cepheids are very valuable stars in astronomy because they can be used to measure distances. This is possible because the period of a cepheid — the length of time it takes for one whole pulsation — tells how bright it is. This is a general property of cepheids; all stars that have the same period have the same brightness. For example, every cepheid that has a five-day period is 2,000 times as bright as the Sun, while every cepheid with a ten-day period is 4,000 times as bright as the Sun. These brightnesses are, of course, the real brightness of the star; how bright it looks will depend on how far away from us it is. The relation between the pulsation period of a cepheid and its brightness is called the period-luminosity relation. It can be displayed as a graph that shows the brightnesses of

LIGHT CURVE OF DELTA CEPHEI

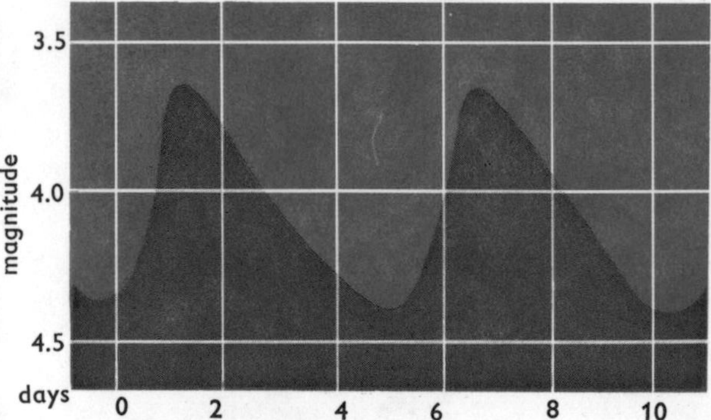

cepheids of each period length. When an astronomer has measured the period of time that a cepheid takes to make one whole pulsation, he can read from the graph how bright the cepheid really is.

Once the luminosity — or real brightness — of a cepheid is known, its distance can be found by seeing how bright it looks. Just as a distant searchlight looks faint because it is far away, so a distant cepheid looks faint because of its distance. Because the astronomer knows how bright the cepheid really is, he can tell how far away it must be to look so faint.

Cepheids are actually very bright stars, so they can be seen a long way off. They can even be seen in other galaxies, and finding the distances of the cepheids tells us how far those galaxies are from us. In this way cepheids have been used to explore and measure a large part of the universe.

CEREALS are plants of the grass family that produce a dry fruit or grain used as food. Cereals have been important since ancient times and are sources of protein, oil, and

John Strohm

This man is farming rice, the basic food of people in southern Asia.

vitamins as well as starch and sugar. Most cereals have been grown so long that their wild ancestors are no longer known. Maize or Indian Corn was widely used by Indians in the Americas long before the arrival of European explorers. Barley, wheat, oats, and rye were cultivated in the Mediterranean area in ancient times. Rice has been a basic food of people in southern Asia for centuries. Most cereals are now grown throughout the world. Barley and rye grow best in northern regions; wheat in temperate regions; rice in the tropics. Maize, the most adaptable, is a tropical plant that grows well in temperate climates. Wheat is the most important of the cereals in Europe, North America, and parts of South America. Rice feeds half of the world's population. Vast quantities of cereals are used for the production of breakfast foods. Nutrients lost in the manufacturing are replaced and supplemented with others in the final products. Most cereals are processed to be eaten cold with milk and sugar (many are now sweetened in the manufacturing process). Fewer kinds are used as quick-cooked hot cereals. (See BARLEY; MAIZE; MILLETS; OATS; RICE; WHEAT.)

CHERRIES (*Prunus* spp.), members of the rose family, grow abundantly in cool areas of the Northern Hemisphere. Some of the nearly 200 species are prized for their

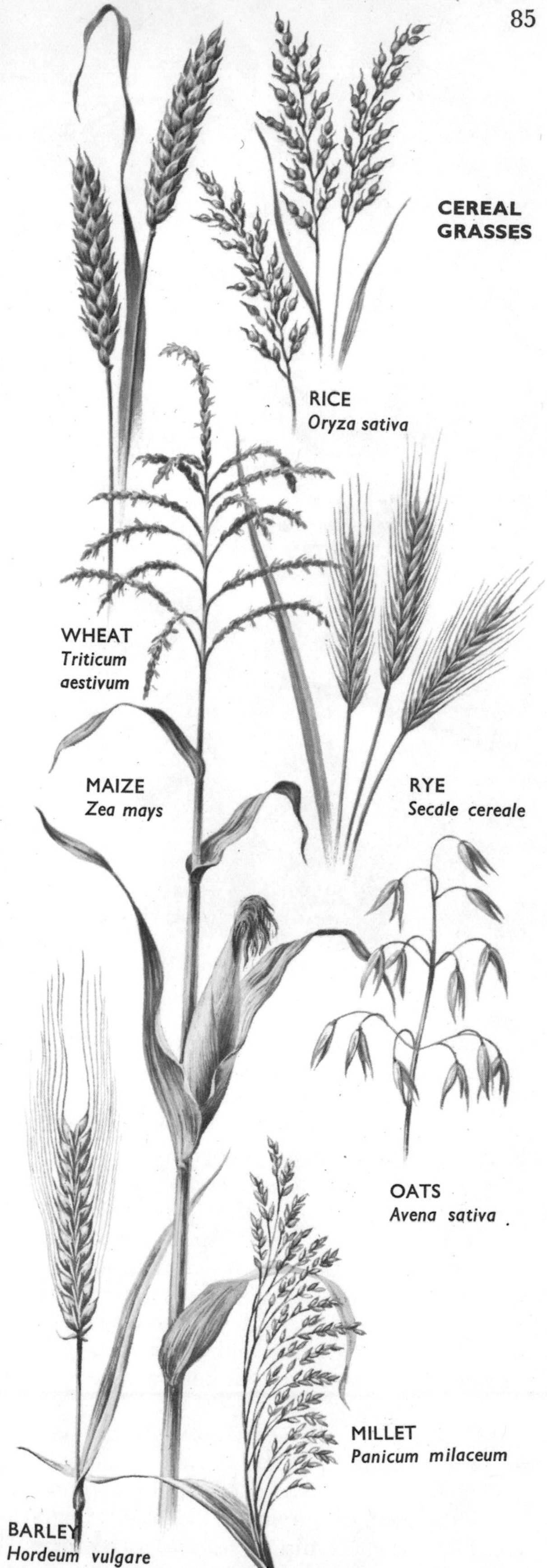

CEREAL GRASSES

RICE
Oryza sativa

WHEAT
Triticum aestivum

MAIZE
Zea mays

RYE
Secale cereale

OATS
Avena sativa

MILLET
Panicum milaceum

BARLEY
Hordeum vulgare

ROYAL ANN
(sweet)

MONTMORENCY
(sour)

TARTARIAN
(sweet)

SWEET CHERRY
in flower

COMMON VARIETIES OF CULTIVATED CHERRIES

MORELLO
(sour)

delicious fruit. Others are planted as ornamentals or are valuable for their wood. Cultivated cherries originated in the area of the Black and Caspian seas. In England, Kent has always been associated with the growing of cherries but other producing areas are in Gloucestershire, Worcestershire and Herefordshire. Two types of cherry are grown: the sweet cherry, a dessert cherry of which there are many varieties, and the sour cherry which are eaten when cooked or used for making jams and conserves. The Morello is perhaps the best known variety of the sour cherries.

Many species of *Prunus* adorn our gardens as ornamentals for their showy blossom in spring or their colourful foliage in autumn. Of the former, the Japanese Flowering Cherries *(P. lannesiana* and *P. serratula)* and their varieties, and of the latter, *P. sargentii* whose leaves turn deep crimson in early September, are the best-known and most showy.

Two of our native species, the Bird Cherry *(Prunus padus)* and the Gean *(Prunus avium)* are sometimes used as stocks on which dessert cherries and ornamental varieties can be grafted.

CHICKWEEDS have spread around the world, mainly in temperate regions. They are common but attractive weeds. Many species have weak stems which sprawl along the ground. These modest, inconspicuous

COMMON CHICKWEED
Stellaria media

BOG STITCHWORT
Stellaria alsine

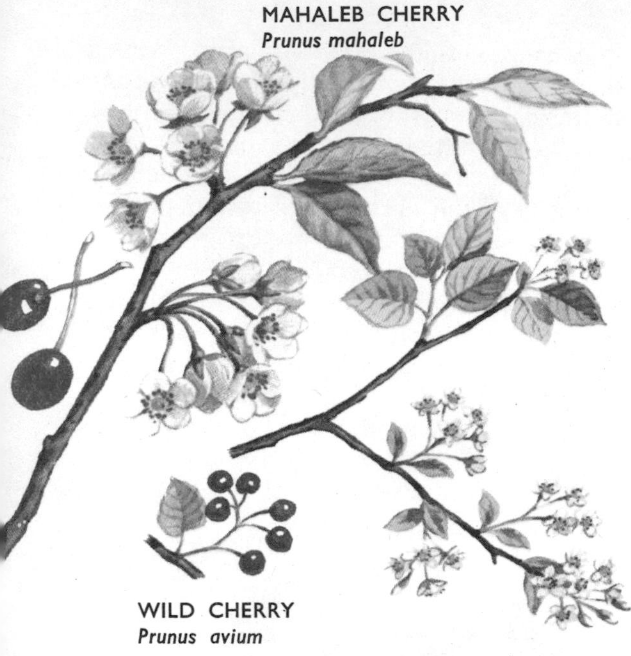

plants belong to the carnation or pink family. The petals of the Common Chickweed's small flowers are split like the points of tiny stars. This gave the plant the scientific name *Stellaria*, which means star-like. In its native Europe, the leaves of the Common Chickweed are eaten in salads or are cooked like spinach.

About 50 other species of chickweeds grow in the British Isles. Snow-in-Summer *(Cerastium tomentosum)*, a pretty European species, is sometimes planted in gardens.

CHICLE is the gummy latex of the Sapodilla *(Achras sapota)*, a tree native to Central America, the West Indies, and South America. Unflavoured latex was chewed by the Indians long ago. The chewing gum industry can be traced to General Santa Ana, famous Mexican president and a military leader. Exiled from Mexico in the 1850s, he sought refuge in New York. There he continued to chew the gum — chicle — popular in Mexico. An American who saw the pleasure Santa Ana got from his chicle gum conceived the idea of manufacturing chicle chewing gum.

Chicle is collected by natives called 'chicleros'. During the tropical rainy season when the latex flows freely in the trees, they go into the jungles of Honduras, Guatemala, and Mexico to find wild Sapodilla trees. Deep gashes are cut in the bark so that the latex flows down the trunk. It is collected in bags at the base. Most of the latex flows out of the tree within a few hours. Several years must elapse before the same tree can be tapped again.

The chicle is boiled in large kettles to concentrate the liquid. While still hot, it is poured into brick-like moulds. These dried blocks of chicle, each weighing 20 to 25 pounds, are shipped to manufacturing plants where the chicle is cleaned and combined with sugar and flavouring to make chewing gum.

Sapodilla trees may grow to a height of 100 feet. They bear a delicious sugary fruit, and are planted for the fruit alone. (See TROPICAL FRUITS.)

Tapping a tree to get latex for chewing gum.

CHICORY *(Cichorium intybus)*, a native of Europe, can be found along roadsides and in fields in many parts of the country. It is a weed-like plant with beautiful blue blossoms, strongly resembling a dandelion, which stay open for only a couple of hours on sunny days. This is why Chicory is not planted in gardens in spite of its very attractive flowers.

Roasted roots of Chicory are ground and added to coffee or are used separately to make a drink like coffee. The leaves of Chicory, though slightly bitter, are used in salads, both green or in a bleached form, which is produced by covering the plant with a container.

Endive or Escarole *(Cichorium endivia)* may

have originated in the eastern Mediterranean region where the Romans used it both as a salad vegetable and as cooked greens. Like chicory, the leaves, high in vitamin A, add a slightly bitter taste to green salads. Endive and chicory are closely related, and the leaves of both are frilled along their edges.

CHLOROPHYLL is the green pigment possessed by most plants. There are four kinds: chlorophyll a, b, c and d. These chlorophylls are composed of carbon, oxygen, hydrogen, nitrogen, and magnesium in slightly different compounds. This green pigment may be masked by two other pigments such as carotene (orange) or xanthophyll (dark brown). Chlorophyll is generally found in plant cells in definite bodies, called chloroplasts, which are of a variety of shapes.

The elements that form simple plant sugar or glucose ($C_6H_{12}O_6$) are carbon, hydrogen, and oxygen. The plant obtains carbon and some of the oxygen from the air in the form of carbon dioxide. It gets the hydrogen and some oxygen from water drawn into the plant through the root system or, in some cases, from moisture in the air. These are combined in the presence of chlorophyll and with energy supplied by light from the sun to form sugar. Further processes in plants or animals convert basic sugar into more complex sugars or into proteins, starches, and other building blocks of all living matter. Scientists consider chlorophyll to be the link between the sun, the source of all the world's energy, and all living matter, past or present.

CHROMITE, the only ore of chromium, is found in lens-like granular masses, scattered grains, or small eight-sided crystals in serpentine with which it is almost always associated. Less commonly it is found with platinum. Chromite has a metallic lustre and is black with a dark-brown streak. It is slightly magnetic. Crocoite is a bright orange-red lead chromate found where chromite and lead minerals occur together.

Chromite is the source of chromium, the shiny metal used as an alloy of steel to give it strength, toughness and hardness. It increases the resistance of steel to breakdown by electricity and high temperatures and to corrosion by weather elements. Because it also increases shock resistance, it is added to steel used as armour plating, jet engines, gas turbines, and high-speed tools. Chrome plate — the bright, shiny protective coating on metal — is a familiar use for chromium. Nichrome wire (60 per cent nickel, 14 per cent chromium, 15 per cent iron) is used for the heating elements in electric heaters; chromium oxide for bricks that line steel and copper furnaces because they will withstand corrosion and sudden temperature changes. Chromite is used to make brilliant yellow, green, and red pigments for paints and also in tanning leather.

Brian J. Green

A shiny protective coating of chrome plating has been used on the bumpers of these cars.

Chromite occurs in Sweden, Finland, Germany, U.S.S.R., Turkey, Rhodesia, India, the Philippines, and New Caledonia. In the United States it is found in small amounts in several states.

CHRYSANTHEMUMS (*Chrysanthemum* spp.) are popularly called 'mums' by many people. Chrysanthemum (kriss-ANTH-uh-mum) means 'golden flower'. The many fine varieties known today have been created by combining plants that came from China and other countries of south-eastern Asia.

Chrysanthemums are admired in many lands. They rank second only to roses in world popularity. Almost everyone likes the giant yellow, bronze, or pink flowers, the many coloured little pompons, and the numerous in-between sizes. Most of the hundreds of varieties are hardy perennials.

Chrysanthemums are best loved in Japan, the country that did the most to bring the flowers to their present state of perfection and beauty. Japanese gardeners have worked

PAF International

for centuries to produce better chrysanthemums. They succeeded so well that Japan has adopted the chrysanthemum as its national flower. Japan has a chrysanthemum holiday, and the flower appears on Japanese stamps.

The delicate, white or pink-flowered pyrethrums are also in the chrysanthemum group. These plants are the source of pyrethrum, an insecticide prepared from the dried flowers. Feverfew, an old-fashioned favourite and several other garden flowers belong in the large and complex chrysanthemum clan.

The common White Field Daisy or Oxeye Daisy, abundant throughout Britain, is one of the wild species of chrysanthemums. Luther Burbank, the great plant breeder, is said to have used the White Field Daisy, to produce the Shasta Daisy, a popular ornamental flower. (See DAISY.)

Small quantities of cinnabar are used in the manufacture of many of the insecticides which are used so widely in modern agriculture.

USDA

CINNABAR

CINNABAR is the only common mercury mineral. Deposited from alkaline solutions in low temperature veins, it is found as bright red, fine-grained crystalline crusts or coatings in veins or is spread throughout sandstones. It has a scarlet streak, brilliant lustre, and one perfect cleavage. Cinnabar is very heavy and melts at a low temperature. Mercury or quicksilver is a good electrical conductor and is used in switches and control instruments. It is the only common metal that occurs as a liquid. In mining operations it is used in the recovery of gold and silver. Mercury boilers are more efficient than steam boilers for generating power, but the large amount of mercury needed makes their cost very high. Small amounts are used in mercury vapour lamps, thermometers, drugs, dental fillings, and in insecticides. An anti-fouling paint used on ship bottoms contains mercuric oxide, which reacts with sea water to form mercuric chloride that kills barnacles and seaweeds. Mercury is also used in manufacturing explosives. Cinnabar comes from Italy, Spain, Yugoslavia, China, Japan, Mexico, and the U.S.A.

CITRUS FRUITS (*Citrus* spp.) are believed to have originated in China and south-eastern Asia and Polynesia. Oranges were known in China by 2200 B.C. and the citron about two thousand years earlier. One by one citrus fruits were introduced to Europe through the Mediterranean region. Citrons were first — about 300 B.C.

Columbus brought seeds of oranges, lemons, and citrons to Haiti in 1493. A few years later, Spanish and Portuguese explorers carried citrus fruits into various parts of North, South, and Central America. Citrus fruits are grown in many parts of the world, but

All kinds of citrus fruits are popular. They are eaten raw, used in fruit juices and to flavour food. They are one of the best sources of Vitamin C.

the United States leads as grower and consumer.

Citrus trees vary in size, but all are relatively small. Many types have spines. Sweet Oranges may reach a height of 35 feet, but most mature citrus trees are from 15 to 20 feet high. Lemon and limes are more shrub-like, seldom taller than 15 feet. Citrus flowers are attractive and fragrant. All citrus fruits are a special type of berry, a hesperidium, which consists of eight to fifteen segments that contain the juice sacs or pulp. In many varieties these segments are easily separated, making the fruit easy to eat when peeled. Usually the inside of a citrus rind is white and very bitter; the outer surface varies in colour. Most people associate a yellow colour with lemons and grapefruit, green with limes, and orange with oranges. Some varieties of grapefruit have pinkish skins, however; tree-ripened limes may be yellow, and some Mandarin Oranges are reddish. Skins of oranges are coloured artificially to give them a more uniform, eye-appealing colour. The smell of a citrus fruit comes from oil glands in its skin.

Oranges, grapefruit and tangerines are eaten as table fruits, while limes and lemons are used chiefly in beverages or for flavouring. Some of the many citrus fruit products are: frozen and heat-processed juices, tinned fruit segments, alcoholic drinks, essential oils used in flavouring, perfumes and soaps, pectin, candied citrus peels, jellies and marmalades, and cattle feed. Citrus fruits are one of the best sources of vitamin C and have recently been recognised as a source of vitamin P.

Sweet oranges include such varieties as the Common Orange, Navel Orange, and Blood Orange. Navel Oranges have a navel-like marking at their apex (the point opposite where the fruit is attached to the stem). Blood Oranges have reddish-coloured flesh. Valencia, Jaffa and Outspan are some of the commercial varieties either eaten fresh or squeezed for their juice.

Seville or sour oranges have rougher peels and more seeds than sweet oranges. Large quantities are used to make marmalades,

Vitamin C, found so abundantly in citrus fruits, is essential for the healthy development of children.

Walter Chandoha

orangeade, and candied peels. An oil is also extracted from sour oranges.

Mandarin Oranges are sometimes called kidglove oranges because they are so easily peeled. One type has an orange-yellow skin; another, called Tangerines, has a reddish-orange skin. Tangelos, a cross between a tangerine and a grapefruit, were developed in Florida U.S.A. They are larger than most oranges but peel like tangerines.

Lemons are grown in frost-free regions such as in the Mediterranean. Lemons are picked green and cured in storage rooms before shipment. Ethylene gas is sometimes used to hasten their ripening. Lemon juice is used in beverages and salads and to flavour fish and other foods; slices are used as a garnish. Oil extracted from lemon skins is made into lemon extract, perfumes, and soaps.

Limes were introduced to the West Indies by the Spaniards and spread from there into the Florida Keys and Mexico. These were the small lemon-yellow limes now known as Mexican, West Indian, or Key Limes. They now grow wild in these areas but are difficult to grow and harvest. The Tahiti or Persian Lime is the common lime now grown in Florida and California. This lime is larger, resembling a lemon in size and shape. It is harvested and marketed while still green. Most limes are very sour (acid) and are used like lemons. Sweet limes, grown in Egypt and parts of Asia, are a variety highly prized in Latin America. British sailors were called 'limeys' because they ate limes to prevent scurvy, caused by vitamin C deficiency.

Grapefruit apparently originated in the West Indies. Housewives prefer them seedless as fresh fruit, but the canning industry favours seedy varieties because of their better flavour and because their segments remain intact better when tinned. Grapefruit are a good source of thiamin and ascorbic acid but have less vitamin A and sugar than oranges.

Citrons are cultivated chiefly in Corsica, Sicily, Greece, and the West Indies. This fruit resembles a lemon with a thick skin. Citron peels are candied and used in cakes or as a confection.

Kumquats *(Fortunella)* also belong to the citrus fruit group.

head of Buddha
4th—5th centuries

Victoria & Albert Museum, London

CIVILISATION. Ants, termites, bees, gorillas, and many other animals live in social groups that are highly organised, but civilisation applies only to human societies that have an advanced method of communication and the specialisation of labour and skills made possible by the existence of cities. Where these exist, generally there is government, progress in technology, and extensive development of the creative arts.

To say that a society has a civilisation is different from saying that it has a culture. All peoples have cultures, but only those cultures with the above characteristics are called civilisations. Despite this, most primitive peoples have complicated codes of etiquette, strong moral ideas, and conceptions of duty, loyalty, and hospitality.

Civilisations never appear before the use of agriculture. Without farming there would not be enough surplus food to feed city people working at their specialised occupations. Until about 3500 B.C. there was no culture that could be called 'civilised'. The discovery of agriculture made possible the earliest civilisation, that of the Sumerians.

A bison painted on the wall of a cave in Spain about 25,000 years ago, during the Palaeolithic period.

OLD WORLD CIVILISATIONS. The world's first civilisation grew in the fertile lowlands between the Tigris and Euphrates rivers. In this same region, known as Mesopotamia, man had even earlier moved from the Old Stone Age into a time of settled rural life, practising agriculture. Between 4500 B.C. and 3500 B.C., the earliest cities of the world appeared in this area. The people who built them were the Sumerians. Sumerian city-kingdoms, such as Ur and Babylon, were surrounded by great walls built of mud bricks. Inside the walls were the houses and shops of workers and businessmen as well as huge temples.

The Sumerians were the first to use writing. They studied the heavens, and they developed business and banking methods. The first complete law code ever drawn up was made by the emperor Hammurabi.

Several thousand years before the great civilisation of Egypt, there were Stone Age peoples living in the Nile Valley. Around 4500 B.C. they learned to make tools of copper. In following years, the foundations were laid for the great Egyptian civilisation.

Until 3200 B.C. there were two separate kingdoms in the Nile Valley. When these were united under the same ruling dynasty, a period of rapid progress began. The civilisation of Egypt suddenly bloomed.

By 3000 B.C. the Egyptians were using the plough, weaving linen, and making excellent pottery. Important crops were wheat, barley, dates, and honey, along with several meat animals. Fine craftsmen were working with copper, gold, and precious stones. Glassmaking had been invented. Writing by means of hieroglyphics was well developed. Scrolls were written about diseases and their treatment. Religion and government became well organised. In later centuries the huge stone buildings were built for which Egypt is famous, such as the enduring pyramids and temples.

Chinese civilisation can be traced to the Shang Empire, which lasted from 1766 B.C. until 1122 B.C. During this period, writing by means of picture characters developed. People lived mainly in villages. Examples of excellent craftsmanship in metal have survived. The bow and arrow was used in warfare along with bronze weapons. In battle, nobles drove chariots drawn by two horses. The rural villages were governed by councils composed of the family heads. The Chinese realised that education was the core of

This Sumerian stele (3,000 B.C.) is one of the earliest depictions of agriculture and animal domestication.

British Museum, London (Draeger)

Colorphoto — TWA

Hieroglyphics decorate the mighty columns of Hypostyle Hall in the temple at Karnak, Egypt. This imposing structure was completed by King Rameses II about 1200 B.C.

This gold portrait mask of King Tutankhamen (King 'Tut') of Egypt covered the face of his mummy.

Cairo Museum: Colorphoto — TWA

Metropolitan Museum of Art — Fletcher Fund, 1940

This Chinese scroll painting on silk from the Sung Dynasty (A.D. 960—1279) shows the emphasis on family life.

their greatness. Scholarship was honoured in court circles and by government officials and private citizens.

Chinese life has always been rooted in the family. The great values have been those of family loyalty and respect for family authority. Beyond the immediate family are organisations of kinsmen upon whom one depends. Even religion is a family affair, and the worship of ancestors is widely practised.

Before 3300 B.C. another great civilisation had appeared in the Indus Valley of north-western India. Two great cities, Harappa and Mohenjo Daro have been found. These cities must have rivalled those of Mesopotamia and were almost as old. Their inhabitants seem to have lived mainly from farming and dairying. By 2300 B.C. Indian merchants were trading in the Sumerian cities. The wheel and the loom for weaving were known very early in India. Cotton and cotton cloth originated in this region. These early Indians had excellent houses built of red brick and baths and drainage systems.

Several factors helped to give Indian life its own particular character. Hinduism appeared and became immensely powerful. This was not only because it dealt with spiritual matters but because it made daily living a part of religion.

Another great civilisation began when a wandering people we now know as Greeks settled down on the shores of the Mediterranean and Aegean Seas. In this new land they became farmers and small-town dwellers. They developed great loyalty to their home towns. This was a feeling that people in other civilised regions did not have, and it made a great difference in the way the Greeks behaved.

As villages grew, differences appeared between rich and poor. The rich became noblemen, and in some cities seized all the powers of government. This was the form of government most prevalent, when, in the seventh century B.C. Athens began an experiment. Government was to be by the 'demos', or the people. Laws were passed which practically forced the citizens to take an active part in governing their city. To be sure, the majority of people living in Greek cities were not free citizens. Hence democracy was practised by and for a minority of the people. But it was an important beginning. The Greeks also started Europe along the road to great scientific and medical discoveries and a revival of art and literature.

The Romans are first known to us as a community of farmers and traders settled fifteen miles from the mouth of the River Tiber. By 753 B.C. Rome was a small city-state ruled by a king. In 509 B.C. the Romans overthrew their king and established a more democratic form of government. At the same time they began to build what was to become the most powerful empire the world had yet seen.

The early Romans did not have as highly developed a civilisation as some of their neighbours. Another people, the Etruscans, held much of northern Italy. In southern Italy were cities settled and developed earlier by the Greeks. The Romans conquered both the Greeks and the Etruscans, and Greek civilisation was practically transplanted to Rome.

The Roman Empire lasted more than 500 years. Its peoples were comparatively protected and secure. Gradually, however, the organisation became less efficient.

Greek architecture is admired today in remains like the temple to the goddess Athena Nike, built on the Acropolis in Athens about 426 B.C.

Glyptothek: Munich

Surya, the Sun God, is a commonly depicted form of Vishnu, one of the three principal Hindu gods.

Eliot Elisifon — LIFE

Italian Tourist Office

The Colosseum, built in Rome between A.D. 70 and 82, testifies to the mechanical and technical skill of those times. It was the scene of bloody battles between gladiators.

Various warlike tribes from both Europe and Asia invaded the lands of Rome.

NEW WORLD CIVILISATIONS. The New World civilisations evolved independently of those of the Old World and at a later date. While most of the tribes of American Indians on the continents of North and South America lived a nomadic hunting existence, the mountainous jungles of Central America, the high Andean plateau of South America, and the fertile Valley of Mexico witnessed the rise of civilisations that rivalled those of contemporary Egypt and Greece.

The first great Mayan cities rose in what is today almost uninhabited jungle in Central America. These cities were built in the fourth century A.D. The region of the Maya was very fertile and productive. Farming was the basic industry. They raised corn, beans, tomatoes, and sweet potatoes. Cotton was grown and woven into cloth. Agriculture was carried on by the 'slash and burn' method.

The cities of the Mayas were religious centres. The Mayas were the best sculptors and architects of the New World. They had a system of writing in hieroglyphics and made paper and books. They were also the greatest scientists and mathematicians of the New

Among the many gods of the Maya was Yum Kax, god of corn, believed to have created men and women from this grain.

Peabody Museum, Harvard University; photo by Barry Burstein — Boston

World. The Mayan calendar was superior to anything which had been devised by Europeans up to that time.

Inca civilisation (A.D. 1438 to A.D. 1532) was the last and greatest of a series of civilisations centering in the Andes of Peru and Bolivia. Long before they rose to power the Incas had been settled farming people. Their methods of agriculture were very advanced, with thousands of acres of terraced fields on the mountainsides.

The Incas' temples and forts were built of huge stone blocks cut to fit each other so perfectly that no mortar was needed. The temples were lavishly decorated with gold, silver, copper, and semi-precious stones. No people, except perhaps the Romans, had built a better road system. These roads were narrow, since they were not built for wheeled vehicles. Runners carried messages along them from one relay station to another.

The Inca Empire included numerous tribes in Peru, Bolivia, Columbia, and Chile. It was an excellent example of totalitarian state. All land, minerals, and important domestic animals were owned by the state. Even marriages were arranged by the government. If a particular region needed developing, the government drafted families to move there and work. Life in this empire was prosperous and secure. The government kept huge stocks of food and cloth to distribute as needed.

The Aztecs, a warlike American Indian tribe, settled down in the Valley of Mexico. They overpowered the Toltecs who inhabited the region and established an empire.

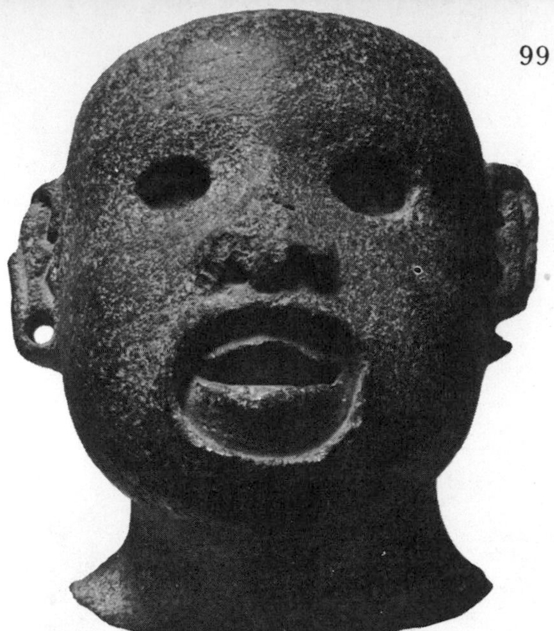

Louise and Walter Arensberg Collection — Philadelphia Museum of Art

The Aztecs made daily sacrifices of human blood to Xipe, their god of fertility.

When Cortes discovered them in A.D. 1519, the Aztecs had recently built their civilisation. Since the Aztecs held many other peoples in their empire by force, they relied on a strong army. Their favourite weapons were heavy javelins thrown with a spear thrower and wooden swords with jagged pieces of natural glass set along the edges. Prisoners of war were often sacrificed to the highest god, the God of War. Capturing a prisoner for such sacrifices brought a soldier higher honour than he achieved by killing enemies in battle.

The civilisation of the Aztecs was built

Serpents were among the gods of the Aztecs, as illustrated by this two-headed snake in turquoise mosaic.

British Museum, London

Clays are used in modern industry to make many useful and decorative products.

without use of the wheel, the arch, or metal, and without the help of draft animals. Yet stone blocks and statues weighing up to 30 tons were transported great distances. They had no coinage but products were bartered throughout the empire.

CLAY is an exceedingly fine-grained mixture of mineral fragments. Kaolinite, quartz, feldspars, and muscovite with some organic matter make up clays. None of these particles is larger than 0.0001 of an inch. They are held together by water. Clay that is almost dry is soft and greasy; wet clay is easily shaped.

Pure clay is white, but most clays contain carbon that make them grey to black. Iron may cause clays to be orange, red, or green.

Clay is formed by weathering of rock. Deposits usually occur in layers and are often found at mouths of rivers. Over long periods of time and under great pressure, clay hardens to become shale. Pure clay — kaolin or China clay — is used for chinaware and pottery. When baked or 'fired', clay hardens and retains the shape into which it is moulded. Less pure clays are used for bricks, tile, and pipe. Clay is added to limestone in the manufacture of Portland cement.

CLEMATIS is a member of the buttercup family. Clematis or Traveller's Joy *(Clematis vitalba)* is usually found growing among thickets, or in actual woodland, where it easily attaches itself to tree trunks and climbs rapidly, due to its leaf-stalks which cling to any available support. These leaf-stalks remain and harden even when the leaves themselves have been shed, allowing the plant to sustain its growth and attain a considerable height. In fact, excessive growth will overshadow to a harmful extent, and

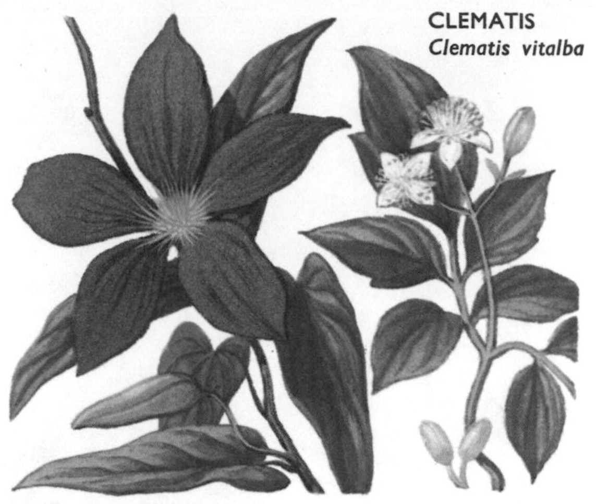

CLEMATIS
Clematis vitalba

even smother completely, other plants in its vicinity. An abundant blossom of white flowers precedes a fruit still containing the pistil, and it is this which then gives the plant a fleecy white appearance. There are about 250 species of *Clematis*. About 50 of these are in cultivation as ornamental garden plants. There are many hybrids. The hybrid *Clematis jackmannii* with its violet-purple flowers is widely grown, long established and very popular.

CLIMATE is the average weather of a region. Climate determines the distribution of plants. *Wet tropical rainy climates* are those in which the temperature of the coolest month is above 17 degrees centigrade (64 degrees Fahrenheit). Included are dense tropical rain forests (see TROPICAL RAIN FORESTS) where the rainfall is heavy throughout the year. These are located near the equator in the Amazon Valley, the Congo Basin, along the Guinea Coast of Africa, and in large parts of the East Indies. Savannas, which have less rainfall, also belong to this group. More open than tropical rain forests, they have a wet season and a dry season. Usually adjacent to tropical rain forests, grassy savannas occur in the Llanos of the

Temperature, caused by unequal heating of land and water masses, is the basis of the world's varied climates.

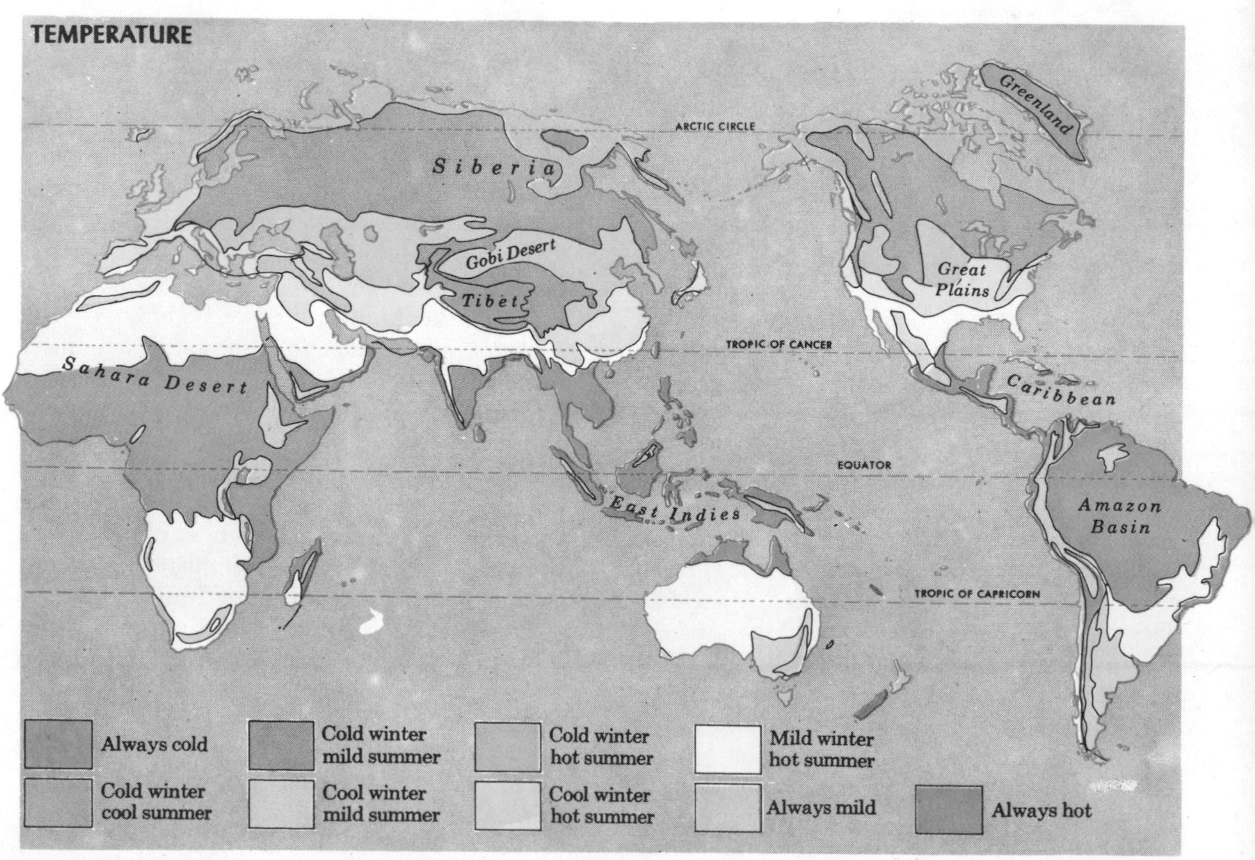

TEMPERATURE

ARCTIC CIRCLE
Siberia
Greenland
Gobi Desert
Tibet
Great Plains
TROPIC OF CANCER
Sahara Desert
Caribbean
EQUATOR
East Indies
Amazon Basin
TROPIC OF CAPRICORN

Always cold
Cold winter mild summer
Cold winter hot summer
Mild winter hot summer
Cold winter cool summer
Cool winter mild summer
Cool winter hot summer
Always mild
Always hot

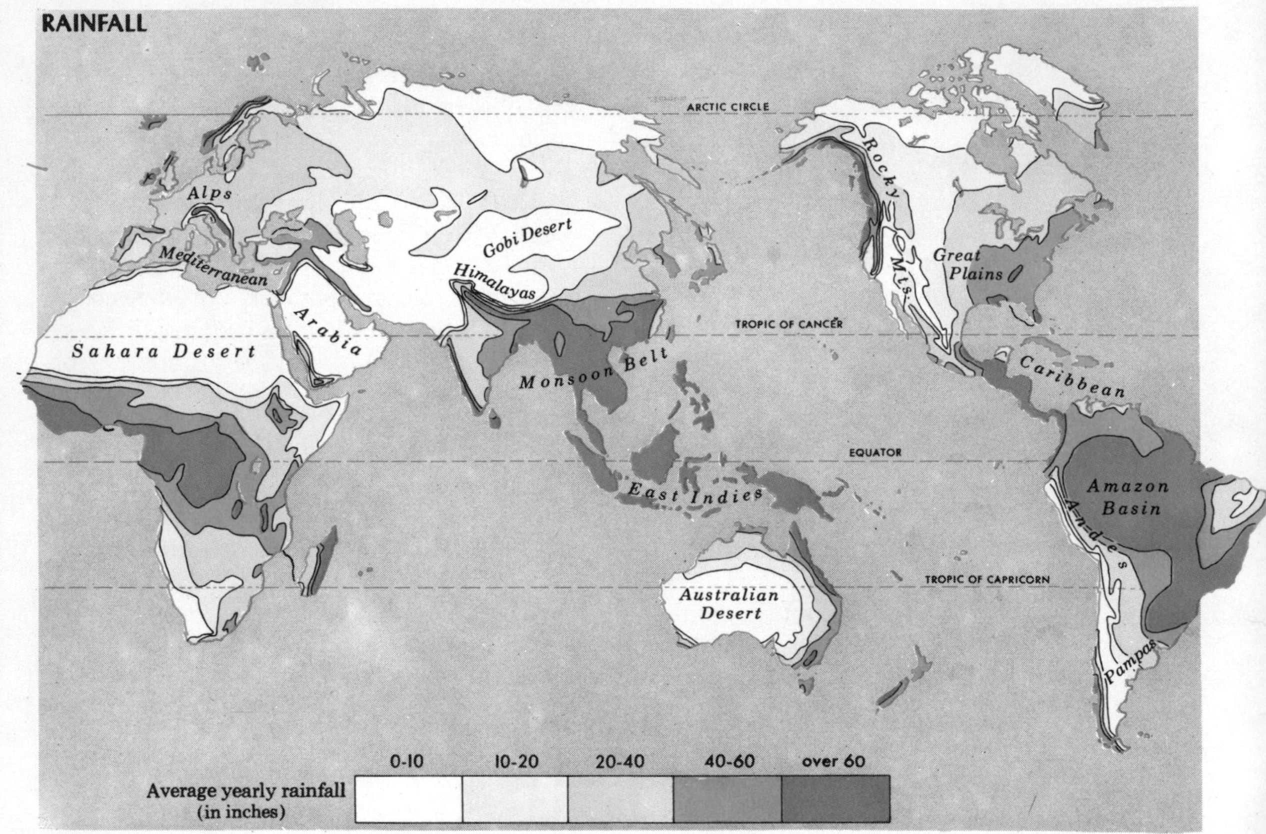

Rainfall modifies the effect of temperature on climate and, with temperature, sets the vegetative pattern.

Orinoco Valley of Colombia and Venezuela, the Guiana Highlands in northern South America, the Campos of Brazil, the Sudan and veld of northern and southern Africa, and the grasslands of northern Australia. (See GRASSLANDS.)

Dry climates are those in which evaporation is greater than the rainfall. These areas are the deserts (see DESERTS), which are dry or arid, and the semi-arid steppes or plains, on which are found short, shallow-rooted grasses. Low-latitude deserts are probably the driest regions on earth and also the most hostile to life. These areas include the Sahara and Kalahari deserts in Africa, Peruvian Desert of South America, Australian Desert, and the Sonora Desert in northern Mexico and south-western United States. Middle latitude deserts and steppes are usually located in the deep interior of continents far from oceans. Asia has the largest area of dry climates; North America is second.

Moderate humid climates are those where the coldest month is between 18 and minus 2 degrees centigrade (64.4 and 26.6 degrees Fahrenheit). Seasons in the tropics are spoken of as wet and dry, but in moderate humid climates, they are summer and winter. These are located along the western and eastern sides of continents but extend inland about 2,000 miles in the Mediterranean region.

Severe humid climates (snow-forests) have cold winters, long frost seasons, and wide temperature ranges. Temperature of the coldest month is under minus 2 degrees centigrade (26.6 degrees Fahrenheit); of the warmest month, over 10 degrees centigrade (50 degrees Fahrenheit). These climates are limited to the Northern Hemisphere except for a small area at the tip of South America.

Polar climates have temperatures no warmer than 10 degrees centigrade (50 degrees Fahrenheit) in the warmest month of the year. These occur beyond the tree limit in the Arctic and Antarctic and at high altitudes in major mountain ranges, such as the Himalayas, Andes, Alps, and Rocky Mountains. (See POLAR LIFE; WEATHER.)

CLOVES are an ancient spice used in China since the third century B.C. They grew originally only on the Spice Islands (Moluccas), between Borneo and New Guinea in the Pacific. Cloves now come mainly from Zanzibar and the Malagasy Republic. Dried cloves are the unopened flower buds and twig tips of the Clove Tree *(Eugenia caryophyllata)*. Whole or ground cloves or clove oil are made by distilling cloves with water. They are used as a flavouring, as a scent for perfumes and soaps, or as a local anaesthetic.

Buds of clove flowers are picked when they turn from green to a bright red. They are then dried in the sun.

COAL, our major fuel, was formed mainly in swampy forests during the Palaeozoic Era 310 to 290 million years ago. Forests of club mosses, horsetails, and ferns grew in the swamps. Many of these plants were tree-sized — 5 to 6 feet in diameter and more than 100 feet tall. Trees that died and did not entirely rot away formed thick layers of plant remains over the bottom of the swamps. Over the years water rose gradually in the swamps and submerged whole forests. Layers of mud and sand settled over the dead plants. Later the water drained away and new forests grew. Then these forests, too, were drowned and covered. This process occurred many times. Gradually the pressure of the many layers of buried trees compressed the plant remains into a solid mass, forming peat and coal. Coal is composed largely of carbon.

Fossil forests can be seen in such places as Swansea Bay; the Island of Lewis; St. Michael's Mount, Cornwall; and at Lulworth in Dorset.

Lignite is the least compressed and lowest grade of coal. It is brown and breaks easily into powdered or flaky fragments. Lignite

TYPES OF COAL

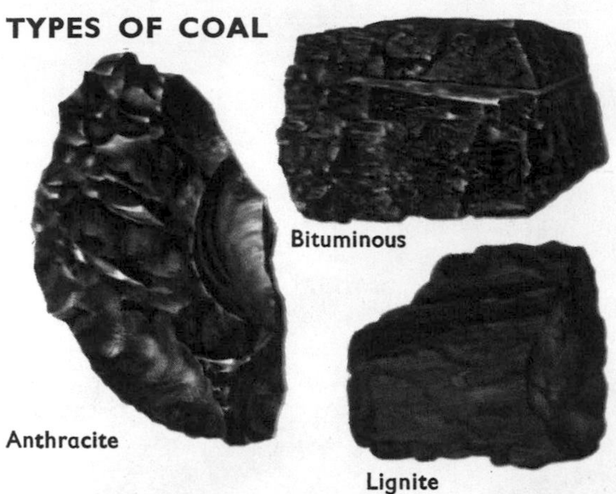

Shift workers leaving the pit head of a modern colliery.

G. M. Dickson, National Coal Board

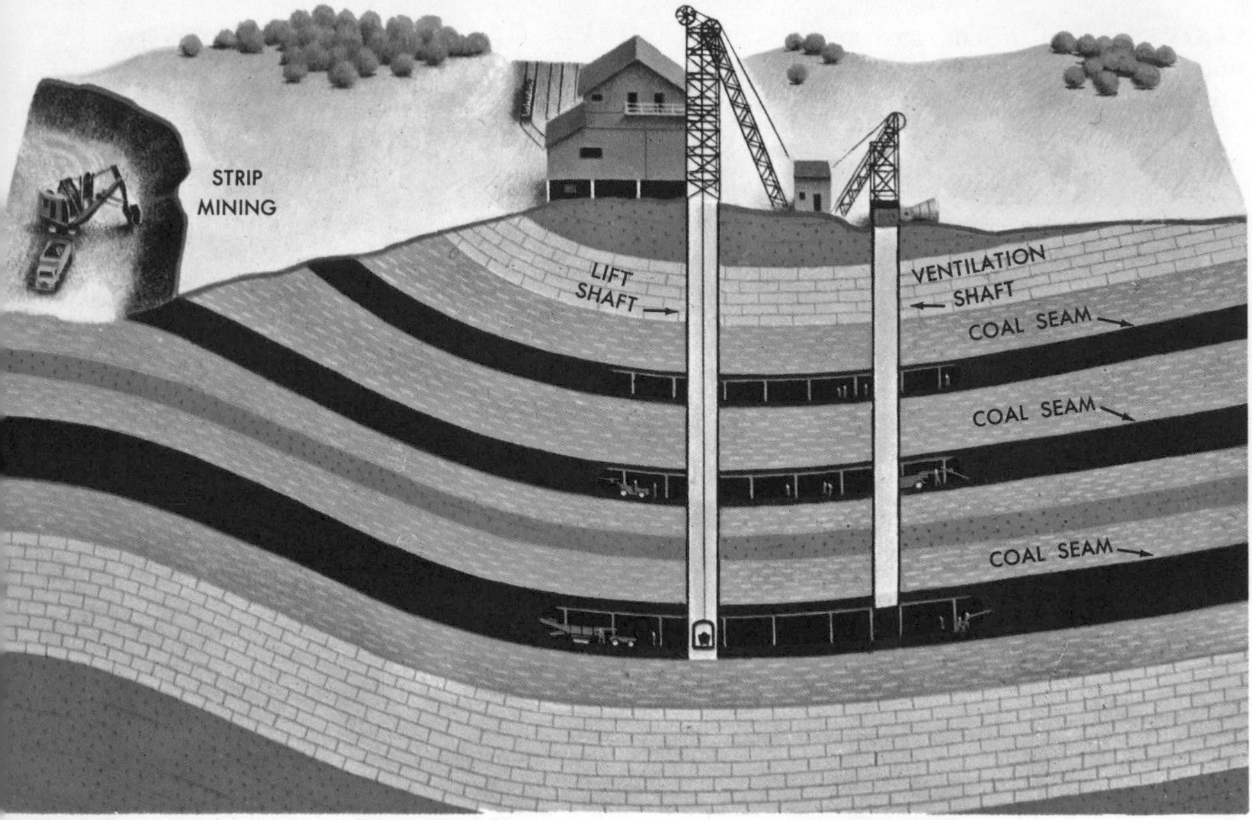

Seams of coal close to the surface are open-cast mined (left), while coal from deep seams is taken through shafts (centre).

also has the highest moisture content of any coal; it gives off the least heat and has a very smoky flame. Bituminous coals are black with a dull lustre. They contain less moisture, break down less in storage, and give off much more heat with less smoke. About 90 per cent of all coal mined is bituminous. Anthracite coal is very hard, black and shiny. It contains the least amount of moisture and gives off the most heat with an almost smokeless flame. It is the cleanest coal to burn. Bituminous coals occur widely in England and Scotland and anthracite in South Wales.

Coal mines are of four basic types. Strip mines are open pits, with the topsoil stripped away. Drift mines cut directly into the vein. Slope mines angle down to the seam below, and shaft mines have a vertical access. Both slope and shaft mines have tunnels spreading horizontally into the coal seams.

The principal use for coal is in producing heat for warmth, and for energy to run engines or industries. Coal-tar, a by-product of coal, also has many uses. It yields such valuable products as ammonia, creosote, carbolic acid, aspirin, various dyes, and saccharine. (See CARBONIFEROUS.)

COBALT, a minor but important metal, comes mainly from two minerals: cobaltite and skutterudite (smaltite). Cobaltite is

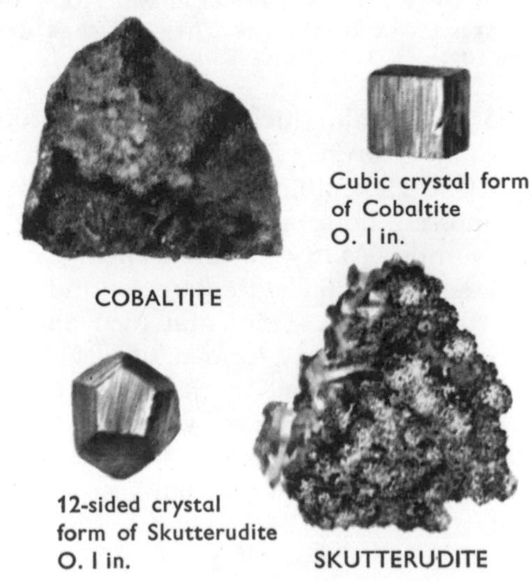

Cubic crystal form of Cobaltite O. I in.

COBALTITE

12-sided crystal form of Skutterudite O. I in.

SKUTTERUDITE

usually found in small, silver-white perfect crystals that have perfect cubic cleavage. It originates in veins of moderate temperature. Skutterudite is found in tin-white, compact, granular masses. It tarnishes to a dull grey.

Cobalt increases the strength of steel. It is alloyed with tungsten to make high-speed cutting tools that retain their edges at high temperature. Cobalt salts are used as driers in paints and varnishes and for ceramic glazes as a pigment. The blue in glass is due to cobalt. Cobalt-60, an isotope, is a replacement for radium in radiographic work. Cobalt minerals are found in Morocco, Rhodesia, the Congo, Ontario and the United States.

COCONUTS are the fruit of the Coconut Palm *(Cocos nucifera)* which grows wild on the coast of most tropical countries. These trees grow 50 to 100 feet tall and are crowned with a cluster of giant feather-like leaves.

John Titchen, AFA Limited

A Hawaiian boy climbs in search of coconuts.

Clumps of the fibrous husked coconuts grow at the point where the criss-crossed leaf stems attach to the trunk. One palm may bear five to ten bunches, each with about a dozen coconuts. Coconuts are the source of valuable oils, 'meat' and juice. Natives

of the tropics depend on them for many of their essentials — food, drink, clothing, shelter, and fuel. From the fibres they make rope, nets, and baskets. Palms — and the Coconut Palm is primary among them — are second only to grasses in importance to Man.

Coconuts are grown on plantations covering millions of acres in numerous tropical regions, including Ceylon, India, the Philippines, and islands of the south-west Pacific. The chief product is copra, the dried meat of the coconut. To obtain copra, the husk is removed from the coconut, and the kernel is broken into small pieces and dried in the sun. Large quantities of copra are shipped to Europe and the United States where coconut oil is removed in huge presses or extracted with a solvent. The oil is used in cosmetics, creams, perfumes, soaps, and margarines. The left-over cake is ground up for livestock feed.

The white meat of coconuts is often finely shredded and used as a topping to decorate cakes.

Oil is also obtained from nuts of the African Oil Palm *(Elaeis guineensis)* and other palms. (See OILS; PALMS.)

COFFEE, native to tropical Africa, was first traded by Arab caravans travelling through the Middle East. It was introduced to western Europe early in the seventeenth century. Coffee houses soon became as popular in France and England as they had been earlier in Arabian towns.

Approximately half of the world's coffee is grown today on plantations in Brazil. Other South American countries, Mexico, Central America, Asia, and Africa also produce coffee. The total world production is more than seven million pounds annually. Americans consume about 50 per cent of this.

The Coffee Plant *(Coffea arabica)* is a

Dried leaves, twigs, and dirt blow away as the worker tosses the coffee beans into the air.

Eric Hess — Triangle

Coffee trees bear when five years old, each producing about one pound of coffee every harvest.

Courtesy of the Pan American Coffee Bureau

Annan Photo Features

Workers spread the coffee beans in the sun to dry on this plantation in the mountains of Colombia. The beans are light grey-green before roasting. If it rains the platforms are rolled under the shed.

shrub or small tree that grows 15 to 40 feet tall. On some coffee plantations, young plants are protected from direct sunlight by planting a rapid-growing crop, such as corn, between the rows. Full-grown trees may be shaded by other kinds of trees. No shade is necessary when the plantations are at high altitudes. Coffee grown at 3,000 to 6,000 feet above sea level has a better flavour than coffee grown at lower altitudes, so owners of plantations in Central America sometimes post signs on their plantations giving the height above sea level.

Coffee berries or 'cherries' are about half an inch in diameter and usually contain two seeds or 'beans'. Ripe fruit are deep red to almost black. All the fruit on a branch do not mature at the same time, and so to get the best quality, they must be harvested individually as they ripen.

Coffee fruits are prepared for market either by the old Arabian 'dry' method or by the modern 'wet' method. In the dry method, the fruits are spread out to a depth of about 3 inches on a hard surface and dried in the sun. If it rains they must be covered. After the coffee beans are dry, they are 'hulled' or cleaned by hand or by machines. In the wet method of processing, the fruits produce a better-flavoured coffee that

Coffee beans are shipped while still green. Before they can be used, they must be blended and roasted. Different grinds and blends are popular with the members of different national groups.

Joe Barnell — Shostal

also brings a higher price. The fruit is first put in water. The ripe fruit sinks, and the leaves, twigs, and green fruit float away. Then the ripe fruit is run through pulping machines that rasp off the skin and most of the flesh. The remaining pulp is removed by placing the fruit in tanks to ferment 12 to 25 hours. They are removed when the proper odour is produced. The fruit is washed and stirred once more to get rid of all the flesh, and then the seeds, still enclosed in their parchment-like coverings, are dried mechanically or in sunlight on paved or tiled areas. Finally the outer covering is removed from the seed, and the coffee beans are ready for shipment to market.

The method used to roast coffee also affects its flavour. Coffee beans are usually ground after they are roasted, but this is sometimes done at the shop when the coffee is purchased, or at home just before the coffee is brewed. Most coffees are blends of several different kinds. Instant or soluble coffee is made from brewed coffee that has been dried and powdered.

The stimulant in coffee is caffeine. A cup of coffee and a cup of tea both contain the same amount of stimulant. Coffee without caffeine is preferred by those who consider the drink too stimulating.

COLA TREE

COLA TREES *(Cola nitida)*, which reach a height of 50 to 60 feet, are native to West Africa. Their star-shaped fruit contain eight irregularly shaped seeds which are used locally and also exported. Natives chew the seeds for their stimulating effect which reduces fatigue and hunger. The seeds contain about 2 per cent caffeine. From the ground seeds they prepare a drink much like brewed coffee. Seeds for export are removed from the fruit, dried in the sun, and bagged. They are used in medicines. Cola trees have been introduced to India, Brazil, tropical Asia, and Jamaica. The chief cola producing areas are in Africa and Jamaica.

COLUMBINES (*Aquilegia* spp.), members of the buttercup family, have been cultivated in Britain for more than 500 years.

Columbines have unusual, dainty blossoms and attractively scalloped leaves. About 100 species grow in the Northern Hemisphere from Europe to Siberia, Japan, and North America, but only one *(vulgaris)* occurs in Britain. It is a local plant of damp, open woodlands. Most columbines prefer cool, moist locations.

Columbine flowers are like miniature lanterns, with long spurs extending backwards. Nectar at the bottom of the spurs attracts bees and butterflies. In European species the spurs are hooked; in some American species

COLUMBINES
Aquilegia

the spurs may be two or three inches long.

Many columbines are just one colour — lavender, white, pink, or blue. One of the prettiest is the large-flowered, long-spurred Blue Columbine. The Columbine with red spurs grading to yellow on the inside of its flowers is much grown in gardens. Garden varieties are hybrids of wild species.

COLUMBITE, the source of the rare metals niobium (columbium) and tantalum, occurs as iron-black, short, tabular crystals in pegmatites and granites. It has a dark-brown streak. Niobium is used to remove gases from vacuum tubes. Alloyed with iron it prevents warping of jet engines at very high temperatures. Columbium carbide makes exceptionally hard cutting tools and fine wire-drawing dies. Tantalite is a similar ore, but it contains more tantalum than columbium. Tantalum is used for pen points and for filaments in rectifier tubes. Principal sources are Australia, Africa, Malaya, and the United States.

COLUMBITE AND TANTALITE

COMET. One of the finest sights in the sky is a bright comet. Its head is as bright as the brightest stars, while its tail streams out to great distances. Halley's comet (1910) stretched more than halfway from one horizon to the other. The shape of a comet makes it look as if it were rushing across the sky, with its tail streaming behind. But this is only an illusion. A comet changes its position among the stars by only a small amount each night, and a bright comet may remain visible for months. Also, the direction of the tail does not show which way a comet is moving; comets move nearly as often tail first as head first.

Every comet travels around the Sun in a perfectly regular orbit. But most comets appear unexpectedly because they have very large orbits that take them far away from the Sun and the Earth for thousands of years at a time. Most of the comets that we see are thus appearing for the first time in modern astronomical history.

Yerkes Observatory Photograph

MOREHOUSE'S COMET, 1908

Some comets, however, travel around the Sun in short-period orbits. The fastest is Encke's Comet, which takes only $3\frac{1}{3}$ years to go around the Sun. But the best-known of the short-period comets is Halley's, which is the only bright comet that returns more than once each century. Halley's Comet has been recorded on every single visit for more than two thousand years. Its orbital period is 76 or 77 years; its last appearance was in 1910, and it will be back again in 1986. Halley's Comet follows a long, narrow orbit around the Sun. The Sun is near one end of the comet's orbit, and so is the Earth's whole orbit around the Sun. The comet rushes around this end of its orbit in a year or so.

A comet is a very different sort of body from a planet, for very little of it is solid. At the centre of its head is a small, solid body only a few miles in diameter. This is called its nucleus, and it is made of frozen gases with pieces of stone and dust mixed in, like a dirty iceberg. When the comet swings in close to the Sun and becomes warmer, gas and dust from the nucleus spread out to form the coma, which may be thousands of miles across. This is what we see as the head of the comet. At the same time material is driven out of the comet, partly by the pressure of sunlight and partly by particles shot out of the Sun. Thus a comet's tail

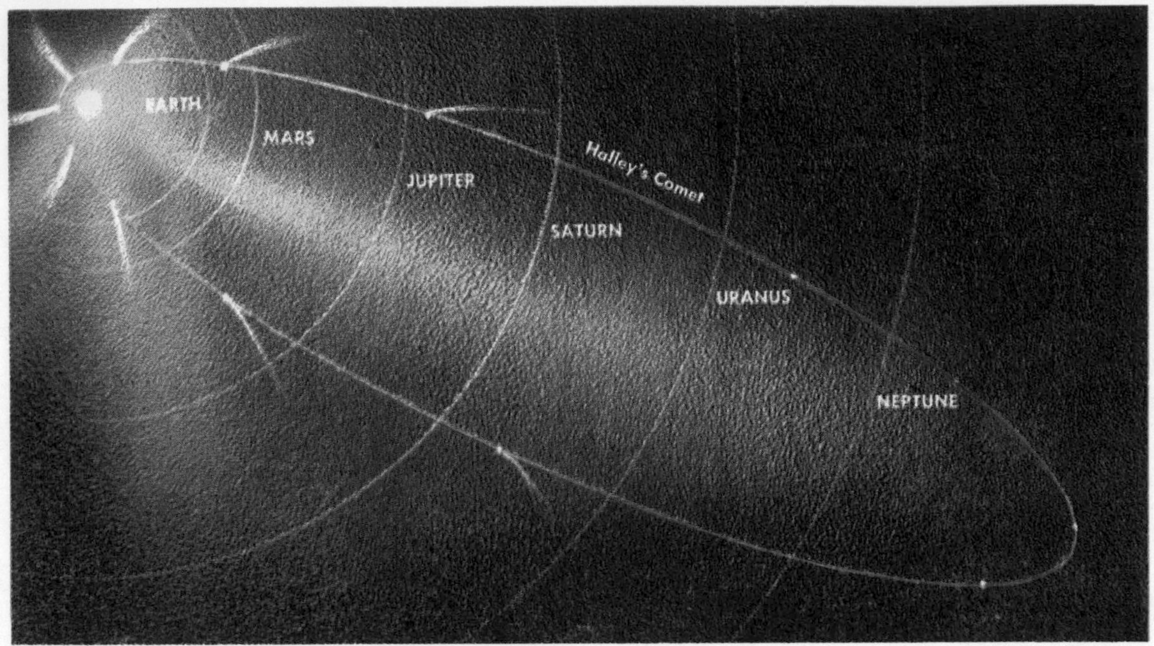

HALLEY'S COMET IN ORBIT

When Halley's Comet appeared in 1910 some newspapers predicted a world catastrophe, but the Earth passed through the tail of the comet without harm. Halley's Comet will be visible again in 1986.

always points away from the Sun. When the comet is approaching the Sun, its tail streams behind it; but as the comet travels away from the Sun, its tail precedes it. Comet tails are millions of miles long.

Some of a comet's light is reflected sunlight, like the light of the planets. But some of a comet's light is a glow in the comet itself, produced by the action of sunlight on the material of the comet. (See ORBIT.)

COMMUNICATION is the exchange of ideas or emotions between individuals or groups.

A variety of methods of communication have been evolved of which that of sound is perhaps the most important. Man has undoubtedly developed this method far better than any other animal, expressing his thoughts by means of his unique achievement called language.

HALLEY'S COMET, 1910

Yerkes Observatory Photograph

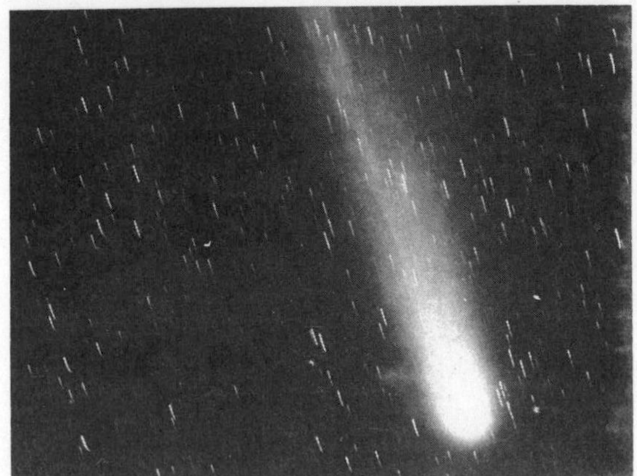

GIACOBINI'S COMET, 1906

Yerkes Observatory Photograph

LANGUAGE is as old as Man himself. It is older no doubt than the use of chipped stone tools. It developed as men came to place meanings on particular sounds made in the throat and mouth. Sounds are combined to make 'words'; words are strung together into phrases, and phrases into sentences. To avoid misunderstanding, every language has rules as to the way words and phrases are strung together to express ideas. These rules are called grammar. There are at least 2,000 languages used in the world today.

SOUNDS AND SIGNALS. Many primitive people have ways of communicating through signals or symbols. Smoke signals, the meanings of which were agreed upon beforehand, were used by American Indians. Aborigines sent messages with sticks in which notches were cut in such a manner as to help the messenger remember his complete message. Many peoples draw pictures in such a way that a long story may be told by them. When peoples with differing languages came into contact, they sometimes agreed upon a system of gestures and words, such as the mixture of French, English, and various Indian languages of the Pacific north-west of America known as Chinook.

A tribal people in Africa, the Ashanti, have been able to talk to one another over great distances by using drums. Many people use a drum to give signals like a telegraph code, but the Ashanti made drums into voices. The Ashanti language gives meaning to different tones of the voice, which English does not. So, by beating out different tones, their drums carried messages on the wings of sound.

Drums are made of various materials and in scores of shapes. Some South American Indians made a drum of a basket turned upside down. Egyptians made a drum of pottery or metal, with a parchment head. A 'water drum' is a container holding water. Drums are even made by shaping sand into a tunnel and then slapping the palm of the

Drums are used to provide the beat for dances and also to send news in the jungles of the Congo.

Hebrew Name	Picture of	Hieroglyph	Phoenician	Hebrew	Early Greek	Roman	Modern
Aleph	Ox			א		A	A
Beth	House			ב		B	B
Gimel	Camel			ג		C	C
Daleth	Door			ד		D	D
He	Window			ה		E	E
Vau	Hook			ו	YF	F	F
Cheth	Fence			ח		H	H
Yod	Hand			י		I	I
Caph	Palm			כ		K	K
Lamedh	Whip			ל		L	L
Mem	Waters			מ		M	M
Nun	Fish			נ		N	N
Ayin	Eye			ע		O	O
Pe	Mouth			פ		P	P
Koph	Head			ק		Q	Q
Resh	Head			ר		R	R
Shin	Teeth			ש		S	S
Tav	Mark			ת		T	T
Samekh	Post			ס	X	X	X
Zayin	Weapon			ז	I	Z	Z

Our English alphabet, of which 20 letters are shown, came from the Roman, which was developed from the Greek. The Greek alphabet, in turn, was influenced by the Hebrew and Phoenician alphabets.

hand against it. A 'friction drum' is one with a string or stick stuck into the middle of the drumhead. The player moistens his fingers and runs them along the string or stick to set up vibrations.

WRITTEN LANGUAGE. Many people, including American Plains Indians and Australian aborigines, drew pictures in such a manner that they represented long and complex accounts of their religious thoughts or their deeds in warfare.

While the use of language was one of the major achievements of early Man, writing is a relatively modern invention. The first

Communication between this man and the horse enables him to teach it simple tricks.

FPG

indications of the use of written characters are from both Egypt and Sumeria, in about 4000 B.C. Writing has since become the principal technique of transmitting and storing knowledge and a foundation of our civilisation.

The ancient Egyptians wrote by drawing pictures to convey their ideas. In one method each picture represented the particular object. This system required many characters and made it difficult to express abstract ideas. In a more advanced form, some pictures or characters represented sounds, as do the letters in the alphabet. For more than 2,000 years the meaning of this hieroglyphic writing was lost to the world. In 1799, the Rosetta Stone found near the Nile River unlocked the secret by showing a message written both in hieroglyphic symbols and in ancient Greek writing, which scholars could read. Picture-writing has been used by many other peoples in the world. The characters in Chinese writing are modified pictures that convey ideas rather than sounds.

Alphabet is the term applied to any set of signs, called letters, that stand for the different sounds made in speaking a language. When we write c-a-t, these signs in our alphabet tell us the sounds to make which result in the word 'cat'. The ancient Hebrews and Phoenicians were the first peoples to give up picture-writing in favour of an alphabet.

PRINTING. The idea of printing probably came to Europe from China. Koreans are known to have used metal type by 1409, a practice re-invented later in Europe. Once craftsmen got the basic idea from Asia, printing developed rapidly. The earliest book production in Europe began in 1447 at Mainz, Germany. Johann Gutenberg was connected with this, but what and how much he invented is unknown.

MODERN COMMUNICATION. Beginning with the printing press, communication became increasingly rapid and far-reaching. Today a printing press can produce millions of copies of a book in the time it took an early scholar to do one copy by hand. As evidence of the spread of printing and its value in our modern world, there are the thousands of public libraries in Great Britain and more than a hundred newspapers are published daily.

Inventions during the nineteenth century made possible the sending of messages over vast distances without actually carrying them. The telegraph and the telephone permitted communication around the world in minutes.

In the 1890s Thomas A. Edison invented the motion picture. Radio and television permit one person to communicate instantly with millions. Radio is the modern version of the 'talking drum', reaching daily into the far places of the earth where even newspapers and books do not go.

CONGLOMERATES are sedimentary rocks composed of gravel cemented together by sand and minerals. Gravels are made up of many kinds of rocks and minerals. Conglomerates may be named for their most abundant or prominent components: granite conglomerate or quartz conglomerate.

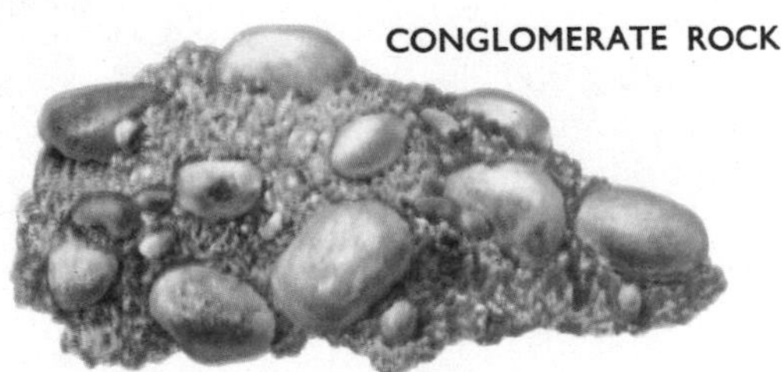

CONGLOMERATE ROCK

They form in fan-shaped deposits at the mouths of steep canyons, on beaches at the foot of sea cliffs, and in river beds.

CONIFERS are the most important members of the group of plants known as gymnosperms, or 'naked seed' plants. They are the oldest seed-bearing plants.

Evergreens (pines, firs, spruces, etc.) are among the more than 500 living species of conifers, which characteristically have cones and scale-like or needle-like leaves. Sequoias and Redwoods, our largest living trees, are conifers. Extinct types include cordaites and seed ferns.

The life cycle of a conifer, though it has no flowers, is similar to the life cycle of a flowering plant. Pollen sacs are produced on male cones, which are modified stems and leaves. Egg cells are enclosed in ovules that eventually develop into seeds. The ovules are produced on scales (modified leaves) of female cones. They are not enclosed in an ovary that develops into a fruit, as in flowering plants.

ENGELMANN SPRUCE
Picea engelmannii
70—120 ft.

About 230 million years ago, conifers were the dominant plant group on Earth, but have declined since Mesozoic times, while angiosperms or flowering plants have become more important.

This fossil Ginkgo leaf is 20 million years old.

Bob and Ira Spring

The Plough in the 20th Century.

The Plough in A.D. 100,000.

At about 40 degrees north latitude the following are considered circumpolar constellations. The Plough (Ursa Major); Little Plough (Ursa Minor); Cassiopeia, the Queen; Cepheus, the King; Draco, the Dragon. To locate these constellations, use the accompanying chart. Facing north, hold the opened book in front of you so that the current month is towards the top. The constellations are now as you will see them during the current month at 9 p.m. To see how they will appear earlier, turn the chart clockwise; for a later time, counter-clockwise. A quarter of a turn will show how much the positions of the stars will change during a six-hour period.

CONSTELLATIONS. Different civilisations have drawn the patterns of constellations in different ways. The set that we use goes back to the ancient Babylonians and has been passed down to us by the Greeks, Romans, and Arabs. We still use the names these people gave to the constellations. Most constellations represent mythological humans or animals, although it often takes a lot of imagination to see the supposed picture.

In the early days the constellations were believed to have an influence on daily life. They were used as a guide for the planting and harvesting of crops and the slaughtering of animals for food. Weather was forecast by the stars, and a person's daily activities were charted by the stars in terms of the constellation of his birth. Each constellation had a story, and different peoples invented different myths about the stars.

The patterns of the constellations have hardly changed since the time of the Babylonians. But as more thousands of years pass and the motions of the stars through space continue, changes in the constellations will become evident. In each constellation, some stars are much farther from the Earth than others, and each star is moving in its own direction. Because of this, the constellations are slowly changing with the passing of the centuries.

Modern astronomers use the traditional

The Sun, the Moon, and the planets, which are called 'heavenly bodies', are said to be within the sign of the Zodiac when they are between that constellation and the observer.

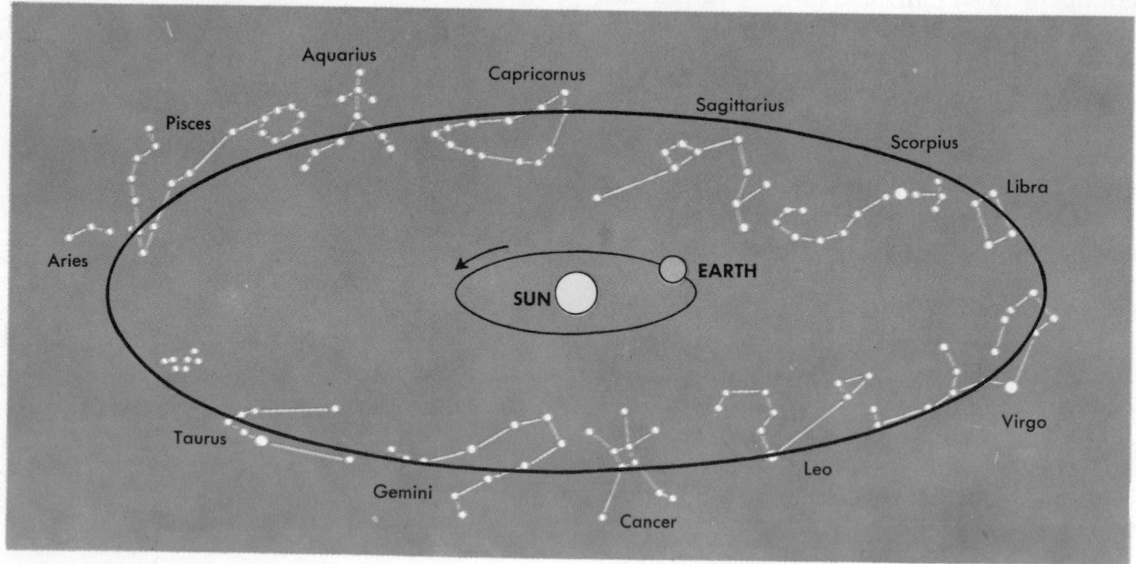

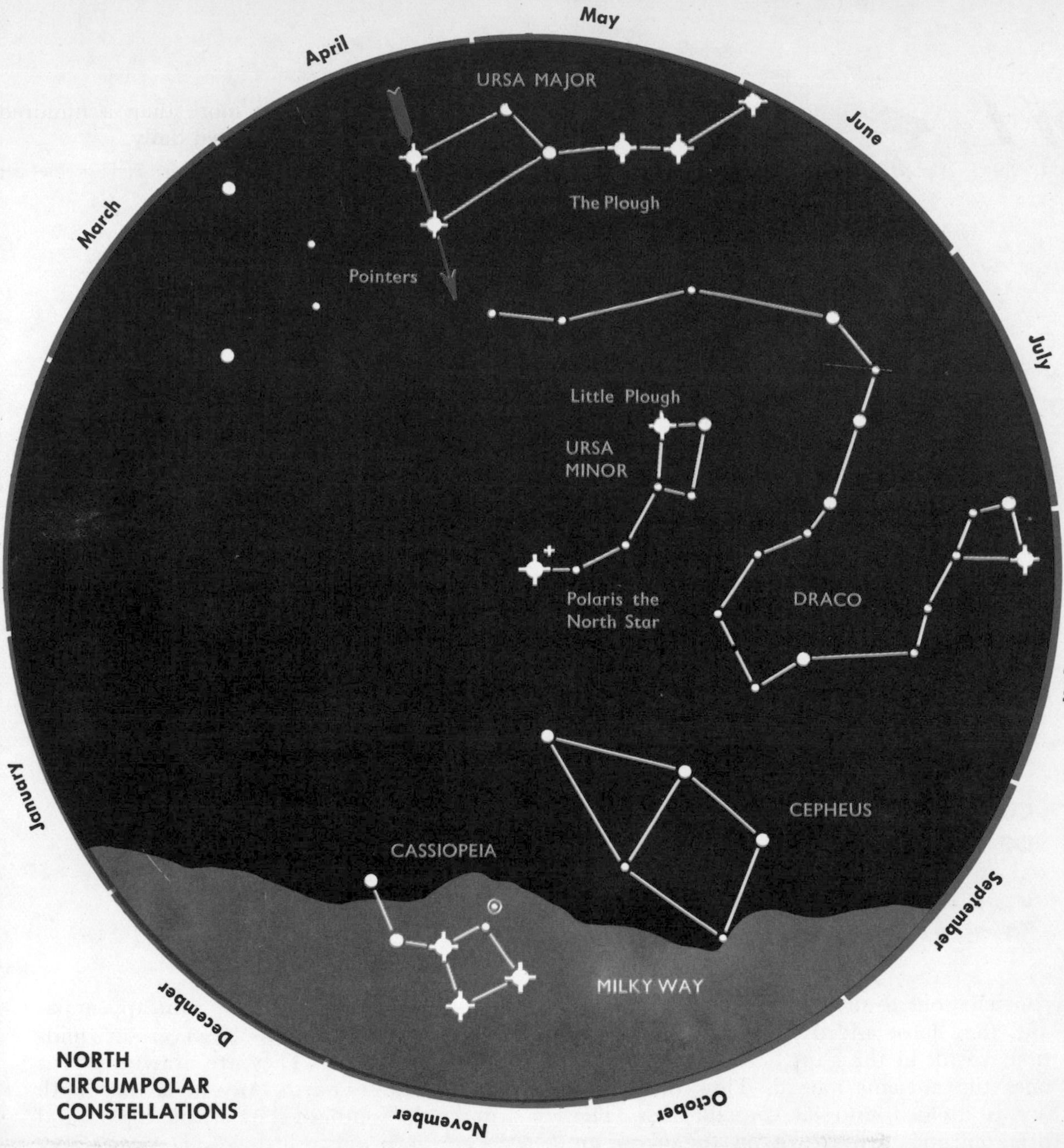

May
April
June
March
July
February
August
January
September
December
November
October

URSA MAJOR
The Plough
Pointers
Little Plough
URSA MINOR
Polaris the North Star
DRACO
CEPHEUS
CASSIOPEIA
MILKY WAY

NORTH CIRCUMPOLAR CONSTELLATIONS

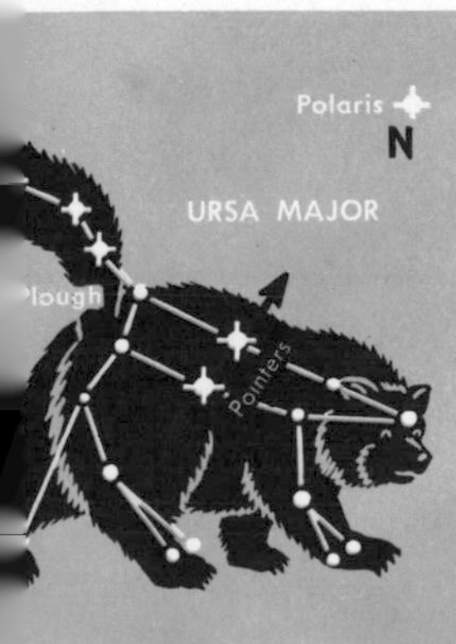

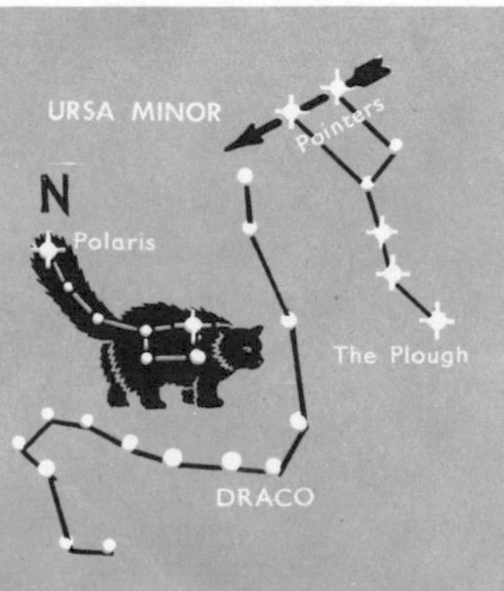

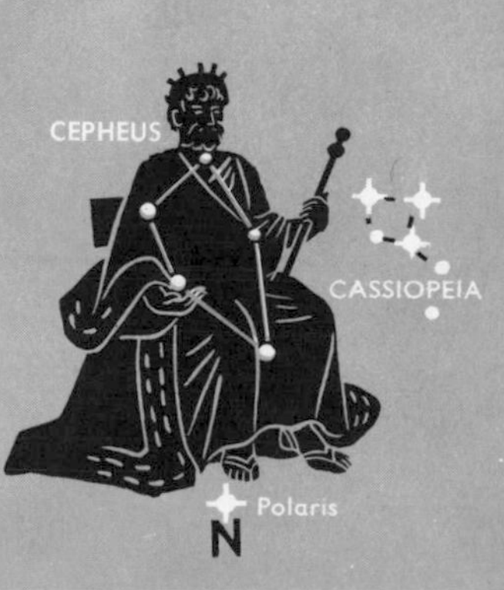

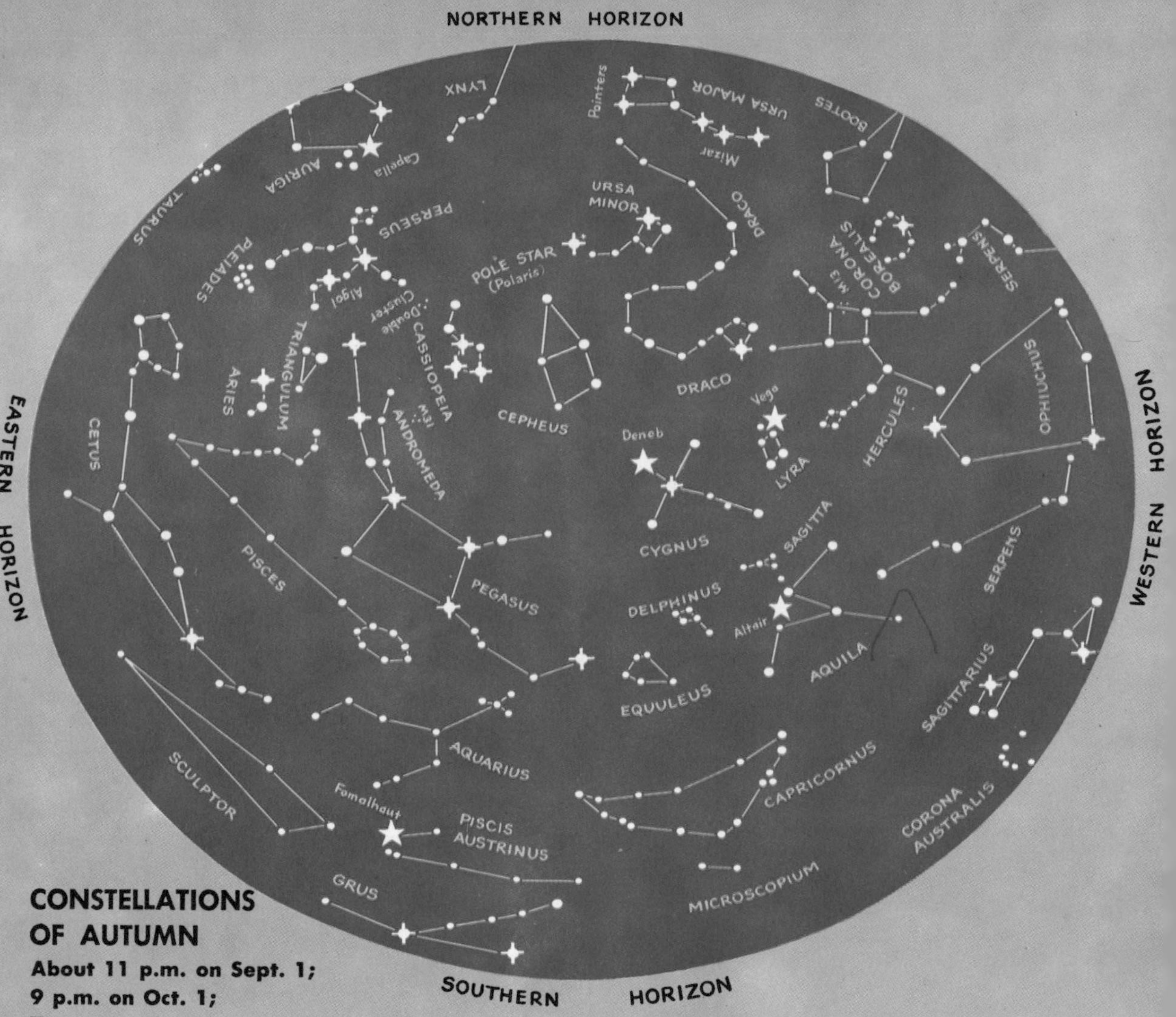

NORTHERN HORIZON

EASTERN HORIZON

WESTERN HORIZON

SOUTHERN HORIZON

CONSTELLATIONS OF AUTUMN

About 11 p.m. on Sept. 1; 9 p.m. on Oct. 1; 7 p.m. on Nov. 1.

constellations to divide the sky into regions, and they have added some faint constellations to fill in the gaps between the bright ones the ancients named. Thus the whole sky is divided into 88 constellations. The brighter ones are shown on the maps on these pages.

These maps show the sky as it appears at different times to an observer in mid-northern latitudes. They are drawn for latitude 40 degrees north. Anyone farther south will see the southern stars a little higher and the northern stars a little lower. An observer farther north will see the northern stars

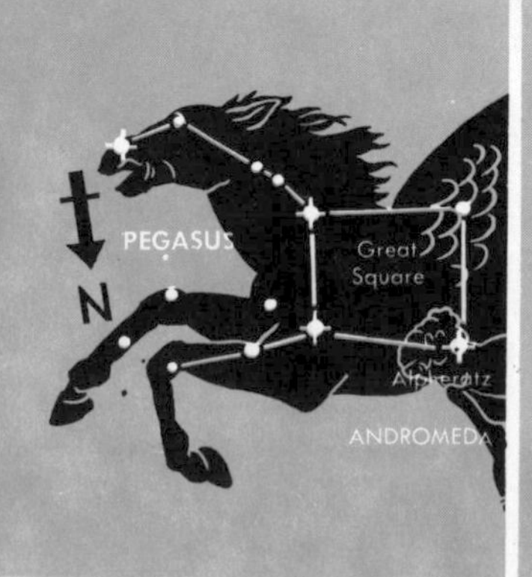

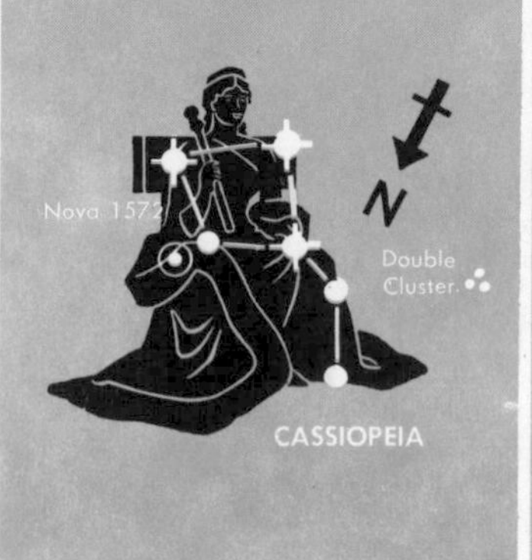

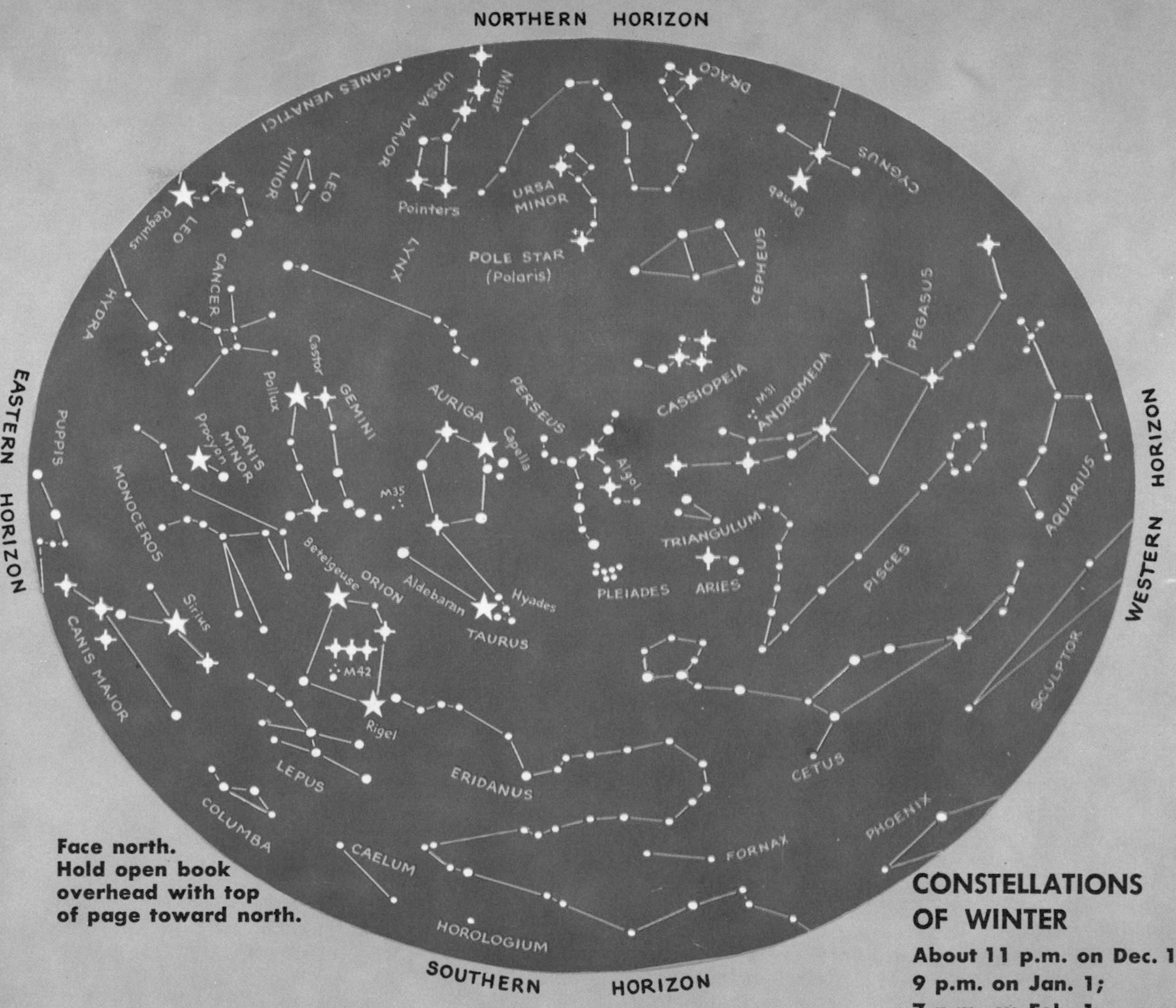

NORTHERN HORIZON

EASTERN HORIZON

WESTERN HORIZON

SOUTHERN HORIZON

Face north. Hold open book overhead with top of page toward north.

CONSTELLATIONS OF WINTER

About 11 p.m. on Dec. 1; 9 p.m. on Jan. 1; 7 p.m. on Feb. 1.

higher and the southern stars lower. Several maps are needed because the Earth's rotation makes the heavens appear to turn about us. (See STARS.) The daily turning carries the stars across the sky, but the next night at the same time they look almost the same again. There is a slow shift throughout the year, however, so that the same view of the heavens comes about two hours earlier each month. Hence the maps have to be labelled with date and time to make them usable.

The apparent turning of the heavens is around a point midway up the northern sky, marked by the Pole Star. Constellations

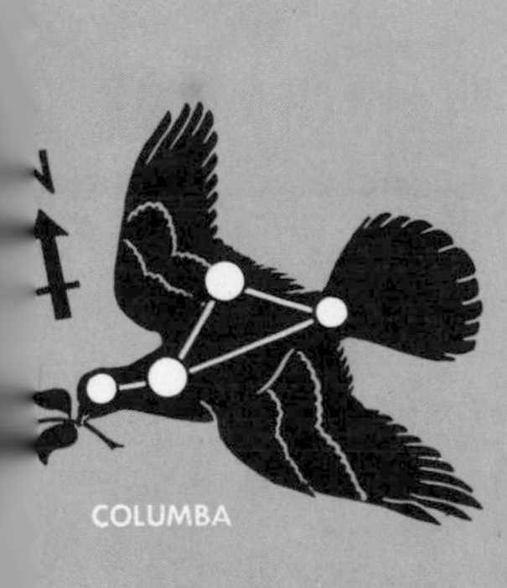

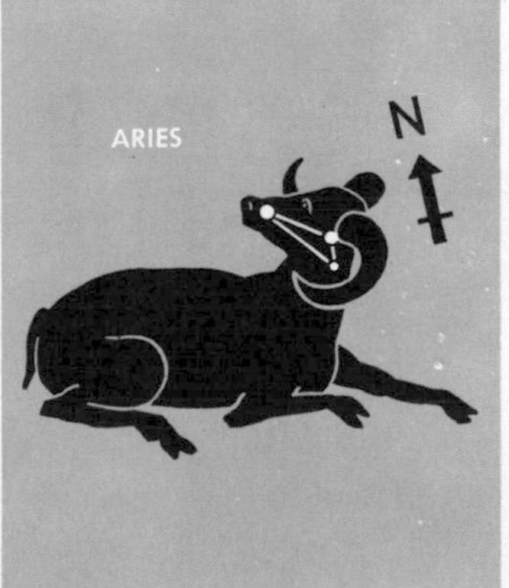

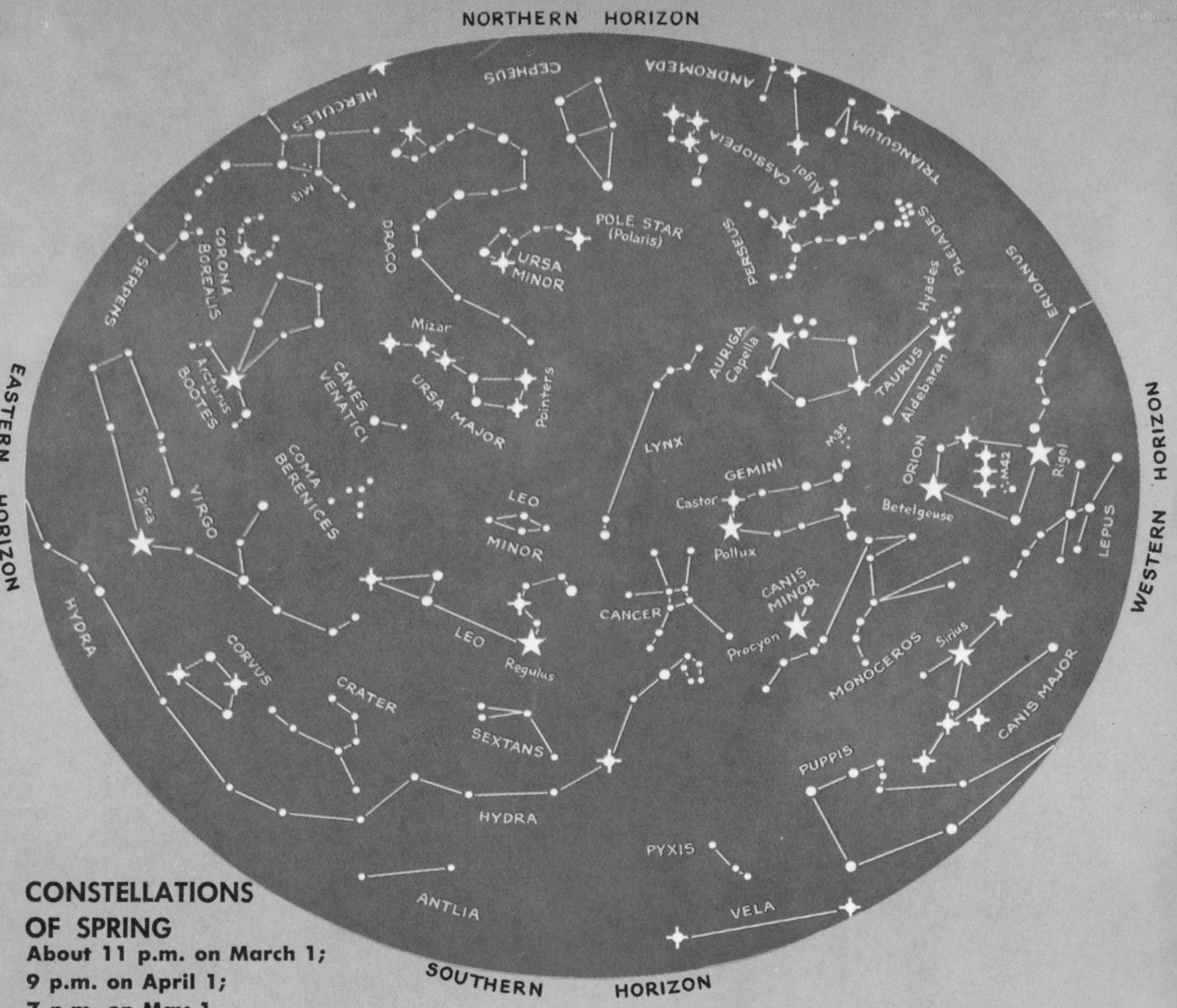

CONSTELLATIONS OF SPRING

About 11 p.m. on March 1; 9 p.m. on April 1; 7 p.m. on May 1.

that are near the Pole Star never set and can be seen on all four seasonal maps. On the other hand, constellations too close to the South Pole of the heavens never appear at all to an observer in the Northern Hemisphere. The map of southern constellations shows constellations that are invisible from middle northern latitudes. Observers farther south – in the south of Spain, for instance – can glimpse some of them on the southern horizon under favourable conditions.

Constellations that completely dominate the South Polar regions are not all visible in northern latitudes. From the equator

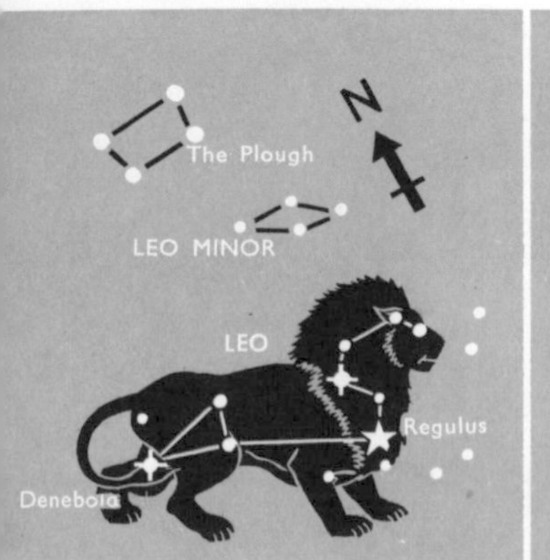

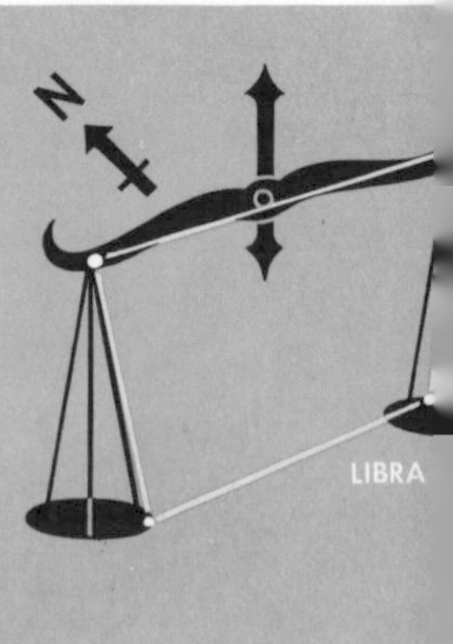

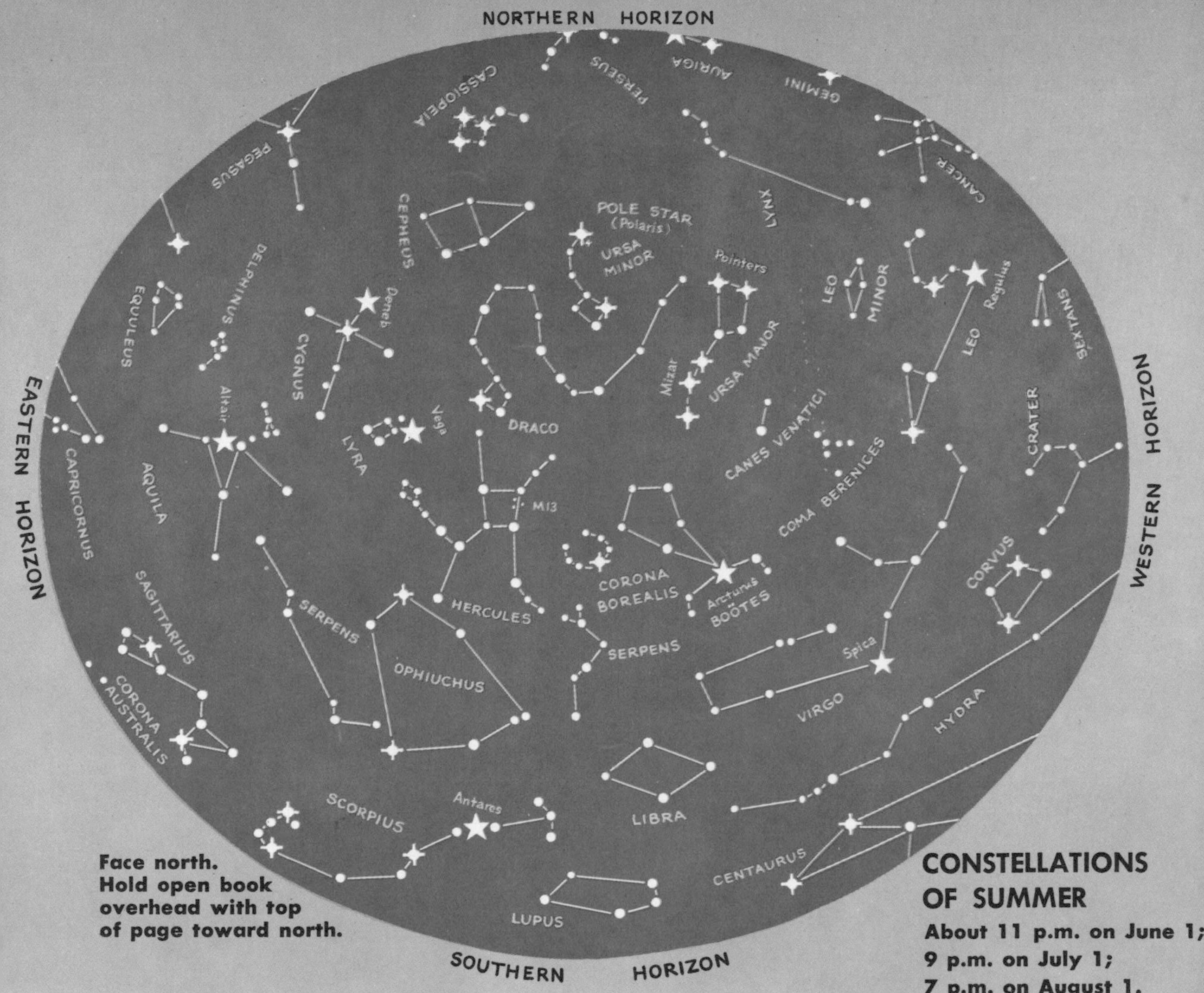

NORTHERN HORIZON

EASTERN HORIZON

WESTERN HORIZON

SOUTHERN HORIZON

Face north.
Hold open book overhead with top of page toward north.

CONSTELLATIONS OF SUMMER

About 11 p.m. on June 1; 9 p.m. on July 1; 7 p.m. on August 1.

southwards these constellations appear higher in the sky as constellations of the Northern Hemisphere sink beneath the horizon.

Unlike the Northern Hemisphere, the Southern Hemisphere sky has no bright star to mark its pole. To find the South Pole of the sky, extend the constellation Crux (the Southern Cross) five times its own length. The true South Pole will then be located on a line between the Southern Cross and the Small Magellanic Cloud, very near the constellation known as Octans. The Magellanic Clouds are clusters of nebulae and stars

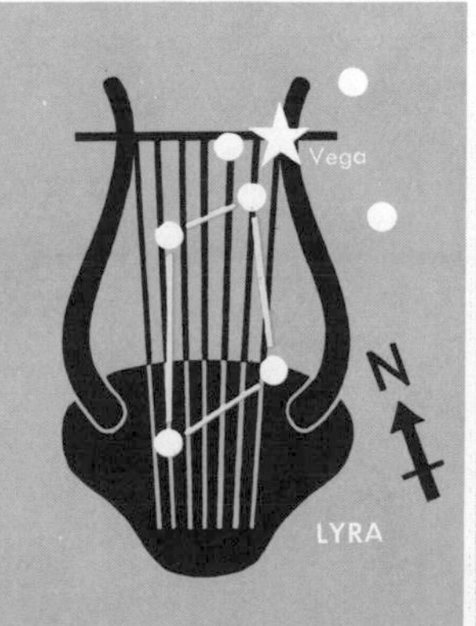

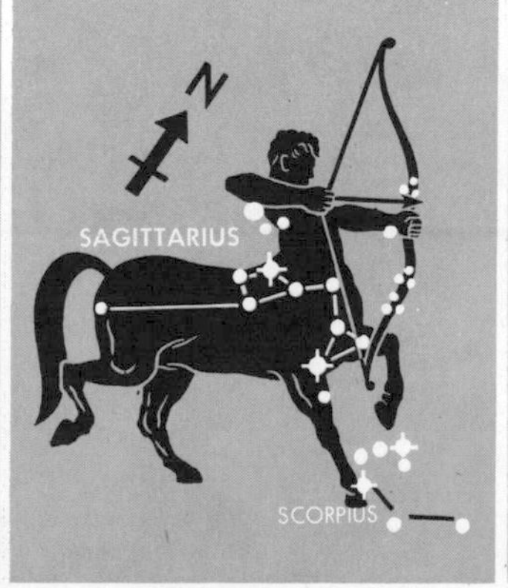

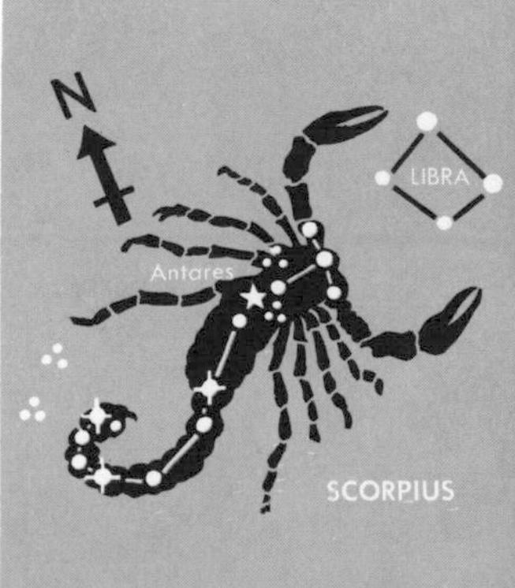

August
July
June
May
April
March
February
January
December
November
October
September
TO SAGITTARIUS
THE ALTAR
MILKY WAY
TRIANGLE
CENTAURUS
PAVO
To Fomalhaut
OCTANS
TUCANA
COAL SACK
SOUTHERN CROSS
SOUTH POLE
TO CORVUS
SMALL MAGELLANIC CLOUD
HYDRUS
Achernar
VOLANS
MILKY WAY
LARGE MAGELLANIC CLOUD
CARINA
DORADO
TO ORION
Canopus

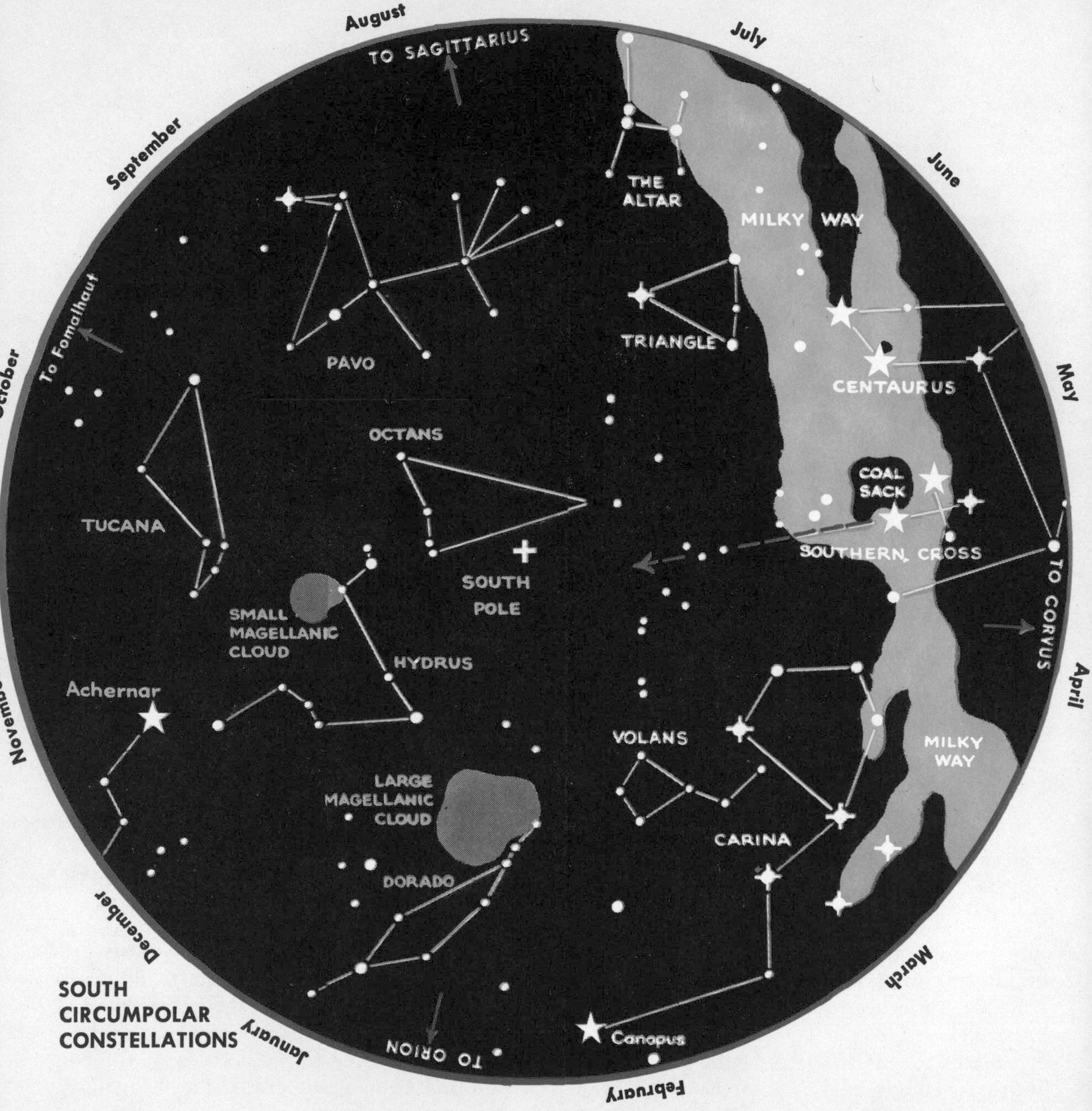

SOUTH CIRCUMPOLAR CONSTELLATIONS

Gacrux
CRUX
Beta Crucis
Acrux
S

CENTAURUS
N
Rigil Kentaurus (Alpha Centauri)
Agena (Beta Centauri)

PAVO
Alpha Pavonis
N

N
CANCER

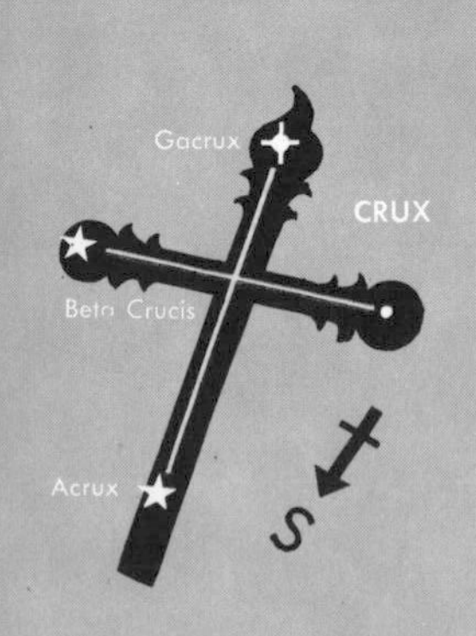

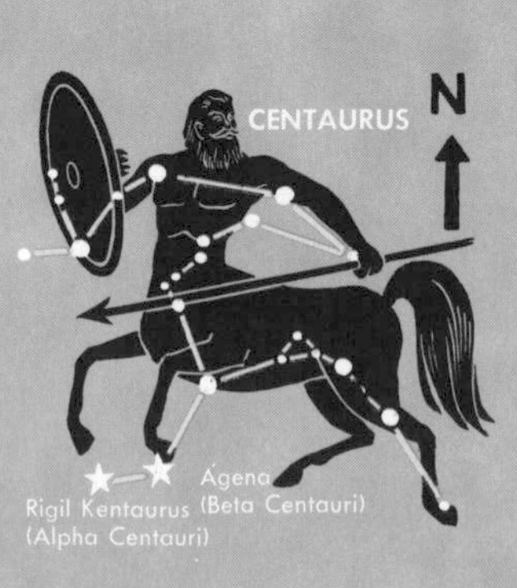

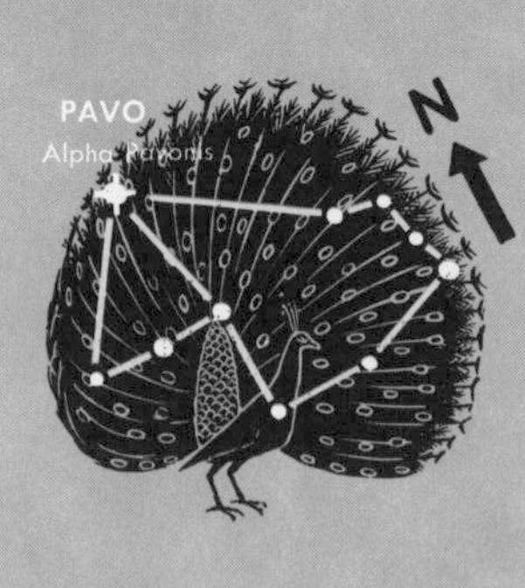

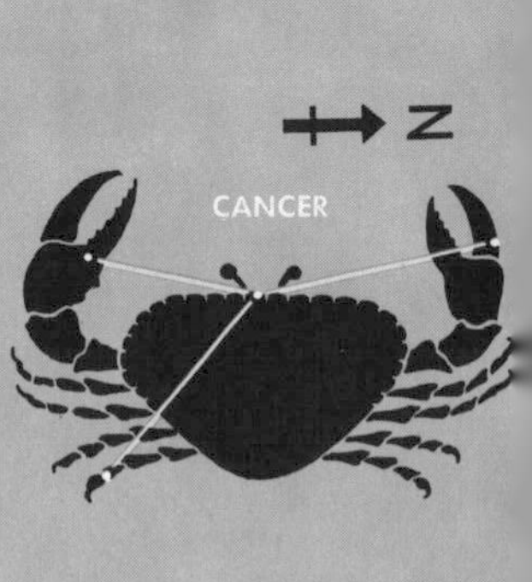

At about 40 degrees south latitude the following are the chief circumpolar constellations: Crux (Southern Cross), Carina (the Keel, of the ship Argo), Volans (Flying Fish), Dorado (Goldfish or Swordfish), Hydrus (Sea Serpent), Tucana (Toucan), Octans (Octant), Pavo (Peacock), Ara (Altar), Triangulum (Southern Triangle), and Centaurus (Centaur).

Near the equator you can locate these constellations with the accompanying chart. Facing south hold the open book in front of you so that the current month is towards the top. The constellations are roughly as you will see them during the current month at 9 p.m. To see how they will appear earlier, turn the chart counter-clockwise; for a later time, clockwise. A quarter of a turn will show how much the positions of the stars will change during a six-hour period.

while Octans is a rather faint group of stars that vaguely resemble some kind of navigational instrument.

As the Earth revolves about the Sun, its brightness hides from us, one by one, a series of constellations. These twelve constellations are called the Zodiac. Each one has its own name, and according to the ancients, its own influence on the lives of those born at the time when the Sun happened to obscure it. The signs of the Zodiac are Capricornus, the Goat; Aquarius, the Water-Bearer; Pisces, the Fish; Aries, the Ram; Taurus, the Bull; Gemini, the Twins; Cancer, the Crab; Leo, the Lion; Virgo, the Virgin; Libra, the Balance; Scorpio, the Scorpion; and Sagittarius, the Archer. This system was devised 2,000 years ago; since then, the Sun's apparent course has changed very considerably, due to constant movement of the Earth's axis.

Today, as in ancient times, some people believe that the stars forming the Zodiac have a great influence on their lives and on the course of events in the world. This pseudo-science, which has no basis in fact, is called astrology. An astrologer plots a person's horoscope on a map of the heavens at the exact time of the person's birth. The positions of the Earth, Sun, Moon, and planets are shown on the Zodiac, with each of its twelve constellations forming a sign or house that exerts a particular kind of influence on the person's life. A horoscope can be used to predict the future, thus being a blueprint for a person's entire life, or it may reflect only day-by-day happenings. This belief still persists and newspapers and magazines regularly publish the predictions of astrologers.

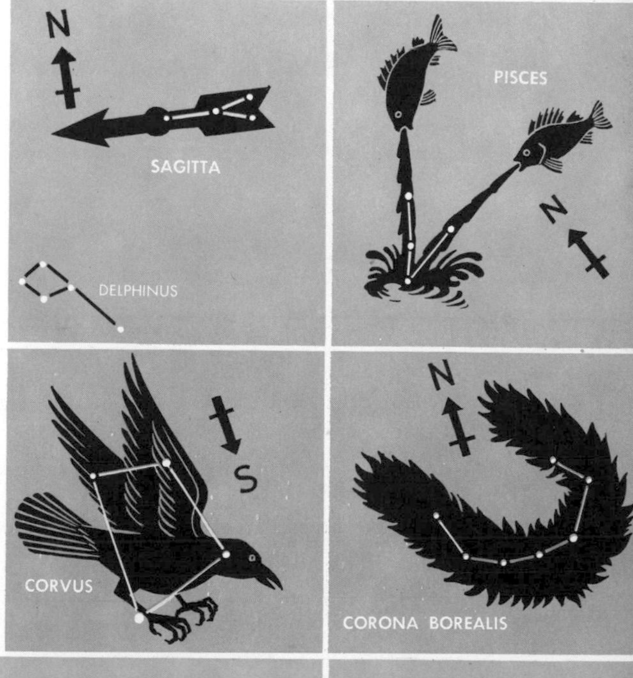

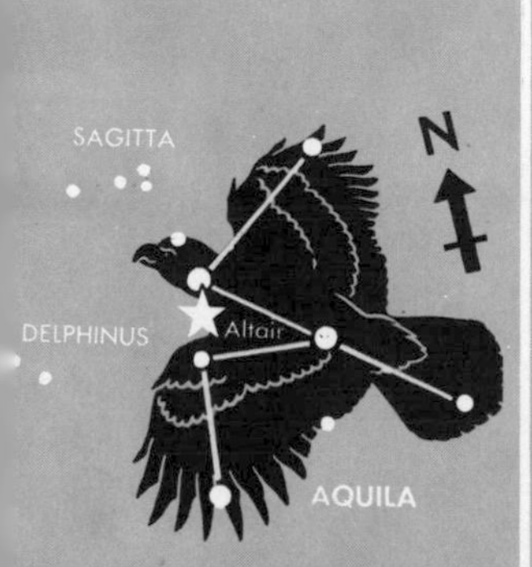

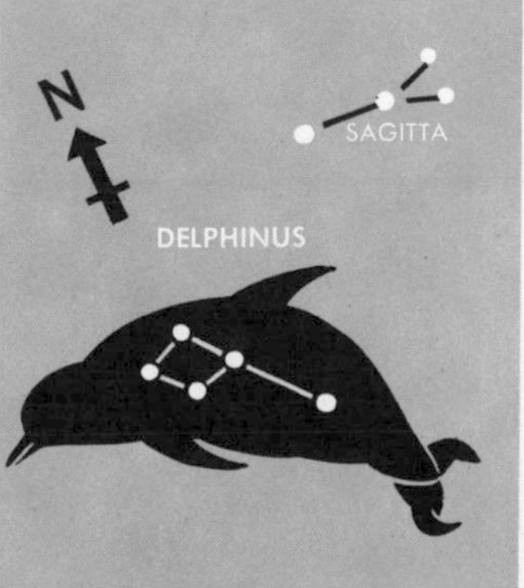

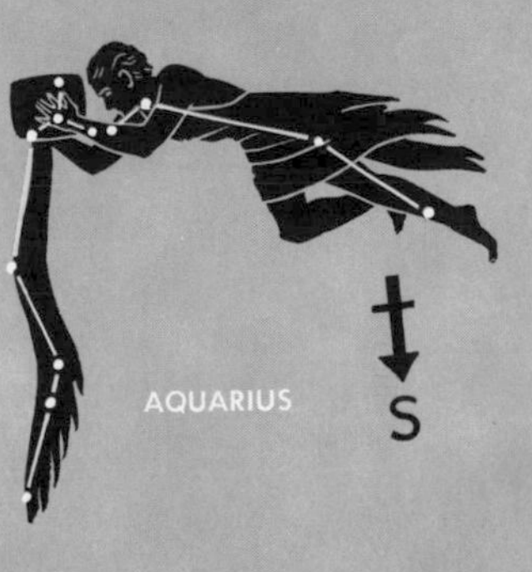

Courtesy of ANACONDA

One of the world's largest open-pit copper mines is high in the Andes Mountains at Chuquicamata, Chile.

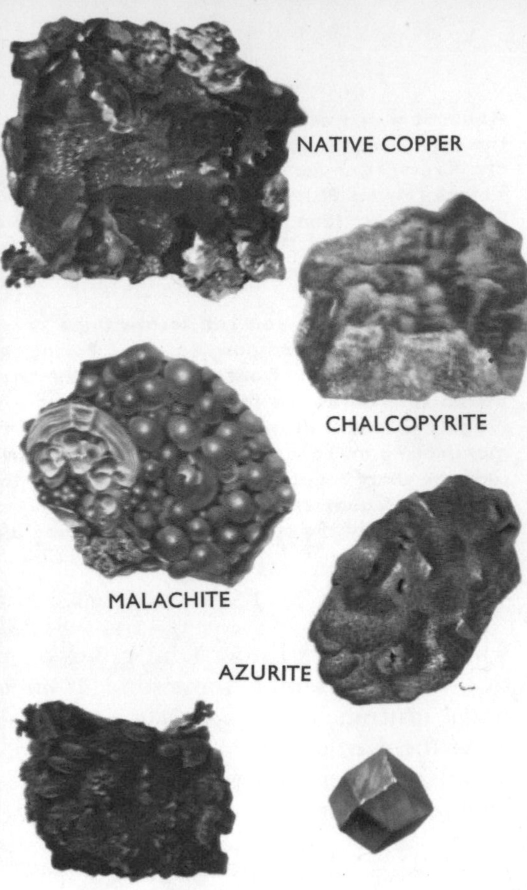

NATIVE COPPER in matrix

Crystal of Native Copper

COPPER occurs in many minerals as well as in pure deposits. Native copper is found in soft, irregular masses, plates, or wires. Freshly exposed, it is a bright copper-red but tarnishes to black or green. Bornite or peacock ore (copper-iron sulphide) occurs in purplish-red, iridescent granular masses; it has a metallic lustre and a black streak. Chalcopyrite (copper-iron sulphide) also has a black streak and is found in compact, brass-yellow, metallic masses. It tarnishes to bronze, purple, or black. Chalcocite (copper sulphide) occurs in dark-grey or black, fine-grained compact masses; it has a black streak. Cuprite (copper oxide) is found in red, fine-grained compact masses or in small crystals. Chrysocolla (copper silicate) occurs in blue or green-blue, smooth enamel-like crusts or masses. Azurite (hydrated copper carbonate) is found usually as azure-blue or dark blue crystals but also occurs in velvety masses or crusts. Malachite (hydrated copper carbonate) commonly is found with azurite but is green.

Copper is one of the most important industrial metals, and a large proportion of the copper used every year is retrieved from scrap. The major use of copper is for wire in the electrical industry.

Brass (an alloy mainly of copper and zinc) also has major uses, as does bronze (an alloy of copper, tin, and zinc). German silver is copper, zinc, and nickel. Manganese bronze, an alloy with great toughness, strength, and resistance to salt-water corrosion, is used for such items as propeller blades and valve stems. An alloy of copper, nickel, aluminium and a small amount of silicon is used as electrical contact springs in business machines.

Copper in small amounts is necessary for plants, but larger amounts are poisonous. Copper compounds may be used both as a fertiliser or as a fungicide. Copper minerals are widely distributed and are mined commercially in Cornwall, Germany, U.S.S.R., Congo, Rhodesia, Australia, U.S.A., and Canada, Chile and Peru.

CORAL REEFS occur mostly on the east side of large islands and continents in tropical waters from latitude 30 degrees north to 30 degrees south. Coral reefs are formed from the 'skeletons' of the stony corals and are also cemented together by coralline algae and the limey shells of other marine invertebrates.

Largest of all coral reefs is Australia's Great Barrier Reef, over 1,200 miles long, and in the United States there are coral reefs along the Florida Keys.

Coral reefs are of three kinds: *fringing reefs*, which lie directly against the land; *barrier reefs*, which are distant from the shore and separated from it by a deep lagoon or channel; *atolls*, which are circular or horseshoe shaped reefs encircling a lagoon. True atolls occur only in the Pacific and Indian oceans. They consist of a broken chain of islands forming an irregular circle, and there is no land in the centre of the lagoon.

BRAIN CORAL

Australian News and Information Bureau

On the cruise of the *Beagle*, Charles Darwin found that atolls were fringing reefs which formed around mountain or volcano tops that began to sink slowly into the sea as the corals grew upwards. According to this theory, the fringing reef eventually would become a barrier reef and finally an atoll as the mountain sank below the waves. Some geologists disagreed with this idea. They thought the reefs formed during a glacial period when the water level was lower, and that the water level rose as the ice melted. Most scientists now believe a combination of methods produced changes that enabled atolls to develop.

CORNFLOWERS (*Centaurea* spp.), like asters, are composite flowers. They are attractive in the garden and are excellent cut flowers because they keep well and have stiff, straight stems. Cornflowers are natives

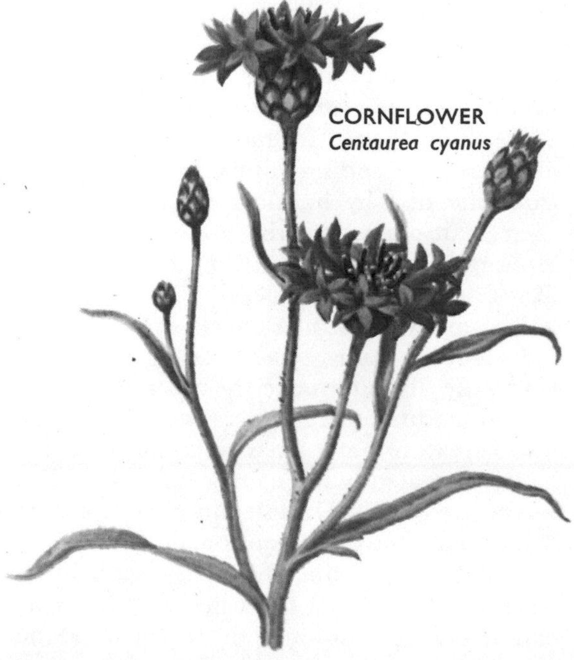

CORNFLOWER
Centaurea cyanus

of Europe, where some still grow wild. They are the national flower of Germany. In North America where they are known as 'Bachelors-buttons', they are garden plants and are grown commercially as cut flowers. A few have escaped flower gardens and now grow wild along roadsides or in open spaces. Cornflowers are close relatives of thistles.

COTTON is the world's most important natural fibre. Cotton cloth was used in India 3,000 years ago, and was used also in ancient Egypt and in China. Spanish explorers found some American Indians wearing cotton garments, and the Incas of Peru wove cotton fabrics.

All the varieties of cotton (*Gossypium* spp.) now grown are a result of centuries of selection. Sea Island Cotton, one of the three major types, produces very long fibres of high quality, but is so susceptible to the cotton boll weevil that it is no longer grown in the United States. Upland Cotton, the type now grown in the Cotton Belt of the United States, accounts for about 95 per cent of the annual production. Another major type is Egyptian Cotton, grown chiefly in the Nile Valley. It is very similar to Sea Island Cotton.

Cotton plants mature in five to six months. Their fruit is a leathery capsule called a 'boll', which opens wide when ripe and exposes a mass of yellowish-white fibres that grow on the surface of the seeds. The fibres are of two types: long, which are called 'lint' or 'staple'; and short, which are called 'linters' or 'fuzz'. In harvesting, the seeds and the surrounding cotton fibres are taken from the boll by hand or by machine and then transported to the cotton gin which separates the long fibres from the seeds. The fibres are cleaned, squeezed into 500 pound bales, and wrapped in coarse canvas.

In cotton mills, machines separate and comb the fibres to make them parallel. Then the individual strands are twisted or spun into thread or yarn for weaving into fabrics. Cotton treated with caustic soda is called mercerized cotton. It is stronger and has more lustre than untreated cotton.

Cellulose is produced from the short fibres which are separated from the seed by a special machine. Cellulose is the basic compound of rayon, plastics, photographic film, guncotton, and many other products. Cottonseed oil pressed from the seeds is used in manufacturing soaps and oleomargarine and as a cooking fat or salad oil. Cottonseed meal, the dried remains, is valuable as a feed and also as a fertiliser. The cotton boll is used as a fuel or in the manufacture of paper and fibre board.

Hal Strong — Shostal

This cotton was grown in Arizona, in the United States, where irrigation has converted the desert into fertile farms.

Mechanical cotton-pickers are rapidly replacing hand labour in the cotton fields of the United States.

USDA

The United States grows approximately half of the world's cotton. Other cotton-producing areas are India, Pakistan, Egypt, China, Manchuria, Brazil, and the southern parts of the Soviet Union.

CRAFTS AND ARTS OF EARLY MAN. Man differs from other animals in many ways, and one of the most obvious of these is his skill in the manipulation of material objects. This talent is not the same as the hereditary ability of such animals as spiders to build webs, termites to build mounds, or beavers to build dams. Man's many skills are learned and must be taught to each generation.

This glass face was made in ancient Egypt.
British Museum, London

Man's handicrafts were developed slowly, though with increasing acceleration as each invention paved the way for a number of others. The basic inventions of language, the use of fire, the domestication of animals, agriculture, basketry, pottery, weaving, the alphabet, and simple metal working were very important advances. These are the fundamental techniques of Man's present civilisations. (See AGRICULTURE; COMMUNICATION; MAN.)

BASKETRY is one of Man's oldest arts, older than either weaving or pottery making. It is a simple form of weaving in which reeds, branches, or various fibres are intertwined. The simplest sort of basketry is that practised by the Fuegians at the southernmost tip of South America. They make a loose, open-weave bag much the same as that used for sacking onions. Another simple method is that of 'wickerwork' or plaiting. This involves running the strands over-and-under-and-over, as children in primary school sometimes learn to do. Some American Indian tribes did very complicated work using the wickerwork method.

The most skilful of all basketry is done by 'coiling'. A long strand is coiled, one layer on top of the other, much as a sailor coils up the rope on the deck of a ship. As they are coiled, the layers may be sewn.

Many primitive peoples make baskets to hold water. Baskets will serve this purpose excellently when tightly woven. They may also be sealed with clay or pitch taken from trees. Wherever Man has not had pottery, basketry has been an essential craft.

POTTERY. One of Man's earliest achievements was the manufacture of hard pottery from soft clay. This skill provided him with vessels for cooking and storing food and for carrying water. Ornaments and works of art were also made of pottery.

Pots are made by shaping soft clay and then drying it. The clay must be first kneaded, and if it is too sticky, animal dung or fine chaff is added. Shaping may be done entirely by hand, or it may be done on a wheel or even in moulds, shaped like the desired pot. Some peoples coil strips of clay, like sausages, layer on layer, pressing each coil gently against the one next to it. Porcelain is a kind of pottery which by a special process is turned into something very much like glass.

If a pot is to be of much use, it must be 'fired'. Firing is simply baking the pot after it has been dried in the sun. The first fired pottery was made about 6500 B.C. in Mesopotamia. Probably the earliest stationary use of the wheel was for shaping pots. In a potter's wheel, the wheel is mounted on the upright end of an axle set in the ground. A piece of clay is thrown on the centre of the wheel, and as the wheel is turned, the potter shapes the clay with his hands. Although the American Indians made excellent pottery, they did not know of the potter's wheel.

WEAVING. Since the New Stone Age, Man has been making cloth by interlacing strands of cord or thread. Cloth weaving grew out of the earlier invention of basketry. Cloth or textiles may be woven from strands of animal fur (wool or hair), from vegetable fibres (cotton, flax, or others), or from an animal product (silk). Even strands of metals, such as silver or gold, can be woven into fabrics. In modern times many chemically-made or synthetic products, such as nylon, are used.

New Stone Age Man grew flax and cotton

One of the earliest human artistic efforts is this Palaeolithic, or Old Stone Age, painting of a horse on the wall of a cave at Lascaux, France. The paint used was red and yellow earth mixed with animal fat.

for their fibres, and kept wool-bearing anials. He mastered the technique of spinning thread from these raw materials, then of combining threads into yarn, and finally of weaving yarns to form fabric. Some peoples, in Australia, for example, have learned how to make thread but have never developed weaving.

Weaving is usually done on a loom, a framework that holds a series of threads taut while the weaver interlaces other threads across and through them. People in southern Peru, however, make a speciality of weaving with their fingers without the help of a loom, although this is not because the loom was unknown to American Indians. Some of the finest weaving ever produced came from the Indians of the Andes Mountains.

Although Europeans never produced more beautiful fabrics than primitive man, they developed techniques for making more cloth with less human effort and skill. During the eighteenth century, the work of weaving was speeded up by rapid advancements in both spinning and weaving. Hargreaves in 1767 found a way for one spinner to control the spinning of many cords at the same time. Many persons contributed to the invention of satisfactory power looms. About 1800 a device was created with which one weaver and his helper could operate five looms at the same time. Further improvements in textile machinery, particularly in England and France, changed textile making from a handicraft to a great industry.

A finely woven Peruvian Inca textile, 1200–1500.
American Museum of Natural History

Denver Art Museum
This clay pot was made by the Zia Pueblos, Indians of south-west U.S. who are famous for their pottery.

Arizona State Museum
Basket storage jar made by Apache Indians on San Carlos Reservation, Arizona, about 1920.

ART. One of Man's unique characteristics is his urge to create art. Other animals use tools, but only man wishes to carve and paint them or to create objects with no purpose except to satisfy his desire for beauty. Thousands of years before writing was invented, men expressed their ideas and feelings

R. Doisneau — Rapho/Guillumette

The Bayeux tapestry, probably woven in England between 1066 and 1082 depicts the Battle of Hastings.

through drawings, sculpture, dancing, music, and other forms of art. Nor has any primitive tribe failed to develop art forms.

Quite early, art became connected with religion and worship, as it still is. The magnificent statues of the Buddha are as inspirational to millions of Asians as are, say, such paintings as Leonardo da Vinci's *The Last Supper* to millions of Christians.

Fine-art goes back possibly 50,000 years, although the earliest great paintings known are the cave art of Cro-Magnon Man created between 12,000 and 20,000 years ago. This prehistoric race left superb paintings on the

Working soft metals was an early development. Gold mask in pre-Grecian style, 1600–1500 B.C.

Department of Antiquities, Ashmolean Museum, Oxford. (Facsimile, original in Athens.)

As early as the 6th century B.C., Persian artists created pleasing bronze castings, such as this Ibex head.

Metropolitan Museum of Art

Nelson Gallery — Atkins Museum (Nelson Fund), Kansas City, Missouri

Stones were among Man's earliest tools and also became a means of artistic expression, as in this Chinese jade carving of 500—300 B.C.

walls of caves in southern France and Spain.

Much more is known of the art of early civilisations. The Sumerians have left us mosaics showing armies marching into battle and others of rich men feasting. The Minoans of Crete expressed themselves in fine pottery and metalwork. By 2500 B.C. Egyptian sculpture and painting were showing exquisite colour and workmanship. Some 5,000 year-old Egyptian sculptures are huge yet graceful in design. The sculpture of the Greeks still provides us with standards of beauty.

Different art styles arise in different societies, since peoples differ in their conceptions of beauty and in the materials with which they work. The art of early Far Eastern civilisations was unlike that of Egypt or Greece. The civilisation of North India produced carved animals and supernatural beings by about 2500 B.C. In China the Shang Dynasty (1766—1122 B.C.) is famous for artistry in bronze, marble, and jade. In the Far East painters emphasised the beauty of landscapes, whereas European artists paid more attention to the human form.

The art of primitive peoples is no less artistic and no less perfect than the art of civilised peoples. To say that a particular art form is more 'advanced' than another is to miss the point that each, in its way, is an expression of Man's urge to create beauty.

CRESS. Several different plants go by the name of cress. Watercress *(Nasturtium officinale)* is a native plant in Britain. It occurs in ditches and at margins of ponds and lakes. When grown as a crop it is cultivated in wide, specially made channels of water and the bed of watercress makes a complete cover. The plant's crisp, round leaves are used in salads or as a garnish.

Cress *(Lepidium sativum)* which is also a land plant, is used as a salad as soon as the seeds have germinated and produced two green cotyledons. It is usually mixed with similar seedlings of Mustard.

WATERCRESS

CRETACEOUS. This most recent period of the Mesozoic era was named for the chalk (Latin, *creta)* which is its distinctive deposit. The Cretaceous, one of the longest periods in the history of the Earth, began about 136 million years ago and lasted about 65 million years. In most parts of the world thick deposits of both marine and non-marine sediments accumulated during the Cretaceous period, indicating repeated rising and falling of land and sea. Towards the close of the period the sea withdrew, and such mountain ranges as the Rockies, Andes, and those in north-eastern Asia and in Antarctica came into existence.

Hundreds of oil and gas fields in the United States and Canada produce from rocks of Cretaceous Age. Rocky Mountain coal deposits of Cretaceous age are second in importance only to those of the Pennsylvanian

TYRANT LIZARD
Tyrannosaurus

At the end of the Cretaceous, the giant dinosaurs became extinct.

Hesperornis **was a large, flightless diving bird, much like a penguin in its aquatic habits.**

(see COAL). Cretaceous strata also produce quantities of copper, bauxite (an aluminium ore), and bentonite (a soft rock used in industry and in the manufacture of such substances as soaps and plaster). In south-eastern England, Cretaceous rocks are important as reservoirs of water.

Rocks of Cretaceous age contain the oldest flowering plants (angiosperms), which by the close of that period had become the dominant plants, and an important new source of food for animals.

The most striking animals of Cretaceous times were the dinosaurs. Their fossils are known from all parts of the world and include many different types. Some of the most distinctive were the horned dinosaurs, such as *Triceratops* and *Styracosaurus*, and the tank-like, armoured *Ankylosaurus*. Among the many kinds of carnivorous dinosaurs *Tyrannosaurus* was one of the most savage. It stood 20 feet high and its skull was over 4 feet long.

Reptiles continued to be common in the

seas throughout the Cretaceous. Ichthyosaurs (fish-like reptiles) declined in numbers and importance. Sea turtles had shells 12 feet long; plesiosaurs were up to 50 feet long; and serpent-like mosasaurs were also common. Many were over 20 feet long. They were among the most savage of all marine reptiles in upper Cretaceous times. They were probably fish-eating carnivores, and were closely related to lizards and snakes.

Best known pterosaur of the Cretaceous was *Pteranodon*, which presumably soared most of the time over the sea. Its body was only about the size of a large goose, but its wingspan was about 20 feet. About half of its huge hammer-shaped head stuck out behind as a great crest. Its long jaws were toothless. *Pteranodon* fossils are found in the Niobrara Chalk of Kansas. (See FOSSILS; JURASSIC PERIOD.)

Foraminifera, ammonites, pelecypods, gastropods, and echinoderms were common in Cretaceous seas.

The end of the Cretaceous was marked by widespread extinction of many groups of animals, including ammonites, dinosaurs, plesiosaurs, and pterosaurs. There is no simple explanation for their extinction.

CROCUS (*Crocus* spp.) is a Greek word meaning saffron, once an important drug and dye. Saffron is made from dried stamens of crocus flowers and is still prepared in Spain. Most crocuses came originally from Asia Minor or southern Europe. They were first cultivated commercially in Holland; hence they are often referred to as Dutch crocuses.

Dainty cup-like crocus blossoms of blue, purple, yellow, or white are surprisingly beautiful, because it is such an unexpected pleasure to see pretty flowers blooming in snow in early spring. Some kinds do not bloom until autumn, just before frost.

Crocuses are attractive, either planted along margins or scattered about lawns. These pretty little plants belong to the iris family.

CRO-MAGNON MAN first appeared in Europe 20,000 or more years ago. Like Neanderthal Man, he was a cave-dweller, but biologically he was a modern man *(Homo sapiens)*. No one knows where he originated but it was probably not in Europe.

The first skeletons of Cro-Magnon Man were found in a cave in France in 1868. Many others have been found since then throughout Europe. Cro-Magnon Man was tall, and he walked erect. His brain was as large and complex as are those of living races.

Cro-Magnon Man left a good record of his culture. Remains of his fine stone and bone tools, including spear throwers, knives, scrapers, and hammer stones have been found in caves in southern France and in Spain. He was also an accomplished artist and left carved and painted scenes on the walls of the caves where he lived. These include illustrations of now-extinct Ice Age animals. He buried his dead, frequently leaving weapons or tools, necklaces, and other ornaments with the body. This suggests that Cro-Magnon Man believed in a life after death. Cro-Magnon Man is a direct ancestor of present-day Man.

Skull, restored head showing facial features, and stone artifacts of Cro-Magnon man.

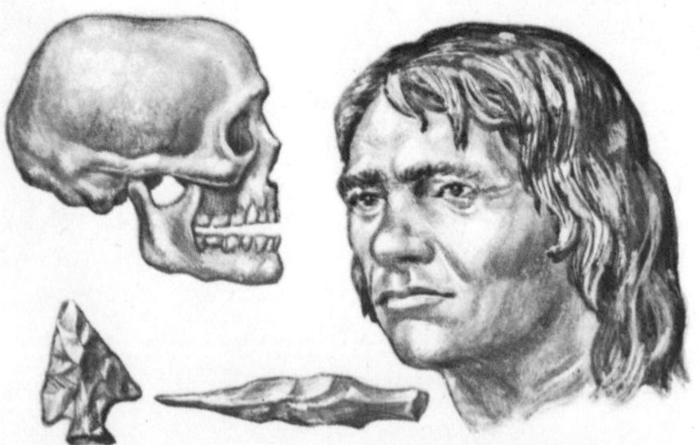

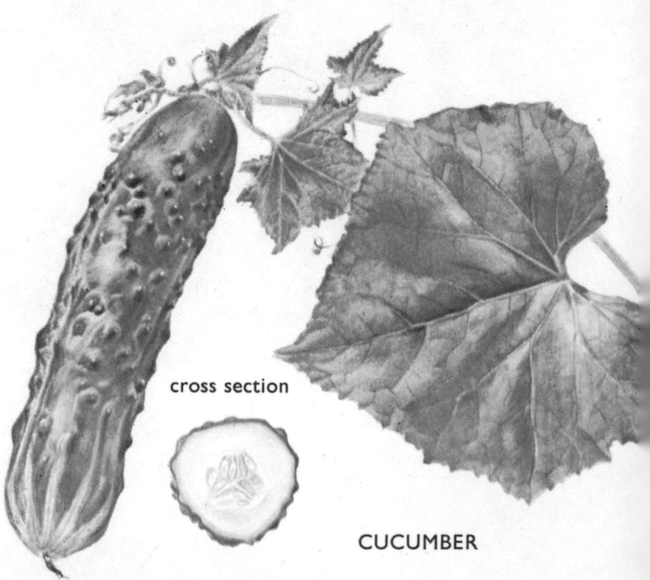

CUCUMBERS *(Cucumis sativus)* are believed to be a native of Africa and the warmer parts of Asia and were carried westward to the Mediterranean region in prehistoric times. They are grown from seed, and their trailing vines produce fruit ranging from 3 inches to 2 feet in length. Cucumbers are harvested by hand as soon as they reach the size desired and are eaten pickled or as fresh salad vegetables. Small ones used in pickles are often called gherkins. True gherkins *(Cucumis anguria)* never grow large. They are native to the West Indies.

Forestry Commission

The straight and stately Italian Cypress *(Cupressus sempervirens)* **can reach a height of 120 feet. It is planted as an ornamental in the British Isles.**

CYPRESS is a name for trees and shrubs of several famlies. The largest group (about 15 species in the genus *Cupressus*) belongs to the cypress family. They grow in western United States, Mexico, China, the Himalayas and the Mediterranean basin. Many are planted as ornamentals, and the wood of some species is valued for timber because of its high resistance to rot. All have scale-like evergreen leaves, which overlap like the tiles on a roof, and small (1 to 1½ inch in diameter), round, woody cones.

The Monterey Cypress *(Cupressus macrocarpa)*, the Arizona Cypress *(Cupressus arizonica)*, the Italian Cypress *(Cupressus sempervirens)*, a native of the Mediterranean, are planted as ornamentals.

Another group in the cypress family includes the Lawson Cypress, and the Nootka Cypress, or Alaska-Cedar (see CEDARS).

The Swamp Cypress *(Taxodium distichum)*, a member of the redwood family, grows 100 to 150 feet tall in the swamplands of southeastern United States. Its trunk is generally swollen and flared out at the base and its branches bearded with Spanish Moss. From its shallow roots, unusual 'knees' stick above the water, often some distance from the trunk of the tree. Pondcypress, a smaller variety, has thin twigs and small scaly leaves.

Closely related and similar to the swamp cypress is the Montezuma Cypress *(Taxodium mucronatum)* of Mexico and Guatemala; but its foliage is evergreen while the Baldcypress loses its feathery, needle-like foliage every winter. The famous Montezuma Cypress of Oaxaca, Mexico, is estimated to be between 4,000 and 5,000 years old. Although the diameter of its trunk (40 ft) is greater than that of the largest Giant Sequoia, it is less than half as tall (141 ft). (See SEQUOIAS.)

D

DAFFODILS are common garden flowers that have a confusing variety of names. They are also called trumpets, jonquils, and narcissus. The generic name *Narcissus* applies to a group of about 50 species, but as a common name, it is used mainly for flowers with white petals.

All members of the daffodil group have a six-parted flower with a cup-like or trumpet-like crown. All are yellow or white, separately or in combinations, and all bloom in spring and grow from bulbs. They have long narrow leaves. Still another characteristic of the whole group is fragrance, particularly noticeable in the white-flowered narcissus. These can be grown indoors in winter by setting the bulbs in a bowl of gravel and watering them regularly. Daffodils have been cultivated in gardens for centuries. The export of daffodil bulbs is also an important business in Holland.

Narcissus pseudonarcissus, our wild daffodil, was once more common. Today it can be found in Gloucestershire, Herefordshire and the Forest of Dean.

The name derives from the medieval Latin *affodilus* and Greek *asphodelus*. The plant was believed to grow in Hades and was prized by Persephone, Goddess of the Underworld.

DAISIES *(Bellis perennis)*, one of the most familiar of wild flowers, got their name from Day's Eye the old English name for this plant with its flower heads opening in the morning, remaining open during the day and closing again at night.

The family *Compositae* in which it is included is often referred to as the 'Daisy family'. This is rather misleading as only some of the included plants have 'daisy-type' flowers with a yellow-disc centre surrounded by a ring of coloured petals. The tall-growing Oxeye Daisy *(Chrysanthemum leucanthemum)* and the Michaelmas Daisy (Aster) have a 'daisy-type' centre to their flowers but the many species of thistles, dandelions and many other related plants included in this family have not.

Horticulturists have, by breeding, produced 'double' forms of Daisies *(Bellis perennis)* the familiar yellow centre being replaced by petals of varying shades of pink and red.

English Daisies *(Bellis perennis)* can be seen in lawns in Europe and Asia, where they are natives, as well as in milder parts of America. They grow only 2 or 3 inches high and have small white or pink flowers.

During the past 25 years, the Transvaal or African Daisy *(Gerbera jamesonii)* has become a favourite flower for bouquets. Those long-stemmed flowers have slender petals of yellow and pink and red. Often the flowers stay fresh for a week or more, making them highly prized commercially.

Another beautiful daisy from Africa is the Swan River Daisy *(Brachycome iberidifolia)* which is rather difficult to grow. In its dainty way, however, this is one of the loveliest of all daisies.

Barnaby's Picture Library

Michaelmas Daisies are pretty late-summer flowers.

DANDELIONS (*Taraxacum officinale*) are European and Asiatic plants that now grow practically everywhere in the world, in towns and cities as well as along country roads and in pastures. Children like dandelions because of their pretty yellow flowers and rich honey-like fragrance. They also like the seeds which fly away on delicate parachutes. But most older people take an unfriendly view of dandelions because they are a nuisance in lawns.

Dandelion flower heads close up at night and on dark days. Then, after the flowers have finished blooming, they stay closed for a while before opening up again to expose the fluffy balls of air-borne seeds. Look at the seeds closely, and you will see one of the reasons for the name dandelion. Near the upper end of each seed are quite a few tooth-like projections. In France the plant was called *dent de lion*, which means lion's tooth. *Dent de lion* became dandelion. Some people make wine from dandelions, and they are also used as a salad green.

DASHEEN AND TARO (*Colocasia esculenta* and *Colocasia antiquorum*) are 'stemless' plants with leaves measuring from 2 to 3 feet in length. In the Orient they are a staple food for millions of people. The starchy roots or tubers are eaten like potatoes — boiled, baked, mashed, or as chips — and are processed into flours, breakfast cereals, and baby foods. Portland arrowroot is also manufactured from the tubers.

Herbert Knapp

Taro grows in moist, fertile soil of the Pacific islands. The root is used for food, and the stem is replanted.

The family to which Dasheen and Taro belong, the *Araceae*, includes the many different kinds of caladiums, colourful broad leaved plants popular for indoor planting.

Both Taro and Dasheen are known as 'elephant ears'.

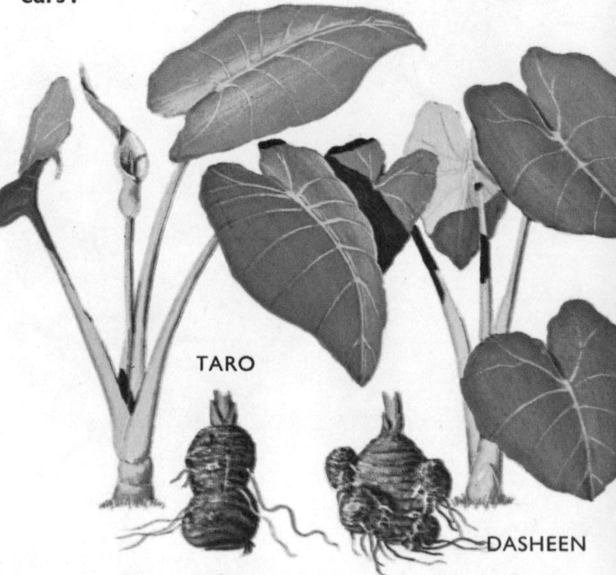

DATES, the fruit of the Date Palm *(Phoenix dactylifera)*, probably originated in the region of the Persian Gulf. The trees are known to have been cultivated in Iraq since 3500 B.C., and dates have served as a staple food for centuries in Iraq, Iran, Arabia, and North Africa. Early Spanish missionaries planted Date Palms around their missions in Mexico and southern California, but not until the present century were dates grown commercially under irrigation in the hot, dry areas of Arizona and California.

Date Palms can be grown from seed or from suckers. Of those grown from seeds, approximately 50 per cent will be males and will not bear fruit. The quality of fruit produced by some seedling female palms may be poor. It is customary, therefore, to propagate Date Palms from offshoots or suckers that develop at the base of young female plants which have produced good fruit. Female flowers are pollinated by tying strands of male flowers into the clusters of females, and to produce top quality dates, the clusters of fruit are often thinned. Since several hundred one-seeded berries may grow in a cluster, the crop remains sizeable after thinning.

A prolific tree may bear 200 pounds of dates a year.

Date palms will often be found at North African oases such as this one at Gabes in Tunisia.

J. Allan Cash

Paper bags are sometimes placed over the fruit clusters to protect them from rain and from birds or other animals.

DAY-LILIES *(Hemerocallis fulva)*. Styles change in flowers almost as much as in clothes. Until a few years ago, the Day-lily had become old-fashioned and lost most of its popularity, but now there is an interest in it again.

DAY-LILY

One reason for the renewed interest in the Day-lily is that during the past quarter of a century it has been improved remarkably. New colours have been added through plant selection, and the blossoms are larger. Now the colours range from clear yellow through various shades of orange or brown to almost reddish brown.

A native of Europe, the old-fashioned Day-lily grows wild in somewhat moist places.

DESERTS are areas where the yearly rainfall is less than 10 inches. They encircle the Earth in two bands — one above and one below the equator. Heat is usually associated with deserts, but the edges of ice caps and permanent snow fields are cold deserts. Nor are deserts all sand. Only about 28 per cent

Sand dunes in Death Valley, with the Grapevine Mountains in the background.
Josef Muench

of the Sahara is covered with sand. Soil over large areas of desert land is rich in mineral nutrients that cannot be used by most plants except after rare rainfalls. Other areas are covered with alkaline soil of such high salt content that plants cannot grow.

People live in deserts in places called oases. These are fertile spots where sufficient water is available for plants to grow and provide food for animals. Some oases are formed or are improved by deep wells that bring water to the surface for irrigation. In Africa and Asia, oases produce fruit, sugar, cotton, dates, and forage crops. In the United

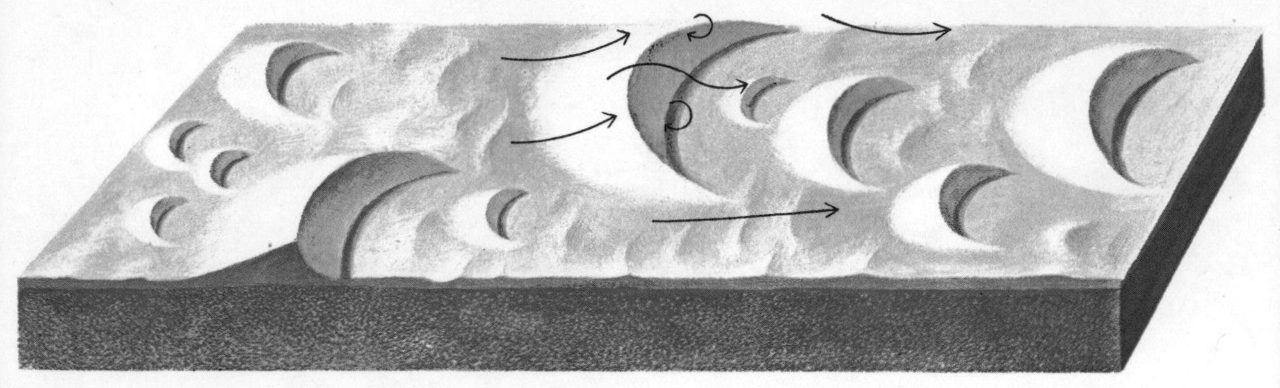

Crescent-shaped dunes are formed by steady winds.

States, some oases are used for agriculture, recreation, and even cities.

All deserts are dry and the evaporation of water exceeds the rainfall. No part of the Earth is entirely without rainfall, although in northern Chile one area has had only three small showers in seventeen years. When rains do come, they are usually violent. Gullies, dry stream beds, and valleys are filled quickly to overflowing. Run-off, soaking into the soil, and evaporation are so rapid that evidence of the rain quickly disappears.

Deserts are usually areas of clear, cloudless skies. The dry air permits an abundance of solar energy (heat and light) to reach the area by day; cooling is rapid at night. Day temperatures may be as high as 57 degrees centigrade (135 degrees Fahrenheit), but night temperatures may be near freezing.

Animals and plants which live in desert regions show many adaptations to this hostile environment. Many plants have a very short life cycle, growing quickly when it rains, flowering and producing seeds in a very short span of time. Such seeds are able to remain dormant for long periods. Other plants are kept alive by storing moisture in bulbous roots, while others, such as cacti, store moisture in their fleshy stems. Some plants have roots which go down into the ground for 50 feet or more in search of water.

In spite of the conditions many animals live in the desert while many others are adapted to living in it for short periods. Most of the animals are only active at night, resting in burrows and under rocks during the day. It has been observed that the temperature 2 feet down in a kangaroo rat's burrow is only 16 degrees centigrade (60 degrees Fahrenheit) while that outside may be over 38 degrees (100 degrees Fahrenheit). Desert animals are frequently light coloured to tone with their surroundings and they also conserve water by losing very little by evaporation and excreting concentrated urine.

DEVONIAN. This period of the Palaeozoic era began about 395 million years ago and lasted for about 50 million years. Named

after the county of Devon, the rocks are widespread and of two distinct types. One consists of marine limestone and shale; the other is usually a red iron-stained deposit that accumulated on land. In Britain these rocks are known as the Old Red Sandstone.

The Devonian was an important period in the development of life. The oldest well-preserved land plants come from Devonian rocks. All were rather simple, primitive plants without well-developed roots or leaves. They did have water-vascular systems like all other land plants, however. Towards the close of the Devonian, forests of large

Fishes, the first animals with backbones, became abundant during the Devonian. Some of the lobe-finned fishes, such as the large-scaled *Osteolepis* (1), ventured on to land as forerunners of land-dwelling amphibians. There were also jawless ostracoderms and many sharks (2).

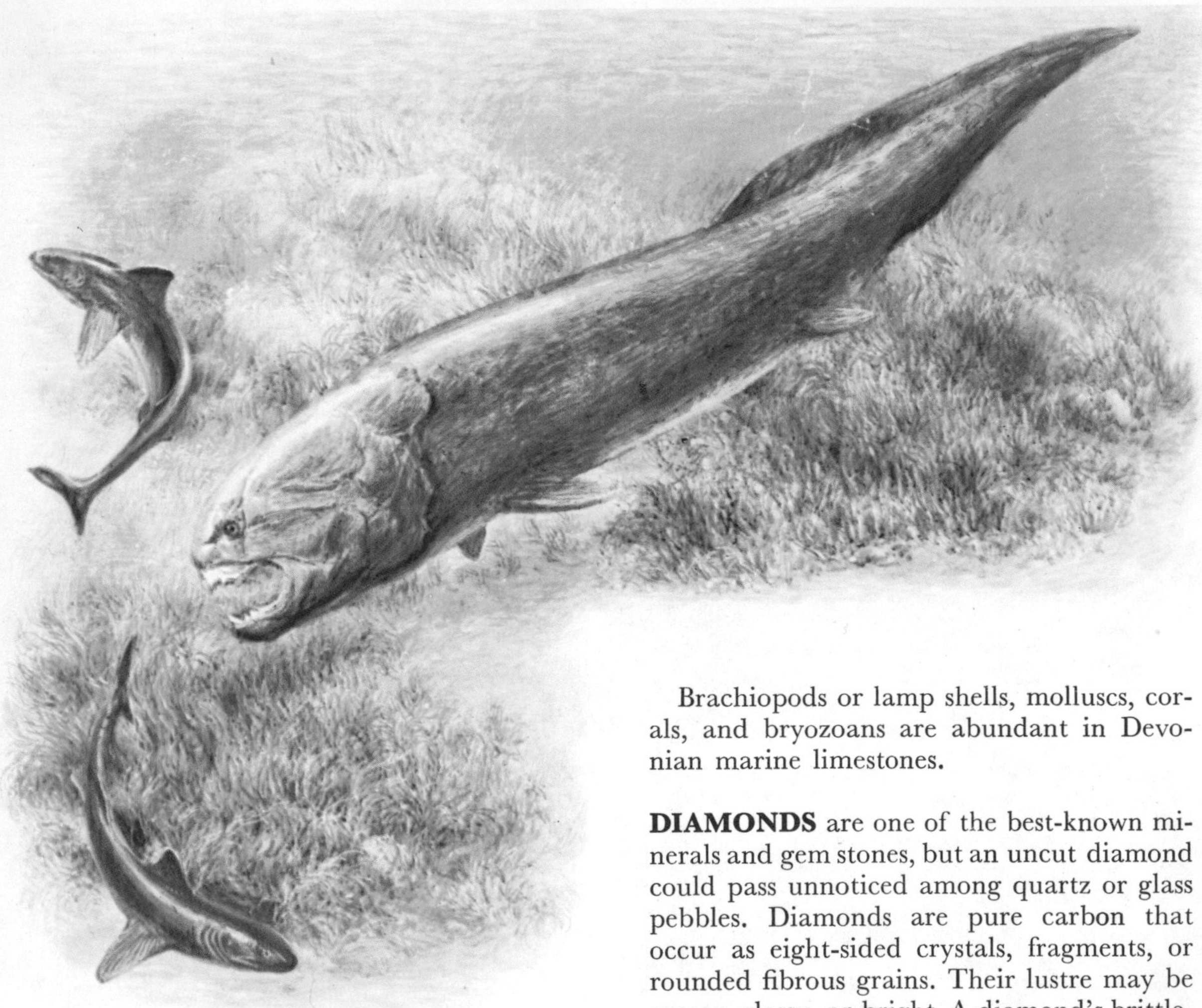

Dinichthys (30 ft.) was the largest animal of its day, some 300 million years ago. It preyed on such unarmoured fish as primitive sharks.

scale trees and seed ferns grew in the many low, moist areas.

Establishment of animal life on land during the Devonian was a second major advance. The most striking of these early land animals were the vertebrates. The oldest amphibians known, are found in upper Devonian rocks of Greenland. Less conspicuous animals — insects, mites, and millipedes — also made their way ashore.

The Devonian is sometimes called the Age of Fishes because of the great increase in numbers and importance of fishes during this period. Ostracoderms, placoderms, sharks, and bony fish, for example, are common in both marine and fresh water deposits of Devonian age.

Brachiopods or lamp shells, molluscs, corals, and bryozoans are abundant in Devonian marine limestones.

DIAMONDS are one of the best-known minerals and gem stones, but an uncut diamond could pass unnoticed among quartz or glass pebbles. Diamonds are pure carbon that occur as eight-sided crystals, fragments, or rounded fibrous grains. Their lustre may be greasy, glassy, or bright. A diamond's brittleness and its perfect cleavage are properties that lower its value both as a gem stone and as an abrasive. Only about 15 per cent of the diamonds produced are of gem quality; many are a yellow or brown colour or have

Diamonds are the hardest known natural substance. They are formed under conditions of great heat and pressure.

flaws large enough to notice in cut stones. A few diamonds of pink, red, yellow, green, or blue colour have an exceedingly high value. Ideally a gem-quality diamond should be flawless, but tiny specks of black carbon or small gas bubbles that cannot be seen with the unaided eye do not interfere with its beauty and fire. Dirty yellow or brown diamonds exposed to radiation in an atomic pile may change to a desirable shade of green.

The common cut for the diamond is the 'standard brilliant', which has a minimum of 58 facets (faces). Many stones are cut in odd shapes to avoid too much loss of weight (hence value) in cutting. These odd shapes are set very artistically in mounts designed specifically to add to the stone's beauty. The value of a diamond is based on the stone's weight, freedom from flaws, and size. Value increases rapidly in stones larger than one carat — a unit of weight for precious stones. If a one-carat diamond is valued at £200, a two-carat stone is worth about £600, and a three-carat stone might be valued at £1200. Paired or matched stones are also highly valued. One of two colourless diamonds of similar size and cut may look like a piece of glass, even though it is a beautiful stone by itself. It may be necessary to compare 50 or more stones before two are found that go well together. The difficulty is magnified when a number of stones are needed for a particular piece of jewellery. Therefore matched stones have a much greater value than the combined values of the stones individually.

Uncut diamonds look like pretty, transparent pebbles.

Constance Stuart — Black Star

Len Sirman — Birnback

Panning river gravel for diamonds in Brazil.

Famous diamonds include the Koh-i-nor and Cullinan, or Star of Africa. The latter is the largest diamond ever found and both were used in the British Crown Jewels. Other notable stones include the Orlor, Florentine, Excelsior, and Star of the South.

Most diamonds are opaque and therefore not of gem quality. These diamonds are used industrially for grinding and cutting, for wire-drawing dies, and for many other uses where hardness is important. For use as abrasives, diamonds are ground to small size. Carat-sized bort and carbonado, fibrous, tough varieties, are set in steel bits used by the oil and mining industries for core drilling. Small pieces, carefully graded in size, are fused into grinding wheels of many kinds.

Diamonds crystallise sparsely in kimberlite, averaging only about 0.2 carat per ton of rock. The rock is mined, crushed, and treated chemically so that the diamonds will stick when passed over grease-covered tables. The waste rock or gangue is carried away by water. The grease, scraped from the tables at frequent intervals is melted to recover the diamonds, which are washed, sorted, and graded. Important diamond yielding areas are South Africa, Congo, and Brazil. Diamonds of small size have also been mined in Arkansas.

Since 1959 small synthetic diamonds have been manufactured in the United States. Several million carats are marketed each year for industrial use. (See GEMS.)

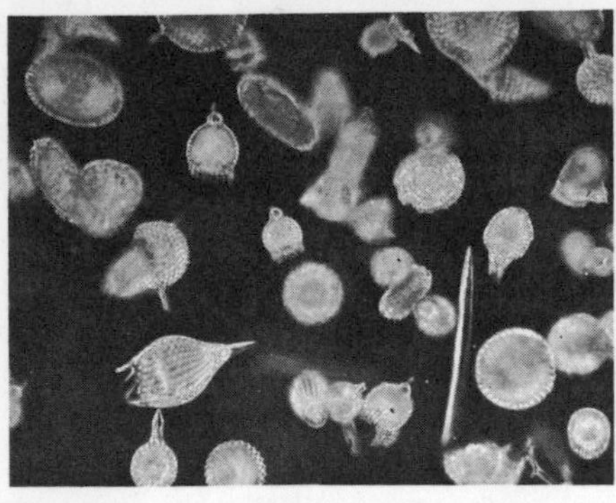

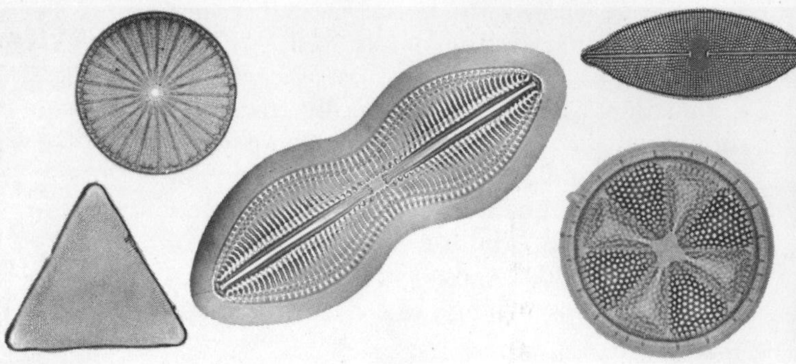

Courtesy of Bausch & Lomb Inc., Rochester 2, N.Y.

Diatoms (microscopic algae) live in fresh water and in the soil but are most abundant and varied in seas.

DIATOMS are a kind of yellow-green algae (see ALGAE). They are one-celled, and the two halves of their cell walls overlap and fit together like the two halves of a pill capsule. Their cell walls contain pectin and other organic compounds but are composed largely of silica (silicon dioxide). The silica is deposited in the cell walls in definite patterns, making diatoms extremely attractive.

Some of the more than 10,000 species are round; others are oblong, square, or triangular. When alive, their yellow or brown pigments usually mask the green chlorophyll. When dead, the organic material decays and leaves the nearly transparent glassy cell wall.

Diatoms, such as *Lichmorphora*, are important food of clams, oysters, and small fishes in the sea.

Dr. Roman Vishniac

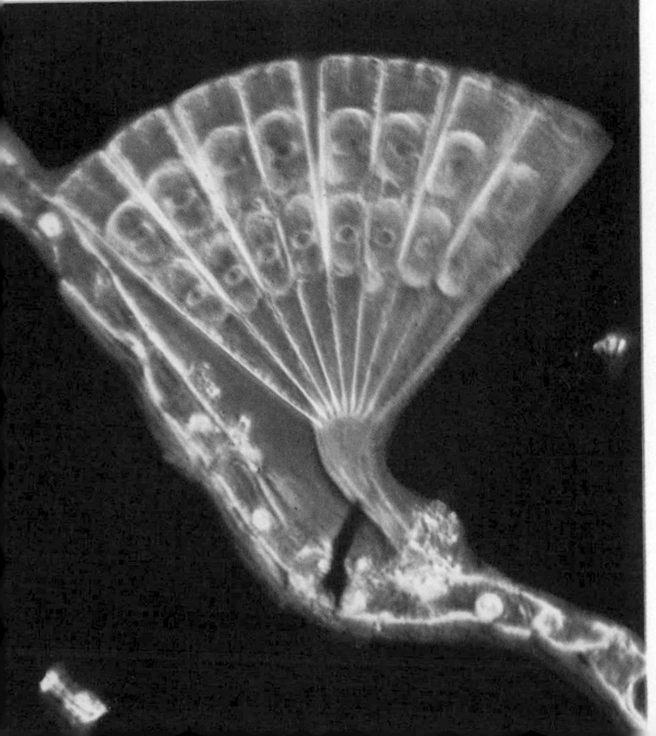

Some diatoms are not able to move; others have complex internal canal systems, resembling the locks in dams, through which protoplasm flows and forces out water. This causes the diatoms to move in short jerks.

Diatoms have a type of cell division which forms two cells of unequal size. One is the same size as the original cell; the other is smaller. If such a process continued, some cells would eventually become too small to survive as individuals. After a cell reaches a certain minimum size, the living contents excape its walls and either grow to the size of the original cell or fuse with the contents of another small cell to form a zygote. This zygote increases to the size of the original cell.

Directly or indirectly, diatoms are the food of many animals. Some kinds of fishes eat diatoms. Others feed on fishes or smaller animals that have eaten diatoms. Clams eat diatoms, then walruses eat clams. The diet of some whales, including the giant Blue Whale, is krill, which consists of small crustaceans that they strain from the water through the whalebone 'sieves' in their mouths. These small crustaceans feed largely on diatoms. On this diet, a Blue Whale calf increases its weight more than 50 tons during the first two years of its life.

Diatoms occur in fresh water and in the soil, but they are most common in oceans and bays, particularly in cool water. When they die, they sink to the bottom, where their soft parts decay. Their 'glassy' cell walls are deposited over the ocean floor.

Over millions of years these deposits become very deep in some parts of the ocean. In areas where the land has since been elevated, exposing the ancient sea floor, thousands of tons of these deposits are mined annually as diatomaceous or Fuller's earth. One of the largest of these mines is near Lompoc, California. Covering about 12 square miles, its layer of pure diatoms is 1,400 feet thick.

Diatomaceous earth is used in nearly all toothpastes and powders, in silver polishes, and in other scouring and polishing creams and powders. It polishes without scratching. Diatomaceous earth is used also for filters in industries where fine screens are needed, as in sugar refining. The diatom skeletons, since they are composed of silica, do not react chemically with the substances being filtered. Bricks made of diatomaceous earth are used to insulate boilers and smelting furnaces. One of the first uses for diatomaceous earth was to absorb nitroglycerin in making dynamite.

Living diatoms store part of their food as oil. Thus diatoms were probably one of the important contributors to the Earth's great deposits of petroleum. Geologists sometimes locate oil wells by identifying the diatoms from sample drillings in oil areas.

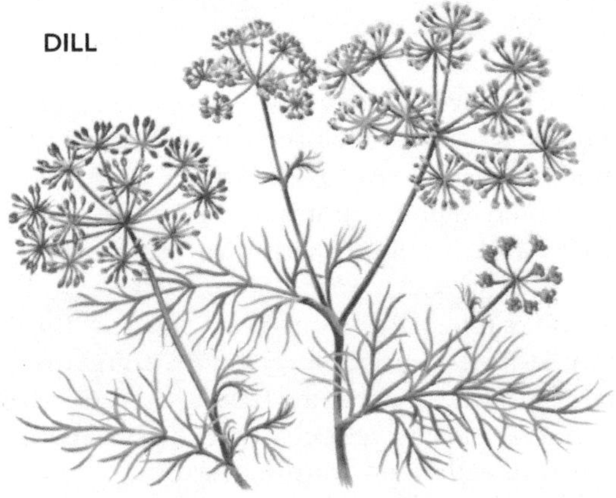

DILL *(Anethum graveolens)* was probably brought to England by the Romans and was a popular remedy for indigestion. It is still sometimes used to flavour salads. Dill is an Umbellifer related to cow parsley. The plants grow 2 or 3 feet tall and have feathery leaves and clusters of small yellow flowers.

DINOFLAGELLATES are microscopic plants that occur in both fresh and salt water. Most of the nearly 1,000 species live in the sea, where they are second in importance to diatoms as food for marine animals (see DIATOMS). Like diatoms, they are one-celled organisms, but each cell has two whip-like hairs (flagella) which are used as swimming organs. The cells are grooved and often have plate-like segments or 'armour' of cellulose. In some groups, the plates are always in a definite number and arrangement. *Peridinium* is an example of this type. Each cell is divided in the centre by a transverse plate, and the upper and lower halves are divided further into smaller plates. Some dinoflagellates contain chlorophyll and thus manufacture their own food. Others lack chlorophyll. Many zoologists classify dinoflagellates as animals.

Dinoflagellates sometimes occur in such great quantities that they colour the water. A reddish marine dinoflagellate *(Gymnodinium brevis)* is associated with the fish-killing red tide of the Mexican Gulf Coast of the United States. Neptune's Triton *(Ceratium)* is a common dinoflagellate that occurs in lakes and other large bodies of fresh water.

Many of the dinoflagellates cause streaks of light and a phosphorescent glow in the water at night. Clams that feed on a species of *Gonyaulax*, a bioluminescent dinoflagellate, are poisonous, and at times when *Gonyaulax* is abundant, signs are posted along beaches on the west coast of North America to warn people not to take clams for eating.

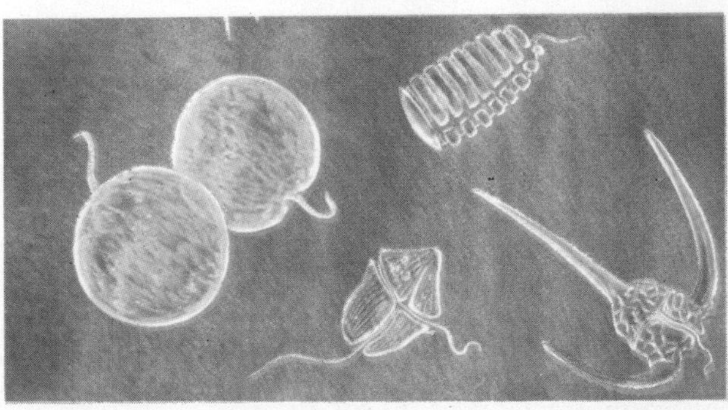

Dinoflagellates, like diatoms, are simple microscopic organisms that occur in large numbers in fresh and salt waters. They are one link in food chains of aquatic animals.

DISPERSAL is a means by which a plant species increases its distribution from its original range. If all seeds or spores fell in the same area in which they originated, the nutrients they need from the soil would soon be exhausted. Spores of many fungi and ferns are spread by the wind. Seeds of berries and some other fruits are distributed by birds after first passing through their digestive tract. The feathery, plumed seeds of such plants as dandelions are carried by air currents. Some seeds are 'shot' from the growing area of the parent plant when the ripened seed pod is touched or becomes dry. Many grasses gradually invade new areas by runners or underground root systems.

Success in dispersal depends on whether the new environment offers what is needed, or how quickly the individuals can become adapted to new conditions. In general, individuals are more successful if they do not move far from the parent population. Spores carried over great distances are less likely to find a favourable environment for germination than those that fall closer to the parent plant. Barriers frequently prevent widespread dispersion. Oceans stop the dispersal of land-dwelling plants; continents are barriers to water dwellers. Mountain ranges stop wind-blown seeds and spores. Deserts interrupt the spread of trees and other plants. On the other hand, Man has taken many plants and animals with him to new lands, thus overcoming natural barriers.

Seeds from the American Milkweed are carried by the wind.

Pansy seeds are released when the seed capsule dries and pops open.

Toothed seeds of sticktights or beggarlice cling to hair or clothing and are carried to new habitats.

DOGWOODS are small trees, shrubs, and herbs that grow in the Northern Hemisphere. Of about 50 species, only one *(Cornus sanguinea)* is found in Britain. It is a small shrub found in hedgerows and damp places and bears small white scented flowers in June. The leaves are thin, 2 - 3½ inches long, oval, slender pointed and silky on both sides. The winter twigs are dull red and often carry small round black fruit.

The Flowering Dogwood *(Cornus florida)* is a slow-growing, small tree that prefers rich, well-drained soil. Its dark, red-brown to black bark is closely ridged and broken into four-sided or rounded scales.

The Cornelian Cherry *(Cornus mas)* is a native shrub of southern Europe and Asia, the Flowering Dogwood and the larger Pacific Dogwood *(Cornus nuttallii)* have white bracts and tight clusters of small red fruits. A variety of Flowering Dogwood with pink blossoms is a common ornamental. *Cornus alba Spathii* is the most beautiful of the yellow variegated dogwoods.

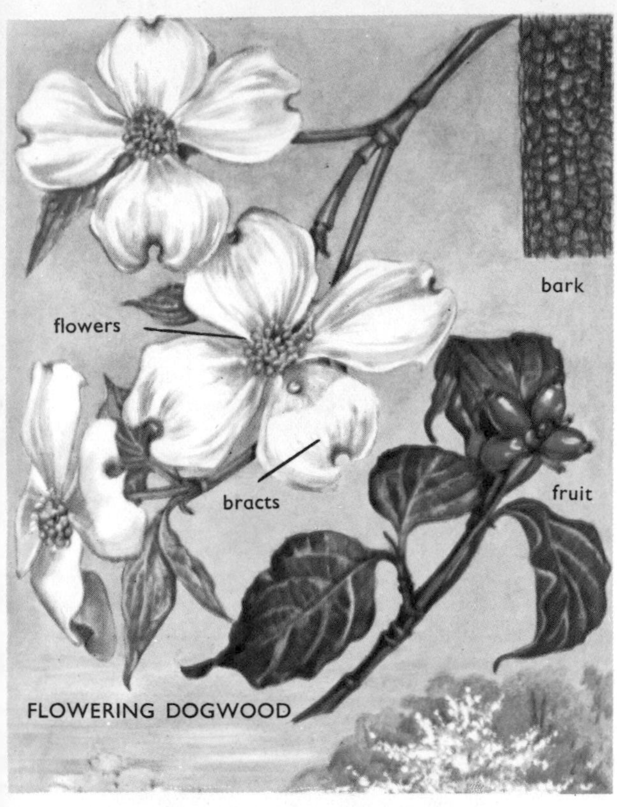

FLOWERING DOGWOOD

DOLOMITE, a calcium-magnesium carbonate, occurs either as white, granular, cleavable masses or as a fine-grained sedimentary rock. In low-temperature veins it may be found in excellent white or pink crystals with curved faces. Dolomite resembles magnesite and has many of the same uses. Dolomite rock is a limestone containing more than 50 per cent of the mineral dolomite. Dolomite is used as a source of carbon dioxide and as a building stone. Dolomite is widespread. Large deposits are found in Switzerland, Britain, Mexico and the United States.

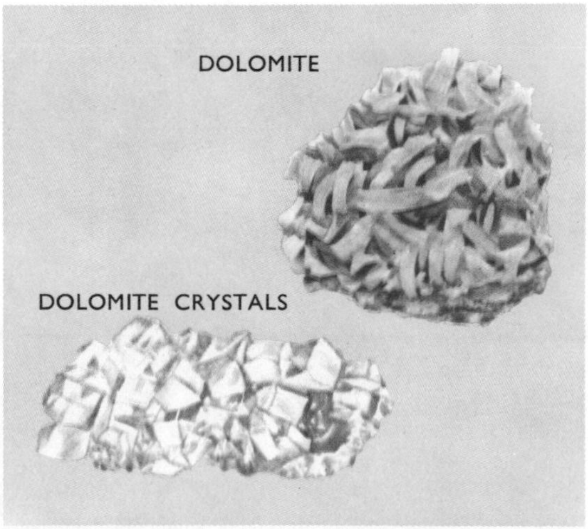

DORMANCY is a period of rest or inactivity. Seeds of most plants require a period of rest before they will germinate or sprout. Usually this is an advantage to plants because the seeds remain dormant during winter when sprouting would result in freezing and death of the plant.

Although dormancy is always accompanied by a decrease in water content, the manner of dormancy varies with different plants. Some, such as English White-clover and lucerne, develop heavy seed coats through which sufficient quantities of water and oxygen cannot be absorbed for germination. Freezing and thawing is necessary to break the coat, or the seeds are scratched by special machines or by threshing to allow water and oxygen to enter so that germination can occur. Some plant embryos complete their development during the dormant period. In others a slow increase in acidity brings about sprouting.

The length of dormancy that is possible varies with the species. Seeds of some orchids and willows remain alive for only a few days. Most seeds will die if germination does not occur within a few years — five to ten at the most. Those of Indian Lotus have been known to retain their ability to germinate for 400 years. Reports that wheat

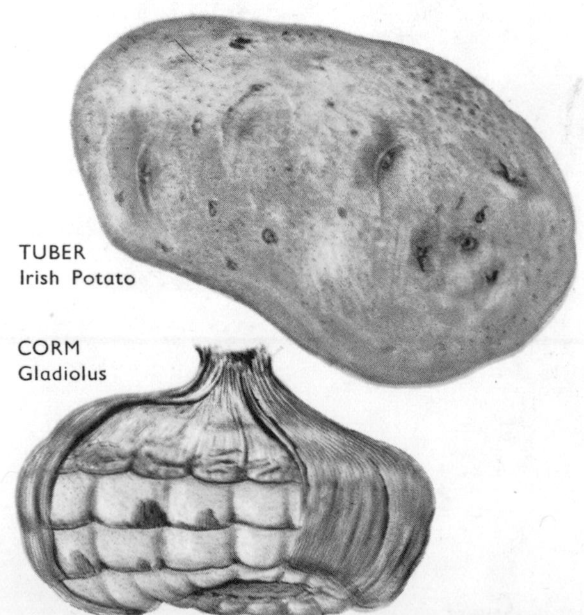

germinated after being taken from ancient Egyptian tombs are false.

Bulbs, tubers, and corms are also dormant phases of plants. They are not seeds but specialised stems. A bulb, as in tulips, onions, and lilies, is really a large bud with a small stem at the bottom. Fleshy storage leaves grow from the stem and surround it. Enough food is stored in the bulb to support growth when the bulb is placed in water or soil. The Potato is a tuber — the enlarged, food-laden end of a stem. A potato can remain dormant for a year or more. When conditions are favourable, their buds or 'eyes' will sprout into new plants. Corms resemble bulbs but are mostly stem with only small thin leaves. Gladiolus and crocus plants produce corms. Resting spores represent still another method by which plants remain dormant in unfavourable conditions. Cells of fungi, mosses, and many bacteria may lose water, form a resistant covering membrane, and then live quietly for varying periods of time. They return to active life when favourable conditions return.

DWELLINGS. Many animals have solved the problem of protecting themselves and their young from enemies and from the rigours of the weather by constructing dens, or by using caves, hollows in trees, or other natural shelters. A rabbit's burrow, a badger's sett, an eagle's eyrie, or a bee's nest in a hollow tree are among the many effective answers to the dwelling problem.

Man is not as well equipped to survive the extremes of weather as are many other animals, and finding adequate shelter has always been one of Man's basic needs for survival. Man's first shelters were probably caves, which are still used as homes in parts of Africa, and Asia. The interlocked branches of fallen trees, supplemented with additional leaves and brush, probably represented

The Cliff-Dwellers of south-western U.S. built their homes on steep rock cliffs of the flat-topped mesas common in the region. They utilised ledges beneath an overhang to shelter them from the weather and protect them from enemies. The inconvenience of having to carry food and water up the steep cliffs was offset by the defensive value of the locations.

Erich Kolmar — Shostal

Circular thatched huts in Sudanese villages of Africa are arranged around a central clearing.

Man's first attempt to move his cave from the hillside into open country.

The simplest shelter is a wind-break. Usually branches or strips of bark are interlaced as a lean-to to break the wind. Sometimes animal skins or palm leaves are strung up on a framework of sticks. When the skin-covered wind-break is developed to give all-around and overhead protection as well, it becomes a tent. Indians of the American Plains built a tent known as the tepee. It was shaped like a cone, with long poles set up so that they met near the top, and over these a soft skin covering was stretched. Eskimos also used hide tents for their summer camps.

Huts are made in all shapes and sizes and of various materials. Grass houses shaped like beehives were the most permanent dwellings of the Shoshone Indians in America just as similar huts are still used in Africa. Wigwams, huts with arched roofs, were of many shapes and sizes. Young trees were set in the ground in a circle or oval and then bent in towards the centre and lashed into place. Strips of bark or mats were placed over this dome-shaped framework. As in the

Where floods or animal prowlers are a problem, houses are built on stilts, as is this one in Malaya.

Margaret Lang — Shostal

less permanent tepee, a hole in the centre let out the smoke.

The Eskimo's winter home, commonly called an igloo, is built up by layers of snow blocks, so that each layer is a little more towards the centre than the next lower one. In this way the Eskimo discovered and used the principle of the dome. The igloo is lined with skins and is quite warm.

Many peoples make a simple house by setting up two lean-tos face to face and joining them along the top ridge. The result looks much like a tent. By setting this framework on walls a sizeable house can be built. Then the lean-tos act as a gabled roof. Walls may be built in many ways. Rows of sticks, blocks of peat, stones with or without mortar, bricks of fired or sun-baked mud, and split or sawn timbers have each been favoured by various peoples in the past and are still in use today. A type of wall construction used widely in the world is wattle and daub.

Pliable sticks or branches are laced between posts driven into the ground so that a sort of cage made of sticks results, with openings for doors. Over the interwoven sticks mud is plastered. A well-made wattle-and-daub house will last many years.

Thatched houses are common in tropical countries, and roofs of thatch are used here and there practically the world over. Thatch is the interlacing of leaves, grasses, or straw.

An entirely different kind of house is one that is partly sunk in the ground. Only the upper parts of the walls and the roof are above the ground surface. Houses of this sort were used by Stone Age Man by about 12,000 B.C. The 'pit house' is widely used by peoples living in cold regions like Siberia.

A. C. Hector

Grass houses thatched on to wood frames were built by some of the Plains Indians of North America.

Thatch-roofed houses on pilings are used by river dwellers in tropical regions, as in north-west Brazil.

Hugh A. Wilmar

Navaho hogans are made of timbers and soil. They have a smoke hole in the ceiling but no windows.

Museum of Navaho Ceremonial Art

John Strohm

Mongol herdsmen of Asia's treeless interior build portable houses or yurts of felt made from wool.

Sometimes the timbers forming the upper part of the dwelling are covered over with earth to seal out icy winds. The 'earth lodge' of the American Indians of the plains was an enlargement of the pit house idea. This type of structure requires little wood for walls and none for the floor. White settlers of the Great Plains often used pit houses roofed with earth.

Great apartment houses or 'pueblos' were built by Indians of the American south-west. These were usually constructed of 'adobe', a sun-dried clay brick. The greatest pueblos were built in the period A.D. 1000 to 1300. Pueblos contained hundreds of rooms and rose often to four stories in height. To the outside, such a pueblo was, in some cases, a great blank wall. The openings all faced inwards on a court where public dances and other ceremonies were held. To enter a pueblo one climbed to the roof on ladders and then came down on interior ladders. Similar buildings were made in caves high up on canyon walls by a long-vanished people whom we call the Cliff-Dwellers.

The Indians of the Pacific north-west drilled holes in timbers and tied them together with deer sinew and cord made of twisted cedar bark. They split logs to use for boards and shingles.

Modern dwellings are usually mere refinements of the permanent homes of early and primitive men. Instead of lashing timber together, we usually use nails. In place of peat or mud, we frequently use planks and a superior type of mud-cement. Bricks similar to those used today were developed in the New Stone Age. Modern houses are not necessarily any better than those of many primitive tribes. They are generally more comfortable, however. For example, central heating (first used in Korea) and glass for windows (invented by the Egyptians) have made European-type housing more pleasant.

An English suburban house of the early 1960s.

Keystone Press Agency Ltd

Snow blocks are good insulators, so the temperature inside an igloo can reach 26 °C (80 °F).

Steve McCutcheon

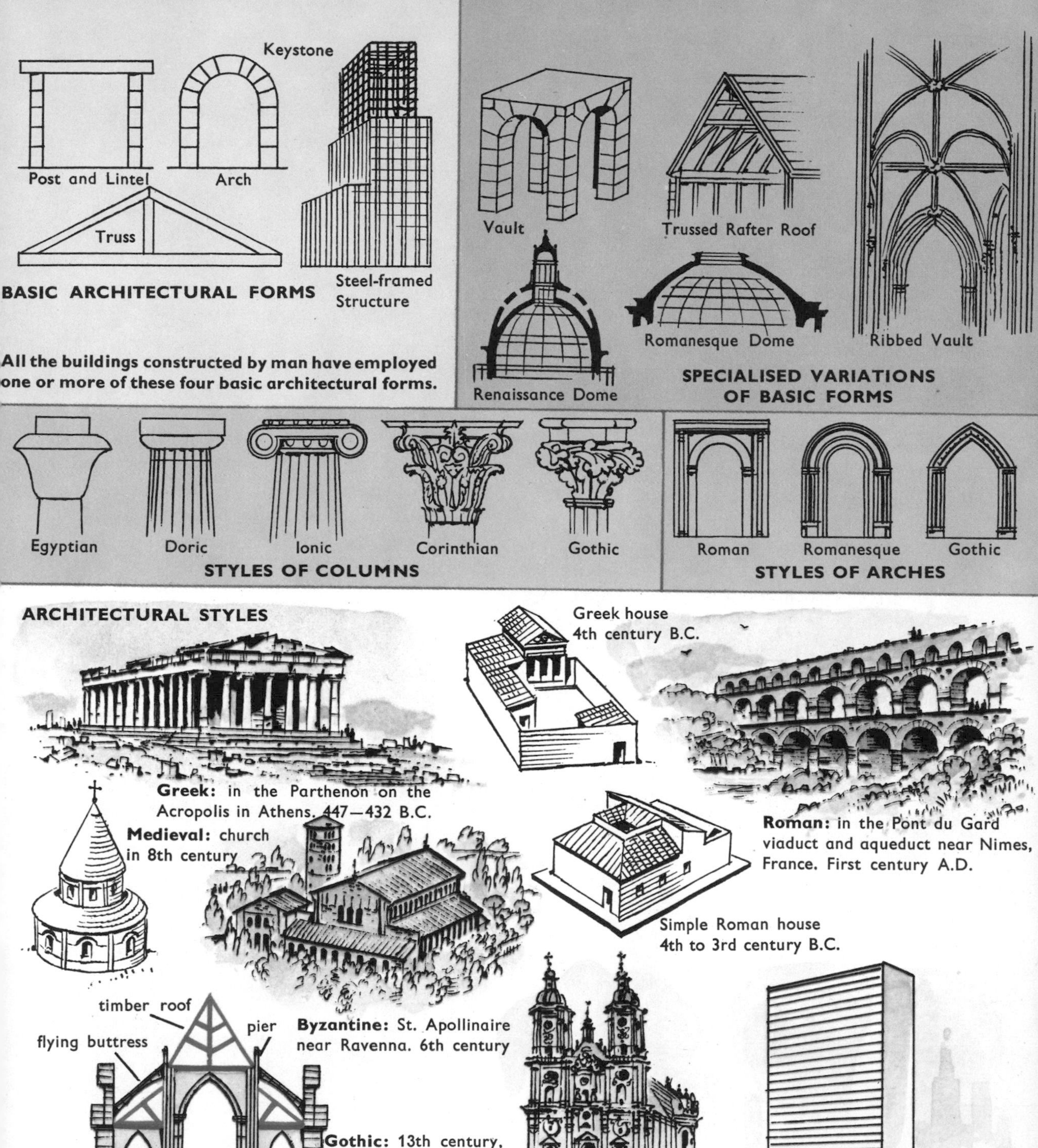

ARCHITECTURE. As Man developed skills in working with the materials best suited to the construction of his dwelling places, such as wood, stone, and brick, he invented techniques of utilising these materials to their best advantage and of building for beauty as well as utility. The combination of knowledge of materials, method, and design is called architecture.

One of the earliest types of construction, and one that is still in wide general use today, is the post and lintel. Two uprights (the posts) are used to support a crossbeam (the lintel). The basic frame of a building consists of a series of posts (usually set around the border of a square or oblong) that support the lintels on which the beams are laid. Materials of lesser strength may then be used to form the walls and the roof.

Although the Romans were the first people to use the arch in their public buildings, earlier peoples, including the Sumerians, employed this method of construction for roofing drains and conduits. In the arch, the shaped blocks fit against one another and cannot fall inwards. The vault and the dome are elaborations of the arch and, like it, require supporting on the exterior of the posts. The high-domed churches of the upper Middle Ages were generally buttressed. In truss roofs, the three sides of the truss are balanced forces with greater resistance to sag than single timbers of far greater weight.

DYES extracted from plants were of major importance for many centuries. In the 1850s an Englishman accidentally produced the first synthetic dye from aniline, a by-product in the distillation of coal. Since then more than 3,000 synthetic coal-tar dyes have been developed that have gradually replaced most natural dyes. Indirectly, these dyes come from plants too.

Indigo, a blue dye extracted from the leaves of *Indigofera tinctoria*, has been used as a dye for over 4,000 years. This plant is native to both the Orient and the New World. Cloth dyed with indigo has been found in Egyptian tombs and also in graves of the Incas of Peru. The famed merchant and traveller, Marco Polo, described the method then used for extracting indigo dye from the leaves of the herb. The leaves were harvested, steeped in water, and allowed to ferment. A blue substance that settled as a sludge in the bottom of the vessel was dried and sold as indigo cakes. By about 1650, indigo had become the most popular dye in Europe. The colour was pleasing and would not fade.

Madder is a red dye extracted from the roots of *Rubia tinctorum* and its relatives. Like indigo, madder was used to dye the cloth in which ancient Egyptian mummies were wrapped. After Vasco de Gama's discovery of a sea route to India around the Cape of

Indigo and woad dyes are made from leaves, madder from roots, and saffron from flowers.

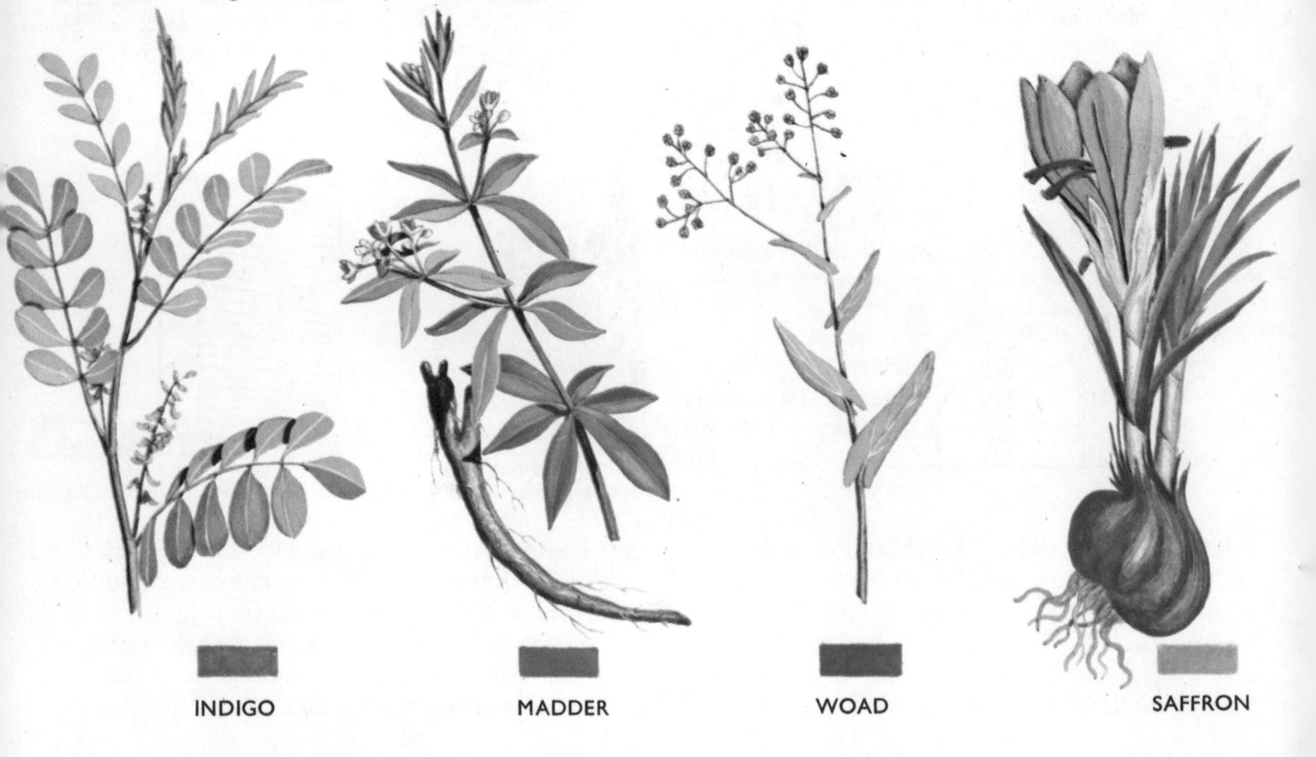

INDIGO

MADDER

WOAD

SAFFRON

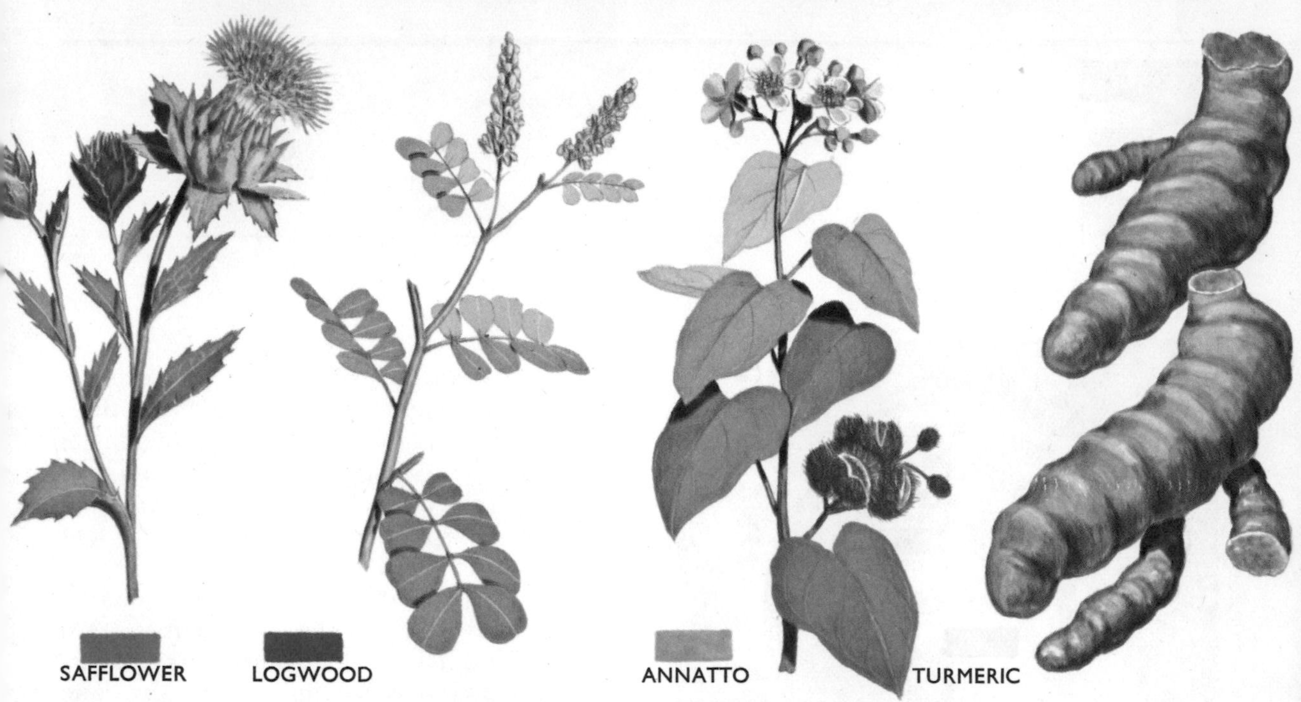

Safflower dye comes from flowers, logwood from heartwood, annatto from seeds and pulp, turmeric from roots.

Good Hope, much of this dye was imported to Europe. The famed Redcoats wore coats dyed with red madder. Madder is cultivated today on a limited scale for use by artists who prefer this natural pigment to synthetic dyes.

Woad is a blue dye extracted from the leaves of *Isatis tinctoria* a native to Europe, where it was a prized colouring for cloth. When Julius Caesar's armies invaded the British Isles, they found people called Picts or Painted People, who slashed their bodies and then rubbed woad dye into the wounds to make coloured designs. Woad was later much used throughout Europe for dyeing fabrics. Such a foul odour is produced when the leaves of the plant are fermented to make the dye that it was once declared unlawful to ferment woad within five miles of the estate of Queen Elizabeth I. Before indigo was brought in from India, a university was established in Erfurt, Germany, solely from profits made on woad. Many artists of the Renaissance period used woad as a pigment in painting now-famous masterpieces.

Saffron, the chief yellow dye of the ancients, is too expensive to be widely used today. Saffron is extracted from the female part of the flower of a crocus *(Crocus sativus)*. About 4,000 flowers are needed to produce an ounce of dye.

Safflower, another yellow dye, is extracted from flowers of a thistle-like plant *(Carthamus tinctorius)*. This plant is still cultivated for dye in India.

Logwood dye, one of the few natural dyes still used extensively in the New World, is extracted from the heartwood of a large tree *(Haematoxylon campechianum)*. A native of Mexico, the tree is now grown in many other tropical and sub-tropical regions. Haematin, derived from logwood, is a reddish stain used for dyeing microscopic sections of plant and animal tissues, and in the manufacture of ink.

Annatto is an orange dye made from the seeds and pulp of *Bixa orellana*, a South American tree sometimes called the Lipstick Tree. The tree is now planted in tropical areas throughout the world. The dye is often used as a food colouring for cheese, butter, and margarine and as a condiment on rice. A small amount is used in lipsticks.

Turmeric is another natural yellow or orange dye used in foods and condiments. It is extracted from the tubers of a herb *(Curcuma longa)*, a native to India and China. Turmeric was once used as a fabric dye.

E

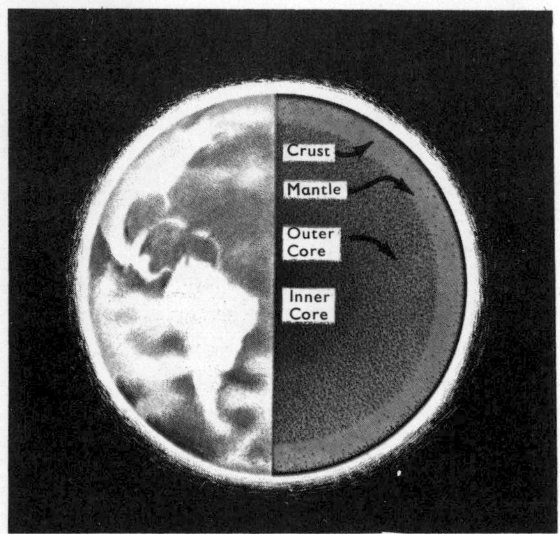

EARTH. We live on the Earth, one of the nine planets that go around the Sun. The Earth is third in distance from the Sun and fifth in size. (See PLANETS.) It has a moderately dense atmosphere, and usually about half its surface is covered with clouds. About three-quarters of the Earth's surface is covered by oceans. This is unique, for no other planet has bodies of water. The Earth is also the only planet with a large amount of oxygen in its atmosphere. Both features make the Earth the only planet on which we could live without special breathing apparatus and water supply.

The Earth's diameter at the poles is 7,900 miles, while at the equator it is 7,926 miles. This means that the centre of the Earth is about 3,900 miles below us. The Earth's circumference at the equator is about 24,900 miles. The Earth is therefore not perfectly round. Its shape is an oblate spheroid, which means that it is flattened, like a pumpkin. The flattening is very slight, however. The Earth's diameter is only 26 miles less through the poles than through the equator. We say either that the Earth is flattened at the poles or that it bulges at the equator. In either case, it is very nearly round.

The Earth's mass is about 6,000 million,

Studies of earthquake waves have furnished evidence that the Earth's interior varies in density. This illustration shows that waves travelling through the Earth's mantle move in smooth arcs, covering the distances indicated by the elapsed time. When they hit the dense core, they are bent or refracted and move more slowly until they come again to the less dense rocks of the mantle. Sensitive instruments record their path.

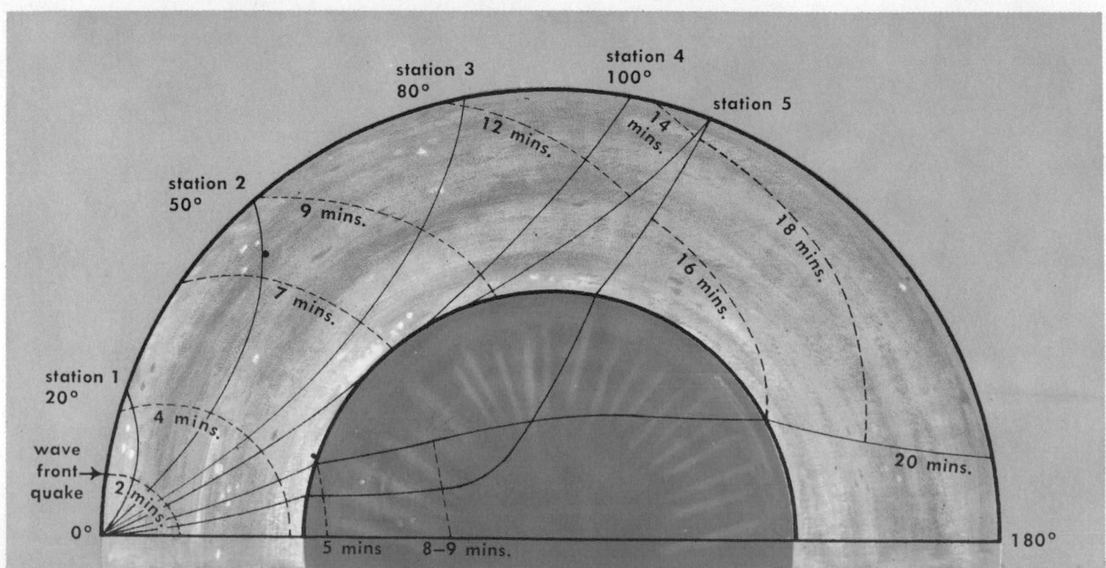

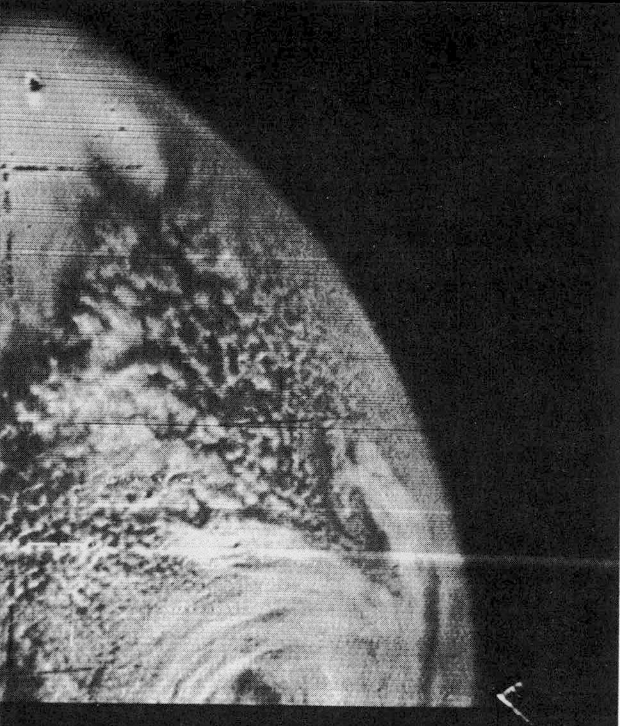

A cyclonic storm appears as a fluffy mass of clouds that are centred over Alaska.

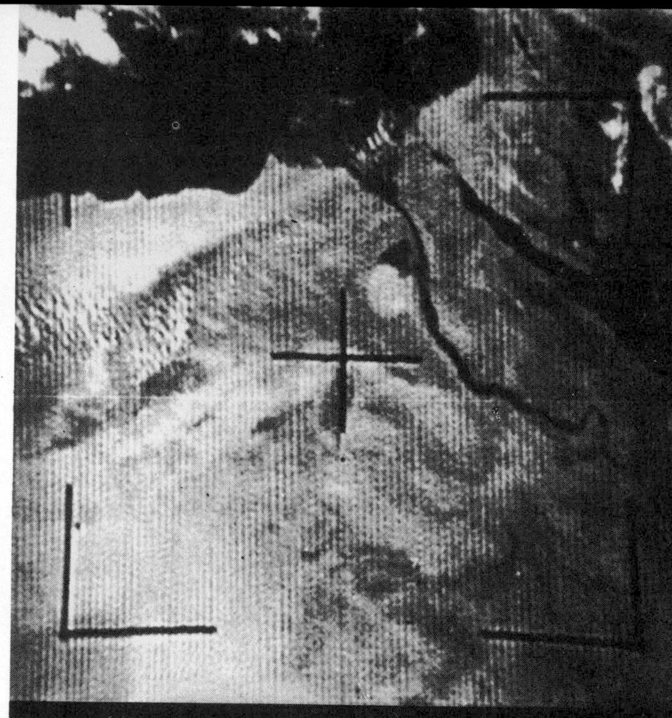

The south-eastern Mediterranean Sea and the Nile River are dark areas at the top of this picture.

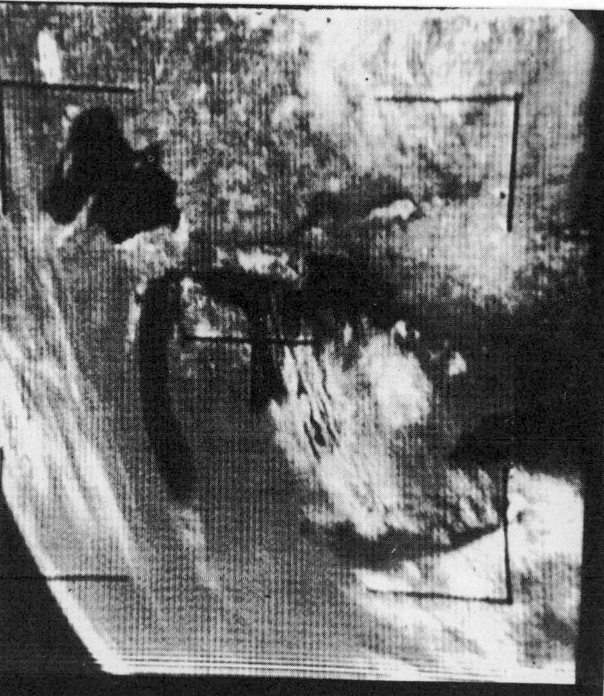

In the centre of this space photograph are the Great Lakes of North America, with storm clouds over Ontario.

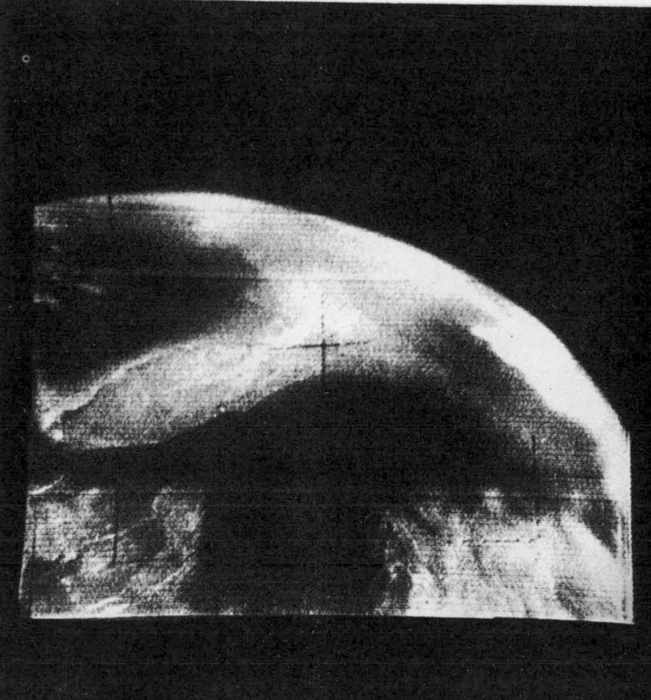

Florida, the Gulf of Mexico, and the Atlantic coast of the U.S. seen between storm clouds.

PHOTOGRAPHS OF THE EARTH FROM SATELLITES

Photographs taken by cameras mounted in artificial satellites have given man his first global-scale view of continents, islands, and bodies of water. Details of cloud formations, the sources of rain, snow, and storms, have also been recorded by the scanning cameras of these astronomical weather stations and observatories as they orbit the Earth. Such pictures from orbiting satellites will aid greatly in weather forecasting in the future.

million, million tons. Such a large body exerts a strong gravitational force on objects near its surface. (See GRAVITATION.) The force of gravity gives objects weight and pulls them towards the centre of the Earth. Because of the flattening at the poles, objects weigh slightly more at the poles than at the equator. A man who can throw a ball 190 feet at the north pole could throw it 191 feet at the equator.

The Earth is the only planet whose interior we can study. We cannot drill holes deep enough to explore the Earth directly, but the study of earthquakes provides a wealth of information about its interior. Every time an earthquake occurs, the shock causes waves to travel through the Earth, just as they do through a bowl of jelly. These waves can be detected all over the Earth and are recorded on instruments called seismographs. The speed of the waves and the direction in which they travel both depend on the characteristics of the material inside the Earth. From these waves we find that the interior of the Earth consists of four layers: crust, mantle, outer core, and inner core.

The crust is made of low-density rocks like those that we find on the Earth's surface. It is only 10 to 30 miles thick. The mantle is 1,800 miles thick and extends nearly half way to the centre of the Earth. It is made of denser rock. At the bottom of the mantle the rock is much denser, because it is compressed by the weight of the hundreds of miles of rock above. The Earth's core is even more dense and is very probably made of iron. Furthermore, the outer core is liquid rather than solid. The inner core has a slightly higher density and may be solid.

The temperature inside the Earth is much higher than on the surface. Just below the surface the temperature rises 10 or 20 degrees Fahrenheit for each 1000 feet of depth. The temperature rises much more slowly in the mantle, until in the core it may reach 5,500 to 8,250 degrees centigrade (10,000 to 15,000 degrees Fahrenheit).

Surrounding the Earth's surface and extending upwards for hundreds of miles is the atmosphere. It is a mixture of gases, mostly nitrogen and oxygen, and is dense near the surface but thins rapidly with height. The atmosphere warms the Earth.

Popperfoto

Earthquakes can cause great damage and loss of life. In August 1968 an earthquake lasting nearly one minute struck Manila in the Philippines. Shown above is some of the resulting devastation.

It protects us from meteors and radiation and supplies the gases that animals and plants need to breathe (see ATMOSPHERE).

The Earth's surface seems firm and stationary, but actually the Earth is in rapid motion. Its two prinicpal motions are a rotation on its axis every day and a revolution around the Sun every year. These two motions of the Earth are directly responsible for the periodic changes that we call days and years.

The Earth turns on its own axis from west to east. Thus the Sun, Moon, planets, and stars seem to rise in the east and set in the west. The most prominent heavenly body is the Sun. When the Sun is above the horizon, we call the time day; the time when the Sun is below the horizon is what we call night. We even set our clocks by the rotation of the Earth, for time signals sent out by various observatories all depend on observing the moment when certain stars cross the central meridian of the sky. (See CELESTIAL SPHERE.)

Although we do not feel any motion, the Earth's rotation carries us along rapidly. At the equator every point of the Earth's surface is travelling eastward at 1,000 miles an hour. At 40 degrees north latitude, the speed is 800 miles per hour. At the poles it is zero.

The Earth's revolution around the Sun seems slower, since it takes a whole year. But actually this motion is very rapid – 18½ miles per second. The trip around the Sun takes so long only because it is such a long trip. As we travel around the Sun, the seasons change. The reason is the tilt of the Earth's axis. As the Earth goes round its orbit, the Northern and Southern Hemispheres are alternately tilted towards and away from the Sun. When our hemisphere is tilted towards the Sun, we receive more light and heat, and it is summer. In winter we receive less light and heat, because our hemisphere is tilted away from the Sun. (See SEASONS.)

The path that the Earth follows around the Sun is called its orbit. Year after year it travels along this same path, and only over thousands of years does the orbit change appreciably. The average distance of the Earth from the Sun is 93 million miles, but the actual distance varies from one time of the year to another because the orbit is not a perfect circle. In January, when it is at perihelion or its closest point to the Sun, the Earth is 1½ million miles closer to the Sun than average. In July, at aphelion or the farthest point, it is 1½ million miles farther than average.

AGE OF THE EARTH. Written histories go back a few thousand years, and man has existed for a million years. But the age of the Earth is measured in thousands of millions of years. Scientists are able to measure ages over such a long period of time by studying the gradual changes that take place in rocks.

The best method uses radioactive atoms, which disintegrate and change into atoms of another kind. Radioactive atoms continue to disintegrate at the same rate regardless of their surroundings so that at any time the age of a sample can be measured by seeing how much of the original material is left. Uranium is the most useful for dating rocks. It turns into lead, but so slowly that even after millions of years some of the

The Earth's most ancient rocks are the 'shields' that form the cores of the continents. In most regions these rocks of Pre-Cambrian age are covered by layers of younger rocks.

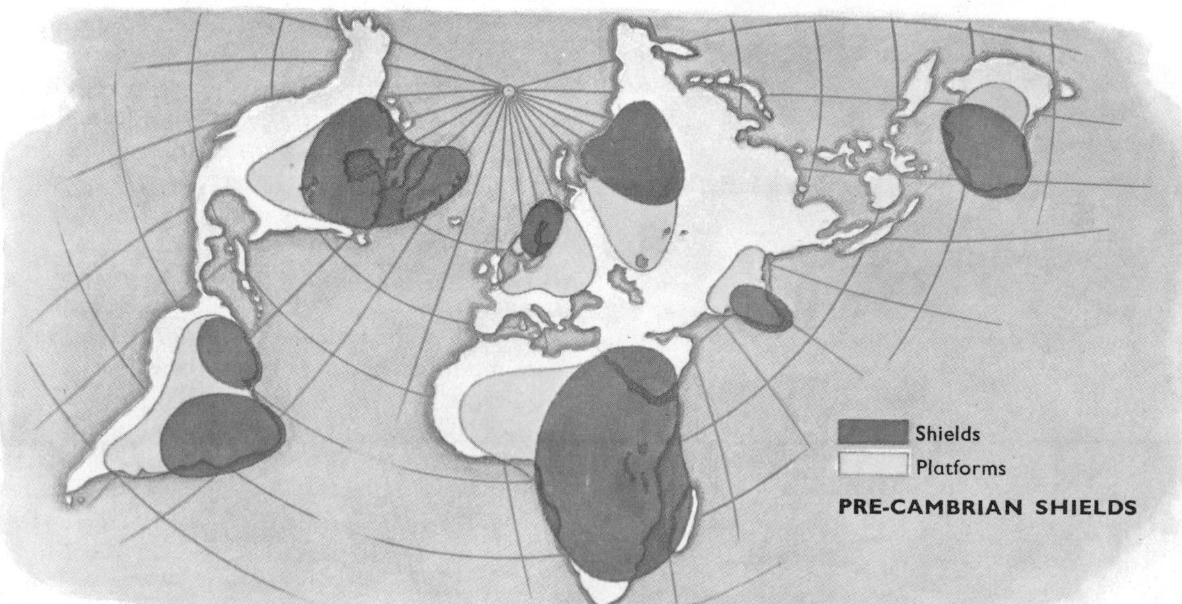

original uranium can be measured by comparing the amount of uranium in it with the amount of lead. A rock that has much more uranium than lead is young; there has not been enough time for much of the uranium to disintegrate. But a rock that has more lead than uranium must be old enough for most of the uranium to have disintegrated. This kind of measurement depends on very accurate chemical analysis as the amounts of uranium and lead are exceedingly small.

The oldest rocks that have been dated by these methods are possibly 3,0000 million years old. The Earth must therefore be older for these are certainly not the oldest rocks.

When the Earth was first formed it was completely barren, and it remained barren for a long time. The earliest known fossils are around 2,700 million years old. They gradually evolved into more plants and animals, until the seas of 600 million years ago became filled with all sorts of creatures. Animals first crawled out on to land about 425 million years ago, and dinosaurs lived from 160 million to 60 million years ago. Since then mammals have been dominant, and for the last million years Man has become more and more important. (See CIVILISATION; FOSSILS; GEOLOGY; LIFE'S ORIGIN AND DEVELOPMENT.)

EBONY is a wood that comes from tropical trees closely related to persimmons. (See PERSIMMONS.) Some of the nearly 200 species are found in temperate regions of Asia, North America, and around the Mediterranean.

True ebony wood is black, often with irregular brown streaks; it is very heavy, fine-grained, and even-textured. It is commonly used for piano keys and also for canes, heads of golf clubs, and carvings. The trees which supply ebony wood grow in Ceylon, India, the East Indies, and West Africa. The various species of ebony are members of the genus *Diospyros*.

ECLIPSES. As the Moon goes around the Earth, once each month, it usually passes above or below the Sun. We do not see it in the bright day-time sky, but on occasions when the Moon passes directly between the Sun and the Earth, it hides the Sun. This is called an eclipse of the Sun.

The Sun is 400 times as large as the Moon, but it is also 400 times as far away, so they look nearly the same size. The distances of the Sun and Moon from the Earth vary with the time, so sometimes the Moon looks a little larger than the Sun and can hide it completely. Then the Moon can produce a total eclipse. When the Moon looks smaller, it cannot eclipse the Sun completely, and a bright ring of Sun shows all around the edge of the Moon. This is called an annular eclipse. At the time of either a total or an annular eclipse, anyone who is not directly in line with the Sun and Moon sees only a partial eclipse; one edge of the Sun is hidden, the other visible.

During an eclipse of the Sun the Moon's shadow touches the Earth. Its shadow has two parts. The umbra is completely dark; it narrows with increasing distance and tapers to a point at about 230,000 miles from the moon. The penumbra contains some sunlight. This part of the shadow widens with distance and extends indefinitely far from the Moon. At the time of an eclipse the Moon's penumbra sweeps across the Earth in a path 4,000 miles wide, and anyone in this path sees a partial eclipse of the Sun. But at the Earth's distance from the Moon, the umbra tapers down to a tiny point. If

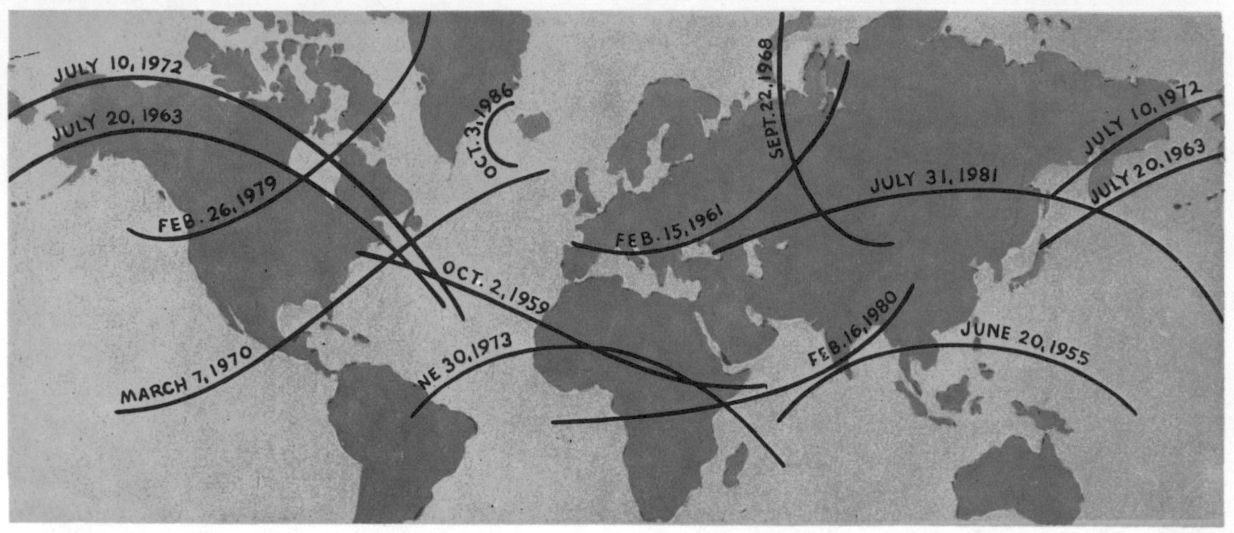

The paths of total eclipses visible in the Northern Hemisphere are plotted on this map for the years 1955 to 1980.

it reaches the Earth's surface, then a total eclipse of the Sun can be seen inside the narrow track that the umbra traces out as the Moon travels along. If the umbra does not reach the Earth's surface, then an annular eclipse is seen instead, also along a narrow path.

As the track of the Moon's umbra across the Earth's surface is never much more than 150 miles wide and usually is much narrower, it is rare to see a total eclipse of the Sun. Although nearly every year a total eclipse occurs somewhere on Earth, most of the eclipse tracks cross remote lands or the ocean. At any given point of the Earth's surface, a total eclipse of the Sun occurs on the average only once every 350 years.

A total eclipse of the Sun is an unforgettable sight even though it lasts only a few minutes. The partial eclipse begins almost two hours before totality when the first nick appears in the western edge of the Sun. The Moon itself remains invisible, but its progress is clear as a larger and larger portion of the Sun's face is blotted out. At last the Sun dwindles to the narrowest crescent. The light is much dimmer but it is still daylight. The eclipse is still only partial. Then suddenly the last crescent of sunlight vanishes and in that instant daylight turns into darkness. The Sun appears transformed, and around the black disc of the Moon glows the pearly white of the Sun's corona. The illumination is only as bright as moonlight, and the stars shine clearly. Usually after a minute or two, a crescent of dazzling light suddenly appears at the other edge of the Sun. It is daylight again, and the total phase of the eclipse is over. All that remains is for the Moon gradually to move clear of the Sun during the next two hours.

Astronomers often travel to the far corners of the Earth to observe total eclipses of the Sun, for some observations can be made only

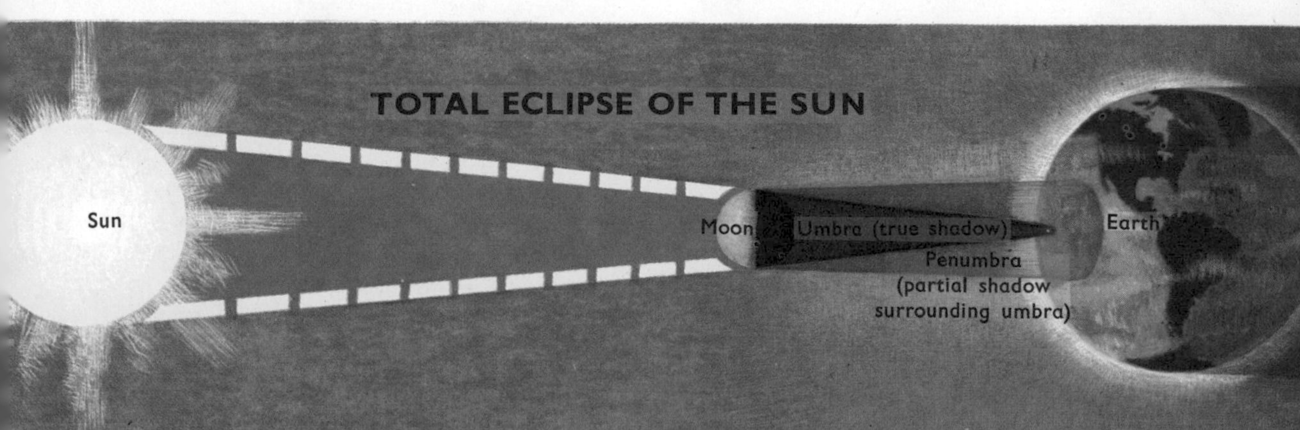

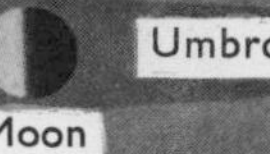

The Moon, Earth's only satellite, is located in the Earth's shadow, during a total eclipse of the Moon.

at those times. Foremost is the study of the outer parts of the Sun. The layers just above the Sun's surface are best studied as the Moon covers them one at a time, and the outer parts of the corona are too faint to be seen except during a total eclipse (see SUN). Eclipse time is valuable, for the period of totality is never longer than $7\frac{2}{3}$ minutes and is usually only 2 minutes or so. If an astronomer could travel to every eclipse, a lifetime would provide him with only 3 hours of totality — even if cloudy weather did not make many trips a total loss!

By comparison with a total eclipse of the Sun, an eclipse of the Moon is a pale event; but by way of compensation, eclipses of the Moon are easier to see. In an eclipse of the Moon, the Moon passes into the Earth's shadow, and this can be seen by everyone on the side of the Earth from which the Moon can be seen at that time. The Earth's shadow is large enough to envelop the Moon completely, and when the Moon passes completely into the Earth's shadow, we see a total eclipse of the Moon. The Moon becomes very faint but does not disappear completely, for the Earth's atmosphere bends some sunlight into the shadow. This light is reddened, like the rays of the setting Sun, and the Moon takes on a deep red colour when totally eclipsed. An eclipse of the Moon is a leisurely event. The Moon takes an hour to go into eclipse and an hour to come out. The period of total eclipse may last for as long as an hour and forty minutes.

Every year eclipses occur, some of the Sun and some of the Moon. Although the occurrence of eclipses is determined by the motions of the Earth and Moon, exact predictions involve long computation. There are some simple rules, however. One is that eclipses occur only at certain times of the year. At least one eclipse of some sort must occur in each eclipse season, perhaps on the opposite side of the Earth from us. The seasons occur about 19 days earlier each year.

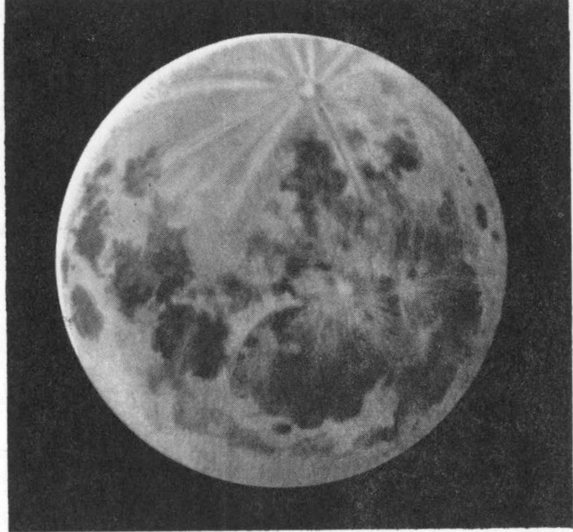

During an eclipse of the Moon the Moon's surface is a copper red colour due to light reflected from the Earth.

In an annular eclipse, the Moon does not hide the Sun, and its shadow or umbra does not reach the Earth.

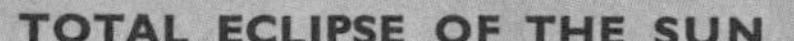

TOTAL ECLIPSE OF THE SUN

This remarkable multiple-exposure photograph, taken by an amateur, shows several stages in a total eclipse of the Sun. At lower left, the Sun is partly covered by the Moon. Its crescent shape becomes progressively smaller until it is completely covered and shows only as a glowing ring. In similar stages the Sun reappears and is almost full again in the photograph in the upper right.

Colour photo by Mel Tinklenberg, St. Paul

SHAGGY INK CAP — 4–8 in
Coprinus comatus
Europe, North America

COMMON MUSHROOM — 2–6 in.
Agaricus campestris
Europe, North America

HONEY FUNGUS — 2–4 in.
Armillaria mellea
Europe, North America

COMMON EDIBLE MUSHROOMS

A few of the several hundred species of edible mushrooms of Europe and North America are illustrated here. By comparison, the number of poisonous species is small, but the poison they contain is powerful and may cause death. Do not eat any mushroom if there is any doubt about its being an edible species.

A mushroom, also called a 'button', is the above-ground fruiting body of a fungus. It bears the spores by which the fungus is spread. Beneath the ground is a mass of thread-like filaments (the mycelium) that mushroom growers refer to as the 'spawn'.

CHANTERELLE — 4–6 in.
Cantharellus cibarius
Europe, North America

EDIBLE FUNGI. Few kinds of fungi are poisonous. Most arc either edible or too woody to eat. There is no way to tell a poisonous fungus from an edible one except by identifying the species. If you are not absolutely sure that a fungus is edible, do not eat it. Most coral fungi, morels, puffballs, and truffles are edible, but all *Amanitas*, pink spored *Agarics*, *Clitocybes*, and all species of *Cortinarius* and *Inocybe* should be avoided. (See MORELS; TRUFFLES.)

A variety of the Field Mushroom *(Agaricus campestris)* is cultivated in Western Europe and the United States. Large quantities are grown in caves, cellars, or special buildings (see MUSHROOM GROWING). The Field Mushroom and the Horse Mushroom *(Agaricus arvensis)* grow wild in moist lawns and pastures.

Truffles (*Tuber* spp.) are rounded underground fungal bodies grown in association with oak trees in France, but occurring in beechwoods in southern England. The Truffles, up to 5 inches across, are searched for by trained pigs or dogs.

The Oyster Mushroom *(Pleurotus ostreatus)* is one of the best-tasting of the wild gill fungi. Found on decaying wood, it has a shell-shaped cap and white gills and spores.

The Parasol Mushroom *(Lepiota procera)*, one of the favourite of the edible kinds, has white spores. Morgan's Lepiota *(Lepiota morgani)*, a poisonous member of the same genus, is easily confused with the Parasol Mushroom but has green spores.

The Shaggy Ink Cap *(Coprinus comatus)* occurs in rich soil, in gardens, by roadsides, and in woods, and the black spores are suspended in an inky fluid. It is edible before it becomes inky.

MOREL — 2—6 in.
Morchella esculenta
Europe, North America

EDIBLE BOLETUS —3—7 in.
Boletus edulis
Europe, North America

HORN OF PLENTY — 3—5 in.
Craterellus cornucopioides
Europe

BLEWIT — 3—6 in.
Tricholoma personata
Europe, North America

WARTED PUFFBALL — 1—12 in.
Lycoperdon perlatum
Europe, North America

GIANT PUFFBALL — 3 in.—4 ft.
Calvatia gigantea
Europe, North America

Most members of the genus *Boletus* are also edible, but a number of them are poisonous. All are stalked. On the under surface of the cap are numerous closely packed tubes that open through tiny pores that are usually easily separated from the rest of the cap. *Boletus chrysenteron* is a common but variable species. Its cap varies from yellowish-brown or reddish-brown to brick red, tawny or even carmine red. The flesh is yellow but often changes to blue where wounded. Tubes are greenish-yellow, but when wounded they first change to blue, then greenish. *Boletus edulis*, the most desirable of the boletes, is more common in Europe than in the United States.

The Giant Puffball *(Calvatia gigantea)* and smaller puffballs are good to cook providing they are gathered while young and firm.

The Orange Milk Cap *(Lactarius deliciosus)* produces orange-coloured milk that quickly turns green when exposed to the air. All parts of the mushroom are coloured orange or greyish-orange.

The Chanterelle *(Cantharellus cibarius)* has narrow, thick gills that extend down the stem. The gills often branch and join. When fresh, the fungus has the odour of apricots. The Shaggy Chanterelle *(Cantharellus floccosus)* has an elongated funnel or trumpet-shaped fruiting body with narrow, thick gills that form regularly and often join.

The Blewits *(Tricholoma personata* and *Tricholoma nuda)* are collected to eat in England and Europe but not so much in the United States. They grow in woods and pastures and often form fairy rings. (See FAIRY RINGS.)

The Flat-capped Mushroom *(Agaricus placomyces)* has gills that are first white, then pink, and finally blackish-brown. The spores are purplish. The stem has a bulbous base.

The Savoury Pleurotus *(Pleurotus sapidus)* is closely related to the Oyster Mushroom, differing chiefly in the pale-lilac colour of the spores. The stem is usually also slightly longer than the Oyster Mushroom's stem.

The Beefsteak Mushroom *(Fistulina hepatica)*, one of the pore fungi, has a short lateral stem or has no stalk. The skin is dark red and usually movable like the skin on the back of the hand. The yellowish or pink tubes are free from one another. It is common on chestnut or oak stumps.

EGGPLANT or **AUBERGINE** *(Solanum melongena)*, a member of the potato family, has been cultivated since prehistoric times. During the Dark Ages, a variety of this plant was brought from its native India to England and soon became known as 'eggplant' because of its small egg-shaped fruit. Improved varieties grown now have much larger fruit. Botanists of the sixteenth century called it the 'mad apple' because they thought eating it caused insanity.

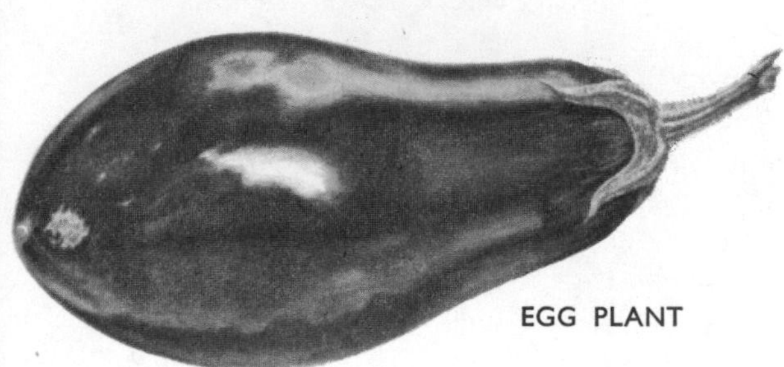

EGG PLANT

Eggplants may be yellow, purple, red, white, green, or striped. They also vary widely in shape.

AMERICAN ELM

ELMS are popular shade and ornamental trees. About 35 species are native to Europe, Asia, and eastern North America. They have simple, alternate leaves with coarsely toothed margins. Each seed is enclosed in a wafer-thin papery wing. Elm wood, which is strong and tough but coarse-grained, is used for such items as furniture frames, barrels, crates, boxes, and rough flooring. Many elms in America have been destroyed by the Dutch elm disease introduced from Europe years ago.

The Wych (or Scotch) Elm *(Ulmus glabra)*, one of the most common, is native to Europe and central Asia. A cultivated form of this species, known as Camperdown Elm, or Umbrella Elm, has long, drooping branches.

COMMON ELM
Ulmus campestris

The English Elm *(Ulmus procera)*, a native of Britain and France, has a large, rounded, wide-spreading crown. Its twigs and smaller branches also have corky wings. Dwarf Asiatic Elm *(Ulmus pumila)* and Chinese Elm *(Ulmus parvifolia)* are two small trees with leaves less lopsided at their bases than other elms.

The elm family includes hackberries and 13 other groups of trees and shrubs totalling about 150 species. Most are native to north temperate regions of the world; a few grow in the tropics at high altitudes where it is cooler.

EMERALD

EMERALD, the most expensive of the gem stones, is a beautiful green and rarely found without flaws. It is a form of beryl (see BERYL). Emeralds come from Colombia, Ceylon, U.S.S.R., and Brazil.

EMPRESS TREES *(Paulownia imperialis)* look much like the catalpa. Their fragrant flowers, which bloom before the leaves develop, are purple rather than white, and their woody seed capsules are oval instead of long and bean-like. Often planted in parks and gardens, especially in the south and west, the fast-growing Empress Tree, a native of China, belongs to the snapdragon family.

EMPRESS TREE

EOCENE, which means 'dawn of recent', was that portion of the Tertiary period that began about 54 million years ago and lasted about 16 million years. Eocene rocks were first described in the Paris Basin but are also well-developed in Belgium, Germany, and southern England. Both marine and freshwater deposits of Eocene age are found in southern England. In the north were vast lava flows, famous now for the regular columnar jointing to be seen at Fingal's Cave, Staffa and the Giant's Causeway, Antrim.

Most Eocene plants and invertebrates were fairly modern in appearance. Their distribution was quite different from today, however, because of the warm climate that prevailed during Eocene times. Palm trees grew as far north as Alberta, and Greenland and the plants in southern England resembled those of present day Malaysia. In late Eocene times the climate became too cool for such tropical plants to grow in northern latitudes. Among the most abundant of the invertebrates were shell-bearing one-celled animals, the foraminifera. These included the large *Nummulites* which are abundant in the rocks of which the Egyptian pyramids are built.

Many mammals were ancient types that became extinct at the close of Eocene. Among these were the creodonts, condylarths *(Phenacodus)*, uintatheres, amblypods *(Coryphodon)*, and some of the carnivores, such as *Oxyaena*. Newcomers, distinguishing Eocene mammals from those of the preceding Palaeocene epoch, included ancestral horses, camels, elephants, rhinos, rodents, and primates. During the Eocene, the pouched mammals (marsupials) were already becoming secondary in importance to the more modern placental mammals. Among other outstanding Eocene animals were carnivorous, ground-living birds, one of which *(Diatryma)* stood 7 feet tall. The ancestors of many of the groups of present day birds first appeared during the Eocene epoch.

The reptile life of Eocene times differed greatly from that of the preceding period. Dinosaurs and other giants of the reptile clan had disappeared (see DINOSAURS). However, because of the warm climate, crocodiles and turtles were common in the lakes and rivers of many regions, including

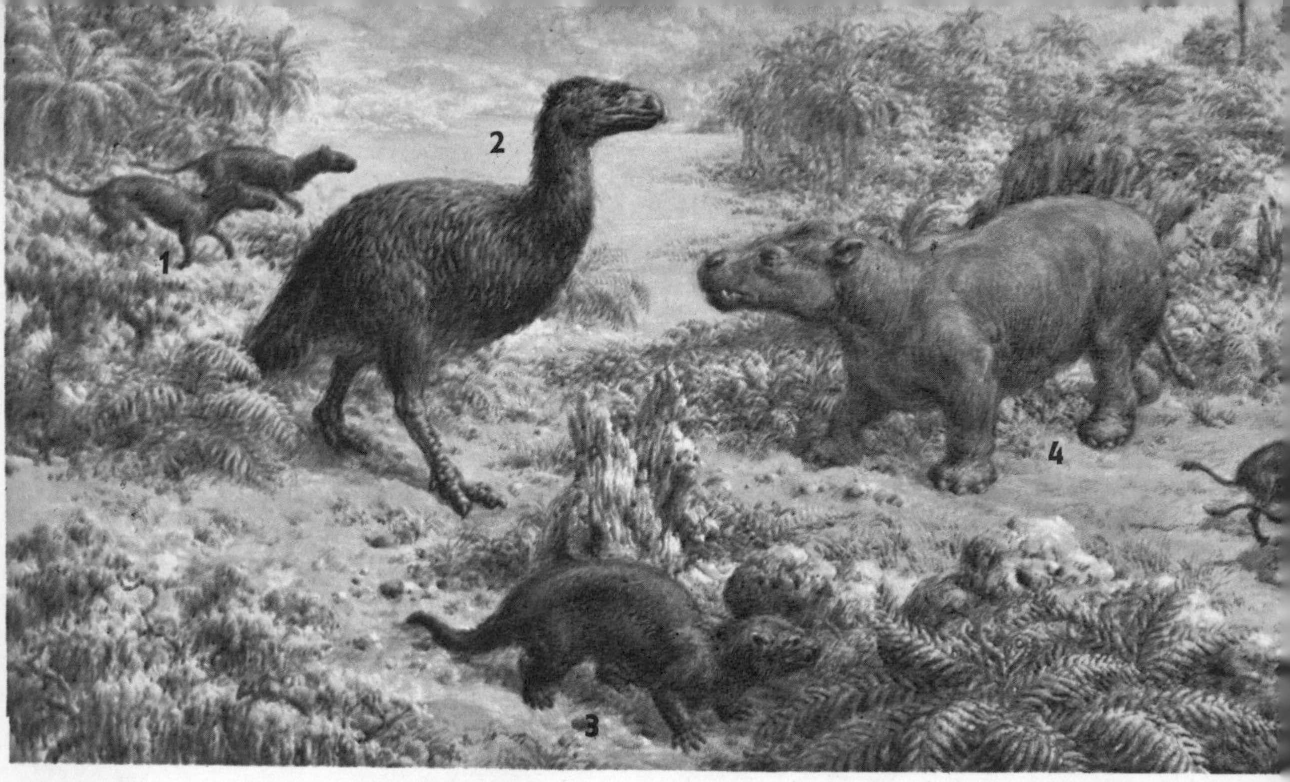

Among the animals of Eocene times were: *Phenacodus* (1), a primitive ungulate or hoofed mammal; *Diatryma* (2), a giant flightless bird; *Patriofelis* (3), a powerful cat-like carnivore; *Coryphodon* (4), a stumpy-legged tapir-sized ungulate that had long canine teeth despite its vegetarian diet; *Eohippus* (5), forerunner of the modern horse; *Eobasileus* (6) and *Uintatherium* (7), rhinoceros-sized hoofed mammals that became extinct before the end of the Eocene epoch.

England. The fish of the period were in most respects the same as those swimming in the seas of today.

EPIPHYTES have no root connections to the soil. They use plants, poles, and other objects for support — but not for nutrition. They are not parasites. Most kinds have chlorophyll and manufacture their own food by absorbing moisture and gases from the atmosphere.

Many kinds of epiphytes grow in the tropics and sub-tropics. By growing high on the branches of trees they get sunlight. Orchids, Spanish Moss and many members of the pineapple family are epiphytes. Sometimes tangled growths of Spanish Moss become so dense that they break the branches of trees, but otherwise they do no harm. Many mosses, lichens, liverworts, and ferns are epiphytes too. Lichens are common as a greenish or bluish-white crust on rocks, tree-bark, shingles, and fence posts. They are not single plants but an association of green or blue-green algae with fungi. The fungi receive food from the algae and aid the algae by absorbing and retaining water and also by providing them with physical support. The algae found with lichens can be more easily grown without the fungi than the fungi can be grown without the algae. (See LICHENS.)

Some plants, such as the Strangler Fig, start as epiphytes but eventually develop roots and become attached to the ground. (See FIGS.)

WILD PINEAPPLE
Tillandsia fasciculata

CLAMSHELL ORCHID
Epidendrum cochleatum

BALL MOSS
Tillandsia recurvata

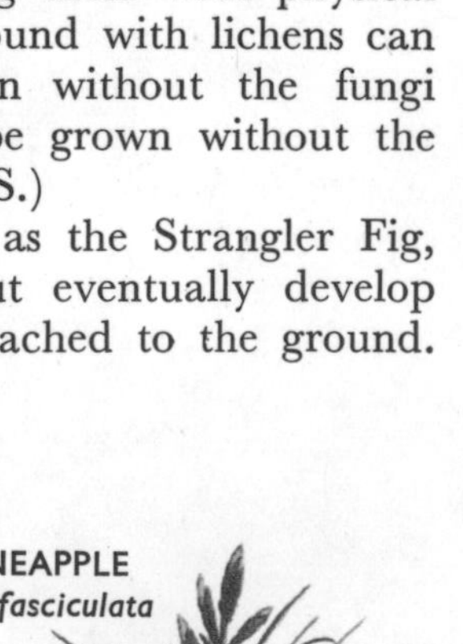

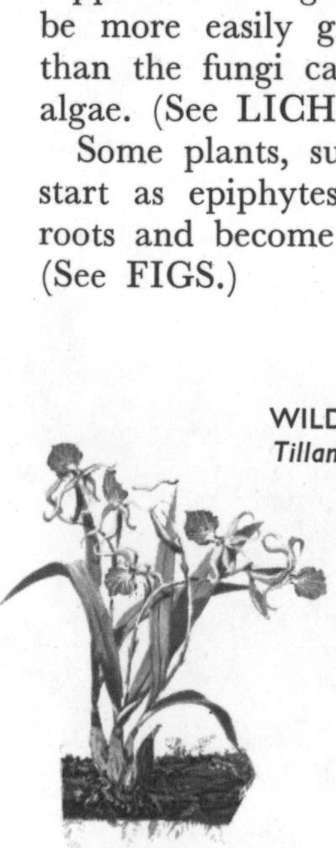

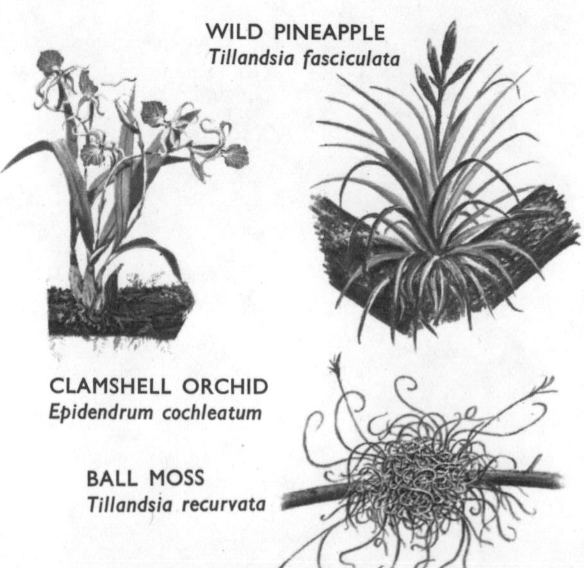

EUCALYPTUS trees are a genus of nearly 600 species in the myrtle family. They are natives to Australia but have been planted throughout the world for wind-breaks. In Britain, a few species are planted as ornamentals in mild localities.

Eucalypts are the dominant trees in Australia. Some grow in the mountains where in the harsh winds, heavy snows, and intense cold, they develop grotesque shapes. Others are found only in tropical rain forests, and many only along streams in semi-arid regions.

Some eucalyptus trees are tall and straight, their trunks free of branches for many feet above the ground. The Blue Gum *(Eucalyptus globulus)*, one of the most commonly planted eucalypts in the world, grows 100 to 140 feet in height. The Mountain Ash *(Eucalyptus regnans)*, of Victoria and Tasmania, is the tallest Australian tree and the tallest of the world's hardwoods. Many are much smaller, with short trunks and wide-spreading crowns.

As a group, the eucalypts are easy to recognise, but the various species are not easy to identify. Their bark, particularly important in field identification, varies in colour and may be smooth, dimpled, furrowed, scaly, flaky or stringy. The colour of their wood and odour of their leaves are also distinctive features. These are the basis for such group names as gums, iron-barks, stringy-barks, mahoganies, boxes, peppermints, blackbutts, scaly-barks, and ashes.

Eucalyptus leaves are evergreen, greyish in colour, leathery in texture, and smooth-margined. In most species the leaves are long and narrow (3 to 8 inches) tapering to a point. Their small flowers are in loose clusters, and their unique fruit — bell-shaped 'pods', called gum nuts — open at the top to release numerous, minute seeds.

FAIRY RINGS are formed by gill fungi. People used to believe that fairies danced in circles on the grass in the moonlight. Mushrooms that grew in rings were thought to be seats for the elves.

A fairy ring is formed of the visible, reproductive structures of an underground fungus. A fungus spore germinates and the mycelium or body of the fungus grows steadily outwards to form a circle that may grow, after some years, to many feet in diameter. The distance depends on the moisture, temperature, nature of the soil, and the kind of fungus. The fruiting bodies grow at the rim of the ring. They only appear each year if conditions are favourable. Sometimes it takes centuries to form a large ring. The Fairy Ring Mushroom *(Marasmius oreades)* is the most common of a number of kinds of gill fungi that form fairy rings.

The kind of fairy ring that has attracted most attention has three concentric circles — an outer and an inner zone of darker coloured grass and a middle zone that is bare.

As the mycelium grows some proteins are changed into amino-acids and ammonia. Decayed mycelium and other organic matter in the soil is changed by certain bacteria into ammonia. Other bacteria convert the ammonia into nitrates. These nitrogeneous materials make the grass and other plants grow larger and greener.

What causes the bare zone is still a debatable issue. Some have suggested that the fungus infects and kills the roots. Others say the mycelium packs the soil so tightly that water cannot penetrate it so that the roots die from lack of water. We still do not know the answer.

FAIRY RING MUSHROOM

FELDSPARS are an abundant group of minerals widespread in igneous rocks and less common in metamorphic rocks. They are rare in sedimentary rocks. All have a hardness of about 6, and two good cleavage faces. All are aluminium silicates with one or more other metals. The orthoclase group (potash feldspars) contains orthoclase and microcline; the plagioclase group consists of albite (sodium feldspar), oligoclase, andesine, labradorite, bytownite, and anorthite (a calcium feldspar). The intermediate members from albite to anorthite contain decreasing amounts of soda and silica and increasing amounts of calcium. Orthoclase, often flesh-pink, is characteristic of granites and syenites and is not found in pegmatites. Microcline, found in pegmatites and in lesser amounts in granites, may be white, red, or green (Amazon stone). Albite and oligoclase are found in granites, syenites,

ANORTHITE

LABRADORITE

monzonites, and diorites. Feldspars containing more calcium are more abundant in diorites, gabbros, and their fine-grained equivalents. Feldspars weather chemically to form kaolin and various other clay minerals.

Only potassium and sodium feldspars are used in ceramics. Some is added to glass to make high aluminium glass. Others are used for pottery, enamel (mixed with kaolinite and quartz), low-voltage electrical porcelain, grinding wheel cement, white ware, and sanitary ware. Small amounts are used as gem stones; examples are Amazon stone, moonstone with opalescence, and labradorite with its attractive iridescent play of blue, green, yellow, and red colours.

Feldspar crystals come mainly from pegmatites and some porphyries. Orthoclase feldspars are commercially exploited in Cornwall, Sweden, Norway, Italy, U.S.A., and Canada. The tips of the china clay industry of Devon and Cornwall are well known.

FERNS are the best known and largest group (about 9,000 species) of the nonseedbearing vascular plants. Ferns are common in wooded areas, along banks of streams, and in open pine lands. Most ferns grow in the soil. Some are epiphytes, growing on the limbs or trunks of trees but manufacturing their own food. Several are aquatic, either free-floating or rooted in the mud with their leaves floating on the surface. Others grow on rocks, and some occur only in lime sinkholes.

Ferns are an ancient group. Many fossil ferns are found in coal, shale, and other sedimentary rocks. They were prominent in the Coal Age. Many were small, but some were tree-like. Tree ferns 50 feet tall are still fairly common in the tropics. Some present-day ferns are climbers, crawling up trunks of trees. Others are less than half an inch tall.

Ferns differ in several ways from all other non-seed vascular plants. Their sporangia or spore cases are produced in groups (called a sorus) either on the underside of the leaves or on a special spike-like section of a leaf. In some ferns the sorus has a cover that folds back when the spores are mature. Others have no cover. Spore-bearing leaves generally look like other leaves, but those of Royal Fern, Adder's Tongue, and others are

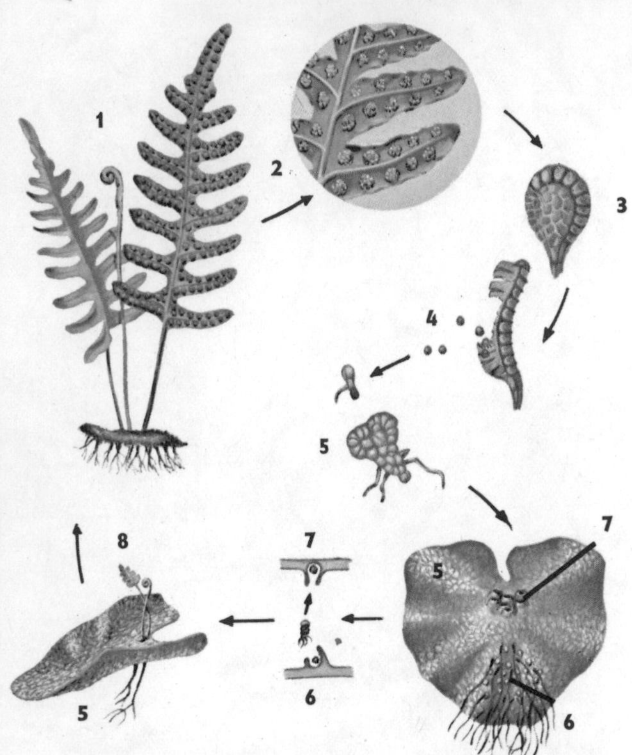

The sporophyte generation of the fern plant (1) is the familiar leafy plant of woods and gardens. It produces spore cases (2), or sori, on the underside of the leaves. Each spore case (3) ruptures, scattering minute spores (4) that develop into the gametophyte generation, called the prothallium (5). This supports the antheridium (6) that produces the male cells that find their way into the archegonium (7) that contains the egg cell. From this union, the new fern develops. (8)

different from the vegetative leaves. Spore cases of the so-called water ferns are in hard-coated structures called sporocarps.

The life cycle of a fern is similar to that of a moss. Ferns are much more advanced, however. The common fern plant grows from a fertilised egg cell and produces spores when it is mature. It has roots, stems, and leaves and also vascular tissues. The fertilised egg forms in a smaller plant, the gametophyte. This is green and is an independent plant. It is rather inconspicuous and varies in size from about 1/16 of an inch across to slightly less than the size of a sixpence. Called a prothallus, the gametophyte is more or less heart-shaped and has no roots, stems, or leaves. It grows flat on the surface of a rock, soil, tree, or flower pot and is anchored by thin threads. In many ways it resembles a small liverwort. On its underside are the sex organs where the gametes (eggs and sperm) are produced. When there is rain or a heavy dew so that a film of water surrounds the gametophyte, the sperm unites with each egg. The cells produced by these unions are called zygotes, and they grow into the spore-producing plant.

At first the sporophyte is dependent on its female parent. Later it produces roots, stems, and leaves of its own and becomes an independent fern plant. Eventually it forms spore cases on the back of its leaves. If several mature spore cases are scraped on to a slide and examined under a microscope, their opening can be observed. As soon as they dry, they spring open suddenly and catapult their spores into the air.

Fibres of the Royal Fern *(Osmunda)* and

others are used in growing orchids and other epiphytes.

The Walking Fern *(Camptosorus)* is an interesting fern that is cultivated in some gardens and is a native of America. The Walking Fern produces spores as do all other ferns, but also has another means of reproduction. The tips of the young tapering leaves grow into new plants wherever they touch the ground. These new plants produce more narrow, tapering leaves that also take root at their tips. Thus the fern 'walks' along.

One of the most beautiful ferns is the Maidenhair Fern *(Adiantum)*. Its spore-bearing bodies (sori) are protected by the in-rolled margin of the leaves.

The Bracken *(Pteridium)* grows in open fields and woods, sometimes covering large areas. Fertile leaflets, like those of the Maidenhair Fern, are turned under at the margin.

The Polypody Fern *(Polypodium)* usually grows as an epiphyte on the branches of oaks or other trees in warm climates. One species *(Polypodium vulgare)* is a native of the British Isles and can be found in abundance in western districts.

The Osmunda family is represented in the British Isles by one species only, *Osmunda regalis*, the Royal Fern. It is a stately fern which grows to a height of 8 feet in favourable conditions. Unfortunately it is becoming very scarce as a wild plant in Britain, mainly because of the drainage of bogs and the collection of plants by gardeners. It is now only found in the south-west and Ireland. Sporangia, or spore cases are produced only in a spike-like portion at the top of the leaf.

The Holly Fern *(Polystichum)*, a rare species in mountain districts, has leaflets toothed at the edges.

Spleenworts *(Asplenium)* grow on shady moss-covered rocks and in walls. These dainty, little ferns have leaves 3 to 8 inches long and dark purple or black leaf stalks.

Moonwort *(Botrychium)* and also Adder's Tongue *(Ophioglossum)* grow in grassy places. Both have a single, divided leaf. One branch looks like an ordinary leaf, while the other is spike-like and bears spore cases.

The Hart's Tongue Fern *(Phyllitis)* is common in woods, hedgerows and walls. Its leaf is quite different to other ferns in being undivided.

The Staghorn Fern *(Platycerium)* is a large epiphytic fern from tropical Africa and Asia and temperate Australia. It has two types of leaves. The sterile leaves are flat, rounded, shield-shaped, undivided, and parchment-like. They clasp the tree or whatever support

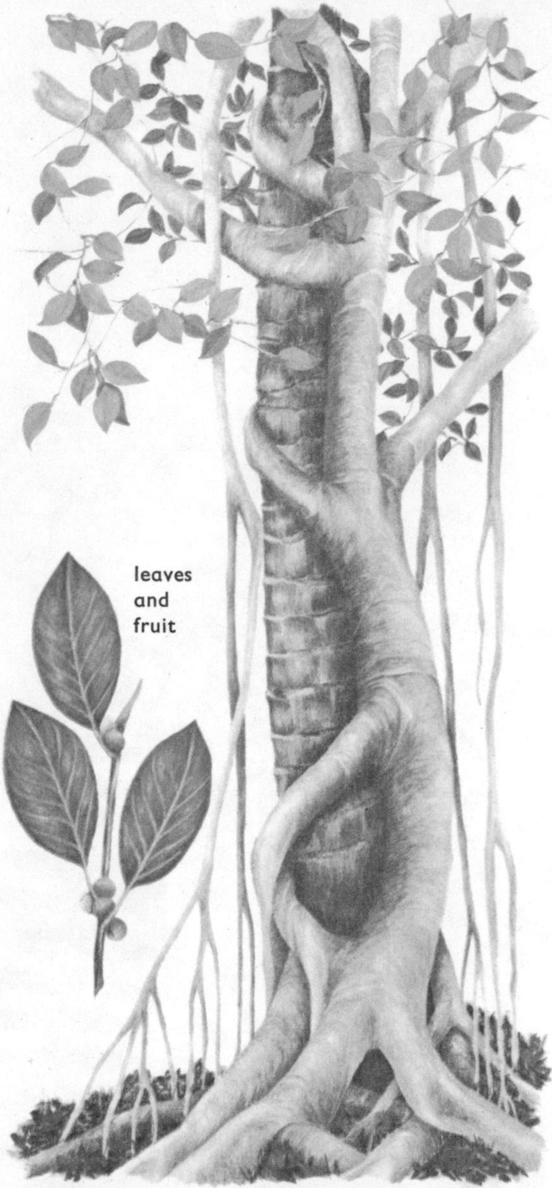

The Strangler Fig *(Ficus aurea)* often grows 60 feet tall. Usually it begins as an epiphyte, when a seed dropped by a bird lodges in the crotch or bark of another tree. The Cabbage Palm is a common victim. The long, vine-like roots of the Strangler Fig grow into the ground and rob the host tree of its nourishment, while the spreading crown blocks out the light from its leaves. In time, the host tree dies.

on which the fern is growing. The other type of leaf grows erect and bears sori on their underside.

The so-called water ferns *(Azolla)* differ from other ferns not only in being aquatic but also in having two kinds of spores. *Azolla* is a small, floating plant which can cover the surface of ponds. Pillwort *(Pilularia)* is also a small water plant, occuring on the edge of ponds. Its leaves are undivided and rush-like and the spores are borne in globose structures at the base of the leaves.

Tree Ferns are majestic plants found only in tropical areas.

FIGS. More than 600 species, chiefly tropicals, form this group in the mulberry family. A familiar species is the India Rubber-tree, a common potted plant in homes and hotel lobbies. The Bo Tree of India is sacred to Buddhists. Under the sheltering branches of a Bo Tree, Buddha spent many years of his life in deep meditation.

Many figs, like the Banyan, send air roots from their branches to the ground. These take root so that eventually the tree produces a grove of stems around its main trunk. Some species sprout from seeds which become lodged in the crowns of other trees, on rock ledges, or other points of elevation. Roots from these plants eventually reach the

The edible fig is a tree about 25 feet tall. The fruit is borne at the base of the flat, divided leaves.

ground, often winding around the host tree's trunk. Eventually they 'strangle' their host by monopolising the light and soil nutrients.

The flowers appear in a vase-shaped receptacle which broadens and folds inwards at the top. The fruits, also produced in this receptacle, become sweet and fleshy when ripe. A specific type of wasp is necessary to pollinate some kinds. All figs have a milky juice in their trunks, branches, twigs, and leaves. Some kinds, such as the India Rubber-tree, are a source of low-grade rubber (see RUBBER PLANTS).

Most figs are marketed as dried or canned fruit. In Mediterranean countries figs are a basic part of the diet and are even fed to livestock. They have a high sugar content when dried.

Figs are mentioned frequently in the Bible and have been cultivated throughout the Mediterranean region since ancient times. Spain leads the world in fig production, but the Smyrna figs of Turkey are the most famous.

Smyrna figs are pollinated by a unique process called caprification. The caprifig, original wild type, is host to a wasp that is essential for pollinating the flowers. For this reason caprifigs containing the immature wasps are hung in the Smyrna fig trees. The wasps develop in the caprifigs but also visit the flowers of the Smyrna fig and pollinate them.

FIR. True firs (*Albies* and *Picea* spp.) are beautiful evergreen trees with dense, usually conical crowns and stiff, erect tips. Many are important sources of timber and paper pulp; others furnish balsam and oils used in medicine and technical work; and some are popular as ornamentals and Christmas trees. Their needles, usually flat and widened at the base like suction cups, leave conspicuous round scars on the twigs. Cones of true firs stand upright on the branches and fall apart when mature. Only the slender core of the cone remains on the branch after the ripe seeds are shed.

About 35 or 40 true firs grow in various parts of Europe, Asia, North Africa, and North America. Balsam Fir, most common of the North American species, is found in south-eastern Canada and in the United

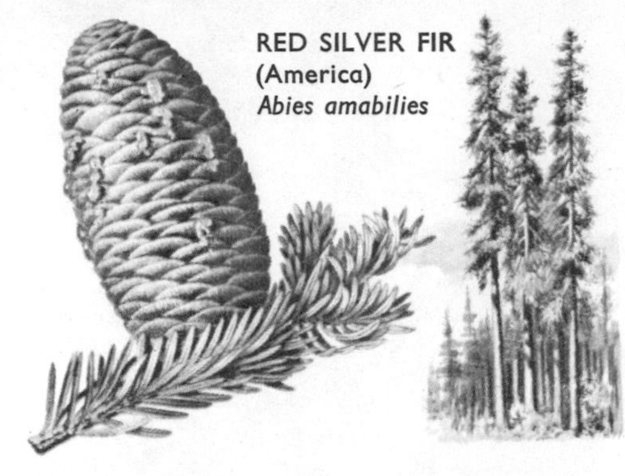

RED SILVER FIR (America) *Abies amabilies*

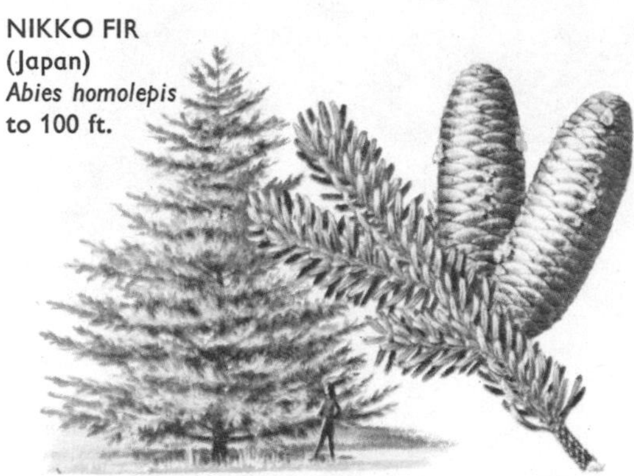

NIKKO FIR (Japan) *Abies homolepis* to 100 ft.

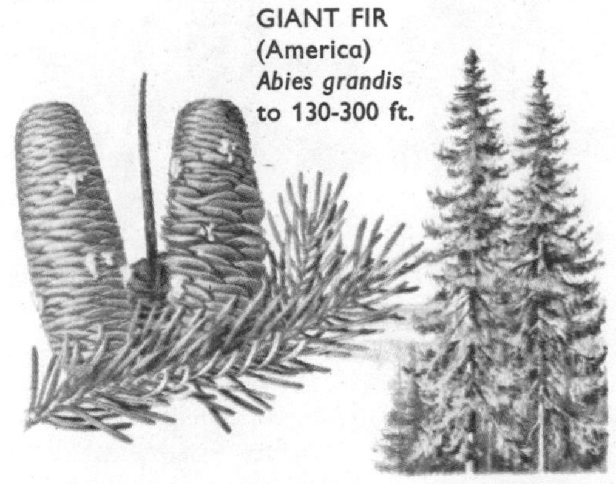

GIANT FIR (America) *Abies grandis* to 130-300 ft.

CAUCASIAN FIR (Black Sea region) *Abies Lasiocarpa* 60-100 ft.

ALPINE FIR
Abies lasiocarpa
60—100 ft.

CHINA-FIR
Cunninghamia lanceolata
to 80 ft.

NOBLE FIR
Abies nobilis
to 200 ft.

States. Principal species planted in Britain are *Picea abies*, Common Spruce and *Picea sitchensis*, Silver Spruce. Both are widely grown as timber trees and also furnish vast numbers of our familiar Christmas trees. Himalayan Silver Fir, of northern India; Momi and Nikko firs, of Japan; Siberian Fir, of the Soviet Union; and Nordmann Fir, of the Black Sea region are among the many species grown as ornamentals.

The Douglas-Fir *(Pseudotsuga douglasii)*, which grows from the Rockies to the Pacific and from Canada to Mexico, is 'king' of the forest in the Pacific north-west. It is often more than 200 feet tall and 6 feet in diameter. A tree cut in 1895 stood 417 feet tall, and many others have exceeded 300 feet in height. The Douglas-Fir's wood is used for a wide variety of purposes. This handsome tree is also a beautiful ornamental grown in the British Isles.

Douglas-Fir needles, although flat like true firs, are narrow at the base rather than widened. They leave a small, raised leaf scar on the twig. The tree's cones, also different from true firs, hang rather than stand upright and do not fall apart when mature.

The China-Fir *(Cunninghamia lanceolata)*, a timber tree of western China, belongs to the sequoia family. Occasionally planted as an ornamental in the British Isles, the China-Fir has stiff, sharp-pointed, evergreen needles which are dark-green above and have two silvery bands below. The China-Fir's round cones have sharp, prickly scales.

FISHTAIL PALMS (*Caryota* spp.) grow in the foothills of the Himalayas, in India, and south through Malaya. They are the only palmst hat have leaves divided twice (bi-pinnate leaves). Though not hardy, they are favourite indoor palms in large rooms, where space permits them to grow naturally. The pith of fishtail palms makes an edible flour, the leaves are used for cordage, and the sap can be boiled to produce sugar.

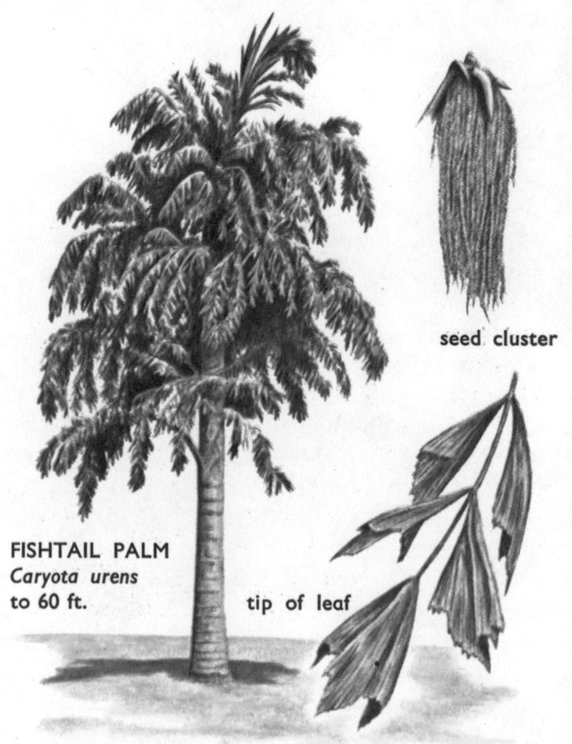

FISHTAIL PALM
Caryota urens
to 60 ft.

Linseed oil is produced by squeezing the oil from ripe flax seeds. The oil is sometimes boiled.

FLAX *(Linum usitatissimum)* is a straw-like annual that grows from 1 to 4 feet high in the three to five months before it is harvested. Linseed oil is obtained from the seeds, and linen fabrics are made from the fibres. Linen products range from such fine fabrics as cambric and damask to the coarse heavy-woven linen used in fire hoses and the strong twines used in sewing shoes.

Flax fibres are dried in the field, then cleaned and sorted for spinning. This field of flax is in Formosa.

Hamilton Wright Organization, Inc.

When flax is grown for fibre, the plants are pulled from the soil by hand or by machine. The stems are submerged in water or spread out in fields to rot from exposure to dew. This is called 'retting'. After a time, the stems are dried and run through rollers to break the woody centres so they can be separated from the bark containing the fibres. Bundles of flax fibres are then carded and combed into fine fibres that can be twisted into thread or woven on a loom into fabrics.

The use of flax is ancient. Egyptian mummies were clothed in linen cloth made of flax, and paintings on the walls of tombs show the culture and preparation of flax fibres.

Russia and the Baltic countries are now the major flax producers. Ireland is the leading manufacturer of linen products.

In addition to Common Flax, from which linen fibres come, there are many other kinds of flax plants, a few of which are planted in gardens.

FLOWERS may be composed of as many as four different sets of parts. Taking them from the outside to the centre of the flower, they are sepals which are often green; petals which are generally coloured; stamens which are the male sex organs and pistils which are the female sex organs. These separate parts of a flower may be attached at different levels on a somewhat elongated receptacle or in whorls on a flattened receptacle. There are however many variations and exceptions to this general pattern. When all the sets of parts are present the flower is considered complete; conversely, if one or more sets are absent, incomplete. If the flower lacks either stamens or pistils it is said to be imperfect. When both stamens and pistils are present, the flower is considered to be perfect whether or not petals or sepals are present. Imperfect flowers are of two kinds, those bearing stamens but not pistils (male flowers), and those bearing pistils but not stamens (female flowers). Sometimes male and female flowers are born on the same plant (cornflower);

Rutherford Platt

Wild flowers are abundant in summer meadows.

sometimes on different plants (willow). The flower is thus the part of a higher plant or angiosperm which is concerned with sexual reproduction. Flowers lead to the production of fruits and seeds; a means to propagate themselves. Flowers which have neither stamens or pistils are said to be sterile as in the marginal flowers of the cultivated hydrangea. Most plants reproduce sexually by the fusion of male and female cells. Only in the flowering plants are the female cells (ovules) in a protective organ (the ovary), which is found at the base of the pistil and which, after fertilisation, matures to become the fruit. Extending from the top of the ovary is a finger-shaped style which has a somewhat enlarged and sometimes branched tip, the stigma. The male cells are contained in the pollen, which is the familiar yellow powder to be found on ripe anthers, the pouch seen at the top of stamens. Fertilisation is achieved when pollen is transferred from the anther to the stigma; the process in which this is done is called pollination.

POLLINATION. Soon after a pollen grain lands on the stigma, the flattened and often sticky top of the pistil, it develops a tiny tube that grows downwards into the base of the pistil. Through this tube passes the male cell which fertilises the egg. The fertilised egg is the very first stage of a new plant. Finally, most parts of the flower dry up and fall off, leaving only the pistil with its fertilised ovules. These develop into seeds which in proper conditions sprout and become new plants.

Many plants are capable of fertilising themselves, but in cross-pollination the plants produced are different from both parents. These variations may enable some plants to survive in conditions which neither parent could tolerate. Cross-pollination produces the greatest variety of colours and forms.

Most pollen grains are transferred either by the wind or by insects. Flowers pollinated by the wind often produce many millions of pollen grains, for the chances of a grain of pollen reaching another flower of the same kind are indeed slim. Pollen grains carried by the wind have shapes that help keep them air-borne and they may drift many miles. Few wind-pollinated flowers are showy or fragrant, as this would have no advantage to the plant. Their stigmas are generally broad with a hairy or sticky surface. Grasses and many kinds of trees are pollinated by the wind.

Flowers that depend on insects to pollinate them often have bright petals and pleasant odours. Many kinds of insects — bees, wasps, moths, butterflies, beetles, flies, and others — may transfer the pollen from one flower to another. They do not visit the flowers for this purpose but come for the sweet nectar, which is a food for them. Bees, however, also use the pollen for food.

Flowers that depend on insects to pollinate them do not produce as much pollen, but the pollen grains are larger. Often the grains are sticky or have hooking devices that cling easily to an insect's body. Many flowers have unusual arrangements which help bring about pollination by insects. An example is salvia (see SAGES), a common flower of European and American gardens. Its flower petals are shaped in such a way that, when a heavy insect such as a bee, alights on the lower petal, it pushes against a lever that lowers the anther and dusts off pollen on its back. The bee brushes the pollen off on the stigma of the next flower as it enters, as the drooping stigma scrapes its back.

The colour of flowers may attract insects. Often the colour of flowers range into the ultra-violet end of the spectrum. These short rays are visible to insects but not to the human

Buttercup
Bulbous Crowfoot
Ranunculus bulbosus

Cornflower
Centaurea cyanus

eye. Thus a flower that appears white to a human may be blue or violet to a bee or other insect visitor.

Some night-blooming flowers depend on insects for pollination. Colour is of no value in the dark, so it is not surprising that night-blooming flowers are yellow or white. Instead, their fragrance guides moths or other night-flying insects to them.

Some flowers are constructed to discourage visits by insects that would steal nectar without transferring pollen. Ants, for example, are not good pollinators, nor are most beetles. They have smooth bodies to which the pollen does not cling. Stems of many flowers are covered with a dense growth of hairs or bristles so that it is hard for these crawling insects to get to the flowers.

Man, the horticulturist, is a pollinator, too. He creates new flowers by transferring the pollen from one flower to another, forming hybrid or cross-bred flowers of new colours, sizes and shapes. The hybrid flower may be far more beautiful than the original. Most cultivated flowers are a result of hybridising.

FORMS OF FLOWERS. Flowers may be symmetrical like a rose, asymmetrical like a pansy; they may have their petals free like a buttercup or joined together like a snapdragon. The arrangement of a large number of small flowers to form what is commonly considered to be a single flower is characteristic of the daisy family. The head has one type of flower, ray florets (male flowers) on the outside and disc florets (female flowers) on the inside. Variation in the general appearance of a flower is also due to the arrangements of the flowers on a common stalk — variation in the type of inflorescence. Flowers can be arranged on a spike or raceme as in the delphinium; to form a flat platform or umbel as in the Sweet William, or to form a head as in the cornflower. The form of the flower, the number and nature of its various parts and the type of inflorescence are important factors when identifying a plant and deciding to which family it belongs.

FLOWERS AS FOOD. When we eat a cauliflower and a pineapple we are eating an

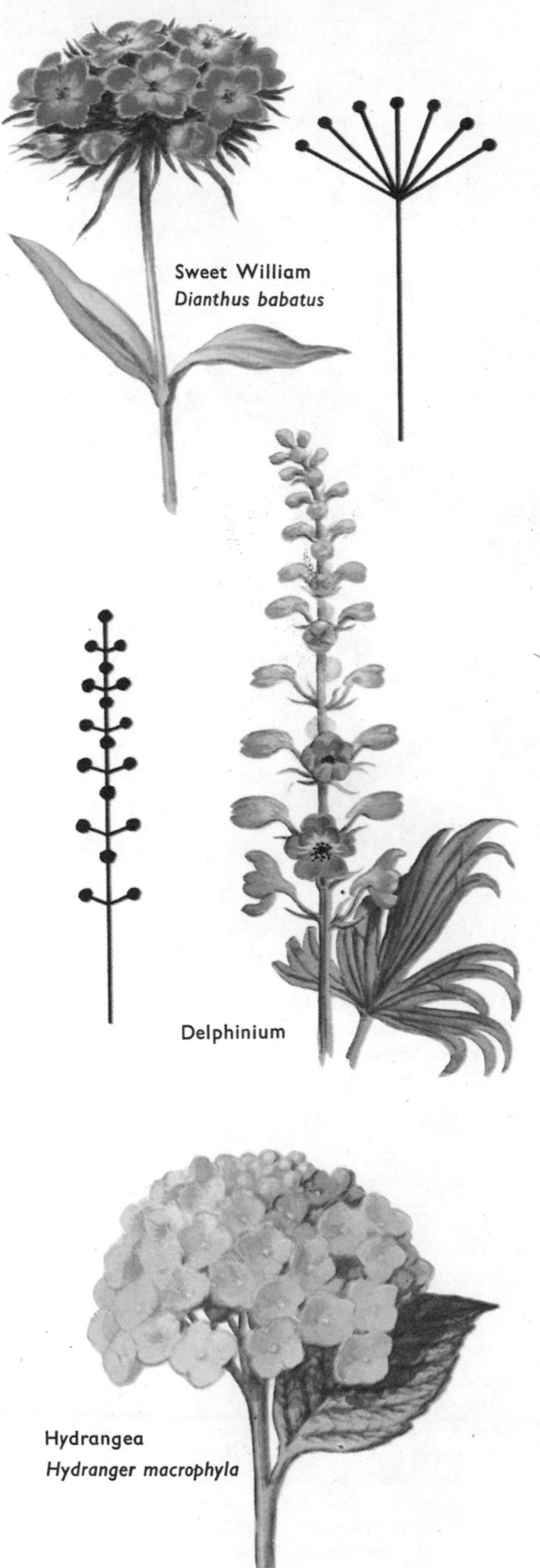

Sweet William
Dianthus babatus

Delphinium

Hydrangea
Hydranger macrophyla

ORIGIN OF SOME COMMON GARDEN FLOWERS

(1) Rhododendron, (2) Louisiana Iris, (3) Snapdragon, (4) Pansy, (5) Wallflower, (6) Crocus, (7) Anemone, (8) Tulip, (9) Chinese Aster, (10) Japanese Iris, (11) Zinnia, (12) California Poppy, (13) Carnation, (14) Regal Lily, (15) Dahlia, (16) Marigold, (17) Cosmos, (18) Sweetpea, (19) Candytufts, (20) Oriental Poppy, (21) Hollyhock, (22) Poinsettia, (23) Morning Glory, (24) Canna, (25) Bird-of-Paradise Flower, (26) Lobelia, (27) Strawflower, (28) Nasturtium, (29) Petunia, (30) Fuchsia, (31) Gladiola, (32) Geranium, (33) Calla Lily, (34) Hibiscus, (35) Chrysanthemum.

inflorescence. Apples, oranges, grapes are obvious fruits; peas, beans, tomatoes, marrows are not. Cereal grains, wheat, barley, oats, corn are seeds.

We also crystallise flowers — the violet and a number of fruits for use in decorating food.

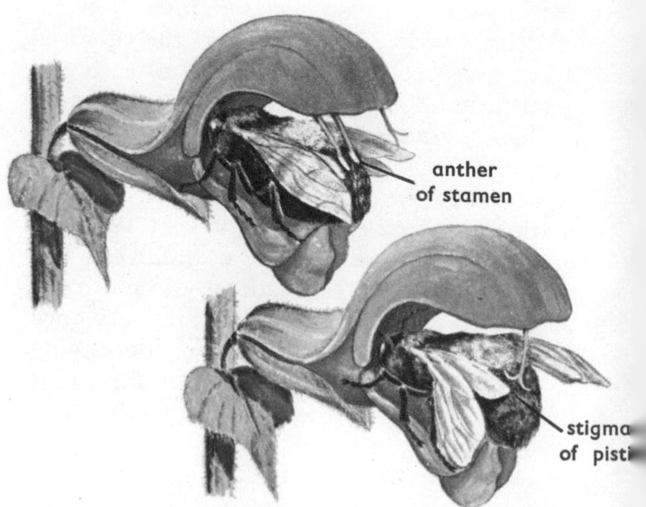

When a bee enters a young salvia flower (left), it pushes against the base of the stamens and causes them to pivot forward, the anthers depositing pollen on the hairs of the bee's back. Later the bee visits an older flower (right) in which the stigma has developed and bent downwards. Pollen picked up earlier from younger flowers is deposited on the stigma of the pistil, thus accomplishing cross-pollination.

WIND POLLINATION OF FLOWERS

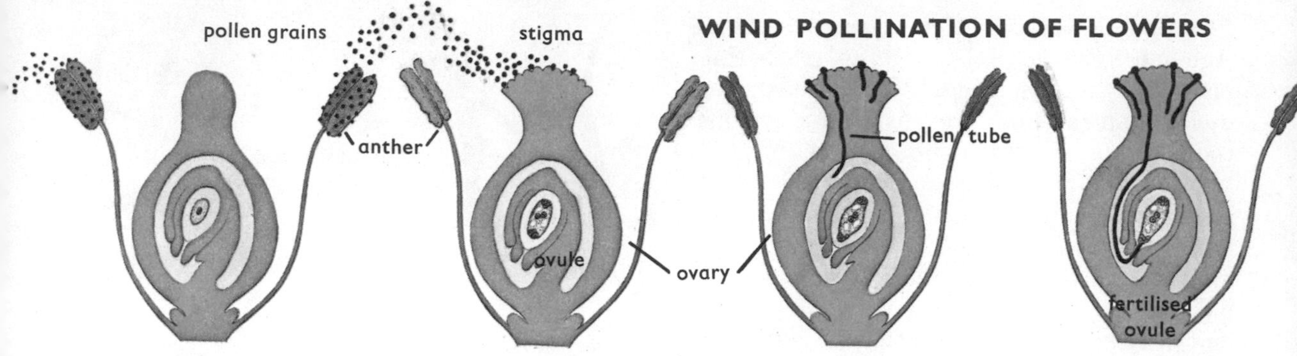

Cross-pollination by the wind is a common way in which flowers are fertilised. Pollen is shed from the anthers when they are ripe (1). At this stage, in most flowers, the pistil has not yet matured. The pollen is blown by the wind and lands on the roughened or sticky stigma (2) of another flower in which the anthers have withered and the pistil has matured. In this flower, the ovary is ripe, and the ovules are ready to be fertilised. The pollen grains germinate, the tubules growing down through the style towards the ovules (3). Male cells unite with the ovules, which will ripen as seeds. The fruit consists of the seeds surrounded by the fleshy parts of the ovary.

FLOWERS FOR PERFUMES. Chemically produced perfumes are now being introduced but most perfumes still come from flowers and fruits such as roses, lavender and citrus fruits. The latter are the most vital, providing a variety of commercially important essential oils widely used in perfumery.

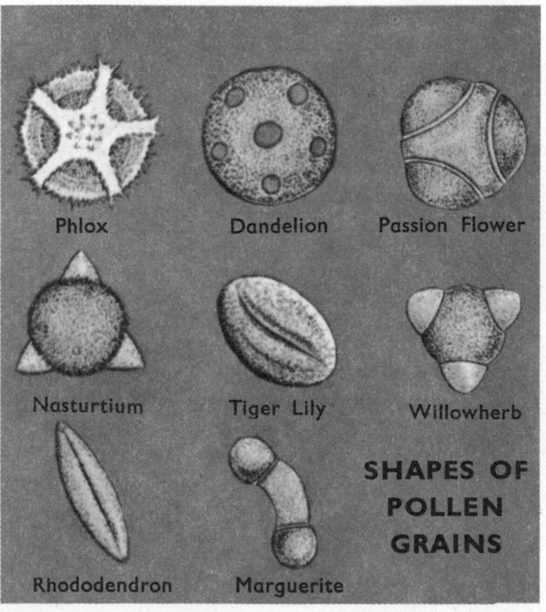

SHAPES OF POLLEN GRAINS

FLUORITE, a calcium fluoride mineral, sometimes called fluorspar, occurs in cubic crystals, or cubes with bevelled corners. Though its usual colour is purple or green, it may be colourless or any colour. It has a colourless streak and a vitreous lustre. Fluorite usually is found as a hydrothermal replacement mineral and occurs in both igneous and sedimentary rocks. Because it makes slag more fluid and helps to remove phosphorus and sulphur, fluorite is added to iron ore in open-hearth smelting to make steel and also in the smelting of other ores. Hydrofluoric acid — made from fluorite — is used to dissolve silica or to etch glass. Freon gas, also made from fluorite, is a refrigerant in electric refrigerators. Some telescope and spectroscope lenses are made of clear, flawless fluorite because of its low index of refraction and dispersion. In Derbyshire, where it is associated with lead, the mineral is known as Blue John and has been mined for centuries. It is made into ornaments. The mineral is associated with tin in Cornwall, and with limestones in the north of England.

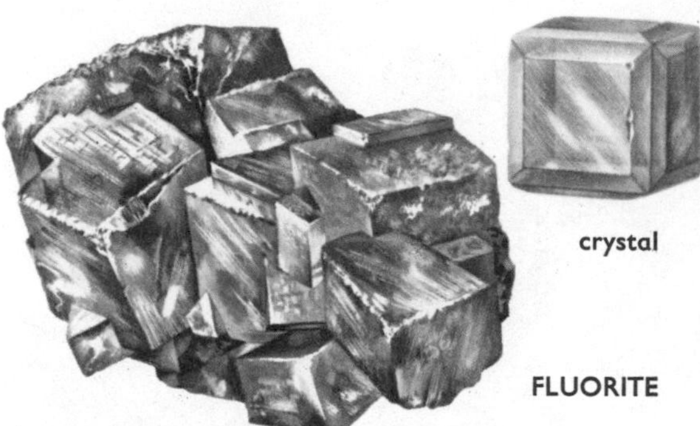

FLUORITE

FOODS OF MAN. Men of the Old Stone Age got their food by digging, gathering, trapping, and hunting. Meals must have included meat from various animals, fruits, roots, grubs, shellfish, and carrion.

Hunting and food gathering peoples must know much about their environment. To find wild roots and edible seeds and to trap food animals for takes knowledge of their habits, the seasons, the favourable places, and ways of preparing and preserving what is found. Devices must be made for digging the roots and for catching the game. To bring down his game, primitive Man devised clubs, spears, arrows, darts, traps of all kinds, nets, hooks, axes, knives, and poisons. To approach his game he learned how to stalk and also how to use boats and to ride horses. The tracking and stalking of game were developed into a real science. Eskimos dress in sealskin clothing and approach the seal by imitating its movements. Hunting certain animals calls for group action. In hunting the American bison or buffalo, the Indians not only organised for the hunt but had a police force to see that everyone did his job as expected. Africans, too, conduct skilful and courageous group hunts in trapping such fierce animals as the elephant. Usually, hunting tribes divide up into small bands, each roaming its part of the tri bal territory. When the game in one place runs out, they move on for better hunting.

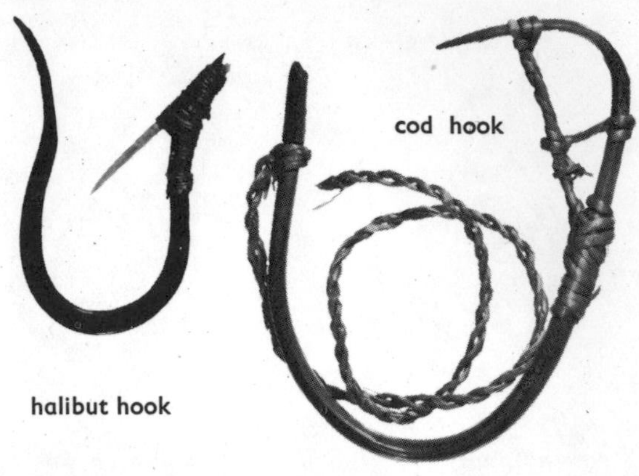

American Indians made fishhooks of wood, bone, and horn.

FISHING. Angling, or catching fish by hook and line, is an ancient art. Fish-hooks made of bone have been found with the remains of Old Stone Age Man. A later improvement

These American Indians are netting, trapping, and smoking salmon during a spawning run at a falls in the Pacific north-west.

Safari Productions-Photo Researchers

Fishermen are using a trap or weir made of rushes to catch fish from this lake in Uganda in equatorial Africa.

in the fish-hook was the barb. This prevents the fish from slipping off the hook after it has been hooked. The 'gorge' was probably used even before the hook. This is a sharp instrument of stone or metal fixed inside the bait at the end of a line. It lodged crosswise in the fish's gullet when the bait was swallowed and the line was pulled taut.

Nets have been made in many shapes and sizes, each designed for a specific kind of fishing. Modern nets do not differ greatly from nets made and used by primitive Man. Fish may also be captured by shooting them with a spear or arrow, by trapping them and even by doping and by tickling them. A Chinese system of fishing is to train cormorants to bring in the live fish. South American Indians used crushed derris roots (rotenone) to poison fish without making them inedible.

Frequently, several methods of fishing are used at the same time. Thus the Indians of the Pacific north-west built dams across streams to slow down the salmon as they

The American Pomo Indians of coastal California were experts at making nets, and used to catch birds as well as fish.

swam upstream to spawn. When the salmon got stalled below the dam, the Indians could spear or net them easily.

TRAPS. Since the early Old Stone Age Man has used traps to catch animals less clever than himself. All recent primitive peoples and many civilised ones use traps for getting food, skins, and other useful products and also to do away with undesirable animals.

The simplest trap is a pit dug along an animal trail and hidden by branches. Sometimes sharp posts are set in the bottom to pierce the animal when it drops in. 'Deadfalls' are traps in which the animal pulls the enclosure down over him when he tugs at a bait.

'Snares' catch animals as they move forward. The animal pushes his head into a noose which tightens and holds him. A 'spring trap' is a noose tied to a bent tree or a branch. The branch is weighted down, but when the animal is inside the noose, the weight is released so that the bent tree straightens up suddenly and the animal swings into space.

Many peoples trap fish. One method involves the use of a large basket. A funnel, with its large opening towards the outside, is fitted into one end of the basket. Fish find their way into the basket through the big end but rarely find the opening to escape.

Before Man developed the skill that made him a formidable hunter, he had to rely on food that could not run from him. Insects, molluscs and the products of the plant kingdom were of greater importance to him than the animals that he could not catch.

Fruits, berries, roots, and succulent stems must have been available everywhere. The first human groups probably resembled those of the present-day Australian aborigines. They were wandering family units that subsisted on whatever food chanced their way, and they returned each season to former camps near to some ripening wild crop or easily harvested grain.

The art of cooking increased the scope of Man's diet. Heat renders many plant products soft and palatable that are useless when raw, and increases their digestibility.

Recognition of the connection between the seed and the plant led early Man to propagate desirable species. In his wanderings, the more edible plants became spread over wide areas in this fashion. Agriculture, the careful planting and tending of crops, was a much later development in the history of the human race. (See AGRICULTURE.)

One of the by-products of efficient transportation on land and on the oceans was the spread of useful plants. Emigrants carried familiar species to their new homes, and explorers scoured new lands for potentially valuable plants. People of today may choose from a world-wide garden.

FORESTS are communities of trees and shrubs, but they are also communities of flowers, fungi, insects, reptiles, birds, mammals, soil, moisture, and air. Trees are, however, the dominant type of life in forests.

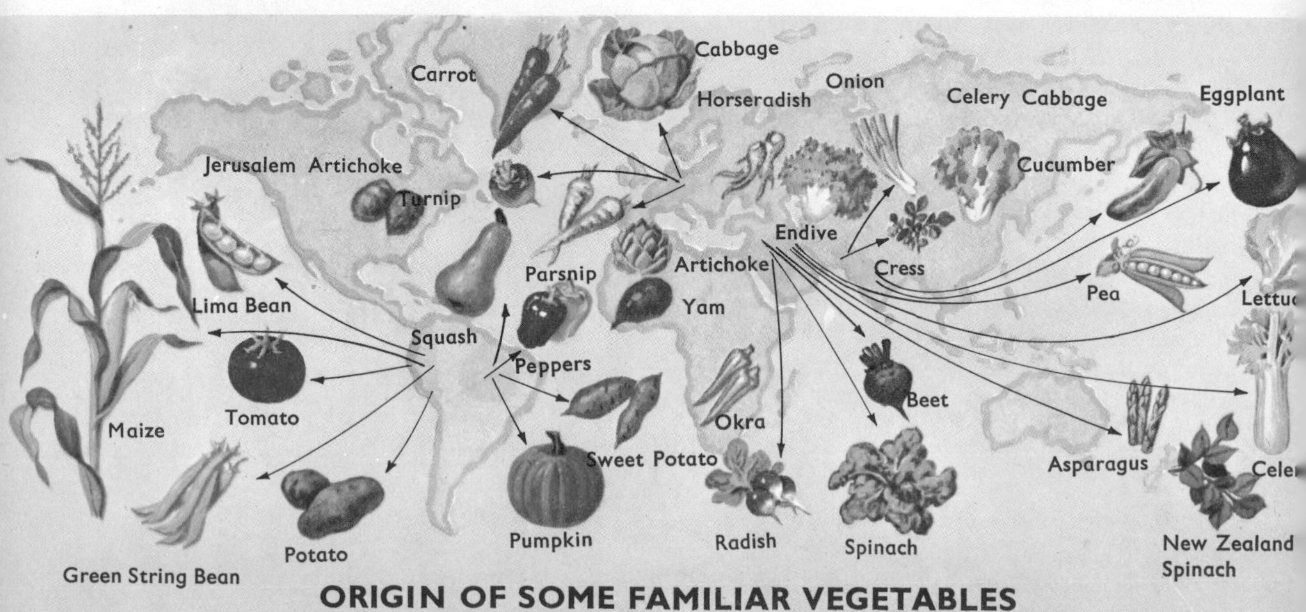

ORIGIN OF SOME FAMILIAR VEGETABLES

Phot. Jacque Bauguet

The Sun's rays scarcely penetrate the luxuriant vegetation of the equatorial forest which is broken only by a few clearings. In this dark, humid kingdom there is an intense, teeming life.

Forests of the world are divided into three broad classes: boreal conifers, temperate hardwoods, and tropical hardwoods. Boreal conifers (cone-bearing trees) are located in cool temperate climates. They form a belt encircling the Earth just below the treeless arctic tundra. In the northern part are chiefly spruces and firs. The southern part contains also pines, larches, and hemlocks.

Temperate hardwood forests are made up of deciduous trees — including ash, beech, birch, elm, maple, and oak. Hardwoods also grow in tropical lowlands and include such valuable and beautiful trees as ebony, mahogany, and rosewood.

Forests provide timber for construction and wood pulp for paper. They regulate and conserve water necessary for other plants, for animals, and for irrigation, power, and drinking water supplies. They reinforce the soil and decrease the force of rainfall and run-off, thus helping to prevent erosion. Forests also affect temperature, preventing it from dropping too low at night or rising too high during the day as in grasslands. They also serve as wind-breaks. Forests convert tremendous amounts of sun energy into food, thus serving as the first link in the food chain of plant-animal communities. Few animals live in deep forests, however. The greatest variety and abundance of animal life is at the forest edge. (See TREES.)

FORGET–ME–NOTS (*Myosotis* spp.) have been admired for centuries. They are mentioned often in legends and in poetry and are regarded as symbols of friendship and trust. There are about 50 species adapted to a wide range of habitats in temperate climates.

Several species occur in Britain and cultivated varieties often escape from gardens. Some species grow in swampy areas, even partly submerged in water. Others are common on dry, bare or disturbed soil.

Their usual colour is pale blue with a white or a white-and-yellow centre, but some are white, pink, or even yellow. Low-growing cultivated varieties are used to decorate borders in gardens or along paths and pavements.

FORGET-ME-NOT
Myosotis scorpioides

FORSYTHIA
Forsythia intermedia spectabilis

FORSYTHIA (*Forsythia* spp.) is native to south-east Asia and the several species are widely cultivated as ornamental shrubs. They produce their flowers before the appearance of the leaves in early spring. The golden-yellow flowers have four strap-shaped petals united at the base into a short tube. Some grow tall (8 to 10 feet) and erect, others have droopy, willowy branches. Often these popular shrubs are planted to form a flowering hedge. Forsythia is a member of the olive family which includes such other shrubs as lilac, jasmine, and privet.

FOSSILS are the remains of prehistoric animals and plants or some direct evidence of their existence. They may be bones or shells of animals, imprints of leaves and stems of plants, or just trails or borings made by worms in wet mud or sand that was later changed into rock.

In rare cases whole animals have been preserved. In 1846, a young Russian surveyor was exploring the Indigirka River in Siberia. As his party reached a place where a stream, swollen by recent heavy rains, had undercut the river bank, he noticed a huge, dark object floating in the water. It was a Woolly Mammoth. Its heavy tusks still preserved, its eyes still open, its shaggy coat still soft, its trunk swaying in the water. This creature had lived 10,000 years ago, when most of northern Europe was covered by glaciers.

A party of 50 men and their horses managed to drag the great beast on to the bank. They found that even the contents of the animal's stomach had been refrigerated in the frozen ground of the arctic country.

Since the first discovery numbers of other animals have been found similarly preserved by deep freezing in Siberia and Alaska. In Galicia, Poland, a complete Woolly Rhinoceros was discovered, the soft parts of its body preserved in the oil-soaked ground.

Spectacular as these examples are, they are very rare. The soft parts of most fossils either are not preserved at all or are preserved only as films or impressions. In dry caves in Nevada and Patagonia, remains of Ground Sloths have been found with dried skin, hair and tendons preserved. In parts of western Canada, the delicate patterns of dinosaur skin have been preserved as impressions in sandstone, formed from sand that covered the dried-out carcasses.

Amber, the fossil resin of trees, sometimes contains perfectly preserved insects and leaves. Most of these come from the Baltic region of Europe.

The soft tissues of most fossils are preserved only as dark films of carbon or, more often, as black outlines on the rock. Leaves of trees which made up the mighty coal-forming forests are preserved in this way, as are some small marine animals.

But all these examples are rarities. Usually fossils represent only the hard parts of ancient animals and plants, whose soft parts decayed soon after their death. In a few cases these hard parts are not much altered. In the famous Rancho La Brea tar pits in Los Angeles, California, bones of many ice-age animals were preserved by burial in asphalt, which sealed and protected them. It is not difficult to imagine how the cries of a Mammoth caught in the tar would bring Sabre-Toothed Cats or carrion-loving condors

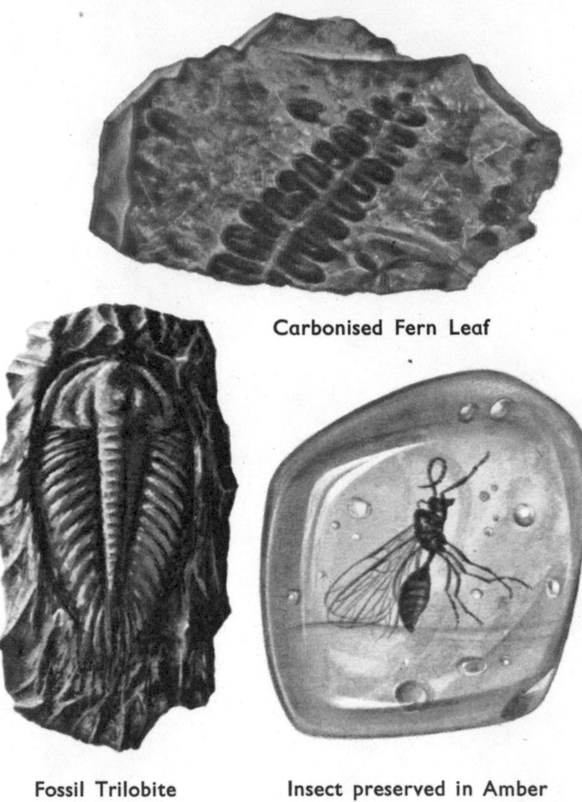

Carbonised Fern Leaf

Fossil Trilobite (cast)

Insect preserved in Amber

A frozen Woolly Mammoth, found in Siberia in 1900.

The remains of many Ice Age animals have been found in the La Brea Tar Pits in Los Angeles, California.

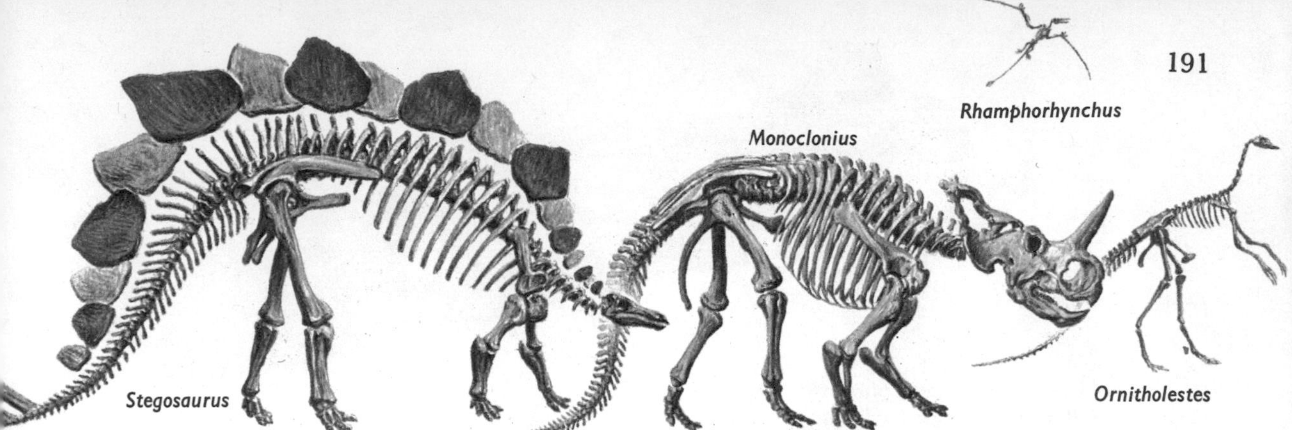

quickly to the scene. And then they, too, would become engulfed in the clinging asphalt. Even mice, small birds, and plants were trapped in the treacherous, seeping tar.

Not all fossils with unaltered hard parts were preserved under such dramatic conditions. Bivalves and gastropods left their shells as records.

More commonly the pore spaces in wood, bone, and shell are filled up by substances, usually silica deposited from water filtering through the sand and mud in which they were buried. Sometimes all the original material is dissolved and is completely replaced by these new materials. Usually this destroys whatever fine structure the original may have had, but occasionally even the most minute cellular structures are preserved. This is how the beautiful specimens of petrified wood were formed in Arizona, where forests of conifers were buried in sands and muds rich in silica waters from ancient volcanoes. In time percolating waters dissolved the original wood but replaced its every detail by a tracery of silica which can be seen in polished pieces of these fossil logs. Although not as spectacular as the Arizona trees the various submerged forests around the British coasts are of considerable interest and prove the relatively recent submergence of the land. They appear, usually at low tide, as stumps and roots. The south coast has a number of examples: Dover, Hastings, Bexhill; while others are found further west, and in Wales, northern England and Scotland.

In other cases, the hard parts of plants or animals have been replaced by iron pyrite or calcium carbonate.

Other fossils may be moulds or casts of shells and other hard parts, which have themselves been dissolved. Often the inside of a hollow snail shell will become filled with mud, which is preserved as a hard spiral internal cast, long after the shell itself has disappeared.

Other kinds of indirect evidence of prehistoric life are footprints and trails. Wastes (coprolites) of some animals and stomach stones (gastroliths) of others are occasionally found.

USING FOSSILS. Fossils help solve one of the most important and common problems in geology: comparing ages of rocks in one area with those in another. Called 'correlation', this is an everyday problem in petroleum and mineral exploration, mining development, surveys for dams, and construction work. Rocks of the same age can be identified by their fossils, for those deposited at the same time and under the same environmental conditions generally contain similar fossils.

Both coal and oil are formed of the remains of once-living plants and are often spoken of as fossil fuels. Carnotite, one of the most important uranium ores, is found with fossil logs in Colorado and Utah. Diatomite and some iron ores are also formed of fossil remains. In some regions fossil shells are so common they are used for lime burning or for road construction.

By studying the distribution of fossils it is also possible to reconstruct the outlines of ancient lands and seas. Sometimes ancient climatic conditions and directions of ocean currents can also be determined. The study of fossil spores and pollen grains has revealed much about climatic conditions in Ice Age times and about the kinds of plants that grew then.

Fossils are the only source of information about the long history of life on Earth. Those

PETRIFIED WOOD

Cells of the wood of auracaria pines that grew more than 150 million years ago have been replaced by silica, preserving details in agate.

many millions of years are no less a part of history and of no less importance than the record of the past few thousand years when our history was written.

ROCKS THAT CONTAIN FOSSILS. Virtually all fossils are found in sedimentary rocks, such as limestone and sandstone. These rocks are formed from sand, mud, and other sediments eroded from the land, or they are deposited from solutions. They are usually found in layers or strata. Sediments that make these rocks may accumulate in many different areas — in deserts, swamps, at the

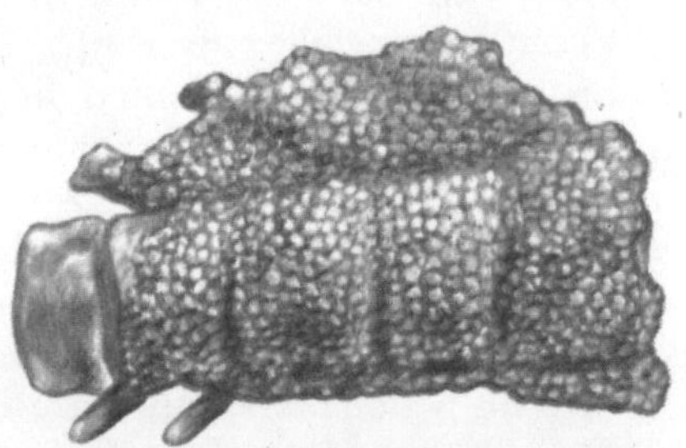

Impression of dinosaur skin in sandstone.

noses of glaciers, in lakes, in valleys along rivers, at the foot of mountains. Many are carried by wind, ice, gravity, or running water and are finally deposited in deltas, lagoons, tidal zones, or on ocean bottoms.

Sandstones are formed by the wearing away of older rocks by ice, flowing water, or wind. The fine particles — mostly of quartz or silica — are cemented together when they are deposited, which is generally in shallow seas. Shales are formed of hardened clay and mud. Limestones consist mostly of calcium carbonate which comes mainly from marine plants or animals. Often limestone rocks are made almost completely of fossil shells. Any bones, shells or other hard parts of plants or animals in the sediments are transformed with them into sedimentary rocks. The chances of some animals or plants becoming fossils are much greater than others. A bird, for example, is much less likely to be a fossil than is a shellfish living in the shallow sea where sediments are deposited rapidly.

Many sedimentary rocks remain deeply buried. Others are lifted up by movements of the Earth and are eroded and exposed on the land. Much of the Earth's surface is covered with sedimentary rocks, and from the fossils they contain, palaeontologists (scientists who study fossils) are able to piece together the story of life of the past.

Because of their origin, the other two groups of rocks — igneous and metamorphic — only very rarely contain fossils. Igneous rocks are formed by the cooling and hardening of molten material (magma), from deep below the surface. Metamorphic rocks, such as slate and schist, are formed by alteration of older igneous or sedimentary rocks. Often this involves intense heat or pressure.

FINDING FOSSILS. Fossils can be found in nearly all sedimentary rocks. Some fossils remain buried below the surface; others are exposed as the rock surrounding them is worn away. Good places to look for fossils are in cliffs along coasts and streams, on rocky hillsides, in quarries, along ditches, railway and road cuttings or wherever there has been an excavation or erosion of the soil to expose the rocks.

Marine invertebrates are by far the most common fossils and so are easiest to collect. These animals lived in conditions that aided fossilisation. Some limestone rocks consist almost entirely of fossils. Land-dwelling

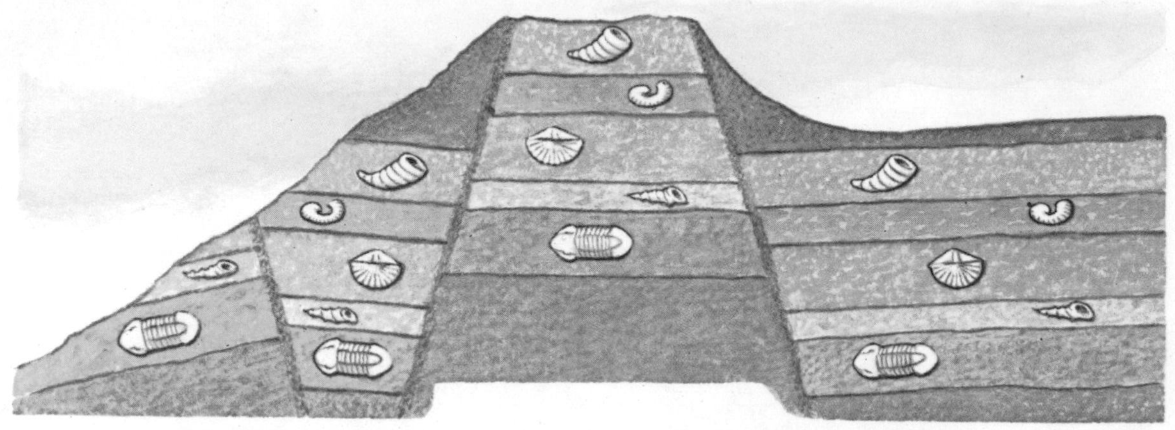

Strata containing identical fossils are of the same age even though they may occur far apart or at different depths due to Earth movements.

animals, such as birds and mammals, and also plants that grew on the land are less common. Fossils of such large animals as dinosaurs are rare and are collected successfully only by expert palaeontologists.

Amateur fossil collecting does not require elaborate and expensive equipment. A hammer, a chisel, paper for wrapping and labelling, and a knapsack for carrying specimens are all that a collector needs.

In most cases it is best not to separate the fossil from the rocks in the field. This can be done at home where the rock can be broken carefully, and the fossils examined with a lens. All fossils should be labelled. Each label should identify the fossil, give details of the locality at which it was found and if possible, information on the geological horizon.

The kind of fossils found in any rock depends partly on its geologic age, and partly on the environment in which it was formed.

A scientist examines fossil-bearing sediment cores taken from the bottom of the sea.

Lamont Geophysical Laboratories

Oil is formed by fossil plants and animals. Fossils in drill samples are the clue to oil deposits.

Sinclair Oil Corporation

SEDIMENTARY ROCKS CONTAINING FOSSILS

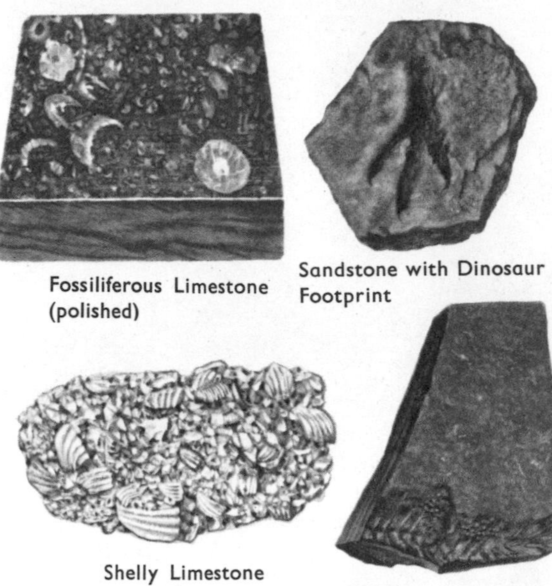

Fossiliferous Limestone (polished)

Sandstone with Dinosaur Footprint

Shelly Limestone

Oil Shale with Fossil Fish

Maps prepared by geological surveys are available for most regions. They show each kind of rock outcropping and the age of the rock. By studying these maps and using an identification manual a collector can soon learn to know the kinds of fossils that might be found in an area.

Ordovician seas covered much of the United Kingdom and Eire 480 million years ago, depositing sand, mud, and lime. These sediments contain such marine fossils as graptolites, corals, trilobites, and brachiopods or lamp shells. Ordovician rocks are exposed in many regions and, in the British Isles are common in Wales, Scotland and northern England. A fossil hunter in a region of Ordovician rock outcroppings would never find a dinosaur. Fossil fish have been found in Ordovician rocks in Colorado, but are rare. Fossil hunting for invertebrates in Ordovician rocks would be highly rewarding and graptolites are abundant in some shales and slates.

In England there are fairly large areas of

Portion shown in photograph
limestone
sandstone
Permian
shale
sandstone and shale
Miss.
limestone
Devonian
quartzite
shale
sandstone
Cambrian
Colorado River
shale
black schist
granite
Pre-Cambrian
Josef Muench

Layer upon layer the geology of the past is revealed in the Grand Canyon, where the Colorado River has cut down through many thicknesses of sedimentary rocks to the underlying granite.

Mesozoic and Cenozoic sediments. Some are of continental origin in which fossils are not common. In the Jurassic deposits of Lyme Regis, Dorset, the remains of many ichthyosaurs have been found. It was here, as a girl, that Mary Anning (1799—1847) discovered the first reasonably complete ichthyosaur skeleton. In 1824 she also found the first almost complete skeleton of *Plesiosaurus*. Very few dinosaur fossils are found, of course, and the collecting equipment needed for one of these giants far exceeds the hammer, chisel, and knapsack that are adequate for the amateur. The skull of a dinosaur, for example, may weigh half a ton. Scientists sometimes spend many months carefully removing the bones of a dinosaur. Their study of the position of the bones may give a clue as to how the animal died. Also, scientists want to find all the bones they can so that they can have as complete a skeleton as possible. Sometimes many tons of rock must be moved to uncover a complete skeleton.

Bones exposed after burial for millions of years are sometimes fragile and will crumble quickly if not handled gently. They are commonly coated with shellac and encased in plaster before they are transported to a museum. At the museum the bones are reinforced, then put together to reconstruct the skeleton. If bones are missing, the scientists may be able to match them with bones in a similar skeleton or determine their probable size and shape by studying the anatomy and structure of related animals.

When the skeleton is finally put together in a life-like pose, scientists can use it for study purposes, and people who visit the museum can see what the prehistoric animal looked like. Sometimes the animal is fully restored from the skeletal remains, giving it the form and appearance the experts believe the animal had. Some of this must be done by guessing, but most restorations are based on knowledge of conditions and anatomy. Bits

Plaster bandages protect large fossil bones made ready for shipment to universities and museums.

Fossils may become brittle when exposed at the surface and must be removed with great care.

of skin impressions in sand have been discovered and also nests of dinosaur eggs. All this information is used by the scientists in deducing what these animals looked like and how they moved and acted in life. The habitat scenes of dinosaurs and other animals and plant life in these books are artist's concepts, based on facts which fossils themselves have disclosed about life of the past.

In contrast to such giant fossils as dinosaurs are microfossils. These are the microscopic remains of whole plants and animals or of their parts, such as the scales of fishes. Microfossils are rarely collected by amateurs, but they are of great interest and importance to scientists. Hundreds of perfect specimens may be found in one small sample. Microfossils are especially useful in correlating rock strata.

FOSSILS AND TIME. Calendars of geologic time allow us to date such events as the rise of a mountain range or the occurrence of certain fossil groups. This system gives

At the museum a skull is removed carefully from the protecting plaster and the remaining rock clinging to it (left). Large bones are supported with steel rods or frames, such as the frame being attached to the fossil dinosaur skull below.

PITCHBLENDE
(uranium ore)

only relative age. Geologists speak of a fossil as late Cambrian, meaning that it was found in rocks about 520 million years old. Or an early Cretaceous dinosaur is one that lived about 125 million years ago.

Most early attempts to measure ages of rocks or the age of the Earth were largely guesswork. As early as 450 B.C., however, Herodotus suggested that the rate at which sediment was deposited indicated that thousands of years had been necessary to build the broad delta at the mouth of the Nile.

Various estimates of the age of the Earth were made during the nineteenth century. These were based on the total thickness of sedimentary rocks and the salt content of the oceans. A maximum age of about 100 million years was arrived at by these methods, but the many corrections in these calculations all tended to increase the Earth's age greatly. It was the discovery of radioactivity in 1896 that provided a basis for a reliable geological clock.

Uranium and other radioactive minerals, although they occur in small amounts, are widely distributed in igneous rocks. All have unstable atomic nuclei and continuously break down into other, more stable elements. Uranium, for example, slowly breaks down into lead and helium. This process is totally independent of all known physical and chemical changes in the environment. Although the rate of breakdown or disintegration is very slow, it can be measured accurately. Measurements show that 1 gram of one type of uranium disintegrates into 1/7,600 grams of lead every million years. Therefore, the age of a rock can be determined by the ratio of lead to uranium still in it. Other radioactive decay processes, for example rubidium-strontium, potassium-argon, and carbon isotopes, are also used in this manner to measure geologic time. Carbon-14 disintegrates more rapidly. Half of any given quantity will disintegrate in 5,568 years. For this reason it is most useful in dating younger

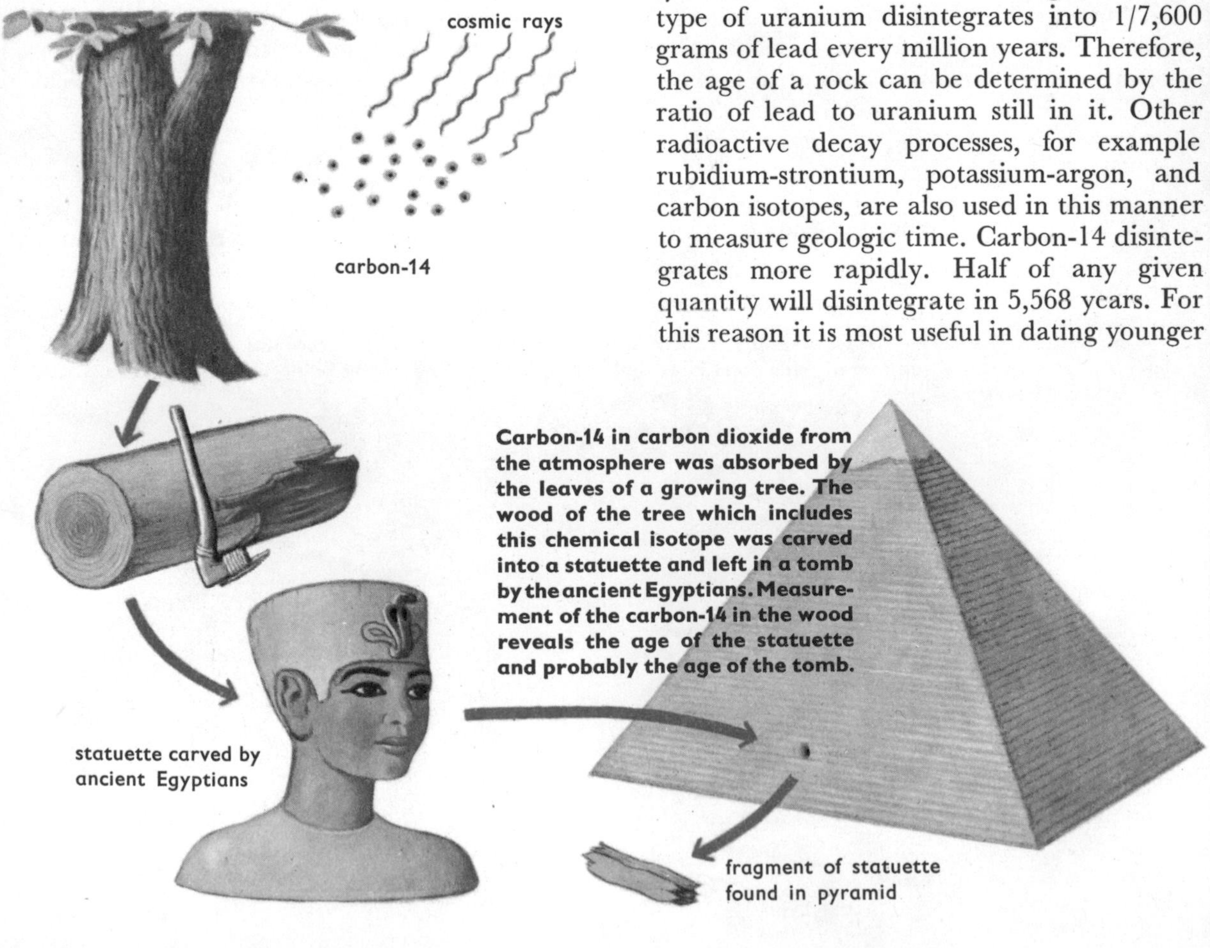

cosmic rays

carbon-14

Carbon-14 in carbon dioxide from the atmosphere was absorbed by the leaves of a growing tree. The wood of the tree which includes this chemical isotope was carved into a statuette and left in a tomb by the ancient Egyptians. Measurement of the carbon-14 in the wood reveals the age of the statuette and probably the age of the tomb.

statuette carved by
ancient Egyptians

fragment of statuette
found in pyramid

CLOCK OF THE EARTH'S PAST

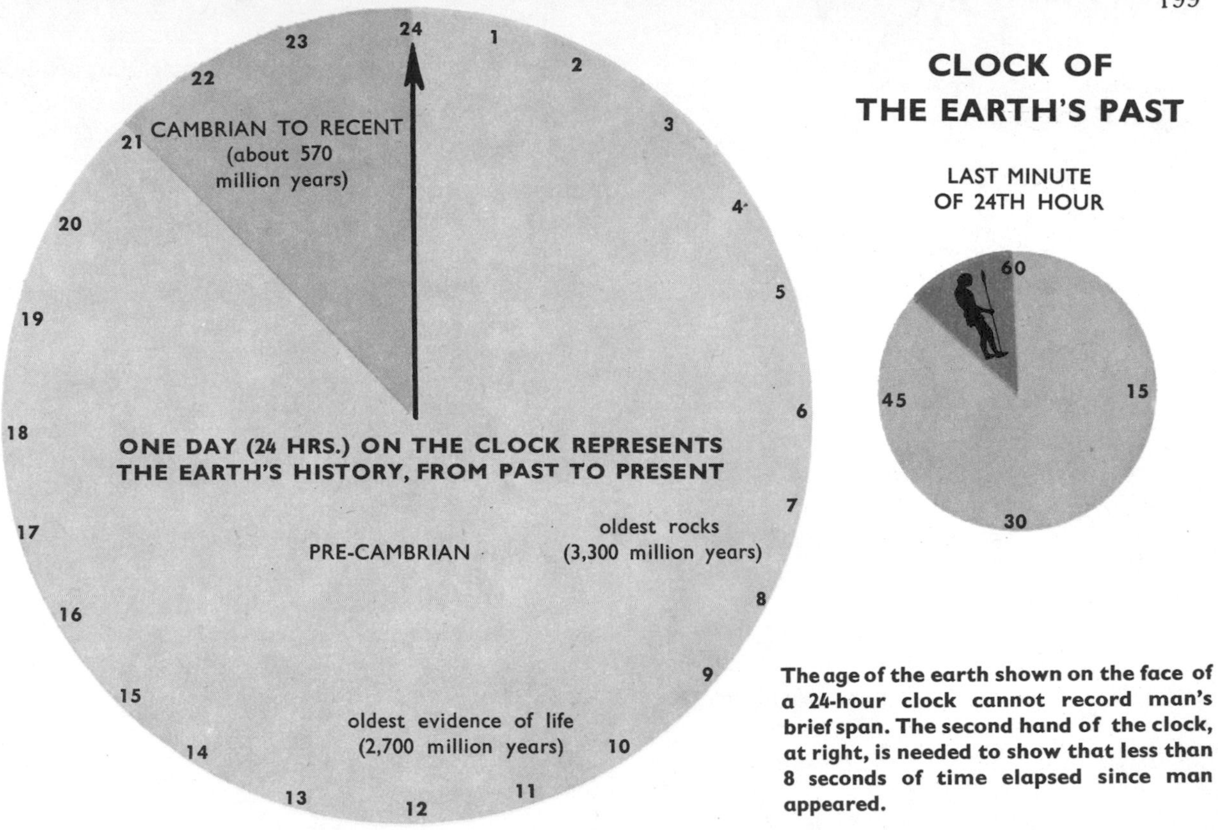

The age of the earth shown on the face of a 24-hour clock cannot record man's brief span. The second hand of the clock, at right, is needed to show that less than 8 seconds of time elapsed since man appeared.

objects, such as prehistoric pieces of wood, charcoal, or cloth. By these methods it is possible to construct an accurate geological time scale.

We now know that the oldest widespread common fossils — those of lower Cambrian age — are about 570 million years old. The oldest fossils (probably algae found in Rhodesia) appear to be more than 2,700 million years old. The oldest rocks so far discovered come from Rhodesia, Wyoming, and Manitoba and are about 3,000 million years old. These rocks do not represent the total age of the Earth, however. The Earth's age is more difficult to determine but is believed to be 4,500 to 5,000 million years. This age has been determined by measuring the rate of expansion of the universe and present distances from the Earth of various outlying galaxies and by studies of rocks, meteorites or shooting stars.

Such vast periods of time are difficult to understand. Suppose an imaginary tree planted at the time of the Earth's origin has since grown continuously at the microscopic rate of 1/10,000 of an inch every year. At that slow rate the tree would now be about eight miles high. A tree planted at the dawn of Cambrian time would be about a mile high. A tree planted when man first appeared would be 2 feet tall, and one planted at the time of Christ would be 1/5 of an inch tall.

Or suppose we show the history of the Earth on the face of a 24-hour clock. If 5,000 million years is used as the probable age of the Earth, each minute represents 3,470,000 years. Pre-Cambrian time would take up 21 hours of the 24. The oldest known rocks were formed between 7 and 8 o'clock, though it is assumed that older ones lie below them. Primitive forms of life appear between 10 and 11 o'clock, about 2,700 million years ago. Man appears in the last 7 or 8 seconds before the hour of midnight. All of recorded history is compressed into one-half of a second, just one tick of the clock of Earth's long history. (See LIFE'S ORIGIN AND DEVELOPMENT.)

These tremendous periods of time are of great importance to us in understanding the significance of fossils. Only by appreciating this time scale can we recognise the nature of the far-reaching changes that have taken place in the life of the Earth.

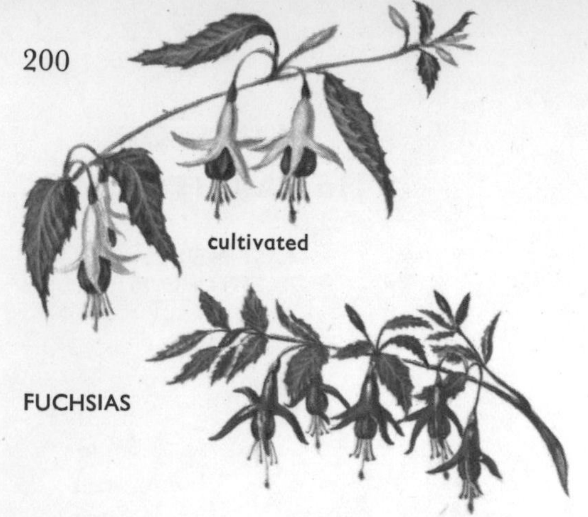

FUCHSIAS (*Fuchsia* spp.) were named after Leonhaard Fuchs, a sixteenth century German botanist. There are about 100 species native in Central and South America and very many cultivated varieties.

The brightly coloured pendant flowers of varying size, form and shades of red, purple and white make them popular ornamental shrubs. The flowers usually have a very brightly coloured calyx tube with sometimes reflexed sepals.

The petals at the mouth of this tube are often of a contrasting colour. The stamens and style are long and prominent. The species which is commonly grown as a hedge and naturalised in parts of Britain is *Fuchsia magellanica* which as its name suggests comes from South America.

FUNGI are one of several groups of organisms believed to be plants, which contain no chlorophyll and many of these organisms are microscopic in size. Since they are unable to carry out photosynthesis and manufacture their own food, they must obtain it from other organisms. In this respect the nutrition of these several groups is very similar. Some, known as saprophytes, feed on dead remains of organisms; some, the parasites, can attack living organisms; some can survive on decaying remains and attack a suitable living host if it is present.

The three groups of organisms concerned are the Bacteria *(Schizomycetes)*; the Slime Fungi *(Myxomycetes)* and the True Fungi *(Eumycetes)*.

For some time many thought that the bacteria were closely related to the true fungi. This was based on the fact that most bacteria and all fungi lack chlorophyll, produce little or no starch, and their cell walls are materials other than cellulose.

Recent studies have shown that bacteria are closely related to the blue-green algae, and that these two groups lack certain features which are found in all other organisms. Thus they cannot be related to the fungi.

In the Slime Fungi *(Myxomycetes)* the fungal body consists of naked protoplasm containing many (but sometimes one) nuclei during some of the stages in the life cycle. Many kinds, like microscopic animals, are capable of absorbing solid food particles.

True Fungi *(Eumycetes)* have rigid cell walls, and the vegetative body, or mycelium, generally consists of many fine branched hollow filaments, or hyphae. As these grow through their food material they produce

A fungus spore first grows a single thread, or hypha. Many of these threads form the mycelium. In time, spore-producing or fruiting bodies develop from the mycelium. Mushrooms are the fruiting bodies of a large and extensive mycelium that grows underground or in rotted wood.

enzymes, which digest the material which can then be absorbed in solution.

Fungi form spores, or small reproductive bodies, produced either by the separation of fragments of hyphae, or as the result of a sexual reproductive process. Fungal spores are very small, and often are carried by wind high in the atmosphere and above the oceans. When they land on a source of food material, they will germinate if there is sufficient warmth and moisture present.

Maytag Dairy Farms, Inc.

BLUE CHEESE
flavoured by a mould

A great many fungi are microscopic in size, but one sub-group the *Basidiomycetes* contain many kinds that are characterised by large reproductive bodies, such as the Mushrooms, Toadstools, and Bracket Fungi.

The more than 100,000 kinds of fungi — almost a third of all the kinds of plants known — are an important group. Their greatest value is the part they play in maintaining the balance of nature. Fungi and bacteria are responsible for the decay of all plant and animal remains.

Fungi or their products are used practically every day. Bread is baked with yeast, a fungus that causes the bread to rise and be fluffy and soft. Blue cheeses, such as Roquefort, get their consistency, flavour, and colour from blue and green moulds.

All alcoholic drinks are fermented by yeast. Among the organic acids produced by fungi are gallic acid used in dyes, citric acid used in soft drinks and medicines and gluconic acid used in medicines. Fungi are used to tan leather and are the source of some vitamins.

Fungi produce antibiotics such as penicillin and streptomycin, the so-called miracle drugs. Yeast is effective in treating acne, and puffball spores are sometimes used by veterinarians to stop bleeding.

Fungi associated with the roots of many plants, particularly trees, form a symbiotic relationship called mycorrhiza. The fungi get their food from the roots, and the roots in turn are able to absorb more water and minerals by the aid of the fungus.

Fungi are also harmful to Man's interest. Cloth, fruits, and vegetables are quickly rotted by fungi. Decay of timber and wooden buildings is caused by fungi, mostly belonging to the pore fungus group. These fungi can soon destroy sidings, sills, or floors. To prevent this from happening, building timbers are well dried. Any parts that might come into contact with the soil or any moisture are treated with a preservative that keeps the fungus from growing.

Fungi also causes diseases. Certain yeasts cause skin diseases in man. Wheat rust, apple scab, carnation wilt, mango anthracnose, and withertip of citrus are a few of thousands of plant diseases caused by fungi. Downy mildew causes late blight of potatoes and tomatoes.

Fungi also cause athlete's foot, ringworm, and many internal diseases of humans. Spores of fungi produce allergies, causing hayfever type breathing difficulties. Some people sneeze violently when entering a room where there are moulds or mildews.

Many kinds of fungi are edible, but some are poisonous and may cause death.

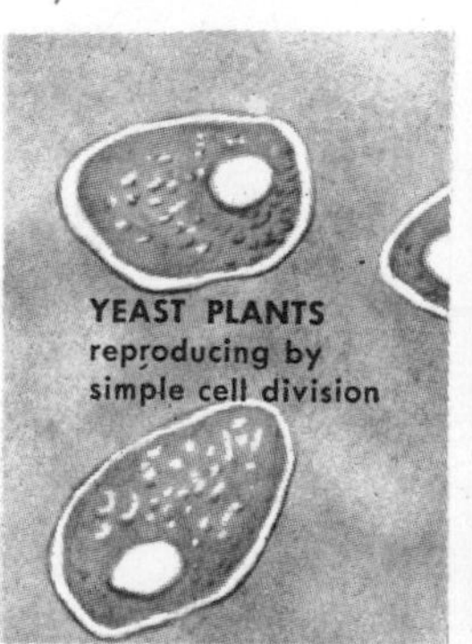
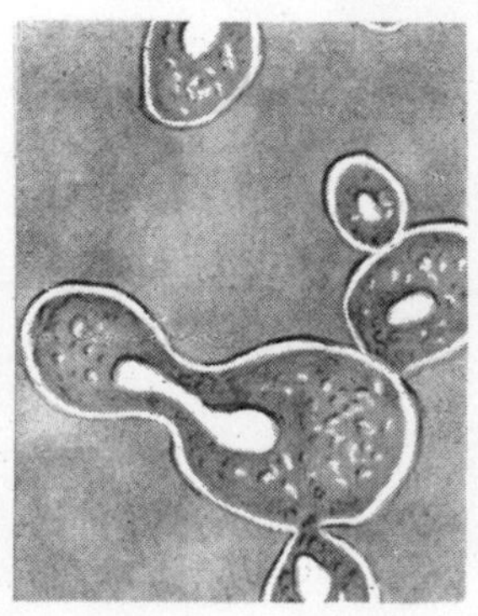

YEAST PLANTS
reproducing by
simple cell division

G

GALAXY. The stars are all around us. Some are bright and nearby, but larger and larger telescopes reveal fainter and more distant stars until it seems as if there were no end to them. Nevertheless, the system of stars that we live in does have a limited size, even though it is very large. Such a system is called a galaxy, and our own galaxy is called the Milky Way (see MILKY WAY), after the faint band of light that circles the sky. The Milky Way contains 100,000 million stars of which our Sun is just one.

The Milky Way is a type of galaxy called a spiral, which consists of three parts: the disc, the spiral arms, and the halo. Most of the stars are scattered through the region of the disc, which bulges at the centre and tapers down at the edges. Embedded in the disc are the spiral arms that wind out from its centre. Often there are two arms opposite each other, but some galaxies have many more. The spiral arms contain a large amount of gas and dust in the space between the stars, and they also contain the brightest stars in the galaxy. The third part of the spiral, the halo, is not flattened like the disc. The halo surrounds and extends right through the disc.

An astronomer studies the heavens.

Mt. Wilson and Palomar Observatories

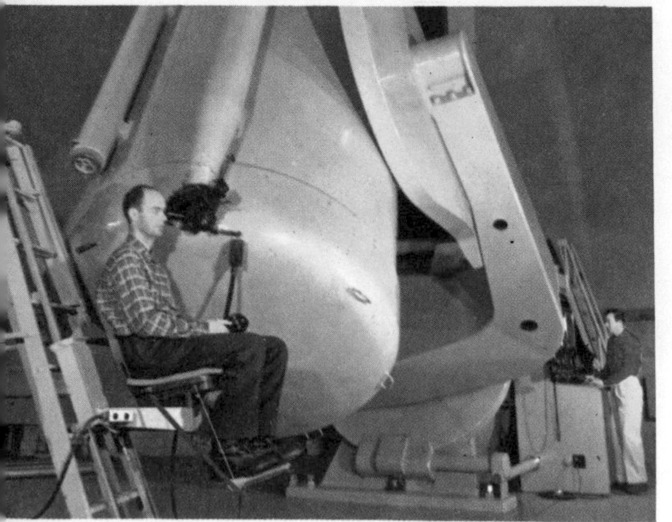

Another type of galaxy is called elliptical. In this type the stars are arranged uniformly throughout, but there are more stars near the centre than towards the edges. Most elliptical galaxies look like nothing more than fuzzy blobs of light. They are so far away that we do not see their individual stars but only the combined light of all their stars. Irregular galaxies, a third type, have the greatest amount of interstellar gas and dust. Many bright new stars are formed from this material. Spirals have somewhat less gas and dust, and it is collected in their spiral arms. New stars form in the spiral arms and gradually spread throughout the rest of the disc, which consists of older stars. Elliptical galaxies have very little insterstellar material and contain only old stars.

Galaxies contain from a million up to hundreds of thousands of millions of stars; the diameters, from 1,000 up to 50,000 parsecs (each parsec equals 3.26 light years). The Milky Way is larger than average but is not the largest galaxy that we know. Galaxies are spread through the universe about a million parsecs apart — some singly, others in groups. The Milky Way, for instance, has two companions, the irregular galaxies called the Magellanic Clouds. They are easily visible to the naked eye and look like two patches torn out of the Milky Way. They can be seen well only from the Earth's Southern Hemisphere because they are so close to the South Celestial Pole.

Besides double and triple galaxies there are larger groups too. The Milky Way, for example, is part of a small cluster made up

Mt. Wilson and Palomar Observatories

The great spiral nebula M 31 in Andromeda is similar to our galaxy. Each contains hundreds of billions of stars. The Andromeda galaxy is six hundred thousand parsecs away and is seen through a sprinkling of foreground stars in our own galaxy. The two small bright blobs near it are its companion elliptical galaxies.

of a dozen and a half galaxies within the space of less than a million parsecs. Besides the Milky Way and the Magellanic Clouds there is one other triple system — the great spiral galaxy in Andromeda with its two elliptical companions. Also included in the group are one more spiral, two irregulars, and nine small elliptical galaxies. Other small galaxies could easily have escaped the notice of astronomers.

There are many other small groups of galaxies like the one to which the Milky Way belongs and also much larger clusters. The Virgo cluster, for example, includes

This is our galaxy, viewed from the side and top. The position of our solar system is marked by the white cross.

Strong radio signals led astronomers to discover this pair of colliding galaxies in the constellation Cygnus.

Mt. Wilson and Palomar Observatories

many of the brightest galaxies in the sky. It has hundreds of galaxies in a diameter of about a million parsecs. The Coma cluster, although more distant and therefore less conspicuous, has over 1,000 galaxies crowded into a diameter of a million parsecs. Other clusters are scattered through the universe in every direction. Not all galaxies are in clusters, though; many of them have no near neighbours.

All galaxies are in motion. Many rotate about their own axis, and the stars move back and forth. But each galaxy is also moving along as a whole — usually at a speed of 50 to 100 miles a second. Even so, the distances between galaxies are so large that most neighbouring galaxies take a 1,000 million years to move past each other.

Besides these individual motions, the distant galaxies have a rapid motion in common. They all seem to be moving away from us, and the more distant ones appear to be moving faster than do those nearer our own galaxy. This is called the expansion of the universe.

As far as we can see into the distance, the universe is filled with galaxies. It is true that in some directions we see no galaxies, but this is only because the dust clouds of the Milky Way hinder our view. About a hundred million galaxies can be photographed with our largest telescopes, and with larger telescopes the number would be even greater. Since each of these galaxies contains many thousands of millions of stars, the number of stars in the part of the universe that we can see is truly tremendous (see STARS; UNIVERSE).

GALLS are abnormal plant growths that arise as the result of a parasitic attack. Although the most familiar are produced by insects that lay their eggs in the tissue of the plant and develop inside the gall, galls can be produced by bacteria, fungi, eelworms and mites. Exactly what causes the gall is not known. Each species of insect always produces the same type of gall on a particular type of plant. If different species of gall-makers deposit eggs on the same type of plant, each forms its characteristic kind of gall. The members of five orders of insects — Diptera, Hymenoptera, Coleoptera,

Mt. Wilson and Palomar Observatories

Arms of a barred spiral galaxy begin at the ends of a straight bar through the nucleus.

Mt. Wilson and Palomar Observatories

Most elliptical galaxies are so far away that their stars seem to blend into a solid patch of light.

In this nearby elliptical galaxy, large numbers of individual stars can be seen.

Mt. Wilson and Palomar Observatories

In spiral galaxies, the trailing arms are prominent because they contain bright stars.

Mt. Wilson and Palomar Observatories

Lepidoptera, and Hemiptera-Homoptera — form galls.

One of the most familiar galls, the oak apple, is produced by Gall-wasps. A wingless female inserts numerous eggs in the base of an oak bud, which is almost severed from the twig in the process and most of which is lifted off by the rapidly swelling gall in early May. When mature, in June-July, the oak apple is spongy and often rose-pink in colour. Several oak apples may be clustered together. In summer, adults escape through special exit-holes. The dark coloured, shrunken remains of the gall persists through the winter.

The best known bacterial galls are the small root nodules on leguminous plants in which live colonies of nitrogen-fixing bacteria *(Rhizobium)*. Black-wart, a disease of the roots of potatoes is caused by the fungus, *Synchitrium endobioticum*.

GARLIC *(Allium sativum)* is native to central Asia but has been cultivated in countries bordering the Mediterranean for over 2,000 years. Garlic belongs to the same group of plants as onions *(Allium cepa)*. It is used both fresh and dried as a flavouring for meats, soups, pickles, and salads. Garlic bulbs separate easily into segments called cloves or toes.

GARNETS are a group of silicate minerals that have excellent crystal form. They have conchoidal fracture and a glassy lustre. Most garnets are of metamorphic origin; their outstanding crystals develop by crowding aside the surrounding minerals. Garnets, which may vary greatly in colour due to impurities, are usually grouped by chemical composition.

Almandite (an iron and aluminium garnet) is red-brown or dark red. It occurs in schists, gneisses, and sometimes in pegmatites. Some almandite crystals from the Adirondack Mountains in the United States have grown over a foot in diameter.

Grossularite (a calcium and aluminium garnet) may be brown, yellow, or colourless. It is found in marble, schists, and nepheline-syenite. Pyrope (a magnesium and aluminium garnet) is deep red. It occurs in igneous rocks as rounded grains rather than crystals. Rhodolite (a magnesium, iron, and aluminium garnet) is rose-red or purple and is

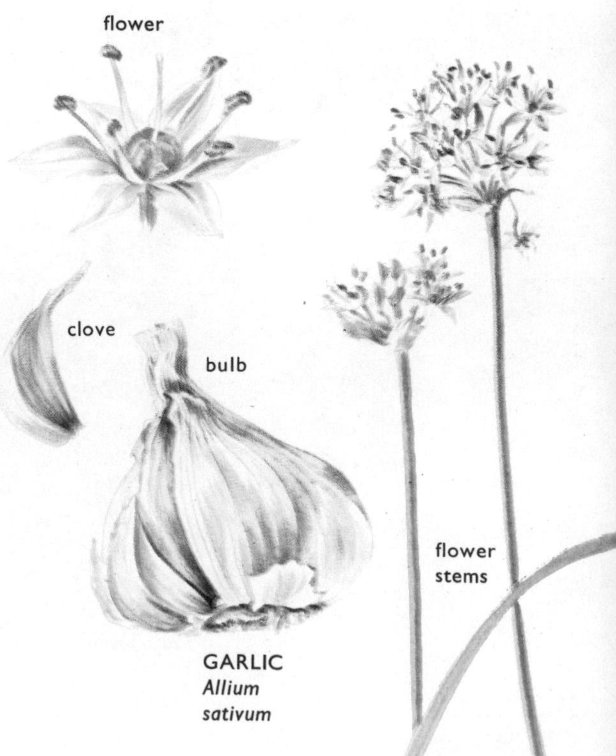

GARLIC
Allium sativum

found in schists. Spessartite (manganese and aluminium), a red or brown garnet, occurs in granites. Andradite (a calcium and iron garnet) is brown, yellow, or sometimes green. It occurs in syenite and also in such rocks as marble and schists. Uvarovite (calcium and chromium) is an emerald-green garnet that occurs in marble, gneisses, and serpentine. It is rarer than the other forms.

Transparent garnets may be used as gem stones. Darker ones are cut as cabochons and paler ones faceted (see GEMS). The principal use of garnet is as an abrasive and depends on its toughness, hardness, and the ability of the grains to break with sharp cutting edges. As garnet paper or cloth these abrasives are used for woodworking, leather and plastic finishing, and other grinding operations. Granular garnet is used for plate-glass and optical-lens grinding, metal polishing, and sand blasting. If garnet is roasted for several hours at 800—900 degrees centigrade, the toughness and sharpness of fracture of the gem stone is greatly increased.

Garnets are world-wide in occurrence in metamorphic areas. The main localities are India and Ceylon for almandine, Malagasy Republic, South Africa and U.S.A. for pyrope. Ceylon also yields grossularite and spessartite and Malagasy Republic rhodolite. Other localities are Brazil and Australia.

Garnet crystals are common, ranging in size from as much as 12 inches in diameter to no larger than a pinhead. Few are of gem quality.

GEMS are minerals, rocks, or man-made substances used as jewellery. Practically all hard minerals with pleasing colours can be gem stones. Quartz, which occurs in many colours and patterns, is the most common gem stone. (See QUARTZ.)

The value of gems is determined by their beauty, durability, rarity, and popularity. Beauty is based on colour, variation in colour, lustre and, in the case of transparent light-coloured stones, brilliance. Brilliance is determined by the way light is bent as it passes through the stone, and this can be emphasised by the cut of the stone. Durability is the stone's hardness and toughness. Gems worn in a ring, for example, should have a hardness of 7 or greater because quartz dust is present everywhere and will abrade anything softer. Toughness is important when stones are being mounted. Pressure is applied to the metal prongs bent around a stone, and greater care is necessary to prevent brittle stones from being damaged or chipped.

Gem stones are worked by three common methods: tumbled to make baroques, cut as cabochons, or faceted. Translucent, dark-coloured, badly flawed, or opaque minerals are tumbled in water with an abrasive. After a week or two, the stones are washed carefully to get rid of the abrasive and then returned to the tumbler. Sometimes a detergent is added. About two weeks later the stones become highly polished. The finished baroques are irregular in shape.

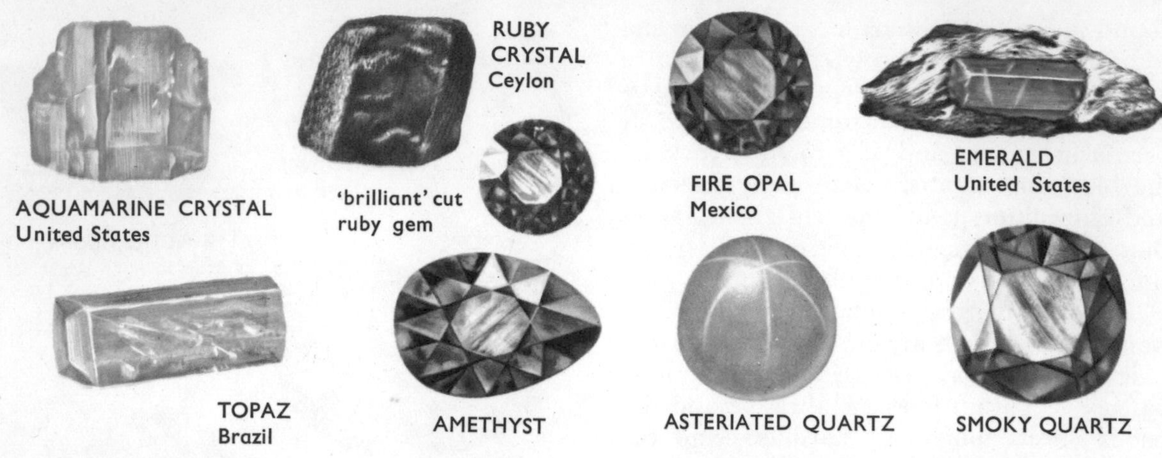

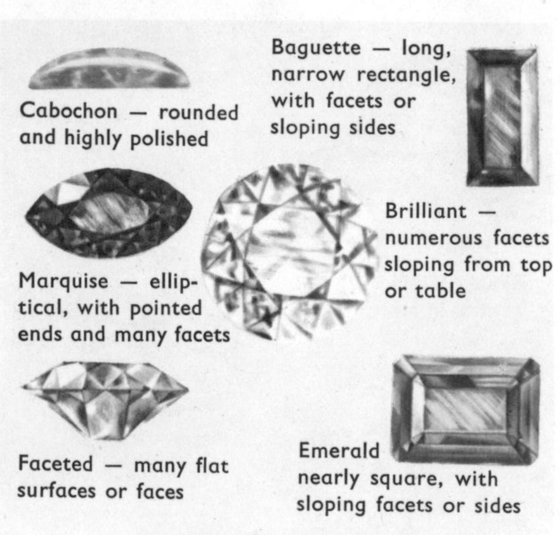

STYLES OF GEM CUTS

Cabochons are stones cut and polished with rounded surfaces. They are usually cut in the rough with a diamond saw from opaque minerals that have pleasing colours or patterns. Then the stone is mounted with special adhesive (dopping wax) on a special stick (dop stick) and carefully shaped on successively finer abrasive wheels. Finally the stone is polished.

Faceted stones are those cut with many flat faces. Gem stones used for faceting are transparent, colourless, or light-coloured. Those with the fewest flaws are the most valuable. The facets are cut at definite angles so that light enters the stone and is reflected from facet to facet and finally comes out through the top (table) of the stone. This gives the stone its brilliance. To get maximum brilliance, it is important that the facets are absolutely flat and highly polished.

Some gem stones are cut as cameos, on which an artist engraves a raised figure of a lighter colour standing above a darker, lower layer. In an intaglio the figure is cut into the dark lower layer, the reverse of a cameo. Intaglios were used as seals when it was the custom to seal letters with sealing wax.

SYNTHETIC GEMS. Synthetic gems resemble natural stones physically and chemically. Synthetic corundum and spinel have been produced cheaply and in large quantities for more than 50 years. They are more nearly perfect than most natural stones, and it is difficult to see the curved lines that distinguish fused synthetic gems from the natural stones. Synthetic corundum and spinel are produced by dropping the pulverised chemical through an intense flame that fuses the powder. The drop of molten material falls on to a support where it crystallises. More molten material is added and the fresh material orients its molecules with those of the already solidified mass so that the stone grows. The synthetic mineral is allowed to grow into a pear-shaped boule of 25 to 1,000 carats in weight (1 carat = 0.2 grams). The pure synthetic gem is colourless. Small quantities of impurities are added to produce colours and shades to imitate ruby, sapphire, emerald, peridot, topaz, alexandrite, amethyst, aquamarine, garnet, kunzite, morganite, and others. Synthetic corundum is also made into rods that are cut into jewels for watches and scientific instruments. Synthetic rutile, marketed as 'titania', has unmatched brilliance, but is yellowish and relatively soft. Synthetic emeralds have been manufactured for 30 years in sizes suitable for use, and large synthetic quartz crystals are produced for use in radio transmitters. Synthetic diamonds are competing now with natural diamonds as abrasives, and gem quality synthetic diamonds will probably be manufactured in the near future.

GEOGRAPHICAL DISTRIBUTION OF MAN. Prehistoric man — where he lived and what he looked like — is known only by his fossil bones, tools, paintings and other evidence of his existence, which are found scattered over Europe, Asia and Africa.

For hundreds of thousands of years Man was a wanderer, gathering what foods nature provided. New Stone Age peoples began domesticating animals at about the same time they invented agriculture (see AGRICULTURE). These two important discoveries made it possible for Man to settle in places most favourable for cultivating the soil or the herding of flocks. Thus, people did not become spread evenly over the world. They prospered more in some regions than in others, and in these different climates, social as well as physical, there arose the variety of peoples that now inhabit the Earth. (See MAN.)

The early history of Man is largely a record of the impact of wandering tribes — hunters and nomadic herders — upon settled agricultural peoples. The barbarians — the Celts, Goths, Vandals, Huns, Slavs, and Mongols — all appeared out of Asia to menace the agricultural civilisations that had developed in the Mediterranean Basin.

In some cases, the invaders displaced the inhabitants and obliterated their culture. In recent historical times, the European settlers

A brilliant diamond is cut in nine stages. The rough stone (1) is sawed in two parts (2). Cutting of the larger part proceeds with rounding or girdling (3). Lopping begins (4), producing the first facet. Further lopping produces 4 main facets (5) and then 12 (6). The main facets are finished (7), then tiny star facets are added (8). The finished gem (9) has 58 facets or flat faces to reflect the light and give the diamond its sparkling brilliance.

In this synthetic gem apparatus, the alumina (Al_2O_3) sifts into a very hot oxyhydrogen flame and forms a slow-growing 'boule' at the end of a ceramic rod. Pigments are added to imitate the colour of the natural gems.

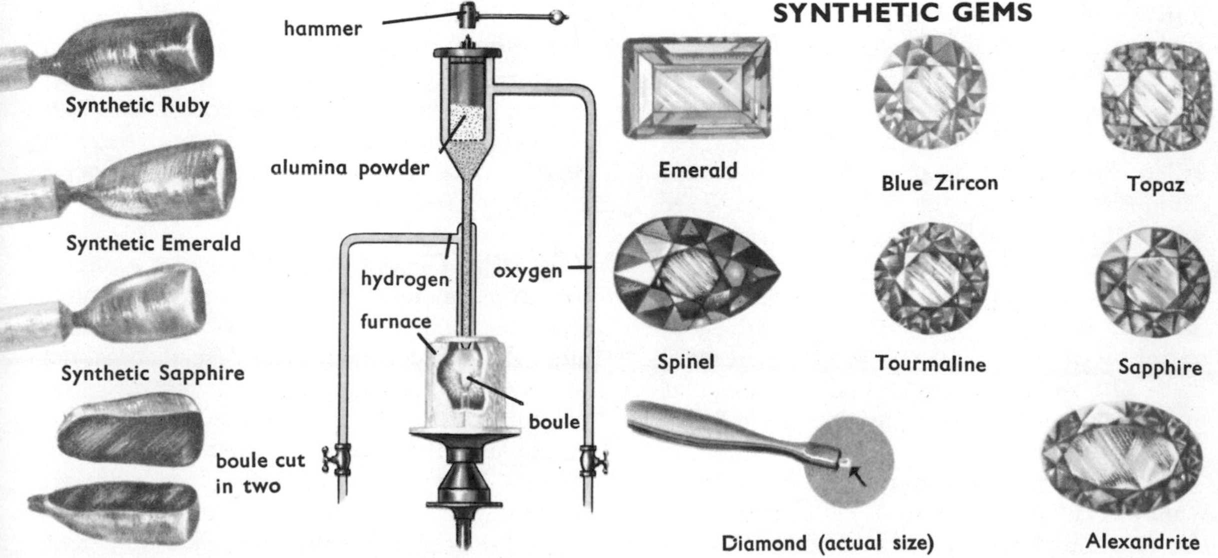

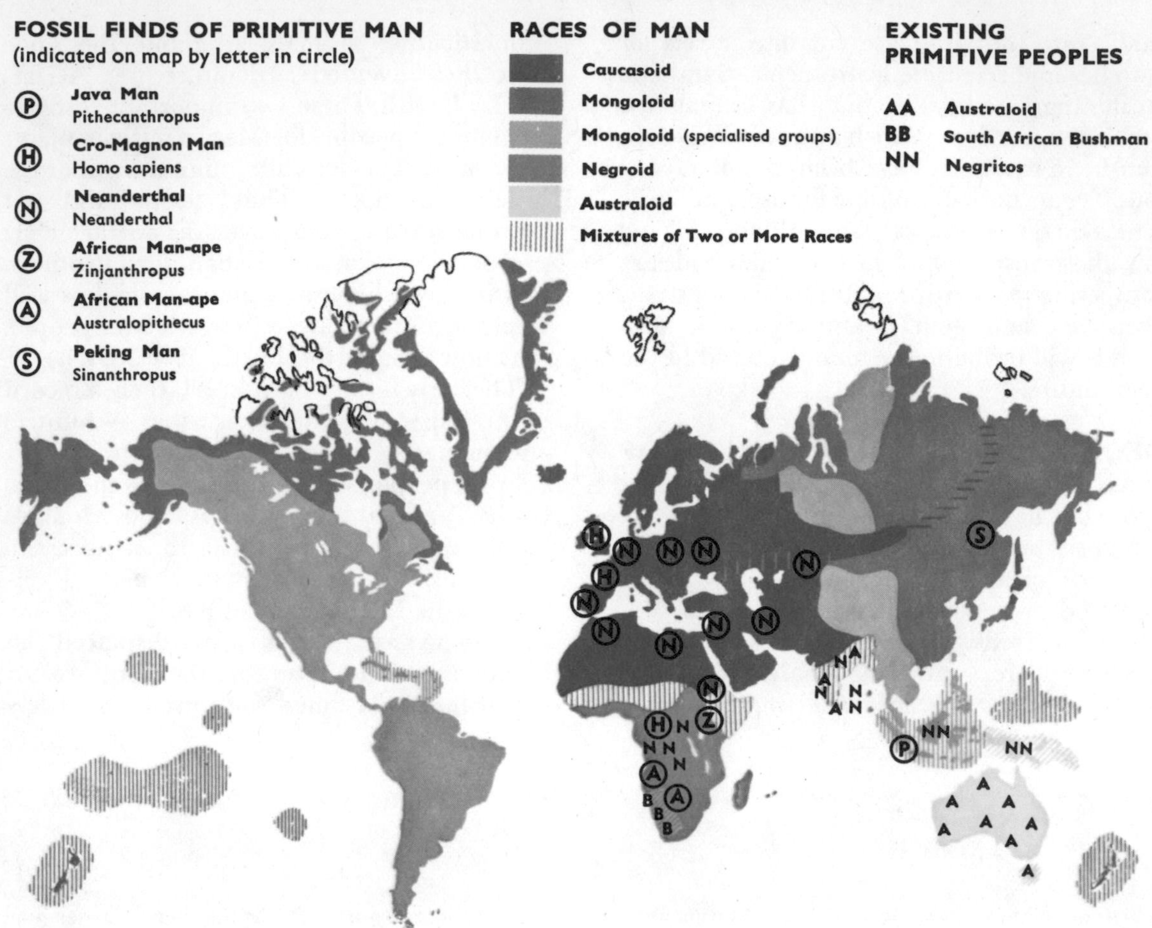

This map shows the distribution of the principal races of man before the year 1400. It also indicates, by means of the circled letters, in what parts of the world fossils of primitive man have been found. The most primitive groups of man in existence today are shown by the small, uncircled letters.

in North America nearly exterminated the native Indian tribes. The population of South and Central America, however, is still largely Indian, especially in mountainous and jungle regions.

Before A.D. 1000, when Eric the Red sailed his Viking ship to Greenland and established a colony, the Western Hemisphere was occupied only by Eskimos and American Indians, both of Mongoloid origin. Asia was occupied by people of the Mongoloid race; Europe, by people of the Caucasoid race; and most of Africa, by people of the Negroid race. The world population at that time was about 100 million, compared to over 3,000 million now.

Exploration and colonisation on a large scale began with the voyages of Columbus in the late 1400s. Since then, the distribution of the basic racial and sub-racial types has changed considerably, although their original concentrations are still much in evidence. Modern transportation and communication systems have done much to bring the many peoples of the world together, and there is reason to believe that in time both social and physical differences will be dissolved.

EUROPE. Geographically, Europe is one of the largest peninsulas of Asia. It is the only continent joined by land to another, and often the two continents are described as one — Eurasia. Europe's boundaries are the Atlantic Ocean on the west, the Arctic Ocean on the north, the Mediterranean Sea on the south — three distinct natural boundaries. Eastern Europe is separated from Asia by the Ural and Caucasus mountains, which are considered the dividing line between predominantly Western culture traced to Greece and Rome and the Eastern cultures spread westward from China and northward from India and the Middle East. Through history, this cultural dividing line has fluctuated considerably, most notably in the fourteenth century with the Mongol conquest of Russia and in the fifteenth century when the Turks menaced Vienna and lands to the west.

Europe is largely mountainous. The Sierra Nevada mountain range in Spain meets the Pyrenees near the French border, and the French Massif Central swings eastward to the Alps. This rocky central core of Europe is divided into the Apennines which extend the length of Italy, into the Balkans which reach the tip of Greece, and into the Carpathians which form a wide arc to the Black Sea. Several mountain ranges are found on the Scandinavian Peninsula, mainly along its western edge.

North of the Alps, from the Spanish border of France across Germany, Poland and Russia to the Ural Mountains, stretches the Great Plain of Europe. European Russia is, for the most part, a low-lying and level terrain, although several ranges of low hills extend south of Moscow to the Sea of Azov.

Neanderthal and Cro-Magnon were early types of Man that inhabited Europe. They were replaced by or merged with wanderers from the plateau of Central Asia in a series of migrations that began many years before recorded history. Conquerors, such as the Arabs who invaded and controlled Spain from the eighth century to the fifteenth century, upset the political controls of their day but did not result in the wholesale displacement of populations.

Patrick Morin — Monkmeyer

Icelanders, like these children, are typical Scandinavians, with blue eyes and blonde hair.

Italians are largely of Mediterranean stock, with light skin and dark hair. These men are in Naples.

Max Tatch — Shostal

Slavic peoples of eastern Europe are stocky, broad-faced people and usually have a dark complexion.

Paul Byers — FLO

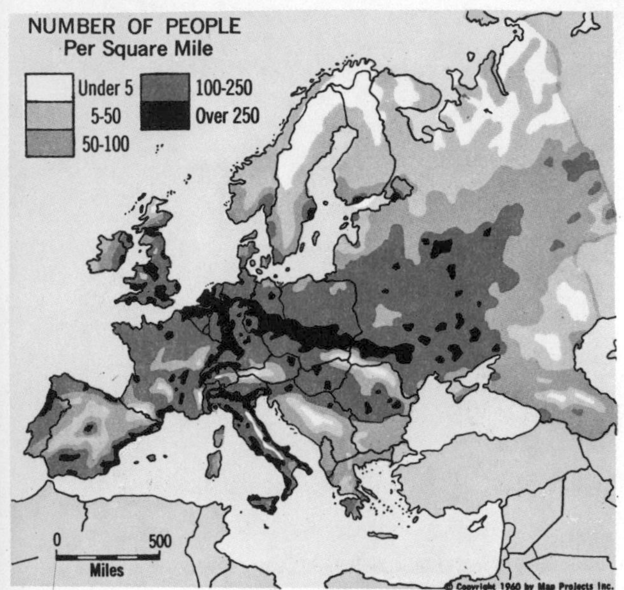

Europe's population is most dense in industrial areas, lightest in the mountains and in the Arctic.

Europe's combination of long, high mountain ranges, deeply indented coastlines, and diverse strains of migrants has permitted the development of numerous cultural and linguistic islands on the one continent. Nearly constant warfare and continually improving methods of exchange of goods have maintained contact between the peoples of Europe, and the rate of cultural growth has been relatively uniform.

At its peak the Roman Empire absorbed all of the Mediterranean Basin, the Danube Basin, the south bank of the Rhine, and even part of the British Isles. With the collapse of the Roman Empire, Christianity began its spread beyond the shrinking boundaries of Imperial Rome. In the Middle Ages, the Roman Catholic Church was the greatest link between the various geographical areas, though it became less so with the dawn of the Protestant movement in the fifteenth century. Without the protection of the Roman legions, the people living in the farm regions of Europe were left to the mercies of northern barbarians, now known to us as the Goths, Visigoths, Vandals, Franks, Lombards, Burgundians, and Slavs. These peoples settled among the remnants of the earlier population, and eventually the social structure of feudalism evolved, taking the place of both the imperial organisation of Rome and the tribal loyalties of the barbarians. At the top of the feudal structure was the king. The nobles were his 'vassals', who owed him allegiance in return for his protection. The nobles, in turn, had 'villeins' or 'serfs' under them. These were the common people who farmed the land or worked in the lord's household or stables. The lord, or 'liege', protected his serfs in time of war and permitted them to farm land for their own uses. In payment, the serfs gave part of their farm produce to the lord or worked for him directly.

The rise of the modern nation-state from the fourteenth through to the seventeenth century ushered in the colonial period, in which Europe established political domination over most of the world. The social organisation of Europe underwent major changes in the eighteenth and nineteenth century, with the Industrial Revolution and the spread of democracy. Europeans were the discoverers of the New World, and they populated both North and South America.

Today, nearly 600 million poeple live in Europe, making it the most densely populated of the continents. In race, the people are largely Caucasoid, but there are many sub-racial groups in the more than 30 countries. Europeans represent three basic origins, as determined by their physical features and their language similarities: the Romanic group, whose language was derived from Latin and whose people live principally in southern Europe (French, Spanish, Italian, Greek, and others); the Germanic group, who are the people of northern and western Europe (British, German, Dutch, Danish, Swedish, and others); and the Slavic group, who live in eastern Europe (Czech, Polish, Russian, and others).

ASIA. More than half of the world's population lives in Asia, the largest continent. Here live large numbers of Mongoloid and Caucasoid peoples. In some regions these races are mixed and in still others they are mixed with Negroid sub-races. In way of life, Asia is even more varied than in race. Reindeer herders of the North have little in common with rice farmers in the tropics. Neither of them lives, thinks, nor acts like the industrial workers of Tokyo, Shanghai, or the Soviet oil fields.

Julien Bryan — Photo Researchers

Men of Afghanistan show a mixture of sub-racial features. All are swarthy and have dark hair.

Asia may by divided roughly into six great cultural regions or realms.

The Middle East is predominantly Moslem. This common faith has a great binding force among the numerous nations of the region. It is a region generally of desert and semi-desert lands. Farming is difficult, and many people live as nomadic herdsmen. Except for Israel, it is an area of much poverty and few industries. However, great oil fields are scattered throughout the region. Although it was there that the earliest city civilisations appeared, the vast majority of people are still dependent upon farming and herding. Israel and Lebanon are the only important countries with dense population. The much larger areas of Saudi Arabia and Iran are very thinly populated. Here there are many miles of desert with few densely settled fertile spots.

The Indian Realm contains Pakistan, a Moslem country; Nepal and Ceylon, with many Buddhists; and India, which is predominantly Hindu.

With nearly 500 million people, India is by far the largest country of the region. The population of surrounding areas totals more than 100 million. In race, the region is mainly Caucasoid. Towards the north-east, however, people are more Mongoloid and in southern India there is much mixture of Caucasoid peoples with races whose ancestors lived in this region in prehistoric times.

The fertile Ganges Valley of northern India is one of the most densely populated areas in the world. Although India has several

An old lady of Peking holds her grandchild, one of 55,000 babies born every day in China.

John Strohm

Koreans are closely related to the Chinese. A distinctive costume is the black horsehair hat and white robe.

Edmund N. Paige — Shostal

PEOPLES OF ASIA

Asia's crowded lands sent waves of people into Europe. Hungarians (1), Ukranians (2), Poles (3), Finns (4), Lapps (5), and Russians (6) have retained features showing their Asiatic origin. In Asia's Middle East live the Arabs (7), Bedouins (8), and Kurds (9), while to the west are the Turkmen (10) and Afghans (11). Indians (12), Nepalese (13), and Sinhalese (14) are among the many peoples of the Indian Realm, where divisions are more along religious than racial lines. South-east Asia is a great mixture of sub-races, including the Burmese (15), Malayans (16), and Javanese (17). The west coast of Asia, considered the homeland of the Mongoloid race, is inhabited by the Chinese (18) and Japanese (19). Many tribes live in central Asia. Among them are the Kirghiz (20), Karagass (21), Mongols (22), Yakuts (23), and Evenki (24).

industrial cities with over a million people, most Indians live in rural villages surrounded by the fields they cultivate. Four-fifths or more of the Indian region's population farm for a livelihood. Rice is the most important single crop and in some areas it is viewed as the 'staff of life'.

Southern Asia is a sprawling region extending from the Indian border to the Philippine Islands. It includes mainland countries like Thailand, once called Siam, and thousands of islands strung out in a 2,500-mile-long chain. Living in this region are 250 million people. They are scattered over a land area less than half the size of the United States. These people are mixtures of Mongoloid with Caucasoid, with many subracial groups, including Negrito.

Today most of the mainland South-east Asians are Buddhist, while those of the islands are Mohammedan. Throughout the entire region, rice is the major crop and the basic food. In addition to rice, which is often grown on irrigated lands, the drier highlands produce vegetables and grains like millet and corn. Commercial agriculture is found in certain parts of the region, especially where Europeans have developed rubber and other plantation crops.

The largest of the south-eastern Asian countries, in both land area and in population, is Indonesia. The Indonesian Republic, with its numerous islands, contains about one-third of the region's land and about 40 per cent of its population. Almost two-thirds of Indonesia's 100 million people are crowded onto the island of Java, which produces rubber and palm oil.

The Chinese Realm is the homeland of peoples of the Mongoloid race. Most of the countries included in this region have from time to time been considered outlying territories of China. Japan and Korea, however, have been distinct societies for centuries. On the Asian continent, population is concentrated where rainfall is adequate for farming. The lands of Tibet, Sinkiang, and Mongolia range from deserts to semi-arid plains and towering mountains. Eastern China is the most densely settled region, although China as a whole, with about 700 million persons, has easily the largest population of any

Herbert Knapp

This young Buddhist monk is from Thailand.

Tibetans are mainly Mongoloid, like Koreans and Chinese, but have features distinct from other Asians.

George Holton — Photo Library

country in the world. Although great efforts have been made in recent years to industrialise the country, about 80 per cent of the people are farmers. In the thinly settled outlying regions, people depend on cattle, sheep and goat herding. In some regions rice is the most important food crop; elsewhere it is wheat or other grains.

Japan is the only country of the Far East that is not mainly rural. In recent years it has become an industrial nation with a large city population. In yield per acre, the Japanese are now the world's most efficient farmers.

Numerous languages and hundreds of dialects are spoken throughout the Chinese realm. Customs of the nomadic tribesmen of the deserts are utterly different from those of southern Chinese farmers or the fishermen of Japan. Yet, throughout much of this realm people have been influenced by the same great religious leaders and by similar artistic, literary, and even political ideas.

Siberia is a vast region once held by various Mongoloid tribes. The northern fringe is arctic in climate. South of this is a great belt of cold forest land. Still farther south there are semi-arid plains and difficult mountain ranges. While most of Siberia is not of great economic importance to the Soviet Union, it holds growing industrial centres, mines, oil and timber.

Soviet Central Asia includes several republics, the largest of which is Kazakhstan. Kazakhstan is nearly as large as India in area but is much more thinly populated. It is a region of dry plains and high mountains, with some fertile, irrigated valleys and oases. Cotton is an important crop. Samarkand, one of its cities, was once an important centre along caravan routes connecting Asia with Europe. It was also a centre for Mongol tribesmen in their conquest of southern Asia and much of Europe during the Middle Ages. Mohammedanism is the principal religion.

AFRICA. The African continent covers one-fifth of the entire land surface of the Earth. Although its area is so large, its population is only around 300 million. It is a continent of great mineral resources but of very difficult climates. Hundreds of different primitive tribes have made satisfactory lives in harsh deserts and jungles, and civilisations have arisen in various parts of this continent.

Historically and geographically, Africa is divided by the Sahara Desert. North of the Sahara are the Arabic-speaking peoples of Morocco, Algeria, Tunisia, Libya and Egypt. The countries in this narrow strip of land along the Mediterranean are largely desert,

PEOPLES OF AFRICA

North Africa is inhabited by Berbers (1), Tuaregs (2), Egyptians (3), and Arabs (4). A sprinkling of Europeans live in the coastal cities.

Along the Guinea coast, the dark-skinned people (5) are mainly farmers, while those of the Sudan grasslands are cattlemen (6). Many of the numerous tribes are mixtures of Caucasoid and Negroid races. A similar mixing of races occurs in the Abyssinian Highlands, east of the Sahara. This is the land of the Ethiopians (7) and the Somali (8). The peoples of the great drainage basin on the Congo and along the western coast of Africa are Negroid. Here live the Negritos or Pygmies (9), Bantu (10), Mukamba (11), Watusi (12), and Masai (13). Those of the forest live by farming and hunting; those of the drier highlands to the east are hunters and herdsmen.

In the dry lands of southern Africa live the Bushmen (14) and such tribes of the Bantu as the Barotse (15), Zulu (16), Basuto (17), and Hereros (18). The people of the Island of the Malagasy Republic (19) show race relationship to the Negroids of Africa and to the Mongoloids of southern Asia.

Elliot Erwitt — Magnum; Courtesy of Holiday Magazine; © 1958 The Curtis Publishing Co.

Moroccan tribesman at the pastime known as 'Powder Play', which is a test of their horsemanship.

and all are poor. The region is mainly Caucasoid in race and Moslem in religion. In ways of life this region has always been in close contact with the civilisations of the Mediterranean and the Middle East. North Africa produced the great early civilisations of Egypt and Carthage.

The Berbers are the principal people living in the Sahara Desert. In earlier times, the Tuaregs, a fierce nomadic tribe of Berbers, policed the caravan routes. Berbers are a mixed Negroid and Caucasoid people. Like their neighbours to the north, along the Mediterranean, they are Moslems.

East of the Sahara and the Nile are the Abyssinian Highlands. Ethiopia is a country of this region. Racially, the population is mixed: skins are dark, while lips and noses are shaped like those of Caucasoids. These people have an ancient civilisation and they have been mainly Christian since the third century.

South of the Sahara are peoples who are mainly Negroid in race. Negroid Africans may be divided into three major groups: 1) the Guinea and Sudanese; 2) the Bantu; and 3) the Pygmy, Bushmen and Hottentots.

The Guinea and Sudanese live in the Sudan region, south of the Sahara Desert. These peoples include many different tribes. Typically, the Guinea practise farming. On the semi-arid grasslands of the interior, the Sudanese live mainly by cattle raising and dairying. In the high-rainfall belt near the equator cattle raising is practically impossible because of the tsetse fly, which transmits sleeping sickness and other serious diseases. Here, the people of the jungle subsist on the cultivation of bananas, yams, manioc, palm oil, and cocoa.

South of the Sudan is the land of the Bantu. The Bantu number over 60 million persons, living from just north of the equator southwards. The many different tribes and nations which make up the Bantu peoples live chiefly by farming or dairying. On the grassy highlands of East Africa, cattle raising and dairying are common. Today, most of the industrial workers in the cities of South and East Africa are Bantu.

Pygmies live in the rain forest of the Congo River basin, the heart of tropical Africa. In height, pygmies average about four and a half feet. They live primarily by hunting and by gathering nuts and roots in the forest. Generally, they trade meat and other jungle products for bananas and manufactured items produced by their neighbours, the Bantu.

Related to the pygmies are the Bushmen and the Hottentots. The Bushmen are a little taller than the pygmies. They too are nomadic hunters and food gatherers. Both are expert in tracking and stalking game. The Bushmen, however, live on the edge of the Kalahari Desert in South-west Africa. Hottentots were once hunters but for a living now depend largely on cattle and sheep.

Negroid Africa has developed a number of important civilisations. In East Africa, there was the great kingdom of Uganda, northwest of Lake Victoria. A complex government spread the rule of a king over a large area.

Another great kingdom was that of Dahomey on the west coast. It was from this region that many Negroes were taken to America. Dahomean society had a highly organised government. In arts and crafts, the African kingdoms produced work as skilful as that found in the great periods of European art.

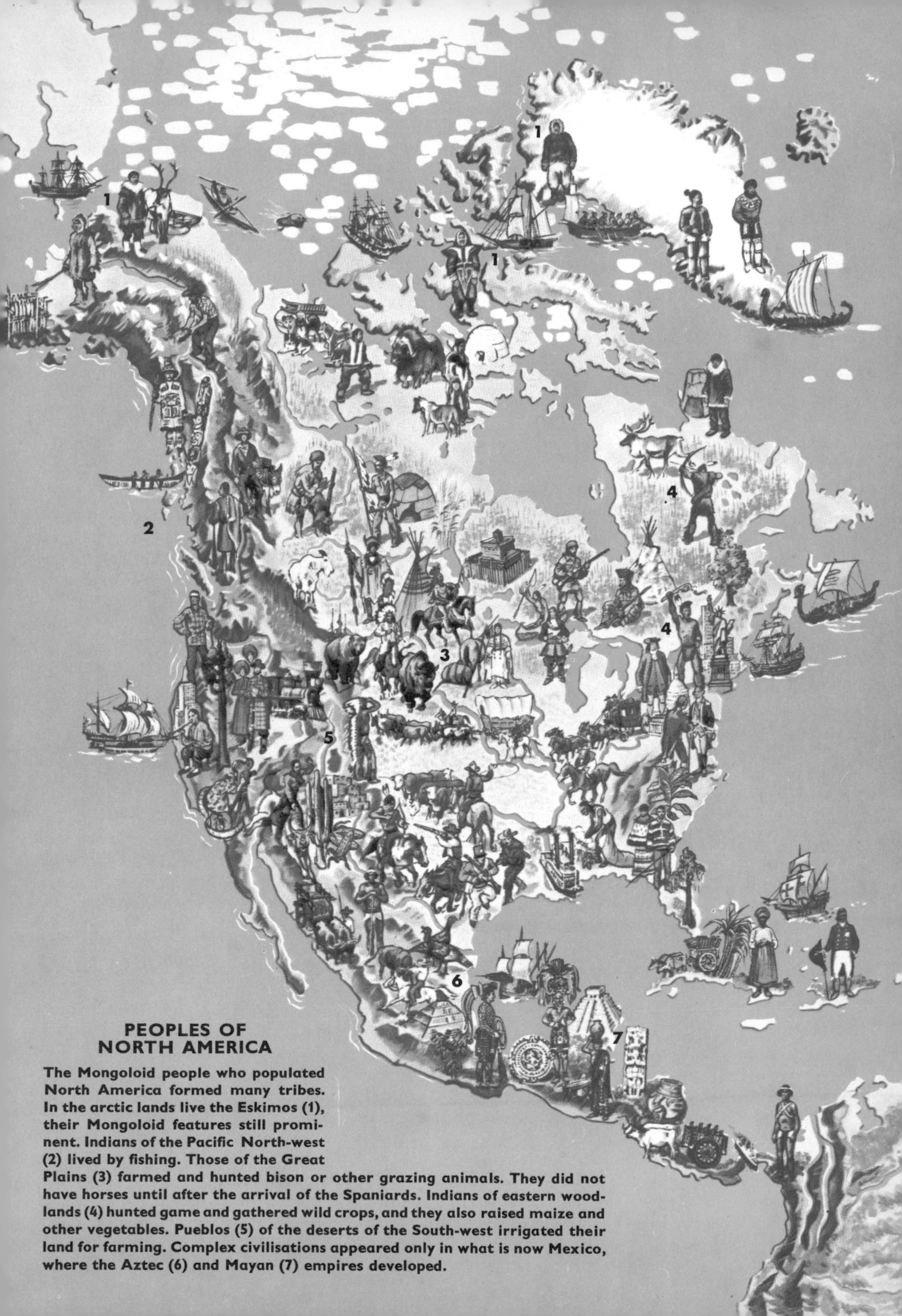

PEOPLES OF NORTH AMERICA

The Mongoloid people who populated North America formed many tribes. In the arctic lands live the Eskimos (1), their Mongoloid features still prominent. Indians of the Pacific North-west (2) lived by fishing. Those of the Great Plains (3) farmed and hunted bison or other grazing animals. They did not have horses until after the arrival of the Spaniards. Indians of eastern woodlands (4) hunted game and gathered wild crops, and they also raised maize and other vegetables. Pueblos (5) of the deserts of the South-west irrigated their land for farming. Complex civilisations appeared only in what is now Mexico, where the Aztec (6) and Mayan (7) empires developed.

At work on the range, an American cowboy about to throw his lariat.

NORTH AMERICA. When Columbus sailed west, he hoped to reach India. Thinking that the New World was really India, he misnamed the inhabitants 'Indians' and the name stuck.

These first settlers in America came from Asia by way of the Bering Strait 15,000 to 20,000 years ago. Before that time there was no human life in either North or South America. The migrations continued for thousands of years.

In the New World these Stone-Age travellers spread throughout North and South America, where they developed into hundreds of tribes having different languages and ways of life. Agriculture was invented independently of the rest of the world by Indians in northern South America or in Mexico. They developed many important crops, such as corn, potatoes, kidney beans, pumpkin, rubber, and tobacco. In Mexico and in the Andes Mountains of South America complex civilisations appeared.

When the white man reached America, the Indians and Eskimos had adapted themselves in many different ways to the varying natural living conditions of the New World. Along the Arctic Ocean the Eskimos had acclimatised themselves to their extremely difficult environment.

Eskimos still live in small groups generally consisting of close relatives. They hunt caribou, seals and walruses and also catch fish and birds. Their most important weapon was the harpoon, but many of them have now adopted the gun. Tinned food, radio, and other goods introduced by white men are also now in common use. Eskimos sometimes live in temporary snow houses but also build homes of skins stretched over a framework of whalebone; both are called igloos. Where materials are available they may also live in log cabins, canvas tents, or other shelters. Many Alaskan Eskimos have frame homes with modern conveniences.

To the south were Indian tribes that wandered the forests of the North, fishing and trapping. They practised no agriculture, since they had ample food from game, salmon, and wild berries and fruits.

Many agricultural tribes lived in what is now the north-eastern United States. In upper New York State the Iroquois Confederacy linked five important tribes into a 'united nations'. The Iroquois were excellent farmers and also skilled hunters and fishermen. The Indians of the south-east were mainly farmers. Early travellers marvelled at the great size of the corn-fields they saw in this region.

Before the white man came, the Indians of the Great Plains were farmers, living along the river valleys. Their way of life was disrupted when the Spanish brought horses to America. There were no horses in the New World before this time. When the Plains Indians discovered horses they left farming to become buffalo hunters.

In the dry south-west lived the Pueblo tribes, famous for their huge apartment-house dwellings. These peace-loving peoples grew maize in a region of terrible drought. They learned to irrigate their land to grow crops. Near them lived the Navaho and Apache, who became sheepherders and skilful weavers of wool.

In some regions the white man treated the Indians honourably. More often the Indian was treated with cruelty and injustice. The Indian Wars, through which the white settlers took over North America from the Indians, did not end until 1892. Even then harshness and injustice continued. Indians were herded on to reservations — land set aside by the government for their use. While reservations in desert regions were being 'given' to the Indians, their good land was being taken from them elsewhere. In recent years more has been done to improve the Indians' condition, but injustices remain to be corrected.

After 1500, North America was explored and colonised rapidly by Europeans. The Spanish and Portuguese settled in Central America, Mexico, and parts of what is now the southern United States, while the English and the French settled in the northern part of the continent. Negro slaves were introduced, and the three races of man are now represented in large numbers. The Indians are now a minority group, and Negroes compose about 12 per cent of the total population.

SOUTH AMERICA. The waves of wanderers that crossed the Bering Strait from Asia and inhabited North America continued south, over the Isthmus of Panama. The chain of the Andes Mountains, running from the northernmost point to the frozen wastes of Tierra del Fuego, separated the dry Pacific coast from the hot, steaming basin of the Amazon and Orinoco rivers, the temperate pampas along the Rio de la Plata, and the windy, barren plains of Patagonia.

The degree of culture developed by the many tribes had depended considerably on the environment in which each had lived. The people of the cold lands of Tierra del Fuego and Patagonia were simple, nomadic hunters. The now extinct Indians of the pampas were also nomadic hunters but practised some agriculture. Those of the jungles of the east and the north-east employed a slash-and-burn agriculture.

In the north-western corner of the continent, where the modern nations of Columbia, Ecuador, and Peru are today, a number of tribes developed a high degree of civilisation. The principal crop was maize, which they may have originated, and the llama was the main source of meat, wool, and hides. During the centuries preceding Spanish conquests, the Incas secured dominion over the others in this region. The main cities of the empire were connected by a marvellously engineered road system. Mountainsides were terraced to increase the scanty acreage of arable land. The government was paternalistic, with a well developed noble class. The empire of the Incas dissolved a few years after the first contact with the white man.

Christopher Columbus sailed along the north-east shores of South America in 1498. Spanish, Portuguese, French, and Dutch explorers visited the eastern tip of the continent, and the Portuguese settled the region after 1530. Spanish efforts were concentrated in the northern areas, first around Panama, then down the Pacific coast in the former territories of the shattered Inca empire.

In each region, the Indian inhabitants were reduced to a status verging on slavery,

Len Sirman — Birnback

Indians of the Amazon Valley live as hunters and food gatherers, and are in constant struggle with the jungle.

The Indian tribes of the Peruvian Andes have kept their ancient language, costumes, and customs.

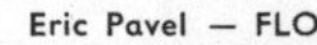

Eric Pavel — FLO

PEOPLES OF SOUTH AMERICA

The native peoples of South America are Indian, as in North America, and there are a great many tribes. Those of the Amazon Basin (1) are mainly hunters but practise some farming. Indians of the plains (2) were wanderers, moving wherever the hunting was good or nature's crops bountiful. Those who lived in the mountains (3), such as the Incas, developed good systems of agriculture, with terracing, irrigation, and stock raising. Indians who lived at the southern tip of the continent (4) spent their days in ceaseless search for edible plants or animals in the cold, desolate region.

though most of the tribes were not exterminated, as were those of North America. The plantation economy of tropical north-eastern South America demanded vast numbers of workers, and African slaves were imported to fill this need.

Nearly all of the nations of Europe contributed numbers of immigrants to South America. Most of the modern nations of the continent, who won their independence from Spain and Portugal in the early nineteenth century, have populations that are a mixture of Indian, Negro, and European white.

OCEANIA. Scattered through the vast South-west Pacific are countless islands. Thousands of them are coral rings, or atolls. Hundreds of them are fertile and are large enough to be settled by man. Here also is the smallest continent, Australia, and near it is the second largest island in the world, New Guinea.

This South Pacific world may be divided into four regions: (1) the continent of Australia; (2) Melanesia, a region which includes New Guinea and many other islands bordering Australia; (3) Micronesia, an area of hundreds of tiny islands north of the equator; (4) Polynesia, the eastern part of Oceania, forming a great triangle with points in New Zealand, Hawaii, and Easter Island.

Polynesians are tall, with light brown skins. While racially mixed, they are mainly Caucasoid. Probably there were several waves of migrants out of Asia, each having somewhat different sub-racial origins. In the islands they intermarried to form the present population. Micronesians are racially similar to the Polynesians.

A sub-race of man known as Australoids is found in Australia. The Australoids are believed to be a mixture of various Negroid and Caucasoid sub-races. Some Australiods look like African pygmies. Probably the pygmies — or Negritos — were the earliest to reach this continent in some prehistoric migration.

The peoples of Melanesia are much more Negroid in appearance and origin than are the Polynesians. They are a mixture of Negrito (pygmy), Polynesian, Mongoloid, and early white races.

In ways of life, the native peoples of Oceania are even more varied than they are racially. The aborigines are literally an Old Stone Age people. Their tools are

Frank Newton — FPG

Fiji islanders have dark skins and frizzy hair.

Natives of New Guinea live in a Stone Age culture.

Bips — Photo Researchers

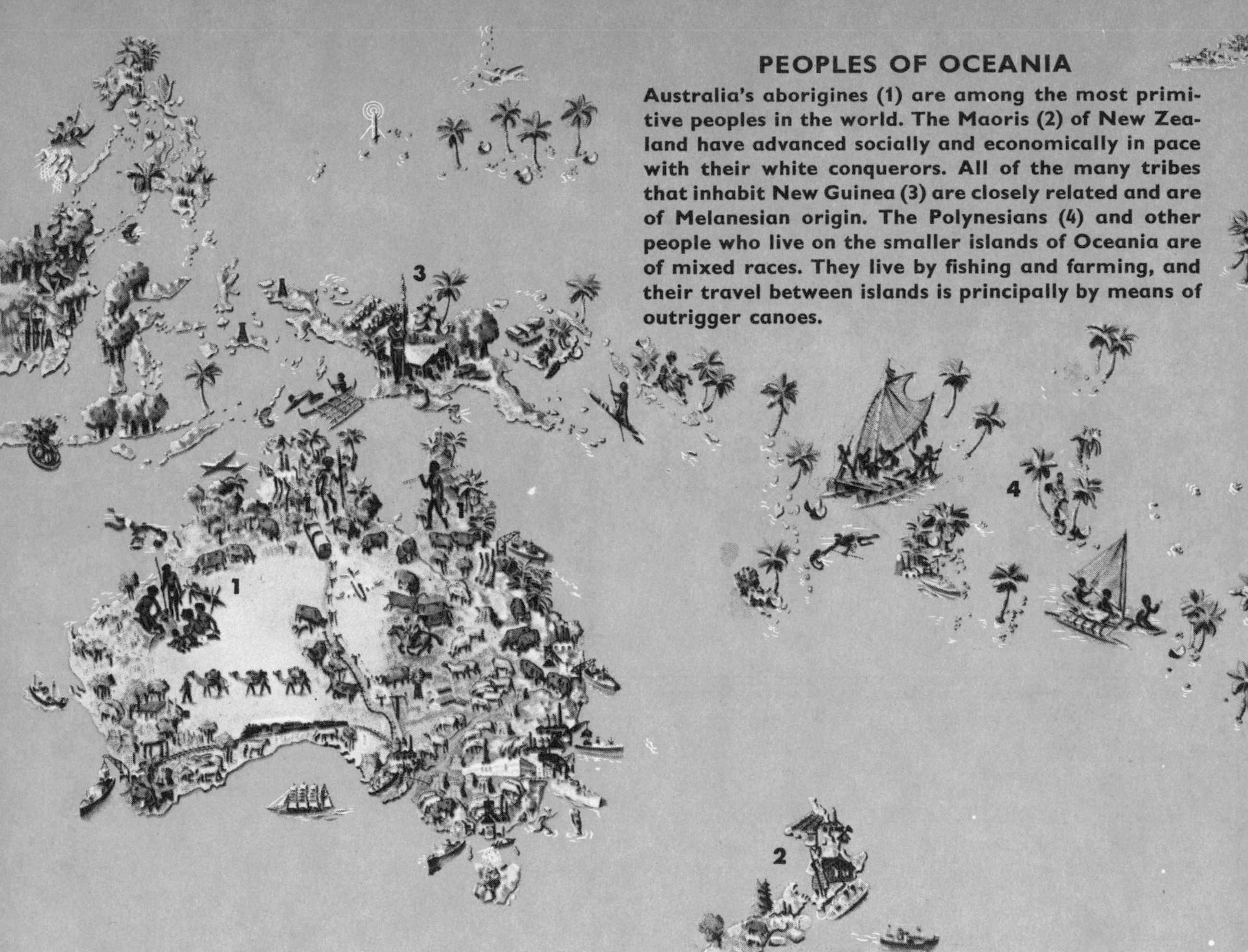

PEOPLES OF OCEANIA

Australia's aborigines (1) are among the most primitive peoples in the world. The Maoris (2) of New Zealand have advanced socially and economically in pace with their white conquerors. All of the many tribes that inhabit New Guinea (3) are closely related and are of Melanesian origin. The Polynesians (4) and other people who live on the smaller islands of Oceania are of mixed races. They live by fishing and farming, and their travel between islands is principally by means of outrigger canoes.

crudely made of stone. There is no pottery or carving, and this is the only part of the world in which the bow and arrow is unknown. People live in low domed huts or simply in wind-breaks made in hit-or-miss fashion. Government is little developed among them. However, regarding marriage and family organisation, the Australian aborigines have perhaps the most complex culture in the world. They also have rich religious ceremonies and a wealth of ideas about supernatural powers. Their art work is colourful, and full of action.

On the islands the people live chiefly through fishing and agriculture. Throughout the South Pacific coconut palms abound. These trees provide nuts for food and oil, wood for building and for fires, and leaves for thatching houses.

The science of sailing is highly developed. The Maoris of New Zealand made dugout canoes of huge size. Sometimes large boats were made by lashing several dugouts together. The outrigger canoe was invented in this area.

Europeans began to visit the Pacific islands after the voyage of Magellan in the early sixteenth century. Spanish and Portuguese sailors were followed by Dutch, French, and English. By the end of the eighteenth century Europeans had visited nearly all of the important islands. On island after island, Europeans and Americans abused the natives. The Westerners introduced new diseases, alcohol, opium, and forced labour that amounted to slavery. In some places missionaries and government officials protected the islanders and helped them. Generally whites became rich from their cruel abuse of the natives.

Australia and New Zealand have had modern histories very different from most of the Pacific islands. Both of these areas have been settled by Europeans, especially the British. The aboriginal Australians were slaughtered or driven into isolated areas; the native population of Tasmania was entirely wiped out. The Maoris, however, are today an important group in modern New Zealand. Both Australia and New Zealand are modern nations of the European type, with great cities as well as rich farming regions, though the development of Australia has been limited by the fact that most of the interior is desert.

Throughout history, men from many countries have claimed that their own people are more civilised, or even more human, than all the others. In Europe, theories of racial superiority have been with us for several centuries. An amusing illustration comes from a Chinese historian writing 2,000 years ago. 'The barbarians of the north have yellow hair, green eyes, and prominent noses and are just like monkeys from which they are descended.'

The many attempts to classify man in a scientific way began with Carolus Linnaeus (1707–1778). He divided mankind into four 'races'. These were White, Red, Yellow and Black. He also added, however, psychological and sociological notes. For example, Whites were inventive while Red Indians were governed by custom. There is, in fact, no scientific evidence that peoples vary in their average potential intelligence, personality, or temperament. If there are any differences, we can be sure that the variety within any one people is far greater than the difference between peoples.

From the idea of the many different human 'races' it is a short step to thinking of 'racial' types. A famous example is that of the Nordic – tall, long-headed and very light colouring. This name was first used to describe the people of northern Europe, among whom such features were common but certainly not universal. There are dangers in thinking in these terms and there are many illustrations. For example, in Hitler's Germany the myth of racial 'superiority', was used as an excuse to enslave and kill millions of so-called 'inferior' peoples – mainly Jews.

GEOLOGY is the study of the Earth, its history and its present form as revealed through its rocks and minerals and the forms in which they occur.

Man lives on the Earth's crust. Composed of a variety of rocks and minerals, this outer shell averages only about 20 miles thick – perhaps as much as 50 miles over high mountain ranges and less than five in deep ocean trenches. Oil wells have been drilled nearly four miles into the Earth's crust, and mine shafts have been dug about two miles deep. But these borings and diggings tell us little about what is inside the Earth, for it is about 3,900 miles from the Earth's surface to its centre. What lies beneath the Earth's crust is more of a mystery and less explored than outer space.

Studies of seismic or earthquake waves, tidal movements, and the composition of meteorites give scientists clues to what the inside of the Earth is like. The very centre, forming the Earth's core, is thought to be a ball of heavy metal – probably iron and nickel. The core's temperature is believed to be as much as 8,250 degrees centigrade (15,000 degrees Fahrenheit) and the heavy pressure due to the tremendous weight of the surrounding materials must be about 25,000 *tons* per square inch, compared to the atmospheric pressure of 15 *pounds* per square inch at sea level. The Earth's core is about 2,000 miles thick.

Surrounding the Earth's core is the mantle, about 1,800 miles thick, consisting of such elements as iron, magnesium, silicon, and oxygen. Where these have cooled near the surface they are combined to form a dense rock. Both heat and pressure are much greater in the mantle than at the surface. When disturbed, the materials that make up the mantle bend or move, although they are not in a liquid stage. They emerge from fissures or volcanoes as hot lava. Earthquake waves seem to originate in and are transmitted rapidly through the mantle.

Outside the mantle is the Earth's crust. Its principal rock is granite on the continents, although the composition varies from place to place. Over millions of years rocks that contain plant and animal remains and sediments produced from weathering have been added to this bedrock. Metamorphic rock, a third type, was produced by changes in pre-existing rocks by heat, pressure, and liquids.

Many of the rocks and minerals that make

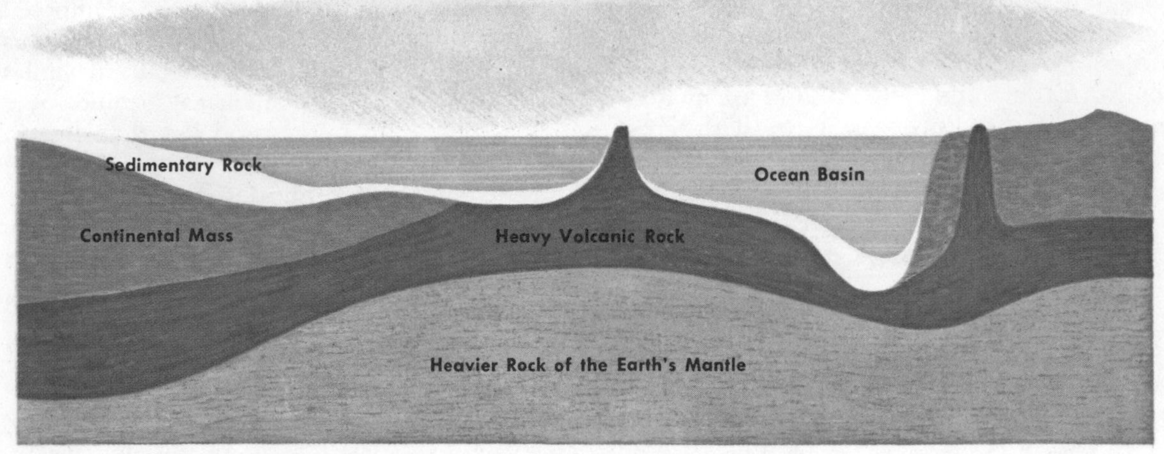

The Earth's thin crust, which overlies the mantle, is composed of many different types of rock.

up the crust of the Earth are described in separate articles in this volume. (See MINERALS; ROCKS; and Index for separate entries.)

THE EARTH CHANGES. The Earth is changing continually. Man lives such a short time that he does not see many changes in the surface of the Earth during one lifetime. Few alterations, such as those caused by volcanoes, earthquakes, floods, and landslides are sudden and spectacular enough to be seen. Other changes take thousands or even millions of years.

Two kinds of forces are active in changing the Earth: those that wear it away and those that build it up. These two, in continual action, rearrange the Earth's surface and aid in the formation of new rocks or minerals. Sometimes they alter the rocks or minerals already present; sometimes they simply move debris from one place to another and in this process may bring about the formation of new sedimentary rocks. Thus, the same forces that wear away the Earth may also build it up. Water, wind, ice, for example, are the principal agencies that decompose, wear down, and remove the rocks of the Earth's crust. In this role they are destructive agents. But where wind, water, or moving ice

Movements of the Earth's crust and the work of the forces of erosion give the surface its uneven form.

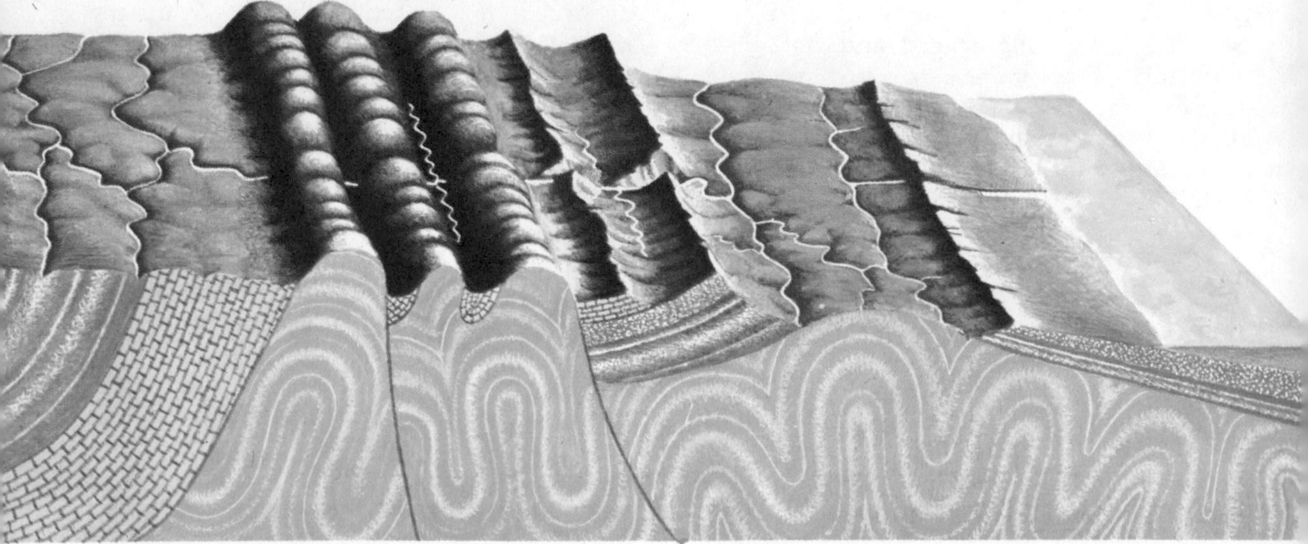

deposit rock, sand, and other debris they act as builders — constructive agents.

Wind-borne deposits include loess (glacial dust) and sand dunes. Water-carried debris forms flood plains, bars, deltas, and beds of sand, mud, and clays in lakes, swamps, and shallow ocean basins. Glacial deposits form moraines, kames, and drumlins. They dam streams and create waterfalls and lakes in which varied clays may be deposited.

The action of destructive forces reduces mountains and levels the land. The splitting action of ice freezing in the cracks in rocks and the slow erosion by stream-borne pebbles is hastened by the action of living things. Roots of plants grow in the fissures of rocks and help to break them apart, as do the acids produced by plants as they grow or when they decay. Earthworms, and other soil organisms help in breaking down rocks and forming soil.

As mountains are being worn down in one region, new mountains may be forming in another. Layers of rock, sometimes many thousands of feet thick, are elevated slowly to form plateaus. Sometimes the layers may be tilted upwards or tremendous force may fold them — crushing and breaking the more brittle rock layers. Movements of rocks along great cracks or faults is a common part of mountain building. Mountains are also built by lava flowing from volcanoes or from great vents in the Earth's crust. Or mountains may be formed by wearing away of the land, leaving resistant rocks standing high above the new surface.

WEATHERING. Rocks are weakened and broken into pieces by the process of weathering. There are two types of weathering, chemical and mechanical, and they often work together.

In chemical weathering, the elements in the rocks and minerals combine with water, carbon dioxide, and oxygen to form new minerals or are dissolved and removed in solution. For example, water and air acting on feldspar minerals form kaolinite.

Rocks are also weathered physically. Abrasion is one of the common methods. Sand and gravel rolled over and over in a current of water strike rocks and grind away pieces as they also become rounder themselves. Roots grow in cracks and lift or split rocks and minerals. The most powerful physical force is the freezing of water in the cracks in rocks. The force of water as it expands to form ice equals about one ton per square inch. Frost-wedging is an especially active and important force in high mountain country and in cold latitudes. In many cases the addition of elements in chemical weathering increases a rock's volume. As a result of this swelling, layers of rock flake off, a process

Florida News Bureau

Central Florida in the United States is covered by miles of sand deposited in shallow, ancient seas. Much of the state's citrus crop is grown here.

The rock debris in this photograph is a glacial moraine at the edge of an ice sheet in Greenland.

Rutherford Platt

Josef Muench

Erosion shaped these spectacular peaks and pinnacles in America's Bryce Canyon National Park in Utah.

called exfoliation. Several forces of weathering may be at work at the same time on a rock. A crack caused by exfoliation may be widened by the wedging effect of the roots of a growing plant. Moisture that collects in the crack freezes in winter and may split the rock apart completely.

SOILS. Soils produced by weathering cover most of the Earth's surface. Soils are portions of the crust that can support growing plants. Young soils are much like the rocks from which they came. Later, as the soils mature, they take on characters determined by the climate and the kinds of plants that have grown in them.

Soils develop three zones: the topmost portion or 'A' horizon contains remains of plants and animals and in moist regions is more or less leached by seeping ground water. The 'B' horizon has little organic material but has been enriched by materials carried down from the 'A horizon in ground water. The 'C' horizon, lowest of the three, is original weathered rock material.

Some soils are many feet thick. This depends on how rapidly the soil forms and how fast it erodes. Tundra soil, which forms at high altitudes and in polar regions where the subsoil remains frozen throughout the year, is nearly unaltered rock debris. A little further towards the equator, where rainfall is moderately heavy but evaporation limited, podsols are formed. These are well leached light-grey clay soils. In middle latitudes, soils are darker because they contain more organic materials. Known as brown earths, they merge with leached soils called red-and-yellow earths. Red-and-yellow and brown earths are the world's agricultural lands.

In tropical rain forests are very red soils (laterites) which are leached of all minerals but limonite, kaolinite, and quartz. Some are rich enough to be mined as iron ore, and the world's aluminium deposits are in laterites.

Because of the organic matter in the soil and climatic conditions, generally dry summers and frosty winters, the upper layers of the soil in some areas are black. These are known as chernozem after the Russian which means black earth. Such soils are found in southern U.S.S.R., India, Canada and the U.S.A. Desert soils are light in colour and rich in lime and other salts up to the surface. Desert soils range from powdery to gravelly. When irrigation water carries away the salts in solution, desert soils grow excellent crops.

Often the physical and chemical activities of centuries result in a layer of soil only a few inches deep. The deepest soils are about a hundred feet thick, and the average depth is a foot or so. Erosion is responsible for the removal of much of the topsoil and its deposition in the world's oceans. Man has accelerated this process through an imperfect knowledge of good agricultural methods.

Left, Tropical Red Soils are well-drained. Their colour results from a chemical action of rain and air on iron minerals. Right, Residual Soils form as the parent bedrock decays. The many types of these soils vary with the rock and with the local climate.

Left, Transported Soils develop from silt and alluvium carried by wind and deposited in valleys. Right, Northern Forest Soils are grey and acid. They form slowly under conifers in cool regions.

The soil, shown left, developed from a bedrock of limestone. Its dark 'A horizon' or topsoil is formed from the decayed remains of plants and is heavily leached by surface waters. Some of this organic material is deposited in the 'B horizon' or subsoil below. The 'C horizon' consists of partially decayed bedrock. The forest soil on the right is formed from a granite parent rock and shows similar zones. Soil continues to form by the addition of organic material at the top and by a continual breakdown of the bedrock below.

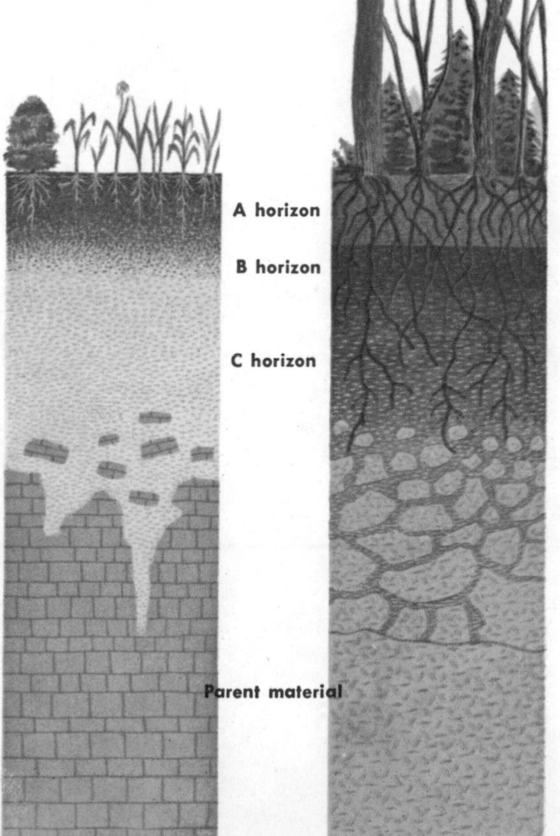

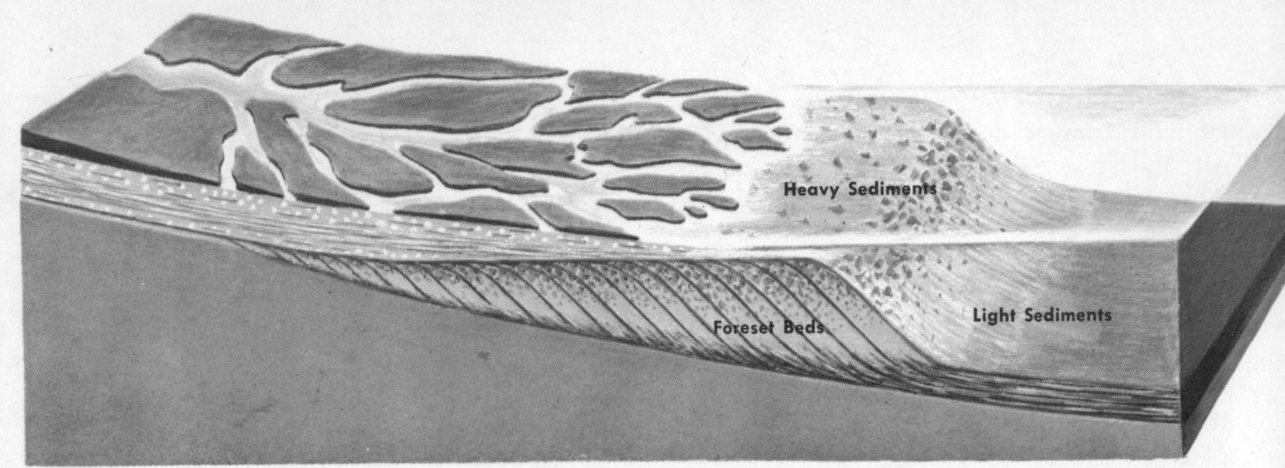

A river drops its load of sediments at its mouth as its speed is checked when it enters the ocean. Heavier sediments settle out first, then the finer silts. These triangular-shaped deposits are called deltas.

RUNNING WATER. The land is shaped largely by running water that carries away materials loosened and broken up by weathering. This is called erosion. Soft rocks weather and erode more quickly than harder or tougher rocks.

As erosion cuts down the land, hard ridges of tougher resistant rocks remain with the valleys between cut into the much softer rock.

Flat resistant layers of rock form plateaus. The great Colorado Plateau in New Mexico and Arizona is an example. Plateaus are cut away gradually as rivers and tributaries carve deep valleys and canyons. Large isolated, flat-topped remnants of plateaus are called mesas, and when the flat tops have finally been cut away, they become steep-sided buttes.

Streams drop their sediments when they slow down. These deposits form alluvial cones and fans at the foot of steep slopes. Clays are also deposited on flood plains during high water, and fine sands build natural levees at a river's edge. When a stream flows into the quiet water of a lake or the sea, the muds and sands it carries are dropped as deltas. Examples are found at the mouths of such rivers as the Ganges-Brahmaputra and the Indus in India, the Nile in Egypt, the Rhine in Belgium and Holland, the Yukon in Alaska, and the Mississippi in southern United States. Most rivers do not form deltas because their loads of silt are swept away by ocean currents that flow alongshore and across the river's mouth.

A STREAM'S CYCLE. Some of the water that falls on the land evaporates; some is absorbed by the soil and rocks; most of it moves across the surface of the land, first as brooks or rills and then as streams and rivers which cut and broaden their valleys on the way to the sea. A stream cuts downward until it reaches base level. This is sea level, but lakes or resistant rocks may serve as

The Mississippi Delta is one of the world's largest. Its

temporary base levels. As a stream nears its base level, it moves along more slowly, turning from side to side as it meanders. As it turns, the force of its current is thrown against one bank, and a cut-bank develops. Rocks and soil slide into the stream from the walls of the cut-bank and force the stream towards the opposite bank. Thus by meandering from side to side a stream widens its valley and develops a broad flood plain which becomes covered with water during high-water stages. Flood plains continue to widen and eventually merge with those of other streams to form a broad flat area called a peneplain that slopes gently to the sea. Peneplains are evidence of the old age of an area. The streams are broad and shallow and have numerous cut-off meanders that form oxbow or horseshoe lakes.

The stages in a stream's erosion cycle represent the work that has been done compared to the amount of work necessary to change the area to a peneplain. This is not related to the stream's age in years, for a stream cuts slowly through resistant rocks but rapidly through sands or clays. Also, a small

sediments are from a million-square-mile watershed.

Freeport Sulphur Co. — FLO

STAGES IN A STREAM'S CYCLE

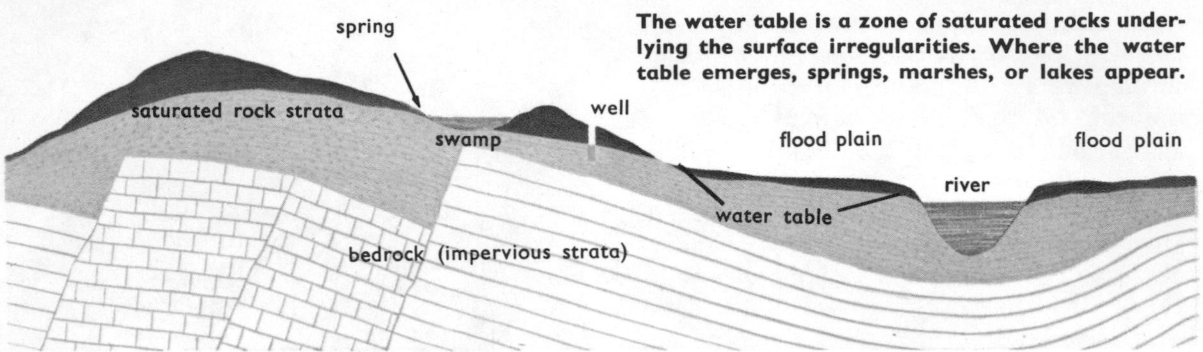

The water table is a zone of saturated rocks underlying the surface irregularities. Where the water table emerges, springs, marshes, or lakes appear.

stream does the work of erosion much less rapidly than a large stream, and in an area high above sea level there is more work to be done than in an area that is only slightly above sea level.

If a stream's erosion cycle is interrupted by a new uplift of land, the cycle commences again.

GROUND WATER. Water in the soil and in the pores and cracks of rocks below the surface is called ground water. Most ground water is rain water containing dissolved carbon dioxide and oxygen, a little is that which was trapped in the original sediments and a very small amount is water that comes up from magmas from deep inside the Earth.

The top of the ground water is the water table, which is not a flat surface but rises somewhat under hills and goes down under valleys. During wet weather the water table moves upwards; during dry weather it sinks and flattens out as the water flows slowly from higher to lower elevations. The level of lakes and permanent streams represents the water table in moist regions. Water that collects above the water table on an impervious layer of rock, such as clay or shale, for

Columbia Glacier in Alaska combines the ice from tributary glaciers to make a front 5 miles wide and 200 feet high by the time it reaches the Pacific.

example, is called a perched water table.

The amount of ground water in a region depends on the amount of rainfall and also on the porosity of the rock. Ground water usually moves less than 10 feet a day. The rate depends on the slope of the water table and also on the nature of the rock or soil. Movement will be more rapid in a sandy soil than through a clay.

Springs occur where the water table comes to the surface. Artesian wells are those in which the water is under pressure and rises towards the surface when the impervious overlying rock is broken. Water tables at or near the surface also form marshes or swamps.

As water trickles down towards the water table through cracks in limestone, it gradually dissolves the rock. The solution process stops only when all of the carbon dioxide in the water is used up. Solution holes are openings that have been formed by dissolving of the rocks. If the walls slump or the ceilings collapse, open sink holes are created. Caves are formed when the water dissolves channels that are more or less horizontal to the surface. Caves may extend for miles and may have several levels. Carlsbad Cavern in New Mexico in the United States, has several levels and also the largest known cavern room — 4,000 feet long, 600 feet wide, and 300 feet high.

GLACIERS. Moving bodies of ice are called glaciers. They are formed when more snow falls over a succession of winters than can be melted during the following summers. As a consequence, the snow accumulates year after year. Snow that melts partially and then freezes again becomes granular. This granular snow, called névé, is squeezed into a compact mass by the pressure of the ice above. Water from melting ice and snow seeps down and refreezes the névé, changing the grains into solid ice. After many years the accumulation of ice becomes so heavy that it overcomes friction and begins to move, then glaciers move down slopes or are squeezed out at their base by the weight of ice above.

Valley glaciers act very much like rivers of ice. They deepen and carve the valleys and smooth rugged rocks. Ice freezes in the cracks in the mountain wall and pulls out chunks of rock when the glacier moves away. In this manner the glacier eats into the mountain. Rocks within the glacier scour the valley floor.

US Navy: American Geographical Society

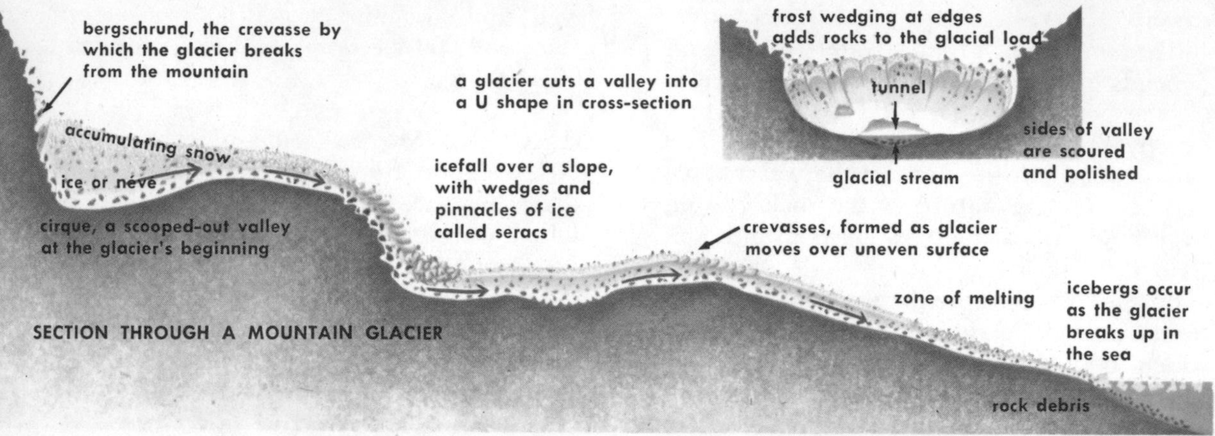

Valley glaciers scour off the ends of the ridges between valleys and leave sharply cut spurs of land. If glaciers attack a mountain on several sides, they leave a sharp-pointed peak or horn. If glaciers are at work on both sides of a mountain range, they create a jagged, irregular ridge known as an arete.

Moraines, sometimes called till or drift, are deposited by the glacial ice when it melts. The debris in moraines ranges in size from fine clay to blocks many feet across. The farthest advance of the glacier is marked by a terminal moraine.

Continental glaciers form in large areas where it is warm enough for abundant snowfall yet cold enough to prevent complete melting of the snow in summers. After the ice is piled high enough, it begins to push out in all directions from its base and in the course of centuries may spread over vast areas.

Continental glaciers that formed during Pleistocene times must have been more than 10,000 feet thick.

In Europe the continental glacier was mainly centred in Scandinavia. Ice spread over northern Russia on the east, northern Germany on the south, and westward over the North Sea, England, Scotland, and Ireland. Not all of England was ever covered by the ice. Very approximately it did not come further south than a line drawn from the Thames estuary to the Bristol Channel. Most of Canada was covered by glacial ice that extended southwards to Long Island, which is a terminal moraine. The southern limit of the glaciers is marked by the Ohio and Missouri rivers, whose valleys were dug along the ice front. Only minor areas of continental glaciation developed in Siberia where there was less snowfall. In the Southern Hemisphere, glaciation during the Pleistocene epoch was confined to valleys (see ICE AGES). Most of Greenland and all of Antarctica are still covered by ice caps, and there is a small remnant in central Norway.

Under the ice centres the glaciers first picked up loose materials and then scoured the land to bedrock, leaving striations,

Winds move sand dunes five or six feet a year, covering buildings or trees in their path.

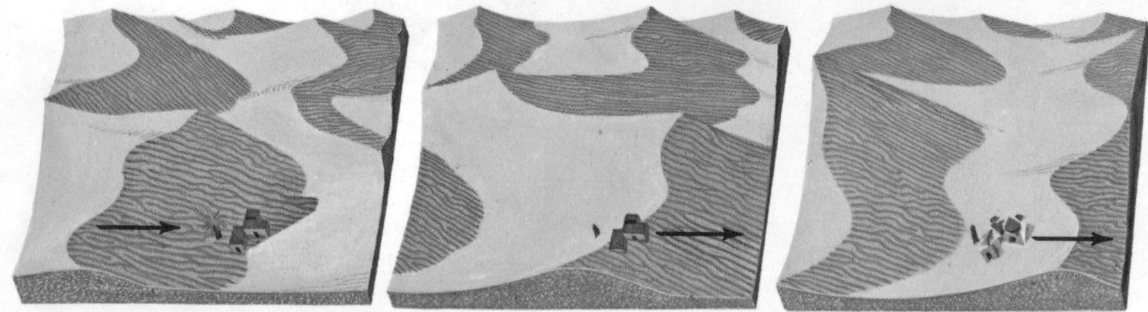

scratches, and glacial pavements that show today after 10,000 years of exposure to weathering. The ice dug more deeply into soft rock and formed valleys. Hills facing the advancing ice were cut down to gentle slopes, and their lee sides were sheered by the moving ice, making them steep. The general effect of continental glaciation during the Ice Ages was to smooth the land, by scraping the mountains into the valleys.

THE WIND. Sand and silt are made of particles small enough to be blown by the wind. Very fine materials may be suspended in the air as a dust cloud. Fine sand is rolled or bounced along the surface. Left behind are coarser sands, heavier gravels, and bare rock.

Sand piles up in dunes when the velocity of the wind is checked. Transverse dunes, formed at right angles to the prevailing wind, are found where there is a large amount of sand and the velocity of the wind is moderate — 5 to 10 miles per hour. In time, or with higher wind velocities (10 to 20 miles per hour), longitudinal dunes form parallel to the prevailing wind. Barchans, crescent-shaped dunes with their convex side facing the wind, rae created if the amount of sand

Harold Wanless

Winds cross-bedded desert sands millions of years ago consequently forming 'frozen dunes' in America's Utah sandstone.

is small and the winds moderate. U-shaped dunes, their concave side facing the wind, develop from a transverse dune when the wind becomes concentrated at one place and digs a hole, called a blow-out.

Sands form dunes along shore lines of

Active volcanoes, such as Izalco in El Salvador, are builders, adding lava and ash to the Earth's surface. Lava plateaus may cover thousands of square miles.

David-Forbert — Shostal

Mountains may form when lateral pressures cause a buckling of rocks in the Earth's crust, as in these folds making Mt. Timpanagos, Utah, U.S.A.

Harold Wanless

Bob and Ira Spring

Crater Lake in Oregon, in the United States, was created about 12,000 years ago when the volcano Mt. Mazama collapsed, leaving a saucer-shaped crater or caldera 6 miles long, 4 miles wide, and 4,000 feet deep. Wizard Island, in the centre, is the cone of a recent volcano.

lakes and seas. Dunes also occur in continental interiors where very soft sandstones have been weathered to sand or where sand is blown from dried-up river channels. Sand is most abundant in deserts where all kinds of rocks have been weathered into small pieces. The great deserts in the Northern Hemisphere are the Sahara, Arabian, Gobi, Takla Makan, and Sonoran; in the Southern Hemisphere, the Kalahari, the 'Dead Heart' of Australia, and the Atacama.

Sand dunes migrate 5 or 6 feet a year with a rolling motion. The sand is blown up to the top on the windward side and rolls down the lee side. If the climate becomes more moist, vegetation grows over the dune's surface and stops its migration.

Sand dunes make up a very small per cent of a desert's total area, however. Most sand in deserts is transported by running water, for when rains come in deserts, large volumes of water fall in a short period of time.

The most common type of oasis in a desert is the area next to rivers that flow into the dry areas from rainier regions. Most desert rivers disappear quickly by seeping into the sand. A few rivers are large enough to flow completely through the desert, as do the Nile, Tigris-Euphrates, and Colorado rivers.

Loess is silt-sized particles carried by wind. It has been deposited in thick layers east of the central Asian deserts in China and also in the United States over large areas of Iowa, Missouri, and Illinois. Eroded loess gives the yellow colour to the waters of the Yellow River of China and the Yellow Sea.

Unlike other loose materials, loess forms gullies with vertical walls. These gullies develop quickly when farming exposes the land to erosion. Loess deposits form the bluffs along the east side of the Mississippi River valley in Tennessee and Louisiana.

Mountain making may involve complex movements in the Earth's crust. Some are formed by a squeezing or folding pressure, others by a shifting or tilting of great blocks of rock. Buttes and mesas remain where erosion has removed most of the rock laid down in flat, sedimentary layers.

Mountains formed by Folding and Thrust-faulting

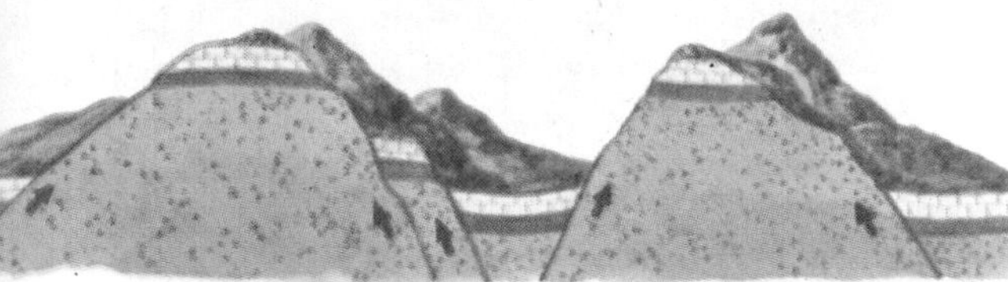

Mountains formed by Block-faulting

Mountains formed by Erosion

MOUNTAINS. Mountains are land masses that stand above the surrounding landscape. They often have steep sides and a small summit. Mountains are formed in three principal ways: as cones built up as volcanoes, by the erosion of fault blocks (formed by vertical shifts of the Earth's crust) and as crumpled or folded layers of rock.

Volcanoes are formed by an outpouring of fragments and molten lava. Lava may spread over great areas and form broad plateaus before solidifying. The Deccan of India is a lava plateau.

Each of the Hawaiian Islands is formed from a piling-up of lava. These are known as shield volcanoes. Thicker lava piles up in and near the opening from which it comes. Finally the pressure of the magma below blows away the material violently enough to shatter it and scatter it in all directions as volcanic blocks, lapilli, ash, and dust.

The most common type of volcano is built

Tremendous pressures pushed sedimentary rock strata to the surface to form the Front Range of the Rocky Mountains in Colorado, in the United States.

State of Colorado

of alternate layers of lava and fragmental materials. This is called a composite cone, and volcanoes of this type are found all over the world. Famous ones are Vesuvius of Italy; Fujiyama, Japan; Mt Mayon, Philippines; Cerebus, Antarctica; Popocatepetl, Mexico; Mt Shasta, California; Mt Hood, Oregon. Cinder cones are small volcanoes with steep sides. They are composed almost entirely of fragmental materials. Crater Lake in Oregon is an example of a volcano that blew away its top leaving a large crater in the centre. This type of crater is called a caldera. Another caldera is Monte Somma at Naples, Italy, which exploded in A.D.79 burying the city of Pompeii. Then it began rebuilding, and Mt Vesuvius rose in the crater.

Other mountains are formed by an uplifting of layers of segments of rock. These are called fault-block mountains. Commonly, because of tilting in the uplift, one side is steep and the other is gently sloped. The eastern slopes of the Sierra Nevada Mountains in the United States, for example, drop sharply nearly two miles to the desert floor, while the western side slopes much less steeply towards the sea.

The most common Earth movement forming mountains is folding. This takes place when pressures in the Earth's crust cause the layers of rock to fold and buckle and lift above the surrounding land. The Scottish Highlands were formed in this manner. Their cycle is typical of folded mountains. It began when a large trough of land, called a geosyncline, sank below sea level. Sediments from adjoining land masses were deposited in the shallow waters of the trough. Their weight caused the floor to sink slowly, and the sinking continued for millions of years as thousands of feet of sediment piled up in the basin. It stopped only when the surrounding lands were eroded to base level.

When the crust of the Earth was squeezed in the folding process, the soft sediments in the trough were a weak place, and they arched upwards in simple and complex folds. Mountains were formed as the more resistant rocks were left standing while the softer sediments eroded. In some areas the crumpling has been complicated by later folding and faulting as in various areas of Scotland and Wales.

Mountains may be formed, too, when the surrounding land is eroded away, leaving resistant rocks standing high above the surrounding landscape. Buttes, mesas, and plateaus of western United States are peaks or mountains that were formed in this manner.

The heat and pressure of mountain building often forms metamorphic rocks — changing shale into slate, limestone into marble, and granite into gneiss. Long-buried rocks and minerals are brought to the surface. These changes in the Earth's crust — the building of mountains and their wearing away to level again — give a landscape its character.

Depth soundings reveal peaks, ridges and plains — a continuous variation in the bottom of the sea. This profile was made by a ship that travelled the course shown by the red line, from St. Augustine, Florida, via Bermuda to the Mid-Atlantic Ridge.

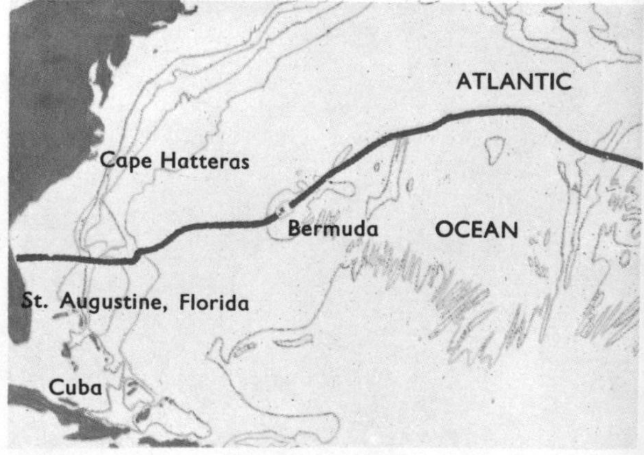

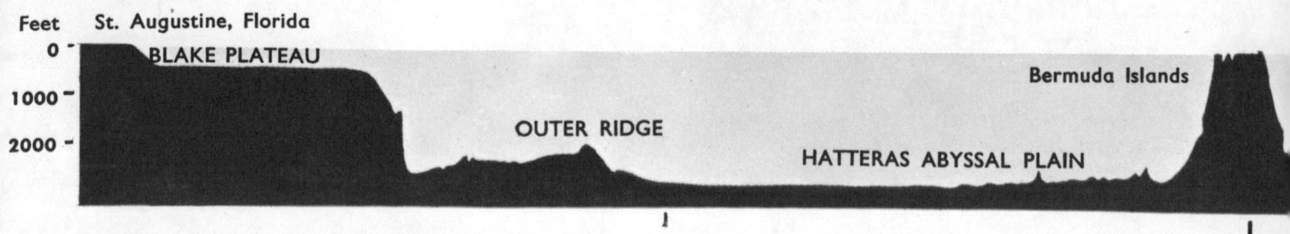

OCEANS. Most minerals taken from the land eventually are carried by rivers to the sea. There they are deposited as sediments on the bottom or are dissolved in the water. Other minerals are produced in the sea by the plants and animals that live there. Animals with shells, such as coral, oysters, and clams, deposit large quantities of lime, as do some kinds of algae. Oceans are the main source of bromine, salt, and magnesium. Many mineral deposits on present land areas of the Earth's crust represent the location of ancient seas. Deposits of salt, borax, and gypsum now obtained from the land were laid down in the past in shallow seas.

In the future we will probably convert salt water of the sea into fresh water and will turn to the oceans more and more to obtain minerals and metals as these resources are exhausted from the land. Some substances dissolved in sea water can be extracted chemically. Magnesium is now produced commercially in this manner. Manganese, iron and other metals deposited in ores on the sea floor may in the future be mined or dredged, and large amounts of oil are obtained now from off-shore wells.

An oceanographer on the Canadian HMS *Oshawa* lowers a corer into the sea to get a sample of the bottom sediments to study the composition.

Francis P. Shepard

Using this corer, scientists on the Swedish Deep Sea Expedition sampled sediments in the open Atlantic where sediments deposited are as much as 12,000 feet thick.

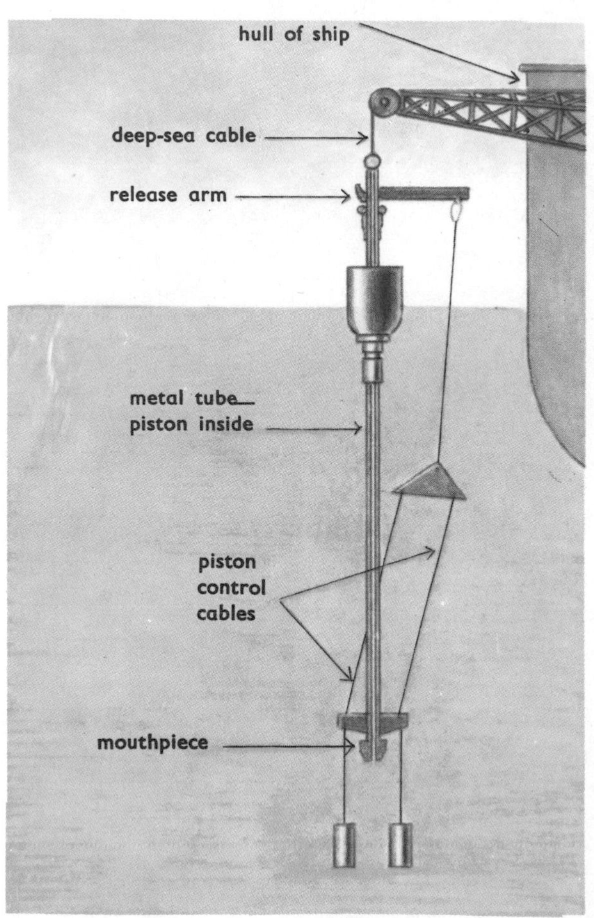

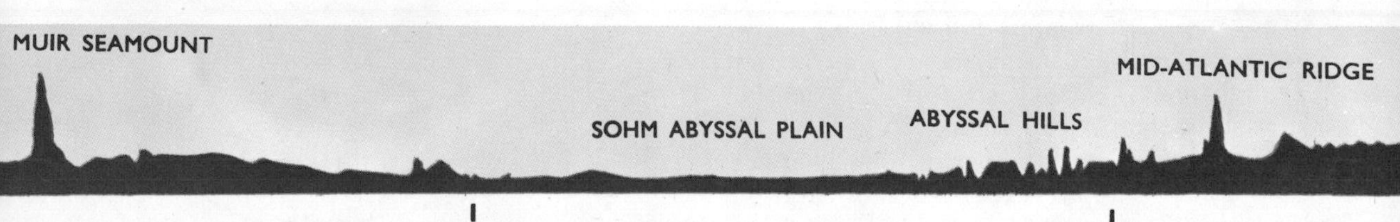

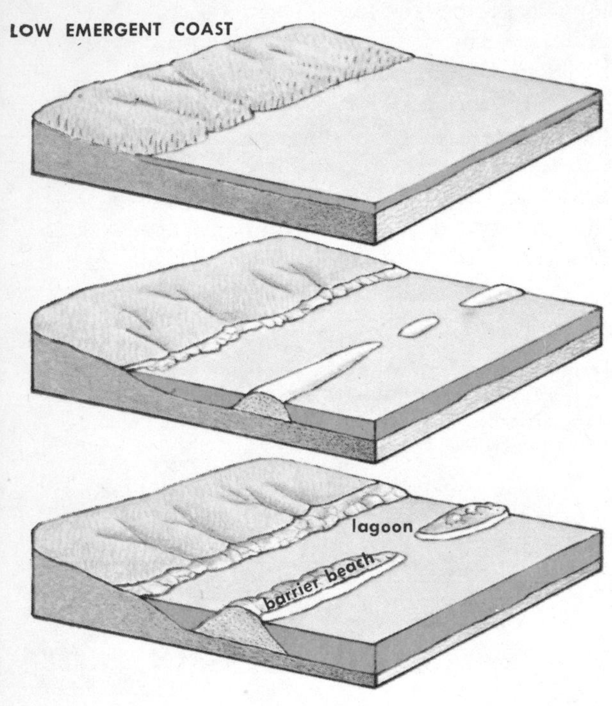

Seas are divided into distinct zones. The beach is the sandy or gravelly area above high tide. The area covered by high tide and exposed at low tide is called the foreshore, and from it a gently sloping, smooth continental shelf extends into the sea as much as 100 miles and to depths of about 400 feet. Most of the loose material eroded from the land is deposited on the continental shelf. The bottom drops off steeply at the continental shelf to the abyssal zone, which makes up most of the oceans with depths of thousands of feet.

Submarine canyons, with rock walls and tributaries but submerged under hundreds or several thousand feet of water, cut through the outer margin of continental shelves. Narrow steep-walled troughs in the abyssal zone are called trenches or deeps. Near the Philippine Islands in the Pacific is a trench nearly seven miles down. This is the Mindanao Deep, the deepest known spot in the ocean. Other deep trenches are the Bartlett Trough near Puerto Rico and the Aleutian Trench in the North Pacific.

Cores taken from the ocean floor in quiet, deep areas of the sea reveal much of what the sea floor is made of in the depths. Far from shore, sedimentary deposits are limited and thin layers in the cores represent long periods of geologic time.

Waves continually wear away the land. Along steep shores, they form narrow beaches with a wave-cut bench stretching out under the water as a ledge. Along gently sloping shores the waves break before reaching the shore because of friction on the bottom, churning up the sand and moving it towards the shore.

Shore currents help the waves in their endless task. When there are headlands and the general drift of the material is along the shore, spits and bars will form. A spit terminates in open water and may be straight or have a hooked end. A good example of the latter is Spurn Head. Barrier spits are well developed on the east coast. The outflow of both the Yare and Alde rivers has been diverted for a considerable distance to the south. The most famous bar in the British Isles is Chesil Beach which stretches for more than sixteen miles along the Dorset coast.

In time an uneven shore tends to become straightened by the actions of the waves and currents. The headlands are hardest hit by the waves while at the same time the bays

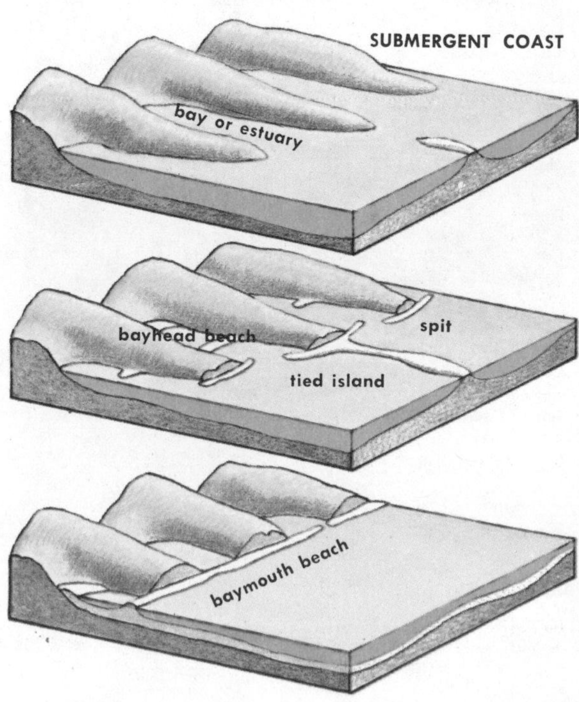

Frank Newton — FPG Leon Deller — Monkmeyer

The aerial view above shows coral reefs fringing a tropical island in the South Pacific. Left is an atoll, coral islands surrounding a lagoon.

tend to fill with sand that is deposited by the slowing of the waves caused by the beach.

In shallow, warm seas, such as parts of the Pacific and Indian Oceans, the Gulf of Mexico and around some of the islands of the West Indies, coral polyps attach themselves to the submerged rocks and build fringing reefs that are in contact with the shore. If conditions permit, for coral growth the water must be clear to allow the sunlight to penetrate and always above 20 degrees centigrade (68 degrees Fahrenheit), the reef grows upwards as well as outwards and forms an offshore barrier reef with a lagoon between it and the land. Circular reefs around a central lagoon where an island has submerged form a ring of coral called an atoll. (See CORAL REEFS; SEAS.)

GERANIUMS are two distinct but related groups of flowering plants that belong to the same family. One group of geraniums is referred to by the genus name *Pelargonium*. Many beautiful cultivated varieties have been developed from these wild plants of South Africa.

Pelargonium geraniums rightly deserve to

The ocean bottom has ridges, valleys, mountains, and plains, similar to landscapes seen above the water.

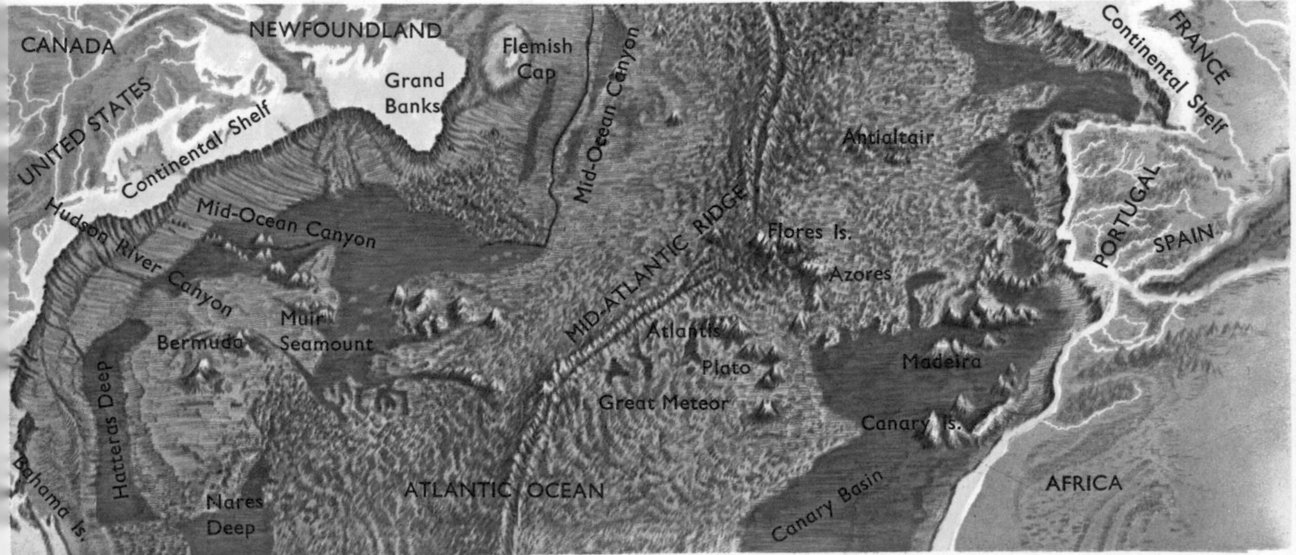

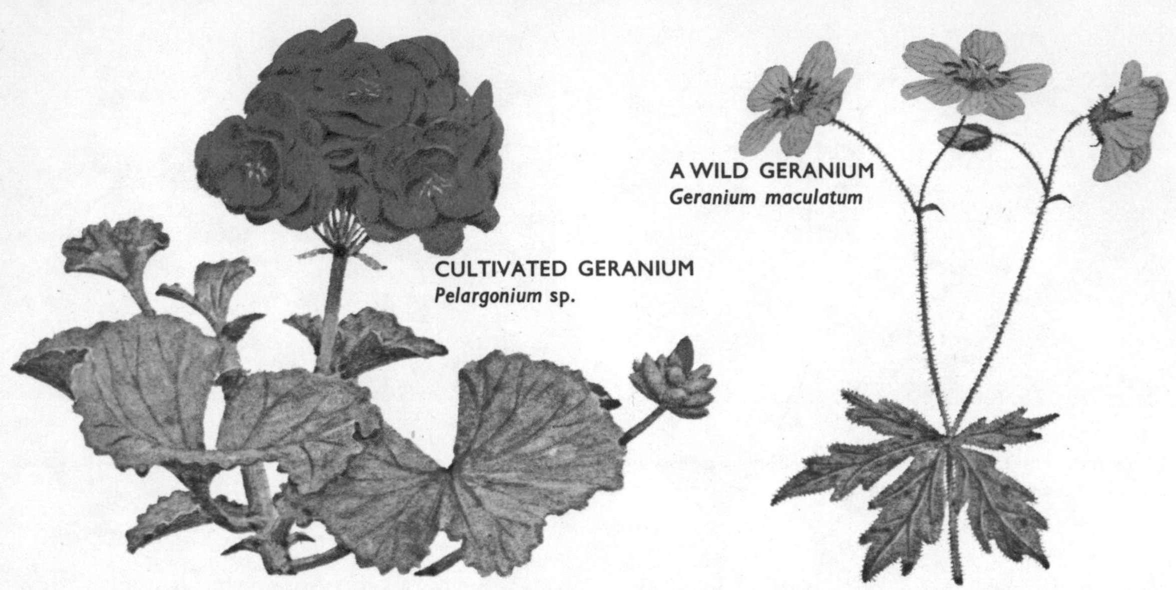

Cultivated geraniums are easily propagated by root cuttings and grow well in pots or in window boxes. If kept warm, they bloom all year. Wild geraniums are common spring flowers of open woods.

be one of our most popular cultivated flowers. They have bright, beautiful blossoms and attractive, scented leaves. They bloom in summer, but if the climate is warm, they will bloom all year round. The flowers are white, pink, or red. *Pelargonium* geraniums grow easily from cuttings.

The common Zonal Geranium *(Pelargonium hortortum)*, which has unusual colour patterns in its leaves, is the best known of this group. In northern areas it is grown as a potted house plant. More attractive is the Martha Washington Geranium *(Pelargonium domesticum)* with its large two-coloured flowers. The Ivy Geranium *(Pelargonium peltatum)* has shiny leaves and a vine-like habit. Several of these geraniums have leaves marked with interesting colour patterns. Most have scent glands, and some, like the Lemon Rose Geranium *(Peltatum limoneum)*, are especially fragrant.

The other group of geraniums, most of which are wild, are the true geraniums. Their common name is the same as their scientific name — *Geranium*, e.g. our common Herb Robert *(Geranium robertianum)*. Other smaller, wild geraniums are often weeds of pasture fields and gardens. The flowers usually have five petals and ten stamens. The colours vary from pink, lavender, blue and purple to white.

The lowest blooms in a gladiolus spike open first, then those directly above. The last to open are those at the top.

GLADIOLUS is a scientific name (a genus) that has become a common name. *Gladiolus* means dagger or sword in Latin and describes the swordlike leaves.

Each flower has three petals and three sepals united into a coloured tube at the base. Around this is a green sheath.

Gladioli originated in South Africa, and the wild forms there are quite different from the large-flowered, frilled, and colourful varieties that we know today.

They are easy to grow. The corms are planted 3 to 6 inches deep in spring, and with adequate watering they soon sprout. Corms can be bought in selected colours and in rainbow mixtures.

GLAUCONITE, a complex hydrated potassium-iron-aluminium silicate, is an olive-green mineral occurring as granules in sandstones, making the so-called 'green sands'. It originates under marine conditions, probably from an alteration of biotite or of sediments rich in iron. Glauconite is found in rocks of all ages but most plentifully in rocks of the Cretaceous period. It is worked as a source of potassium in the U.S.A. and U.S.S.R.

GNEISS (pronounced *nice*) is a banded metamorphic rock formed from granites, other coarse-grained igneous rocks, and also sedimentary rocks. Pressure and heat, such as occur during mountain building, change these rocks into gneiss. Some gneisses may develop when the squeezing of a magma forces its minerals into parallel bands. Injection gneisses were formed by the instrusion of a fluid magma between the thin layers of another rock.

Gneiss is a rock containing large grains of quartz, feldspar, and mica. The common varieties of gneiss are given names that refer either to their origin, as in *granite* gneiss and *injection* gneiss; to their composition, as in *biotite* gneiss and *muscovite* gneiss; or to their structure, as in *augen* gneiss. Augen gneiss has prominent minerals or mineral aggregates spotted throughout the rock. The lens-like shapes are stretched in parallel formation and the grain of the rock weaves and swirls around them like the grain in wood.

MUSCOVITE GNEISS — GRANITE GNEISS

HORNBLENDE GNEISS — INJECTION GNEISS

Gneisses are common metamorphic rocks found all over the world. The cores of the Himalayas are thought to be gneiss. Outcrops can be seen in Scotland. Many granite buildings and monuments are actually constructed of granite gneisses.

Gneiss does not take a fine polish, but because of its pleasing patterns, gneiss may be used in building.

Harold Wanless

Scottish Field

A prospector searches for some of the small quantities of gold which can be found even in the Scottish and Welsh mountains.

GOLD has been cherished for thousands of years, and the search for gold has led Man to all parts of the Earth. Most gold is found in nuggets, or grains. Soft and easily shaped, the native metal is golden-yellow, as is its streak. Gold occurs widely in hydrothermal veins associated with igneous rocks. When veins containing gold weather, the heavy metal may be left as a residue or carried away and deposited elsewhere as a placer deposit. Sometimes it is found as rounded masses called nuggets. One found in Australia in the nineteenth century, and called the Welcome Stranger nugget, was worth £10,000. The gold tellurides are Sylvanite, found as silver-white plates or granular masses; Calaverite, occuring as brass-yellow granular or bladed masses with a pale yellow streak; and Petzite, in steel-grey or iron black compact masses; and Nagyagite.

Nearly 90 per cent of the world's gold is in storage in government reserves. It stabilises the paper money used in trade. The purity of gold is expressed in parts per thousand and is referred to as 'fineness'. Gold with 20 per cent impurities has a fineness of 800. The purity of gold in the jewellery trade is designated by carats. Pure gold, for example, is 24K (carat). Most gold is alloyed with copper or other metals. Gold used for jewellery, for example, is 14K. Dental gold is about 22K. Gold-filled jewellery is made by placing a sheet of copper between sheets of 10 or 14 carat gold and pressing it together under rollers until it becomes a single sheet of the desired thickness. The sheets are then cut or stamped into the shape needed for the jewellery to be manufactured. Some metals are gold plated by placing them in a solution of gold chloride. Gold leaf is made by pounding sheets of gold between 'gold beater's skins'. An ounce of refined gold can be pounded into 100 square feet of gold leaf which is used for stamping titles on book covers, for gilding the edges of book pages, for the gilt in churches and other buildings, and for statues. The different colours of gold in jewellery are made by adding alloys: white gold consists of 15 per cent nickel or 10 per cent palladium; green gold, 70 per cent silver; red gold, 50 per cent copper; blue gold, 25 per cent iron. Gold lace is made by winding very fine gold wire around silk thread. Ruby glass is a lead or barium glass with 0.1 per cent gold.

In hard-rock gold mining the ore is crushed and the gold recovered by mixing it with mercury or dissolving it in a cyanide or a chlorine solution. Placer gold is usually

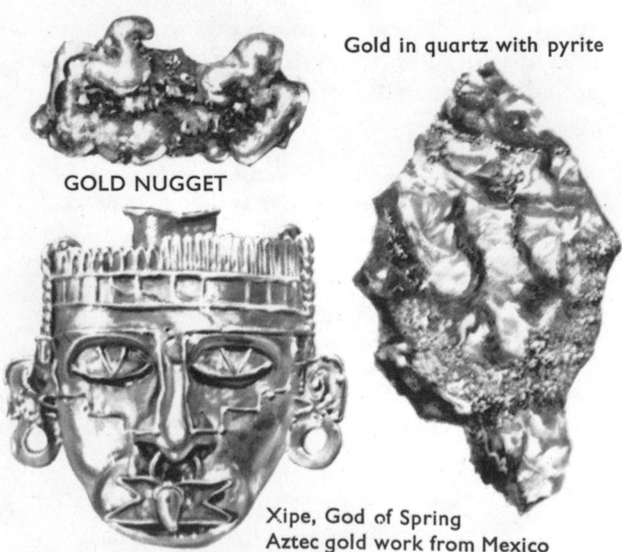

Gold in quartz with pyrite

GOLD NUGGET

Xipe, God of Spring
Aztec gold work from Mexico

GOLD CRYSTAL
0.1 in.

GOLD ORE

Some granite quarries have been cut 350 feet deep. The rock is cut with drills and sawed into blocks weighing several tons.

Rock of Ages Corp., Barre, Vt.

recovered by panning or sluicing to wash away lighter materials.

South Africa, the U.S.S.R., and Canada are the world's leading gold producers. Other important producers are Malaya, the Phillippines, Australia, Ghana, Congo, Rhodesia, Guyana, Chile, and Peru. In the United States, South Dakota, Utah, California, and Alaska are the major producers. Very small deposits of gold can be found in some rivers of the United Kingdom, and gold has been mined in Wales and Scotland. Elizabeth II's wedding ring is made of gold from a mine near Dolgellau, Merionethshire.

GRANITE is a coarse-grained igneous rock; its interlocking grains and crystals are usually uniform throughout. Some granites have small grains. Feldspar and quartz are the most common minerals in granite. Often micas, hornblende, or other minerals are present. Biotite granite and hornblende granite are so-called because they contain noticeable quantities of these minerals. When some crystals are larger than others, the rock is called porphyritic granite; if the larger crystals are numerous, the rock is

Granite is usually formed of about 60 per cent feldspar and 30 per cent quartz. The remainder consists of either mica or hornblende.

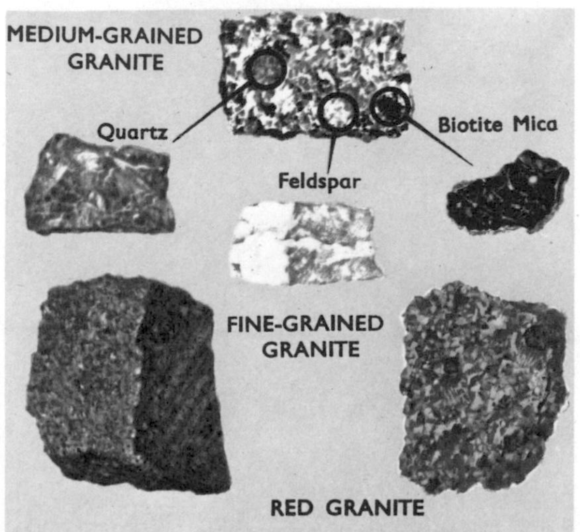

called granite porphyry. Large crystals occur because most granites formed from magmas that cooled slowly beneath the Earth's surface. The crystals could grow quite large before the entire mass solidified.

Most granites appear in such instrusive formations as batholiths and laccoliths. There are, however, large masses of granite that show no displacement or pushing aside of the surrounding country rocks. One explanation for these formations is that some sedimentary rock may have melted and later solidified as granite. Where sedimentary rocks show a complete graduation through schists and migmatites (metamorphic rocks) to unquestioned granites, this appears probable. Another explanation is that such deposits were formed by granitisation. This is the invasion of rock by granitic materials that gradually replace its original minerals. Proof of this process is found in formations where there is a gradual increase in the number and size of feldspar and quartz crystals surrounding a granite mass. At first a few isolated crystals appear, then larger and larger ones. Finally the whole mass becomes granite with only vague traces of the original rock.

Feldspars in granites contribute to their normal pink or light grey colour. Quartz, which is usually colourless, adds a glassy lustre or sometimes a white or red tinge. Dark-green grains indicate the presence of hornblende and black or white flakes are mica.

Few rocks are as strong or widely used as granite. An average granite block can withstand a pressure of 20,000 pounds per square inch. Granites are excellent for buildings and monuments. Their colours are pleasing, and they take a high polish. Granites are not fire resistant, however; they crack, flake, and crumble under great heat. Syenite is more satisfactory in this respect, for it contains no quartz — the weakening agent.

Granite forms three well-developed sets of joints. Two are nearly vertical, and the third horizontal. The size of blocks that can be quarried is determined by the spacing of these joints. Granites occur throughout the world — from cores of mountains to masses once buried deep under stratified rocks and now exposed at the surface.

France is the most important wine producing country in the world. No other country can rival her in the variety and abundance of her vines.

Phot. J. Niepce—Rapho

GRAPES (*Vitis and Muscadinia* spp). Old World grapes are believed to have originated in the area of the Caspian and Black seas, for grape seeds have been found in ancient Egyptian tombs and the earliest known Hebrew writings refer to grape wine. The native American species grew wild and in such abundance that Norwegian explorers called the new-found land Vinland.

Early settlers in the United States tried to introduce Old World grapes for wine making, but the East Coast climate was too cold and wet. Spanish colonists succeeded in introducing European varieties to Mexico, New Mexico, and California, where the dry growing season and mild winters resemble more closely the climate of the Mediterranean area. Today many European grape growers propagate their vineyards by grafting the desired varieties onto rootstocks of hardy American varieties of grapes.

Each of the many varieties is grown for one specific use, and may be classified accordingly. The categories are those of

The Stark Delicious is a superior table grape.

FORD ALMANAC, 1958

wine grape, table grape, raisin grape, and sweet juice grape. While any variety is satisfactorv for each of these purposes, each one has its best use.

Wine grapes are mainly of European derivation, and are marketed under the name of the wine rather than the name of the grape.

Home made wines are becoming popular in this country. The method for grape wine making is very easy and the equipment inexpensive.

Table grapes may be of European stock, but American varieties are also popular.

Raisin grapes include Thompson Seedless and Muscat.

GRAPHITE is a soft, black mineral formed as the end product of the metamorphism of plant or animal remains. Small amounts of carbon are also found in granite pegmatite, syenite, and basalt, where they are believed to have originated from gases formed when the magma intruded a sediment containing carbon. Like diamond, the hardest of the minerals, graphite is pure carbon. It may occur as crystals spread through rocks that originally were carbonaceous sediments. The heat of metamorphism caused the carbon particles to migrate to one another, building graphite crystals and removing the black colour from the surrounding rock. Graphite that occurs in bedded layers was originally a bed of peat which metamorphosed through coal to graphite. When found in veins, the carbon is probably from surrounding rocks.

Graphite's principal use is for the inside of moulds in foundries and crucibles because of its resistance to high temperatures and its chemical inertness. It helps prevent metal from sticking to the moulds. Pure graphite is an excellent lubricant, either alone or in oil, and is used also as a pigment or polish on metal surfacs. Carbon electrodes are made of artificial graphite, as is the graphite used in atomic piles to slow down neutrons. Graphite is found in Austria, Germany, Italy, England, Norway, Ceylon, Malagasy, Ontario, Mexico, Korea and in several states of the U.S.A.

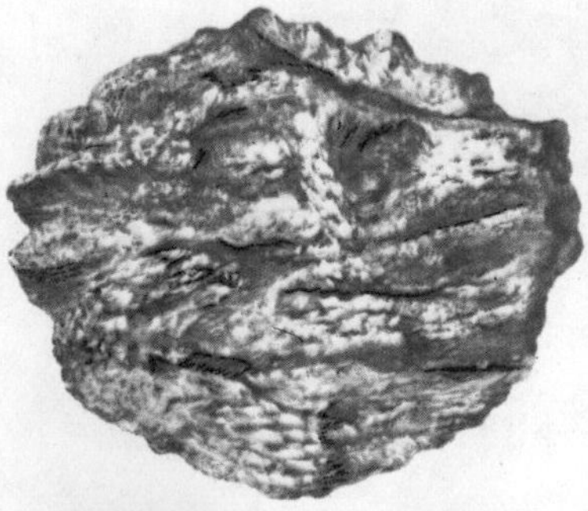

MASSIVE GRAPHITE

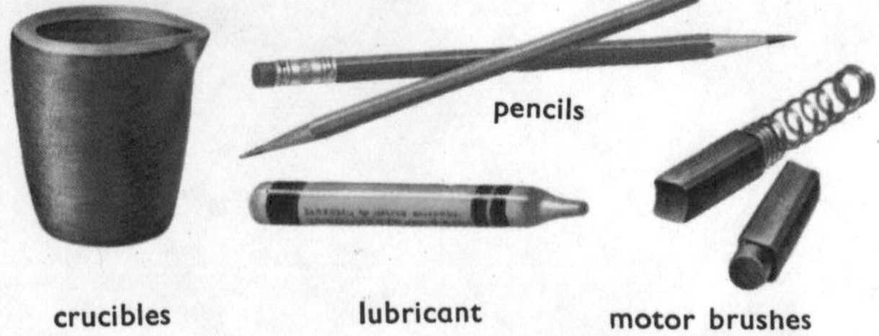

Some of the many uses of Graphite

pencils

crucibles

lubricant

motor brushes

GRASSES, of the large Gramineae family, are among the most widely distributed and most useful plants known to man. There are several thousand species, including cereals or grains, many forage crops, ornamental grasses, bamboos, and sugar cane. Even wild grasses are valuable forage for wild and domesticated animals.

All grasses have similar structure. Their stems are usually hollow, except at joints or nodes. A few such as maize, have solid stems. Leaves of most grasses consist of two parts – a sheath and blade. The sheath is often quite long and surrounds the stem, thus protecting tender tissues located just above each node or joint. The blade is commonly long and narrow and has parallel veins. Many grasses have flowers grouped together to form a long finger-like structure called a spike. Each spike is composed of numerous groups of small flowers called spikelets. Some grasses, instead of producing spikes, produce branched clusters of flowers. The seeds or fruits of grasses are called grains and are mature ovaries. Many are tufted with hairs or have wings and are blown easily by the wind or float in water. Grasses also spread by runners from their roots.

Cereals of grains are a basic food, and include such grasses as wheat, rice, oats, barley, rye, maize, sorghum, and millets.

Both wild and cultivated grasses are important forage and hay crops. (Forage crops are those consumed without harvesting;

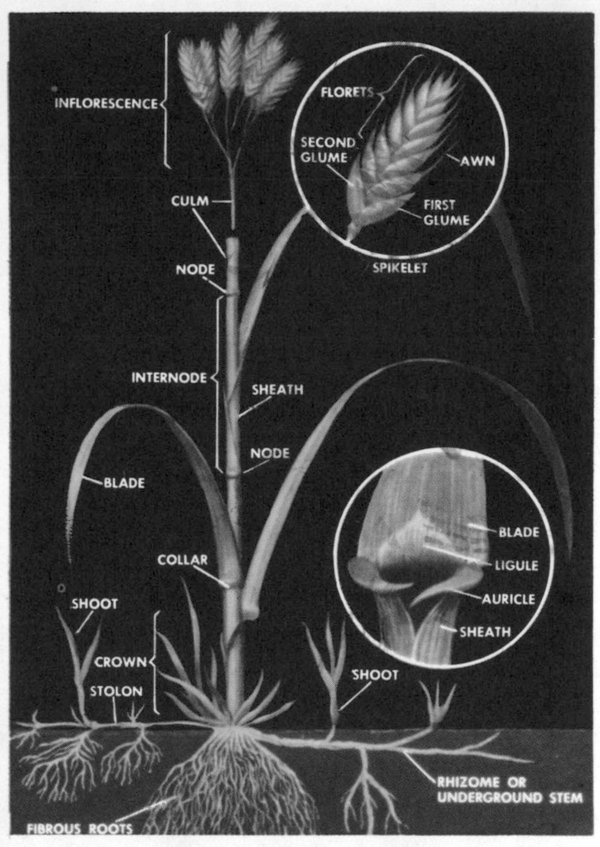

© Phillips Petroleum Co

hay is the dried grass.) Supplies of meat, milk, butter and cheese are dependent largely on grasses eaten by livestock. Many grasses important as grain crops, such as oats, barley, rye, wheat, sorghum, maize, and millets, are also used as forage crops. Others are grown only as forage or hay crops. Timothy *(Phleum pratense)* native to Europe and western Asia, is also a widely cultivated grass for hay in North America.

GRASSLANDS. Plains, prairies, and savannas cover large areas in the interiors of all continents except Antarctica. These flat or gently rolling natural grasslands once occupied about 25 per cent of the Earth's land area. They occur wherever the rainfall is more than enough for desert life but not great enough to support forests.

Prairies are lands of tall grasses in temperate climates. A seasonal rainfall of 20 to 40 inches, deep humus, and moderate temperature make prairie lands ideal natural pastures. Most natural prairie lands have been ploughed and are used for growing crops.

Plains lands are used mostly for grazing livestock. Crops can be grown in plains country, but the land must be irrigated in dry seasons. Dust storms are common when the grass holding the loose soil is removed for raising crops or by overgrazing, exposing the land to wind erosion.

Tropical savannas are grasslands with scattered trees. They occur in regions with 40 to 60 inches of rainfall and prolonged dry seasons. Savannas occupy large areas of South America, Australia, and Africa. Such grasses as Bluejoint or Beard Grass, Old Witch, and millets grow luxuriantly in savannas during the rainy season but turn brown during the dry season. This promotes fires. Baobabs, acacias, palms, and spurge trees are scattered through the grass, but often only one kind of grass and one kind of tree grow in an area.

GRAVITATION. The force that governs the motions of the planets and also the motions of the stars is gravitation. The law of gravitation says that every particle of matter attracts every other particle. The strength of the attraction depends on the size of the bodies and on how close together they are.

We do not notice the attraction of everyday objects on each other because gravitation is in most cases a weak force. Only very massive bodies, like the Earth, exert strong gravitational forces on objects near them. The attraction of the Earth on objects near its surface is called gravity. It holds objects down and gives them weight. All other large bodies have a sizable force of gravity at their surfaces, but its strength is usually different from that of gravity on the Earth's surface. You would weigh only a sixth as much on the Moon and would be able to jump great distances. But on Jupiter you would weigh $2\frac{1}{2}$ times as much as on the Earth and would find it hard even to stand up.

Although gravitation is mainly a weak force, it is important in astronomy because the planets and stars move in empty space where no other force affects them. Gravitational forces control their motion completely. In many cases one large body controls the motions of other bodies near it. In the solar

Space Photographic Inc

This picture of an American astronaut engaged on a 'space walk' clearly shows the effect of weightlessness. The Gulf of Mexico can be seen below him.

system this is the Sun, which is much more massive than all of the planets put together. The force the Sun exerts on a planet is much greater than the force of the planets on each other, so each planet travels around the Sun. The path of a planet is called its orbit, which changes only very slowly over the years. Even though the Sun is always pulling on it, a planet will never fall into the Sun because a moving body tends to keep moving. The Sun's gravitational force keeps the planet from flying away, and the planet's motion keeps it from falling into the Sun. The two opposing forces remain in balance. (See ORBIT.)

GROUNDSEL *(Senecio vulgaris)* belongs to a genus of widely distributed plants. Some species of *Senecio* are woody or semi-woody perennials several feet in stature. The common Groundsel is an over-wintering annual weed of disturbed soil in the British Isles. Flowers can be found in every month of the year.

GUMS are vegetable substances used in medicines and in making adhesives. They are collected and transported by methods little changed in twenty centuries. Gum arabic, gum tragacanth and karaya gum are all obtained by tapping trees or shrubs. Dried gum is collected from the bark surface as it runs out of injured areas. The sun-bleached gum is carried to market by camel.

Gum arabic is obtained from a small thorny tree *(Acacia arabic)*, native to northern Africa. A large tree *(Sterculia urans)* grown in India produces karaya gum. Gum tragacanth comes from a low shrub *(Astragalus tragacantha)* grown in dry regions of Iran and Turkey.

GYPSUM, a hydrated calcium sulphate, usually occurs as white, cleavable, earthy or silky masses. It is found also as colourless, tabular crystals known as selenite. Gypsum originates as an evaporation product of sea water. If the temperature of sea water rises above 34 degrees centigrade as it evaporates, anhydrite is deposited rather than gypsum. Both are deposited when the original volume of water has been reduced to about half. Halite is much more soluble and is not precipitated until the water is evaporated to about 10 per cent of the original volume. Anhydrite may change to gypsum if the water content is increased.

Evaporation of sea water in sufficient quantities to deposit these minerals must take place in warm, sub-tropical regions where there is little rainfall. As evaporation takes place the more concentrated water settles and finally becomes so concentrated that gypsum begins to precipitate.

Gypsum is used as a retarder to slow down the setting rate of Portland cement. Plaster of Paris is made by heating gypsum to drive off about 75 per cent of the water of crystallisation; when water is added, the powder recrystallises as gypsum, which is the setting of the plaster. Alabaster is a translucent variety of gypsum, and satin spar is a silky variety. Both are used for carving ornamental objects, such as bookends, ash trays, and lamp stands.

Gypsum and anhydrite are widely distributed on all continents. Large deposits are found in Greece, Switzerland, France, Italy, Spain and the U.S.A.

HALO. Sometimes when the sky is covered with very thin clouds a large ring or halo can be seen around the Sun or Moon. Halos belong not to astronomy but to meteorology, the science of the weather. They are caused by ice crystals in the clouds, which reflect light in special ways. All ice crystals are six-sided, and when a ray of light passes through an ice crystal and is reflected at two alternate faces, it comes out with its direction changed by about 22 degrees. So a bright ring appears around the Sun or Moon, 22 degrees away on all sides. Sometimes it is more complex consisting of numbers of concentric and tangential rings. Other kinds of internal reflection in ice crystals sometimes produce a 46-degree halo, as well as bright spots called sun dogs.

AMERICAN ASHE HAWTHORN
Crataegus ashei
10—25 ft.

ENGLISH HAWTHORN
Crataegus oxyacanthoides
10—25 ft.

WILD HAWTHORN
Crataegus spathulata
10—25 ft.

AMERICAN SCARLET HAW
Crataegus pedicellata 15—20 ft.

HAWTHORN (*Crataegus* spp.) is the common name for more than 1,000 species of small trees and shrubs in the rose family. Widely distributed in Europe, Asia and North America, the many species can be difficult to identify. They usually have thorny twigs and alternate, conspicuously toothed or lobed leaves. Clusters of white, pink, or red flowers develop into small, apple-like fruits. These are eaten by birds, which also nest in the thorny branches. The wood, although hard and heavy, has little commercial use except for mallets, tool handles, and similar items. Hawthorns can be grown to form a tight hedge, and are often used for such in Britain. The familiar May or Hawthorn of the countryside is regularly cut and layered to form impenetrable hedges to protect farm animals. Jellies are made from the fruit of some varieties, but most hawthorns are of ornamental value only.

HEATHS AND HEATHER (*Calluna vulgaris* and *Erica* spp.) are low, evergreen shrubs which, in late summer to spring, bear spikes of pink, white, or flesh-coloured flowers. In northern Europe and Asia, heather grows wild on peaty moors, often being the principal vegetation or cover.

Cornish Heath *(Erica vagans)* and Dorset Heath *(Erica ciliaris)* grow wild only in these counties. Ling *(Calluna)*, Bell Heather *(Erica cinerea)* and Cross-leaved Heath *(Erica tetralix)* are common on the sandy ridges of the British Isles. The Winter Heather *(Erica carnea)* is popular for the winter garden and many other species including Tree Heathers *(Erica arborea)* are grown here. South Africa has many wild species of Erica, often very highly coloured.

The heaths and heathers are usually plants of acid soils and when grown in the garden thrive best where plenty of peat has been added to the soil. Although many of them are low shrubs, some will grow into small 'trees'. *Erica mediterranea* is such a species and will grow best in alkaline soils. A heather garden can be so arranged that different species are flowering all through the year. In addition to their value as ornamental plants they produce excellent honey.

HEATHER
Calluna vulgaris
Erica scoparia

The root of *Erica arborea* is used for the manufacture of briar pipes.

HELIOTROPES (*Heliotropium* spp.) of more than 250 species grow in warm climates around the world. Common Heliotrope or Cherry Pie is an old-fashioned garden favourite that came originally from Peru. Its purple flowers have a fresh, vanilla-like scent. Others have a narcissus odour. The plant is shrub-like in appearance, growing to between 1 and 3 feet tall. In Britain, seeds are sown each year in March or cuttings are taken in September.

HELIOTROPE
Heliotropium peruvianium

HEMLOCKS are a group of about a dozen species of evergreen trees in the pine family. They are not to be confused with the very poisonous herb of the carrot family. Tree hemlocks are important sources of timber and paper pulp and are also planted as ornamentals. They have lacy foliage and graceful, conical crowns with weak, nodding tips.

Needles of most hemlocks are flat, soft, and marked on the underside with two silvery bands. They are attached by slender stems to small woody 'cushions' on the twigs. When

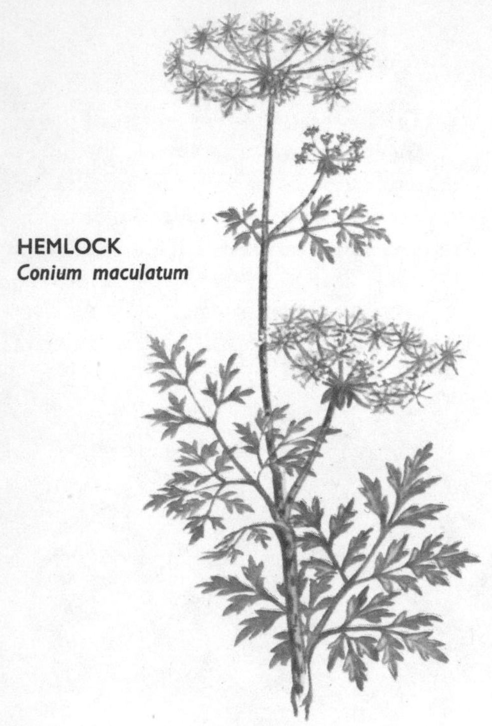

HEMLOCK
Conium maculatum

the needles drop, the 'cushions' remain on the twigs and give them a slightly rough appearance. Small round or oblong cones hang from the tips of the branchlets.

The Eastern Hemlock *(Tsuga canadensis)* and the larger Western Hemlock *(Tsuga heterophylla)*, both from North America, were first introduced into England in 1736 and 1851 respectively. They were at first planted in parks and gardens as ornamental conifers but now are grown in plantations for their timber.

A Chinese hemlock and two species from Japan are commercial timber trees in their native lands and are also planted as ornamentals in other countries.

HEMP
Cannabis sativa
5—8 ft.

cross section of stem showing fibres

female flower

male flower

seed

HEMP *(Cannabis sativa)*, apparently a native of Asia, is a bushy plant that grows 5—8 feet in height. Its fibres were used for weaving fabrics more than 4,000 years ago. Today the plant is also a source of drugs, and oil from its seeds is used in paints and soaps. The seeds were eaten by Europeans during the Middle Ages. Now they are used as bird feed. Hemp grows in temperate regions throughout the world. Russia produces and uses the largest quantity.

Hemp fibres occur in the plant's bark. Some bundles of fibre cells are as much as 15 feet long. When the plants are cut to obtain the fibre, the stems are generally left in the field for several weeks; less often they are collected and covered with water. Either method allows the softer plant tissues to decay from the fibres. Then the stems are run through rollers to crush them. This breaks the core of the stem and is called 'scutching'. Finally the fibres are cleaned, brushed, and combed.

Hemp is used today for rope and twine, carpets, sacks, and webbing. Other fibres are even better for these uses, however, and are gradually replacing hemp.

Manila hemp or abacá is obtained from the leaf stock of the Abacá Banana *(Musa textilis)*, which resembles the Common Banana but produces inedible fruit. The plant grows about 20 feet tall, and its leaves are 2 feet long.

HIBISCUS (*Hibiscus* spp.) although a native of India and China, is now widely cultivated in Europe.

The flowers of varieties of hibiscus grown as ornamentals may measure nearly 6 inches

Picturepoint — London

Hemp has been used for these long lengths of mooring ropes.

LIGHTERAGE COMPANY

Richard D. Westcott

More than 700 varieties of hibiscus are grown in tropical and sub-tropical areas.

across. Some are brilliant red, and others are pink, white, or yellow — or combinations of these colours. Growers have also developed some fancy double-flowered forms of hibiscus. In Britain the three most important garden species are the half-hardy annual *Hibiscus trionum;* the big bushy shrub *Hibiscus syriacus;* and the tender greenhouse shrub *Hibiscus rosa-sinensis.*

Hibiscuses are members of the mallow family. The family includes, in addition to hollyhocks and other plants grown solely for their flowers, such important and useful plants as cotton and okra. (See COTTON; HOLLYHOCKS; MALLOWS.)

HOLLIES (*Ilex* spp.) grow in both temperate and tropical regions everywhere in the world except western North America, Australia and its neighbouring islands in the Pacific. There are nearly 300 species, both trees and shrubs.

The familiar holly has red berries and leathery evergreen leaves with large spiny teeth. These are used for Christmas wreaths as both the leaves and berries hold their

ENGLISH HOLLY
Ilex aquifolium
10—30 ft.

colours and do not drop quickly. Several other kinds of hollies are not evergreen and not all produce red berries.

English Holly, native to Europe, western Asia, and China, is a popular ornamental which grows to about 30 feet in height. It has very spiny evergreen leaves and clusters of small white flowers that produce an abundance of bright red berries.

The leaves of a native South American holly are used to make Paraguay tea or *hera de mate.*

HOLLYHOCKS (*Althaea rosea*) because of their tall, stately form, are particularly attractive along a fence or beside a building. Their large frilled blossoms can be red, pink,

HOLLYHOCKS

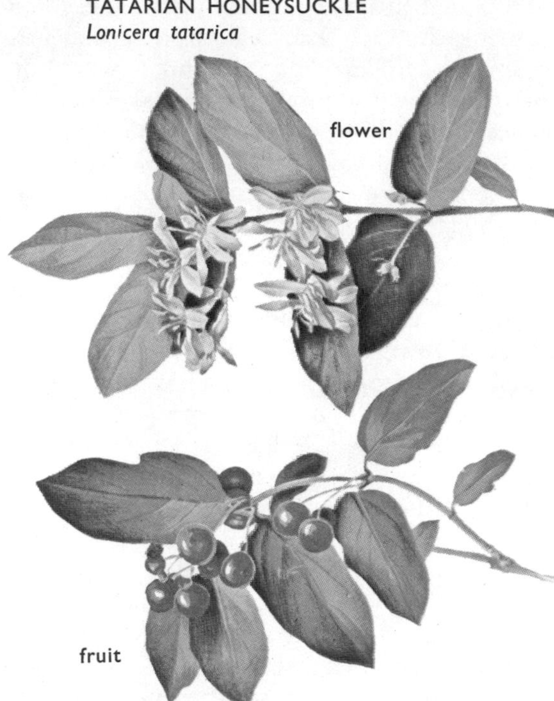

white or yellow. There are ruffled double forms as well as singles.

Hollyhocks are believed to be one of the oldest cultivated flowers. From their native China, hollyhocks travelled to Europe and then were carried to America by early settlers bound for New England.

Two years are required to grow flowering hollyhocks from seed.

HONEYSUCKLES (*Lonicera* spp.) are shrubs or climbers with fragrant flowers. In Britain they need sunny positions to flower well. The most common shrubbery species in gardens is *Lonicera tatarica* which has pink flowers. The yellow climbing honeysuckle of our hedgerows is widely grown usually in one of its varieties, 'Late Dutch' or 'Early Dutch', as a wall plant or on trellises or fences. There are also climbing species with red flowers, and others which have insignificant flowers but produce brightly coloured berries.

HOPS are the dried female flowers of a vine *(Humulus lupulus)*. Cultivated vines are trained to grow on strings. Harvesters pick the crop which is kiln-dried and treated with sulphur. Hops add flavour and sparkle to beer and prevent its decomposition. Prior to commercial yeast cakes, yeast for making bread was grown in a solution of hops and water. Hops are native to and cultivated in Europe, North America and Asia. They are grown as a crop in South America and in eastern Australia.

HORSECHESTNUTS are deciduous trees and shrubs. Their leaves are opposite, long-stemmed, and compound, the leaflets (5 to 9) radiating from the centre. In spring they bear large, bell-shaped flowers in showy

John Topham Ltd

Although machines are widely used, much hop-picking is still done in the traditional way by hand.

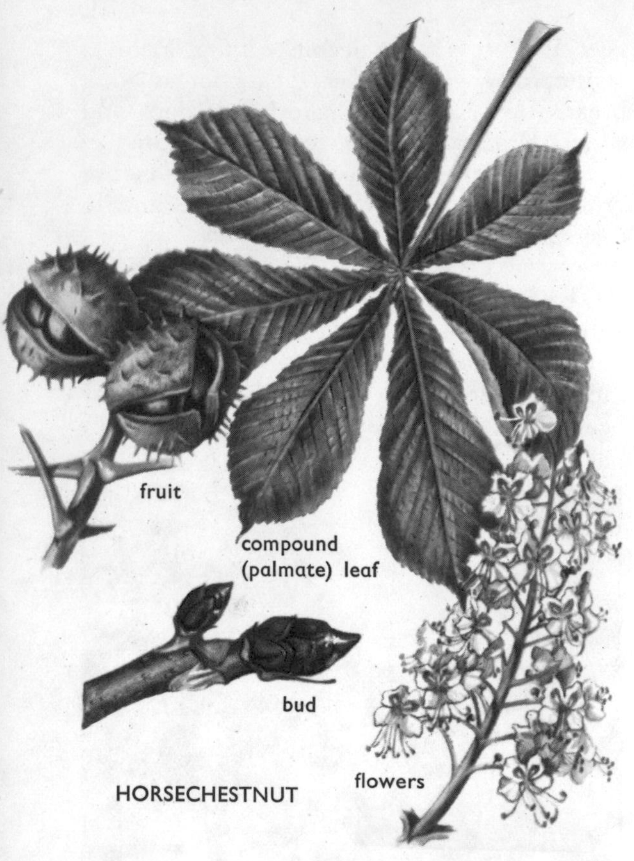

HORSECHESTNUT

clusters. The round, chestnut-brown, inedible 'conkers' are enclosed in thick, leathery husks which split open when ripe. Twigs in winter have large, dark, sticky buds.

Most common is the horsechestnut *(Aesculus hippocastanum)* a native of southern Europe and Asia. Its white flowers are spotted with yellow and purple, and the husks around its seeds have soft spines. These trees are not related to chestnuts of the beech family.

HORSETAILS or Scouring Rushes were once among the dominant plants on earth. Today there are only about 25 species, all of the genus *Equisetum*, which means 'horse bristle'. Some kinds of horsetails were used by Europeans and Americans in past centuries for scouring household utensils. Even today isolated groups of American Indians use these scouring rushes or horsetails to polish shafts of arrows or for similar work.

Equisetum differs from all other plants in having grooved or ribbed stems which are joined and contain silica. It is this sand-like compound, also found in diatoms (see DIATOMS) that makes the plants useful for scouring. At each joint of the stem a sheath of small scale-like leaves forms a whorl or collar around the joint. These leaves can be seen more easily when a stem is pulled apart.

All horsetails have underground stems that live many years. In some species the upright stems are annual, dying back each year; in others they are perennial, living year after year. In the Field Horsetail *(Equisetum arvense)* the upright stems have whorls of branches, giving the plants a horsetail appearance. Some plants have two types of aerial stems. In early spring, a short, unbranched stem, lacking chlorophyll, emerges from the soil producing a conelike structure at its tip. This is called the fertile shoot, and it soon disappears. Later a green branched stem arises. It is called the sterile vegetative shoot because it produces no spores. These last throughout the growing season dying back in the autumn. Species of horsetails occur everywhere in the world except in Antarctica, Australia, New

FIELD HORSETAIL
Equisetum arvense
8—30 in.

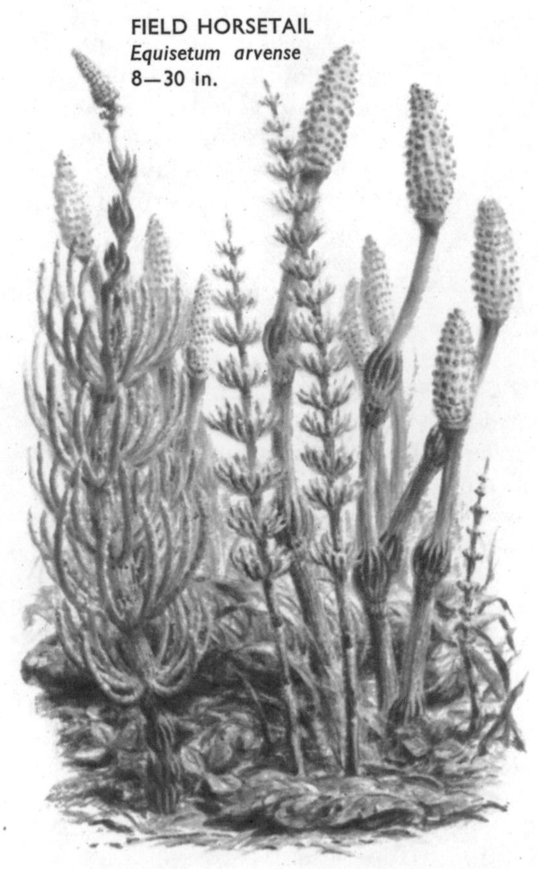

GIANT HORSETAIL
Calamites to 100 ft.

Zealand and the islands of the South Pacific.

All species of *Equisetum* have alternation of generations. Their life cycle is much like that of ferns. Spores, which are produced in the cones, are all alike. They are wind-blown, finally settling to the ground where they germinate and grow into small independent plants of the gametophyte generation. Some produce eggs; others produce sperm.

During the Coal Age horsetails were very abundant. One of these giant horsetails *(Calamites)* grew about 100 feet tall and had a trunk as large as 3 feet in diameter. (See CARBONIFEROUS.)

HYACINTHS (*Hyacinthus* spp.) combine beauty of form and colour with as sweet a fragrance as can be found anywhere in the flower world. In Europe, perfume is made from hyacinths. From the plant's wild parents in western Asia, specimens were brought into cultivation many centuries ago, and from these a wide range of beautiful garden hybrids have been raised.

The world's main source of hyacinth bulbs (also daffodil, tulip, and other bulbs) is Holland where the soil and climate are unusually favourable for their growth.

Bluebells of the south of England, *Endymion nonscriptus*, are closely related to hyacinths and occur in several varieties other than the well known blue form, the pink and white being particularly attractive. Confusion sometimes occurs because bluebells of the north of England, *Campanula rotundifolia*, are called harebells in the south.

The many cultivated varieties of hyacinths range in colour from white to red and blue and are both single and double-flowered. They are not related to the Camass or Wild Hyacinths.

DUTCH HYACINTH
Hyacinthus orientalis

CAMASS OR
WILD HYACINTHS
of the U.S.A.
Camassia quamash

I

ICE is a mineral that is best known as a fluid, namely, water. Its crystals are flat, triangular, or six-sided, but it is usually found in white (because of gas bubbles) or green-blue masses. It floats when solid and melts at 32 degrees Fahrenheit or 0 degrees centigrade. Ice is found everywhere, but in solid form is confined to the polar regions and high mountains. If all this ice were melted it is estimated that the sea level would be raised more than 200 feet.

ICE AGES have occurred several times during the history of the Earth. The most recent began about 3 million years ago (in the Pleistocene) and ended about 11,000 years ago. Four times during this period ice sheets advanced and retreated. The ice covered more than 7½ million square miles in Europe, Asia, and North America, and at least another 5 million square miles in South America, Africa, Australia, and Antarctica.

Ice sheets covered much of the continents of North America, Asia, and Europe during the glacial period.

New lakes were created by the glaciers. The Great Lakes of North America for example, were formed then. Glaciation changed the courses of rivers, modified the topography of the land, and in some places deposited great thicknesses of glacial sand and gravel (drift). There were great differences in sea level between the glacial and inter-glacial periods; during the former it was lower and Britain was joined to the Continent, during the latter it was higher. These changes are indicated by various features such as drowned valleys and raised beaches.

Many animals migrated to escape the glaciers. Plants not adapted to the cold died and some large mammals that had existed for long periods became extinct. Between each glacial period plants and animals again inhabited the areas from which they had been driven, and each time some were destroyed and others forced out by glaciers.

There have been several periods of glaciation in the past. In Pre-Cambrian, Cambrian, late Carboniferous and possibly Cretaceous times, various parts of the world have suffered the advancing ice.

Variation in solar radiation received by the Earth is one of the many explanations suggested for these changes in climate. The rise of new mountain ranges or changes in ocean currents are others. It has also been suggested that changes in the position of the Earth's axis or the position of continents with respect to the Poles may have caused glaciation. We do not know the real cause, but one of the reasons suggested, variation in amount of solar radiation from the sun is the most probable.

At present we are living in an immediate post-glacial period. If it is a truly post-glacial period, the temperature should become increasingly warmer. There is some evidence that this is taking place, and if this trend continues, ice caps existing on Antarctica, Greenland, and various high mountain ranges will melt. Eventually, over thousands of years, the sea will rise about 200 feet, bringing drastic changes to our coast lines. If we are in an inter-glacial period, we can expect ultimately renewed advances of continental ice sheets.

The American Mastodon, extinct relative of modern elephants, foraged in the swamps of North America in Ice Age times, 10,000 to 15,000 years ago. It was a browser. Modern elephants are largely grazers, as were the mammoths from which they developed.

AMERICAN MASTODON
Mastodon americanus
10 ft. at shoulder

INSECTIVOROUS PLANTS. Insect-eating plants are among the most amazing, most interesting plants in the world. These carnivorous plants digest and absorb nourishment from the bodies of their insect prey. Like other green plants, they manufacture most of the nourishment they need. The insects they 'eat' balance their diets by providing them with nitrogen, not otherwise available in their boggy homes.

Several hundred kinds of insect-eating plants are found in the world, and they are especially abundant in south-eastern Asia. More than 50 kinds occur in North America, and of these the various pitcher plants *(Sarracenia)* are the largest and most conspicuous. Venus flytrap *(Dionaea)*, Sundews *(Drosera)*, and Bladderworts *(Utricularia)* are among the other kinds. In Britain there are 13 kinds of Bladderwort, Sundew, and Butterwort *(Pinguicula)*.

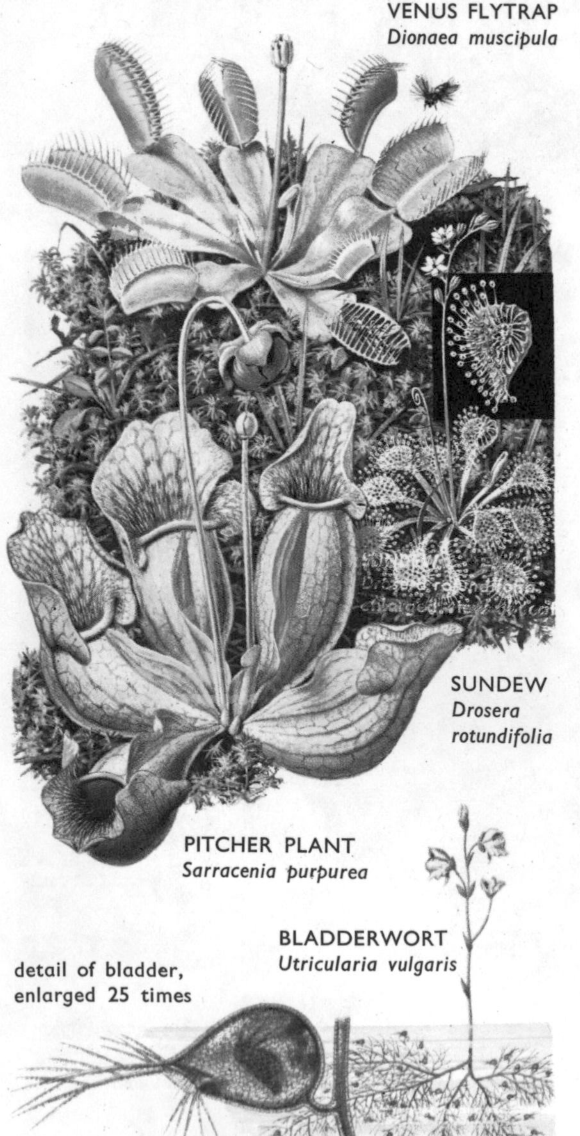

VENUS FLYTRAP *Dionaea muscipula*

SUNDEW *Drosera rotundifolia*

PITCHER PLANT *Sarracenia purpurea*

BLADDERWORT *Utricularia vulgaris*

detail of bladder, enlarged 25 times

Pitcher plants have peculiar, hollow, tube-like leaves — their 'pitchers'. Tropical pitcher plants *(Nepenthes)* are generally climbers, with pitchers formed from leaves at intervals along the vine. Some pitcher plant leaves form a special landing platform for the convenience of insect guests that are attracted either by the bright colours of the leaves or by the sweet smells from inside the pitcher. The inside of the pitcher is covered with a thick growth of stiff hairs, all slanting downwards. Insects crawl into the pitcher easily, but are unable to come out against the hair bristles, especially since the lower part of the pitcher is often slippery. Eventually they fall into a liquid at the bottom and drown. The liquid consists partly of water and partly of a digestive juice which absorbs the soft parts of the insects.

Venus flytrap, a very curious type of carnivorous plant, grows in coastal sections of North and South Carolina in the United States. The outer end of its leaves are divided into folding halves with stiff spines along the outer margin. In each half are several stiff 'trigger' hairs. When an insect touches these hairs, the halves close in seconds, often trapping the visitor between them. The under surface of the leaves is frequently red, the colour of the digestive glands.

Another type of insect trap is developed by the Sundews, which have a sticky, glistening, dewlike secretion on their hairy leaves. Insects that alight on the leaves are trapped. A gland in the leaves then secretes a digestive juice which absorbs the soft parts of the insects. Sundews are widely distributed in Europe, Asia, and North and South America. Some grow high up on mountain slopes.

Bladderworts are aquatic plants which catch their insects in bladders in their leaves. These are closed off by trapdoor-like openings which spring open when an insect or other creature touches certain bristles on the leaf. The interior of the bladder is under tension and water is sucked in, carrying the insect with it.

INTERSTELLAR GAS AND DUST. Scattered through interstellar space are clouds of gas and dust. So thinly is the material spread that a cubic mile of interstellar space contains less material than a thimbleful of air. Nevertheless, the distances between the stars are so great that when all the interstellar material around us is added up it is equal to the amount of material in the stars.

Interstellar material exists in two forms – gas and dust. Dust consists of grains of finely divided solid material; gas is completely fluid, and is mainly neutral or ionised hydrogen, with the individual atoms and molecules moving past each other freely. The gas and dust show up in several different ways in different situations. In some places in the sky we see hazy bright patches called bright nebulae. They usually consist of glowing gas in the space surrounding a hot star, but some bright nebulae are dust clouds that are illuminated like fog around a street light. In other places the dust clouds are so dense that they hide the light of the stars behind them. These dark nebulae leave 'holes' in the Milky Way. An example is the Horsehead Nebula in Orion. The gas also shows up in the spectrum of distant stars, for as the starlight passes through the gas, certain wave lengths of light are removed so that additional dark lines show up in the spectrum. Finally, hydrogen gas in interstellar space emits radio waves of a frequency that can be detected with radio telescopes. Since most of the interstellar gas is hydrogen, radio observations are very useful in locating the gas. (See NEBULA; RADIO ASTRONOMY.)

In observational astronomy interstellar material is the greatest single hindrance to studying our galaxy – the Milky Way. Dust clouds scattered through the plane of the Milky Way obscure the light of nearly all distant stars. This interstellar absorption not only hides many parts of the Milky Way completely but also makes it difficult to measure the distances of the parts that we can see. (See MILKY WAY.)

Interstellar material plays an important role in the birth of stars, for new stars are created as condensing clouds of interstellar gas and dust. Thus new stars are being born continually in irregular galaxies or in the spiral arms of galaxies like the Milky Way where there is plenty of interstellar material. In regions where there is no interstellar material, only old stars exist. (See STARS.)

The Horsehead Nebula, a cloud of dark gas near Orion, is visible only with a telescope.

Mt. Wilson and Palomar Observatories

This Gaseous Nebula can be seen with binoculars in the sword of the constellation of Orion.

Mt. Wilson and Palomar Observatories

IRISES (*Iris* spp.) are named in honour of Iris, Greek goddess of the rainbow, because of the variety of colours in their flowers. Some people call them Flags or Fleurs-de-lys.

More than 100 species of wild irises grow in Europe, Asia, Africa, and North America. Most wild irises have blue, purple or yellow flowers and have either erect sword-like leaves, or narrow grassy ones.

From the many wild irises in the world, new and more gorgeous garden hybrid irises have been developed continually over the centuries.

The most common garden type is the tall, large-flowered Bearded or German Iris. Three of its petals arch upwards over the centre of the flower, and are called standards. The other three curve downwards and have a dense hairy beard near their base and are called 'falls'. Bearded Irises can be propagated by simply breaking off a piece of the thick rootstock, and planting it an inch or so deep. New varieties are raised from seed.

Other popular cultivated irises are the Beardless, Japanese, Spanish and English. Spanish and English are grown from bulbs, rather than from rootstock. Orrisroot, which is obtained from the roots of several kinds of European irises, is used in making perfumes, sachets, and toothpastes. The seeds of the Bog Iris serve as a substitute for coffee. Another European iris once furnished a pigment used by painters under the appropriate name of 'irisgreen'.

A certain amount of mythology surrounds the iris. In Ireland the Common Yellow Flag *Iris pseudocorus* is hung in branches outside the doors on the feast of Corpus Christi to avert evil.

The most ancient kings of France were depicted as holding a Flag in blossom instead of a sceptre. This custom lead to irises becoming the armorial figures of France. In pictures relating to the legend of St. Clotilda (sixth century, France) she is represented as attended by an angel holding a shield on which are three Fleurs de Lys. Louis VII of France assumed the Fleur de Lys as his device in 1137. It was thus incorporated in the arms of France and formed one of the embellishments of the crown.

The Fleur de Lys is one of the most famous of symbols.

IRON, one of the most abundant metals in the Earth, has been more highly prized than gold and is surely more useful. It is the backbone of modern civilisation. The rise of modern world powers is related to their access to large deposits of iron and coal. Meteorites are composed almost wholly of iron, but this type of iron is of interest only to scientists.

Hematite (iron oxide), most important of the four common iron ores, is found as dull-red or metallic-grey masses. One kind is found as layers of small, round grains and is referred to as oolitic. Hematite has a dark red streak and contains about 70 per cent iron.

Limonite (hydrated iron oxide), sometimes called goethite contains about 60 per cent iron. It is brown, as is also its streak. It may be found as fibrous, radiating stalactites or in soft, earthy masses.

Magnetite (iron oxide), containing about 73 per cent iron, is found in coarse, granular masses or in eight-sided crystals. It is iron-black in colour and streak.

Siderite (iron carbonate), about 48 per cent iron, is found in brown, cleavable masses or curved, irregular crystals. It has a pale streak and a pearly lustre.

Pyrite (iron sulphide) is about 47 per cent iron and is found in various ore veins. It is bronze-yellow in colour and because of its resemblance to gold is often known as fool's gold. Sometimes it does in fact contain gold. It is not used as an iron ore but for sulphur and for the production of sulphuric acid and sulphate of iron. Marcasite is also an iron sulphide and is sometimes called white iron pyrites. Another iron mineral is pyrrhotite (magnetic pyrites) which often contains nickel. It is mined for this valuable metal in Sunbury, Canada.

Iron is smelted in a blast furnace, which is a steel tower about 150 feet tall lined with fire brick. It is filled with alternating layers of coke, iron ore, and limestone. A blast of hot air is blown in at the base of the furnace. As the material burns down more is added at the top. Molten iron and slag drip into a pit under the furnace. Periodically the iron is drawn off and cast into ingots — pig iron. This is also known as cast iron. It is weak and brittle. Wrought iron is iron that contains

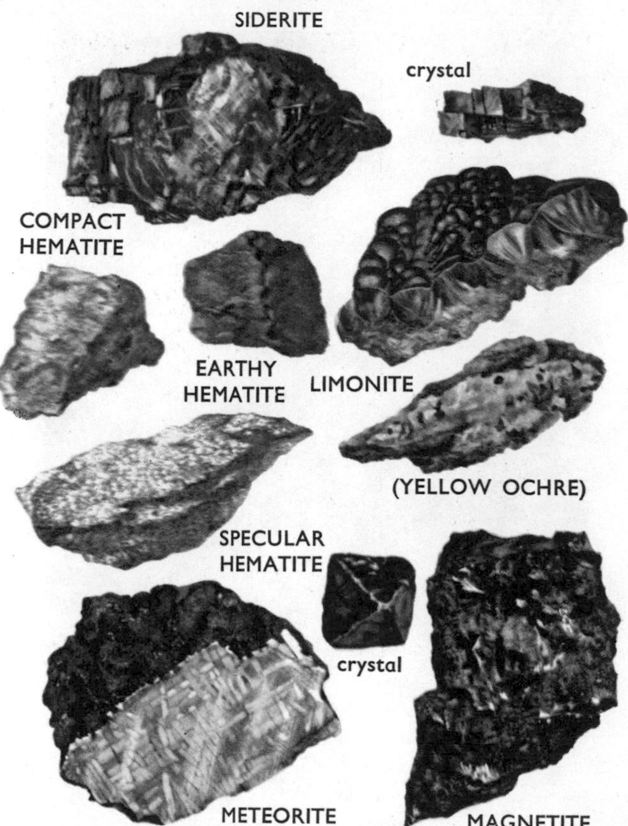

some slag; it is more resistant to corrosion and is tougher than cast iron. Steel is made by heating pig iron in an open-hearth furnace or a Bessemer converter to remove silicon, phosphorus, sulphur, oxygen, and nitrogen. Alloying metals are usually added to give it desired qualities. The slag drawn off above the iron is used in the manufacture of Portland cement. A blast furnace is operated constantly until the lining burns out (usually two or three years). Then it must be rebuilt.

Iron minerals are well distributed over the world. Commercial amounts are produced in Great Britain, France, Germany, Austria, U.S.S.R., China, Australia, India, Algeria, Morocco, South Africa, Brazil, Venezuela, Canada and several states of the U.S.A.

ISLANDS are bodies of land surrounded by water. Many are so completely isolated from mainland masses that they form unique habitats for plants and animals. Islands, such as Malagasy, the British Isles and New Guinea were once joined to the continents to which they are now closely situated. They

Keystone Press

Colourful, soft tweeds are woven in the Hebridean Islands in Scotland.

became islands when the connecting land strip sank and was flooded. Oceanic islands, such as the Hawaiian Islands, the Azores and Canaries, arose in the middle of the oceans. The Hawaiian Islands are volcanoes built up from the ocean floor.

Plants and animals isolated on islands may develop differently from their relatives on land. Some plants and animals may be introduced after the islands have been formed. The mixing of island and continental plants and animals depends on how far the islands are from the mainland and also on the kinds of plants and animals. Man has introduced numerous plants and animals to islands, or has taken them from islands to the mainland.

Island isolation often results in species found nowhere else. The farther an island is from the mainland, the greater the number of its native forms of plants and animals.

Basalt columns form the Giant's Causeway in Ireland.

Many animals and plants now present on islands belong to primitive groups. Changes in climate and the development of new and numerous enemies have brought death and extinction to similar or related species on continental land massses. Islands, with their stable climates and lack of aggressive forms, serve as refuges where primitive types may flourish.

Island plants follow essentially the same

Peter Beighton

Easter Island, discovered on Easter Sunday 1772. Some of the centuries-old statues are 40 feet high.

pattern as animals in tending to have a character of their own. Spores and seeds that are carried long distances by winds and waters or by animals account for the occurrence of plants from continents on remote oceanic islands. Many native island plants are ancient forms, and many are larger than mainland relatives. Some of the islands of the North Atlantic (the Azores and the Canaries) still have laurel forests, which have long been extinct in Europe. Silverswords and tree plantains of the Hawaiian Islands are primitive plants found nowhere else in the world.

Both plant and animal evolution on islands goes on independently of continents and their influences. Island plants and animals which were similar to continental ones millions of years ago now show little similarity.

Lt. Alan Lisle

This remarkable photograph shows the birth of an island near the island of Fayal in the Azores in September, 1957. Lava and smoke are rising from an eruption that in a few days had formed land where previously there had been only open sea. In time this island on the Atlantic might be populated with plants and animals, or might disappear into the sea before living things become established there

J - K

JADEITE

PINK JADEITE

CARVED JADE
early Chinese

JADE has been a highly prized gem for thousands of years, especially in the Orient. Prehistoric jade ceremonial vases, bowls, dishes, and images have been found in Asia, Europe, Africa, South and Central America. In many cases the original source of the jade is still unknown and may have come from great distances as trade items. Two minerals, jadeite (a pyroxene) and nephrite (an amphibole), are known as jade (see AMPHIBOLES; PYROXENES). Both are usually green, tough, and fibrous. They are metamorphic minerals associated with serpentine. Jadeite, the better of the two kinds, occurs in many shades, varying from green to yellow, pink, brown, purple, and white. Skilful artists have carved vases decorated with flowers, leaves, fruit, and stems in their appropriate colours. Apple-green jade is the most highly prized today. Jadeite is found in Burma and the U.S.A.

JOSHUA TREE

JOSHUA TREES, or **YUCCA,** are weird-looking members of the lily family that grow in the deserts of America. Many are protected in the Joshua Tree National Monument near Indio, California. Although found in the southern States, some species are hardy in mild parts of the British Isles.

JUPITER is the largest of the nine planets — in fact larger than all of the others put together. Jupiter has a diameter of 88,700 miles, which is 11 times the diameter of the Earth but still only a tenth of the diameter of the Sun. Its mass is 318 times that of the Earth or 1/1000 of the mass of the Sun. Jupiter is the fifth planet in distance from the Sun — 484 million miles or 5.2 times the Earth's distance from the Sun. It takes nearly 12 years for Jupiter to go around the Sun. Jupiter is the fastest rotating planet, taking only 9 hours and 50 minutes to spin once around on its axis.

At such a great distance from the Sun, Jupiter is naturally cold — about minus 130 degrees centigrade (200 degrees Fahrenheit below zero). It has a thick atmosphere full of clouds that never lets us see Jupiter's surface. At such a low temperature the clouds cannot be water droplets, like those on Earth; instead they are droplets of ammonia. The whole atmosphere of Jupiter is

The path of a satellite crossing Jupiter is shown in these illustrations. In the first two, both the satellite (white) and its shadow (dark) are visible. In the last two, the satellite is invisible, but its shadow is seen.

very different from ours. Most of it is hydrogen and helium gases, which are very rare in the Earth's atmosphere. There are also large amounts of methane as well as ammonia, both of which are poisonous to us. Besides the belts of light and dark clouds, Jupiter's atmosphere has contained a large red spot for nearly 100 years.

Jupiter has an average density only $1\frac{1}{3}$ times that of water and is probably composed of hydrogen and helium in solid form as the result of great pressure.

Of all the planets, Jupiter is richest in satellites or moons. Twelve have been found so far. Four of these are large and bright; they go around Jupiter at distances of $\frac{1}{4}$ million to a million miles, with periods of $1\frac{3}{4}$ to 17 days. The other eight known satellites of Jupiter are smaller and fainter.

In spite of Jupiter's great distance from us, because of its size, it always looks brighter than any star and all the other planets except Venus. It is the easiest planet to observe satisfactorily with a small telescope, and its four Galilean satellites can be seen even with binoculars. With greater magnification the cloud belts parallel to the equator are visible, and motions of the satellites can be followed. The times of the appearance and disappearance are listed in almanacs. The other satellites can be seen only with powerful telescopes. One of these is very close to its mother planet but the others range as far out as 15 million miles. (See PLANETS.)

JURASSIC PERIOD. This middle period of the Mesozoic era began about 190 million years ago and lasted about 59 million years. It was named after the Jura Mountains on the borders of France and Switzerland.

The surface of Jupiter is partially hidden by heavy cloud belts parallel to its equator. Shown are four of the planet's twelve moons and, on its face, the red spot.

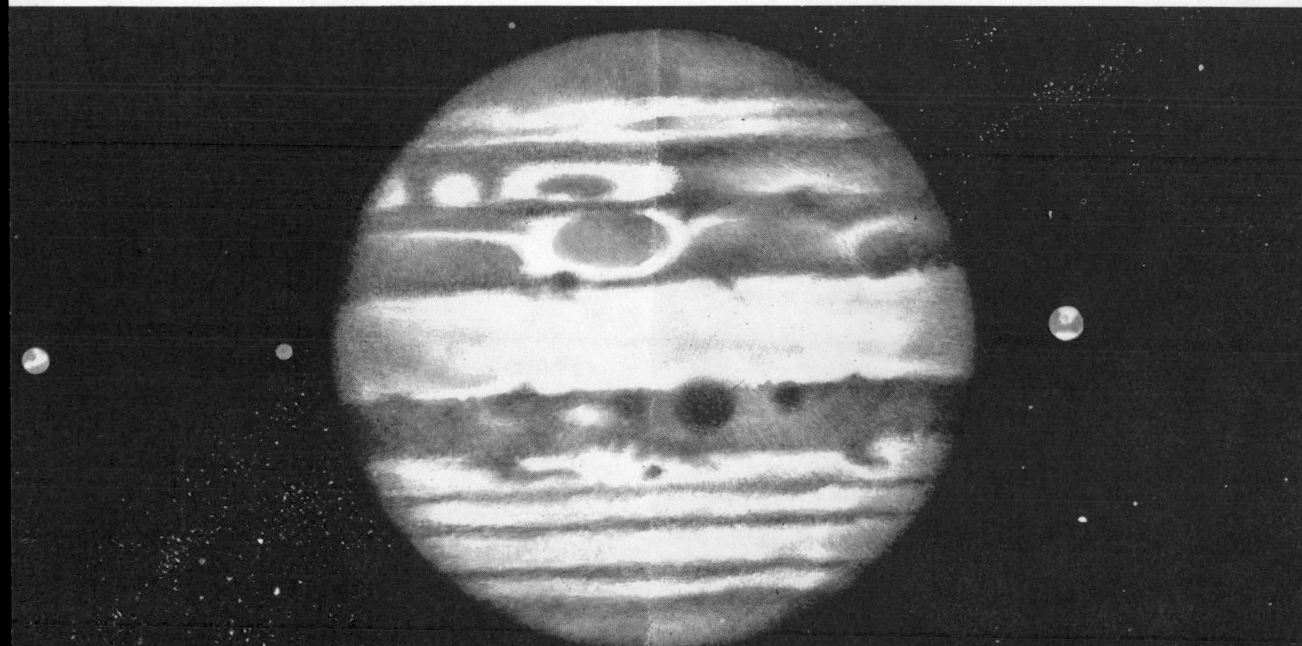

During much of the Jurassic time a shallow sea stretched across Britain. Owing to earth movements the seas were continually changing. Jurassic rocks are found in Britain and form such areas as the Cotswolds, Northampton Uplands and Lincolnshire Edge.

There were many distinctive Jurassic plants including cycadeoids, conifers, ferns and ginkgos, and the earliest flowering plants which were to change the whole pattern of vegetation in later periods.

Most characteristic animals were the

Allosaurus, **about 35 feet long, preyed on the huge vegetarian** *Brontosaurus*, **which was approximately 80 feet long and weighed 40 tons. Both lived in the Jurassic Period, between 180 and 135 million years ago. In the background is** *Camptosaurus*, **a small vegetarian.**

reptiles. On land, dinosaurs were most common. These included the giant carnivorous *Allosaurus* and *Diplodocus*, the 85-foot vegetarian. However, some dinosaurs were only about a foot long. (See CRETACEOUS; MESOZOIC ERA; TRIASSIC.)

Reptiles were equally dominant in the seas. Ichthyosaurs and plesiosaurs reached their peak. There were also many turtles and geosaurs, which were sea-going reptiles that resembled modern crocodiles.

Pterosaurs and pterodactyls were flying reptiles that also appeared during the Jurassic and became extinct in the Cretaceous. These varied from about the size of a robin to others with wingspans in excess of twenty feet. Most Jurassic pterosaurs were similar to *Rhamphorhynchus*, a creature which had a wingspread of about two feet. The wing structure suggests they were gliders rather than fliers. Many bones in the skeleton were hollow, others were fused. Their legs were not suitable for walking — they evidently used all four limbs in an awkward shuffle — although they could well be used for clutching in a rather bat-like fashion. Most probably they were fish eaters.

The oldest fossil birds are found in the Bavarian Solenhofen limestone of Jurassic age. Three well-preserved specimens of *Archaeopteryx* (which means 'ancient wing') with even the impressions of feathers have been found in these rocks. This crow-sized bird was a striking mixture of bird and reptile. It had feathers, but it also had teeth (no living bird has teeth). It had typical bird-like feet but a reptilian tail. It had a wishbone and wings, but there were claws on the leading edge of its wings. If feathers had not been preserved with *Archaeopteryx*, this bird would probably have been classed as a reptile, for it was remarkably similar in appearance to small lizard-like, tree-dwelling reptiles from which it evolved.

In this very pure, fine-grained Solenhofen limestone, used for lithographic engraving, the fossil remains of over 450 species of animals have been collected. Most of them are in an excellent state of preservation. They include such fossils as crustaceans and ammonites, 8 kinds of jellyfish, over 100 insect species, and 29 species of pterosaurs.

Early mammals roamed the land during

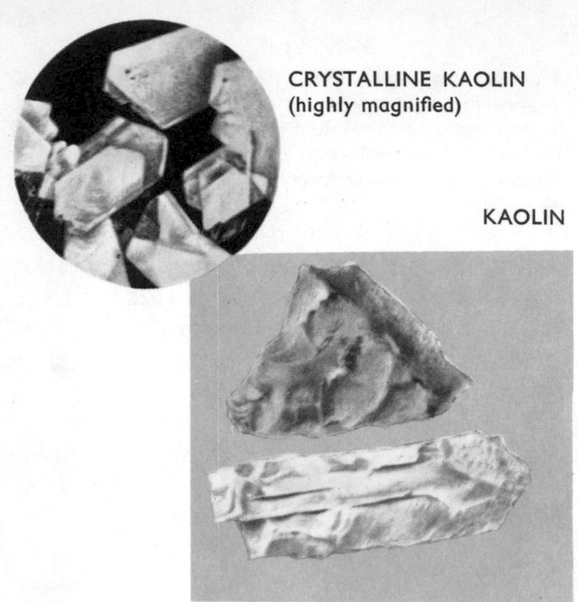

CRYSTALLINE KAOLIN (highly magnified)

KAOLIN

this time. They were no larger than present-day mice and shrews and probably looked like them. A number of insects, snails, and other small animals without backbones have been found in rocks of Jurassic age.

Jurassic seas contained a great variety of animal life well represented by fossils. There were both ammonites some six feet in diameter and belemnites; numerous bivalves, echinoids, crinoids, brachiopods, and various marine arthropods.

KAOLINITE is one of the many clay minerals, all of which are exceedingly fine-grained and easily shaped when wet. One of the most widespread of all minerals, kaolinite has been used by man for thousands of years because it moulds easily and fuses at a low temperature. Pottery made of kaolinite by primitive man is one of the best sources of information about early cultures. Today kaolinite is used in the manufacture of chinaware, bricks, tiles, electric insulation, Portland cement, and moulds. It is used also as a filler in cloth, rubber, paper, linoleum, and wallpaper to add weight and body. Kaolinite is as world-wide in distribution as mud and shale. It is formed from aluminium silicates acted upon by rain water or hot water from magmas. Fine quality chinaware is made from pure kaolinite, which is less widely distributed. China clay is exploited in Cornwall and Devon. Few visitors to the area around St. Austell can have failed to notice the immense waste tips which have been made up of the grey residue after the clay has been refined. Other well-known deposits occur in France, Germany, Czechoslovakia, Italy, Japan and several states of the U.S.A.

Kelp being gathered in Co. Clare, Eire.

Bord Failte Photo

KELPS are a large kind of seaweed. They belong to the algae group of plants, are brown, and are the largest of the thallophytes. Some reach 300 feet in length. A kelp consists of a holdfast, a long stem-like portion, and a flattened blade. The blade may be solid or divided. Most kinds grow in fairly deep water — at least beyond the low-tide mark. Some have air bladders that help keep them afloat.

Kelps grow only in cool or cold seas. Off the coasts of North America they are more abundant in the Pacific than in the Atlantic. Several kinds are used as food in Asia and Europe. In the Orient the dried plants, called kombu, are cooked with meat, used in sauces, made into a drink, or eaten like sweets. Kelps are sources of algin. Iodine has been extracted from several species.

Laminaria has a long, flat leathery blade, a short stem-like portion and a branched holdfast by which it attaches itself to rocks. *Macrocystis* and *Nereocystis* are large, well-known Pacific kelps. *Macrocystis* has many blades arising from a long stem and an air bladder at the base of each blade. *Nereocystis* has a holdfast, a long cord-like stem, and a large air bladder from which arise numerous narrow blades.

KUDZU *(Pueraria lobata)* is a rapid-growing legume believed to be native to Japan and China. In one season it may grow as much as 50 feet. This makes the vine a pest in some parts of the tropics and subtropics, as it crawls over everything in its path, but it is valuable cover on eroded land. It also serves as forage and is cut for hay. Kudzu seeds or beans can be eaten, and a starch is extracted from the roots.

KYANITE is an aluminium found in fibrous aggregates of slender blue or white crystals. It is formed from shale or slate by moderate temperature and intense pressure. Kyanite has two distinct hardnesses — 4-5 parallel to the long axis and 6-7 across the long axis. Kyanite and sillimanite are used for the manufacture of spark plug porcelain. Blue transparent kyanite is used as a gem stone. It is found in the U.S.S.R, Czechoslovakia, Switzerland, and eastern United States.

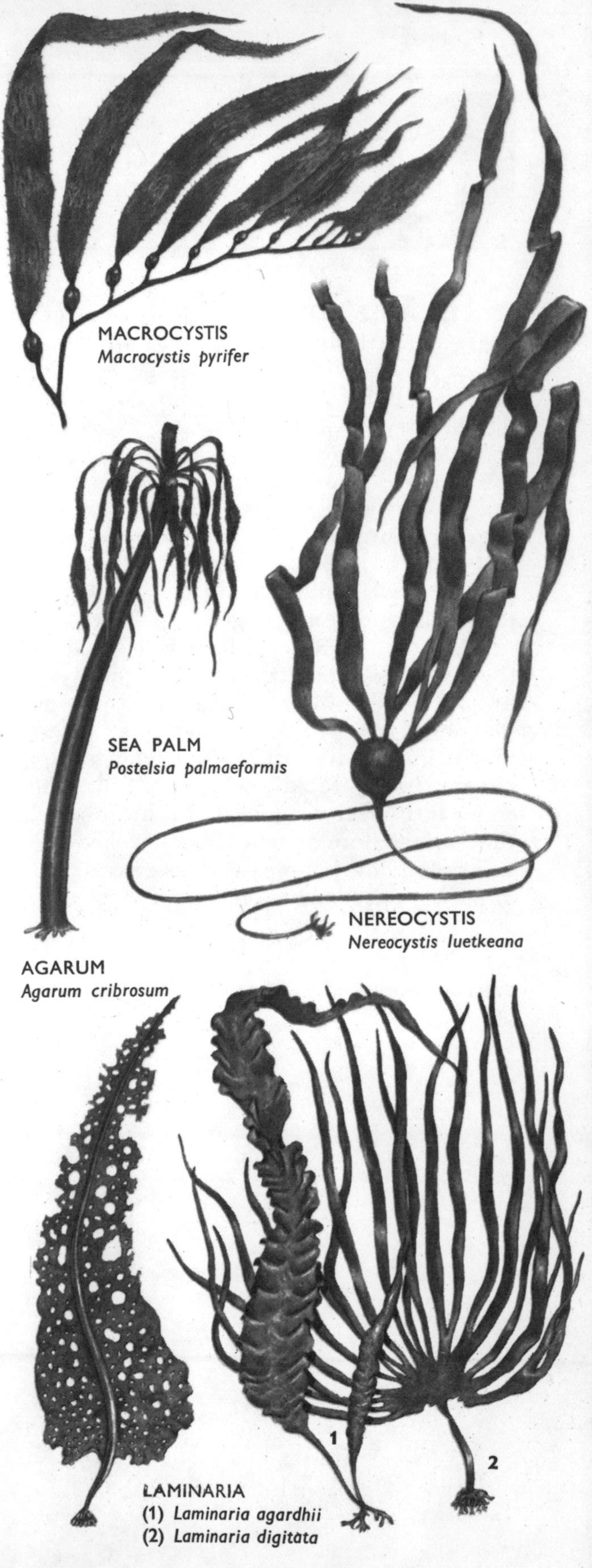

L

LAKES AND PONDS are bodies of standing water. Although the distinction is not precise, a lake is usually a large body of water; a pond is a small one. Ponds frequently dry up in summer.

Water becomes heavier as its temperature decreases, reaching its greatest density (weight) at 4 degrees centigrade (about 39 degrees Fahrenheit). As the water becomes still colder, it becomes lighter. Ice floats because it weighs less than water at a temperature of 4 degrees centigrade.

The water in a deep, fresh-water lake in the temperate zone consists of three layers: an upper warm layer circulated by wind and wave action; a lower cold, quiet layer; and an intermediate layer where temperature changes more rapidly. Twice a year, the water turns over completely. In the autumn, the surface water cools, becomes heavier, and sinks to the bottom. The less dense water at the bottom comes to the top. In the spring, when the ice melts, the surface water warms to 4 degrees centigrade (the temperature at which it is heaviest) and sinks to the bottom. It is replaced by the warmer water from the bottom. Animals usually seek warmer surface waters in the spring, but in summer are found most abundantly in cooler, deeper

In the deep water of a lake the temperature is low.

Coniston Water in the Lake District.

Colour Library International

Phot. Jacques Bauguet

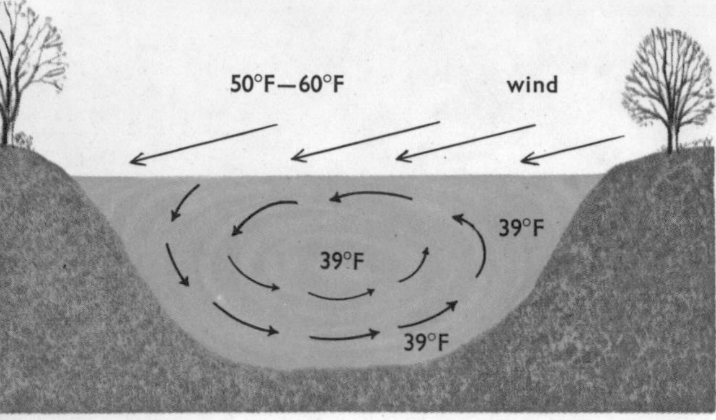

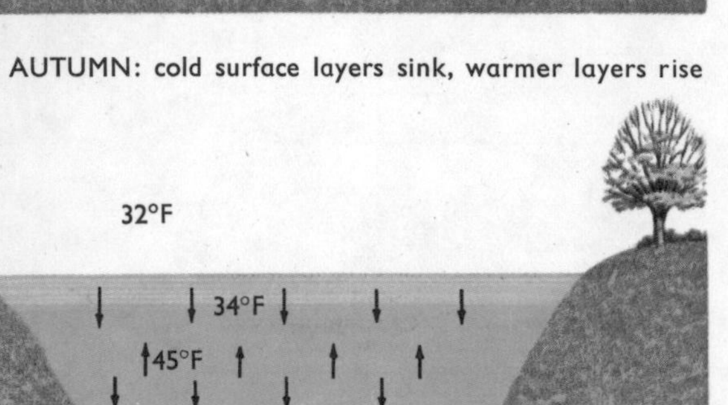

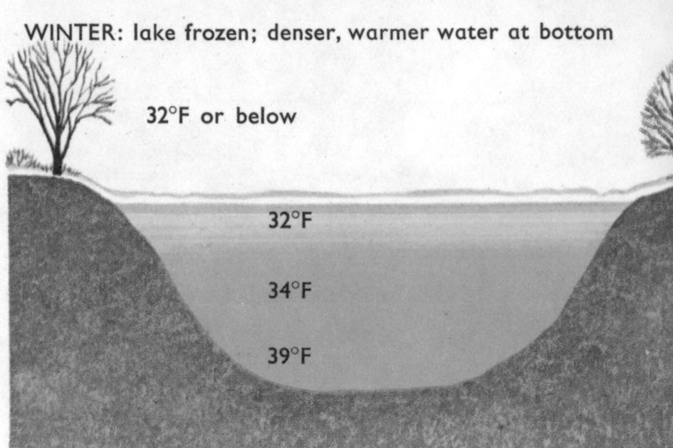

In temperate climates the water in a lake or pond circulates twice a year, in the spring and in the autumn. This occurs when the surface water becomes cold in autumn and sinks to the bottom, the water at the bottom coming to the top. The cycle is repeated in the spring when, as the ice melts, the surface water again becomes more dense.

waters. They are less frequently found in the bottom layer where plants are absent and oxygen is low.

Light is most intense close to the surface and decreases with depth. Light penetrates deeper in clear lakes than in muddy ones or in those where the water is coloured by iron or other chemicals. In a lake as on land, however, the ultimate source of energy is the sun. Sunlight is the energy used in photosynthesis by water (and land) plants to produce sugars and starches.

Vast numbers of algae, diatoms, bacteria, protozoans, rotifers, small crustaceans such as water fleas and aquatic insects make up the plankton life at or near the surface of lakes. In summer, the plankton forms an almost continuous layer of food near the surface. When winter comes, active plankton disappears. Water fleas produce batches of winter-resistant eggs. In spring, eggs hatch and plants and animals emerge, thus replenishing the food supply.

In the deep water of a lake, the water temperature is low and light is either absent or so greatly reduced that plants are unable to live. Oxygen is used in the decay of organisms, and carbon dioxide is high

ANNUAL LARKSPUR
Delphinium ajacis

because it is produced during the process of decay.

LARKSPURS (*Delphinium* spp.) are a group of plants that are annuals — that is, they grow just one year and then must be replanted by seed. Perennials of the same genus are called delphiniums. Both are popular garden flowers.

Annual larkspurs are easy to grow and bloom over a long period. Their blossoms are clustered close to the central stalk. There are both single and double-flowered larkspurs with colours ranging from shades of purple and red to pink and white. Larkspur leaves are so finely divided they appear lace-like, and this is the easiest way to tell them from the lobe-leaved delphiniums.

LAURELS, in ancient Greece, were sacred to Apollo, and garlands of their leaves were presented to heroes and athletes. This shrub is thought to have been the evergreen Sweet Laurel or Bay *(Laurus nobilis)*, native to Europe.

Many shrubs, similar in leaf structure, colour, and growth habit, are also called laurels. Among them are several members of the genus *Prunus* of which the Cherry Laurel *(Prunus laurocerasus)* is the best known of the ornamentals.

Duncan Edwards — FPG

Lava from Sicily's Mt. Etna is used as building stone.

The Spurge Laurel *(Daphne laureola)* is a well-known small shrub of English and Welsh woods on calcareous soils.

LAVA is magma that has reached the Earth's surface in a molten state. Lava flows are usually black, but they weather quickly to brown. When the surface of a lava flow consists of sharp, jagged blocks, it is called *aa* (ah-ah). Smooth and ropy lava is known as *pahoehoe* (pah-hoay-hoay), a Hawaiian name referring to the glistening surface of the flow. Volcanoes are formed when lava piles up around a central vent. More commonly, lavas have oozed from great fissures and covered large areas to depths of several thousand feet. Many lava flows spread under the seas have rolled into round masses known as pillow lavas. Flows may travel at speeds of 50 miles per hour at the moment of eruption. Their speed diminishes rapidly as the slope of the ground lessens. Across flat country, speeds of 5 miles per hour have been noted. Lavas rich in silica flow like molten glass. They move slowly and tend to pile up near their vents. When a flow stops moving, sometimes only the surface solidifies. Then

Oregon State Highway Department

These beds of cinder ash and lava were blown out 12,000 years ago by the now-extinct Mt. Mazama, U.S.A., which formed Crater Lake when it collapsed. Deep layers of ash and cinders were deposited. Running water has carved this soft rock into towers and pinnacles, some of them 200 feet high.

the end or side of the flow may break open, and molten lava will drain from beneath the crust leaving a 'lava tunnel'. Scoria is a rock formed from cooled lava in which the gases have expanded to form large pores. In pumice, the pores are small, while obsidian and basalt are non-porous. (See BASALT; GEOLOGY; OBSIDIAN; VOLCANOES.)

Ropy pahoehoe lava at Craters of Moon in Idaho, U.S.A.

Josef Muench

LAZURITE is a deep azure-blue metamorphic mineral that occurs as fine-grained masses in marble. It is often spangled with pyrite (see PYRITE). Lazurite is found in Iran, Afghanistan and Chile. Two blue igneous minerals — sodalite and lazulite — are frequently confused with lazurite. Lazurite is not a common mineral, and richly coloured varieties are valued highly as gem stones or for mosaics, vases or other ornaments. Lapis-lazuli is a rock rich in lazurite and is used for gems and inlaid objects. During biblical times, lapis-lazuli was a highly prized gem.

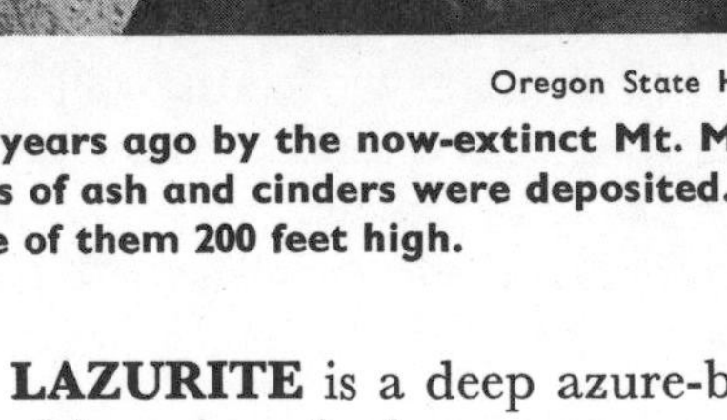

LAZURITE

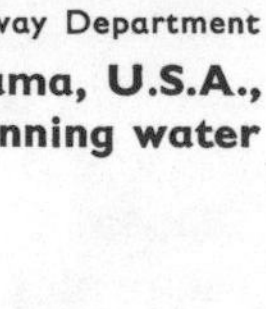

LAPIS-LAZULI

LEAD is produced mainly from galena, a lead sulphide, found in metallic lead-grey cubes or masses with perfect cubic cleavage. Galena has a grey-black streak and is a mineral of hydrothermal origin. Two other lead minerals — cerussite (lead carbonate) and anglesite (lead sulphate) — usually occur with galena. Cerussite occurs as white fibrous masses with good cleavage. It is formed when waters containing carbon dioxide act on galena. Anglesite forms white concentric layers around galena or separate nodules. It has a bright resinous lustre and forms when sulphuric acid from decomposing pyrite acts on galena.

Lead is a soft metal, easily moulded or shaped. It has a low melting point and alloys readily with other metals from which it is also easily recovered. Lead resists corrosion and is impenetrable to gamma rays. These properties and its low cost make lead highly valuable in many industries. Large quantities are used for cable coverings where telephone and electric cables are laid underground or underwater. In many cases the covering is a lead pipe containing nitrogen gas under slight pressure; this keeps water out and also makes it easy to detect leaks. Lead used for bearings is alloyed with copper to make machine brass and bronze and with other metals for making type metal and babbitt. Sheet lead and lead pipe are used in the construction of buildings.

Solder, a mixture of lead and tin, melts at a lower temperature than lead alone. About one third of the lead produced each year is used for plates in storage batteries. White lead (75 per cent lead sulphate, 20 per cent lead dioxide, and 5 per cent zinc oxide) and several other lead compounds are used for paint pigments. Tetraethyl lead is a compound added to petrol to make the burning more uniform in an engine. This increased efficiency is estimated to save about 4,000 million gallons of petrol annually. Lead is also used for shields against X-rays and in nuclear reactors.

Lead ore (galena) is smelted in blast furnaces or in open hearths. First the lead combines with oxygen in the air to make lead oxide; then the lead is freed from the oxygen which combines with coke. The sulphur dioxide produced in the first stages is made into sulphuric acid. Crude lead may contain some copper, tin, arsenic and antimony. These can be removed by an oxidizing process. Silver and gold are valuable impurities also found in lead ore. All impurities are skimmed off the top of the molten lead.

Lead minerals are widely distributed throughout the world, and may be found also as good crystals. Famous lead mining areas are New South Wales, British Columbia, and the states of Colorado and New Jersey. Lead was previously mined in Cornwall, Derbyshire and southern Scotland.

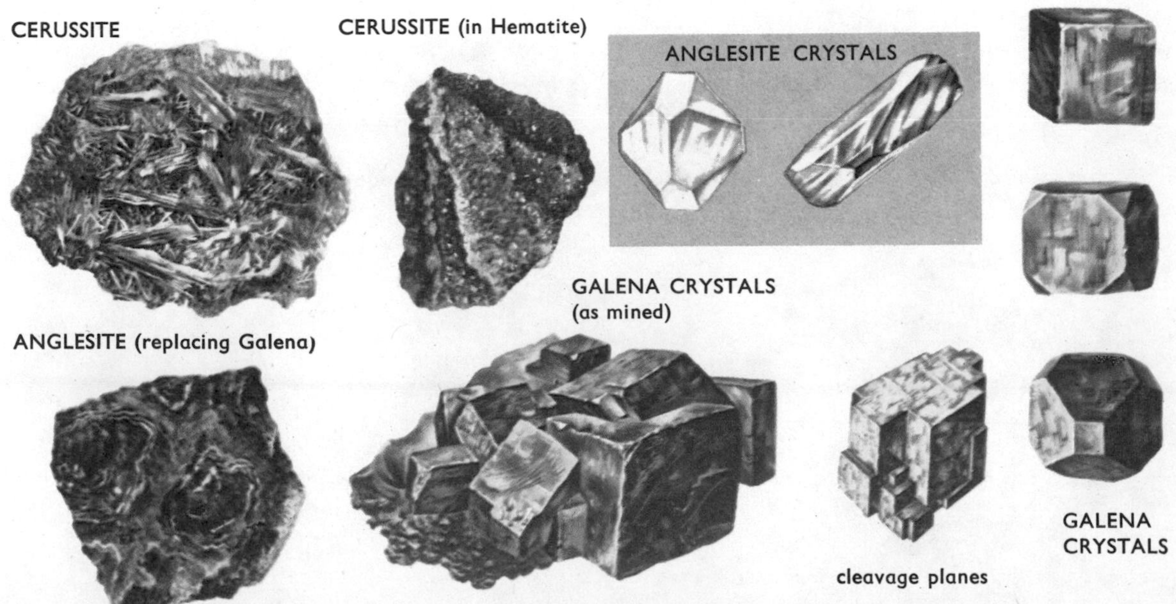
CERUSSITE

CERUSSITE (in Hematite)

ANGLESITE CRYSTALS

GALENA CRYSTALS (as mined)

ANGLESITE (replacing Galena)

cleavage planes

GALENA CRYSTALS

Thousands of herbs, shrubs, and trees make up the legumes (pea family). They grow in a variety of habitats from the seashore to deserts. Many species are important as forage plants for wildlife; a few are poisonous. All are soil builders, adding nitrogen to the soil.

LEGUMES are pod-bearing plants of the pea family (see PEA FAMILY). The several thousand species of legumes include trees, shrubs, herbs, and climbers. Most legume flowers consist of a broad upper petal called a 'standard', two side petals called 'wings', and two lower petals that are united to form a 'keel'. The stamens and pistil are enclosed in the keel. The pistil develops into a fruit called a pod, in which there is a single row of seeds.

Bacteria that live in swellings on the roots of legumes are able to convert nitrogen from the atmosphere, which higher plants cannot use, into nitrogen compounds that higher plants can use. Some legumes can add up to 150 to 400 pounds of nitrogen in compound form to the soil each year.

In European and American agriculture the clovers, notably White Clover *(Trifolium repens)* and Red Clover *(Trifolium incarnatum)* are widely used to maintain or improve the fertility of pastures. Lupins will grow on poor acid land and are used for reclaiming land of this type. Lucerne *(Medicago sativa)* is widely used in temperate regions to produce hay or forage for cattle. The seeds of peas and beans are eaten green or ripe, and usually contain much more protein than cereal grain. The soybean *(Glycine soja)* and the groundnut *(Arachis hypogaea)* are grown over large areas of Africa, southern Asia and Central America for oil and protein. Several leguminous trees including the Mediterranean Carob Tree *(Ceratonia siliqua)* and the Algarroba *(Prosopis juliflora)* have edible pods that are used in place of cereals. (See CAROB TREES; LUCERNE; SOYBEANS.)

LETTUCE *(Lactuca sativa)* is the world's most popular salad vegetable. It probably originated in southern Europe and western

Lettuce, a low calorie food, provides bulk in the diet and is a moderate source of vitamins.

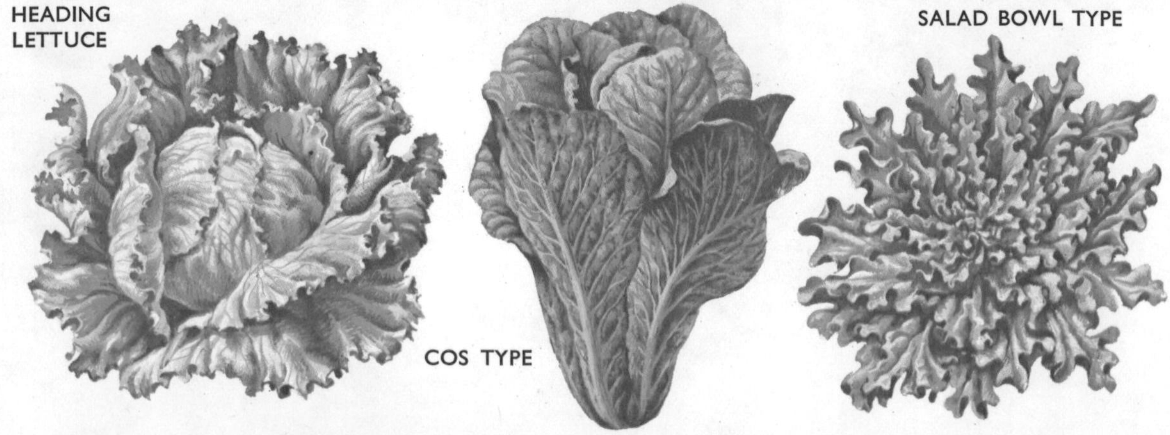

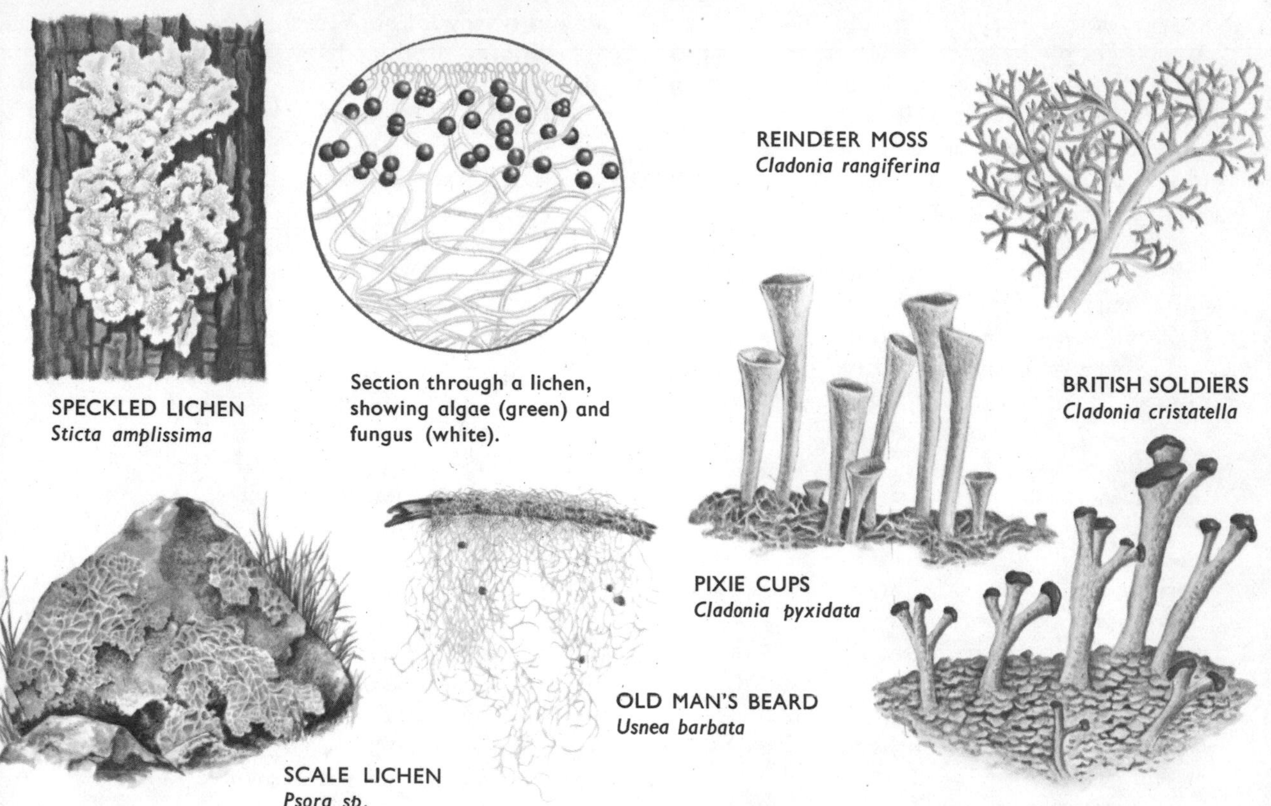

Asia and has been cultivated for over 2,500 years. Like cabbage, present forms do not resemble their uncultivated ancestors.

There are three main types of lettuce grown in Great Britain. The Butterhead type forms hearts, and includes such varieties as May Princess, Cobham Green and Premier; the Curly Crisp group is formed of varieties such as A.I. and Great Lakes; the third type is the Cos, of which Lobjoit's Green and Little Gem are good examples.

Lettuce can be grown in unprotected ground in the summer, garden frames in the autumn and slightly warm greenhouses in the winter. During the summer, lettuce seeds may be sown directly into the position where the plants are to be grown, the seedlings being thinned when an inch or so high to between 12 and 15 inches apart. In late summer and early autumn, lettuce seedlings can be transplanted, either into frames or, in late autumn, slightly heated greenhouses.

Lettuce seedlings transplanted in late spring and summer will 'bolt'. This is a term used to describe a plant which produces seeds instead of its usual expected growth.

LICHENS are a partnership of a fungus and an alga. Some botanists believe these two plants grow together in symbiosis, each benefiting from the other. Others believe lichens are a master-slave relationship. The fungus is the master, giving the alga a home and protecting it from drying out. The alga is the slave and feeds the master the food it manufactures.

A lichen grows as if it were a single plant and is given a genus and species name as if it were one plant. The fungus is usually dominant and makes up most of the body of the lichen, giving the growth its characteristic shape and colour. The alga is either a blue-green or a green. In some cases the fungus and the alga can be separated, and each will grow by itself. Probably in most cases they cannot grow separately. The algae lie just beneath the surface of the lichen. Thus, they get light which they need for photosynthesis but are protected by the fungus from drying out.

Lichens of some 6,000 kinds grow all over the world, from the arctic to the tropics. Usually they grow where there is little competition from other plants. Often they are pioneer plants, growing on bare rocks and helping to break them into particles to form soil. Acids secreted by lichens dissolve the rock surface. Also, as the lichens die, they add organic matter to the rock particles. Mosses, ferns and seed plants then grow in this new soil.

Lichens are the only plants that grow in some parts of the arctic. Reindeer Moss *(Cladonia rangiferina)* is eaten by reindeer and other arctic animals. Other lichens grow in deserts, and many are found on the bark of trees. Some kinds, such as species of *Parmelia*, grow as flat crusts, clinging so tightly to rocks or bark that they appear to be embedded. Others, less firmly attached, resemble fallen leaves. Some types grow upright and have many braches. Old Man's Beard *(Usnea barbata)*, a shrubby lichen, grows over the branches and trunks of trees in coniferous forests in cool climates. Its branched threads hang from the trees like the Spanish Moss of southern United States of America.

The fruiting bodies of lichen fungi are sometimes small, flat cups, occasionally stalked. Pixie Cups *(Cladonia pyxidata)* have long, funnel-like fruiting bodies. British Soldiers *(Cladonia cristatella)* have bright-red or light-brown knobs at the top of the stalks. The spores produced by the fungus part of the lichens are not very important in reproduction. The lichens usually reproduce by forming tiny clumps of fungus mycelium around a few alga cells. The clumps are so small that they appear to be dust particles. They are easily blown by the wind, and, when they land in a suitable place, they form a new lichen plant. Some grow rapidly, though a large patch of lichens may be over a hundred years old.

Most lichens are grey-green, but some are brown, black, yellow, white, or even red. Lichens are sources of certain dyes. Litmus paper, used to determine whether a solution is acid or alkaline, gets its colour from a lichen, as do Harris-tweed fabrics. Some lichens are used for human food, although most kinds are too bitter. The biblical manna is thought to have been a lichen *(Lecanora)* carried by the wind to the area where the hungry Israelites gathered this miraculously supplied food. This lichen grows in mountainous regions and is blown loose into the lowlands where the plants pile up in small heaps in the valley. As late as 1891 there was an abundant fall of this manna in Turkey. It is still used today by desert tribes, who mix it with meal to one third of its weight.

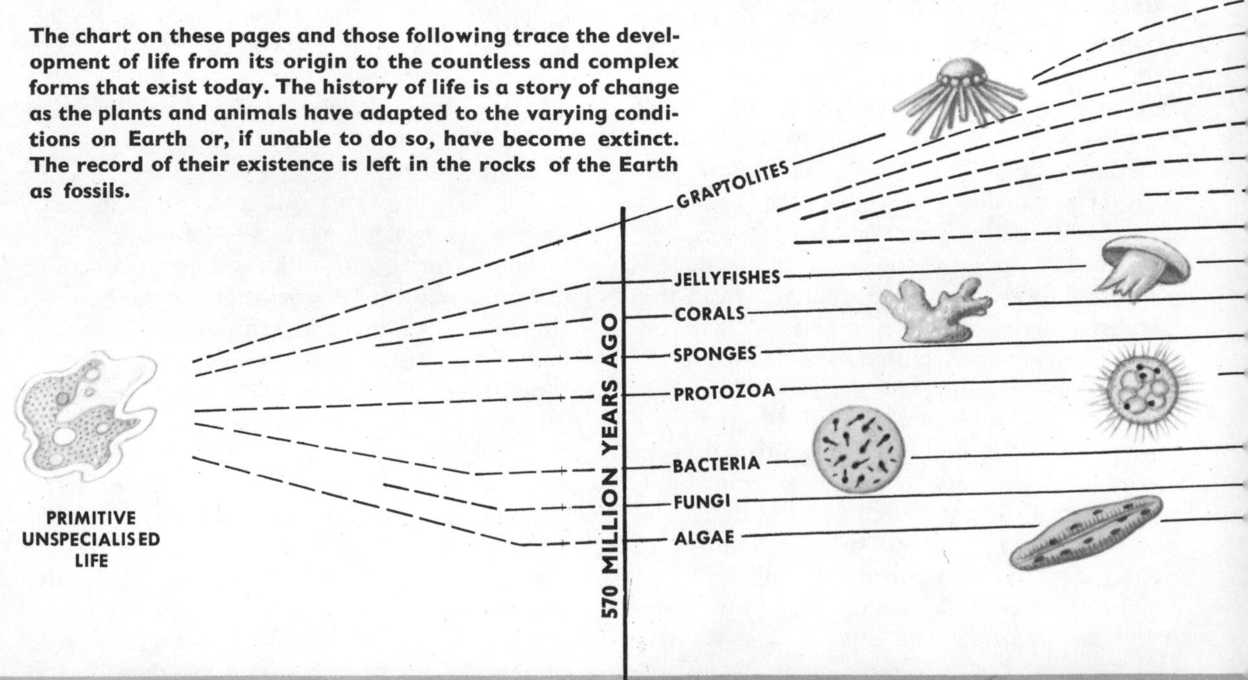

The chart on these pages and those following trace the development of life from its origin to the countless and complex forms that exist today. The history of life is a story of change as the plants and animals have adapted to the varying conditions on Earth or, if unable to do so, have become extinct. The record of their existence is left in the rocks of the Earth as fossils.

In Iceland, Norway, and Sweden, another lichen *(Cetraria islandica)* is commonly mixed with cereals and mashed potatoes to make a healthful bread. In Japan, a delicacy known as 'rock mushroom' is a lichen *(Umbilicaria esculenta)*.

Lichens are used as fodder and for grazing. The domestic raising of reindeer is often dependent on lichens. In Lapland, the lichens are collected by hand and dried as fodder. The wise Laplander, each of whom may own a herd of several thousand reindeer, harvests only about a fourth of the crop and leaves the rest. In Norway, rakes are used in harvesting. Two thirds of the supply may be harvested at a time, and it may require as long as 30 years to replenish the supply.

LIFE'S ORIGIN AND DEVELOPMENT. How life began is still a mystery, but we know that it has existed for over 2,500 million years.

Evidence indicates that all plants and animals alive today developed over long periods of time from ancestors that were often quite different. It seems certain that the earliest living things on Earth must have been very simple. The oldest fossils so far known come from rocks of Pre-Cambrian age. They include algae, fungi, jellyfish, worms, and some sponge-like animals. All were very simple but were already far advanced from the lowly single cells which might be called the first living organisms. It is unlikely that fossils will ever be found that carry us back into the first 2,000 million years of the Earth's history.

The first atmosphere of the Earth probably consisted mainly of methane gas (CH_4), water vapour (H_2O), and ammonia gas (NH_3). These substances contain all the chemical elements needed to make amino acids — the building blocks of protein, which is the basis of life. Recent laboratory experiments have demonstrated that a mixture of these gases subjected to an electric discharge will produce amino acids. Some scientists believe that lightning in the early atmosphere may

AGNATHA (OSTRACODERMS)
PLACODERMS
INSECTS
TRILOBITES
WORMS
MOLLUSCS
AMMONITES
BRACHIOPODS
STARFISHES
JELLYFISHES
CORALS
SPONGES
PROTOZOA
BACTERIA
FUNGI
ALGAE
MOSSES
HORSETAILS
FERNS
SCALE TREES
500 MILLION YEARS AGO
440 MILLION YEARS AGO
395 MILLION YEARS AGO
345 MILLION YEARS AGO
ORDOVICIAN PERIOD
60 million years
SILURIAN PERIOD
45 million years
DEVONIAN PERIOD
50 million years
345 MILLION YEARS

ANKYLOSAURUS
an armoured dinosaur

have assisted in bringing about such a reaction. From amino acids to proteins is a long step, and it is a still longer one from proteins to the simplest living cells. But this discovery makes it possible to imagine a series of steps by which the earliest life may have originated.

The odds are indeed many against having the proper circumstances for the beginning of life in this manner, but conditions necessary for this development of life must have existed on Earth for perhaps as long as 2,000 million years and over enormous areas of the Earth's surface. There is no proof that life did originate in this or in any other particular way. As life did evolve, however, creatures gradually developed hard parts and provided a record of their existence in the form of fossils.

The chief ingredient in evolution is time. Only against a background of about 3,000 million years of life does the process of evolution become clear. Science is concerned largely with the question of *how* this came about.

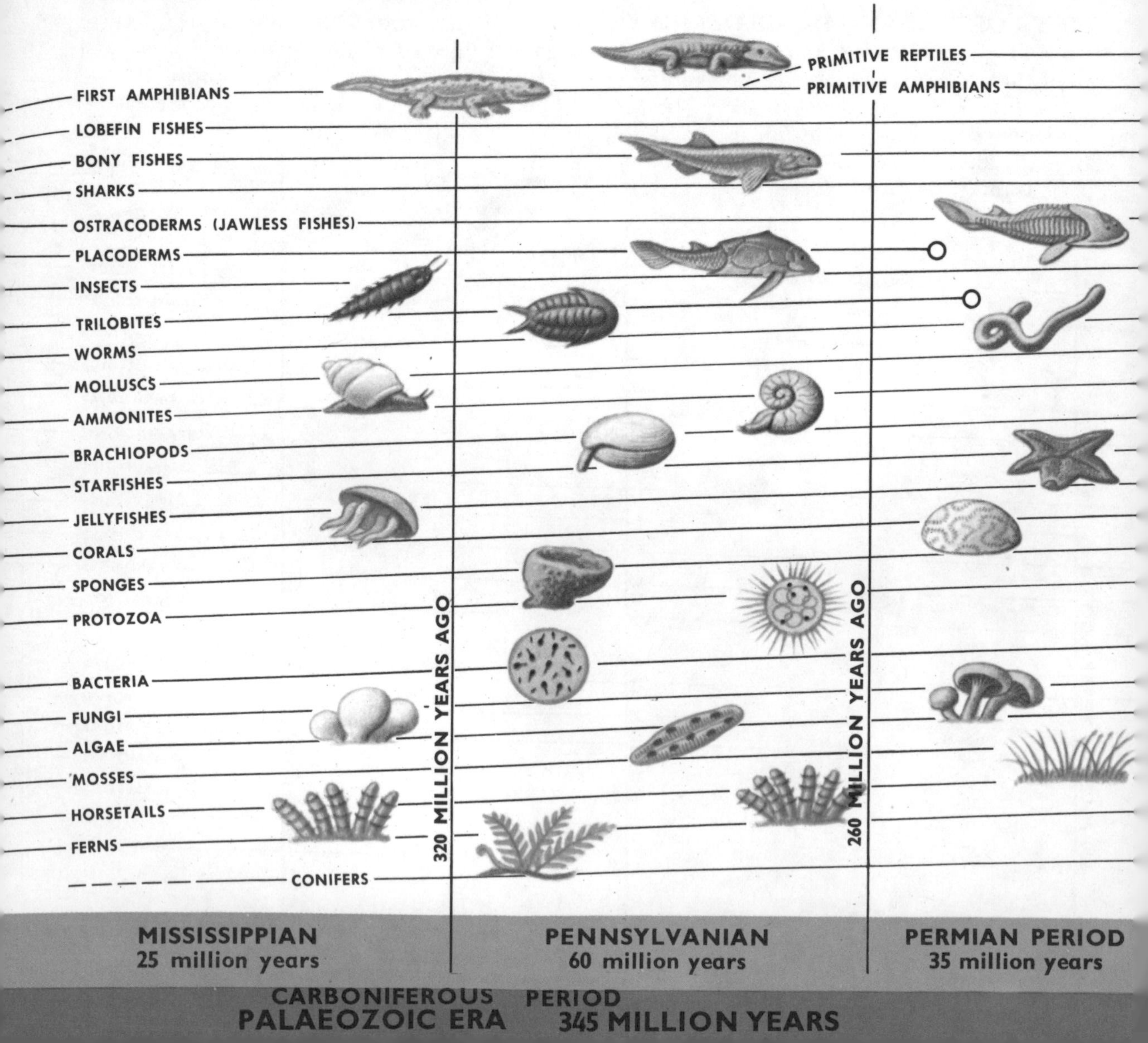

PRIMITIVE REPTILES
FIRST AMPHIBIANS
PRIMITIVE AMPHIBIANS
LOBEFIN FISHES
BONY FISHES
SHARKS
OSTRACODERMS (JAWLESS FISHES)
PLACODERMS
INSECTS
TRILOBITES
WORMS
MOLLUSCS
AMMONITES
BRACHIOPODS
STARFISHES
JELLYFISHES
CORALS
SPONGES
PROTOZOA
BACTERIA
FUNGI
ALGAE
MOSSES
HORSETAILS
FERNS
CONIFERS

320 MILLION YEARS AGO
260 MILLION YEARS AGO

MISSISSIPPIAN
25 million years

PENNSYLVANIAN
60 million years

PERMIAN PERIOD
35 million years

CARBONIFEROUS PERIOD

PALAEOZOIC ERA 345 MILLION YEARS

The Earth, too, has changed in its long history. Most present-day features of the Earth's crust are comparatively recent in origin. The Pacific Ocean seems to have persisted unchanged for the longest time. The Alps are 40 million years old, the Appalachians of North America about 225. Only 11,000 years ago most of northern Europe and North America were covered by ice sheets.

LIFE IN ANCIENT SEAS. During the whole of the Cambrian and Ordovician periods and most of the Silurian (a total of 175 million years, starting around 570 million years ago) many kinds of creatures thronged in the shallow seas. These periods show a great variety of animal and plant life, all of which show considerable advancement over creatures of the Pre-Cambrian and are far evolved from the first living things. It seems probable that there were no living things on land and possibly none in the existing streams and lakes. The land areas must have been unbelievably desolate wastelands of bare rock, sand, and mud, without a single bird, mammal, insect, tree, grass, or flower.

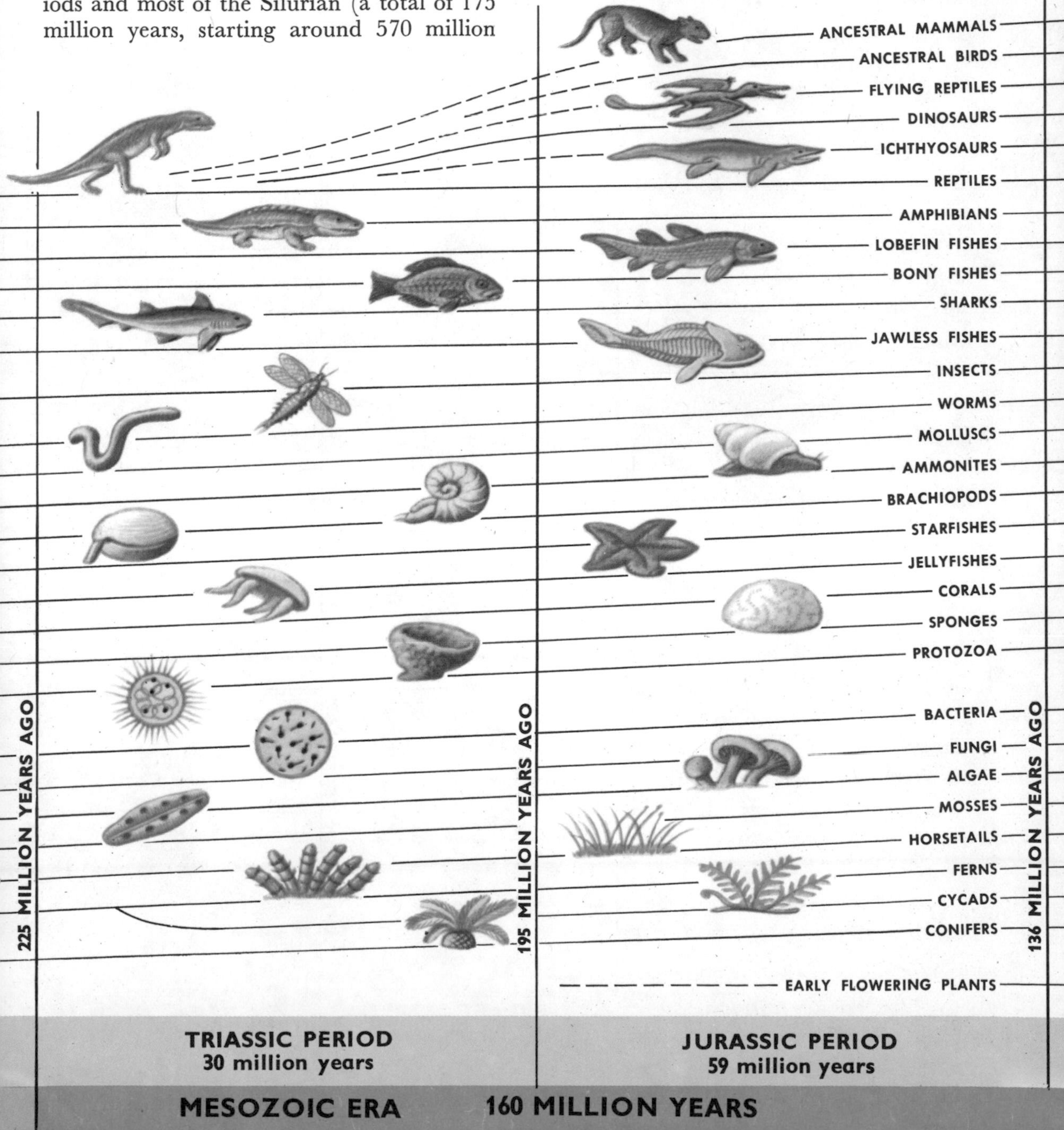

THE COLONISATION OF LAND. The oldest well-preserved land plants come from the upper Silurian of Victoria, Australia. By Devonian times land plants had become common and are known from such scattered areas as Britain, Norway, Czechoslovakia, Wyoming, and China. Most were small and primitive, but by upper Devonian times there were forests of scale trees in some areas. These trees, which became extinct during the Palaeozoic era, were the forerunners of those forming coal swamps of Pennsylvanian times.

The oldest undoubted fossil record of

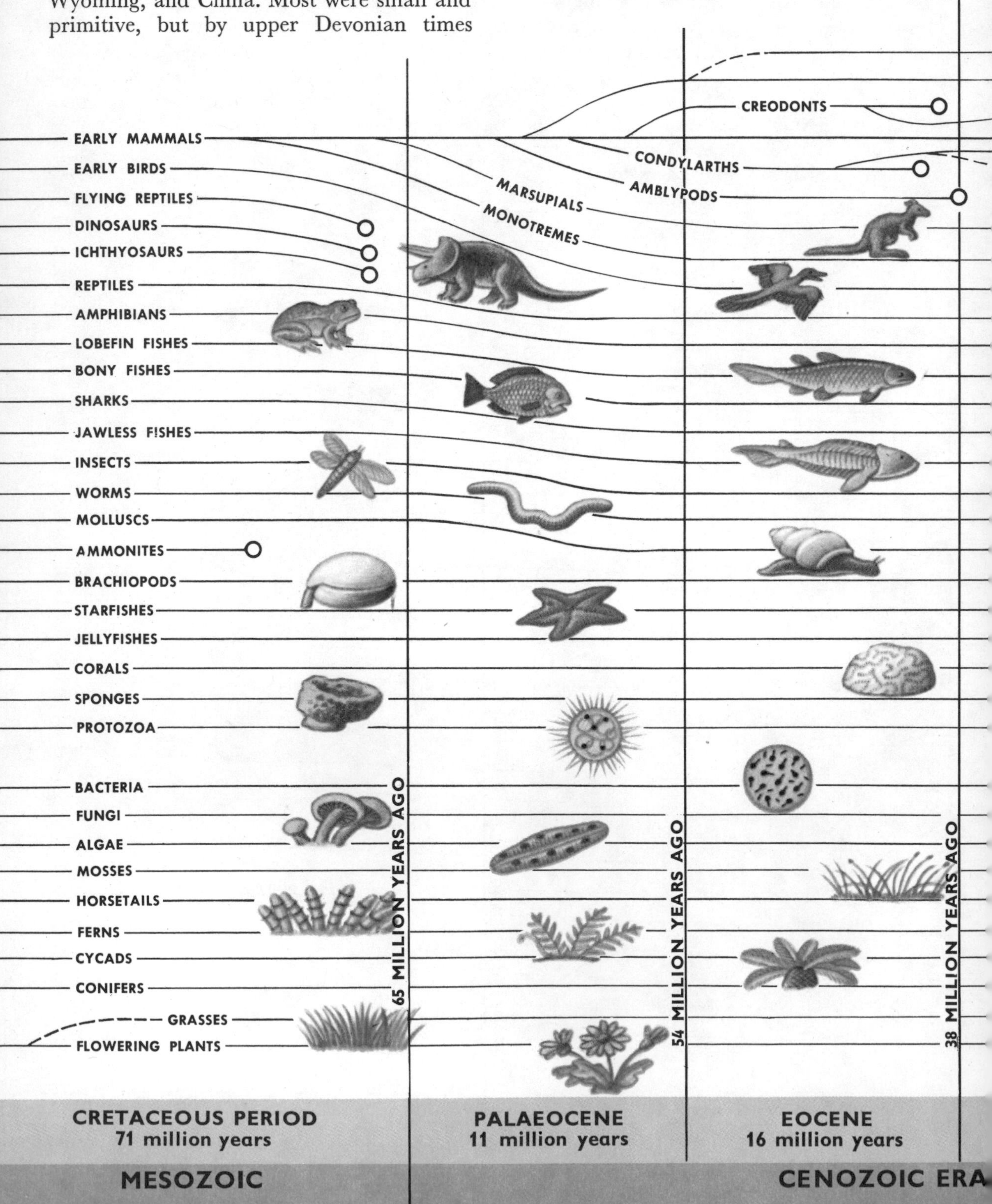

animal life on land comes from Devonian times when arthropods, including spider-like and tick-like animals, were established. Several kinds of insects had appeared by upper Devonian times. During the Mississippian period air-breathing scorpions and true spiders appeared. Land snails are known

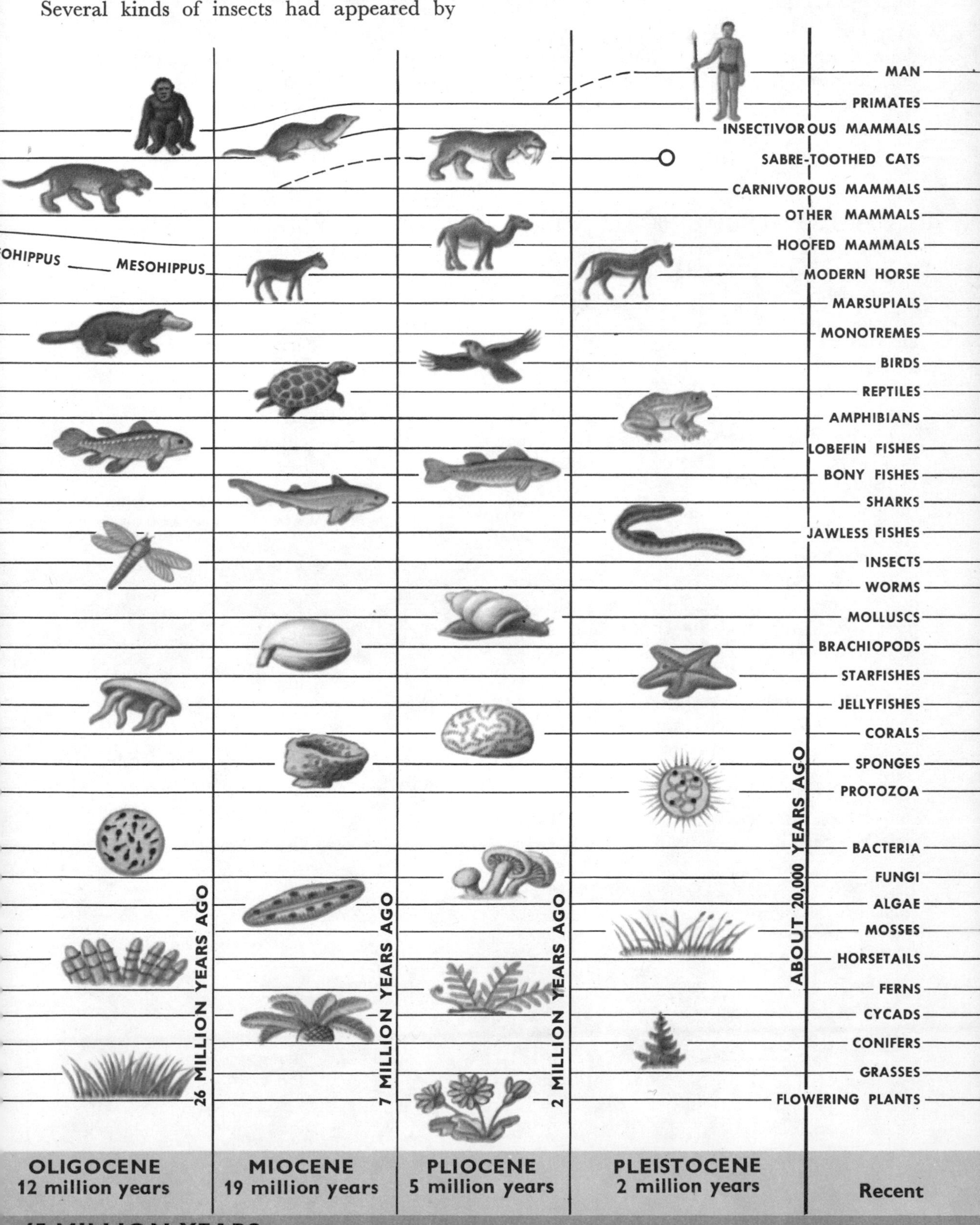

from Pennsylvanian rocks in Canada, preserved with fossil trees.

Early land animals were directly or indirectly dependent on land plants for food. Many years later some land plants came to depend on animals for pollinating flowers and for seed dispersal. The appearance of both land plants and the land animals at roughly the same geologic time is a reminder of this basic interdependence of all living things.

ANIMALS WITH BACKBONES. The oldest fossil fish are preserved as small bony fragments in middle Ordovician rocks in the Rocky Mountains. From then until upper Silurian times fossil fish are rare, but by the Devonian they were important both in seas and in fresh waters. All major groups of fishes were well established and flourishing.

Lungfish were probably already partly independent of water in the Devonian when they were a widespread group. Found today in South America, Africa, and Australia, they and their ancestors were adapted to survive dry periods buried in the mud. A related group of fresh-water carnivorous fishes (crossopterygians) were strikingly like the earliest amphibians in the structure of their limbs and fins, backbone and skull. Remarkable fossils of primitive amphibians show a mixture of characters of both groups.

Amphibians were still tied to the water by their need to lay their eggs there. Though incomplete, their liberation from water was a landmark in life's history, for amphibians later gave rise to other vertebrates that were completely adapted to life on land. These were the reptiles.

THE REIGN OF THE REPTILES. The ancestors of living reptiles ruled land, sea, and air for almost 130 million years — almost the entire span of the Mesozoic era. In the 80 million years that amphibians were dominant they never completely escaped from a dependence on water, but reptiles succeeded inspreading far inland. In some ways they were better adapted to life on land than were the amphibians. Notable among these advances was a leathery outer covering that protected their eggs from drying. In some the young developed inside the mother's body and were born alive. Likewise, the scaly skins of reptiles were not affected by dry air, while the moist skins of amphibians confined them solely to moist surroundings.

The oldest fossil reptiles come from Pennsylvanian and Permian rocks. Some Permian forms, such as *Seymouria*, were much like amphibians, suggesting their recent rise from this group. During the Mesozoic, the Age of Reptiles, they underwent great expansion

Some ichthyosaurs measured 10 feet from the tip of their beak to the last vertebra in their long tail.

ICHTHYOSAUR

fossil skeleton

and developed in a number of directions.

Most spectacular of all the reptile groups were the dinosaurs. They existed on every continent. But the range of reptiles extended beyond the land. Mosasaurs, Cretaceous sea serpents, were carnivores. Crocodiles, too, existed in Mesozoic times.

Having spread across the land, reptilian groups successfully invaded the seas. Turtles (some of them 12 feet long), streamlined ichthyosaurs, plesiosaurs (the largest 50 feet long), ponderous placodonts, and serpent-like geosaurs and mosasaurs swept through the oceans. Reptiles even extended their dominance into the air. The first birds developed in Jurassic times.

The close of the Mesozoic saw the decline of the reptiles. Dinosaurs, flying pterosaurs, and great sea-going reptiles — all became extinct. Snakes, lizards, turtles, crocodiles, and the Tuatara *(Sphenodon)* are remnants of a line that has known greater days.

***Calamites*, extinct relative of modern horsetails, grew to height of present-day trees in coal-forming swamps.**

FLOWERS AND FUR. Flowering plants and mammals became important during the Cenozoic. Both had been in existence for a long time. The oldest fossils of flowering plants are found in rocks of Cretaceous age, and the group had expanded greatly before the end of that period. Beeches, birches, oaks, maples and walnuts are among the kinds of trees that existed then and are still alive today. Flowering plants transformed the face of the Earth and influenced the history of development of many animals.

Mammals existed as a small, rather insignificant group for at least 100 million years of Mesozoic time. The earliest mammals were small, shrew-like creatures that probably arose from the mammal-like reptiles. Some were plant eaters (condylarths); others ate flesh (creodonts). With the decline of reptiles, mammals underwent considerable expansion. They replaced and excelled reptiles.

Cenozoic mammals showed even greater diversity than did the reptiles of the Mesozoic. Many were large, and had more complex brains than any animals that existed before them. In the Cenozoic, too, swampy forests were converted into upland grass-covered prairies. Many Miocene mammals became grazers on these vast grasslands rather than browsers on leaves and twigs in the forests. Changes in their teeth and limb structure show this clearly.

In Cenozoic times the major features (mountains, canyons, etc.) of the Earth's crust developed as we know them now. The last great physical event of the Cenozoic era was widespread glaciation of northern continents in the Pleistocene. During the past 2 million years four great advances of ice have buried a large part of the Earth. This, too, affected life greatly. Many large mammals became extinct, and those that survived became more restricted in distribution.

In this frozen world Man emerged as a tool-making and tool-using animal. Man's brain set him apart in the animal world. For the first time in the long history of life a species has developed with the power to control to a large degree the future pattern of life. Man alone has this most awesome responsibility.

LIGHT is one form of radiant energy. The radiant energy spectrum is a broad band extending from very short waves a few trillionths of an inch long to waves hundreds of miles long. Beginning with the shortest and finishing with the longest, they are known as cosmic, gamma waves, X-rays, ultra-violet, visible light, infra-red (heat), micro-waves (radar communications), radio and TV waves. Still longer waves exist but are not used at the present time.

Visible light waves, a small part of the entire electromagnetic spectrum, are those from about 1/62,000 to 1/36,000 of an inch in length. The shortest waves of visible light are the blues, followed by greens, yellows, oranges, and reds, which are the longest.

Light is essential to all plants that manufacture their food by photosynthesis. Some plants require long days and short nights for flowering; others, short days and long nights (see PHOTOPERIODISM). Red light stimulates growth of reproductive structures — flowers and fruit. Blue light stimulates growth of vegetative parts — leaves and stems. Some plants, such as grasses, sunflowers, goldenrods and tomatoes, are sun lovers. Others, such as ferns, mosses and woodland flowers, grow best in the shade and are retarded in growth or killed by bright sun. Light causes the stomata on the leaves of plants to open; this increases the plants' internal temperature and their loss of water by evaporation. Plants growing in shade have larger, more watery leaves than those growing in the sun.

Direct exposure of protoplasm to light causes death. Animals and plants must be able to use light but at the same time be able to prevent it from destroying them. Pigmentation does much to protect them. *Euglena*, a protozoan, possesses a small, red eyespot in ordinary light, but if light intensity increases, the red pigment spreads to cover the body and decreases light penetration. Albinos are not successful in direct sunlight because they lack the protection of a dark pigment.

Small surface plants — mostly algae — are inhibited in growth by intense light. Their growth is slowest during midday.

LILACS (*Syringa* spp.) are woody shrubs that have been popular ornamentals for centuries. In early spring they bear dense clusters of fragrant purple or white flowers. Plant breeders of France contributed most in developing handsome varieties by combining various species that grow wild in Europe and Asia. In European countries they are forced to bloom in winter for cut flowers.

Some plants, such as goldenrods, require full sunlight and do poorly in the shade. Others, such as primulas are shade-loving plants and do not grow well in the sun.

LILIES (*Lilium* spp.) are the symbols of purity seen on stained-glass church windows and religious decorations. Their floral parts are arranged in threes and sixes. The three sepals and three petals look alike, and there are also six stamens. The stigma is divided into three parts.

There are roughly 80 species of *Lilium*, divided into 3 groups. These are based on the flower shape, which is either trumpet-like, pendant with reflexed petals or erect and bowl-shaped. The main colours are white, yellow, red or orange sometimes spotted black. The most common species in gardens are the Regal Lily with large, white trumpets, the Madonna Lily, the Tiger Lily which is orange with black spotting, and the Martagon or Turkscap, a species from the mountain woods of Europe, that are shaped like turbans.

Lilies are raised from seed which usually takes several years to flower but the Easter Lily will sometimes produce its huge white trumpets only 6 months after sowing the seeds.

Most lilies are not very easy to grow, particularly the wild kinds. Their soil, water and light needs are very critical. Lilies are also susceptible to many diseases.

Tulips, hyacinths, bluebells, and onions are also members of the lily family, which contains more than 2,500 species. Water-lilies have 'lily' as part of their names but are not true lilies (see WATERLILIES).

LILIES-OF-THE-VALLEY *(Convallaria majalis)* are old favourites known throughout the world. They are easily grown in bowls indoors in winter. In outdoor beds they spread rapidly in shady spots with rich soil, becoming an attractive ground cover. The crowns should be dug and split apart after several seasons. Lilies-of-the-valley are rare wild plants in woods in the British Isles but are more common in mountainous regions of Europe, Asia and America.

LIMESTONE. Any rock that contains more than 50 per cent calcium carbonate is limestone. Limestone rocks make up about 15 per cent of the Earth's land surface. The calcium carbonate in limestone is usually in the form of the mineral calcite. Calcite adapts to physical and chemical changes more than any other rock-forming mineral. It dissolves quickly, recrystallises easily, and can be replaced rapidly by other minerals. Thus limestones have a wide range of textures, content, and structure. Calcite is normally colourless, white, or grey. Other minerals, such as dolomite, quartz, glauconite, kaolinite, and siderite, are present as impurities and may stain the limestone buff, brown, yellow or red.

All sea water contains dissolved minerals. When some of the sea water evaporates, the amount of minerals the water can hold in solution is reduced. Some of the calcium carbonate precipitates or drops out of solution and is deposited on the bottom. Much

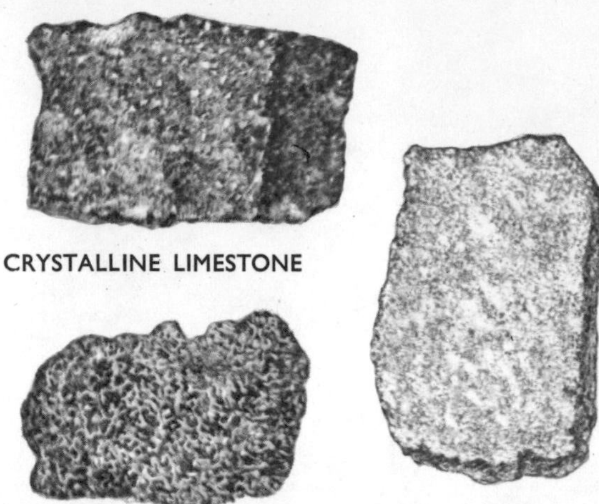
CRYSTALLINE LIMESTONE

TUFA

OOLITIC LIMESTONE

calcite is precipitated when aquatic plants take carbon dioxide from the water and use it to manufacture food. There it collects in thick beds and consolidates finally into a fine-grained rock. Marine plants or animals that die and drop to the bottom are incorporated in the rocks as fossils.

Limestone develops also in fresh water. It forms in springs where calcite collects as a crust on plants, twigs and debris. It occurs on land where wind-blown grains of calcite are deposited in dunes.

Two very common impurities in limestones are chert and flint, which are cryptocrystalline varieties of quartz (see QUARTZ). They occur as nodular concretions or beds that were formed when the limestone muds were deposited, or they may have been brought in later by silica-rich water percolating through the rock replacing part of the original mass. Flint was much used by primitive man to make arrowheads and knives.

Water containing dissolved carbon dioxide dissolves the calcite and rapidly hollows out a limestone formation. Caves such as those in Derbyshire and Yorkshire were formed in this manner. Solutions dripping into these same caves lose their calcite as the water evaporates. The calcite crystals form icicle-like stalactites that hang from the roof and stalagmites that build up from the floor. When joined they form columns.

Coquina limestone is composed of loosely cemented shell fragments. Shell limestone resembles coquina but has nearly whole shells firmly cemented together. 'Eggstone'

Shells of large one-celled animals (Foraminifera) form the limestone rocks of which the great pyramids were built. This 3-inch wide species, ***Nummulites leavigatus*****, occurs in rocks found in northern France.**

Steven Celebonovic

R. J. Fish

In this cave in Agen Allwedd, Breconshire, calcite crystals have formed icicle-like stalactites.

and 'peastone' are familiar names for oolite and pisolite. These are limestones in which the round grains of calcite look like tiny fish eggs (oolite) or like peas and larger balls (pisolite). Chalk is an extremely soft and porous limestone composed of shells of one-celled marine animals. Marl is a fine mixture of calcium carbonate and clay (kaolinite). Marls are rich sources of fossils. Lithographic stone is almost pure calcite. This stone is so tough and smooth that it was once used to make the blocks for engravings of pictures and maps.

Tufa is a very porous limestone deposit that forms in springs. Elaborate terraces at Mammoth Hot Springs in Yellowstone National Park, Wyoming, are tufa. Tufa gradually becomes travertine as more calcite is deposited. Travertine may be white but is usually tinted yellow, brown, pink, or green. It is widely used for ornaments or as a decorative stone. Stalactites and stalagmites are travertine. Mexican onyx, a banded and

The White Cliffs of Dover are formed of chalk, the skeletal remains of one-celled animals that lived in the sea 100 million years ago.

Ewing Galloway

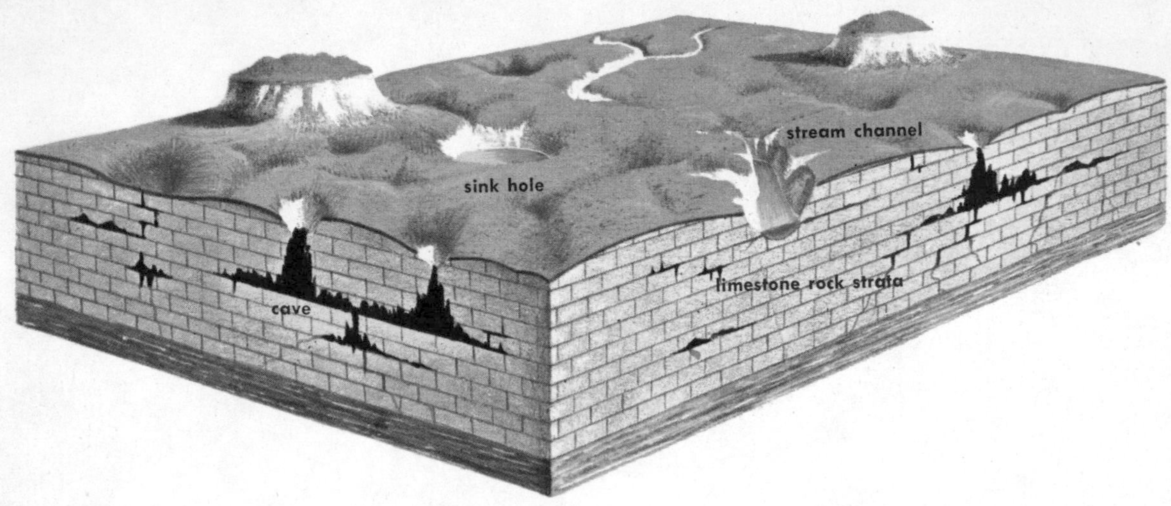

Water has formed sinkholes, caves, and channels for underground streams in this bed of limestone.

mottled variety of travertine, takes a high polish and is used for pen stands, lamps, and vases.

Limestone in which the original calcium carbonate has been changed to large calcite crystals with noticeable cleavage is known as crystalline limestone. Because it takes a high polish, crystalline limestone is known in the building trade as marble, but true marble contains no visible fossils (see MARBLE).

Limestone makes excellent building stones because blocks can be cut easily and are strong enough to stand heavy loads. Many quarries are found in Europe and the United States. Roman walls built of travertine are still standing after almost 2,000 years. Crushed limestone is used for road beds and is spread over farm lands to neutralise acids and 'sweeten' the soil. Portland cement is about 80 per cent limestone and 20 per cent clay (see SHALE). Large quantities of limestone are used in the manufacture of pig iron. Oil reservoirs also occur in limestone deposits.

LOTUS *(Nelumbo lutea)*. The American Lotus or Duck Acorn, with pale yellow flowers, grows along the east coast of North America as far north as Connecticut. American Indians called the plant Chinkapin and obtained a starchy food from its coarse underwater tubers. They also ate its ripe seeds. The leaf stalks and the young leaves are also considered edible. Other species of the genus grow in Asia and Africa.

Members of the waterlily family, lotus leaves are large and circular, often a foot or more across, and are attached like umbrellas to their stems. The beautiful pink Asiatic Lotus *(Nelumbo indica)*, once considered sacred by the Hindus, is often grown in ponds and heated pools in Europe and America.

The famed lotus of ancient Egypt *(Nymphaea lotus)* also belongs to the waterlily family (see WATERLILIES).

1 AMERICAN LOTUS *Nelumbo lutea* 2 EGYPTIAN LOTUS *Nymphaea lotus*

The 'Lotus-eaters' were a Mediterranean people who ate the fruits of a shrub also called Lotus (*Zizyphus* spp.).

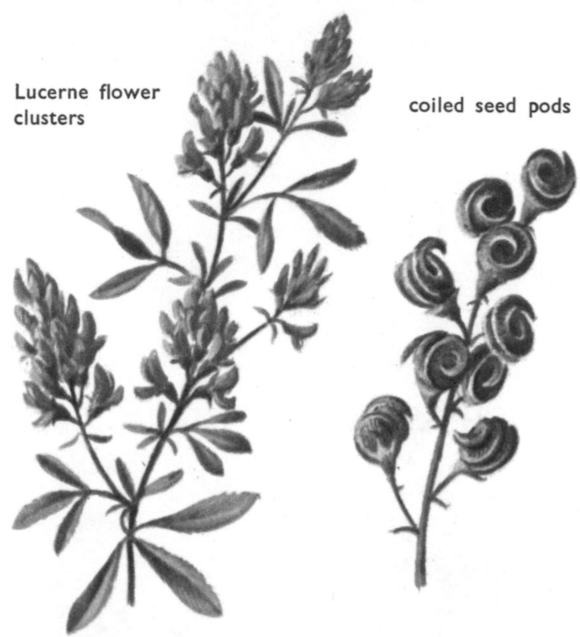

LUCERNE *(Medicago sativa)* was one of the first forage crops grown by man. A native of south-western Asia, it is an important crop throughout the world today. Like other legumes or members of the pea family, lucerne enriches the soil by adding nitrogen.

Lucerne is a hardy plant. It grows in a variety of soils and survives dry, hot spells because its taproots grow deep into the soil where moisture is more plentiful.

Lucerne plants attain a height of 2—4 feet. Because new stems and leaves regenerate rapidly after a cutting, several crops can be harvested in one season.

Lucerne flowers are purple or sometimes yellow. They discharge their pollen explosively when bees separate the flowers' wing-shaped petals. Tightly coiled, spiral seed pods develop at maturity. Lucerne intended for drying and stacking as a winter feed for livestock is cut before it flowers. In some areas crops are allowed to flower as a source of nectar for honey bees.

A Lucerne crop is being harvested for winter feed.

Ford Motor Co: Ford Almanac 1962

LYCHEES are fruit held in high esteem for centuries in China, believed to be the plant's native home. A 'lychee nut' is not a true nut but a dried lychee fruit just as raisins are dried grapes. The fruit is round to oval and about the size of a plum. At maturity, the rough, rather woody skin is usually brilliant red, like a strawberry. The juicy flesh has an excellent flavour, similar to a good grape. The trees are sub-tropical evergreens that frequently grow 40 feet tall. Many varieties are grown commercially in China, India, South Africa, Australia, Hawaii, and Florida.

MAGNESIUM is a light metal obtained from the sea and also from three common minerals. Magnesite (magnesium carbonate), most abundantly used magnesium mineral, is found in dull-white, compact masses or veins; it has good conchoidal fracture, resembling porcelain. It also occurs as clear crystals that have three perfect cleavages. Magnesite is closely associated with serpentine from which it is formed by the action of carbon dioxide in water. It is found also in sedimentary beds. Brucite (magnesium hydroxide) is a translucent to transparent mineral found as white leaf-like masses. It has a pearly lustre and one perfect cleavage. The other important magnesium mineral is dolomite, a calcium-magnesium carbonate. (See DOLOMITE.)

Magnesium bars are attached to steel boilers, ships, and pipelines because the magnesium corrodes and leaves the steel untouched. It is used as a reducing agent in smelting titanium and zirconium. Since it is one third lighter than aluminium, it is being used for ladders, business machines, artificial limbs, lorry bodies, and other places where lightness is important. Because it burns with an intensely white flame, it is used for flares and incendiaries and may be used as a rocket fuel. Magnesia bricks are used to line furnaces because they do not react with molten metal and can withstand high temperatures. Magnesium cement, which is made with magnesium chloride, sets hard and may be laid over large areas without cracking. Other magnesium compounds are used in industry and in drugs. Magnesite comes from the U.S.S.R., Austria, Yugoslavia, Greece, Manchuria, Australia, Quebec, Ontario, and Washington. During times of emergency, magnesium compounds

Magnesite and dolomite are the ores of magnesium.

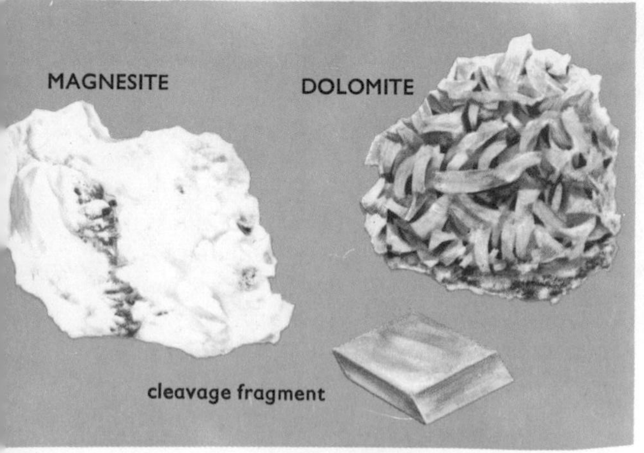

STARRY MAGNOLIA
Magnolia stellata

are produced in the United States from sea water in Texas and California and from brine wells in Michigan.

MAGNOLIAS are beautiful trees and shrubs widely planted as ornamentals. They have showy flowers and oval leaves. When ripe, their large red seeds hang by slender threads from upright, cone-like clusters. About 35 species of magnolias are native to North and Central America and eastern Asia.

The Southern Magnolia *(Magnolia grandiflora)*, a handsome evergreen tree, has fragrant flowers with 6 to 12 waxy white petals. The Cucumber Magnolia *(Magnolia acuminata)*, a large deciduous tree, has cup-shaped flowers with greenish-yellow petals. The Sweetbay *(Magnolia virginiana)*, a shrub or small tree, has fragrant and creamy-white flowers. Less common American species are Bigleaf *(Magnolia macrophylla)*, Umbrella *(Magnolia tripetala)*, and Fraser *(Magnolia fraseri)* magnolias, small deciduous trees.

Several oriental species, all of which bloom before their leaves develop, are planted as ornamentals. Most common is the Saucer Magnolia *(Magnolia soulangeana)*, a tall shrub which has tulip-like flowers usually white with a purple case. The Kobus Magnolia *(Magnolia kobus)*, a small tree from Japan, and the Starry Magnolia *(Magnolia stellata)*, an early blooming small tree or shrub, have small white flowers.

MAHOGANY is a name given to many trees and shrubs in several families, but genuine mahoganies grow only in the American and African tropics. A West Indies mahogany occurs as far north as the Florida Everglades.

Both West Indies and African mahoganies

AFRICAN MAHOGANY

WEST INDIES MAHOGANY

have pinnately compound leaves much like those of ashes (see ASHES). Their small, white flowers are tubular. The West Indies species (*Swietenia* spp.) are evergreen; the African (*Khaya* spp.) are semi-deciduous. Both have flat, winged seeds borne in hard, woody capsules, either pear-shaped as in West Indies mahoganies or round as in African species. Large trees (up to 180 feet high; 6 feet in diameter), they have straight trunks free of branches for many feet above the ground. The wood, which is of many different colours, is used for high-quality furniture and cabinet work.

Philippine mahogany (*Shorea* spp.) comes from several different trees of the lauan family. These are among the most important trees in the tropical forest of the Indo-Malayan region. Philippine mahoganies, which vary greatly in strength and durability, are used for general construction as well as for doors, veneers, and panelling. The beautifully grained and figured wood ranges in colour from yellow to dark reddish-brown.

Philippine mahoganies are all large, broad-leaved evergreen trees (often 150 feet high; 6 feet in diameter).

Among other plants referred to as mahogany are the Prima Vera or White Mahogany (*Tabebuia donnel-smithii*), an important timber tree of tropical Mexico and Central America; several eucalyptus trees, native to Australia (see EUCALYPTUS); several shrubs and small trees of the rose family; and Mahogany Sumach (*Rhus integrifolia*), an evergreen shrub or small tree of the cashew family.

MAIZE (*Zea mays*) is the only important cereal that originated in the Americas. In the United States it is called corn; in other countries corn is a term used for other grains as well. The exact origin of maize remains a mystery. When the white man arrived in America, he found the Indians growing various types of maize for food. It is generally believed that one form originated in the Andes in South America. Through a series of crosses with its relatives, the many kinds of maize that we know today were eventually developed.

Maize is a member of the grass family. The tassel that develops on top of the maize stalk consists of male flowers; female flowers

Maize is one of the world's major food crops. Some of the many varieties were developed for livestock feed, for starch, for flour, or for edrly or late harvest.

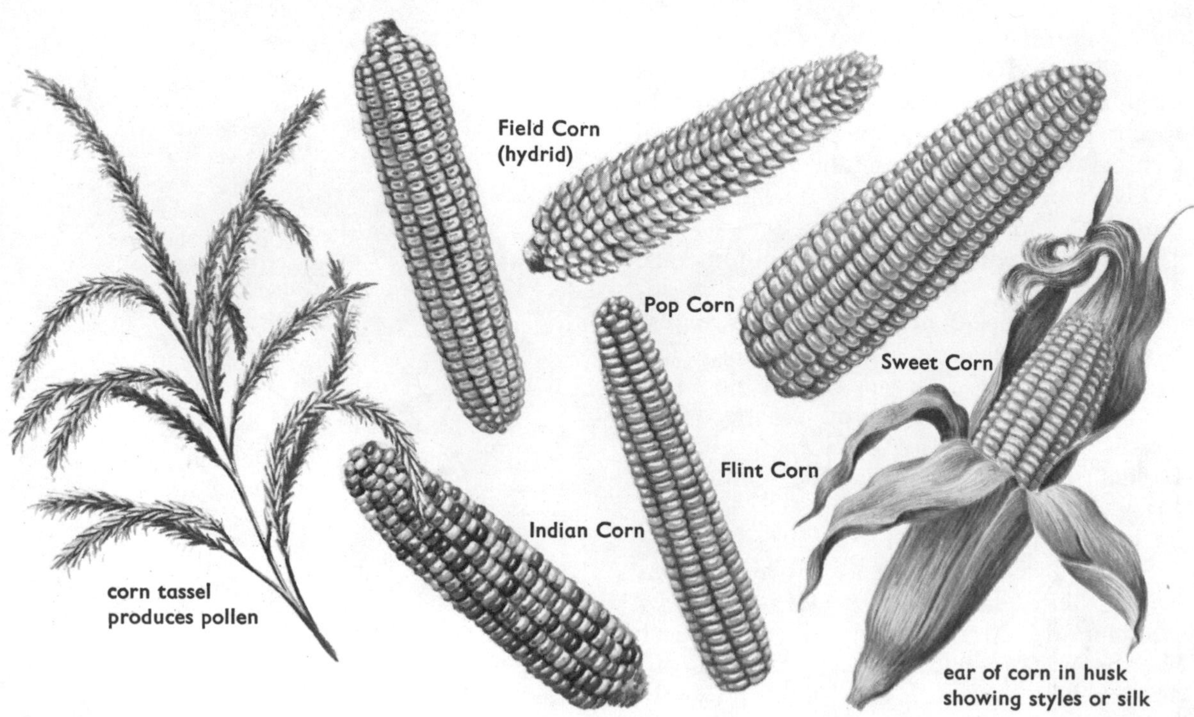

are produced lower on the plant on the so-called cob within the corn husks. Each kernel on a cob of corn is the ovary of a flower, and each has a long thread, the style, that protrudes from the end of the husk. These threads or styles are called cornsilk. Mature kernels may be white, yellow, red, or purple and are arranged regularly or irregularly on the cob.

In America approximately half the maize produced is used as livestock feed. In addition to sweet corn, eaten as a vegetable, people eat maize as cornmeal, breakfast cereals, cornflour, corn syrup, and corn oil. Maize stalks are used in making paper and yarn; the pith in the manufacture of explosives; corncobs as a mulch and in the manufacture of pipes.

In Britain maize is occasionally grown as a feed for cattle.

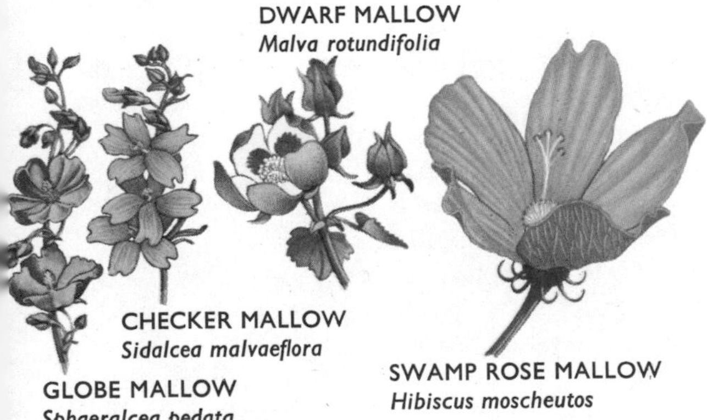

MALLOWS. All the many tiny stamens of a mallow flower are united into a chimney-like tube from the top of which the upper parts of the five or more pistils stick out. Only the mallow family has this unusual arrangement. Their seeds are clustered in a structure from which wedges like slices of cake can be removed. Each contains one or more seeds. The mallow family contains more than a thousand species, most abundant in warm climates.

The Common Mallow *(Malva sylvestris)* is 2 to 3 feet high, bearing purple-rose flowers in the summer.

MAN. The earliest men appeared 500,000 or more years ago, but the species we call modern man is about 25,000 years old. Like other animals, man has been 'in process' for many millions of years. Only about one million years ago, the animal that was to become modern man set out on its own path of development. Man evolved along his pathway while apes, monkeys, and other animals evolved along their separate ways. Along the road of human evolution numerous varieties of men have appeared and disappeared. Some of these differed considerably from modern man and belonged to different human species. Modern man, however, is one species — *Homo sapiens*. Of course, living men differ in race, but all living races belong to the same species. They have few differences but many similarities. All are equally evolved; each is different from all other animals. (See CRO-MAGNON MAN; NEANDERTHAL MAN; PEKING MAN.)

A few general statements can be made about man as a biological animal. He lives

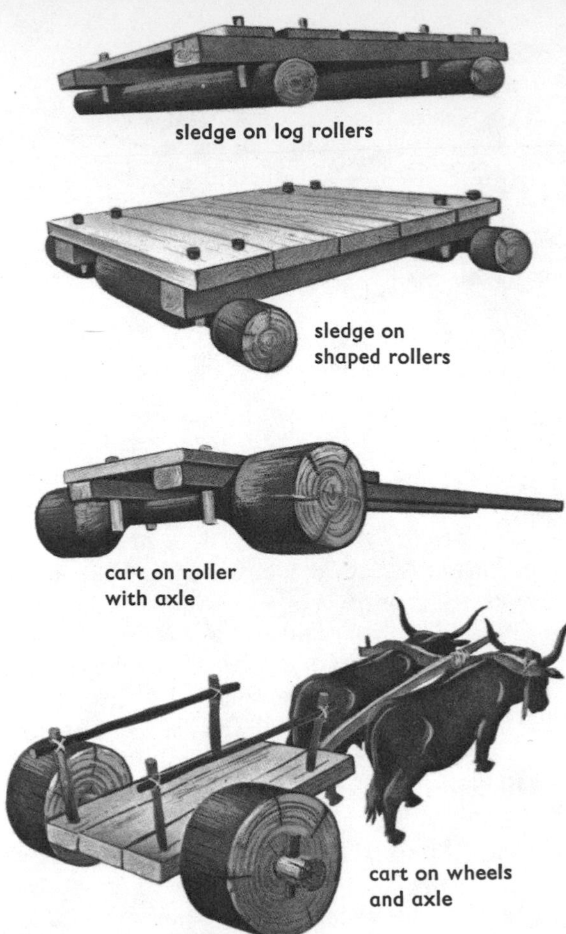

The evolution of the wheel is an illustration of applied intelligence. Each vehicle is an improvement.

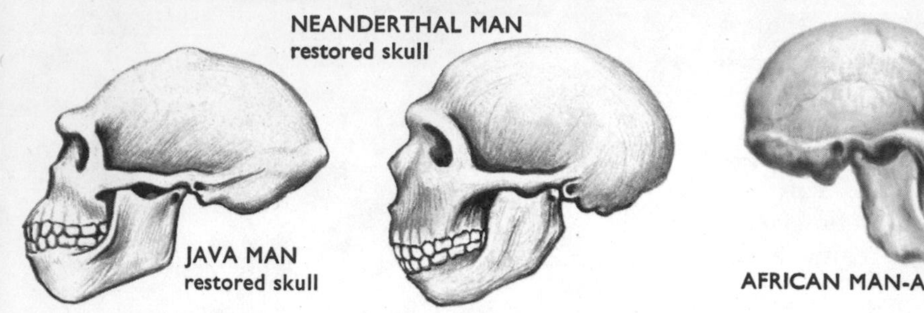

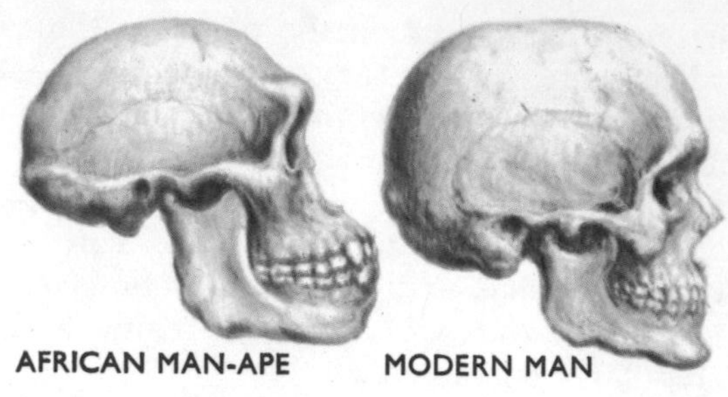

Primitive African man-apes had protruding jaws and much smaller brains than modern man.

in a greater variety of climates and environments than any other mammal. He is not very strong for his size, but he has enormous endurance. He is communal; that is, he lives in groups. He eats almost everything that is digestible and not actually poisonous.

Man's biology has given him some great advantages over other animals. He has the most highly developed brain. Consequently he can learn more and can solve more complicated problems. He is also capable of speech — a gift which no other animal possesses. Speech is possible because of his excellent brain and also because of his unusual mouth and vocal cords. Man also has an erect posture; standing easily on his 'hind legs' he has two useful arms and hands to do his work. Man's use of tools depends upon his ability to grip with his unusual hands and to hold objects between thumb and forefinger. With these and other gifts of nature, man has made inventions and discoveries. His ability to speak and develop language allows him to share this knowledge with other men. His gift of speech is perhaps the greatest single advantage he possesses.

Biologically man has changed little for at least 20,000 years. Men in the heart of Asia are physically much like men in the heart of Africa or Britain. Yet man's way of life has constantly changed and customs in the heart of Asia are very different from those in Africa or in Britain. Differences in man's way of life have changed far more rapidly than has his biology.

Man's ability to change his way of life so rapidly and so completely stems from the fact that little of his behaviour is instinctive. He does not have instincts in the sense that other animals do. An instinct is a complicated way of acting that is inborn and hence unlearned. A wasp in search of food does not need to learn how to sting a particular kind of spider in a particular part of its body. Man, like the wasp, needs food; but unlike the wasp, man must *learn* how to capture his food. There is nothing inside him that tells him how to go hunting or fishing or shopping in a super-market to get his food. This apparent disadvantage is actually

The knife (below) and the bow (in the cave painting to the left) were two of man's earliest and most useful tools and weapons. The knife evolved from a chipped stone blade to one of sharpened metal. The bow extended man's striking power for many yards beyond the reach of his arms.

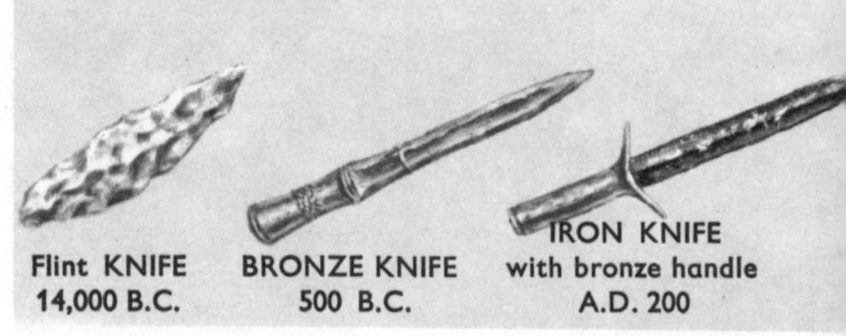

Sunday Times

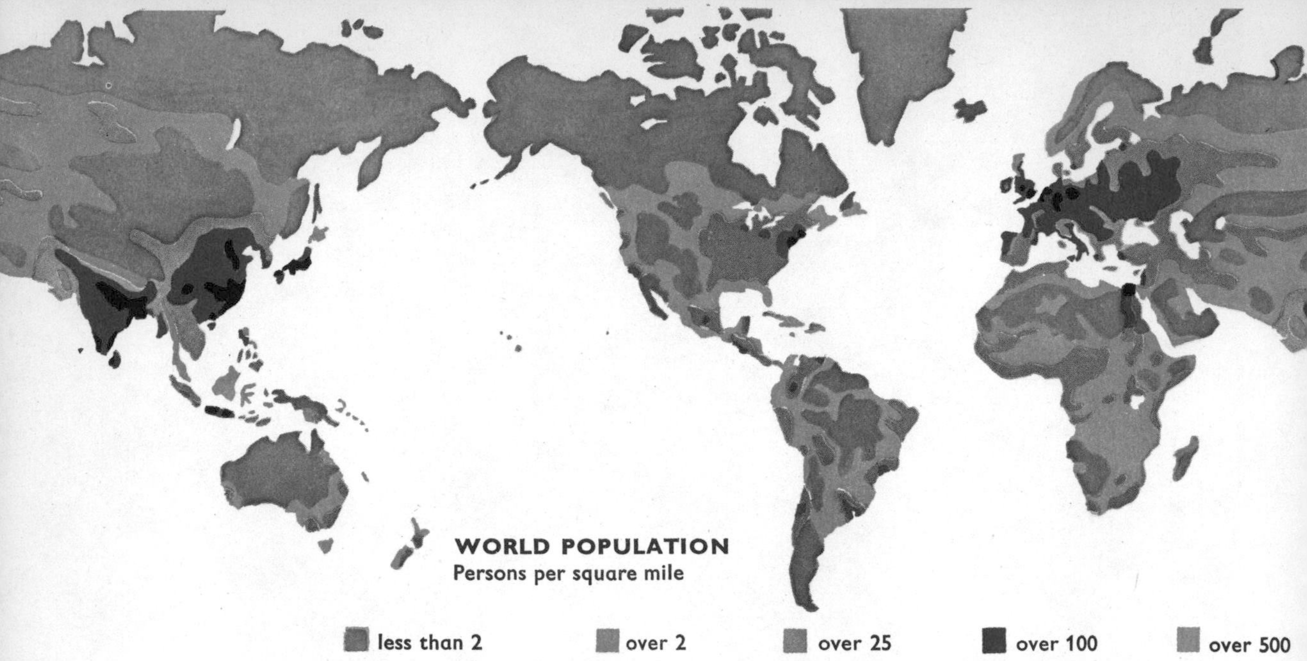

an enormous advantage. Knowledge, once acquired, can be passed on from generation to generation. In this way it accumulates and is improved upon. A child today inherits the learning and wisdom that rest on the foundations laid by Java Man.

Every human being is born into a society of people. Every society has its own way of life. Hence every human being is born into his society's man-made environment of customs, rules, morals, tools, and knowledge. This is his culture. Society — or certain members of it — passes on this great body of ideas and knowledge to its next generation.

The study of mankind as a whole is called anthropology. As a science it is divided into several fields of study. *Physical* anthropology is the study of man as a biological animal. *Cultural* anthropology deals with the works of man — his customs, tools, and beliefs. Archaeology, also a part of anthropology, is the study of the remains of vanished cultures. By careful excavations and reconstructions, archaeologists have uncovered facts about man's daily life long before there were records.

RACES OF MAN. All mankind belongs to the same species (*Homo sapiens* — 'knowing fellow'). Hence, all men have far more in common with each other than they have differences in physical make-up. Every variety of man can breed successfully with every other variety. Yet mankind may be classified into several large groups, each distinguished from the other by certain inherited physical traits. Such large groupings are called races. All living races stem from common ancestors who lived more than 20,000 years ago.

The world's population is divided into three racial groups: the Negroid, the Caucasoid, and the Mongoloid.

Caucasoids generally have a light skin colour, wavy hair, and rather narrow noses. Negroid peoples have dark skin, wiry or woolly black hair, and, usually, broad noses and rather thick lips. Mongoloids are midway between Caucasoids and Negroids in skin colour and, while their hair is black as the Negroes', it is straight and coarse. Mongoloid noses are often squat, and their eyes appear to be slanted. Babies of this race have on their rumps a purplish spot, known as the Mongolian patch, that fades gradually after birth.

Generally speaking, the continent of Africa is the home of the Negroid peoples; Asia, the Mongoloid; and Europe, the Caucasoid. Since America was settled chiefly by Europeans, it is largely Caucasoid today. About a tenth of the United States population is of Negro race or partly so. These are the descendants of Africans taken to America as slaves.

Within each major race, there are smaller groupings or sub-races differing somewhat from each other. Thus within the Caucasoid race, certain people, especially in northern Europe, tend to be quite blond and tall. This grouping is called the Nordic sub-race.

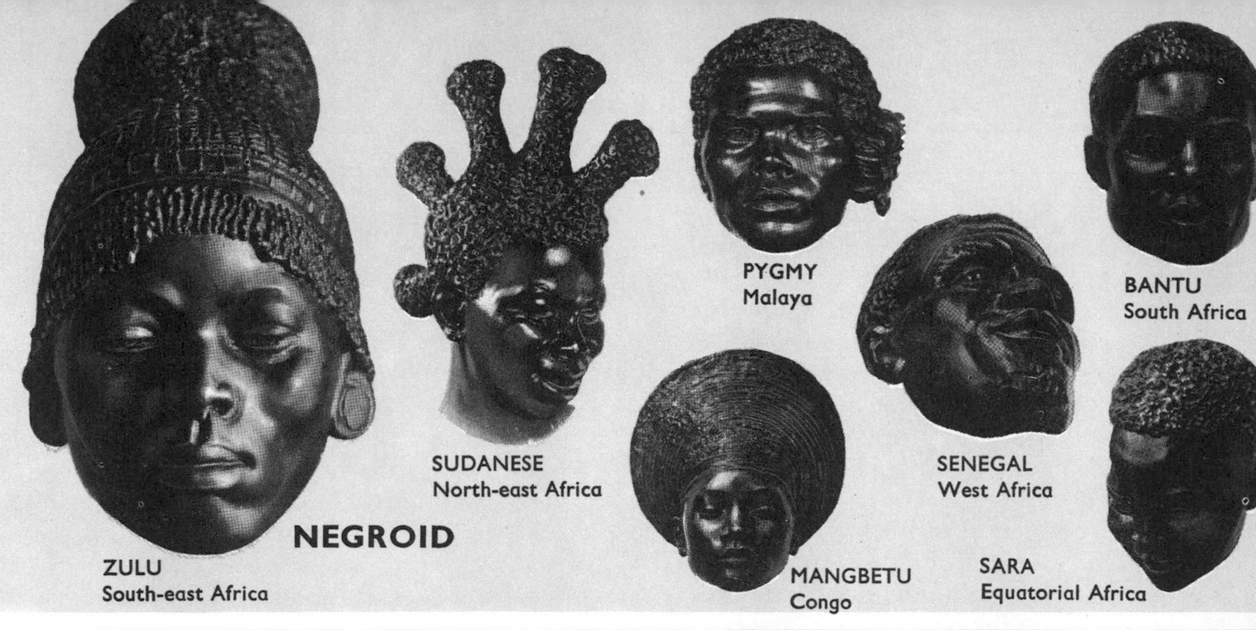

NEGROID

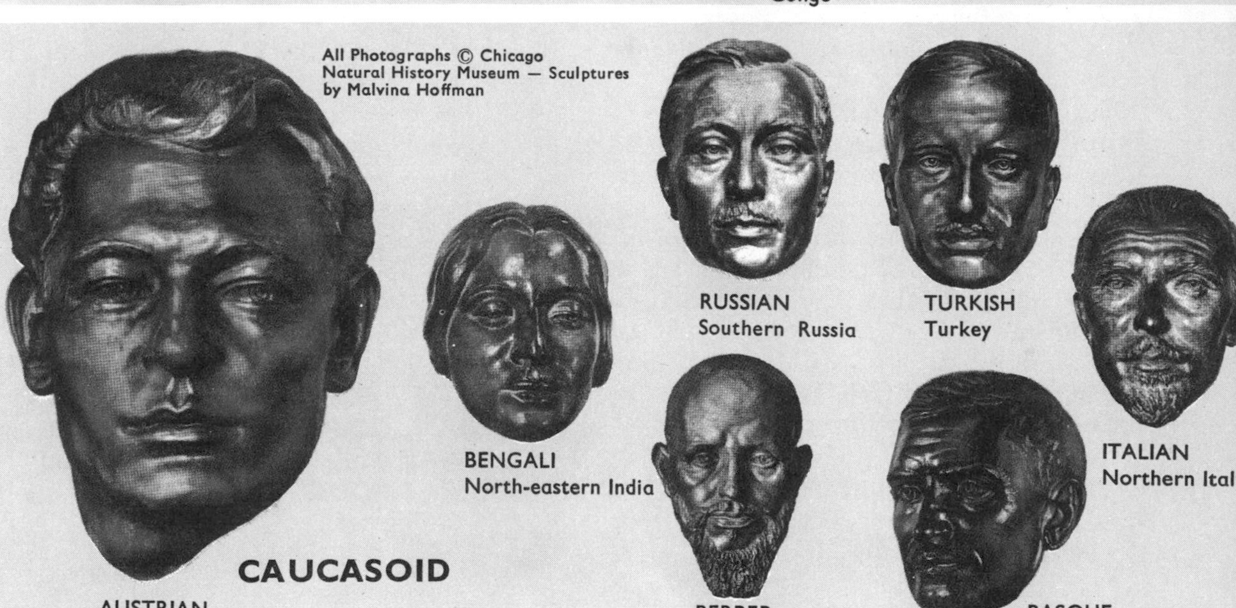

CAUCASOID

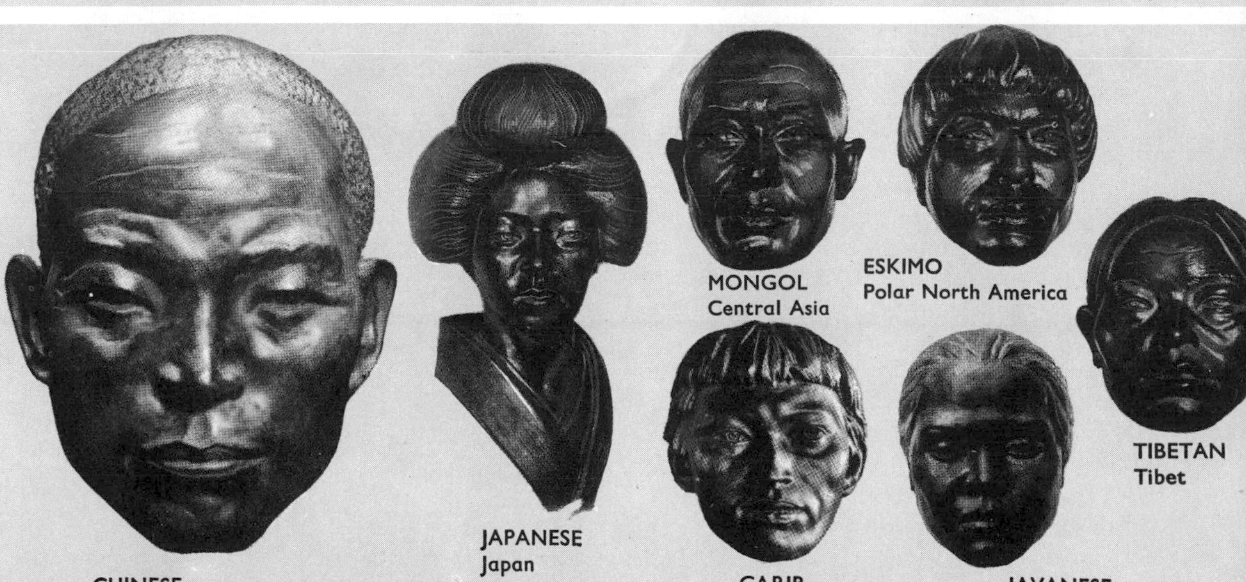

MONGOLOID

Another sub-race is the Alpine. Alpines have a stockier build and a broader head shape than the Nordics. These sub-groupings are not clear-cut today, owing to centuries of intermarriage. Similarly, sub-races exist among Negroids and Mongoloids. The Eskimo, for example, is a sub-race of the Mongoloid, differing in some respects from other Mongoloids living in various parts of China and Japan. The American Indian is also Mongoloid in race, having ancestral roots in Asia.

Large numbers of people in the world do not fit into any of the three main races. The peoples of the South Pacific Islands, for example, are the result of crossings of several Caucasoid, Mongoloid, and Negroid sub-races.

The biological differences among the living races are trifling ones. They have to do with such matters as nose shape, colouring, and type of hair. No one has ever demonstrated any differences in anything which particularly matters. Scientists today are in general agreement that race has nothing to do with one's intelligence or with the amount of progress of a society. Nor does race have anything to do with religion, language, or way of life.

POPULATION OF MAN. The world's population today is approximately 3,000 million persons. This is five times the number of people who lived in the world 300 years ago. At the present rate of growth the world population will be 4,000 million by 1980.

When people lived by hunting and fishing, very few persons could be supported by the environment. Using agriculture, people made the same amount of land and effort yield much more food. Hence, more people were better fed, more babies lived, and the population grew. The New Stone Age, even with its primitive farming, brought large increases in population. Again, about the middle of the seventeenth century Europe's population took a sudden leap forward. Seventeenth-century Europe achieved great progress in science and in machines. Not only was food becoming more abundant but people were learning more about diseases and how to prevent them. This progress in health and in production became more rapid in the following centuries. However, the population of Europe did not keep up its rapid rate of growth. This was because people began to limit the number of children they had.

In the past Asia has grown slowly because death came so early for many people. Today modern health and medical sciences are keeping more people alive. In some Asian countries, population is now growing at nearly twice the speed it grew just 15 years ago. During the next 40 years, the already huge population of Asia will almost triple if it continues at its present rate. Asia must make gigantic advances in the sciences of agriculture and industry if enough food and clothing are to be produced. Probably, however, Asians, like Europeans and Americans, will plan to limit the size of families. This would lessen somewhat their huge task of economic growth.

No one knows how many people can be supported by this Earth. Probably it is several times the number now living on it. It depends on how well we use the resources of the Earth. Constantly we improve our use of resources and find new ones to help us. (See CIVILISATION; CRAFTS AND ARTS OF MAN; DWELLINGS; FOODS OF MAN; GEOGRAPHICAL DISTRIBUTION OF MAN; SOCIAL BEHAVIOUR OF MAN; TOOLS OF MAN.)

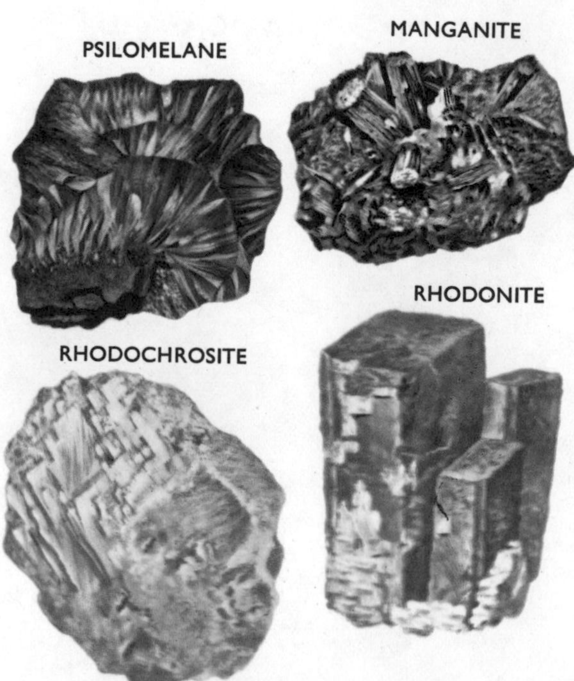

The small, fragrant flowers of the mangoe appear in winter or early spring. The trees bear fruit from May to September.

MANGANESE is a tough metal produced from five minerals — pyrolusite, psilomelane, hausmannite, manganite, and franklinite (see ZINC). Pyrolusite is a widespread sooty-black mineral with a black streak. It may be granular or occur as stalactites that form in low temperature veins or are removed from the water and deposited by bacteria. Psilomelane is found as black, smooth, rounded masses and has a shiny black streak. It is formed in low temperature veins or may be secondary in origin. Manganite occurs as long, dark grey, slender, striated crystals or in cleavable masses. It has a dark red-brown streak. Two manganese minerals are used for gem stones. Rhodonite (manganese silicate) is a pink or rose-red mineral closely related to the pyroxenes. It is formed by metamorphism or is found in veins. Rhodochrosite (manganese carbonate) is also a rose-red mineral. It has three perfect cleavages. It originates in veins as thinly banded masses. In most commercial deposits of manganese the original manganese minerals have been left as residual concentrates or leached away and deposited as nodules on the sea floor. Many sedimentary manganese deposits have been concentrated by the removal of clays and limestones leaving behind the enriched manganese minerals.

Manganese is used in the manufacture of carbon steel to remove oxygen and sulphur. It increases the rolling and forging properties and makes the steel harder and tougher. Manganese steel is used for structural work, ore chutes, bridges, armour plate, safes, rock crushers, heavy gears, ploughs, and power shovels. With titanium, manganese increases the tensile strength of steel by as much as 25 per cent. It may replace nickel and chromium in steel or may be alloyed with other metals, such as copper, aluminium, and magnesium. Manganese oxide is used as an oxidizer in manufacturing oxygen, chlorine, and bromine. It is used with carbon in making dry batteries. Small amounts of manganese added to the soil prevent the shedding of leaves in citrus trees. Manganese was formerly used in the making of glass, but after long exposure to sunlight, manganese glass turns lavender. This pale colour is an aid in determining the age of glass articles.

Manganese minerals are widely distributed but most ores come from the U.S.S.R., South America, South Africa, Angola and India.

MANGOES *(Mangifera indica)* are tropical or sub-tropical evergreen trees that may grow 40 to 50 feet high. The trees are native to India and the Malayan region.

Mangoes are widely grown in many of the tropical and sub-tropical areas of the world. One of the first large orchards of fruit trees ever recorded was a planting of 100,000 mangoe trees made during the fourteenth century in north-eastern India. Horticultural varieties are usually propagated by budding or grafting. The best quality fruit have smooth, yellow to yellow-orange flesh similar to that of the peach and are relatively free of fibres.

This fruit is excellent when eaten raw but may be cooked, frozen, canned, or made into jam. It is a basic ingredient in a spicy condiment known as chutney, which originated in India and was popularised by the British. Most varieties are a good source of both sugar and vitamin C.

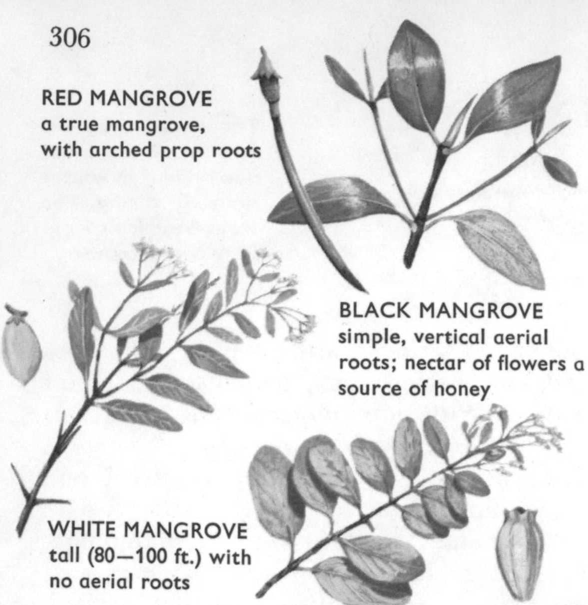

MANGROVES are evergreen trees and shrubs that form forests in shallow, tropical salt-water marshes around the world. A mangrove's main trunk is supported by arching, stilt-like roots that may stand as much as 10 feet above the mud at low tide. At high tide the branches sweep the water. Some mangroves spread by means of branches or aerial roots that grow from the trunk and take root. Their thickets are frequently impenetrable, and they help to bind the marshy soil and thus extend land areas into the sea.

Mangrove seeds germinate while they are still attached to the tree. Slender shoots (1 to 3 feet in length), thicker and heavier at their tips, drop from the tree into the water. They are ready to take root as soon as they touch. The thick, leathery, evergreen leaves are oval and grow opposite on the branches. White to yellow star-like flowers grow in clusters on short stems at the base of the leaves.

Most mangroves are shrubs, but some become sizeable trees.

MANIOC *(Manihot esculenta)*, also called Cassava, or Manihot, is not familiar to many people in temperate zones, yet it is the staff of life for millions in tropical countries where potatoes and cereals will not grow satisfactorily. Large tubers, sometimes weighing 25 to 50 pounds, are the edible portion of the plant. These may be cooked or pulverised and dried to form a starchy meal. The meal is baked into thin cakes that are eaten dry or combined with other foods. Tapioca, used in puddings and as thickening in soups, is made from cassava starch. The stems are replanted after the harvest and grow new tubers.

Harold Schultz, American Museum of Natural History

Manioc roots are peeled and ground up for flour.

MAPLES, widely distributed in the Northern Hemisphere, are among the world's most beautiful and valuable trees.

Both trees and shrubs of the maple group have paired, winged seeds. Their leaves are opposite, simple, and palmately lobed. An

BLACK MARBLE

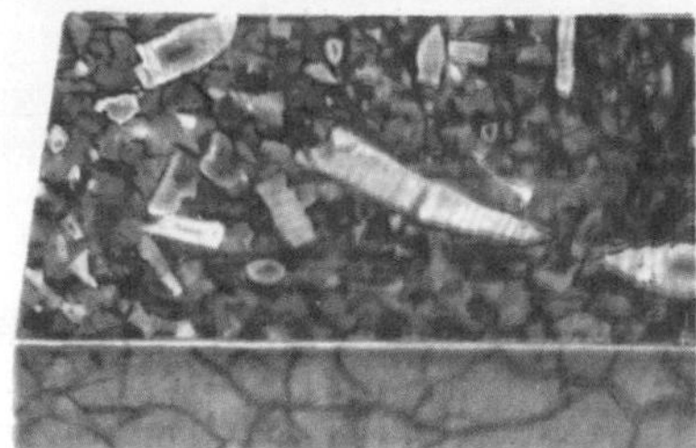

BROWN MARBLE

WHITE MARBLE

Marble may be tinted to attractive shades of pink, yellow, green, or red by iron oxide, carbon, or serpentine.

exception is the Box Elder. Maples are most numerous in central China and the Himalaya Mountains. Thirteen species are native to the United States and Canada. Best known is the Sugar Maple *(Acer saccharum)*, a handsome tree (80 feet high; 2 feet in diameter) with a rounded crown. Its leaves, which turn red or gold in autumn, usually have five toothed lobes. Small clusters of yellowish-green flowers appear with the leaves in spring. Paired, winged seeds ripen in autumn. Maple sugar and syrup are obtained from the sap of this tree.

The Sycamore *(Acer pseudoplatanus)*, native of central and southern Europe and the Near East, has been introduced into Britain, probably in the fifteenth or sixteenth century. Now common in woods and hedgerows, it grows on all but the very poorest soils throughout the British Isles. The Sycamore has broad, five-lobed leaves with coarsely toothed margins. The long wings of its paired seeds are spread at right angles to each other.

A less common tree in Britain is the Norway Maple *(Acer platanoides)*. It has a rounded crown and leaves that resemble those of the Sugar Maple, except that the centre lobe does not have parallel sides. Its paired seeds are spread wide apart rather than being horseshoe-shaped. The Common Maple *(Acer campestre)*, a small tree with a rounded crown, has three to five lobes on its leaves which have wide-spaced, rounded teeth. Clusters of greenish flowers produce paired seeds. It is native in this country, often abundant in woods in central, eastern and southern England.

MARBLE is a metamorphic rock formed from limestone or dolomite. Like its source rocks, marble is composed largely of calcite, but heat and circulating water caused the calcite grains to grow larger, forming the marble. Earth movements, pressure, and hot magmas probably assisted in the change. Crystalline limestone is an intermediate step in the change of limestone into marble. Many geologists do not consider a rock as being marble until all evidence of fossils and bedding planes are no longer visible.

Pure marbles are white, but impurities, such as graphite or iron compounds, commonly stain them grey, black, or shades of green or red. In 'variegated' marbles, these colours are in zones, swirls, or blotches. Marbles are named for their colour or for their use. Sculptors prefer massive white marbles, called statuary marble. These have a uniform texture that makes them desirable for carving. They are quarried in large blocks. Architectural marbles also have uniform texture and colour but come in thinner slabs. Floors, columns, and walls are often 'faced' with these light-coloured marbles. For striking effects or interesting patterns architects use decorative or ornamental marble. Tops for coffee tables and surrounds for fireplaces are also made of these 'variegated' marbles.

Fine white marble comes from quarries at Carrara, Italy. Quarries in Vermont, Georgia, and Colorado, U.S.A., also produce excellent varieties of marble. Belgian black marble is also famous. Verde antique is serpentine. It is sometimes called a marble because it takes a high polish and has a pleasing variegated green colour in wavy bands. The famous Connemara marble is really a serpentine-marble. Most of the so-called marbles found in Britain are not really marbles at all, for example Purbeck Marble.

MARS is the next to smallest of the planets. It has only half the Earth's diameter and a tenth of the Earth's mass. Mars is the fourth planet in distance from the Sun, with an average distance of 142 million miles or 1.52 times the average distance of the Earth from the Sun. It takes 687 days or a little less than two Earth years to go around the Sun.

Mars rotates on its axis in a way very like the Earth. Its day is 24 hours and 37 minutes, and its axis is inclined 25 degrees to the plane of its orbit. Consequently Mars has seasons like ours. However, the distance of Mars from the Sun varies, and this affects its seasons, making them milder in the Northern Hemisphere and more extreme in the Southern Hemisphere.

Mars has two small satellites. They are globes of rock about 10 miles in diameter and are so close to Mars they are hard to see through a telescope. Phobos, the inner satellite, goes around only 3,700 miles above the surface of Mars, completing its orbit in less than 8 hours. As seen from the surface of Mars, it would seem to travel from west to east instead of east to west. Deimos, the outer satellite, is 12,500 miles from Mars and makes its circuit in 30 hours.

Although Mars is small it is always comparable to the brightest stars and when closest to us, it outshines all the planets except Venus. Mars is easy to distinguish from the other planets because of its red colour. How well we see it depends on how steady the air is around us, for this is what limits the magnification that a telescope can use. Under good observing conditions three kinds of regions can be distinguished on Mars. Most of the planet's surface is orange; these are regions of reddish rock and sand. At the

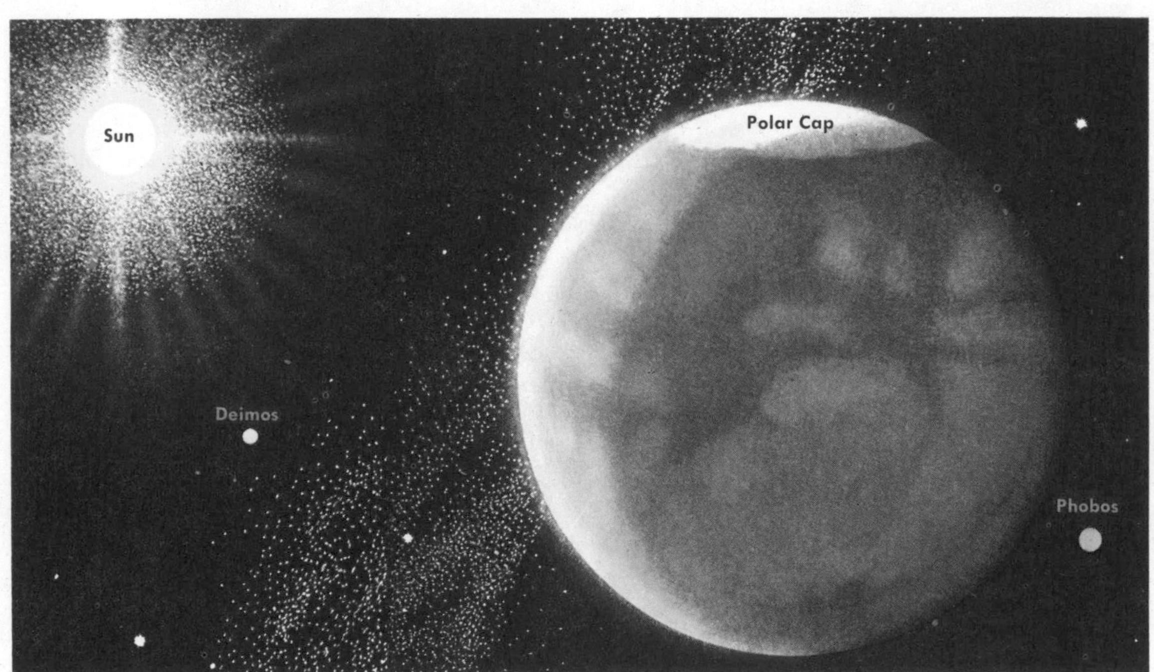

Mars, the reddish planet, is shown with its two moons, or satellites, each of which is about 10 miles in diameter.

The polar caps on Mars shrink and enlarge annually. These changes appear to be on a seasonal basis, because other markings take on a greenish hue as the cap recedes. Some observers interpret the green colour as due to the growth of vegetation. The polar cap shrinkage illustrated here took place over a period of three months.

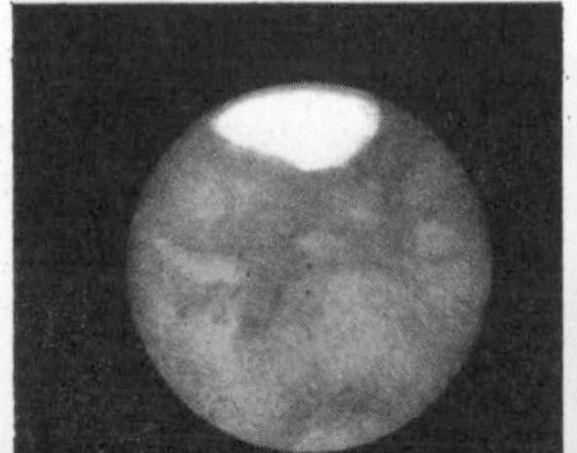
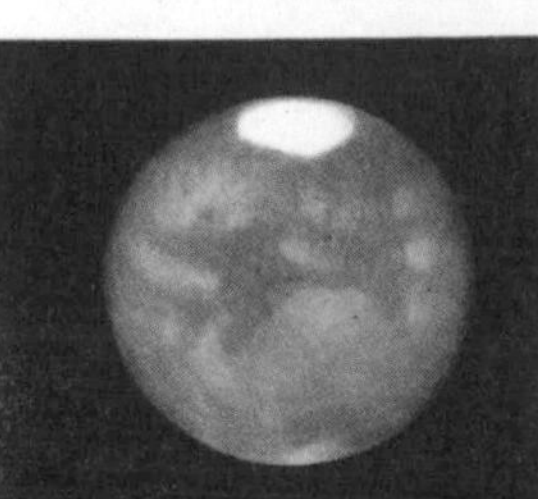
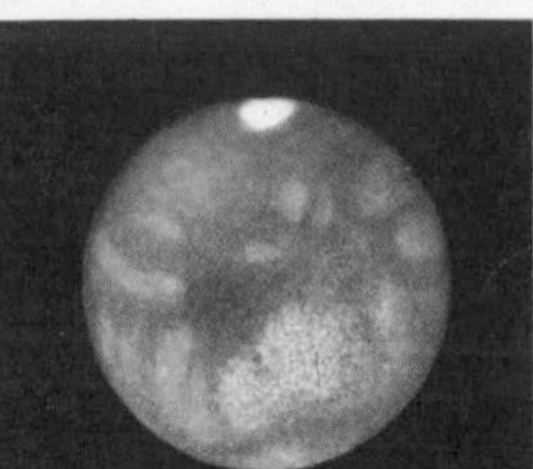

Craters on the Atlantis region of Mars photographed by Mariner IV in 1965.

north and south poles are white areas. These polar caps consist of thin layers of snow or frost. The third kind of regions are called the dark areas and form an irregular pattern through the orange regions. To most people they look dark green, but some careful observers say they are grey and look green only by contrast.

The most controversial features of Mars are the so-called canals. Some observers claim they see a network of fine straight lines connecting the dark areas, but these are not seen in Mariner space craft pictures.

It is an open question whether there is life on Mars. Some astronomers argue that the dark areas are covered with green plants. As evidence they cite the seasonal changes. When spring comes to each hemisphere, the polar cap shrinks, releasing water vapour into the atmosphere, and the neighbouring dark areas change their colour slightly. This may be new growth stimulated by the water, but it is also possible to explain the difference in colour as a change in the colours of rocks.

Living conditions on Mars are impossible by human standards, but some sorts of plants could survive. Mars' atmosphere is a tenth as dense as ours. It is probably made up of a substantial amount of carbon dioxide, the gas that plants need for manufacturing food. There is little or no oxygen, however, and so animals would be unable to breathe. Another problem is water, which has not been detected. The white polar caps are frozen carbon dioxide. The climate on Mars is more severe than in the worst desert on Earth. Clouds are rare, rain never occurs, and great dust storms sometimes sweep over large areas. The temperature is low. Although the ground sometimes warms up to 21 degrees centigrade (70 degrees Fahrenheit), the air stays much colder, and at night both ground and air are well below zero. (See PLANETS.)

MEDICINE AND MEDICINAL PLANTS. Medicine is the knowledge and practice of healing and preventing disease or treating injuries to the human body. All peoples have found means of treating wounds and illnesses, with varying degrees of success.

Many peoples, including New Stone Age men in Europe, practised primitive kinds of

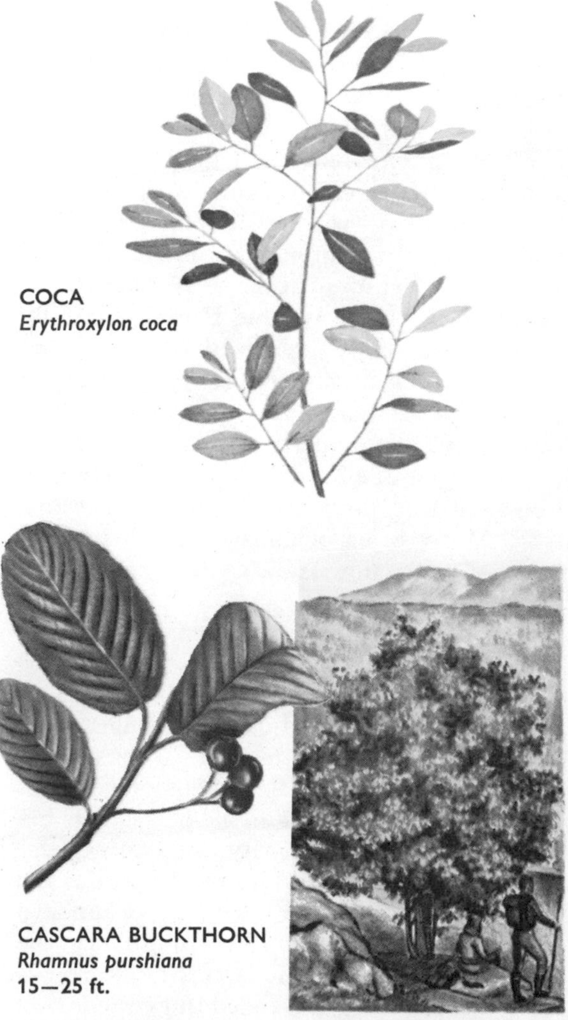

COCA
Erythroxylon coca

CASCARA BUCKTHORN
Rhamnus purshiana
15—25 ft.

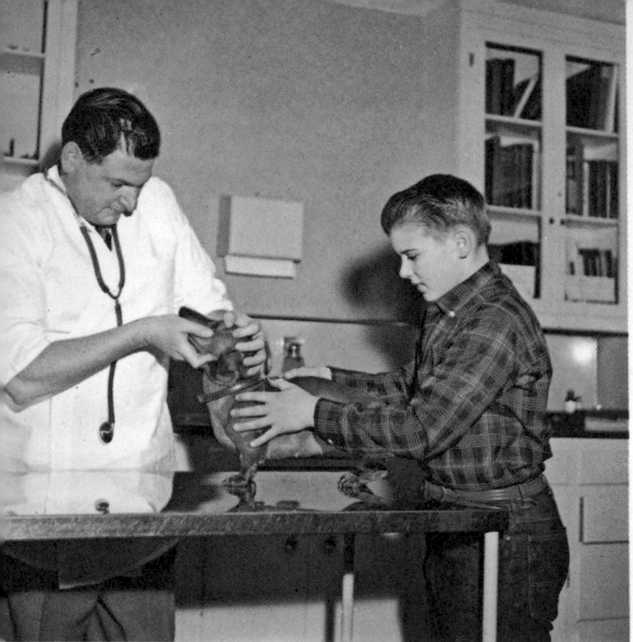

Walter Chandoha

Veterinary surgeons, too, need a wide knowledge of medicine and drugs.

surgery. Appeals to supernatural powers have been made, as well as the use of medicine. Since, as we know today, the attitude of a sick person has much to do with his recovery, rites and prayer may be helpful.

Modern medicine begins with the sixteenth century with the researches then taking place into human anatomy; with the discovery by Harvey in the early seventeenth century of the way the blood circulates through the body; and with the resulting improvements in surgery. In 1796, Edward Jenner discovered a way to prevent smallpox through vaccination. In the mid-nineteenth century anaesthetics first came into use, and Louis Pasteur proved that germs cause disease. Many other scientists have helped to build what we now know as modern medical science and practice.

The history of medicinal plants is largely the early history of botanical science, and Egyptian records indicate established usages of medicines nearly 4,000 years ago. The Greeks gave great attention to medicinal plants and about 75 B.C. Dioscorides produced *De Materia Medica*, a book which became the main authority for many centuries. In the Middle Ages the advent of the herbalists heralded the beginning of modern botany, but they did little to further the study of medicines. The 'Doctrine of Signatures' which they advanced suggested that plants were endowed with shapes and forms that indicated the parts of the human body for which they were to be used. The reddish sap of the Bloodroot was a blood tonic; the walnut kernel was used for brain disorders. Medicinal or drug plants are collected from all over the globe. They are usually dried soon after gathering, and later the active principle may be extracted for use as a drug. Many of these plant drugs are less important than hitherto because chemists have analysed them and found out how to produce them synthetically at a lower cost. Other drugs must still be obtained from plants, but these are now beginning to be grown as crops in fields instead of being collected from wild plants. Atropine is extracted from the belladonna plant *(Atropa belladonna)*; cocaine from the coca tree *(Erythroxylon coca)* in South America; and digitalis, a heart drug, from the foxglove *(Digitalis purpurea)* grown in Holland. Morphine, from the opium poppy *(Papaver somniferum)*, is not only a most valuable pain-killer, but also a drug which those who take it regularly find it difficult or impossible to do without. Opium smoking is illegal in most countries.

Certain medicinal plants are microscopic

In this multiple-exposure photograph, Mercury's transit between the Earth and Sun appears as a black line.

Yerkes Observatory Photograph

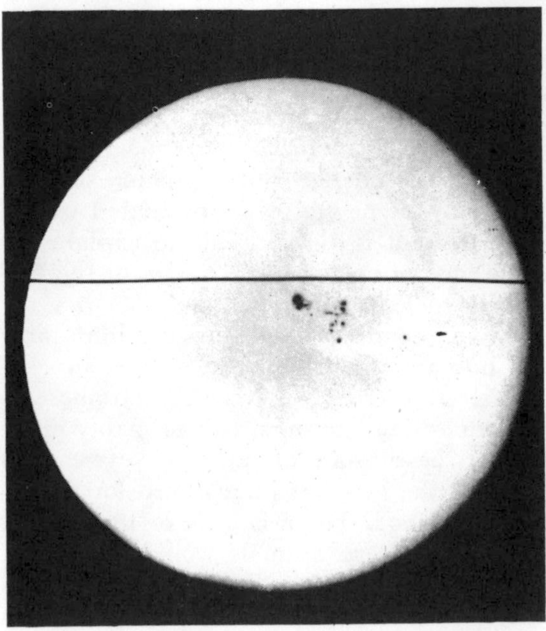

in size — these are the fungi (see ANTIBIOTICS). Their deliberate use is comparatively recent, but the Chinese have long known of the benefits obtained from applying a rotting apple covered with blue mould *(Penicillium)* to certain wounds. (See BACTERIA; QUININE; VACCINES; VIRUS.)

MERCURY, the smallest of the planets, is 2000 miles in diameter — less than half the size of the Earth and only $1\frac{1}{2}$ times as large as the Moon. The mass of Mercury is only 1/20 part of the Earth's mass.

Mercury is only 36 million miles from the Sun, compared with 93 million from the Earth. It is the closest planet to the Sun. It moves faster in its orbit, too, and takes only 88 days to make a revolution around the Sun. Its orbit is less circular than the orbit of any other planet except Pluto and is also more inclined (see ORBIT).

Mercury is very hot — at least on the side that faces the Sun. On that side the temperature is hot enough to melt lead, while the dark side is cold enough to freeze gases. But there are no gases on Mercury, for it is too small to hold an atmosphere. Its surface is just bare rock. To complete the dreary picture, Mercury has no satellites.

Mercury is bright but hard to see. We glimpse it only in the west after sunset or in the east before dawn. It is much easier to see from the tropics or from the Southern Hemisphere.

Through a telescope Mercury does not look nearly as big as Venus, but like Venus it goes through all the phases we see on the Moon. Not much can be seen on its surface, but if it were closer, Mercury would probably look very much like the Moon. (See PLANETS.)

MESOZOIC ERA, the era of middle life, is divided into the Triassic, Jurassic, and Cretaceous periods. It began about 225 million years ago and lasted about 160 million years.

Among marine invertebrate animals of the Mesozoic, the most conspicuous features were the increase of foraminifera, echinoderms, and molluscs. Modern corals, including reef builders, first appeared and expanded rapidly. Many modern crustaceans also became abundant, while brachiopods or lamp shells decreased in numbers. Ammonite and belemnite cephalopods were the most distinctive of all the invertebrates. Their coiled and cigar-like skeletons are found in abundance in Mesozoic rocks throughout the world. Mesozoic insects included flies, butterflies, moths, and other forms. The first mammals and birds appeared during the Jurassic period.

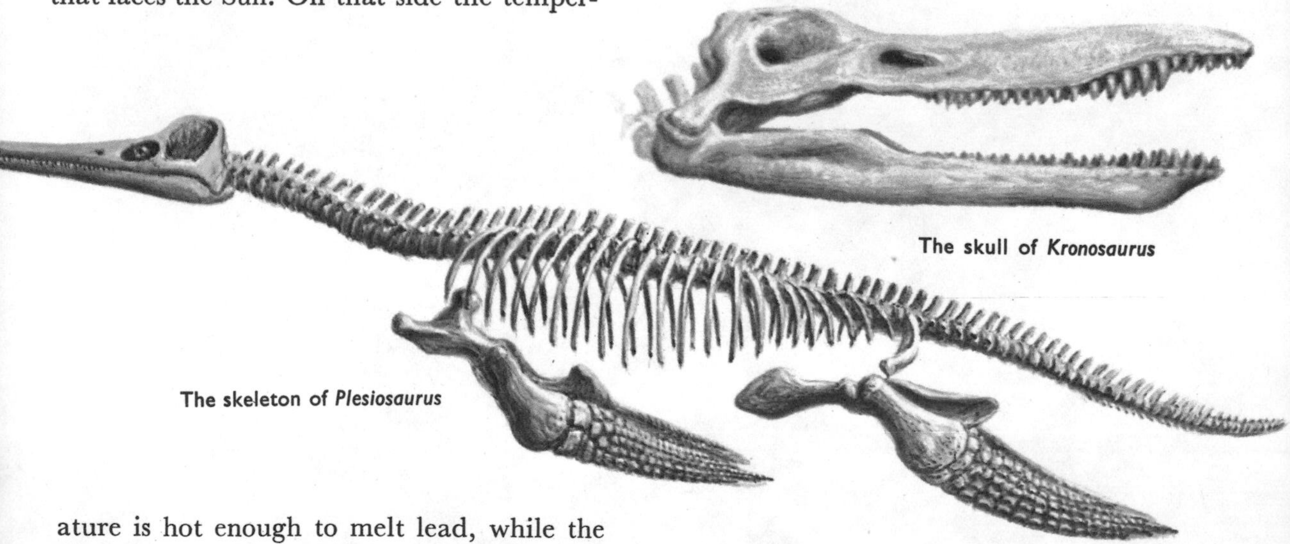

The skull of *Kronosaurus*

The skeleton of *Plesiosaurus*

Bony fish were dominant in Mesozoic seas, although sharks were also common.

Dinosaurs, which means 'terrible reptile', were the supreme animals on land. The largest was almost 90 feet long and probably weighed about 50 tons. Others stood 20 feet

The Mesozoic Era is often called the Age of Reptiles. At least twelve orders of reptiles dominated the life of both land and sea, some of them dwarfing all other living creatures. Some of the dinosaurs were gargantuan combinations of bulk and tiny brain and were the largest land animals the Earth has yet known. Completely overshadowed by these huge creatures were small, reptile-like animals that were developing into the first mammals, whose descendants would inherit the Earth when the dinosaurs had disappeared.

high, about as tall as a two-storey house. Others, much smaller and more delicately built, were very much like birds. Still others had armour of fantastic shapes. Some were savage predators; others were ponderous vegetarians.

One group had hip bones similar in structure to those of modern reptiles. The other group had bird-like hips. But all were reptiles, and shared the reptilian characteristics of 'cold blood' and a relatively feeble brain. *Stegosaurus*, which weighed 10 tons, had a brain about the size of a walnut.

Among the marine reptiles Plesiosaurs

were widespread and common in Jurassic and Cretaceous times. Most kinds had broad, flat bodies with long necks and small heads. Their legs were heavy paddles and their tails were long. They have been described as 'a snake threaded through the body of a turtle'. The largest were 50 feet long.

Plesiosaurs were good swimmers and fed on fish which they caught by rapid thrusts of their long, thin neck. Plesiosaurs moved through the water with paddle-like limbs. Ichthyosaurs, which lived at the same time, moved with fish-like body movements and used their fin-like paddles chiefly for steering.

FORMATION OF A HUGE METEOR CRATER

A meteor one mile in diameter approaches the Earth.

On impact, the meteor turns to gas, and shock waves spread out.

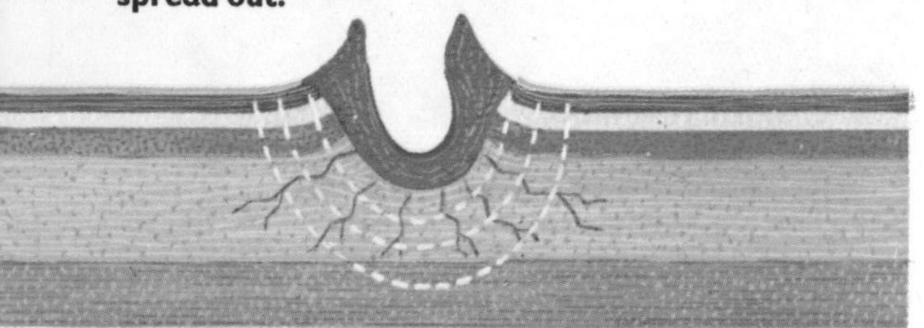

Rocks surrounding the meteor crater melt in the heat or are pulverised by the impact of the striking meteor.

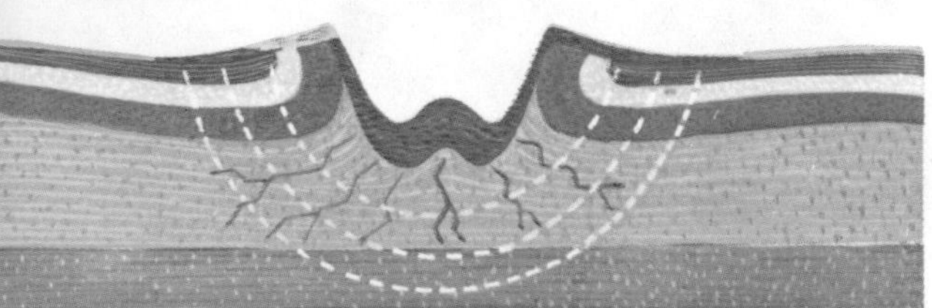

Shattered rock surrounding the crater is folded back.

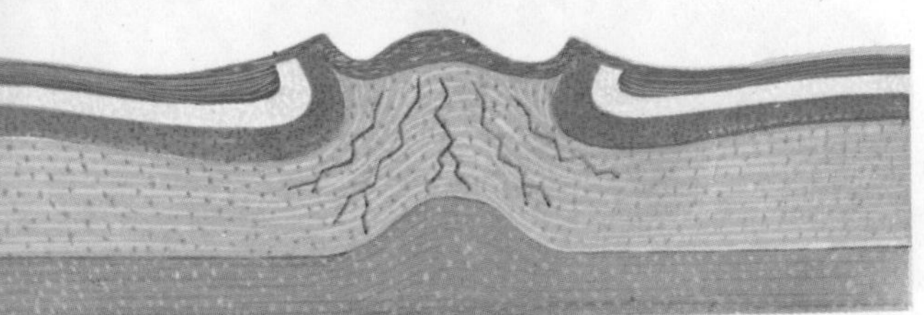

Plug is forced up from mantle rock filling the crater.

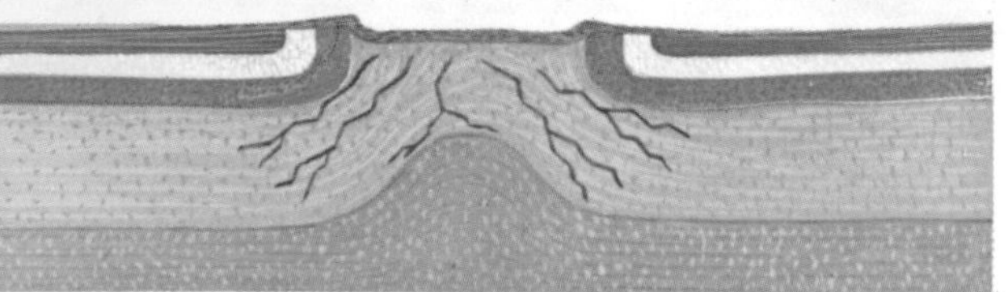

Many years later the location of the crater can be identified by the ring of hills surrounding it and by the shattered rock strata that form them.

Not all plesiosaurs were long-necked, small-headed forms. The necks of some had as few as 13 vertebrae, compared with 76 in the long-necked types, and these forms had larger heads. The head of *Kronosaurus*, for example was 10 feet long.

The Mesozoic is often called the Age of Reptiles.

METEOR. If you watch on a clear, dark night, you will sometimes see a point of light shoot across the sky, as if a star had left its place. Such a body is often called a shooting star or a falling star, but it is not a star at all. Astronomers call these bodies meteors. The stars are very far away, but meteors are often very close to us. They flash through the Earth's atmosphere only about 50 miles above the ground. A meteor is often a tiny particle no larger than a grain of sand, that travels around the Sun in its own orbit in the same way a larger body does. Those we see have had the misfortune to run into the Earth. A meteor strikes the Earth's atmosphere at high speed — usually 20 or 30 miles per second.

Some meteors come at random, and you can generally see one of these every 5 or 10 minutes. Others travel in groups and occur in greater numbers, called showers. Meteors of a shower occur at a particular time of year. For instance, the Perseids come from the constellation Perseus in August, and the Leonids radiate from Leo in November.

Ordinary meteors burn up completely in their first flash. Occasionally a larger body enters the Earth's atmosphere, shining brightly and lighting up the whole countryside for a few moments. Such an unusually bright meteor is called a fireball. The

Meteor Crater, Arizona
500 ft. deep, ¾ mile across

very largest meteoric bodies manage to reach the Earth's surface without burning up completely, and they are then called meteorites. Many have been found and put in museums. A meteorite strikes the Earth with great force, and the larger ones make big craters. Many large craters identified in various parts of the world measure many miles across.

MICAS are a group of silicate minerals with more perfect cleavage than any others. The cleavage flakes of all micas are paper-thin, very flexible, and elastic.

Biotite, one of the common mica minerals, is black or dark green. It is abundant in some granites, gneisses, and schists. Phlogopite is a brown mica found with biotite. Muscovite, also found in igneous and metamorphic rocks, is white or pale brown and is the most common of the micas. Lepidolite is a violet or pink and occasionally yellow mica of both igneous and metamorphic origin. Margarite is a pink mica of metamorphic origin, and, unlike other micas, it is quite brittle. Muscovite and phlogopite are the only micas that do not conduct electricity and are quite resistant to weathering.

A group of similar minerals called the vermiculites contain large amounts of water. They swell into worm-like threads when heated. Vermiculites are formed from biotite and phlogopite, and although they have good cleavage like micas, they are not elastic. Vermiculites are all bronze in colour. They are used as a potting material for rooting plant cuttings, for packing glassware, and for making lightweight, though weak, concrete blocks. They are used for insulation against heat and cold and also as a soundproofing material.

Large crystals of muscovite occur in pegmatites, and most of the commercial production of mica comes from these deposits (see PEGMATITE). Muscovite 'books' are first cleaned of clinging feldspar and other minerals and split into sheets of suitable thickness. Then the flaws are removed and the edges trimmed. Scraps and flakes too small for sheet mica are mixed with shellac or other glue and made into sheets. Small pieces are ground or pulverised to make them of uniform size.

The chief use of mica is in the electrical industry and in telephones. It is used in dynamos, condensers, lightning arrestors, commutators, light sockets, toasters, irons, and heaters. Ground mica may be mixed with shellac or other bonding material and moulded into desired shapes. It is also added to paint, concrete, wallpaper, and roofing paper to make them glitter. Mica is also used in grease or alone as a lubricant.

Micas are world-wide in distribution, but commercial production of muscovite and phlogopite is mainly from India, Brazil, Malagasy, and Canada. Some is produced in North Carolina and New England, U.S.A.

MILDEWS. Three types of plant diseases are called mildews. Powdery mildews on roses, phlox, zinnias, chrysanthemum, apple, and many other plants are caused by these fungi. The spore clusters of *Erysiphe*, *Uncinula*,

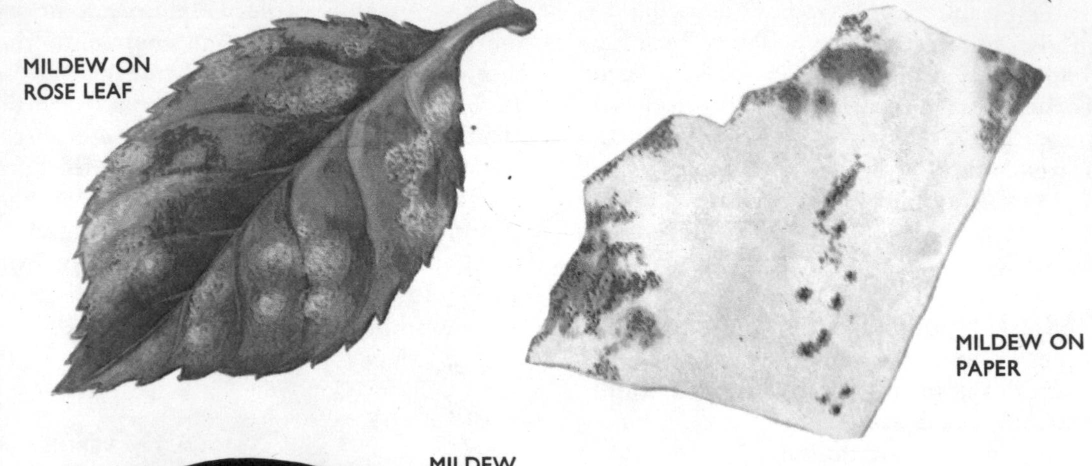

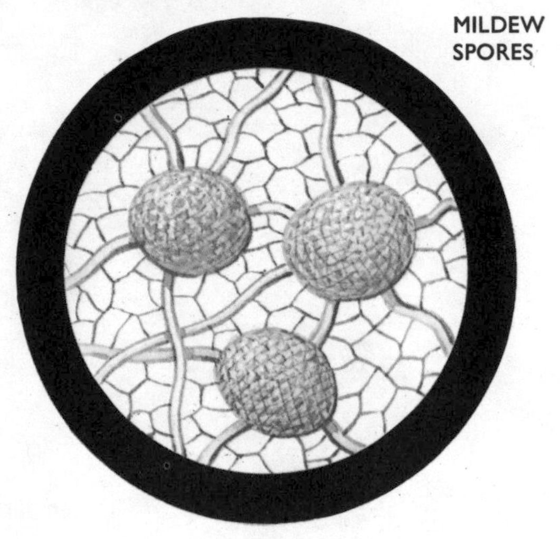

Microsphera, and other powdery mildews look very much alike and form a white powdery mass. A sulphur fungicide will usually kill this type of mildew.

The closely related black mildews, such as *Irene* and *Meliola*, are more common in tropical areas than in temperate regions. They have a black mycelium and dark spores.

Downy mildews are parasites on such plants as spinach, hops, brassicas and lettuce and are closely related to Black Bread Mould. *Plasmopara viticola* is a parasite of grapes, and *Pseudoperonospora humuli* attacks hops.

To most people 'mildew' refers to fungi that make dark mouldy spots on walls and painted surfaces or the pink, black, or greenish spots that spread over paper, tents, sheets and other cloth products. Mildews also occur in leather, as in shoes or belts. During World War II these fungi were a serious problem to the armed forces, for in the tropics much clothing and other cloth material was destroyed quickly by mildews. Even lenses of binoculars, microscopes, and other optical equipment were damaged by fungi that etched the glass.

Fungi which cause this kind of damage include a large number of unrelated species. *Aspergillus* and *Penicillium* are common mildews on leather. *Alternaria*, *Fusarium*, *Stemphyllium* and *Chaetomium* destroy wood, cotton and other cloth products. *Cladosporium*, *Fusarium* and *Monilia* produce yellow, brown, or black spots on paper and may destroy it.

MILKY WAY. The Sun and other stars around us form only a tiny part of the large star system called the Milky Way. This band of stars around the sky is actually an edge view of the galaxy in which we live. The Milky Way is made up of about 100,000 million stars, along with clouds of dust and gas.

Most stars of the Milky Way, including the Sun, are scattered through a large flat disc which is composed of gas, dust and stars. This disc is thicker at its centre or nucleus where the stars are crowded more closely together. In the Sun's neighbourhood — near the edge of the Milky Way — stars are about one parsec apart (a parsec is 200,000 times the distance from the Earth to the Sun). Near the centre of the Milky Way they are ten times closer to each other. The Milky Way measures 30,000 parsecs across — from one edge of the disc to the other. Most of the disc is only about 500 parsecs thick, but at the centre the disc bulges to 1,000 parsecs or more. The Sun is about 10,000 parsecs from the centre of the disc — closer to the edge than to the centre — but it is in the central plane of the disc.

The stars, separated by large spaces, are like grains of sand a mile apart; but the spaces between the stars are not completely empty. In many parts of the Milky Way, interstellar space is thinly spread with gas and dust (see INTERSTELLAR GAS AND DUST). Much of this interstellar material is collected into regions called spiral arms that lie in the disc and wind around and around the centre. The brightest, most massive stars in the Milky Way are also concentrated in the spiral arms. Similar bright stars make the spiral arms of other galaxies prominent.

Not all the stars of the Milky Way belong to the disc or the spiral arms; some are thinly spread through a large region called the halo. The halo is as large as the disc but hardly flattened at all. Halo stars extend 10,000 or 15,000 parsecs in every direction from the centre of the Milky Way. They pass back and forth through the disc but never collide with the stars of the disc because the stars are so small compared with the vast distances that separate them.

The different parts of the Milky Way are inhabited by stars of different types. The youngest stars live in the spiral arms, for it is there that stars are born of interstellar gas and dust. As these stars become older they diffuse out of the spiral arms and spread through the whole disc, which consists of middle-aged and old stars. In the halo are old stars only, for there are no dust clouds there to form new ones. In halo stars, too, the various chemical elements are mixed in a different proportion.

The stars of the Milky Way are in motion and the predominant motion is a rotation around the centre. The whole disc of the Milky Way spins rapidly, with the spiral arms trailing behind as the galaxy turns. The Sun and all its neighbours are thus travelling at a speed of 150 miles per second in a circle around the centre of the Milky Way, but it is so far around the circle that even at this high speed it takes 200 million years to go once around. Besides this rotation in which all the disc stars take part, each star has an individual motion at a speed of 10 or 20 miles per second. These motions carry the stars around in the disc and also up and down through it.

Halo stars have a different sort of motion. Their orbits carry them towards the centre of the Milky Way and far out again. Each star moves on its own. There is almost no tendency for them to go around together.

No one knows exactly how old the Milky Way is. The oldest stars we know are at least 10,000 or 20,000 million years old, but older stars may yet be discovered. Nor do we know much about how the Milky Way has changed with time. Some astronomers believe that the whole Milky Way was once nearly round, like the halo. Then after the halo stars formed, the remaining gas flattened out into the disc where many stars were created immediately and others have been forming every since. Other astronomers dispute this view. Only future research can provide the answer.

Our position in the Milky Way prevents us from seeing its overall shape clearly. To make it worse, scattered around us are clouds of interstellar dust that hide nearly all the distant parts of the Milky Way. What we see clearly is only a small part of the whole system. The stars that we see in the sky at night are mostly within 100 or 200 parsecs of us. This is just a tiny part of the whole Milky Way. The remainder of the Milky

In a dense section of the Milky Way, the stars appear to blend together in one huge luminous mass.

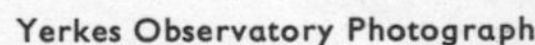

Yerkes Observatory Photograph

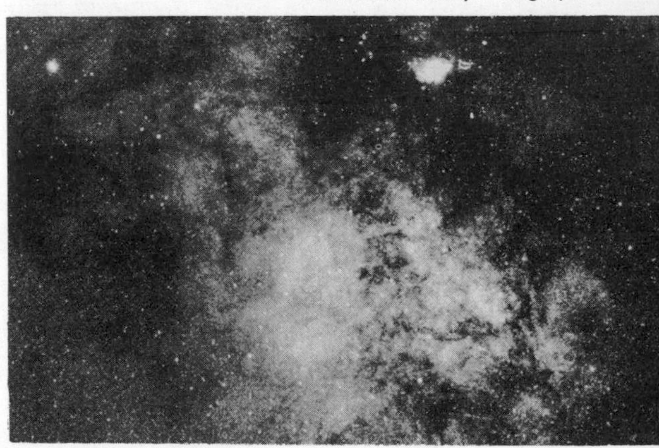

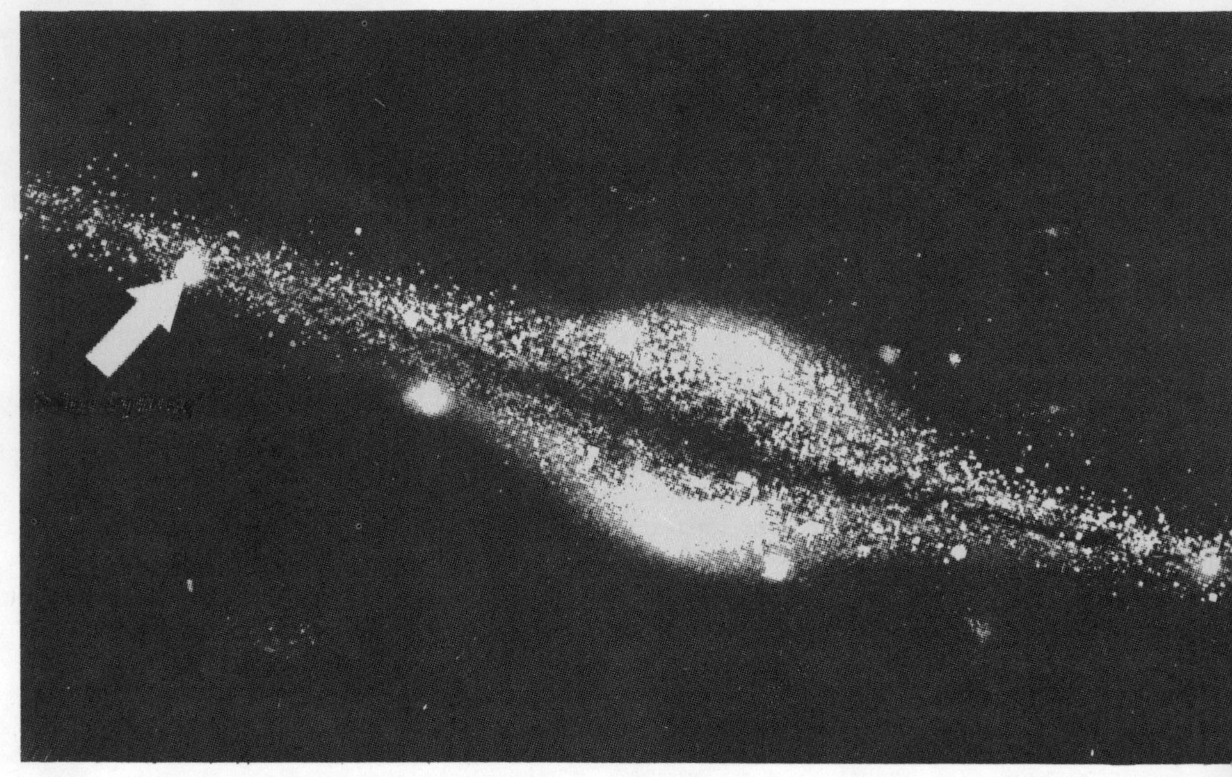

Man has never seen the Milky Way, our galaxy, a flattened spiral star system, from outer space. This is how it probably appears in edge view. Our solar system is an invisible dot near the tip of the arrow.

Way shows up only as a faint irregular white band around the sky, marked on star maps. It is easily visible when the sky is clear and there is no moonlight or artificial light to interfere. In the middle northern latitudes a bright part of the Milky Way is overhead in the early evening in late summer while another part is high on winter evenings. The brightest parts of the Milky Way are best seen from the Southern Hemisphere where they pass overhead on winter evenings. For Southern Hemisphere observers a less bright part is high in the summer sky near the constellations Crux and Aquila.

The light that we see from the Milky Way comes from a large number of faint stars, and marks the direction of the plane of the disc. The detailed appearance of the Milky Way is produced partly by the bright stars of the spiral arms that lie near us and partly by the obscuring dust clouds that seem to cut great holes in the bright band. We live on the inner edge of a spiral arm. Our own spiral arm accounts for the brightness of the Milky Way in the direction of the constellation Cygnus where we look along the arm and see many stars. The brightest part of the Milky Way is in the constellation Sagittarius, nearly in the direction of the centre of the whole system, which is hidden behind many dust clouds and cannot be seen. What we see is the rich star cloud of the next spiral arm — 1,500 parsecs away. This arm sweeps around and away from us in Carina, a constellation in the far southern sky. There we look along the arm, and this may account for the bright patch that we see in that direction. A third spiral arm contributes parts of the brightness of the Milky Way in Perseus and neighbouring constellations. It passes about 2,000 parsecs away from us. All these arms have been traced, and others found, with radio telescopes, far beyond the limits of optical telescopes.

In fact, there is very little that we see directly in studying the Milky Way. We are in a confusing position in the midst of a mixture of disc, spiral-arm and halo stars;

and dust clouds prevent us from seeing much more than our own little neighbourhood. All that we know about the structure of the Milky Way comes from indirect measurements, some of them very complicated. The story of those fascinating techniques makes up a large part of modern astronomy. (See ASTRONOMY.)

MILLETS are a large group of cultivated grasses that produce small seeds or grain. In Europe and Asia they are widely eaten — boiled like rice, ground into flour, or made into porridge. In some regions they are the chief source of starch. Millets are also important forage and hay crops for fattening livestock, their principal use in North America.

Foxtail Millet *(Setaria italica)* is a cultivated grain and hay plant in semi-arid regions of China and the Near East and is also a valuable hay crop in central United States of America. The grain is used for chicken feed. Pearl or Cattail Millet *(Pennisetum glaucum)* is grown during the rainy season in India, Egypt and Africa. Farmers in southern Russia and Asia grow Bread or Proso Millet *(Panicum miliaceum)*. Ragi or Finger Millet *(Eleusine coracana)* is a grain and forage crop in India and Africa, and, like all millets, is cultivated mainly for local consumption. (See CEREALS.)

MINERALS are substances with more or less definite chemical and physical properties found naturally in the Earth's crust. A few minerals are single chemical elements; gold, silver, diamond and graphite (carbon), and sulphur are examples. Most minerals are compounds, that is, combinations of two or more elements. The majority are silicates — the metals combined with silicon and oxygen. Ores are usually made of metals combined with sulphur or oxygen.

Atoms are the building blocks of minerals. The arrangement of atoms and the forces holding them together determine the properties of each mineral. For example, carbon loosely arranged in layers makes soft, metallic, dark-grey graphite; carbon atoms held tightly in groups make hard, colourless diamonds. Because atoms in minerals are arranged in definite patterns, they form crystals when conditions permit. Each crystal is one of the six basic types illustrated overleaf.

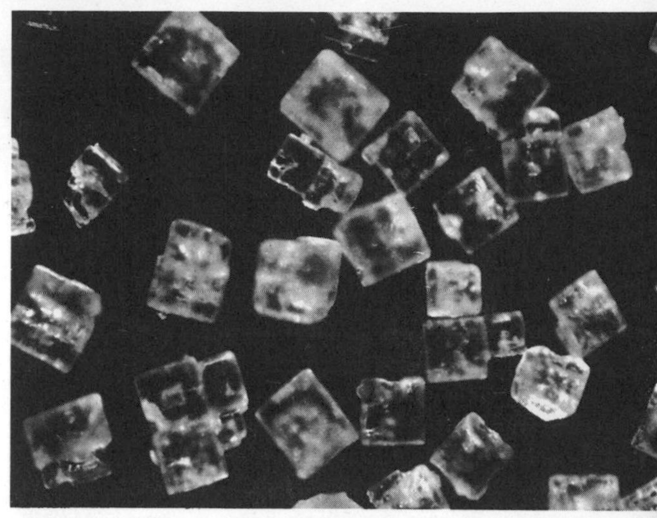

Courtesy Morton Salt Co.

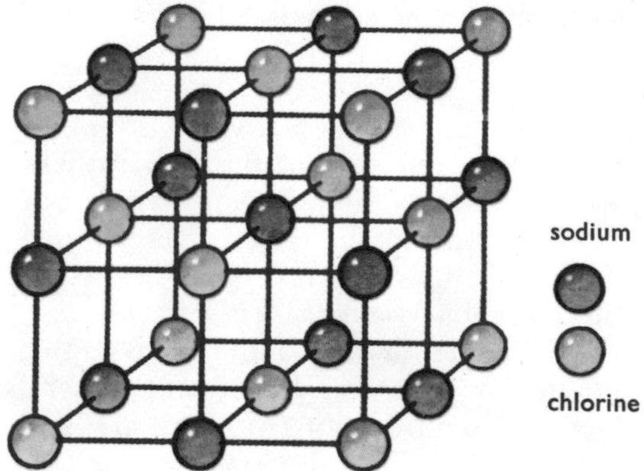

Halite, more commonly known as salt, forms perfect crystals, as shown in the photograph above. The model of its molecular structure shows how the atoms of sodium and chlorine are joined.

Minerals are also identified by such physical properties as lustre, colour, streak, hardness, specific gravity, cleavage, and fracture.

Lustre is the appearance of a mineral due to the reflection of light from its surface. Pyrite, galena, and graphite are minerals that have a metallic lustre. Most minerals have non-metallic lustres, and two thirds of all minerals have a vitreous (glassy) lustre. Examples are quartz, hornblende, apatite, topaz, and olivine. A few, such as zircon and diamond, have an adamantine (brilliant) lustre. Several have a resinous lustre. Others are pearly, silky, dull or earthy, and greasy.

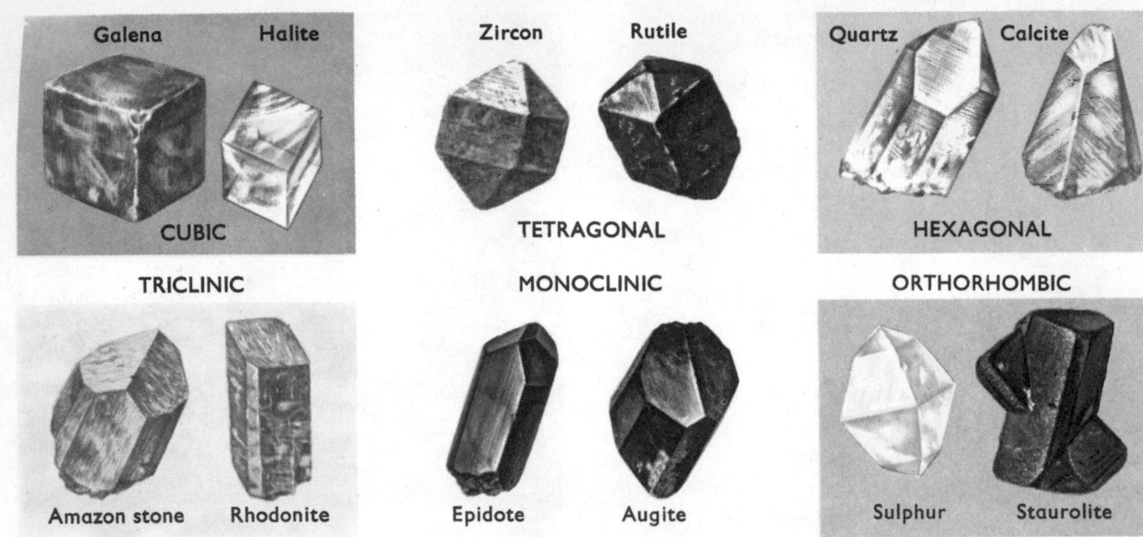

The crystal form of minerals is important in identification. Illustrated above are examples of six basic types of crystals.

Colour of many minerals varies so greatly that colour is not very useful for identifying minerals. Some minerals, however, always have the same colour. Pyrite is always bronze, yellow; galena, steel-grey; greenockite and carnotite, canary-yellow.

Hardness is a mineral's resistance to scratching, and the relative hardness of minerals is useful in identification. Minerals are harder when their atoms are small and closely packed. Mohs' hardness scale is the standard of relative hardness, talc being the softest and diamond the hardest.

1. *Talc*
2. *Gypsum*
3. *Calcite*
4. *Fluorite*
5. *Apatite*
6. *Orthoclase*
7. *Quartz*
8. *Topaz*
9. *Corundum*
10. *Diamond*

Streak is the colour of the mineral as a powder and in a few cases it is strikingly different from the colour of the mineral itself. For example, yellow pyrite has a black streak. Hematite may be red, metallic grey, or black, but its streak is always red. Goethite may be black or brown, but its streak is always brown.

Using a streak plate

Corundum is a mineral that occurs in several colours.

Types of Lustre

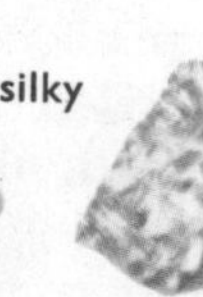

A simple method of testing for hardness.

Try to scratch A with B

Try to scratch B with A

A scratches B

B does not scratch A

Convenient scale of hardness for field use.

Specific gravity is the ratio of a mineral's weight compared with the weight of an equal volume of water. Pure, non-porous specimens must be used for testing to determine the specific gravity of the mineral.

Tenacity is the resistance of a mineral to breaking, bending, or cutting. Most minerals are brittle and shatter when hit. Muscovite is elastic and springs back to its original position after being bent. Gold and copper can be cut or bent. Tough minerals like jadeite do not break or cut readily.

Cleavage is the property that causes a mineral to break along parallel planes. Cleavage directions are parallel to crystal faces, which depend on the atomic structure of the mineral. The quality of cleavage varies from perfect to poor. Biotite and muscovite (micas) have one perfect cleavage. Galena and halite have cubic cleavage; calcite has rhombohedral cleavage.

Fracture is the way in which a mineral breaks other than its cleavage. Most minerals have an uneven fracture. Conchoidal (shell-like) fracture is shown on quartz or obsidian arrowheads. A few minerals break with an exceedingly irregular fracture. This is called hackly. *Magnetism* is a property of some minerals, such as magnetite and ilmenite. Uranium and thorium minerals are *radioactive*. Halite and a few others are soluble in water and have a distinct *taste*. Other minerals fluoresce when placed under an ultraviolet light. For example, willemite fluoresces green; some calcites fluoresce pink.

Blowpipe tests are simple chemical tests useful in making rapid identification. The blowpipe is a tapered metal tube held at the edge of the flame from a Bunsen burner. The temperature of the flame is raised by blowing through the blowpipe, and the mineral specimen, resting on a charcoal block, is held to the flame. The heating may cause changes in the colour or appearance of the mineral, giving a clue to its identity. In a flame test, a clean platinum wire is dipped into the powdered mineral and held in the flame. Many minerals give the flame a distinctive colour, as illustrated on the next page.

A blowpipe test can also be made by mixing a small amount of the powdered mineral with sodium carbonate (washing soda) and

A balance is used to measure the specific gravity of a mineral. This is its weight compared to the weight of an equal volume of water.

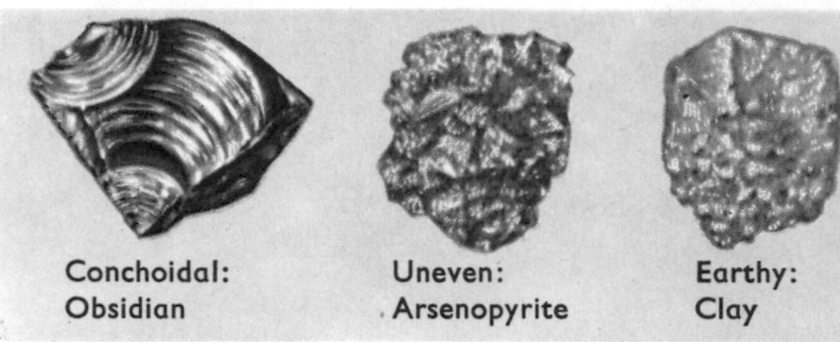

Fracture refers to the way a mineral breaks other than along parallel or cleavage planes.

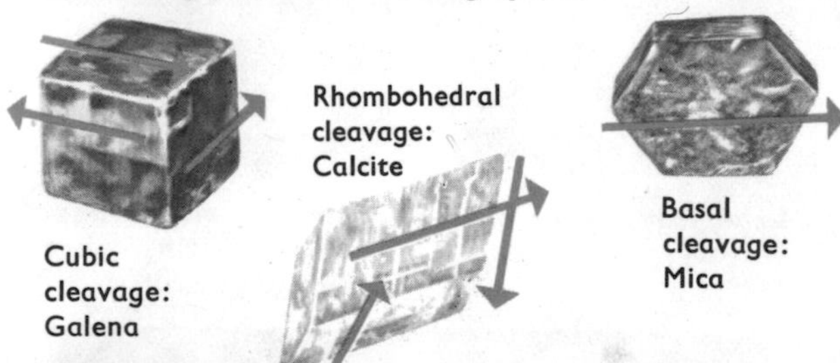

The way a mineral splits along planes (cleavage) is used in identification.

A few minerals are strongly magnetic. This is Pyrrhotite, an ore of iron.

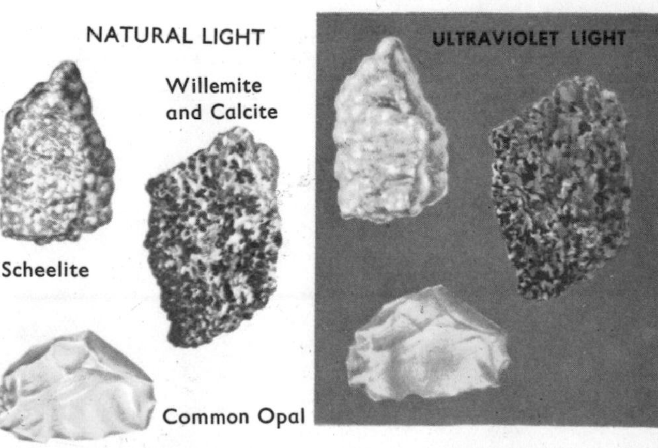

Some minerals emit beautiful colours under the rays of an ultra-violet lamp.

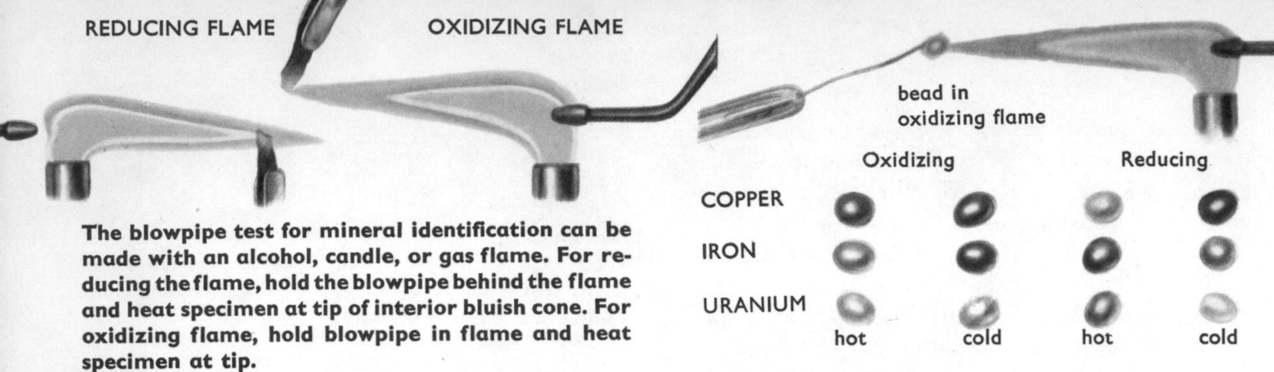

The blowpipe test for mineral identification can be made with an alcohol, candle, or gas flame. For reducing the flame, hold the blowpipe behind the flame and heat specimen at tip of interior bluish cone. For oxidizing flame, hold blowpipe in flame and heat specimen at tip.

Some metals are identified by the borax bead test. Borax powder in a loop of platinum is heated to form a glassy bead which is then touched to the mineral and then reheated in both oxidizing and reducing flames. The colour of the bead is noted when hot and when it has become cold.

In blowpipe test for zinc, ore is heated on charcoal with oxidizing flame.

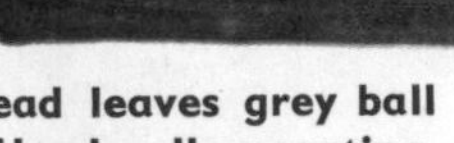

Lead leaves grey ball of lead, yellow coating.

Bismuth, an orange-yellow coating that cools to green.

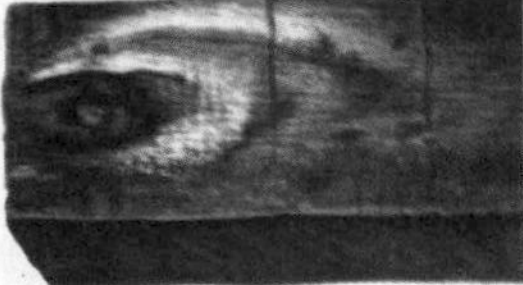

Antimony, a dense white coat with a bluish fringe.

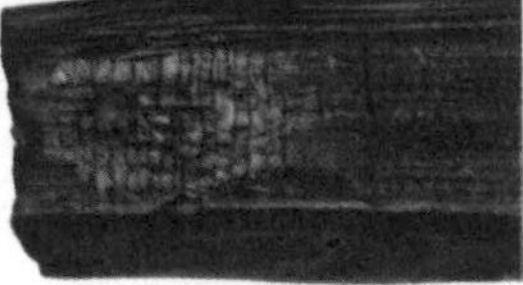

Copper, reddish ball and almost no coating.

In flame tests, a small amount of mineral is placed in the flame. The colour of the flame helps to identify the mineral.

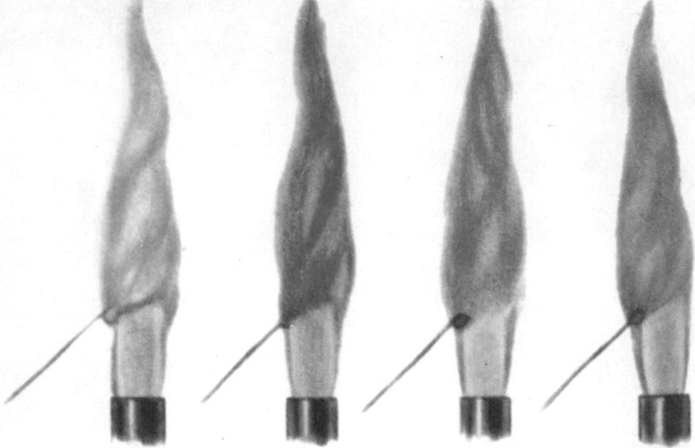

SODIUM strong yellow, invisible through cobalt glass.

STRONTIUM strong, intense crimson-red flame.

COPPER blue with some green, depending on ore.

POTASSIUM violet, appearing as red through cobalt glass.

placing it in a hollow in a charcoal stick. This is roasted in the blowpipe flame until action stops. The residue is a clue to the kind of metal in the mineral.

Still another test can be made by heating a platinum loop and dipping it into borax or microcosmic salt until a clear bead is formed. The hot bead is dipped into a small quantity of powdered mineral and then heated in the blowpipe flame. The colours of the beads are characteristic of elements in the minerals.

A thin splinter of mineral may fuse or melt in a blowpipe flame. Stibnite and a few other minerals will fuse in the heat of a match flame; others cannot be fused at all.

Minerals can also be tested by putting them in either closed or open tubes which are then heated. Some minerals form characteristically coloured residues in the tubes. Or sometimes the mineral powders will react in a definite way with acids or other chemical liquids added to a test tube.

HOW MINERALS ARE FORMED Most minerals crystallise from molten materials called magmas found far beneath the Earth's surface. As a magma cools, the minerals that are least soluble crystallise first. These are called the primary minerals. Minerals rich in iron and magnesium form first, followed successively by those more rich in silicon and oxygen. The order of crystallisation is magnetite, pyrite, augite or diopside, then hornblende and other amphiboles. Next to crystallise are calcium-rich feldspars followed by those with increasing amounts of sodium (oligoclase and albite, for example).

Then potassium feldspar (orthoclase) crystallises, and at the end of the scale is quartz.

As the solid mass of crystallised minerals cools, it contracts and cracks. The remaining liquid magma squeezes into these cracks, and large crystals may form; occasionally some are several feet long. Veins of these large crystals (mainly quartz, feldspars and dark minerals) are called pegmatites. Pegmatites may also contain minerals composed of unusual elements, such as the rare earths (cerium, yttrium, and others), and gem minerals, such as sapphire, ruby, and emerald.

This ideal order of crystallisation is seldom found, however. Magma is very complex, and the formation of crystals is determined by solubility, because magmas are solutions. Some substances are more soluble than others. The temperature and pressure of the magma also affects the order of crystallisation. Some minerals — corundum, magnetite, and apatite, for example — crystallise at very high temperatures and pressures; quartz crystallises at low temperatures. The presence of water (steam), carbon dioxide, nitrogen, sulphur, boron, hydrogen chloride, and hydrogen fluoride also affect the formation of crystals.

As minerals solidify from the magma, the relative proportions of the remaining chemical elements change. Sometimes this new liquid dissolves minerals already formed unless they have settled to the bottom of the magma or have been covered by later-formed minerals. A mineral that has been redissolved may form an entirely new mineral. This occurs with olivine, which crystallises from magma quickly but redissolves readily. The magnesium, iron, silicon, and oxygen of the olivine then combine to form enstatite, a colourful pyroxene.

Minerals also form when liquids from the magma seep into the surrounding rock and combine with already existing minerals. Franklinite, zincite, antigorite, and talc are minerals formed in this manner. New minerals are formed also due to extreme heat and pressure on the original minerals (contact metamorphism). Graphite, epidote, and cordierite are minerals formed by this method. Sometimes the pressure and heat

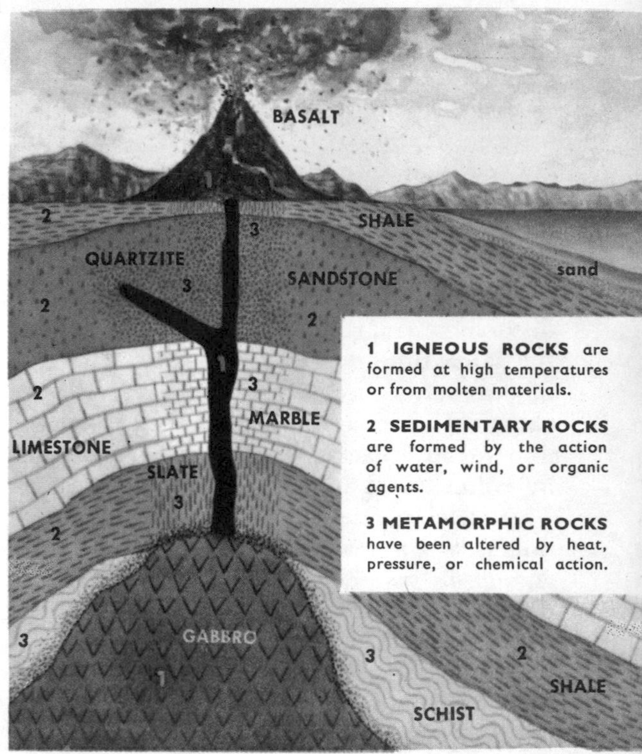

extend over many miles, deep below the Earth's surface. Then new, more complex minerals, such as sillimanite and kyanite, are formed by regional metamorphism.

Many minerals crystallise from gases and water solutions that form from cooling magma. Both temperature and pressure decrease with the distance from the parent magma. Near the Earth's surface, chemical reactions of gases and liquids with the local rock cause minerals to form in veins. Sometimes there is a concentration of one mineral or a group of minerals at a particular place. A bonanza is such a place with a large deposit of a valuable mineral such as gold or silver. Rich pockets of copper, lead, or zinc minerals are also called bonanzas.

High temperature and pressure veins, which have temperatures ranging from 300 to 500 degrees centigrade, yield such minerals as pyrrhotite, ilmenite, tourmaline, and topaz. Veins of moderate temperature (200 to 300 degrees centigrade) and high pressure deposit such minerals as dolomite, pyrite, chalcopyrite, tetrahedrite, and gold. In veins with low temperature (50 to 200 degrees centigrade) and moderate pressure, gold, argentite, galena, sphalerite, amethyst, quartz, calcite, fluorite, barite, and zeolites are crystallised out of the magma.

In hot springs and geysers such minerals as chalcedony (quartz), opal, travertine (calcite), stibnite, and orpiment form. Hot springs and geysers are a transition from mineral veins to surface-water deposits.

Replacement of minerals may take place along any veins. By this process a solution dissolves an earlier formed mineral and at the same time deposits a new mineral. The new mineral may or may not have different chemical composition than the original mineral. Replacement takes place volume by volume without change in size or shape. The varying size of atoms in the different minerals is not a factor because there is no change in volume. The rate of replacement depends on how easily the host rock can be dissolved and also on the supply of new mineral material available. Replacement may start at a centre and the new mineral develop as a perfectly formed crystal. Garnets, tourmaline, and corundum commonly originate in this way.

Minerals are also formed from surface waters in a variety of ways — by chemical reactions, by evaporation, and through biochemical means. A chemical reaction between an iron sulphate solution and calcium carbonate may form limonite. Gypsum or anhydrite followed by the deposition of halite may result from the evaporation of sea water. Bitter salts, such as epsomite and sylvite, are formed by evaporation. Some bacteria are known to deposit pyrolusite, limonite, sulphur, and aragonite. Aragonite, for example, forms around plants. Calcium carbonate in the form of aragonite is the principal material of which shells of sea animals are made, and coral reefs of tropical seas are composed of aragonite. The shells of diatoms are composed of opal (see OPAL).

Surface waters percolating down through mineral veins containing metallic sulphides dissolve the sulphides in the upper portions of the veins and leave a brownish deposit, usually of limonite and quartz. Sometimes these deposits are called an 'iron hat' because of their rusty colour and also because they resist erosion and stand above the surrounding area. As the dissolved material passes downwards through the vein, it oxidises whatever sulphides it contacts, leaving behind such minerals as silver, argentite, copper, cuprite, and hematite. Below the water table (top of water-saturated zone) more reactions with the original minerals cause the solutions to deposit secondary sulphides. This enriched zone contains the original materials plus the materials leached from above. This process, called oxidation and supergene enrichment, has produced valuable concentrations of such minerals as chalcocite, bornite, and chalcopyrite.

Surface or near-surface waters may also deposit new minerals by replacement or petrification. Most fossils, for example, are composed of minerals formed by replacement. Examples are opalised, agatised, or calcified wood in which sometimes even the delicate cell structure of the wood is preserved. In favourable conditions, bones may be preserved in the same way. Cubes of limonite have been found in which all the characteristics of the original pyrite are retained — even the lines on the faces of the cubes.

The rugged Alps of Europe were formed in Miocene times by a great folding of the Earth's crust. In more recent times glaciers have gouged deep valleys and left sheer cliffs.

Courtesy of TWA — Trans World Airlines

MONKEY-PUZZLE TREE

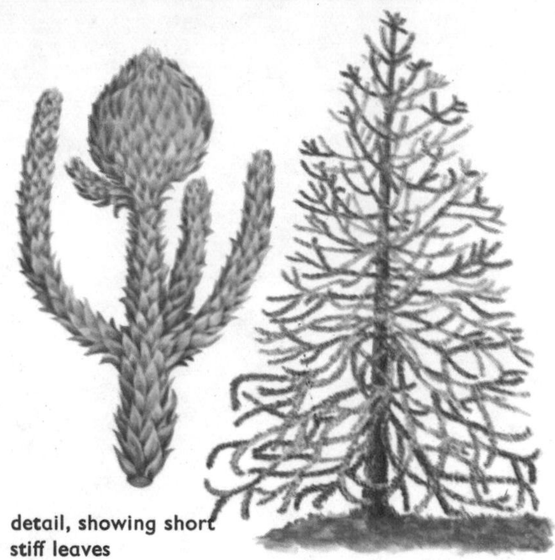

MIOCENE, which means 'less recent', is a period of the Cenozoic. It began about 26 million years ago and lasted 19 million years. Modern mammal groups arose and became supreme in the Miocene. There was a general uplift of land and replacement of lowland forests by open, grass-covered prairies. Many mammals changed from browsing to grazing habits. The change can be seen especially in their teeth and legs.

Miocene deposits in France have yielded primitive rhinoceroses and antelopes. Similar fossil finds have been made in India and Burma.

Miocene plants are very similar to modern forms, as were marine invertebrates. Bony fishes underwent great expansion, and sharks were abundant. One shark *(Carcharodon)* was probably more than 60 feet long.

The Alps and Himalayas were formed during the Miocene period. In Miocene times most of Britain was a land area, and no deposits of Miocene age have survived. The climate changed from sub-tropical to temporate.

MONKEY-PUZZLE TREES *(Araucaria araucana)* are cone-bearing evergreens native to the western slope of the Andes Mountains. Whorls of stiff branches curve downwards or upwards at the ends, like a monkey's tail, growing outwards from the central trunk to form an open crown. The branches are covered with numerous dark green, leathery, sharply pointed, overlapping scales (1 to 2 inches in length). On smaller trees even the trunks are covered with these leaves. The tree's cones are about 8 inches long and are shaped something like footballs. The Monkey-Puzzle Tree, an important timber tree in Chile, is sometimes grown as an ornamental. It is found in South America, Australia, and the Pacific Islands. Kauri pines (*Agathis* spp.) of New Zealand and Australia and the Norfolk Island Pine *(Araucaria excelsa)* are related species.

MOON. Some planets have many satellites; others have none at all. The Earth has just one satellite – the Moon (see SATELLITES). It goes around the Earth once a month. Long ago, in fact, the months were actually marked by the motion of the Moon. The period from new moon to the next new moon is only 29½ days, however, and as the months in our present calendar are a little longer, the phases of the moon do not correspond now to our calendar months. The Moon's orbit around the Earth is not a perfect circle. Every month it passes a point

This picture of the 'other side of the Moon', taken by a Russian lunar probe, shows the same type of landscape as on the earthward side, with seas and craters scattered at random.

Wide World Photo

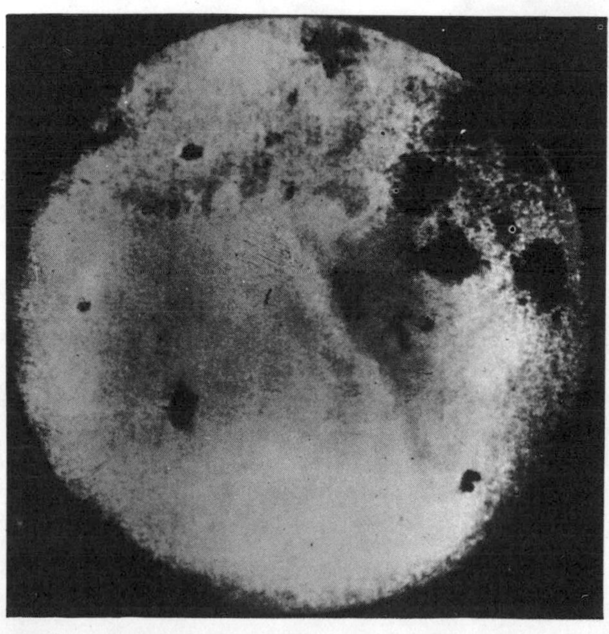

Lick Observatory

SOME IMPORTANT PHYSICAL FEATURES OF THE MOON

Mountains and Valleys
1. Alpine Valley
2. Alps Mountains
3. Altai Mountains
4. Apennine Mountains
5. Carpathian Mountains
6. Caucasus Mountains
7. Haemus Mountains
8. Jura Mountains
9. Pyrenees Mountains
10. Riphaen Mountains
11. Straight Range

Craters
12. Albategnius
13. Archimedes
14. Aristillus
15. Cassini
16. Clavius
17. Copernicus
18. Eratosthenes
19. Grimaldi
20. Plato
21. Ptolemaeus
22. Schickard
23. Theophilus
24. Tycho

Seas
25. Mare Nectaris
26. Mare Foecunditatis
27. Mare Crisium
28. Mare Tranquillitatis
29. Mare Serenitatis
30. Mare Imbrium
31. Mare Nubium
32. Mare Humorum
33. Mare Vaporum
34. Mare Frigoris

Apollo manned landings:
A. 11 Apollo 11
A. 12 Apollo 12

called its perigee, when it is closest to the Earth (226,000 miles). Half a revolution later it passes apogee, when it is farthest (252,000 miles) from the Earth. The average distance from the Earth is 239,000 miles.

The side of the Moon that faces the Sun is lit, while the other side is dark. How the Moon looks to us depends on how the side that faces the Earth is illuminated, and this depends on the direction of the Moon in relation to the Sun. When the Moon is between us and the Sun, the side we see gets no sunlight. Only a little light illuminates the edge, and so the Moon looks like a crescent. On the other hand, when the Moon is opposite the Sun and is in the sky all night, we see it fully illuminated, and the Moon is full or nearly so. Every month the Moon goes through all its phases as it moves around the Earth. At new moon it is invisible, then it is successively crescent, half-moon, gibbous, and full; then it is gibbous, half-moon, crescent, and new again. The half-moon phases are called first quarter and last quarter, because they come a quarter of a month after and before new moon, respectively.

As the phases change, the Moon rises and sets nearly an hour later each day. A few days after new moon we first glimpse the crescent moon in the west just after sunset, and it sets very quickly. By the time it reaches first quarter, the Moon sets at midnight. At full Moon it rises and is in the sky all night, setting at dawn. The last quarter Moon rises at midnight, while the crescent of the old Moon can be seen in the east for only a little while before dawn.

The Moon is 2,160 miles in diameter compared to the Earth's 7,920 miles. Its mass is only 1/80 the mass of the Earth, and the force of gravity is only a sixth as great on the Moon's surface as on the Earth. Visitors to the Moon can move around easily in their space suits in spite of the cratered surface which is rough. It is mainly dust and rock, some of which is shattered, but because there is no atmosphere there is no wind or rain to wear down the rock. The Moon is even rougher than it was when it was created, for the impact of meteors continually causes more damage to its surface, which resembles a lava field.

The lack of an atmosphere makes the surface of the Moon a strange and dangerous place. Men who have landed on the Moon must wear airtight space suits which have a built-in air supply. They also need protection from meteors, ultra-violet light and cosmic rays. The Earth's atmosphere provides us with as much cosmic-ray protection as we would get from a lead shield 3 feet thick. Since the Moon has no atmosphere, shielding is necessary using special materials. Communications are a problem, for without air there is no sound. All conversation has to be transmitted by radio. The sky is really magnificent. All the stars shine in a perfectly black sky whether the Sun is above the horizon or not. When the Sun is in the sky, its corona should be visible to anyone who protects his eyes from the brilliant light of the Sun's face. Since the Moon rotates slowly on its axis, a point on the surface receives brilliant sunlight continuously for 14 days and then passes into darkness for the next 14 days. Without the blanketing effect of an atmosphere, the Moon's rough surface becomes extremely hot 105 degrees centigrade (220°F) in the daytime and very cold at night minus 151 degrees centigrade (−240°F).

An American Apollo Lunar landing craft (an LEM or LM) on the Moon's cratered surface.

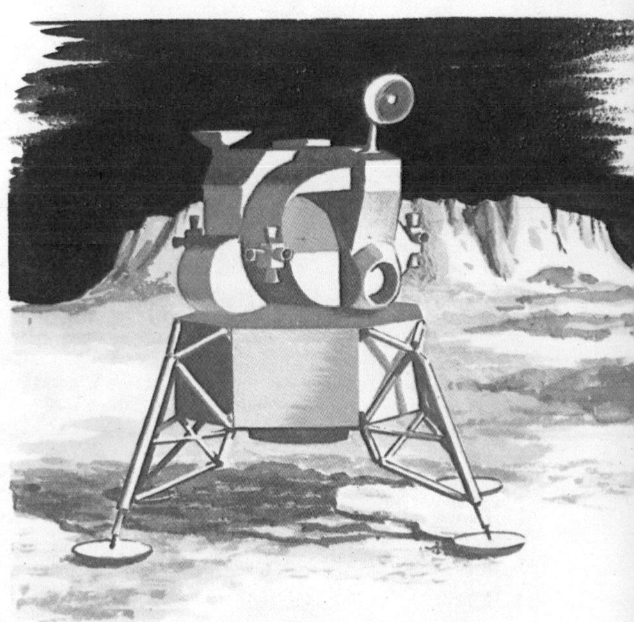

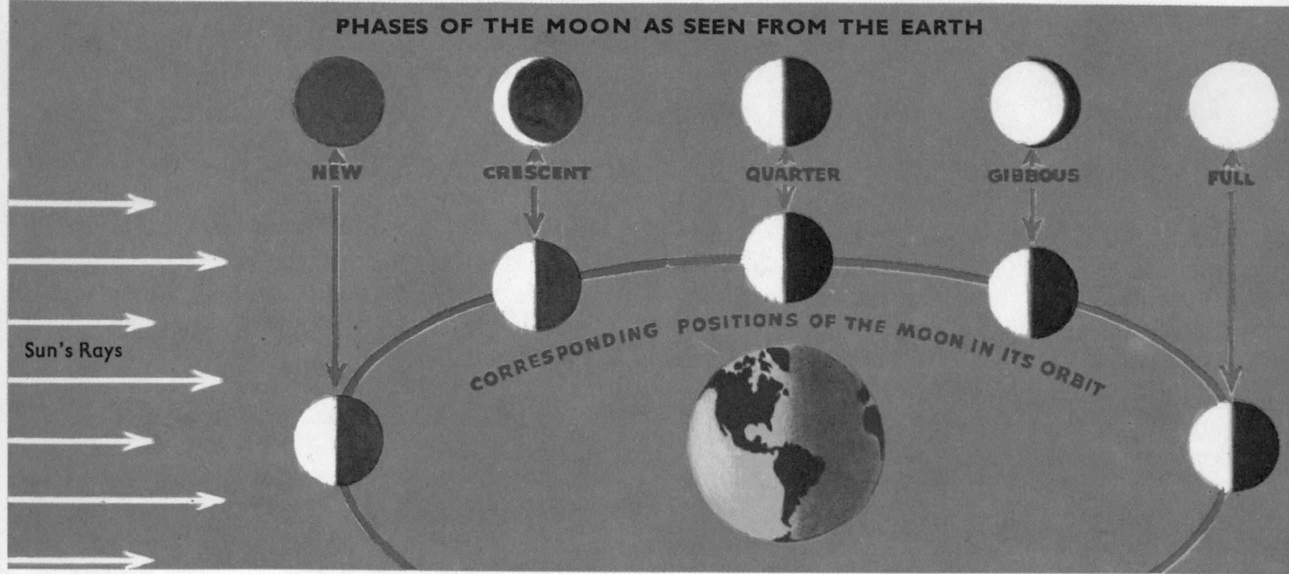

The Moon seen from the Earth has a surface pattern which suggests a face. Even a small telescope shows the true nature of these markings – simply that some parts of the Moon's surface are mountainous, while others are relatively flat. The large, dark areas are level plains called *maria*. They appear darker because the rocks absorb light. The bright areas contain some mountain chains like those on the Earth, but most of their features are craters – the most distinctive part of the lunar landscape. The largest crater on the Moon has a diameter of 150 miles; the smallest are pits too small to see, even with high-powered telescopes.

As the Moon goes around the Earth each month, it also rotates at the same rate; therefore, it always keeps the same face towards the Earth. Because of slight irregularities in the Moon's motion, we often see a little bit around the edge, but 41 per cent of the Moon's surface is permanently invisible from the Earth. The pictures taken by the Russian rocket of October 1959, show that the other side of the Moon is no different from the side we can see. Most of the Moon's surface has been mapped using orbiting space craft.

More than 700 features on the Moon have been named. These are the larger and easily recognisable markings, such as the 'seas', the larger 'lakes', and craters. There are more than 100,000 recorded formations.

The Moon often provides us with light at night, and on rare occasions it eclipses the Sun in the daytime (see ECLIPSES). Its

The flight paths of the American Apollo space craft from the Earth (left) to the Moon (right) and back, that is from blast-off on Earth to landing on the Moon and finally splash-down on Earth.

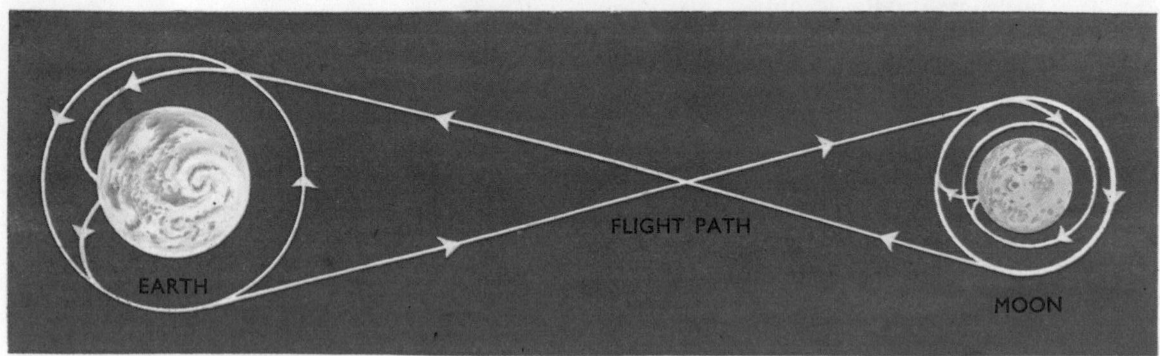

main effect on the Earth, however, is in creating the tides, caused mainly by the Moon's gravitational force that pulls harder on the moonward side than on the opposite side. The result is a stretching effect that causes the water of the oceans to flow slightly towards the point nearest the Moon and also towards the point farthest from the Moon.

MORELS, also called Sponge Mushrooms or Spring Mushrooms, are among the most delicious of all fungi. They are ascus-producing fungi related to cup fungi. These mushrooms have large pitted caps. They may be conical *(Morchella conica)*, cylindrical *(Morchella deliciosa)*, or nearly round *(Morchella esculenta)*. In the Hybrid Morel (*Morchella hybrida)*, the lower half of the conical cap is free from the stem.

Morels appear in early spring in old orchards, in woods and along banks of streams. They often appear in burned-off land. About 200 years ago, it was a custom in parts of Germany to gather great piles of branches, twigs, leaves and shrubs and burn them to provide a suitable place for morels to grow. During and after World War I, the site of bombed houses and trenches no longer used were reported to have produced many morels.

Because morels are among the finest of edible fungi, many attempts have been made to cultivate them. So far, no profitable method has been devised. Putting fragments of morels in a mixture of apple pulp and earth has given promising results.

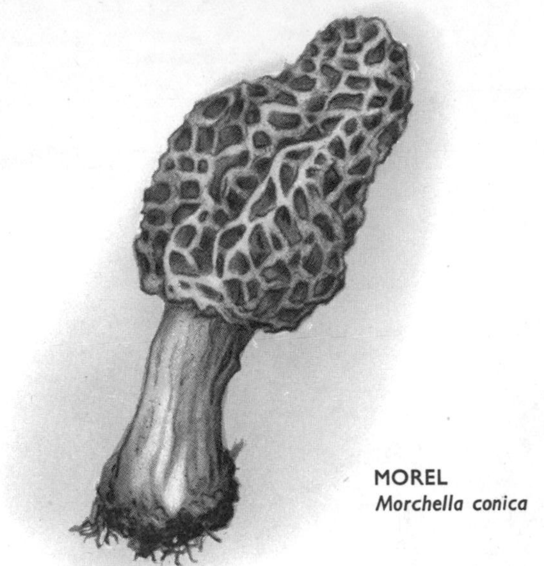

MOREL
Morchella conica

MORNING-GLORIES (*Ipomoea* spp.) are generally much more glorious in mornings than in afternoons, because the blossoms of most kinds do not last long in bright sunlight. Puckered-up remains of dead flowers are typical of late afternoon. Slightly opened flowers show spirally folded pleats. They are closely related to our native bindweed *(Convolvulus)*.

Ipomoeas are most abundant in tropical regions, where there are more than 400 species.

Several kinds of morning-glories have edible tuber-like roots, but the most important is the Sweet Potato (see SWEET POTATO).

MORNING-GLORIES
Ipomoea

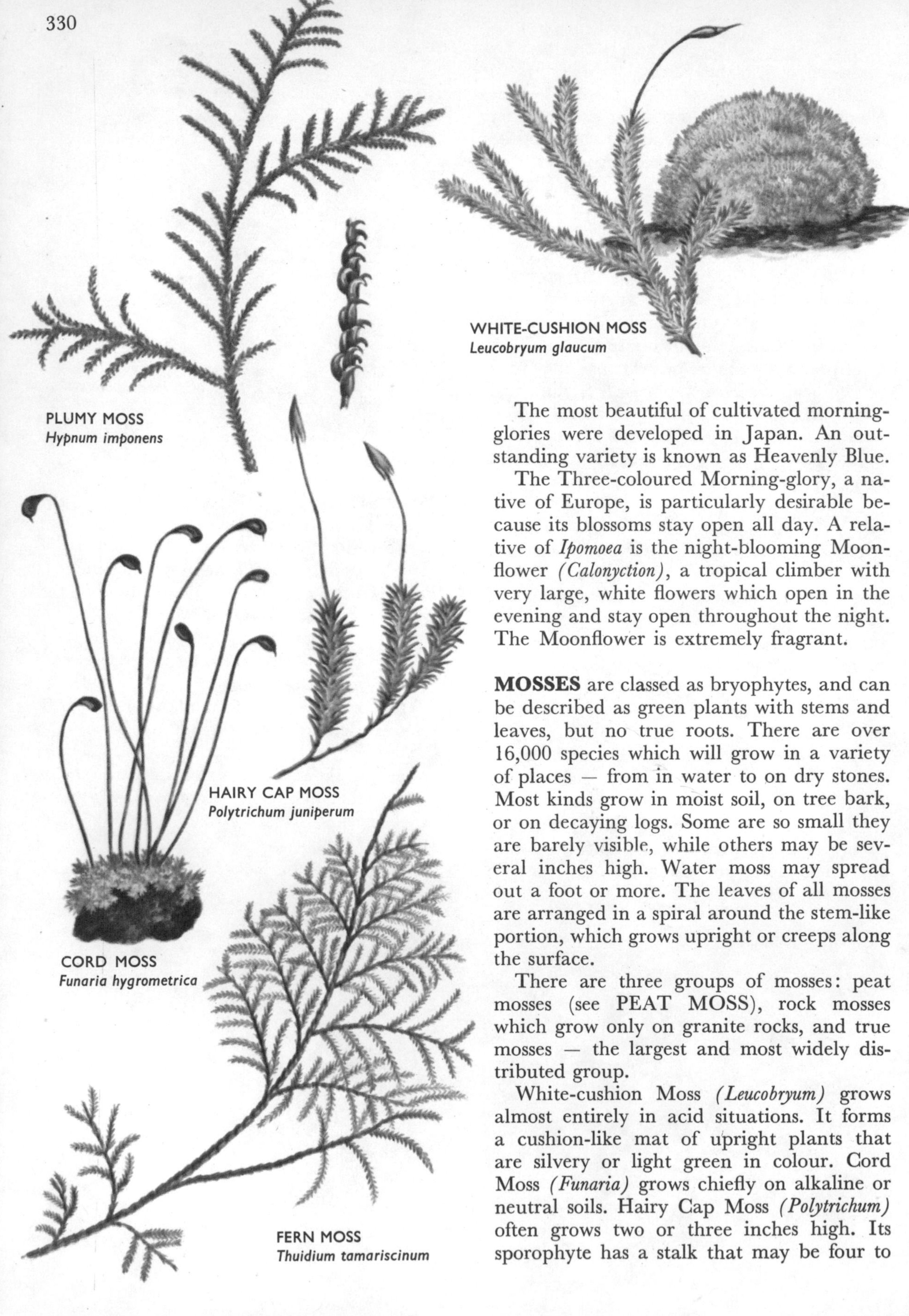

The most beautiful of cultivated morning-glories were developed in Japan. An outstanding variety is known as Heavenly Blue.

The Three-coloured Morning-glory, a native of Europe, is particularly desirable because its blossoms stay open all day. A relative of *Ipomoea* is the night-blooming Moonflower *(Calonyction)*, a tropical climber with very large, white flowers which open in the evening and stay open throughout the night. The Moonflower is extremely fragrant.

MOSSES are classed as bryophytes, and can be described as green plants with stems and leaves, but no true roots. There are over 16,000 species which will grow in a variety of places — from in water to on dry stones. Most kinds grow in moist soil, on tree bark, or on decaying logs. Some are so small they are barely visible, while others may be several inches high. Water moss may spread out a foot or more. The leaves of all mosses are arranged in a spiral around the stem-like portion, which grows upright or creeps along the surface.

There are three groups of mosses: peat mosses (see PEAT MOSS), rock mosses which grow only on granite rocks, and true mosses — the largest and most widely distributed group.

White-cushion Moss *(Leucobryum)* grows almost entirely in acid situations. It forms a cushion-like mat of upright plants that are silvery or light green in colour. Cord Moss *(Funaria)* grows chiefly on alkaline or neutral soils. Hairy Cap Moss *(Polytrichum)* often grows two or three inches high. Its sporophyte has a stalk that may be four to

Photo P. Belzeaux Rapho

Mushrooms are harvested before they expand too much.

five inches long, and there is a hairy cap on its capsule. Fern Mosses *(Thuidium)* have upright, leafy branches that resemble tiny ferns. Plumy Mosses *(Hypnum)* also look like tiny ferns.

Branches of trees in tropical rain forests are often covered with great masses of mosses of various types.

MUSHROOM GROWING. The commercial mushroom is said to be a variety of the Field Mushroom *(Agaricus campestris)*.

Mushrooms are cultivated in specially contructed buildings in which temperature and humidity can be controlled, although deserted mine workings are sometimes used.

Beds are prepared from composted and sterilised manure or rotted straw. After sterilisation the temperature of the beds is lowered to 24 degrees centigrade (75 degrees Fahrenheit), and the spawn is planted. The spawn is a mass of tangled threads of mycelium, the vegetative part of the mushroom. It is prepared by germinating selected spores in a special medium, such as sterilised grain or manure. After the spawn has grown for two or three weeks so that its cottony mycelium has extended through the top 3 inches of the bed, a layer of soil about 1 inch deep is spread over the surface of the bed. The first mushrooms appear about three weeks later. Then the temperature is lowered to 13 to 15 degrees centigrade (55 to 60 degrees Fahrenheit), and the mushrooms continue to develop for two or three months. Mushrooms are harvested when they are 1—3 inches in diameter and before they expand. They are pulled, not cut.

Other kinds of fungus are grown commercially elsewhere in the world. In Japan, Shiitake *(Cortinellus edodes)*, an aromatic species, is grown on logs planted with wedges of spore-inoculated wood. In China, the Jew's Ear Fungus *(Auricularia aricula-judae)* is cultivated on poles of oak, and *Volvaria esculenta* is widely grown in the tropics on beds prepared of rice straw, banana stalks, or sugar cane wastes.

NASTURTIUMS *(Tropaeolum* spp.*)*, like many other plants that we now raise for their beauty alone, were once grown for food. They were called Indian Cress, and the leaves and other parts were used to make tasty salads. Their buds and large seeds were sometimes used in pickles. Cultivated types were developed mainly in Europe where they have been grown as ornamentals for nearly 300 years. About 50 kinds of nasturtiums grow wild in South America, where the plants are native.

These graceful plants produce richly coloured blooms nearly all summer long, and their round, shield-shaped, long-stemmed leaves are attractive, too. Nasturtium plants grow quickly and are ideal as a ground cover or as low climbers. Their blossoms make fine cut flowers for shallow bowls. Trailing varieties can be grown on trellises or on banks or walls.

NASTURTIUM
Tropaeclum majus

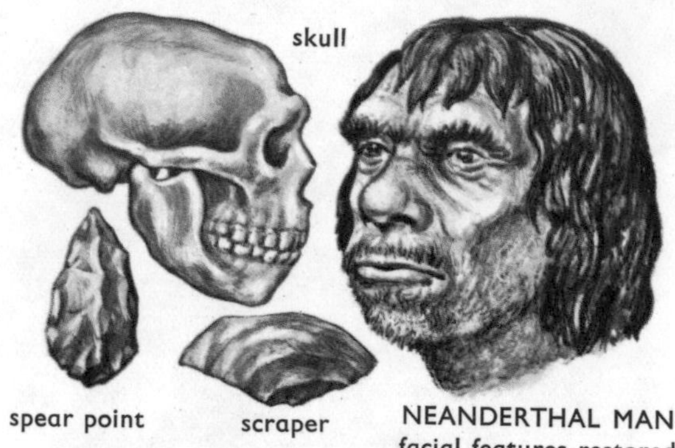

NEANDERTHAL MAN
facial features restored

NEANDERTHAL MAN *(Homo neanderthalensis)*, one of the best known of the prehistoric men, appeared in Europe about 150,000 years ago. Since 1848, remains of nearly 100 Neanderthal men, women, and children have been found in various parts of Europe and the Middle East. Recently a Neanderthal-type fossil skull was found in China.

Neanderthal Man stood only slightly more than 5 feet tall. In brain size he was as well equipped as modern man. He had a heavy brow, a thick neck, and a chinless, projecting face. His walk was somewhat stooped. Neanderthal Man lived in caves, where he also buried his dead. He used well-made stone tools and weapons and knew the use of fire. Possibly he wore simple clothing.

While Neanderthal Man may hardly be considered a direct ancestor of modern man, it is likely that Neanderthals mixed somewhat with early modern-type man. Neanderthal Man existed about 100,000 years. He disappeared as Cro-Magnon Man appeared in Europe, midway through the last glacial period. (See MAN.)

NEBULA. Even in the most powerful telescope, a star looks no bigger than a sharp point of light. But here and there among the

Mt. Wilson and Palomar Observatories

NCG 7293, in Aquarius, is a planetary nebula, a ring or shell of gas that surrounds a very old star.

stars we find hazy bright patches. The astronomers who first observed these called them all nebulae, after a Latin word that means 'little cloud'. Modern astronomers distinguish between two different kinds of diffuse bright objects and use the term nebula for only one of them. Bright patches of one sort are called galaxies; they are great systems of stars so far away that we see only the hazy total light rather than the light from individual stars.

The true nebulae are part of our own Milky Way. Some are irregular in shape and are called diffuse nebulae. Of these, some are clouds of dust illuminated by stars in or near them; others are gas clouds that emit their own light. Even these emission nebulae depend on stars to make them glow, however. The atoms of gas absorb short-wave-length ultra-violet light from the stars that they surround, then they re-emit visible light. Only the very hottest stars have enough ultra-violet light to produce an emission nebula.

Still another type of gaseous nebula is round and smooth-looking, often in the shape of a ring. Such an object is called a planetary nebula and is actually a shell of gas surrounding a very hot, old star. Most planetary nebulae appear very faint.

The Crab Nebula, MI in Taurus, is composed of gases that glow brightly. Photographs taken over the years show that the Crab Nebula is expanding, the result of a supernova that appeared in the year 1054.

Mt. Wilson and Palomar Observatories

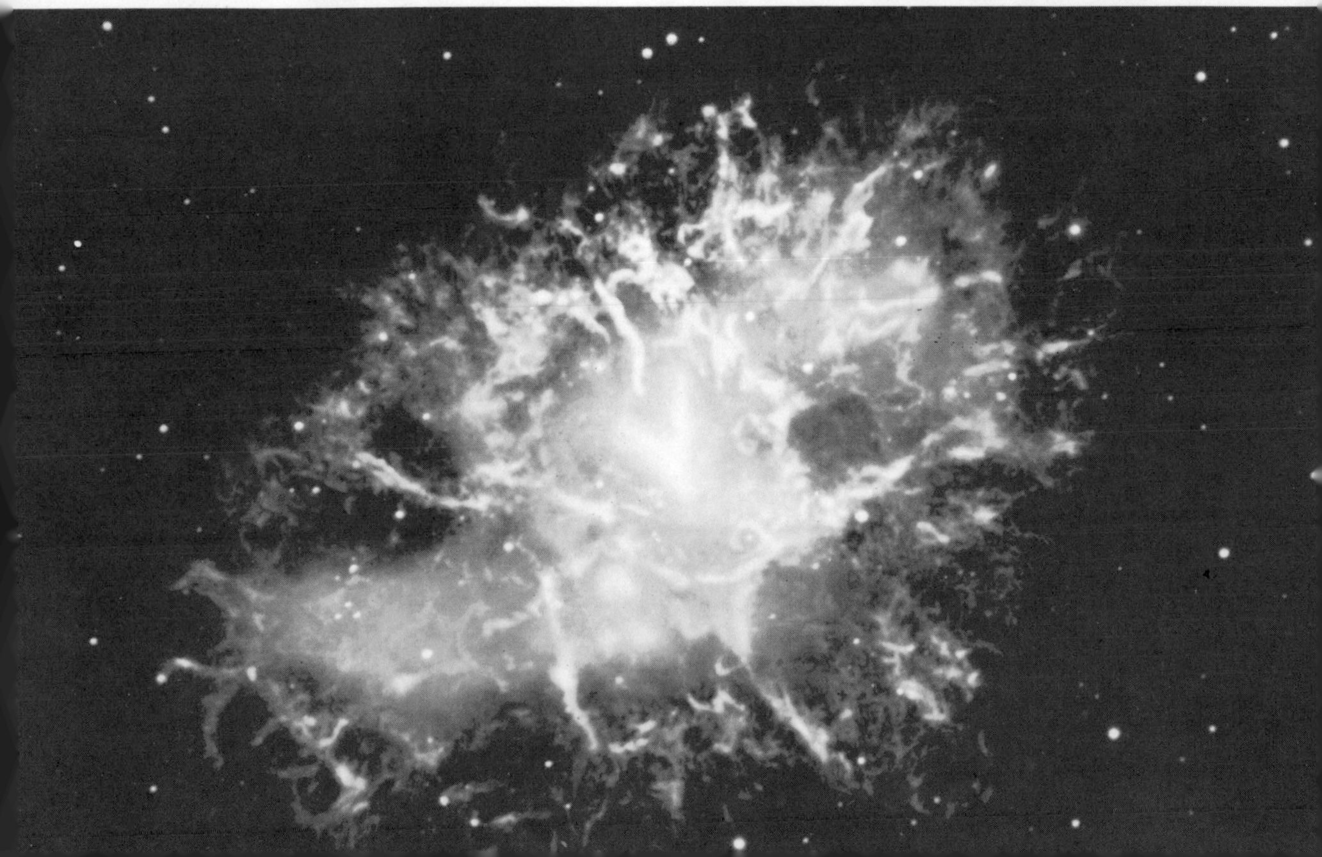

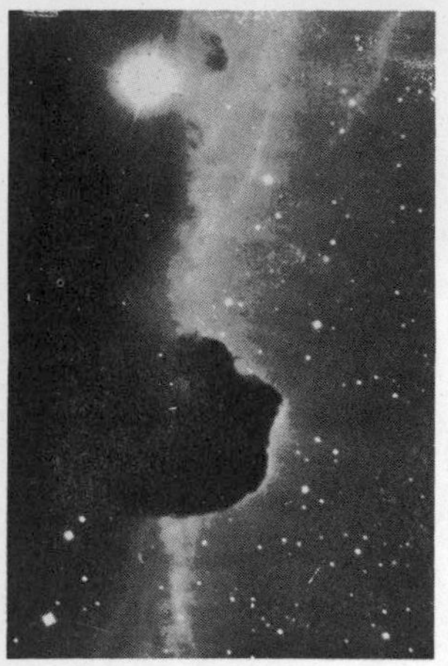
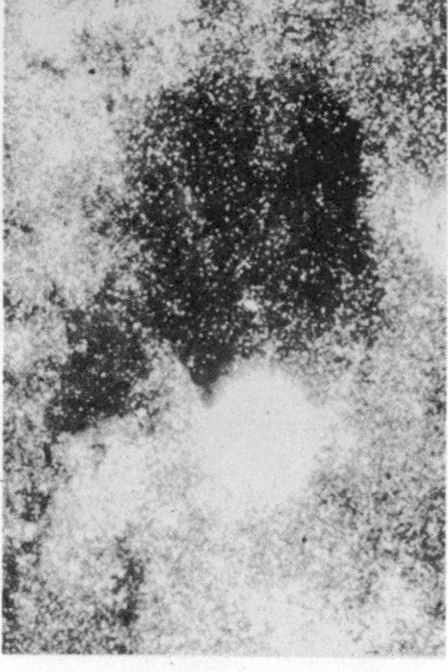

Mt. Wilson and Palomar Observatories

Both the Horsehead Nebula, in Orion, and the Coal Sack Nebula, in Crux, are masses of dust that hide the countless stars behind them.

Besides the bright patches in the sky, we sometimes find dark spots in the Milky Way, where there are many fewer stars than in the surrounding regions. Called dark nebulae, these are caused by dense clouds of dust that hide the light of the stars beyond. (See GALAXY; INTERSTELLAR GAS AND DUST; STARS.)

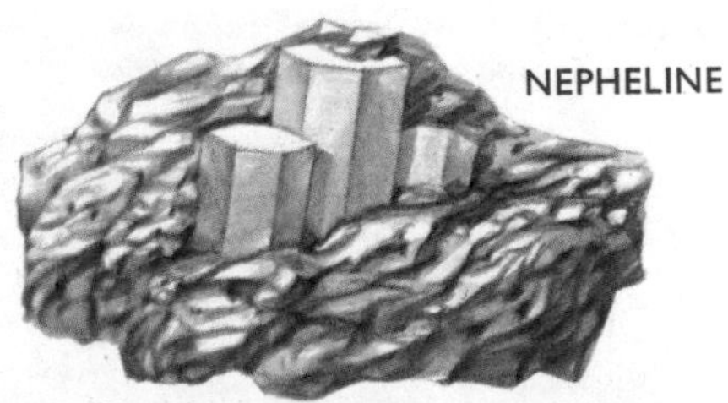

NEPHELINE is an igneous mineral formed, like lazurite and leucite, from magmas lacking silica to form feldspars. Nepheline occurs as grey or red-brown masses with good cleavage or as hexagonal crystals. It has a greasy lustre. Nepheline is used for ceramics. It is found in Germany, Norway, Brazil, U.S.S.R. and U.S.A.

NEPTUNE is the eighth planet in distance from the Sun. Its average distance from the Sun is 2,800 million miles or 30 times the Earth's distance. The planet takes 165 years to circle this large orbit. Neptune is the third largest planet, although it is only slightly more massive than Uranus, which it resembles in many ways. Neptune's diameter is 28,000 miles, or nearly four times the diameter of the Earth. Its mass is 17 times that of the Earth. Being so far from the Sun, Neptune is very cold, with -141 degrees centigrade (-220 degrees Fahrenheit) at its surface. The planet rotates on its axis every $15\frac{2}{3}$ hours and is covered with a dense atmosphere that is probably made mostly of hydrogen and helium. The poisonous gas methane shows up strongly in its spectrum. Neptune has two satellites. Triton is about the size of our Moon, while Nereid is a much smaller body that moves around Neptune in a highly elongated and inclined orbit.

Neptune is too faint to see with the naked eye. It can be seen in a small telescope, but a large magnification is needed to distinguish it from a star.

Neptune was discovered in 1846 as a result of a mathematical prediction. It had been noticed for many years that Uranus was deviating from its predicted orbit because of the gravitational attraction of some unknown body. The problem of determining the position of Neptune from its attraction on Uranus was solved by Adams in England and Leverrier in France. Neptune was found in the position that each had predicted. (See PLANETS.)

NICKEL is important in alloys, especially with iron. Pentlandite, the most important nickel ore, is a compound of nickel and sulphur. Pentlandite is metallic bronze and granular, with a light bronze streak. It occurs in high temperature veins. Niccolite (nickel and arsenic) is found in fine-grained

Neptune (centre) is many times larger than Earth (left) and Pluto (right).

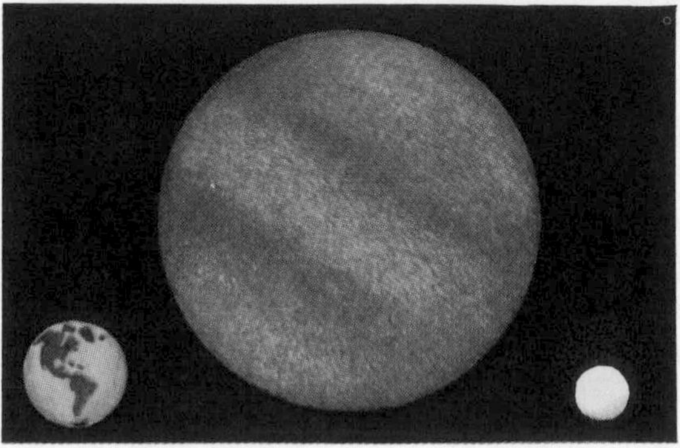

metallic masses that are a light copper-red, commonly tarnished grey to black. Its streak is brown-black. It occurs in veins of moderate temperature. Pyrrhotite, an iron sulphide (see IRON), occurs with pentlandite. It is bronze-red with a brown-black streak, and it tarnishes brown. Pyrrhotite is slightly magnetic. The largest deposits of these ores, which occur together, are found near Sudbury, Ontario. Garnierite, which is found in New Caledonia, is another important source of nickel.

Nickel is alloyed with steel to increase its elasticity. Stainless steel is an alloy of steel, chromium, and nickel. Invar metal is one-third nickel and is used in scientific instruments and measuring tapes, because it is not affected by temperature changes. Some coins are an alloy of nickel and copper. German silver, used for electrical heating elements, jewellery, and kitchenware, is nickel, copper, and zinc. Nichrome wire is used in heating elements. Permalloy (80 per cent nickel and 20 per cent iron) is used for magnets and rapid transmission cable. Monel metal, essentially nickel and copper, is very resistant to corrosion. Nickel is also an important metal in electroplating, making a base for the final coating of chromium.

EVENING PRIMROSE
Oenothera biennis

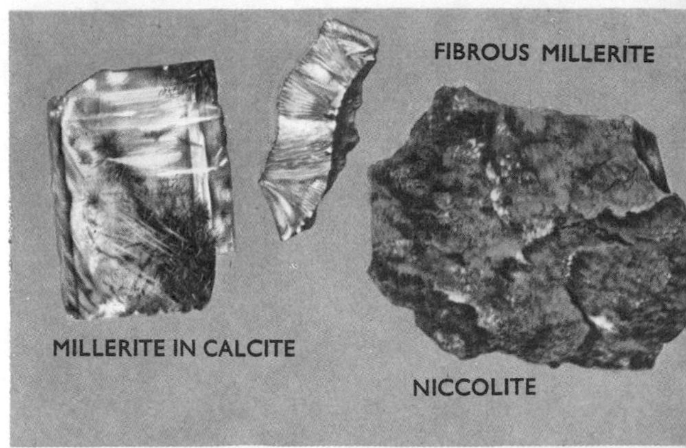

FIBROUS MILLERITE

MILLERITE IN CALCITE

NICCOLITE

NOCTURNAL. Life over much of the Earth is in two parts: one during daylight hours (diurnal) and another during darkness (nocturnal). A third group (crepuscular) is active during twilight hours.

Most plants bloom by day, but some bloom only at night. Examples are Night-flowering Catchfly, Evening Primrose and Night-blooming Cacti. In general, flowers that bloom at night are either white or very pale in colour and are fragrant. Both features make it easier for night-flying insects to find and pollinate them.

In oceans and lakes, plankton animals, such as small crustaceans and rotifers, swim towards the surface at night but move to deeper levels during the day.

NON-FLOWERING PLANTS. Everyone is familiar with large numbers of flowering plants. Broad-leaved trees, shrubs, grasses, vegetables and flowers are all flowering plants. But nearly a third of the plants in the world do not produce flowers. Non-flowering plants are not as well known as flowering types, but they are no less important. Non-flowering plants vary in size from the tiniest bacterium to the Giant Redwood trees, largest of all living things. Plants grow all over the world — from the Arctic to the Antarctic, from deserts to mountain tops, and from the prairies to within the oceans. All of the fungi — the moulds, mildews, mushrooms, bacteria and lichens — belong to this group. All of the algae that grow in ponds and streams and in oceans are also non-flowering plants, as are mosses and their relatives. Ferns, club

Russ Kinne — Photo Researchers

Seaweeds are the largest of the thallus plants. Some float on the surface, others are attached to rocks as much as 100 feet below the surface. Rockweeds *(Fucus)* of several species (above) thrive in the tidal zone.

mosses and horsetails are non-flowering plants, too, as are a small group of seed plants — the cycads and conifers, such as the pines, firs, cedars and spruces.

Lowly forms of non-flowering plants were probably the first living things to inhabit the Earth (see LIFE'S ORIGIN AND DEVELOPMENT). The flowering plants did not appear until relatively recent geological times, and so by far the greatest number of plant fossils are from the non-flowering plant groups. Most of these are of interest primarily to botanists, but some are of great economic value. The world's coal resources are made up of fossilised remains of giant ferns and horsetails that lived about 300 million years ago (see CARBONIFEROUS; COAL). Non-flowering plants of today add the bracing support to coral reefs in warm seas (see CORAL REEFS). Microscopic algae form the basic food in fresh and salt waters throughout the world for animals, and many kinds of algae and fungi are eaten by man. Fungi and bacteria help to keep the earth clean of decaying plants and animals. Bacteria and viruses are the cause of many diseases. The various groups of non-flowering plants and their specific values are treated in separate entries.

The largest, most colourful lichens grow in the Arctic.

Fritz Goro

Some of the simpler non-flowering plants have characteristics of both plants and animals. This is true of some of the algae, such as the green, yellow-green, euglenoids, dinoflagellates, slime moulds, and some of the true fungi.

A thallus is a plant body without roots, stems, or leaves. Sometimes it consists of only one cell; in other cases it is a filament of cells attached end to end, or it may form a large flat plant over a hundred feet long, as in the giant kelps, a type of seaweed (see

KELPS). Not all thallus plants belong to the thallophytes. Liverworts and fern gametophytes, for example, are also thallus types of plants.

Three distinctive characteristics separate the thallophytes and embryophytes. The sex organs in the thallophytes are usually only one-celled, and they *never* have a jacket of sterile (non-reproductive) cells around them. In contrast, the sex organs of the embryophytes are many-celled, and there is always a jacket of sterile cells around them.

The spore-producing organs (sporangia) of thallophytes are also usually one-celled without a jacket of sterile cells, but are many-celled with a sterile jacket in the embryophytes.

The third characteristic has given embryophytes their name. In higher animals and plants an embryo is always formed within the female sex organ. This embryo is an animal or plant in miniature. An embryo is produced by all embryophytes. In thallophytes the fertilised cell falls out of the sex organ before it develops into another plant.

HOW NON-FLOWERING PLANTS REPRODUCE. A characteristic of all living things — both plant and animal — is the ability to reproduce their kind. There are two basic types of reproduction: asexual and sexual. Asexual reproduction does not involve the fusion or joining together of two different cells. Sexual reproduction does. Both methods occur in non-flowering plants, either independently or alternately in the same plant.

The simplest type of reproduction is fission. A cell merely splits into two equal parts to form two cells. Each of the new cells is exactly like the original cell. This type of reproduction occurs in blue-green algae and in bacteria. All of the traits that make an organism what it is are supposedly divided or duplicated in this process. In blue-green algae and in bacteria we cannot observe how

NON-FLOWERING PLANTS

Many non-flowering plants are microscopic in size, but the largest and most massive of all living things is also a non-flowering plant, the General Sherman Sequoia with a weight estimated at 1,180 tons. In numbers of species, the non-flowering plants are fewer than the flowering plants, but they occur in more diverse forms.

SUB-KINGDOM THALLOPHYTA:

plants that are one-celled, threadlike, or flat with many cells (thallus).

BLUE-GREEN ALGAE (Cyanophyta) 1,500 species

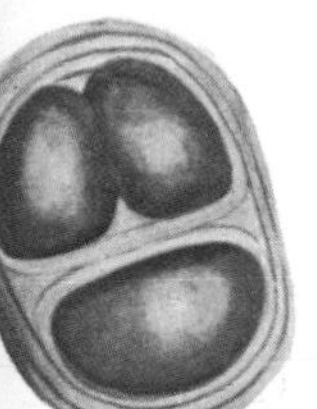

GREEN ALGAE (Chlorophyta) 5,500 species

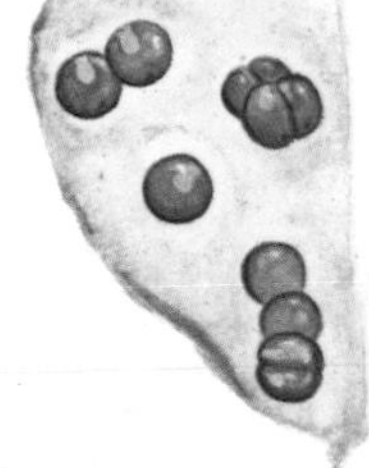

STONEWORTS (Charophyta) 250 species

EUGLENOIDS (Euglenophyta) 300 species

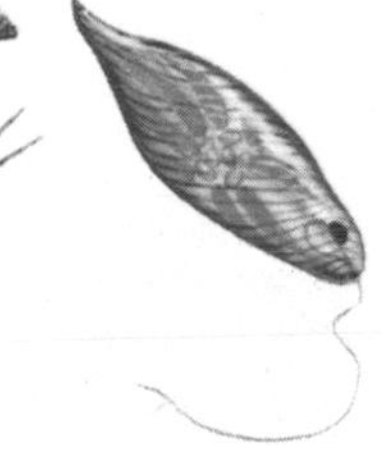

YELLOW-GREEN ALGAE AND DIATOMS (Chrysophyta) 5,000 species

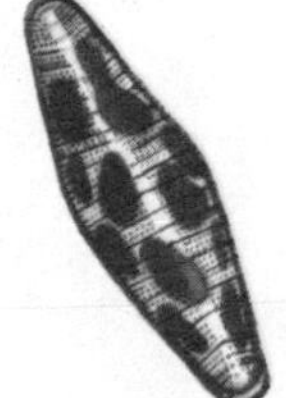

DINOFLAGELLATES (Pyrrophyta) 1,000 species

BROWN ALGAE (Phaeophyta) 1,100 species

SUB-KINGDOM THALLOPHYTA:

plants that are one-celled, threadlike, or flat with many cells (thallus).

RED ALGAE (Rhodophyta) 2,500 species

BACTERIA (Schizomycophyta) 1,400 species

SLIME MOULDS (Myxomycophyta) 500 species

FUNGI (Eumycophyta) 100,000 species

SUB-KINGDOM EMBRYOPHYTA:

plants that produce embryos.

LIVERWORTS, HORNWORTS, MOSSES (Bryophyta) 18,000 species

CLUB MOSSES, FERNS, CONIFERS AND HIGHER PLANTS (Tracheophyta) 200,000 species

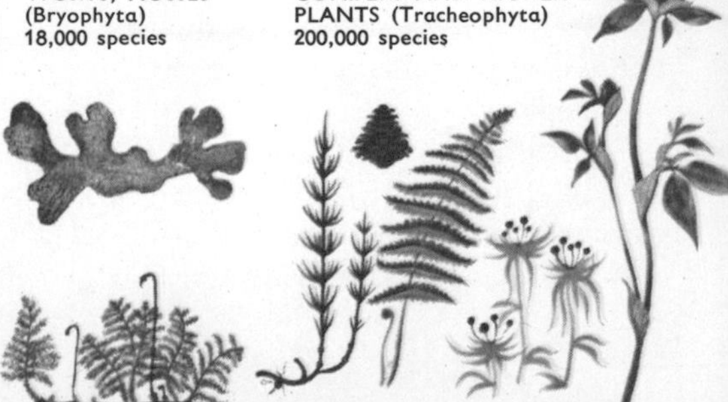

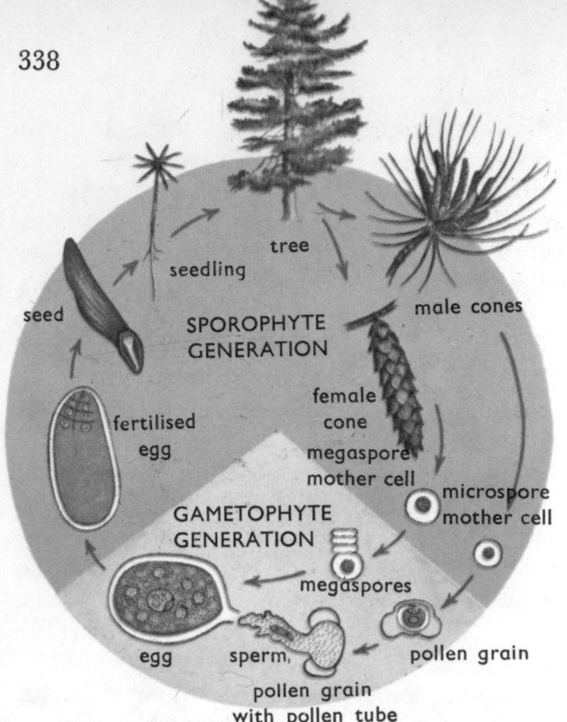

LIFE CYCLE OF A CONIFER

Conifers are highly developed non-flowering plants in which the sporophyte generation is the dominant form.

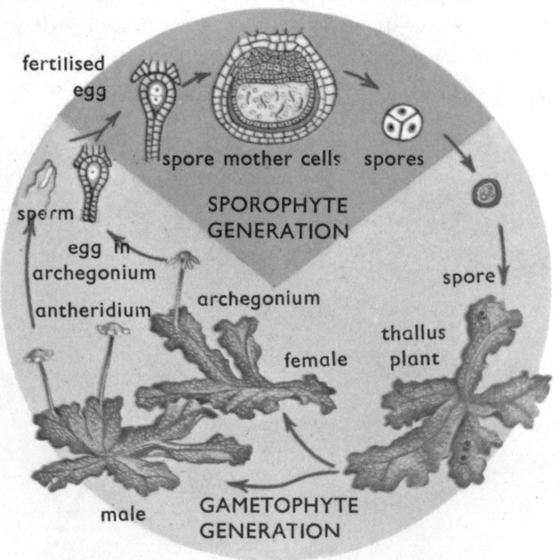

LIFE CYCLE OF A LIVERWORT

In liverworts the gametophyte generation is the dominant visible form, while the sporophyte is barely visible.

this division of nuclear material takes place, however.

Ordinary cell division is similar to fission. Here also a cell divides into two cells that are equal. The nucleus of the original cell duplicates its parts by a process called mitosis so that each of the chromosomes, which carry the traits of the plant, is split or duplicated. This occurs in all growth as new cells are formed. As a young seedling grows from a few inches high to a tall plant, new cells are formed continually in this manner. In the case of single-celled plants or animals, mitosis and the formation of a new cell will result in two new individuals, exactly alike.

The most common type of asexual reproduction in plants is by means of spores, which serve the same function as do seeds. A plant may produce many spores, and each spore can grow into a new plant. In the formation of spores a nucleus divides many times. Each new nucleus gathers a bit of protoplasm about it and forms a cell wall. In most plants, spores are produced in a special spore case called the sporangium. There are many kinds of spores. Most are one-celled, but some consist of several cells. Spores that can move by means of whip-like flagella are called zoospores. The flagellum is a thread-like extension of protoplasm that moves back and forth rapidly in the water. Zoospores are produced by many different kinds of algae and by watermoulds.

Most spores are not able to move by their own power and are blown by the wind. This is true of most fungi, mosses, liverworts, ferns and fern relatives. The green colour of a *Penicillium* mould, often seen on oranges or lemons, is due to the colour of the spores. Brush the growth with your finger and it will be green with the dust-like spores.

Although the simplest algae and fungi reproduce asexually, most algae and fungi and all other plants reproduce sexually. Both plants and animals produce sex cells called gametes. These are produced in sex organs that are one-celled in the thallophytes and many-celled in the embryophytes. In the most primitive type of sexual reproduction the gametes look alike. In many algae and fungi and in all embryophytes, however, the gametes are not alike. The male gamete is called the sperm, and the female gamete is the egg. Usually the sperms can move; they look like small zoospores but cannot grow into new plants. They must first fuse with an egg.

A male and a female sex cell join together to form one cell by fusion or fertilisation. The resulting zygote may develop directly into a new plant. In the embryophytes the zygote develops into an embryo, which is a miniature plant. Some of the algae and all of the embryophytes have an alternation of generations in which an asexual spore-producing generation alternates with a sexual gamete-producing generation. The moss plant that we know is the gametophyte. Attached to it, after fertilisation, is a dependent or parasitic structure, the sporophyte. It consists of only a stalk and a capsule which bears spores.

In the fern, both generations are independent plants. The fern plant with roots, stems and leaves is the sporophyte. The tiny green plant that grows from the spores is the gametophyte. In seed plants, both flowering (angiosperms) and non-flowering (gymnosperms), the sporophyte has roots, stems, leaves and vascular tissues for conducting water and nutrients. The gametophytes are very small, consisting of one to a few cells and are completely dependent on the sporophyte for their nutrition. Thus, in the evolution of plants from lower to higher forms there is a complete reversal in the role of the gametophyte. In the lower plants the gametophyte is the independent, dominant stage. In seed plants the gametophyte is inconspicuous and dependent on the sporophyte.

HOW NON-FLOWERING PLANTS DEVELOPED. Life has existed on Earth for millions of years, but we do not know in what form it first existed. Some believe that perhaps the first living things were bacteria similar to present-day iron and sulphur bacteria. These primitive plants lack chlorophyll, but nevertheless manufacture their own food from inorganic substances. Other scientists believe that the blue-green algae were the earliest living things.

The major groups of non-flowering plants arose independently from a primitive group of algae. Botanists believe that higher plants evolved from green algae.

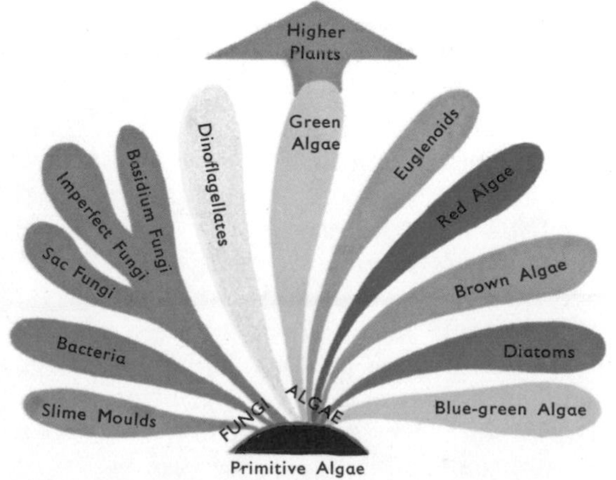

EVOLUTION OF NON-FLOWERING PLANTS

CELL DIVISION OR MITOSIS (1) normal cell at rest; (2) chromosome material forming threads; (3) the material divides into chromosomes, which align on fibres or spindle; (4) chromosomes move to opposite poles; (5) division commences along centre line; (6) daughter cells.

SPORES OF FUNGI

Fruiting body of bread mould before ripening (1), while discharging spores (2) and (3).

All blue-green algae are relatively simple. They are one-celled and do not have well-defined nuclei, as are found in other plants and animals. They manufacture their own food from carbon dioxide and water, using the energy of the sun. Their chlorophyll is not in definite bodies (chloroplasts) as in all other plants that photosynthesise.

At some time, in the distant past, there arose organisms with definite nuclei and chloroplasts. Such organisms were also mobile by means of flagella. They were neither plants nor animals, but had characteristics of both. From this group (flagellates) both plants and animals evolved. Probably the green algae, red algae, brown algae, yellow-green algae, diatoms, dinoflagellates, euglenoids and other algae groups all evolved independently. Only the green algae gave rise to other groups of plants — the liverworts, hornworts and mosses. Many biologists now believe that the hornworts changed over millions of years to form the vascular plants. These plants contain special conducting tissues that transport, from one part of the plant to another, the raw materials (water and nutrients) and food that the plant has manufactured. Vascular tissues are strong and help support the plant.

Hornworts have a thallus gametophyte which is similar to those found in ferns and other lower vascular plants. The sex organs of the two are similar. The most important similarity is found in the sporophyte generation of the plants. The tiny horn-shaped spore stage of the hornwort has a region where the cells continue to divide so that it has continuous growth. In all vascular plants the sporophyte also has continuous growing regions. In the hornworts there is a core in the centre of the sporophyte. This seems to function as a conduction system through which water and food pass. It is believed that this core developed into the vascular or conducting tissue of the vascular plants.

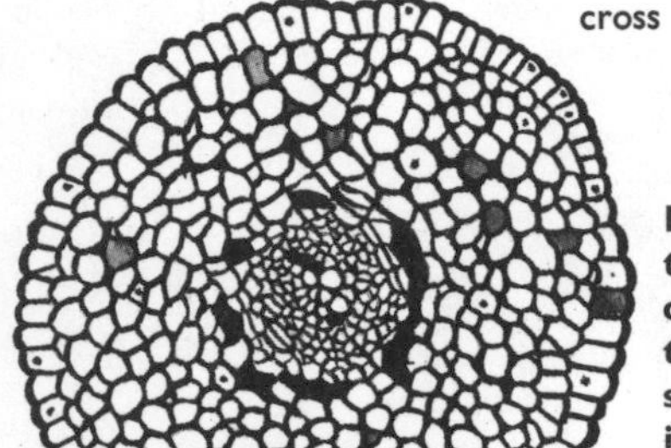

cross section of stem

In psilopsids, the most primitive of the lower vascular plants, the conducting tubes are scattered through the stem, as shown in the cross-section view. ***Tmesipteris tannensis,*** **illustrated, is one of the three living species in this group. It grows as an epiphyte or air plant on the trunks of trees in Australia and on islands in the Pacific.**

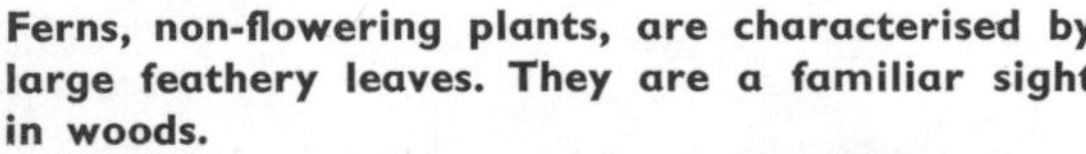

Ferns, non-flowering plants, are characterised by large feathery leaves. They are a familiar sight in woods.

John Topham Limited

Fossils of algae, mosses, hornworts and liverworts are rare. This is understandable, because they have no hard parts to fossilise. Among the oldest fossils of vascular plants are those of *Rhynia* and *Psilophyton*, extinct relatives of the present-day Whisk-broom Fern *(Psilotum)*. It is believed that club mosses, horsetails and ferns developed from vascular plants before or during the Coal Age. Non-flowering seed plants arose several million years later — first the seed ferns, then the cycads, and finally the conifers.

Few fossils of fungi exist, although the mycelium of some parasitic fungi have been found in fossil wood and the fruiting bodies of some of the larger pore fungi have been found attached to fossil tree trunks. Most biologists believe that the simplest of the fungi developed from early flagellates that had lost their chlorophyll. From these simple algal fungi the ascus or sac fungi evolved, and from this group the basidium fungi developed. The origin of the slime moulds is less well understood. Some biologists believe

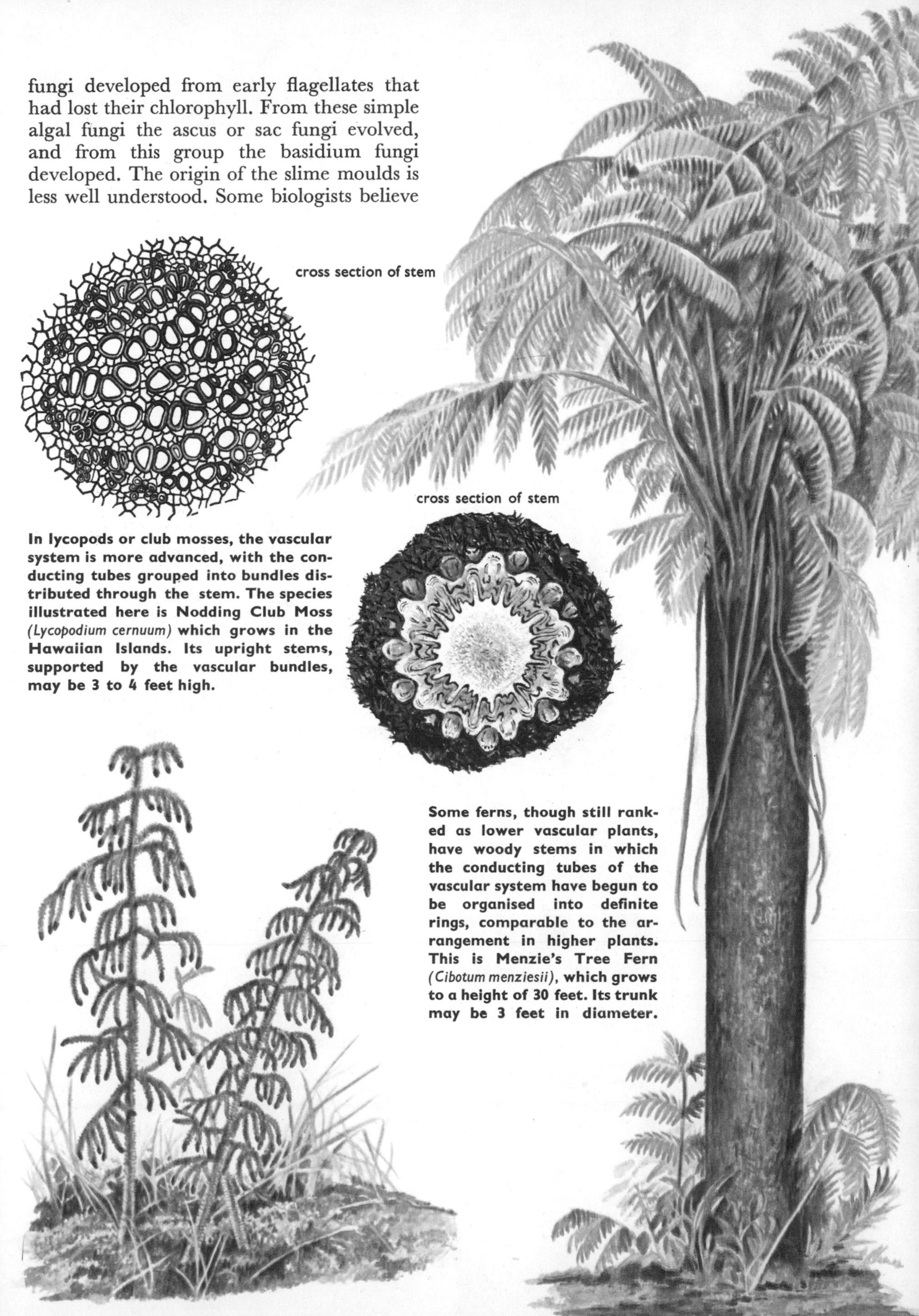

In lycopods or club mosses, the vascular system is more advanced, with the conducting tubes grouped into bundles distributed through the stem. The species illustrated here is Nodding Club Moss *(Lycopodium cernuum)* **which grows in the Hawaiian Islands. Its upright stems, supported by the vascular bundles, may be 3 to 4 feet high.**

Some ferns, though still ranked as lower vascular plants, have woody stems in which the conducting tubes of the vascular system have begun to be organised into definite rings, comparable to the arrangement in higher plants. This is Menzie's Tree Fern *(Cibotum menziesii)*, **which grows to a height of 30 feet. Its trunk may be 3 feet in diameter.**

they were modified from amoebas and thus are more nearly animals than plants. *Vascular Plants.* Plants having special tissues that carry water and food are called vascular plants. Water and minerals pass from the roots to the uppermost leaves through a vascular tissue called xylem. Food manufactured in the leaves is carried to all parts of the plant through phloem, another type of vascular tissue. Phloem is one of the tissues in the tree's inner bark. If a tree is girdled – the bark removed from an area all the way around – the tree eventually dies. Its roots starve, since no food reaches them from the leaves. Veins of leaves have both xylem and phloem.

Vascular tissues make it possible for plants to grow on land areas away from water. Their thick-walled cells give the plants support for growing tall – to heights of more than 300 feet. Bryophytes never grow very tall because they lack vascular tissue. The longest mosses are those that grow in water, which supports them. Since their cells are bathed in water, these mosses do not need cells to conduct water a long distance.

In bryophytes, the independent plant is the gametophyte – the plant that produces sex cells. The spore-producing stage or sporophyte plant is always dependent or parasitic on the gametophyte. In vascular plants the sporophyte is the independent and dominant plant that we see and recognise. It usually has roots, stems and true leaves. Gametophytes of vascular plants are very small, sometimes independent or sometimes dependent or parasitic on the sporophyte.

Vascular plants that do not produce seeds are called the 'lower vascular plants'. There are four main groups: (1) *Psilotum*-like plants, both living and fossil, (2) club mosses and quillworts, (3) horsetails and scouring rushes, and (4) ferns. All reproduce by spores and have an alternation of generations. Their life cycles are all similar although some produce only one type of spores, while others produce two kinds of spores.

Except for *Psilotum* and a few other species,

Bradley Smith/Rapho – Guillumette

Cypress trees are non-flowering seed plants, or gymnosperms. Highly valued for their timber, they are well adapted for growth in a watery environment.

all the sporophyte plants have roots, stems and leaves. Most of them are fairly small, from a few inches to a few feet tall. Some of the tree ferns, however, grow over 50 feet high. In the Coal Age, 230 to 260 million years ago, ferns and their kin were the trees of the swamp forests. Many grew more than 100 feet high. Coal was formed from the remains of these giant ferns and related plants.

Ferns and their kin grow throughout the world but are most abundant in the tropics. Most kinds grow in the shade of trees or along the banks of streams, but some occur in open pastures, in burned-over areas, or on rock cliffs. Still others grow as epiphytes on trees or are climbers. A few float in the water.

Present-day lower vascular plants are of some economic value, but not as much as are those of the past, which are the main source of all coal. Some living forms, particularly the ferns, are cultivated as ornamentals. *Osmunda*, a fern, produces a mass of fibrous roots used in potting orchids. Slabs of tree fern trunks are used to grow orchids and bromeliads. Club mosses of some kinds are also grown as ornamentals, and the spores of some are used in medicines.

Among the non-flowering plants are the biggest and bulkiest of all living things. A Giant Sequoia (right) may weigh 60 times more than a 100-ton Blue Whale, which is the largest animal ever to exist. Bristlecone Pines (below) have exceeded all other living things in age. Some of these gnarled pines on the high slopes of the Sierras in western United States began growing more than 2,500 years before the birth of Christ and have perhaps centuries more growth ahead of them.

Union Pacific Railroad Colorphoto

NON-FLOWERING SEED PLANTS. Algae, fungi, mosses, liverworts, ferns and club mosses do not produce seeds. Spores are their chief means of reproduction. All flowering plants do produce seeds, and there is also a group of plants that produce seeds but have no flowers. Called gymnosperms, they include such plants as pines, firs, cedars, cypress and spruces, as well as cycads and the ginkgo. Gymnosperm means 'naked seed'. The seeds are not enclosed in a fruit, as are the seeds of angiosperms or flowering plants. Seeds of some, such as the podocarps and yews, have a fleshy seed coat and resemble fruits. The seed-bearing cones of junipers and others look like berries. The familiar cones of pine trees are the primitive female flowers that bear the seeds of the pine tree. In the ripe cone, the seeds are exposed to the air, whereas in the flowering plants a layer of cells surrounds them. (See CONIFERS; PLANT KINGDOM.)

Gymnosperms are found everywhere in the world, but are more abundant in temperate regions than in the tropics. The great evergreen forests of Canada and Alaska and cool temperate regions of Europe and Asia are chiefly conifers. Not all gymnosperms are evergreen, however. Cypress and larches are deciduous. (See TREES.)

Giant Sequoias (Redwood Trees) of California and the Montezuma Cypress of Oaxaca, Mexico, are among the oldest known living plants. Some are 3,000 to 4,000 years old. These trees were seedlings when Egypt flourished as a great nation and Babylon was ruled by Hammurabi. By the time Columbus discovered America, these trees were many feet in diameter and 2,500 to 3,500 years old. Bristlecone Pines that grow high on the mountain slopes in the White Mountains of California are even more ancient, some of them estimated to be more than 4,500 years old.

The development of the seed was an important advance in plant evolution. A hard outer coat protects a seed from drying out, from fungi, and from injurious ultra-violet rays of the sun. Seeds can remain dormant for long periods until conditions are just right for their growth. Inside the seed is the embryo, a young plant. Food stored in the seed enables the embryo to live and grow until it can manufacture its own food by photosynthesis. Seeds permit young plants to adapt to a far greater variety of growing areas and under a greater variety of conditions than do spores.

The first seed plants, which looked like ferns, produced seeds at the edges of their leaves. These seed ferns, known only as fossils, lived over 200 million years ago. Many other kinds of seed plants are known only as fossils. Some resembled plants that live today. (See SEEDS.)

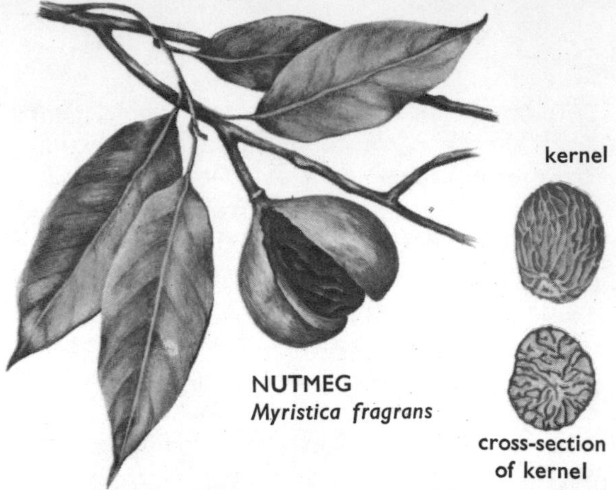

A healthy tree produces up to 10,000 nuts each year, and continues to bear for 20 years or more.

NUTMEG, a common household spice, comes from a tropical evergreen tree *(Myristica fragrans)*, native to the East Indies. The yellow or reddish fleshy outer covering of the tree's round or pear-shaped fruit splits open when mature and exposes a scarlet, fleshy layer beneath. This is the source of mace, used in seasoning meats. Inside the mace is the hard-shelled seed, the kernel of which is the nutmeg. A single tree may bear several thousand fruits in one season.

The Nutmeg Tree (50 or 60 feet high), one of about 80 species of trees and shrubs of the nutmeg family, grows in tropical India, Australia, and various South Pacific islands. Their leaves are highly aromatic. Clusters of small, inconspicuous, pollen-bearing and fruit-producing flowers occur on separate trees.

Several other trees in different families are also known as nutmegs. Most of these trees occur in the tropics, but the California Torreya or California Nutmeg *(Torreya californica)* is an evergreen tree that has needle-like foliage.

NUTS of many kinds are eaten by man and other animals. Botanists define a nut as a dry, one-seeded, hard-shelled fruit, such as hazelnuts or acorns.

All nuts are good sources of fats, proteins, and minerals and may also contain some starch and sugar. Some nuts can take the place of meat in diets; others can be ground and brewed as a substitute for coffee. Most are eaten fresh, roasted, or salted, and are commonly added to cakes, sweets and ice creams. Coconuts and a few others furnish commercial oils.

Chestnuts (several species of *Castanea*) produce nuts in prickly 'burrs'. Chestnuts can be eaten raw, roasted, or boiled; they are added to stuffings for fowl, or are ground to make flour. In some areas of Europe, chestnuts, or marrons, have been used in place of wheat and corn.

Hazelnuts or Filberts (several species of *Corylus*) are grown in Turkey, Italy, Spain, and along the west coast of the United States. The small, round nut is surrounded by a leaf-like structure. Filberts are used largely in sweets and various cakes.

Hickory nuts (several species of *Carya*) are native American nut trees. Only the Pecan is grown commercially.

Macadamia or Queensland nuts *(Macadamia ternifolia* and *tetraphylla)* are native to the rain forests of Australia but are grown now in Hawaii, Florida, California, Africa, and the Mediterranean area.

HAZELNUT
Corylus avellana

Paradise Nuts *(Lecythis zabucajo)* resemble Brazil Nuts and are considered by many to have a better flavour. The hard outer case of this fruit has a lid that falls open and exposes the nuts inside when ripe.

Pinon nuts are the edible seeds of several species of pines *(Pinus)*, native to Mexico and the south-western United States. Indians collect the bean-sized seeds from the ground or extract them from pine cones. Several species of pines of southern Europe also yield edible nuts.

Pistachios or Green Almonds *(Pistacia vera)* are native to the Mediterranean area but are now cultivated in warm climates. The pale green or yellow kernel of the nut may be salted or used plain in ice cream and sweets. (See ACORNS; ALMONDS; LYCHEES; OILS; PALMS; WALNUTS.)

Nuts are so rich in protein they can be used as a substitute for meat in diets.

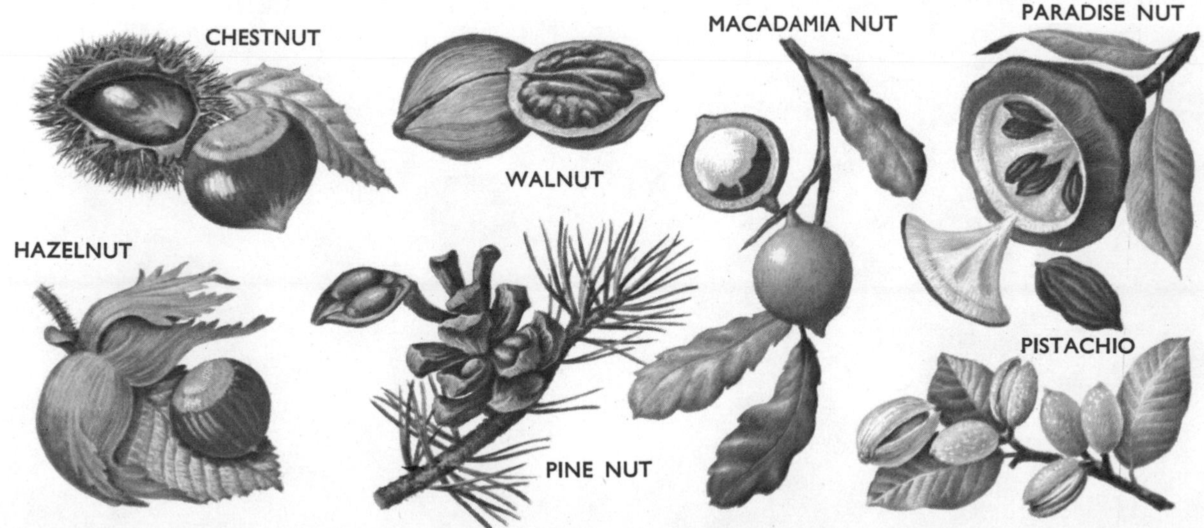

OAKS (*Quercus* spp.) are the most important, most widely distributed, and largest group of hardwood trees in the Northern Hemisphere. Members of the beech family, they are closely related to such familiar trees as the beeches and the chestnuts. Oaks are symbols of sturdiness. Many kinds grow large and reach a venerable age.

Oak wood has many uses. It is especially valuable for flooring, furniture, and barrels. Cork and numerous miscellaneous products are obtained from oaks. Oaks are frequently planted as ornamentals because of their majestic and colourful beauty.

Most oaks are deciduous; some are evergreen. The Evergreen or Holm Oak *(Quercus il x)*, a native of the Mediterranean region, has been introduced into Britain. The Cork Oak *(Quercus suber)* is another evergreen kind; Gerroven Oak is very similar to the above, but distinguished by its thick, corky bark.

Deciduous oaks without their foliage can be recognised by small clusters of buds that occur at the tips of their twigs. Slender catkins of pollen-bearing flowers hang from near the ends of their branches in early spring. Most oaks have lobed leaves, but some have smooth margins, others toothed or holly-like. All bear acorns, a staple food for many kinds of wildlife and also eaten by domestic animals. The oak harbours more insects than any other tree (see ACORNS).

There are two species native to the British Isles. The Common or Pedunculate Oak *(Quercus robur)* is the characteristic tree of clay and loam soils. The Durmast or Sessile Oak *(Quercus petraea)* prefers the damper, more acid soils. The Common Oak can be distinguished from the Durmast Oak by small reflexed auricles, or lobes, at the base of the leaf and the long stalks ($\frac{3}{4}$ inch or more) to the acorns. The Durmast Oak has no auricles to its leaf but does have hairs along the mid rib and veins on the underside of the leaf. The acorn stalks are short, (less than $\frac{1}{2}$ inch).

The Turkey Oak *(Quercus cerris)* has been introduced into Britain from southern Europe and south-west Asia and is sometimes to be seen in avenues or paddocks in southern England. The Scarlet oaks (*Quercus rubra* and *Quercus coccinea)*, with beautiful red leaves in the autumn, have been introduced from North America and are sometimes grown in cultivation.

TURKEY OAK
Quercus cerris

EVERGREEN OAK
Quercus ilex

A number of trees and shrubs not related to the true oaks have 'oak' in their names. Examples are the Australian Silk-oak and She-oak trees and Poison-oak.

OATS (*Avena* spp.) are cereal grasses grown in cool, moist regions of North America and Europe. Some hardy varieties grow almost to the Arctic Circle. The plants are 2—3 feet tall and are easily distinguished from other cereals by their bluish-green leaves. Their fruiting heads may be spreading or one-sided. Like wheat, oats have both summer and winter types and there are many varieties.

Foods made from oats are highly nutritious. In addition to starch, oats contain proteins, minerals and vitamins. A number of dried cereals have an oat base. 'Quick oats', popular because only a few minutes are required for cooking, are dehulled and cracked seeds that have been partially cooked before being rolled. Oatmeal, a European favourite, is made by grinding the oats between stones and flattening them into flakes.

Oats are harvested with a combine. In less advanced areas, the crop is cut, dried in the field, and then threshed. Farmers use oats straw as food and bedding for livestock. The grain is also fed to livestock, especially horses and mules. (See CEREALS.)

COMMON OATS *Avena sativa* — fruiting head may be 8 to 12 inches long

OBSERVATION OF THE HEAVENS. Even with the naked eye the constellations can be identified. Indeed, this is a good first step in observing the heavens (see CONSTELLATIONS). As soon as the constellations are learned, the planets stand out, and it is easy to follow their motion from week to week across the background of the stars.

Soon the observer will want a telescope. Binoculars can be used to see the plains of the Moon, the satellites of Jupiter, the crescent phase of Venus, and a few star clusters, nebulae, and galaxies. But really interesting observations require higher magnification and greater light-gathering power. A suitable telescope for a beginner would be 3 or 4 inches in diameter and should have at least two eyepieces to give different magnifications. A high magnification shows more detail, but a low magnification shows a larger area and also makes objects like nebulae look brighter. Although magnification can be varied, there is a limit to how high a power can be used. The telescope will produce a blurred image if the magnification is more than 50 times the diameter of the telescope in inches. Also, observations with a magnifying power of more than 100 may be hampered by bad seeing — that is, by unsteadiness in the Earth's atmosphere — and by the motion of the rotating Earth.

The solar system is full of interesting objects. The Moon is always worth looking at, and the higher the magnification, the more detail can be seen. Jupiter is a fine sight at any magnification. At low power — even with binoculars — the planet is seen as a disc accompanied by four bright satellites. At magnifications of 50 or more, the cloud belts in Jupiter's atmosphere can be easily seen. Jupiter's satellites provide ever-changing entertainment as they pass behind and in front of the planet. The times of their eclipses and other phenomena can be found in an annual alamanac or in magazines devoted to amateur astronomy.

To a watcher using a small telescope the most beautiful object in the heavens is Saturn, but a magnification of about 75 times is needed to see the rings well. Much higher magnifications — and good seeing — are needed to see the gaps in the rings. Venus, on the other hand, is an easy object. A magnifying power of 5 times will show its crescent phases, and with 30 power all its phases can be seen. Mars, however, is difficult. Even when close to us, a magnification of 100 is needed to see anything more than a tiny orange disc. The best views of Mars are obtained with much higher magnifications and in better than average seeing. Of the other planets, 50 power shows the crescent phases of Mercury; Uranus is a tiny disc at 100 power, as is Neptune above 150 power under good seeing conditions. Pluto is too faint to be seen in small telescopes.

With the aid of positions given in an almanac, an observer with a small telescope can pick out the brighter asteroids, although they look only like points of light. Comets are much more interesting. Nearly every year some comet is bright enough to see with a small telescope, but it is essential to have accurate positions for the comet, night by night, in order to find it. Up-to-date magazines on astronomy give data on newly discovered comets.

Finally, the Sun is an interesting sight. It is best observed by using the telescope to project an image of the Sun on a white card held behind the eyepiece. *(Never look directly*

As seen in telescopes, Mars, Jupiter and Saturn have recognisable characteristics. Mercury and Venus show no detail, though they loom large. Uranus and Neptune appear as small dots. Pluto is not visible with a small telescope.

at the Sun through a telescope.) Sunspots can usually be seen, and their motion can be followed from day to day as the Sun rotates.

Many objects outside the solar system are fascinating to look at, but a prime requisite for finding them is a good star atlas, which lists interesting objects and marks their positions among the constellations. Many double stars can be seen in a small telescope, some with pretty contrasts of colour or brightness. Star clusters, too, are scattered about the sky. Some are open clusters — rich, brilliant collections of stars. Others are globular clusters, really much richer, but faint and hazy looking because of their great distances. Another group of objects are the gaseous nebulae — faint, glowing gas clouds around and between the stars. Some are diffuse nebulae, irregular in shape, while others are the so-called planetary nebulae, which look like neat, round discs or rings. Finally there are the galaxies, great systems of stars so far away that all we see is the hazy combined light of all their stars. So many double stars, clusters, nebulae, and galaxies are within reach of a 6-inch telescope that few amateur astronomers ever reach the end of the list. One thing an observer must be prepared for, however, is that few of these objects look as spectacular as their photographs. The human eye cannot compete with a camera's ability to build up pictures of faint objects in time exposures. (See ASTRONOMY.)

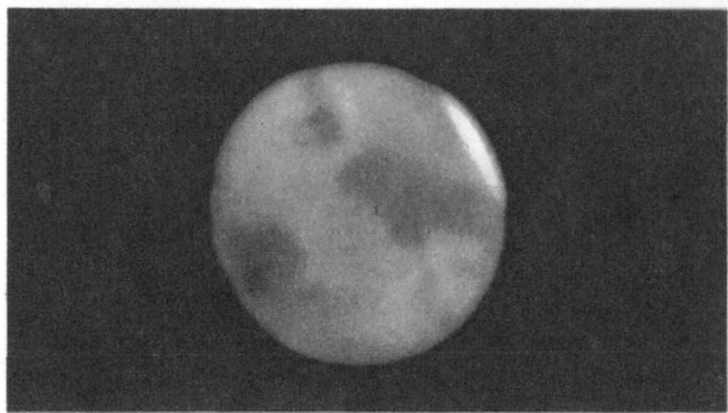

W. S. Finsen, Republic Observatory, Johannesburg

Mars appears reddish, as in this photograph, and its whitish polar cap varies in size with the season.

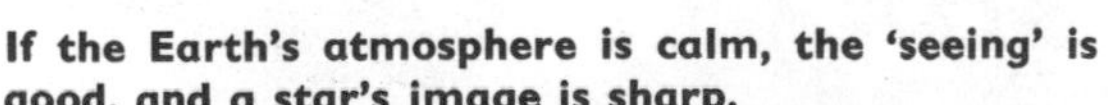

If the Earth's atmosphere is calm, the 'seeing' is good, and a star's image is sharp.

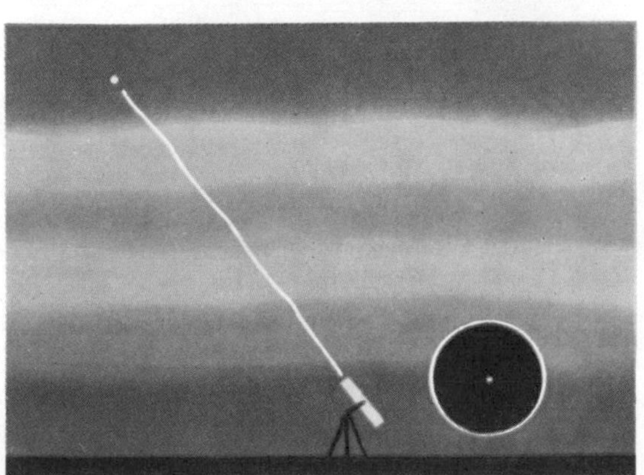

Turbulence in the atmosphere results in poor 'seeing' and a fuzzy star image.

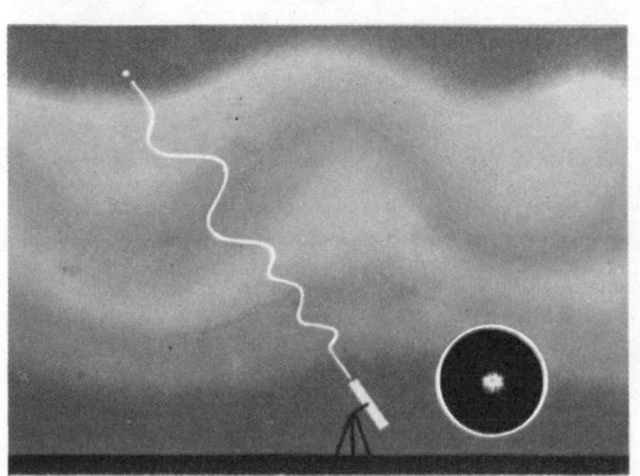

OBSERVATORY. When Galileo first pointed a telescope at the heavens in 1609, he used two small lenses that he had ground himself. Today's astronomer, by contrast, requires larger and expensive telescopes with all sorts of measuring equipment attached. The problems of modern astronomy require detailed analysis of the light of faint stars at the farthest limits of visibility. (See TELESCOPE.)

An optical telescope requires a good climate, and so most major observatories are in desert or near-desert areas where the sky is generally clear. Even more important is the steadiness of the air — what astronomers call the 'quality of the seeing'. The sharp focusing of light by a large telescope is useless if turbulent air currents convert the image of every star into a blur. A large telescope is an impressive sight, and most observatories allow the public to visit at specified times.

This 200-inch reflector-type telescope, the world's largest, is located on Palomar Mountain, California.

OBSIDIAN is a volcanic glass that cooled so rapidly it has no crystals or only a faint suggestion of crystals. Obsidian is generally black with a glassy lustre, but it may be brown or a mixture of brown and black. Thin flakes are transparent or clouded with tiny specks of magnetite. Some fragments of obsidian have sharp, jagged edges that cut like glass. These were used by Indians for arrowheads, spear points, and knives.

The Moon as seen with the unaided eye (inset) and with 7-power binoculars.

Lick Observatory

Pitchstone, a variety of obsidian, contains tiny bubbles of water that give it a dull, pitchy lustre. Perlitic obsidian contains crystals in small angular masses or rounded balls. If crystals have just begun to form radial clusters, the rock is called snowflake obsidian. When large crystals (phenocrysts) of feldspar

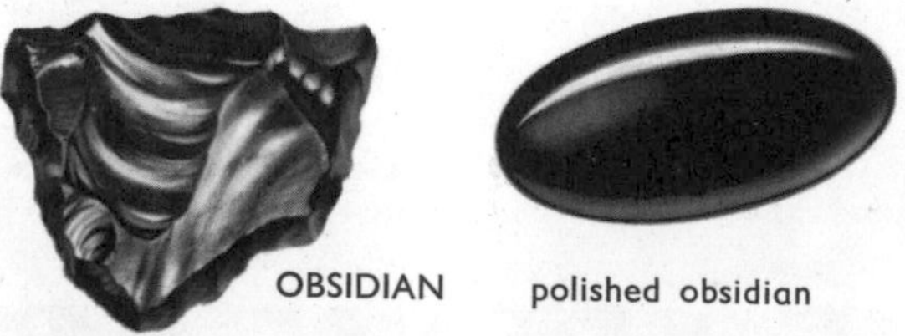

OBSIDIAN polished obsidian

or quartz are found, the rock is known as vitrophyre. These crystals apparently grew before the cooling magma rose to the surface and escaped as lava. The fluid hardened quickly into glass with the crystals still embedded. Obsidian is found wherever there have been great lava flows. Yellowstone National Park, Wyoming, U.S.A. has splendid examples. Varieties are also found in Japan, Iceland, Mexico, Italy and many other places in Europe, and Africa.

OILS obtained from plants are used for cooking, or in the manufacture of such items as soaps, medicines, perfumes, and paints. They are classified either as fatty oils or essential oils. Fatty oils differ from fats in that the oil is at ordinary temperature a liquid while the fat is a solid. Essential oils evaporate when exposed to air and generally have a pleasing aroma or taste.

Fatty oils are most abundant in plant seeds where they are a rich and concentrated source of food for the developing plant. They are extracted either by crushing the seeds or by using a solvent to dissolve the oil.

Non-drying oils remain as a liquid when exposed to the air. Oil from the seeds of the Castor Bean *(Ricinus communis)* is of this type. Produced chiefly in Brazil, Mexico, India, and the Soviet Union, this oil is used as a lubricant and also in medicines, soaps, plastics, paints, and varnishes. Other important non-drying oils are obtained from palms, peanuts, and olives.

Semi-drying oils are a group that dry slowly at high temperatures. Corn oil and cottonseed oil are examples. Corn oil is widely used in cooking. It is extracted from the embryo or 'germ' of corn. Sunflower seeds *(Helianthus)* are also rich in oil.

Major drying oils are linseed or flax, soybean, and tung. These oils oxidise and form a tough outer film when exposed to the air. Linseed oil, obtained from the seeds of Flax (see FLAX), is used in paints, varnishes, soaps, printer's ink, and in the manufacture of leather goods. Tung oil, used similarly, comes from the seeds of the Tung Tree *(Aleurites fordii)*.

The nuts of the Tung Tree are collected, put into sacks, and placed in the crotch of the tree to dry.

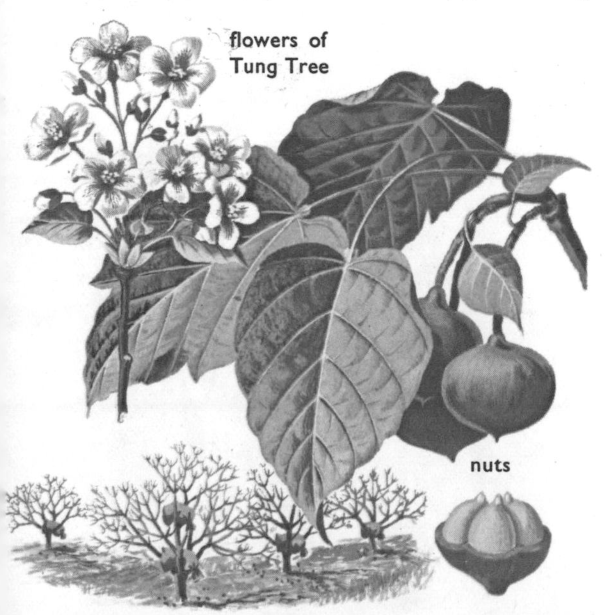

Essential or volatile oils occur in flowers, fruits, seeds, leaves, bark, or roots. These oils are obtained by distilling the plant tissues, by mechanical pressure, or by using chemicals. Essential oils with pleasing odours are used in perfumes and soaps. These oils also give flavour to spices like cinnamon, cloves, dill, hops, and peppermint. Citrus oils have become an important by-product of the citrus canning industry. Most essential oils have been used at one time as medicines. (See COTTON; FLAX; MAIZE; OLIVES.)

OLIGOCENE, a period of the Cenozoic era which began about 38 million years ago and lasted 12 million years. At one stage during the Oligocene, Asia was still joined to North America. Warm, temperate climates were widespread over most of the Earth, but it was cooler than earlier in the Tertiary period.

In the Oligocene there were many large foraminifera, (an order of one-celled sea animals), some of which reached a diameter of 3 inches. Reef-building corals grew in the tropical seas. Sponges, molluscs, and echinoderms were modern in appearance.

In parts of Europe thick forest swamps gave rise to deposits of brown coal (lignite). In the Baltic area pine trees produced resin that became fossilised as amber. It contains beautifully preserved insects that lived in these times. Fresh-water snails and clams were abundant too.

Ancestors of such later carnivores as cats, bears, and dogs made their appearance, as did primitive camels, various piglike animals, and a group that probably gave rise to the hippopotamuses. Various types of rhinoceroses roamed the land. One *(Baluchitherium)* stood 18 feet high at the shoulder. Four-tusked elephants with short flexible trunks and three-toed horses lived during the Oligocene.

Animals of the Oligocene included: *Mesohippus* **(1), a three-toed horse;** *Oreodon* **(2), a sheep-sized grazer;** *Brontops* **(3), a horned titanothere;** *Baluchitherium* **(4), the largest land mammal that has ever existed;** *Protapiris* **(5), a small early-type tapir;** *Hyaenodon* **(6), a creodont carnivore; and some early land tortoises (7).**

OLIVES are the fruit of the evergreen tree *(Olea europea)*, native to Asia Minor. Since ancient times, olives have been cultivated throughout the Mediterranean region. In recent years they have been grown in parts of Latin America and the United States where the Mediterranean-type climate prevails. Olive sprays, branches, and wreaths have long symbolised peace and victory.

Olive trees do not bear fruit for their first ten years. Their small inconspicuous flowers are wind-pollinated.

In addition to their direct use as a food, olives are the source of olive oil, obtained by crushing and pressing almost-ripe olives. The best quality oil from the first pressing varies in colour from clear to golden yellow. Bland in taste, it is used in cooking and salad dressings. It serves as a preservative for such canned foods as sardines, herrings and anchovies. Inferior grades of olive oil are used in making castile soaps and as lubricants.

Spain, Italy, Greece, Portugal, and Tunisia are the world's principal olive producing countries.

OLIVINE, a magnesium-iron silicate, occurs in igneous rocks, especially those of volcanic origin, and occasionally in marble. It never occurs with quartz. It is found in small grains or in granular masses. Dunite is an igneous rock composed of olivine. Olivine is transparent and olive-green. It has a shell-like

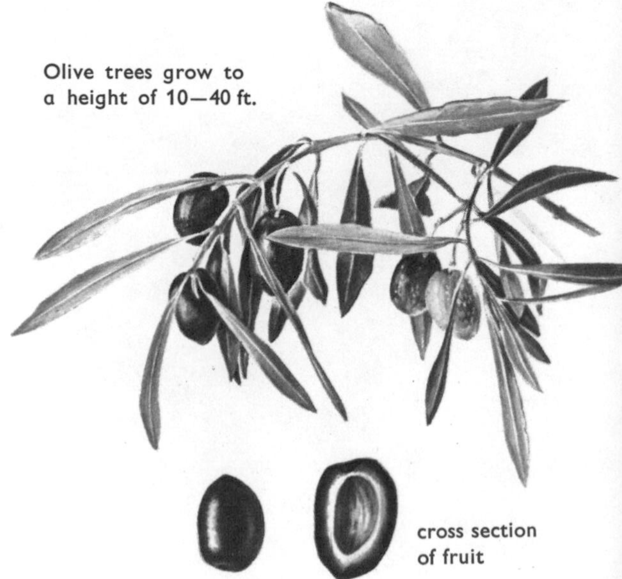

Olive trees grow to a height of 10—40 ft.

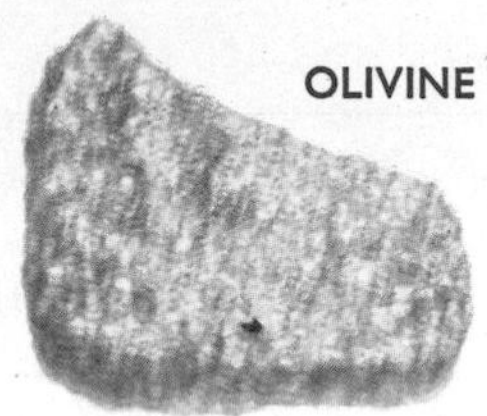

fracture and alters readily so that it may be stained with limonite. Clear olivine is faceted as the gem peridot. Crystals are rare, but large ones, up to several inches long, have been found. Olivine occurs in Norway, Germany, Egypt, Burma, Brazil, South Africa and the U.S.A.

ONIONS *(Allium cepa)* and their close relatives — garlic, leek, shallot, and chive — are members of the lily family. All these species of the genus *Allium* develop bulbs consisting of the swollen colourless bases of leaves, enclosing buds, which are attached to the stem-plate at the base of the bulb.

Onions are grown from seeds or from 'sets', which are very small bulbs produced by sowing seeds thickly. While small, the young plants can be harvested as 'green onions', but later in summer the tops dry out as the bulbs are formed. The onion and related species are native to central and south-west Asia, but they are now widely grown in cooler climates. Bulbs for seed production are planted out in the following spring and produce large umbellate flower heads.

The leek *(Allium porrum)* is grown for its bleached stem-like leaf bases. Like the onion it is a biennial.

The shallot *(Allium ascalonicum)* is perennial and produces clusters of bulbs which resemble the common onion.

Garlic *(Allium sativum)* is a perennial with narrow, flat leaves and small bulbs. It is much more pungent than the onion and is widely used for flavouring by Mediterranean and Far Eastern peoples.

Chive *(Allium schoenoprasum)* is a perennial which produces small leafy clusters of bulbs. It grows wild around the eastern Mediterranean.

Onions and related plants are mainly grown for their pungent flavour and used for seasoning other foods.

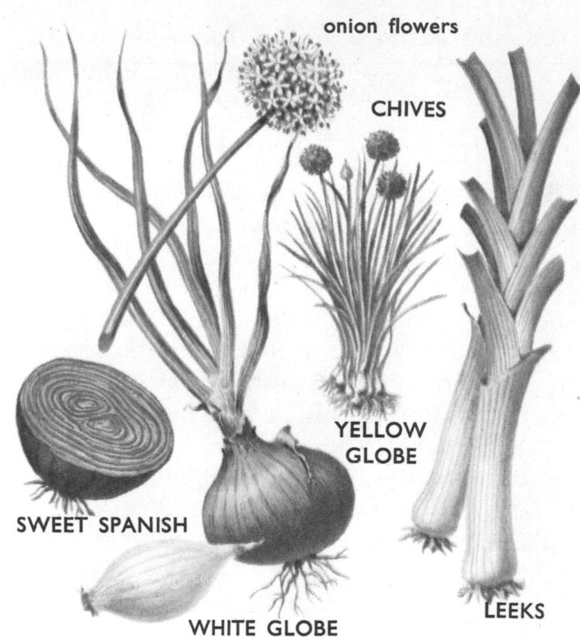

OPAL is a hydrated silicate that does not occur as crystals. It forms as a low-temperature mineral deposit in veins or around hot springs and geysers. Shells of diatoms are composed of opal. Opal is found also as stalactites in cavities of igneous rock masses. Opal has a shell-like fracture. Common opal is milky white. Gem opals are found in a wide variety of colours. Most precious opal comes from Australia. The ancient Romans valued opals next to emeralds and mined

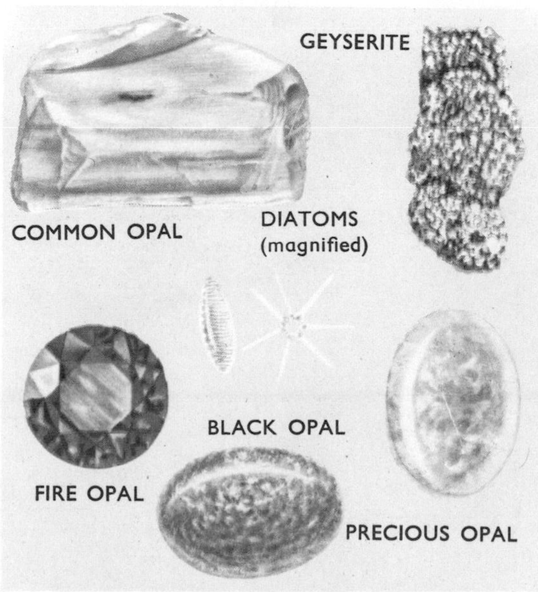

them in central Europe. Today opals are also found, in small quantities, in Japan, Mexico, New Zealand, and the United States.

ORBIT. Year after year the Earth circles the Sun, following the same path or orbit on each annual revolution. The Earth's orbit, or the orbit of any other heavenly body, is a mathematical curve called an ellipse, which is a circle that has been stretched in one direction. The Sun is at one focus in the elliptical orbit of a planet. A long, narrow ellipse is called eccentric, and the more eccentric it is the farther the focus lies toward the end.

Another characteristic of an orbit is that it lies in a single plane. That is, a planet moves around the Sun like a car on a flat track. The plane of the Earth's orbit is called the ecliptic plane, and the orbital planes of the other planets are usually compared to it. The planets have orbits that are nearly circular and slightly inclined to the ecliptic. However, Mercury and Pluto deviate a little more than the others. Asteroids have orbits with moderate eccentricities and inclinations, while comets move in highly eccentric orbits inclined in any of the many possible directions.

Planets, asteroids, and comets follow orbits around the Sun; satellites follow orbits around their planets. Whenever two bodies attract each other strongly and are relatively unaffected by any other forces, they will move around each other in elliptical orbits. The more massive body moves less, and when one body is very much larger, as the Sun is when compared with the Earth, it remains practically stationary while the smaller body moves around it on its regular orbit.

TYPES OF ORBITAL PATHS

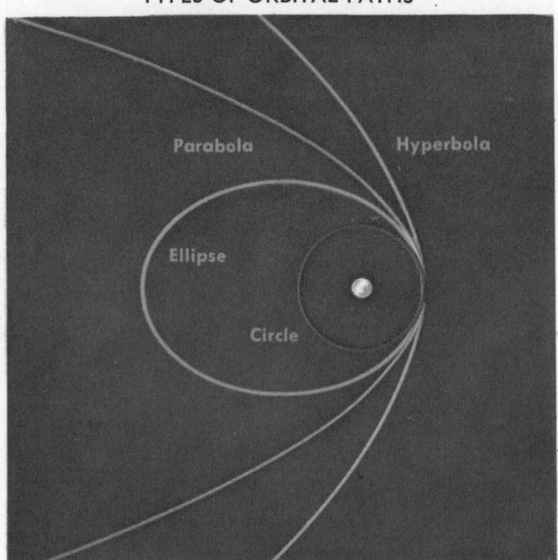

Orbital motion seems strange to us since we are accustomed to seeing falling objects strike the Earth's surface and stop. But the Earth's motion in its orbit *is* its falling motion. Although the Sun attracts the Earth strongly, the Earth does not fall into the Sun because it is moving rapidly in its orbit. The Sun's attraction just balances the Earth's tendency to fly off because of its high speed.

If a rocket were launched towards the Sun it would speed past unless it were aimed at it. The rocket would swing into an orbit around the Sun since in empty space orbital motion is as natural as a falling stone on Earth. (See GRAVITATION.)

ORCHIDS. The beautiful lavender-pink orchid *(Cattleya)* used as a fancy corsage is so familiar that we are likely to think of it whenever orchid is mentioned. But this is only one of about 17,000 species of orchids. Most of them grow in the tropics, but some are found as far north as the Arctic Circle. There are twelve kinds which are native of the British Isles. In addition, plant breeders have produced thousands of hybrids, larger, more colourful and more varied than their wild ancestors.

Orchids are highly developed and specialised in various ways, ranking them high in the plant kingdom. Their curiously formed flowers are specially adapted for pollination by insects, and in many cases each kind of orchid is pollinated by a particular kind of insect. The flowers are so shaped as to provide convenient landing platforms and direction guides for the insects, and their parts are also arranged so that insects cannot make a visit without picking up some pollen as they crawl in to get the sweet nectar deep inside.

Orchid seeds are so small they look almost like powder and will develop into plants only if they become associated with microscopic fungi that provide them with food.

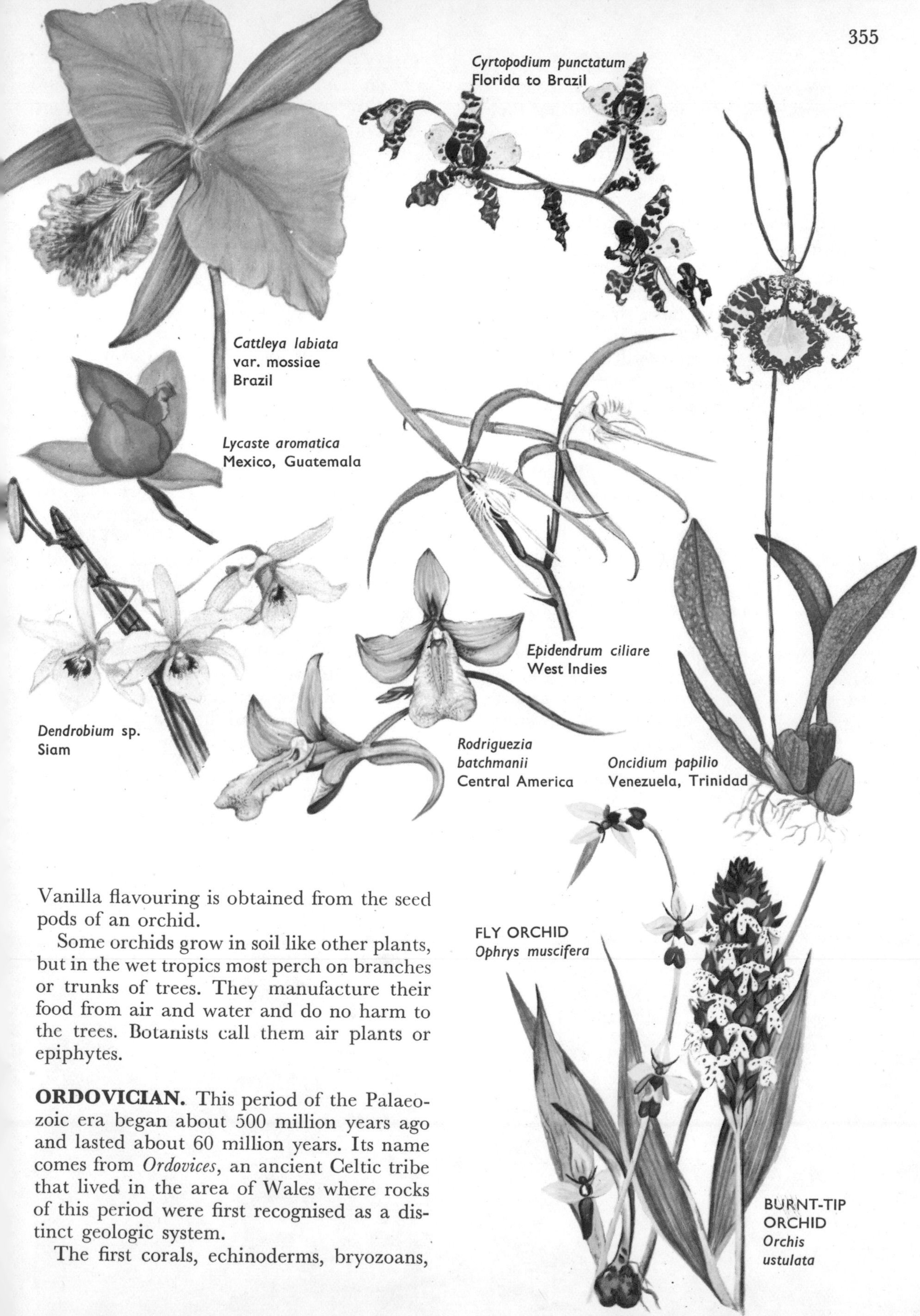

Vanilla flavouring is obtained from the seed pods of an orchid.

Some orchids grow in soil like other plants, but in the wet tropics most perch on branches or trunks of trees. They manufacture their food from air and water and do no harm to the trees. Botanists call them air plants or epiphytes.

ORDOVICIAN. This period of the Palaeozoic era began about 500 million years ago and lasted about 60 million years. Its name comes from *Ordovices*, an ancient Celtic tribe that lived in the area of Wales where rocks of this period were first recognised as a distinct geologic system.

The first corals, echinoderms, bryozoans,

and ostracods are found in Ordovician rocks. Trilobites were very numerous during these times and a wide variety of forms had evolved. Sponges and snails were fairly common in some parts of the sea, and cephalopods increased in numbers. Some cephalopods had straight, conical shells that reached a length of 15 feet. Bivalves (clams, oysters, etc.) appeared but are uncommon in Ordovician deposits. Remains of the earliest vertebrates, fish-like creatures, have been found in sandstones in various states of the U.S.A.

All Ordovocian plant fossils are of various kinds of algae, although there are reports that fossils of simple land plants have been found in Ordovician rocks both in Europe and in western North America.

In both North America and Europe seas covered land areas that had been exposed during earlier Cambrian times. There was considerable volcanic activity in scattered areas. Sea-floor volcanoes were active in central Wales pouring forth lava — these lavas, now much eroded and weathered, form the majestic scenery of the Snowdonia area. There were also Earth movements in parts of eastern North America and the British Isles. Ordovician sediments are widely distributed in Asia but in Africa are found only on the northern edge of the continent. In South America, Ordovician outcroppings are found from Argentina north to Colombia.

ORNAMENTALS. Thousands of trees, shrubs, vines, flowers, grasses and aquatic plants are grown primarily as ornamentals, for their beauty, rather than for their fruit, or other economic value. Many plants now grown as ornamentals were originally cultivated as sources of food or medicine. Some plants, when grown in a garden, are considered ornamentals, but when grown on a large scale may be of agricultural importance for food or fabric.

ORNAMENTATION AND CLOTHING. Of all animals, man has devoted the most time, thought and ability in ornamenting and clothing himself. Decorating the body is one of the most universal practices of human beings. Jewels or rings may be fastened into the ears or nose. Neck rings or chains are also widely worn. Frequently the body or face is painted and the hair dyed, curled, and arranged. In many societies the body is permanently modified through scars, tattooing, tooth pulling or filing, or even by deliberately shaping the head, lips, or feet.

Among the invertebrates that dominated in middle Ordovician times were: *Endoceras* **(1) and** *Sactoceras* **(2), straight-shelled nautiloid types of cephalopods;** *Flexicalymene* **(3), a trilobite;** *Rafinesquina* **(4) and** *Rhynchotrema* **(5), brachiopods;** *Streptelasma* **(6) and** *Favistella* **(7), corals;** *Maclurites* **(8) and** *Cyclonema* **(9), gastropods or snails;** *Byssonychia* **(10), a pelecypod or bivalved mollusc;** *Hallopora* **(11), a bryozoan.**

Arnold M. Davis

An ornamental like Father Hugo's Rose is an exceptionally prolific early spring bloomer.

Painting the skin is as widespread among primitive peoples as it is among modern civilised ones. Usually, body painting is done only for special occasions but in some societies, cosmetics are in daily use.

Body or face paint can be made to last by tattooing it into the skin. Tattooing is done by puncturing the skin with needles carrying an indelible dye. Among Polynesians tattooing was a mark of social importance. Since the Australian aborigines and Africans had such dark skins, they had difficulty in making tattoos that would show. Instead, they cut the skin and rubbed ash and grit into the cut, making a noticeable scar tissue. Scar designs are common among some Africans.

Some peoples seriously deform the body for purposes of decoration. Only in recent years has the practice of ear piercing declined amongst Western women. The Incas of South America and some African tribes not only punctured the earlobe but extended it so that the hole would hold discs up to 6 or 8 inches in diameter.

Women in parts of Burma made their necks longer by means of brass collars. Among the Incas and Mayans, a flat board was bound to the front of the baby's head in order to make the forehead flat and high. Many years ago, the feet of Chinese girls were bound to make them dainty and small. Taking out the canine teeth or filing down the teeth are both practices in which standards of beauty overcome the desire for bodily health. 'Face lifting' and other surgery to beautify the face are modern equivalents of head shaping and neck lengthening practised by primitive peoples.

CLOTHING. There are no peoples who do not ornament their bodies, and there are few who do not wear something that might be called clothing in that it covers part of the body. Man wears clothes for many reasons. He may wear clothes to make himself more beautiful or attractive or to prevent the feeling of shame he may have when unclothed. Clothes may indicate that the wearer is a holy man, a fighting man, or a wise man, or they may distinguish men from women and children from adults. There is nothing natural in man that says he 'should' wear clothing.

While clothing helps man adapt his body to different climates, it is surprising how little relationship there is between climate and the type of clothing worn. For example, people living in the very cold climate of Tierra del Fuego, at the southern tip of South America, wore practically no clothes when first discovered by Europeans. In contrast, the Arabs of the hot North African climate cover their bodies with several layers of clothing. Nor are human beings agreed as to what parts of the body are to be covered. Some peoples believe that a woman's face should be covered. In Tahiti it was not thought immodest if one shed all one's clothing provided one's body was well tattooed.

Animal skins have always been used as clothing by primitive people. Primitive men of the Old Stone Age probably wore animal skins for clothes, and they used bones, shells, and teeth as ornaments. The Shoshone Indians wore rabbit-skin robes as protective clothing. Skin capes are used by African Bushmen and by the primitive people of Tierra del Fuego. Indians of the Andes weave magnificent wool 'ponchos', blanket-like capes that have a head hole in the centre.

Northern Europeans preferred clothing which was made to fit the body, rather than draped over it. The history of dress throughout Western society is one of continuous

change in styles, however. Often the style of clothing worn has to do with the person's status in his society rather than providing comfort. In the 1890s women wore neck-choking blouses and several layers of petticoats beneath ankle-length skirts, even in the heat of midsummer. Thirty years later, the style called for dresses that ended at the knees or above. Styles since then have been between these extremes.

OXYGEN, a colourless, odourless, tasteless gas, is the most plentiful element of the Earth. About 49.5 per cent by weight of the Earth's atmosphere and crust, including the oceans, is oxygen. The world's reservoir of free oxygen is the atmosphere.

Plants give off oxygen as a by-product of photosynthesis — the process by which they use carbon dioxide, water and solar energy to build sugars and starches. In respiration, however, plants remove some oxygen from the atmosphere and give off carbon dioxide. Photosynthesis occurs only in those plant cells that contain chlorophyll (the green pigment) or related chemicals. Respiration — in which oxygen is used to release the energy of stored foods — takes place in every plant and animal cell. Photosynthesis stops at night (when the light-activated cells have released their energy) or in the absence of light, but respiration continues around the clock. (See CHLOROPHYLL; SUN; TREES.)

Plants take in oxygen from the atmosphere through openings in the leaves called stomata (singular: stoma). Gases are also given off through these openings.

Free oxygen is essential to life. Most plants and animals cannot liberate energy from foods without it. Those that can live without free oxygen are called anaerobics. Soil bacteria that cause lockjaw or tetanus and some one-celled animals are of this type. Free oxygen will kill them.

The amount of oxygen available limits both the altitude and depth at which animals can live. No mammals can survive long at altitudes in which oxygen pressure is less than about 45 per cent of what it is at sea level. At 18,000 feet, oxygen is about half as abundant as at sea level. Neither can oxygen-dependent plants or animals survive long in poorly aerated soils. Roots stop growing in soils with less than 3 per cent oxygen. Soil that is constantly water-soaked contains less oxygen because the air spaces between the soil particles are filled with water. Plants die in flooded areas because of lack of oxygen for their roots. Some aquatic plants have special air passages in their stems to bring oxygen from the atmosphere to their roots. Others, such as mangroves, have root branches that grow up through the water into the air where they can 'breathe' oxygen.

Water contains much less oxygen than air, and the supply must be replaced constantly. Some oxygen comes from submerged plants, but most comes from the atmosphere.

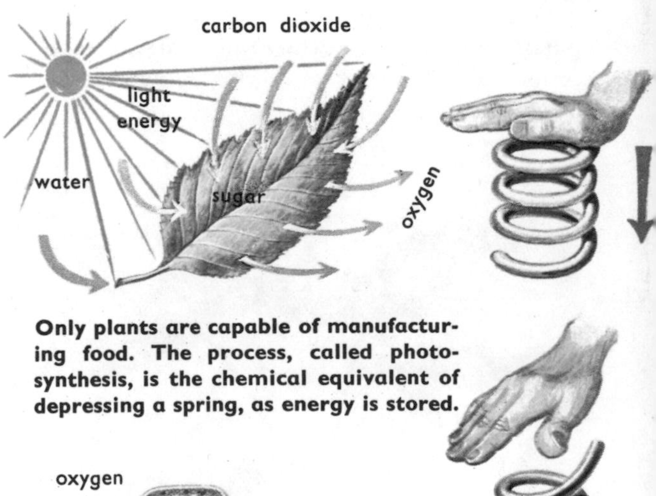

Only plants are capable of manufacturing food. The process, called photosynthesis, is the chemical equivalent of depressing a spring, as energy is stored.

Respiration, in both plants and animals, provides the energy for living. It is the equivalent of releasing a spring, liberating chemical energy.

Fast, cold streams contain more oxygen than do slow, warm streams. In oceans, warm surface waters around the equator contain about half as much oxygen as cooler waters near the poles. As the water gets colder, it also becomes heavier and finally sinks to form vast deep ocean currents that flow back towards the equator. These deep currents of well-oxygenated water supply oxygen to animals living in the ocean depths.

J. Allan Cash

P

PAEONIES (*Paeonia* spp.), members of the buttercup family, have been cultivated for more than a thousand years. Their giant blossoms range from dark red to white and occur in singles, semi-doubles, and full doubles. One variety has a crested yellow centre surrounded by white petals.

There are two types: herbaceous or garden paeonies, which produce new stems from roots each spring, and the old-fashioned Tree Paeony.

PAEONY
Double flowered variety

PALAEOCENE. This oldest period of the Cenozoic began about 65 million years ago and lasted about 11 million years. In the Palaeocene the ruling reptiles of the Mesozoic were replaced by early mammals, including such survivors from Mesozoic times as marsupials and tiny insectivores. Important

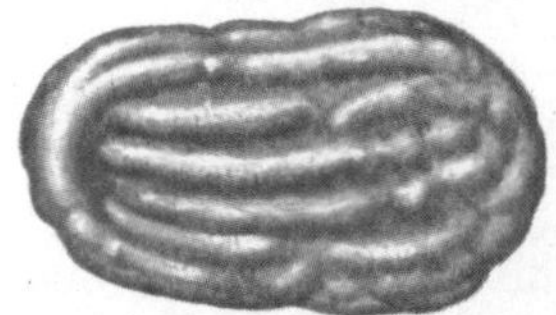

Fossil ostracods (*Bollia*, left, and *Glyptopleura*, right) of the Palaeocene resemble present-day species.

newcomers were creodonts (primitive carnivores), condylarths (primitive hoofed mammals), and amblypods or 'slow-footed ones'. Amblypods were hoofed vegetarians, some of which reached the size of a small pony.

Palaeocene times were marked by the spread of tropical and sub-tropical forests. Plants were much like those of the Cretaceous period.

In North America, Palaeocene rocks are mostly sedimentary and are largely confined to the western part of the continent, although some occur along the Atlantic. In the Rocky Mountain states of the U.S.A. these rocks contain coal. (See LIFE'S ORIGIN AND DEVELOPMENT.)

A Palaeocene landscape, showing a huge carnivorous bird, *Diatryma*; a lemur-like primate, *Notharctus*; and an amblypod *Coryphodon*.

Despite their close relationship, *Dimetrodon* was carnivorous and *Edaphosaurus* was vegetarian. It is quite likely that *Dimetrodon* made an occasional meal of its plant-eating relative.

PALAEOZOIC, the era of ancient life, began about 570 million years ago and lasted for about 345 million years. It includes the Cambrian, Ordovician, Silurian, Devonian, Carboniferous, and Permian periods, each described separately in this book. During the greater part of the Palaeozoic, marine invertebrates were dominant. Brachiopods or lamp shells, trilobites, and graptolites were widespread and abundant. Coiled cephalopods, corals, echinoderms, and molluscs also became abundant in the upper Palaeozoic. By the end of the period graptolites and trilobites had become extinct.

The first vertebrates appeared in Ordovician times and the first land plants in the upper Silurian. Amphibians made their appearance in the Devonian and the first reptiles in the Carboniferous.

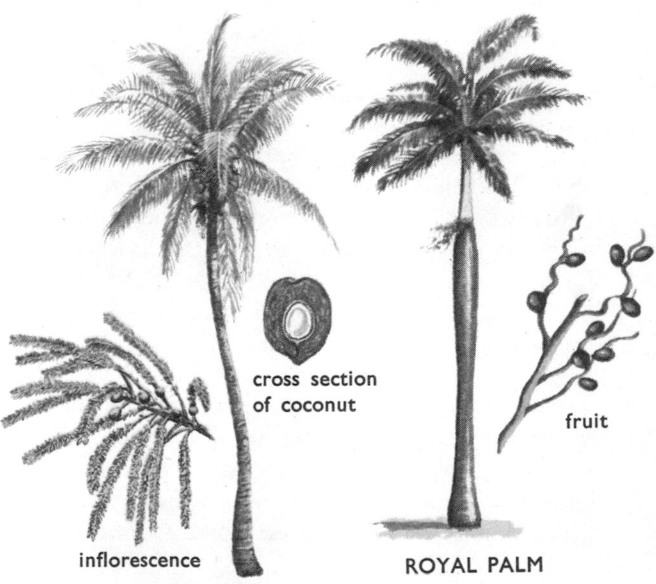

PALMS, which are monocots, vary greatly in size, form, and appearance. Most of the more than 1,000 species are trees; some are shrubs; others, like rattan palms, are vines.

Palms grow most abundantly in the tropics of Asia and the Americas. A small number are native to Africa, and some are found in the warm temperate regions of the Mediterranean, Japan, Korea, and Chile.

Palms are second only to grasses in importance to man. Natives of the tropics use palms for food, drink, shelter, fuel, rope, nets, baskets, brooms, cloth, cooking utensils, and furniture. Dates and coconuts, which are the fruits of the palms, are shipped throughout the world, as are palm oils and waxes.

The wood of palms is soft and spongy, as their stems are composed of irregularly distributed woody fibres. The tall, unbranched trunks of palms are marked on the lower portion with rings, which are the scars of fallen leaves. Palm flowers are usually produced in great numbers, as are their fruits

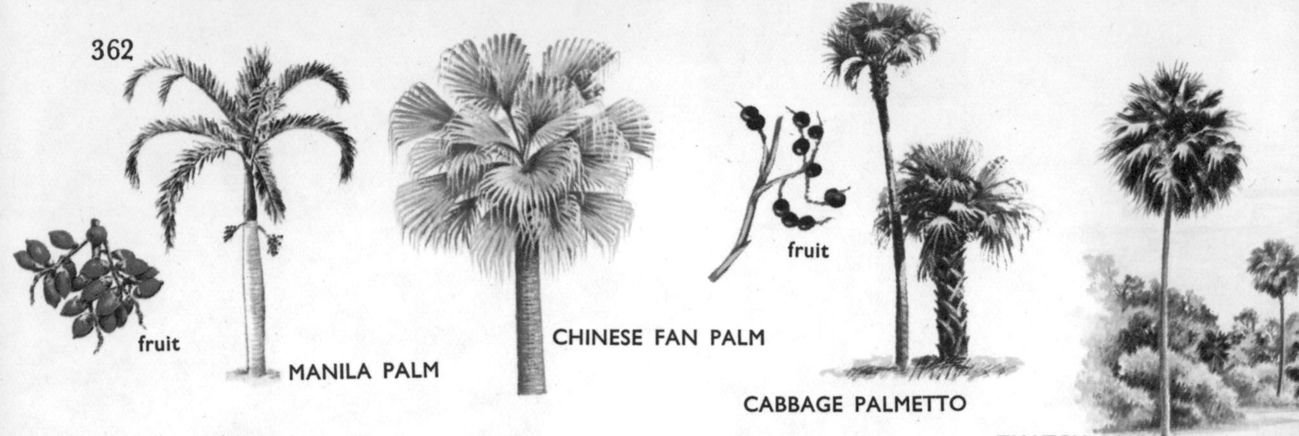

which range from pea size to the coconuts that weigh as much as 40 pounds.

Palms are separated into two broad groups: fan palms, which have the veins and segments of the leaves extending outwards from the centre like the fingers on your hand; and feather palms, which have leaves divided into narrow segments attached at right angles to the leaf stalk.

The Coconut Palm *(Cocos nucifera)*, a native of the South Seas, has a bowed trunk supporting leaves 9 to 15 feet long. The tree is best known for its round, hairy seeds which yield coconut meat (called copra when dried in the shell), oils, and milk. The fibres of the husks are used for mats and coarse textiles, and the shell itself is either burned for charcoal or polished to make containers. Sugar is made from the sap of the Coconut Palm, and its leaves are used for thatching.

The European Fan Palm *(Chamaerops humilis)*, a native of the Mediterranean region, is a bushy palm.

Royal Palms (*Roystonea* spp.) are natives of southern Florida, the West Indies, and Central America. They have spreading leaves divided into narrow segments, and their smooth, whitish trunks look like concrete columns.

Brazil is the native country of the popular Queen Palm *(Arecastrum romanzoffianum)*, while the Manila Palm *(Veitchia merillii)* is from the Philippines and the Bottle Palm *(Hyophorbe amaricaulis)* is from Mauritius.

The Date Palm *(Phoenix dactylifera)* is a native of northern Africa and western Asia. It is a large (25 to 75 feet) feather palm with a dense crown of leaves that arch upwards and outwards from the tip of the slightly bent trunk.

Many kinds of palms produce fruits that contain oils, but most commercial palm oil

WASHINGTON PALM

QUEEN or COCOS PALM

fruit

fruit cluster

inflorescence

BOTTLE PALM

fruit

inflorescence

SAW PALMETTO

PAUROTIS PALM

comes from the African Oil Palm *(Elaeis guineensis)* and the Coconut Palm. The fruit of the African Oil Palm looks like a small coconut, and both its pulp and kernel yield oil. Palm oil is used in the manufacture of soaps, cooking fats, shaving creams, shampoos, toothpastes, perfumes, and printing inks. Nearly 50 million pounds of African Oil Palm pulp oil is used every year, largely in plating tin cans and in sheet roofing where it serves to spread the molten metals.

Two palms native to Brazil, the Carnauba *(Copernicia cerifera)* and the Ouricury *(Cocos coronata)*, are sources of valuable waxes. Leaves of the Carnauba Palm are harvested in the dry season. They are dried and then shredded and beaten to remove the loose, dry wax from their surface. The wax dust is then collected, melted, and poured into moulds for shipment. Carnauba wax was first used in making candles, but large quantities are now used in such products as floor waxes, car polishes, carbon paper, soap, and paint. Wax from the Ouricury Palm, used similarly, is either scraped from the surface of the leaves, or the leaves are crushed and heated to remove the wax.

Other products from palm leaves include baskets and chairs made from leaves of the Raffia Palm *(Raphia ruffia)*; hats from leaves of the Hat Palm; buttons, chessmen, and inlays of imitation ivory from seeds of the Ivory Palm *(Phytelephas macrocarpa)*; and rope from coconut husks. (See COCONUTS; DATES; FISHTAIL PALM; RATTANS; SUGAR.)

PAPAWS are native to tropical America but are now grown commercially in tropical and sub-tropical areas of Asia, Africa, Hawaii, and Australia. The so-called Papaw Trees *(Carica papaya)* are actually giant herbs with crowns of large, deeply lobed leaves. They grow 15 to 25 feet in height and have unbranched, grey-green trunks marked with prominent leaf scars. Papaws bear male, female, and intermediate types of flowers. For this reason a number of plants are usually started and then thinned when they bloom, leaving only fruit-bearing females and enough male plants to pollinate them.

The orange to yellow, melon-like fruit range up to 20 pounds, but average only 3 to 5 pounds. Numerous seeds are clustered around the inner walls of the yellow to pink flesh, which is rich in vitamin A. Papaws are eaten fresh or made into jams, preserves, pies, or drinks. The milky latex of the plant contains papaine, an enzyme used as a meat tenderiser, and in medicines.

PAF International

A reel of newly made paper being lifted from the drying end of a paper making machine.

PAPER is so important today that it is difficult to imagine people existing without it. Yet until the Chinese discovered the art of making paper in the second century A. D., Man wrote on clay tablets, parchment made from animal skins, or tree bark. The paper upon which this book is printed (and all other paper) consists basically of tangled or overlapped plant fibres that have been matted together, pressed into sheets and dried. When paper making was first introduced into Europe, during the Middle Ages, linen rags were commonly used in its manufacture. Although linen and cotton fibres are still used today to make top-quality papers, cellulose fibres from wood chips are the source of most papers. Spruce, hemlock, aspen, pine, and fir trees provide most of the wood pulp. (See TREES.)

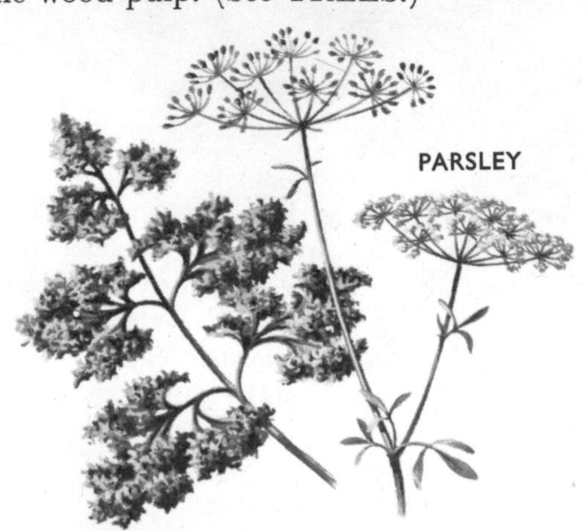

PARSLEY

PARSLEY *(Petroselinum sativum)* is a popular garden herb with greenish-yellow flowers. It is used as a garnish for meats, fish, and salads; as a flavouring for soups, fish, and egg dishes; and in stuffings for fowl.

PEA FAMILY *(Leguminosae)*. One of the largest and most important of plant families, it contains more than 15,000 kinds of plants, including herbs, vines, shrubs, and trees. They grow in temperate and tropical regions throughout the world.

Members of the pea family enrich the soil by transforming atmospheric nitrogen into compounds usable by plants. Nitrogen stored in the nodules on their roots is added to the soil. The leaves of most species are compound; only a few have simple leaves. The most familiar type of flower has butterfly-like petals, as in the sweet pea, but there are several different kinds of flowers in the family. The typical fruit in the pea family is a legume, a pod which carries a single row of seeds and which splits open like the common garden bean or pea. (See LEGUMES.)

Indian, Brazilian, or Honduran rosewood (*Dalbergia* spp.), the trade name varying from region to region, comes from several trees in the pea family, as does African blackwood from East Africa and cocobolo from Mexico and Central America. These dark brown to purplish woods are streaked with various hues and are used for furniture, cutlery handles, or other items where fine grained, beautiful wood is desired. The equally elegant gold, brown, and red woods, known by the commercial name of padauk (*Pterocarpus* spp.) are from African and Asiatic tropical trees in still another genus of the pea family. Zebrawood (*Microberlinia brazzavillanensia*), so named because of its brown colour with darker, fine, vertical stripes, also comes from a tree in the pea family.

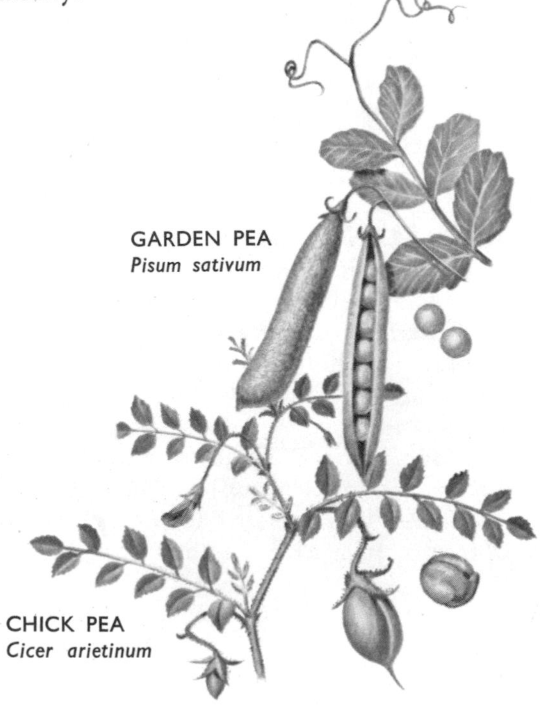

PEARS (*Pyrus communis*), native to western Asia, have long been grown in Europe where many varieties were selected during the seventeenth and eighteenth centuries, and where the majority of the world production of the crop is grown. Many popular varieties of pears grown in the United States were brought from Europe. The flesh of the

PEACHES (*Prunus persica*) are native to western Asia but are now grown throughout southern Europe and in America, South Africa and Australia. In Britain the climate is too cool for them to do well except in seasons when the weather is mild in spring and sunny in summer. They are difficult to keep when fresh but are easily preserved by canning. Nectarines are a small, smooth-skinned variety of peach.

Peaches are generally divided into two groups, either clingstone, or freestone, based on how readily the flesh separates from the stone. Canners prefer the better flavour and firmer flesh of clingstone peaches. Peaches are propagated by budding named varieties on to seedling stocks.

Pears came originally from central Asia and were one of the favourite fruits of the ancient world.

European pear is soft and butter-like, in contrast to the fruit of the Chinese Sand Pear *(Pyrus serotina)* which is comparatively hard and gritty.

Pyrus serotina has been utilised in the United States for crossing with the European Pear to give a range of varieties resistant to 'Fire Blight', a bacterial disease which has largely destroyed European varieties in the eastern areas of that country.

PEAT MOSS or Bog Moss (*Sphagnum* spp.) commonly grows in pools, bogs, swamps, or along the edges of ponds and lakes. Economically, these mosses are the most important of the bryophytes.

Usually a light green in colour, peat mosses grow in mats. Their leaves contain small, green cells that carry on photosynthesis and large, colourless dead cells that have frequent pores or openings, through which water is absorbed and stored in large amounts.

Peat mosses often form quaking bogs and floating islands. Nurserymen wrap plants in peat moss to keep them moist during transportation. The large water-storage cells of peat moss soak up and hold water like sponges. Sphagnum is also used in air-layering, a way of propagating many trees and shrubs. Sphagnum is often added to soil to improve its texture and to enable it to retain moisture. For the same reason, it is used to germinate seeds and root cuttings.

Sphagnum has been used on wounds to absorb blood. It is more absorbent than cotton and also contains an antibiotic that helps to reduce the risk of infection. (See NON-FLOWERING PLANTS.)

PEGMATITE is an igneous vein or dyke rock usually found in and around granite masses. The dykes may be filled with huge crystals — sometimes many feet long. The same minerals found in granite — feldspar, quartz, and mica — are abundant. The crystals are not intermixed as in granite, however. In pegmatite each mineral may form crystals in a different area or layer of the dyke. It is found in Cornwall and the Scottish Highlands and is commercially exploited in Brazil.

PEKING MAN was a prehistoric man whose fossil bones were discovered in the 1920s in a cave near Peking, China. He lived about 500,000 years ago, perhaps a little later than Java Man to whom he was closely related. Peking Man was about five feet tall. He lived in caves and may well have been a good hunter. He made stone tools, kindled fires, and was probably a cannibal. His brain size was smaller than modern man's but larger than that of Java Man. He had heavy ridges over his eyebrows and very little chin. (See MAN.)

PEPPER most commonly refers to one of the oldest and most important spices obtained

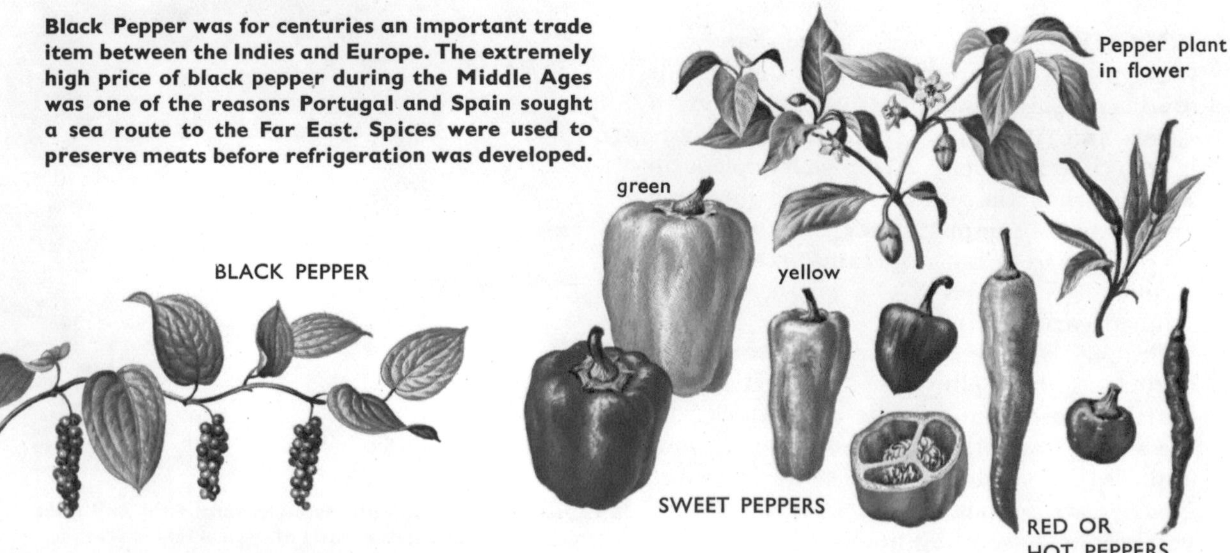

Black Pepper was for centuries an important trade item between the Indies and Europe. The extremely high price of black pepper during the Middle Ages was one of the reasons Portugal and Spain sought a sea route to the Far East. Spices were used to preserve meats before refrigeration was developed.

from the plant *(Piper nigrum)*, native to India and the Indo-Malayan region. It is a climber that produces small, red berries. Picked before they ripen, the berries (peppercorns) turn black when dried. Ground peppercorns are the source of black pepper. White pepper is obtained by grinding the seed of nearly ripe fruit of the same plant.

Early explorers found Indians of the American tropics using an unfamiliar spice. They mistakenly believed this new-found red fruit to be a kind of pepper. Later, as more varieties of these so-called pepper plants were discovered throughout the New World, it was realised that they were all members of the nightshade family and completely unrelated to the prized black pepper of the East Indies. Many varieties of different sizes and shapes of these Red Peppers *(Capsicum frutescens)* are grown throughout the world. Sweet peppers are quite mild and are used both green and ripe in salads and cooked dishes. The small, pointed and very hot Chili Peppers also belong to this group. Dried and ground they become cayenne pepper. Paprika is a spice made from a mild pepper. Pimento, another mild pepper, is also used as a spice. (See SPICES.)

PERFUME OILS are obtained largely from flowers, although the leaves and stems of some plants also contain fragrant oils. The oils are used for perfumes and colognes. Most perfumes are blends of various essential oils dissolved in alcohol or fat, plus a fixative such as ambergris, musk, or a synthetic chemical. The fixatives delay evaporation of the perfume odour.

Essential oils for perfumes are frequently extracted by distillation. The plant material is ground and put in a still. Steam is added, and the oil vaporises in a condenser from which it is collected. This method is used to get oils from roses, geraniums and lavender. Some delicate perfumes cannot be extracted in this manner.

Two other methods used for extracting perfume oils are based on the fact that grease absorbs these essential oils. Grease is spread on both sides of glass panes, and flowers are 'sandwiched' between the panes in stacks. Each day the flowers are replaced with fresh ones until the grease is saturated

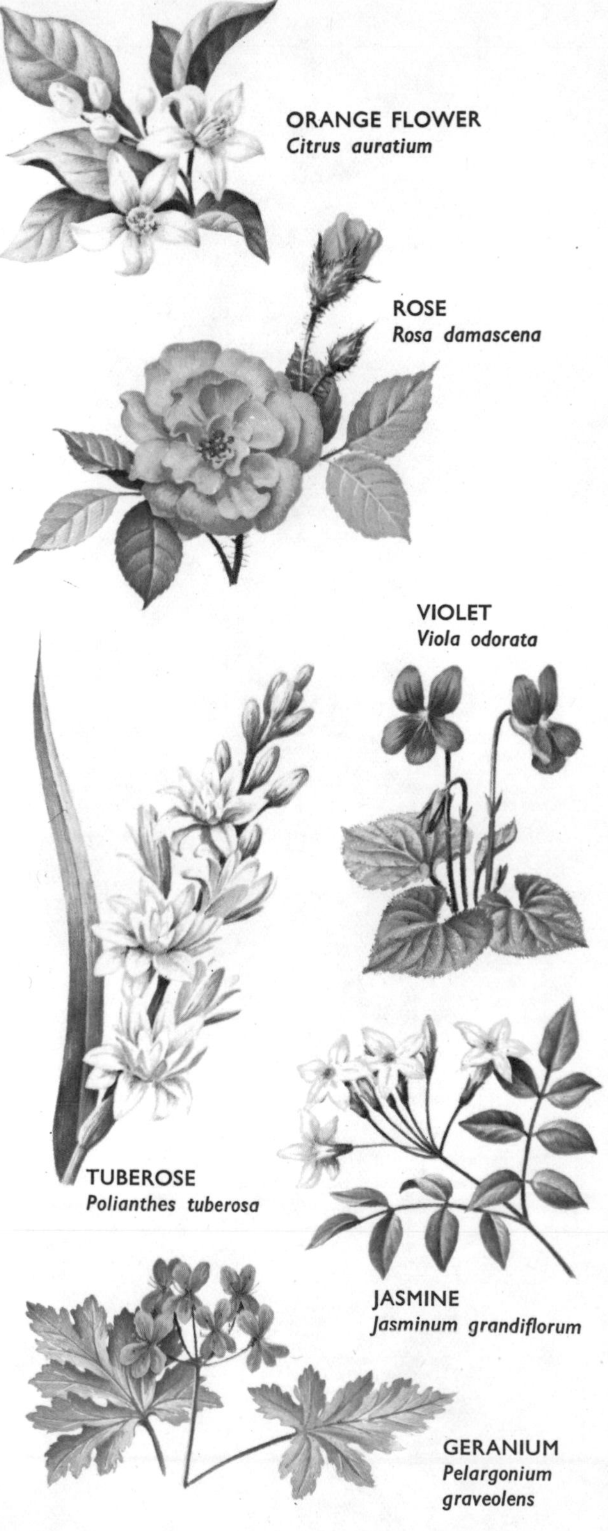

Hundreds of species of flowering plants have been used as sources of oil in the manufacture of perfumes. Here are six of the most common.

with their fragrance. Oils from jasmine and tuberoses are extracted in this way.

Violet and orange oils are extracted by immersing the flowers in melted grease or olive oil. Alcohol is then used to remove the oils from the grease or 'pomade'. This method, however, has now been largely superseded by solution in a spirit solvent such as petroleum ether, which is then removed by evaporation, leaving the perfume behind.

France is the world leader in the manufacture of perfumes, producing more than 500 tons per year. (See OILS.)

PERMIAN, the most recent period of the Palaeozoic era, began about 280 million years ago and lasted about 55 million years. It is

BRADYSAURUS
(a Permian pareiasaur)
about 1 ton

named after the Ural Mountain (U.S.S.R.) province of Perm.

Many marine invertebrates of the lower Palaeozoic became extinct during this period.

Bony fish and sharks were the dominant backboned animals in the seas, although both were rather primitive. Bony fish also lived in fresh water. Reptiles increased in numbers and variety. Most of them seem to have lived in relatively dry regions and included reptiles with bony skin-plates (pareiasaurs) and mammal-like reptiles (theriodonts).

Geographical and climatic conditions were extreme in many parts of the world. In parts of the Northern Hemisphere shallow landlocked seas evaporated, leaving great deposits of salt. In other areas, as in Australia, coal-swamp conditions persisted, and coal was formed. Mountain ranges came into existence in western Europe and in the Appalachians in the U.S.A. In some areas volcanic activity was intense. Continents in the Southern Hemisphere were buried by glaciers. Some geologists believe that during Permian times southern continents were joined together in a huge land area known as Gondwanaland. (See LIFE'S ORIGIN AND DEVELOPMENT; PALAEOZOIC.)

PERSIMMONS (*Diospyros* spp.) belong to a group of about 200 species of trees and shrubs of the ebony family. They grow in the Mediterranean region, various parts of Asia, and North America. Richly beautiful ebony wood comes from several species of related tropical trees of Asia and Africa.

Oriental Persimmons are grown widely in China and Japan and are now cultivated commercially in the Mediterranean area and southern United States. Since the male and female flowers are borne on separate trees, both types of trees must be present to insure having fruit.

Two species of persimmons are native to the United States. The Common Persimmon is abundant in the South and grows as far north as Connecticut and Iowa. The Black Persimmon, which grows in the lower Rio Grande region of Texas and adjacent Mexico, has smaller leaves and black fruit. The Oriental Persimmon, however, is more popular as the fruit is easier to market.

COMMON PERSIMMON
Diospyros virginiana

Petunias range in colour from white to many shades of red, purple, and blue, either solid or mixed.

PETUNIAS (*Petunia* spp.) are one of South America's finest flower gifts to the world. Over a century ago plant breeders began to combine the simple, small-flowered wild species into hundreds of attractive large-flowered types. Brilliant colours today grace the gardens and window-boxes of many homes. Their drooping branches are laden with blooms that keep opening month after month. Petunias are easy to grow from seed. In the United States new plants may be obtained from the scores of seedlings which spring up around the old plants in the spring, but in Britain they are generally raised under glass.

These popular, fragrant, and colourful plants are actually members of the night-shade family and are related to the potato, tomato, and tobacco.

PHOTOPERIODISM refers to the way in which the daily amount of light and darkness affects the growth, behaviour and development of plants.

Flowering plants, in fact, can be classified according to their response to light. Short-day plants, such as asters, cockleburs, chrysanthemums, poinsettias, soybeans, and violets, flower only when daily sunlight is less than 13 or 14 hours as it is in spring and autumn. If artificially subjected to longer hours of light, these plants increase in size but do not bloom. Long-day plants, such as lettuce, beets, spinach, maize, clovers, and gladiolus, flower only when the daily amount of light is more than 13 or 14 hours. Such plants as sunflowers, carnations, dandelions, tomatoes, and beans, bear flowers regardless of the length of day.

Photoperiodism has a great effect on the distribution of flowering plants. Because daylight does not exceed 13 or 14 hours in the tropics and sub-tropics, most plants that grow there are short-day plants. Long-day plants are most abundant in cooler regions north or south of 60 degrees latitude where the length of the day is much longer in summer months. Both kinds grow in temperate zones. Long-day plants flower in late spring and early summer; short-day species bloom in early spring or in late summer or autumn. Intermediate species are distributed widely over the Earth.

The light that brings about photoperiodic

These three petunias each received 8 hours of daylight every day. The plant on the right was then kept out of light, while the centre plant was exposed to 8 additional hours of fluorescent light and the plant on the left to 8 hours of incandescent light. The red in the incandescent light includes the far-red rays which stimulate plant growth. The difference in these three plants demonstrates that the composition of the light as well as the amount is effective in controlling plant growth.
USDA

response is mainly at the red end of the spectrum, and the part of the plant that reacts to promote flowering is the leaf. Flowering will occur even if only one leaf is given proper exposure to light and dark. The leaves form a flower-promoting substance that migrates to the part where flowers appear.

Gardeners and market gardeners make use of this principle. They shade chrysanthemums and poinsettias during a part of long summer days to make them bloom whenever they want them to do so. Or they delay flowering of mature plants by shortening the period of darkness with continuous or intermittent lighting.

PINEAPPLES *(Ananas comosus)* are native to the American tropics. Columbus found pineapples growing in the West Indies, where they had been introduced earlier by the Indians from South America. Both the Spanish and Portuguese planted pineapples in their New World colonies. Pineapple plantations were soon started in tropical regions of Asia, Africa, and the East Indies. Hawaii now produces approximately three-quarters of the world's annual pineapple crop of about 500,000 tons.

Pineapples are short-stemmed plants with pointed leaves, many of which have spines along their edges. The plant's central stock bears dense heads of flowers, topped by a tuft of leaves. The flowers fuse to form a multiple fruit. Pineapples ripened in the field are very juicy and sweet. Their flesh varies from white to yellow. One of the leading commercial varieties, the Cayenne, owes its popularity to its firmness when canned. Pineapples contain bromelin, an enzyme that digests proteins.

Pineapple plants can be started from slips and suckers, or the entire crown of the fruit can be used. Suckers are produced in the axil of the leaves; slips most frequently arise from the base of the fruit stock.

PINES are the largest and most important of the conifers or cone-bearing trees.

Pine timber has been imported into England for centuries. The tall Eastern White Pine *(Pinus strobus)* was especially prized for ship masts, and the best of these trees were reserved for use by the British Navy.

Many varieties of pineapples are grown in the tropics and sub-tropics, but the standby of the pineapple industry of Hawaii and other commercial growing centres is the Cayenne, which has superior canning qualities.

Pines are used even more today. Many kinds yield timber for interior fittings, window and door sashes, matches, crates, railway sleepers, posts, and general construction. Others, and particularly those that grow in south-eastern United States, are most important as sources of pulp for paper. They also yield resin and turpentine, and oils from their needles are used in medicine. Birds and many other animals eat the seeds of pines. Those of the pinyon or nut pines of south-western United States and of the Digger Pine *(Pinus sabiniana)* that grows in the California foothills were an important food of the Indians. Pinyon nuts are sold today as delicacies. Pines are also widely planted as ornamentals.

About 90 species of pines occur throughout the Northern Hemisphere, ranging southwards into the sub-tropics. Thirty-five kinds are native to the United States and Canada. They grow in a wide variety of conditions, but are most common in relatively dry soils.

The Sugar Pine *(Pinus lambertiana)*, a magnificent tree of Oregon and California, is the largest of the pines; its cones sometimes exceed 2 feet in length. Most important and widespread of the western pines is the Ponderosa Pine *(Pinus ponderosa)*.The Lodgepole Pine *(Pinus contorta)*, so named because it was once used by the Plains Indians for tepee poles, often forms dense forests in areas burned-off by fires. Its tightly closed cones open in the heat of the fire and scatter their seeds. In coastal regions the Lodgepole Pine is scrubby, but inland, and especially in the Rocky and Sierra Nevada Mountains, it is tall and shapely. Whitebark and Limber pines are common timber-line trees in western regions. The Bristlecone Pine *(Pinus aristata)* of the Rocky Mountains may grow for 4,600 years. Foxtail pines hold their needles for many years, and their branches become bushy in appearance. Coulter and Digger pines of the dry California foothills have large cones with thick, woody scales that end in pointed 'claws'. The Monterey Pine *(Pinus radiata)* of the central and southern

LONGLEAF PINE
Pinus palustris
80—120 ft.

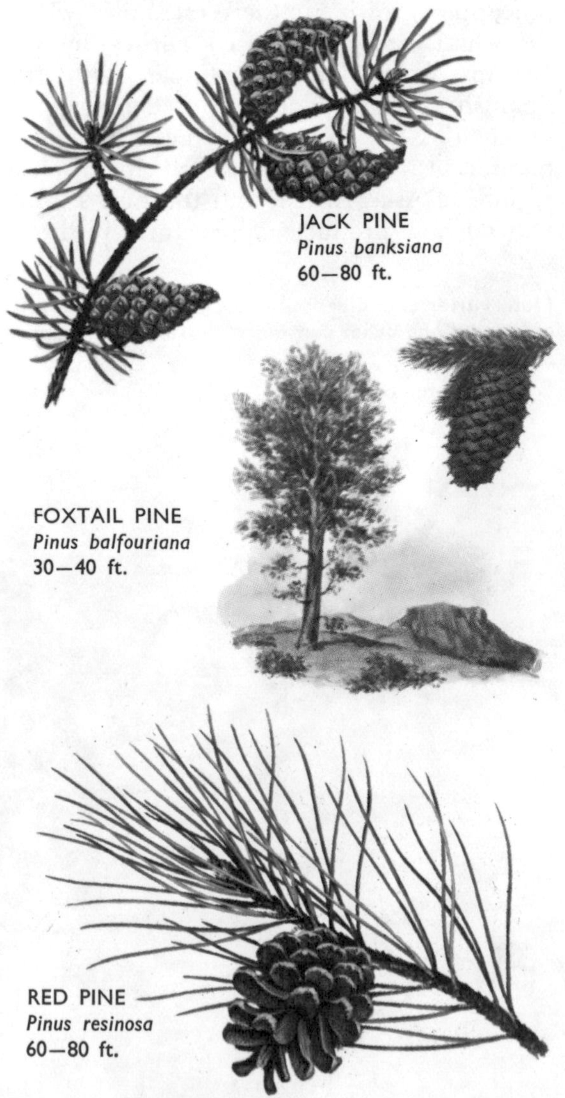

JACK PINE
Pinus banksiana
60—80 ft.

FOXTAIL PINE
Pinus balfouriana
30—40 ft.

RED PINE
Pinus resinosa
60—80 ft.

LODGEPOLE PINE
Pinus contorta
70—80 ft.

SUGAR PINE
Pinus lambertiana
175—200 ft.

California coast has been introduced to Australia where it has become a timber tree.

The Scots Pine *(Pinus sylvestris)* is an important timber tree in Europe.

Several European pines are planted as ornamentals in Britain. They include the Austrian Pine *(Pinus nigra)*, the shrubby Mountain Pine *(Pinus mugo)* from central Europe, and the Maritime and Aleppo pines from the Mediterranean region.

Except for the Single-leaf Pinyon Pine *(Pinus monophylla)* of south-western United States, the needles of all pines are in 'bundles' of two, three, or five. Their cones are composed of woody scales. Some are smooth; others are tipped with a sharp prickle.

Pines have many enemies. Fire, insects, and fungus diseases take a heavy toll. Porcupines kill many pines by eating the bark and girdling the trees.

'Pine' is part of the name of trees in several other families. Most of them have wood which resembles the wood of true pines. Both the Japanese Umbrella-Pine *(Sciadopitys)*, of the Orient, and the King William Pine *(Arthrotaxis)* of Australia, belong to the sequoia or redwood family. The Chile-Pine, Hoop and Bunya Pines of Australia, and several kauri pines *(Araucaria)* of New Zealand and Australia belong to the araucaria family. Black and Brown Pines, Celery-top Pines, and Yellow-silver and Huon Pines *(Dacrydium)* are podocarps. (See MONKEY-PUZZLE TREES; SEQUOIAS.)

EASTERN WHITE PINE
Pinus strobus
90—180 ft.

PLANE TREES (*Platanus* spp.) have mottled greenish-brown bark which peels off in irregular patches exposing the lighter grey-green inner bark. They have large, lobed leaves, and round seed balls which split apart and release many slim, tufted seeds. Their hollow leaf bases cover shiny, brown buds. Planes prefer moist soils and generally

grow along streams; they also do well as ornamentals or shade trees.

Plane trees are native of Canada, United States, Mexico and the Mediterranean. The species so commonly planted in Britain, especially in the towns, is the London Plane *(Platanus hybrida)*. This is a hybrid between the Oriental Plane *(Platanus orientalis)* and the Western Plane *(Platanus occidentalis)* from America.

PLANETS. Going round the Sun are nine bodies called planets. One of them is our Earth. The planets themselves are cold, dark bodies; practically all their light and heat comes from the Sun, which is much larger than any of the planets. As a result, the temperature of a planet depends on how close it is to the Sun. Mercury and Venus, being closer to the Sun, are warmer than we are, while the other planets are colder. Also, the light that we see from a planet is just reflected sunlight, and only the sunward side of the planet is lighted. When Mercury and Venus are nearly between us and the Sun, they dwindle to narrow crescents as seen in a telescope.

As the planets travel around the Sun, they appear to move back and forth among the constellations. The name 'planet', in fact, comes from a Greek word meaning 'wander'. Because Mercury and Venus are closer to the Sun than we are, they are never very far from the Sun in the sky, and we see them in the west after sunset or in the east before dawn. They swing back and forth slowly from one side of the Sun to the other. The times when they pass the Sun are called conjunctions, while the positions farthest from the Sun are called greatest elongation. These and all other positions of planets are called aspects.

The six planets that are farther from the Sun have quite different aspects. Each has only one position of conjunction — when it passes almost directly behind the Sun. But it also has a position in which it is opposite the Sun and can be seen in the sky all night long. In between, some almanacs list two aspects called quadrature, in which the planet is 90 degrees from the Sun. The time it takes for a planet to return to the same relative position is called its synodic period. The planets sidereal period is the time taken for it to complete one orbit relative to the stars.

All the planets go around the Sun in the same direction, in orbits that are nearly circular and nearly in the same plane. The

AVERAGE DISTANCES OF THE PLANETS FROM THE SUN

Mars
Earth
Venus
Mercury
Jupiter
Saturn
Uranus
Neptune
Pluto

0 — 1,000 million Miles — 2,000 million Miles — 3,000 million Miles

THE PLANETS	Mercury	Venus	Earth	Mars	Jupiter	Saturn	Uranus	Neptune	Pluto
Average distance from Sun (in millions of miles)	36	67	93	142	483	886	1,782	2,793	3,670
Distance from Sun (compared to Earth)	0.39	0.72	1.00	1.52	5.20	9.54	19.18	30.06	39.52
Diameter at equator (in miles)	3,000	7,700	7,926	4,200	88,800	75,000	29,300	27,700	3,600(?)
Mass or weight (compared to Earth)	0.05	0.81	1.00	0.11	318.4	95.3	14.5	17.2	0.2(?)
Volume (compared to Earth)	0.06	0.92	1.00	0.15	1.314	744	47	43	0.1(?)
Number of moons (satellites)	0	0	1	2	12	10	5	2	0
Length of day (in hours)	(same as its year?)	(same as its year?)	24	24.5	10	10	10.7	14?	153
Length of year (compared to Earth)	0.24	0.62	1.00	1.9	12	29	84	165	248
Inclination of equator to orbit (in degrees)	(?)	(?)	23.5	25.2	3.1	26.7	98	29	(?)
Weight of an object weighing 100 lbs. on Earth (in pounds)	25	85	100	36	264	117	92	112	0.8(?)

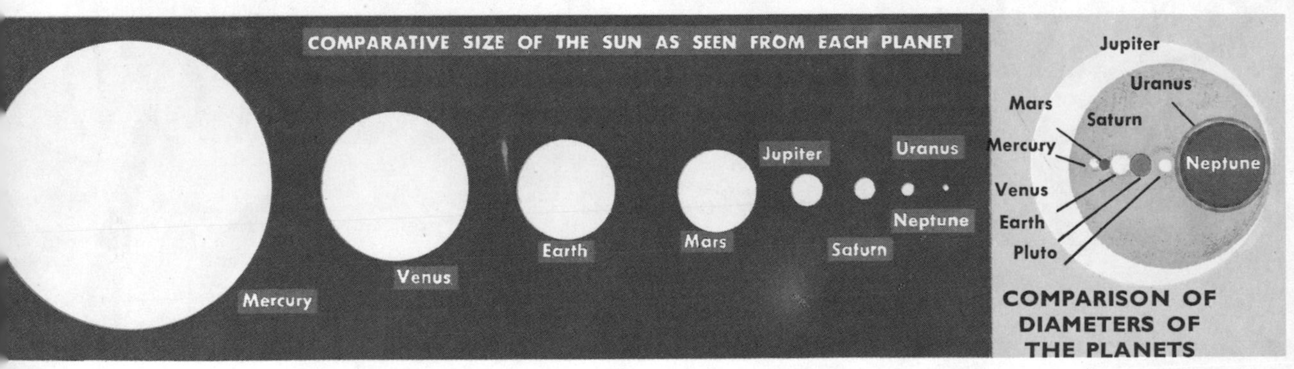

COMPARISON OF DIAMETERS OF THE PLANETS

inner four planets have closely spaced orbits, while the outer five are widely separated. The orbit of Pluto is elongated and overlaps the orbit of Neptune.

In size the planets fall into two groups. The terrestrial planets — Mercury, Venus, Earth, Mars, and Pluto — resemble the Earth. They have moderate atmospheres or none at all, and few or no satellites. They all have high densities, more than rock but less than iron. Mercury is the smallest, its diameter being only about half the Earth's. It is also closest to the Sun. The other group — Jupiter, Saturn, Uranus, and Neptune — are called the Jovian planets. All much larger than the Earth, they have thick, cloudy atmospheres and from two to twelve satellites each. They are made of lighter material than the terrestrial planets, with densities not far from that of water. Jupiter is the largest, with a diameter about 11 times greater than the diameter of the Earth. (Each of the nine planets is discussed separately. See Index.)

There are countless other stars besides our Sun, but we know nothing of any planets that they may have. At such a great distance even a large planet would be lost in the glare of its parent star. Our only way of detecting it would be to notice a slight oscillation in the position of the star caused by the gravitational effect of a planet. This effect may be present in the case of one or two neighbouring stars, but it is far from certain.

PLANT KINGDOM. One of the two big groups into which all living things can be classified is the plant kingdom. In general, the distinctions between plants and animals are clear. Most plants are able to manufacture their own food, using carbon dioxide from the air and water from the soil. By the process of photosynthesis, these simple chemicals are combined into sugars, starches, amino acids and other chemicals which the plants use.

The features that separate plants from animals have many exceptions, especially among the simpler microscopic forms. Some single-celled living things are classified as plants by botanists and also as animals by zoologists. They possess characteristics of both. There are also other living things whose structure is so simple that they can be classified neither as plants nor animals — these are the viruses.

The cell is the building block from which all living things are made. The typical plant cell has a cell wall that contains the chemical

This family tree of plants is a chart representing the probable relationship of the many groups of plants. The simplest and most ancient types of plants are near the base of the tree. Some species have remained unchanged for millions of years; others are comparative newcomers, recently evolved to meet the present conditions for life on Earth.

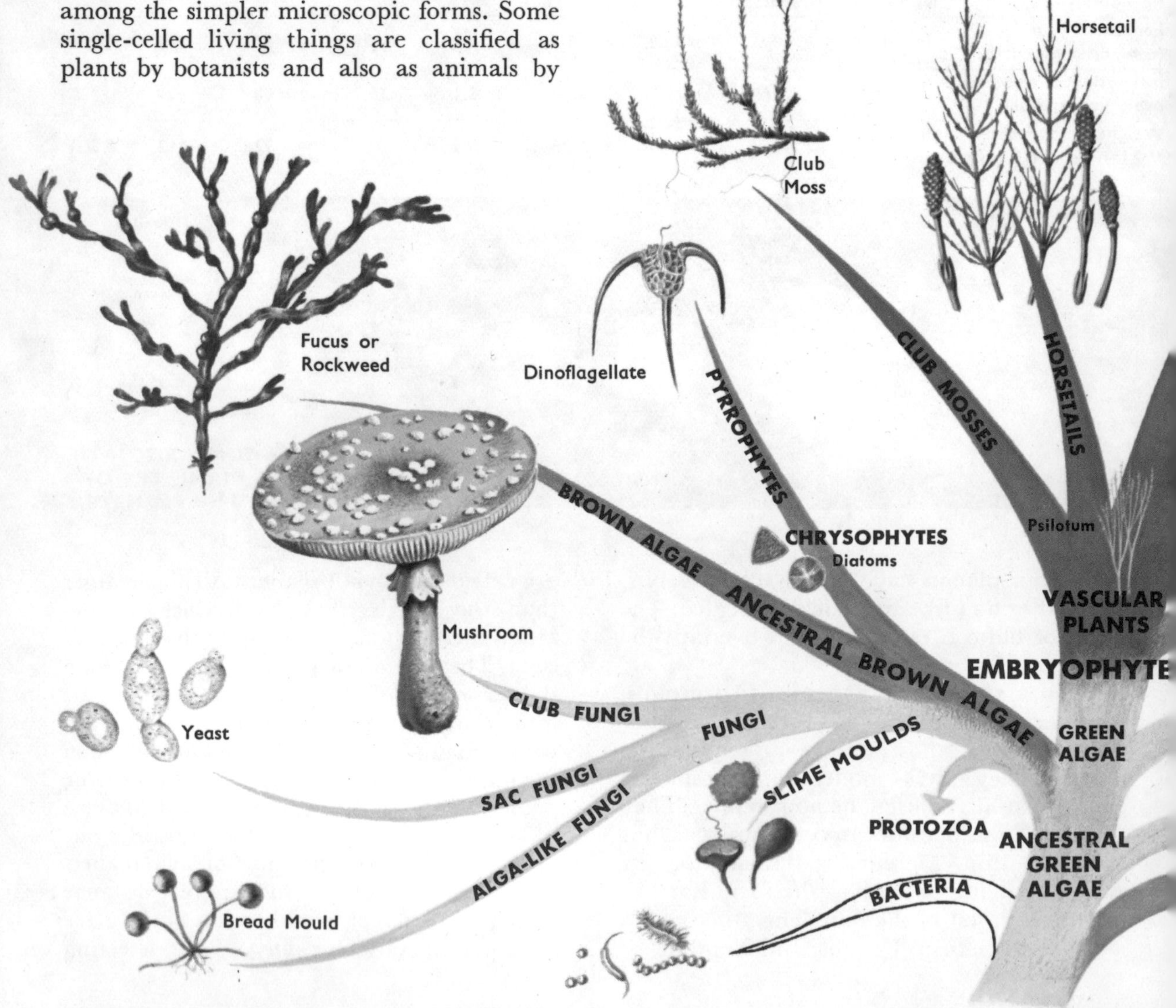

Ginkgo
Pine
Aster
Orchid
GINKGO
CONIFERS
DICOTYLEDONS
MONOCOTYLEDONS
Zamia
Fern
CYCADS
ANGIOSPERMS
FERNS
Hypnum
MOSSES
BRYOPHYTES
LIVERWORTS
Marchantia
HORNWORTS
Anthoceros
Chara
Plumaria
STONEWORTS
Euglena
EUGLENOIDS
RED ALGAE
Gloeocapsa
BLUE-GREEN ALGAE

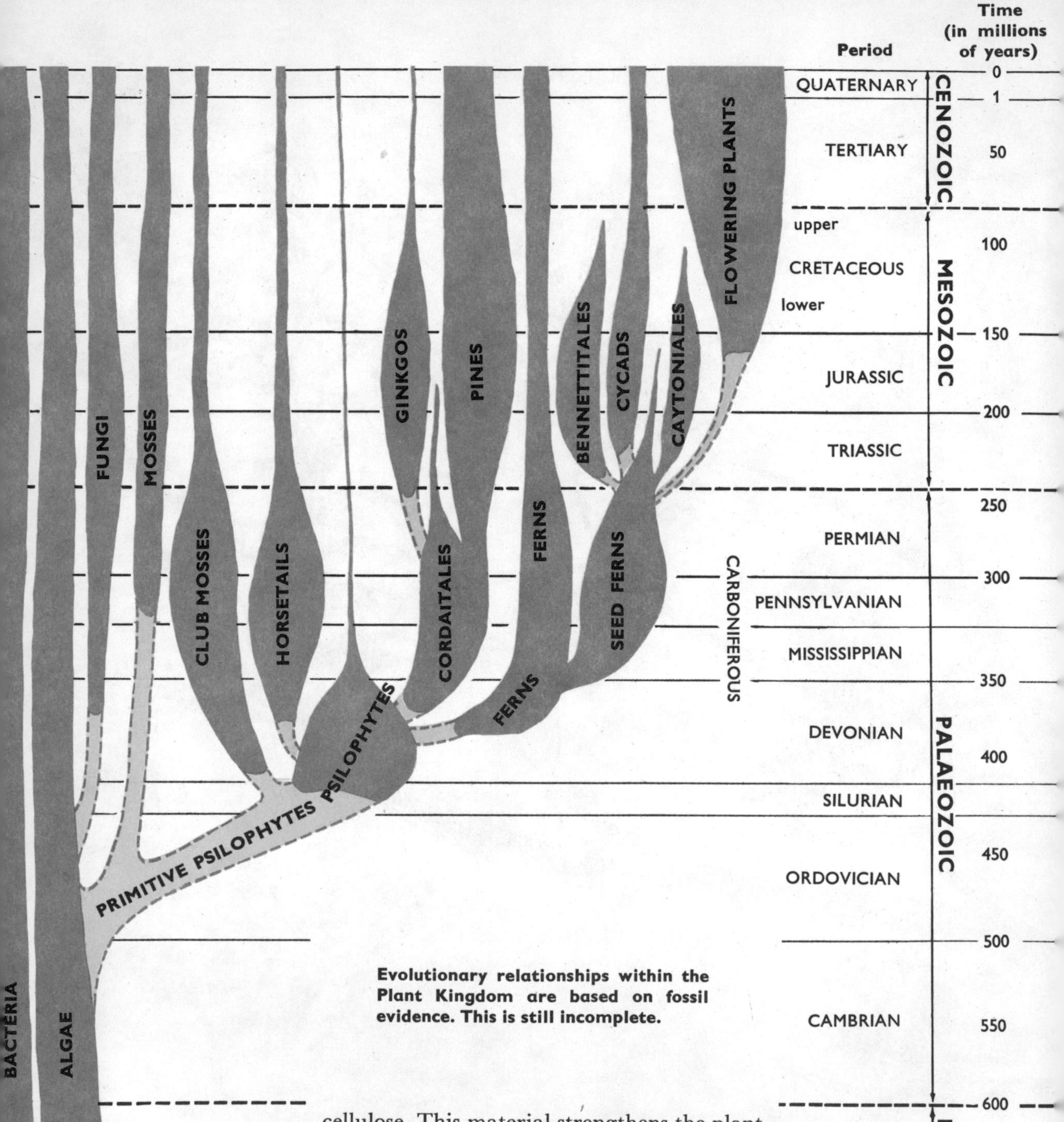

Evolutionary relationships within the Plant Kingdom are based on fossil evidence. This is still incomplete.

cellulose. This material strengthens the plant wall and gives plants their relatively rigid form. Cellulose is almost entirely absent in the animal kingdom. Most plants are stationary. They grow in one place, and their simple movements are limited to changes brought about by growth.

The plant kingdom consists of approximately 350,000 kinds of plants, ranging in size from bacteria very much smaller than a pinhead to giant Redwood trees which can be over 300 feet high.

The plant kingdom has been evolving for millions of years, and as a result many different groups of plants have developed. Each group of plants (phylum, singular; phyla, plural) has certain common characteristics used as a basis of classification. The classification of plants has been changed several times during the past 50 years as new discoveries have been made and as more evidence has turned up on the origin of particular plant groups. The present classification of plants is not perfect, but it represents the best thinking of botanists today. Plants are nowadays classified according to their flowering characteristics. (See NON-FLOWERING PLANTS.)

PLASTICS. A number of organic chemicals can be moulded or spun as fibres and contribute to a large plastic industry. The first plastic was made by combining cellulose nitrate from cotton with camphor to make celluloid. This was in the 1860s. Bakelite, discovered about 1900, was the second. Since then the industry has become gigantic and complex, making its greatest strides since 1940. Wood flour (from sawdust and other waste wood), cotton fibres, soybean meal, and rosin are among the widely used plant materials.

PLATINUM is a rare, silver-white native metal found in igneous rocks. As the parent rocks are eroded, the plantinum may be

NATIVE PLATINUM

carried away and deposited in a new location as a placer. Platinum is malleable (soft enough so that it can be pounded without breaking) and ductile (capable of being drawn into a thin wire). It is highly valuable, and about 25 per cent of the platinum used each year is recovered from scrap. Platinum is used for jewellery, dental fillings and, more importantly today, in chemical and electrical industries. It has a high melting point and does not react chemically. It is used in manufacturing sulphuric and nitric acids, in oil refineries in the manufacture of high octane petrol, and for electroplating, wires, crucibles, and electrodes. Platinum comes from Canada, the U.S.S.R., South Africa, and small quantities from the U.S.A. Large deposits exist in South America.

PLIOCENE. This period began about 7 million years ago and lasted about 5 million years. Its name is derived from two Greek words meaning 'more recent'. The number of plants and animals of modern genera found in Pliocene rocks is considerably greater than in rocks of the Miocene.

Pliocene times marked the transition from the relatively stable climate of the Tertiary to the severe climate of the Pleistocene. In the Pliocene, the broad outlines of the continents as we know them today were developed, and there have been no major changes since the beginning of Pleistocene.

Pliocene marine animals were similar to those still living today, although they include some species now extinct. Land plants were also broadly similar to those of today, though some plants common in Europe during the Pliocene are now found only in areas of Asia and North America. A variety of

Shovel-toothed mammoths, like the *Amebelodon*, lived in late Tertiary and early Pleistocene times.

elephants lived during the Pliocene, as did pronghorn antelopes, the bizarre *Syntheto-ceras* with its forked-horn nose, and the horse *Hipparion.*

PLUMS of various types are grown in many warm temperate areas of the world. The most important type is the European Plum *(Prunus domestica)*, which has been cultivated for over 2,000 years in the Mediterranean area. The Victoria, Damson, and Greengage Plums are commonly grown varieties in Britain. In California, sweet plums of the European type are dried, aged, and glossed to produce the familiar wrinkly-skinned prunes.

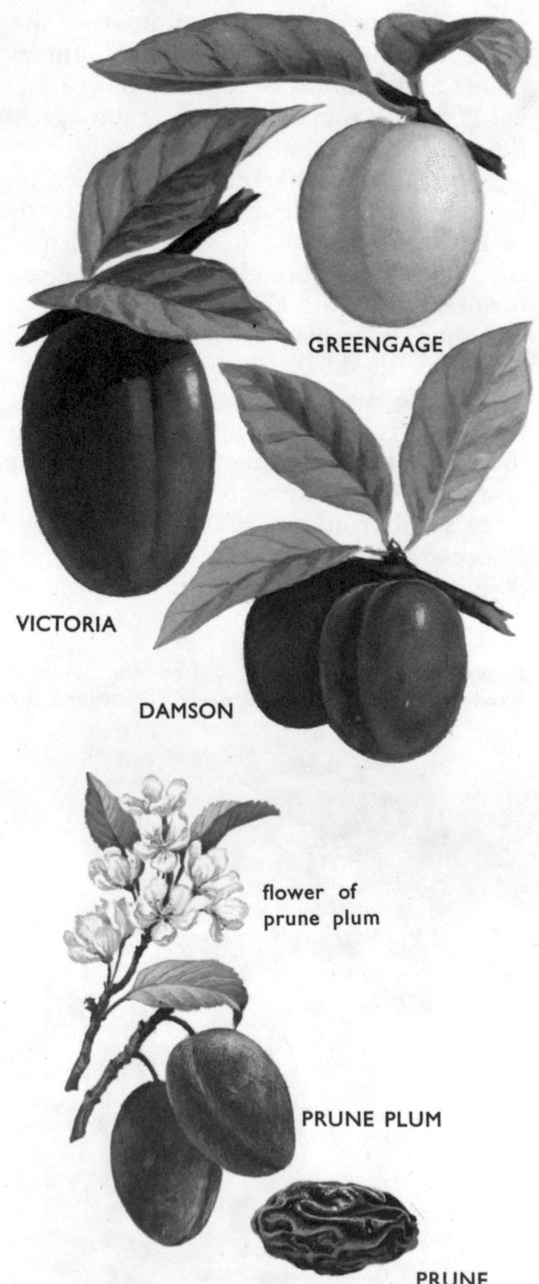

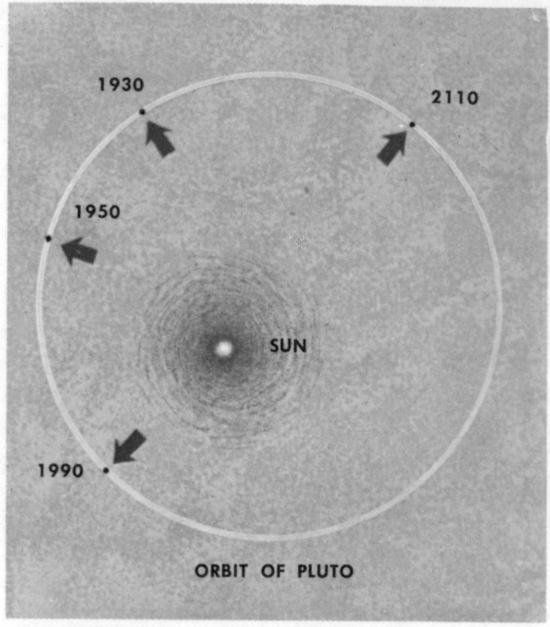

ORBIT OF PLUTO

PLUTO. This most distant known planet was discovered in 1930 as a result of a systematic search begun by Percival Lowell, an American astronomer. It is 40 times as far from the Sun as the Earth is and takes 248 years to circle its gigantic orbit. It is so far from the Sun that it receives very little light and heat, and its temperature averages about −375 degrees Fahrenheit. Pluto is somewhat smaller than the Earth and seems to have no atmosphere. It rotates on its axis every 6⅓ days and has no known satellites. Because of its great distance, it is very difficult to study.

Pluto has a more eccentric orbit than any other planet. At one point it comes closer to the Sun than Neptune. In the past the two orbits may have come very close together, and this has led to the suggestion that Pluto may have begun its planetary career as an escaped satellite of Neptune.

POISONOUS FUNGI cause illness or even death when eaten.

Ergot, a fungus that attacks flowers of

rye and related cereals, replaces the seed with hard, black fungus tissue. As a medicine, ergot is valuable but is dangerous or even fatal if unwisely used. One year in the 1700s many people died in France from poisoning when ergot was ground up accidentally with rye grain to make flour.

Although most mushrooms are edible, a number of species are poisonous, causing anything from mild stomach upsets to death. Most deadly are certain gill fungi *(Amanita)* which have a ring around their stem and a cup at their base. Their spores are white. Some species of the genus *Amanita* are edible, but others are dangerously poisonous. Two pure white species (*Amanita phalloides* and *Amanita verna*) go by the name of Death or Destroying Angel. Fly Agaric *(Amanita muscaria)*, once used to make a fly pioson, has a bright red scaly cap. Among other poisonous gill fungi are species of *Clitocybe*, *Inocybe*, *Lactarius*, *Panaeolus*, *Entyloma*, *Stropharia*, and *Russula*. The Parasol Mushroom *(Lepiota)* is a delicacy, but Morgan's Lepiota, a member of the same genus, is poisonous.

All stinkhorns are poisonous, as are several species of *Boletus*. One kind *(Gyromitra esculenta)* is sometimes deadly poisonous and at other times edible, possibly due to the conditions where it grows.

All hallucigenic fungi are poisonous, causing visions or hallucinations when eaten. Mexican Indians use hallucigenic fungi in their rituals. These fungi can cause death unless used with care. A black-spored gill fungus *(Panaeolus)* that resembles the edible inky caps is hallucigenic. Another kind *(Psilocybe)* has dark brown spores.

Scientists have become interested in the hallucigenic fungi as they believe these fungi might be used to treat certain types of mental illness.

Five main groups of poisons are found in fungi. They are classified according to the nature of their effect on human beings:

1. Poisons which cause cells to break down, particularly cells of the nervous system, liver, kidney, and heart. Their effect is often not evident for several hours or even a day or more. Death results in 50 to 90 per cent of the cases. Death Angel mushrooms are among those with this type of poison.

2. Poisons which cause stomach upsets,

POISONOUS FUNGI

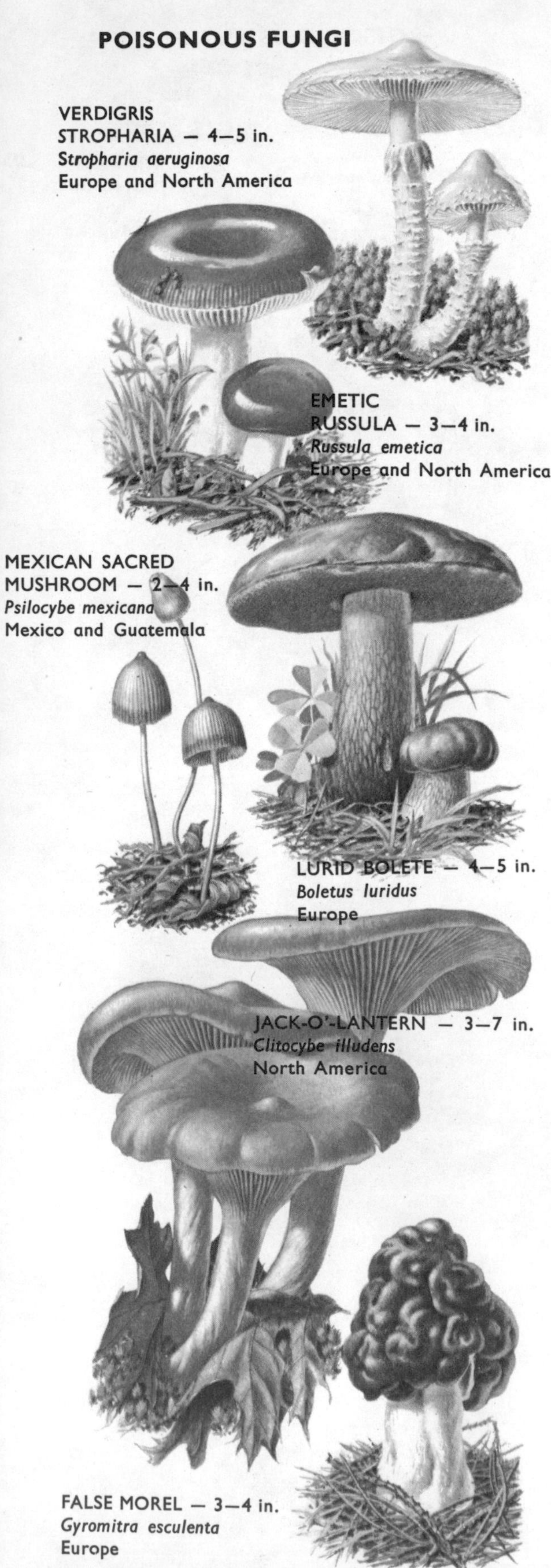

then result in nervous delirium, coma, and often death. Fly Agaric has this effect, as does the Jack-o'-Lantern Mushroom (*Clitocybe*). Poison of this type can be treated successfully with atropin.

3. Poisons which irritate the stomach and intestines, causing vomiting, diarrhoea, and stomach pains. These poisons are fatal only to the very young or to persons who are very weak. The poison can be eliminated by pumping it out of the stomach, and the patient recovers quickly. Morgan's Lepiota (*Lepiota morgani*), Lurid Boletus (*Boletus luridus*), and others belong to this group.

4. Poisons which destroy red blood cells. Several species, such as *Gyromitra esculenta*, are of this type. The poison is helvellic acid which is soluble in water and hence is removed by parboiling.

5. Poisons which cause a staggering gait, exhilarated laughter, disturbed vision, and other symptoms of drunkenness. Hallucigenic fungi are of this sort.

Poisonous fungi can be recognised only by correctly identifying them. There are a number of folk beliefs about how to identify poisonous fungi, but none are valid. The only safe rule is to avoid all wild fungi unless you are absolutely certain the species is edible.

First aid for the person who has eaten poisonous fungi consists largely of helping him to get rid of the unwholesome food. Vomiting is encouraged by giving large amounts of water or emetics. The patient should be kept warm and as comfortable as possible. A doctor should be called to give whatever treatment may be required.

POLAR LIFE. Conditions for life around the South Pole are much different from those around the North Pole. Antarctica, surrounded by the Antarctic Ocean, is a high, ice and snow covered continent of some 5 million square miles. It is the windiest region in the world; wind velocities regularly exceed 130 miles per hour. The temperature may drop to 135 degrees below zero (Fahrenheit), and so all moisture is frozen in this cold desert and of no use to plants and animals. The region immediately around the South Pole has six months without sunshine and six months of constant sunshine. At Little America,

Rutherford Platt

Saxifrages, small flowering plants; grasses; mosses and lichens are typical of plant life on the tundra.

Hunting and fishing are the sole means of subsistence for the Eskimos living within the Artic Circle.

Barnaby's Picture Library

continual sunshine and sunless periods are four months each. In between are periods of two months each when the days have a sunrise and a sunset.

Except for seals and birds that get their food from the sea no higher types of life exist in Antarctica. Some microscopic animals and lichens and moss appear briefly on moist rocks during the brief summer. But the cold waters of the Antarctic Ocean are rich in plant life.

The much milder Arctic region has constant darkness from early December until mid-January and only brief appearances of the sun until the end of May. Then sunlight is constant until July, followed by shortening days and lengthening nights until December. The North Pole is located in the Arctic Sea near such islands as Greenland and Ellesmere, and mainland Alaska and Siberia. Parts of Canada, Alaska, and Asia are within the Arctic Circle. Snow and ice are permanent in the deep polar regions. During the nine-month winters, temperatures may

drop to 62 degrees below zero, but summers are mild. Snow melts in surrounding areas, birds flock in from the south, and plants flourish. Permanent human communities are located along the coasts of the islands. Waters of the rather mild Arctic Sea never freeze over completely. They contain gigantic ice floes that slowly circle the North Pole.

Life in the polar region is characteristic of the tundra, which is a Siberian word meaning 'north of the timber line'. Vegetation includes such permanent growth as Sphagnum and Reindeer Moss, a lichen. With the coming of warmer weather in June, forget-me-nots, lupins, and hundreds of other small arctic plants spread along the shores and across bogs and marches. These are short-lived, however, because winter returns towards the end of August and turns the land into a barren area of snow.

Polar regions are in many ways much like alpine regions which also have a brief spring and summer followed by a long winter. Polar regions, however, have a greater seasonal variation of light, and a richer supply of oxygen in the atmosphere. (See ALPINE ZONE.)

POMEGRANATES *(Punica granatum)*, natives of sub-tropical Asia, are deciduous shrubs or small trees (15 to 20 feet high). They produce round, juicy fruits with thick, brownish-red skins and a pink or reddish, seedy pulp. Their trumpet-shaped flowers are usually orange-red. Leaves are narrowly oblong and glossy-green with curled margins. Pomegranates, said to have originated in Persia, have been a valuable fruit for ages. They are mentioned often in the Bible, and figure prominently in early mythology. The 'apple' in the Garden of Eden was probably a pomegranate. Numerous varieties have been developed and are grown widely in tropical and sub-tropical countries for their fruit or as ornamentals.

POPPIES have beautiful flowers, mainly reddish or orange in colour, which are held high on tall, slender stalks. The bright blooms have wedge-shaped dark markings at the base of their petals. Fat, round buds of poppy flowers are easily recognised, and when the blossom opens, it pushes aside two saucer-shaped protective coverings, the sepals. When the petals fall, all that remains is the circular, ridged seed box.

Poppies come from many lands. Most of the more than a hundred species are natives of southern Asia and Europe, but a number are from North America. Milky juice from the Opium Poppy *(Papaver somniferum)* has long been a source of narcotics — morphine, heroin, and opium. The Common Red Poppy *(Papaver rhoeas)*, which at one time covered the battlefields of France after the First World War, used to decorate cornfields in Britain until the advent of various selective herbicides.

The showy Oriental Poppy *(Papaver orientale)*, and the Iceland Poppy *(Papaver nudicaule)*, are favourite perennials in British gardens because of their bright orange, yellow, pink or white flowers. The annual Shirley poppies and Californian poppies are commonly grown on dry borders in Britain.

PORE FUNGI have conspicuous fruiting bodies with a closely packed layer of tubes instead of gills on their lower surface. The tubes open through small holes or pores. Some are difficult to see without a lens; others are larger, often angular. The inner portion of each pore is lined with club-like basidia, which produces spores. The spores fall from the pore and are blown by the wind. (See NON-FLOWERING PLANTS.)

Fruiting bodies of many pore fungi grow like brackets on the side of a tree, stump, or board. Their tubes hang down. Many kinds (such as *Polyporus*, *Polystictus*, *Fomes*, and *Ganoderma*) are woody or leathery, often lasting for several years. They vary in colour from white, tan, dark brown, or black to bright orange or red, and sometimes are marked on top with different-coloured rings. The Many-coloured Polypore *(Polystictus*

OPIUM POPPY
Papaver somniferum

ROUGH-STEMMED BOLETE — 6 in.
Boletus scaber
North America

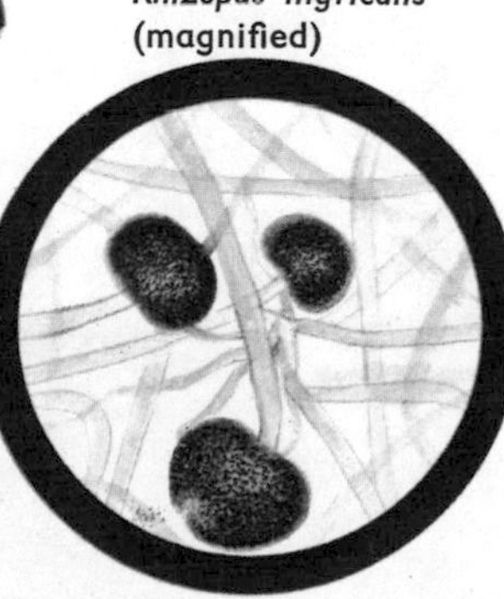

BREAD MOULD
Rhizopus nigricans
(magnified)

RED POLYPORE
Polyporus cinnabarinus
Northern Hemisphere

versicolour) is a relatively thin bracket fungus. Its upper surface is beautifully zoned with various colours — pale tan, grey, green, or violet to nearly black. The under-surface is white with very small pores. It is found throughout the year on dead wood. The Red Polypore *(Polyporus cinnabarinus)* is another bracket fungus common in temperate regions. Its bright cinnabar red colour, both top and bottom, makes it conspicuous. Older specimens fade to white. In tropical and sub-tropical regions a very similar tropical Red Polypore *(Polyporus sanguineus)* is common. Others, especially species of *Boletus* or *Strobilomyces*, have a soft, fleshy central stalk. Some, when bruised or broken open, change from a flesh colour to blue, green, or red as the oxygen in the air oxidises their pigments. Woody and leathery types grow on dead wood and can be found in all seasons. Soft, fleshy types, which usually grow in soil, appear after rains but soon decay.

Dry rot of building timbers is caused by a pore fungus (usually *Merulius* in Europe, *Poria* in the United States). Both kinds can completely destroy beams, rafters, panelling or weatherboard.

One of the most common pore fungi is the Artist's Fungus (*Ganoderma applanatum*, also often called *Fomes applanatus*). These large shelf-like fruiting bodies grow from trees and stumps and may be as large as 1½—2 feet across. The smooth, hard upper surface is tan to dark brown, and the porous under surface is white.

POTATO commonly refers to the White Potato *(Solanum tuberosum)* native to the Andes of South America. This vegetable was introduced into Europe in the latter part of the sixteenth century but did not become an important food until late in the 1700s.

Irish immigrants to America, in 1719, began the large-scale commercial potato planting in the New England states.

In Ireland, the poor people lived almost entirely on potatoes and milk, so failure of the crops due to blight in 1845—47 caused widespread famine.

Potato plants grow about 2—3 feet high.

Varieties of potatoes have been developed to suit different soils, growing conditions, and market demands.

Potatoes became established in North America after several trans-Atlantic trips to and from Europe.

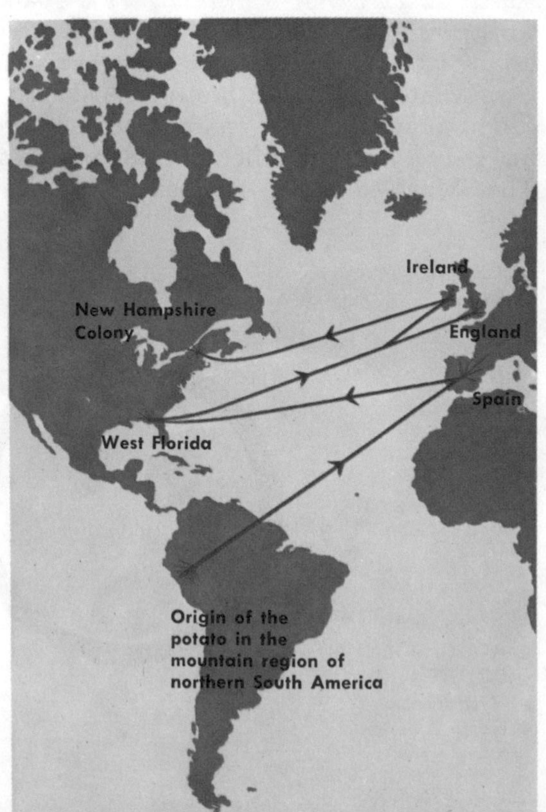

The above-ground portion consists of a stem, leaves, and flowers, and may bear small, seedy green fruit that measure as much as an inch in diameter. Unlike most plants, the potato also has underground stems, and it is the enlarged portions of these stems, called tubers, that are known as potatoes. The 'eyes' of potatoes are actually clusters of buds. Potatoes are propagated by planting small tubers known as seed potatoes. Each contains at least one 'eye'. Seed potatoes are planted in ridges about 2½ feet apart. Potatoes may be dug with a fork or spade, but in large commercial plantings they are usually dug with mechanical diggers. They can be stored about eight months.

Potatoes have become one of the most important vegetables of the world. In Europe and the United States there are many commercial varieties. Some are white-skinned, others red-skinned. Varieties are selected on the basis of resistance to disease, yield, and cooking qualities. Potatoes are also used in the commercial production of potato crisps, starch, flour, and alcohol and as livestock feed. Europe grows about 90 per cent of the world's potato crop. (See STARCH; SWEET POTATO.)

PRE-CAMBRIAN includes the period of time from the origin of the Earth to about 570 million years ago. Since the Earth is probably about 4,500 to 5,000 million years old, Pre-Cambrian time represents about 90 per cent of the long scope of geologic history.

Pre-Cambrian rocks are not nine times more common at the surface of the Earth, however. In many areas these ancient rocks lie deeply buried beneath younger sediments. The original crust of the Earth presumably consisted of igneous rocks, such as lavas and granites, that had solidified from a molten condition. As the Earth gradually cooled, the action of the atmosphere over long periods of time broke down this original crust and deposited sediments in rivers and seas. Pre-Cambrian rocks therefore include both igneous and sedimentary rocks, but both types are often so greatly changed that it is difficult to determine their age and relationships.

Many Pre-Cambrian rocks consist of gneisses, schists, marbles, slate and quartzites, as well as a great variety of granites and other rocks. (See MINERALS; ROCKS.)

The oldest Pre-Cambrian rocks so far measured are pegmatites from South Africa, Manitoba, and Wyoming. Tests indicate that these rocks are about 3,000 million years old.

Pre-Cambrian rocks contain few records of life, but a sufficient number of fossils have been found to indicate that life of a very primitive kind did exist in Pre-Cambrian times. Apparently animals and plants in a wide variety existed. The plants are chiefly remains of calcareous algae. There are also well-preserved remains of other algae and fungi of microscopic size. Several beds of graphite in various parts of the world were

CALCAREOUS ALGA

WORM

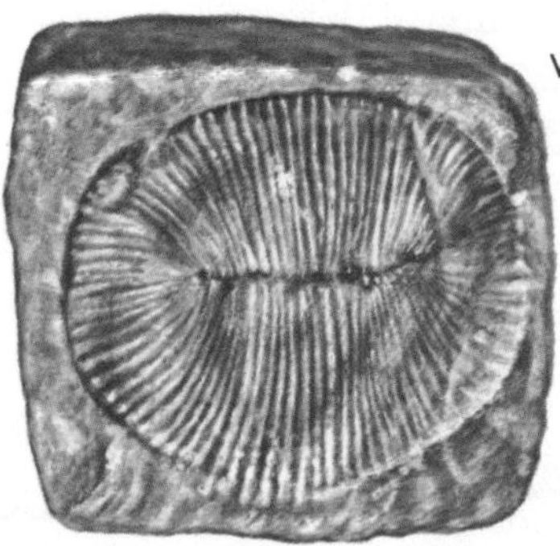

SEGMENTED WORM

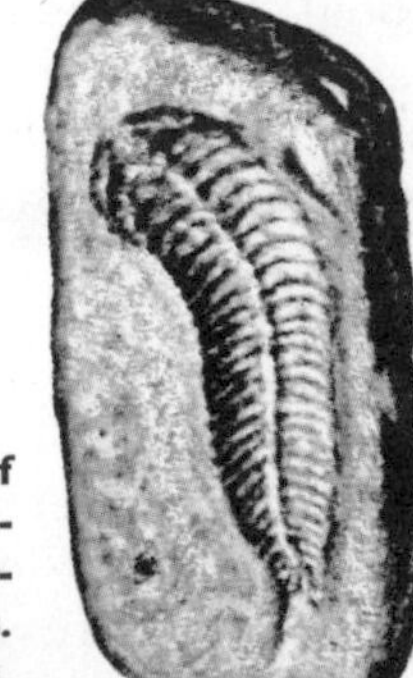

JELLYFISH

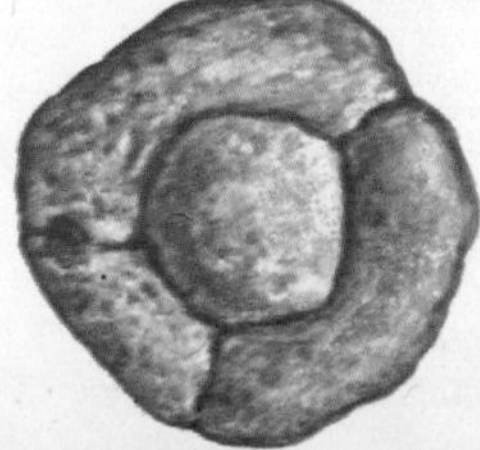

Pre-Cambrian fossils are rarely found. Most life of that period had no hard parts, though limestone-forming algae such as *Collenia* were present. Soft-bodied creatures are known through casts or moulds. The worms and the jellyfish were found in Australia, and are believed to be well over 600 milliony ears old.

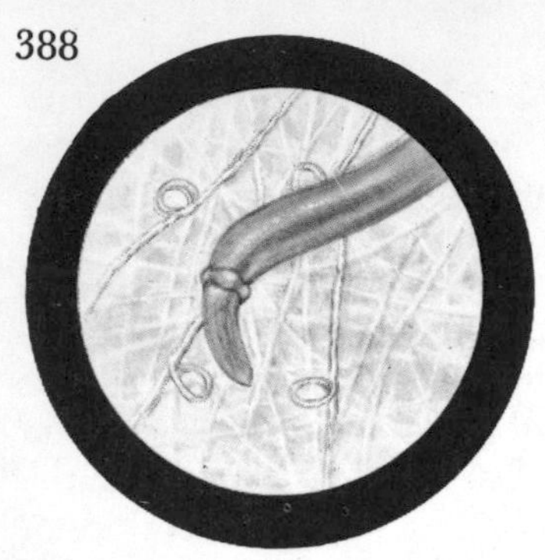

A nematode is caught in the loop-snare of a predaceous fungus. The fungus will grow into the worm's body and digest it.

probably formed from Pre-Cambrian coals.

Tracks and trails of animals have been recorded. The richest finds have been made in southern Australia where more than 500 Pre-Cambrian fossils have been found. These include algae, jellyfishes, corals, worms, and still unidentified types of plants and animals.

Fossils are rare because the animals themselves lacked hard-parts and many of the rocks have been much altered by heat and pressure. (See LIFE'S ORIGIN AND DEVELOPMENT.)

PREDACEOUS FUNGI. Only a few kinds of predaceous fungi have been studied in detail. Some capture nematodes, commonly called 'eelworms'. Some kinds of nematodes, usually less than 1/25 of an inch long, cause root-knot or burrowing nematode disease. Those that live free in the soil are the ones attacked by fungi, however. These fungi grow through the soil with a long mycelium much like other fungi do. At intervals, short branches grow out forming tangles of loops and snarls. In some kinds the loops have a sticky substance on their inner surface. Eelworms become trapped in these loops, and branches of the mycelium grow into any trapped animal, destroy it, and feed on the contents of the body.

PRESSURE. At sea level, air pressure is about 15 pounds per square inch. This is called a pressure of one atmosphere. Air pressure decreases with altitude. At the top of Mount Everest the pressure is about ⅓ of an atmosphere or 5 pounds per square inch. Pressure increases with depth. At 35,000 feet the water pressure in the ocean is about 15,000 pounds per square inch — equal to 1,000 atmospheres.

The effects of low pressure at high altitudes are great, but result mainly from the decrease in amount of oxygen, low temperature and great intensity of light. On the other hand, the high pressure in the depths of the ocean affects plants and animals directly. Regions of extreme high or low pressures are usually permanently cold, but in the salt water of deep oil wells where a few species of bacteria live, temperatures are high — around 107 degrees centigrade (225 degrees Fahrenheit).

Many people live at high altitudes, such as in the Andes and in the Himalayas of Tibet. They raise barley and sheep nearly 15,000 feet above sea level, where the pressure is only about ½ of an atmosphere and the oxygen is reduced to 50 per cent of the amount that is found at sea level. (See ALPINE ZONE.)

The effect of increased pressure in ocean depths is another matter. A human diver in a flexible diving suit with air supplied cannot go deeper than about 300 feet safely. The pressure at this depth is only about 150 pounds per square inch.

A pressure of 10,000 pounds per square inch retards the action of decay bacteria. Dead plants and animals that sift down from surface waters into ocean depths decay very slowly. Amoebas no longer put out their pseudopodia at a pressure of about 3,750 pounds per square inch and will die if kept at 6,750 pounds per square inch for an hour.

The pressure ranges within which life exists.

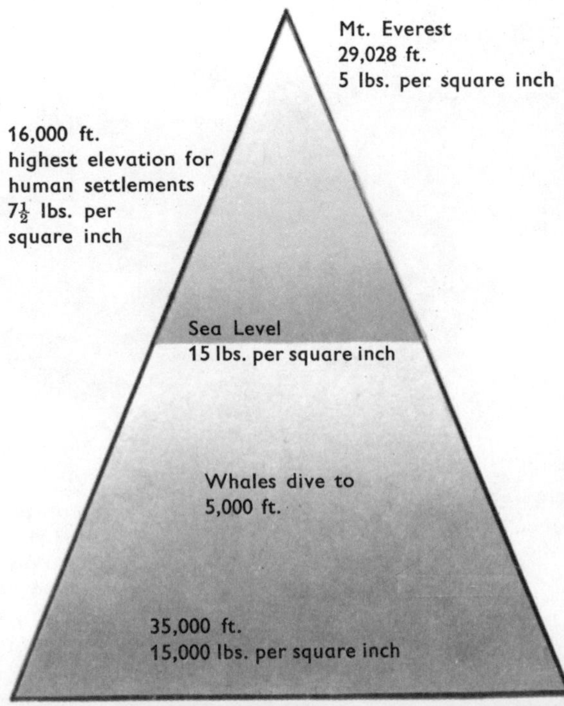

PRIMROSES (*Primula* spp.) Plant breeders have glorified and modernised these old favourites. Hybrid varieties today are almost countless. Large-flowered kinds have short stalks or practically no stalks at all. Colours range from bright blue to yellow and red. Longer-stalked primroses have dainty, smaller flowers, usually lavender or pink. Primroses have leaves clustered at the base of the plant.

COMMON PRIMROSE
Primula vulgaris

PROPAGATION OF PLANTS — vegetative methods. The plant breeder attempts to grow as many new types as he can so that useful kinds can be selected. Plant growers wish to raise many plants of the *same* type, and not to lose the characteristics which have made it useful. Some plants are easily propagated by growing from seed and more or less 'breed true'. These include annual plants such as wheat and other farm crops, onions and many vegetables, and some flowers.

However, many perennial plants are not satisfactory when grown from seed. Either seedlings take too long to mature, or the majority of seedlings will revert to inferior types. In these cases, including potato, where the tubers provide a natural method, and in fruit trees, plants are propagated vegetatively. Vegetative propagation means that the new plants are produced by taking pieces of stem, root, or leaf and a complete new plant is induced to grow from this part.

If the part is severed from the plant before regeneration of the missing parts takes place it is known as a cutting. If the part, generally the stem, is left attached to the plant while it is induced to form roots, it is known as layering.

If a piece of stem with buds is joined on to an existing rootstock, in such a way that the two unite, it is known as grafting. A special type of grafting, known as budding, consists of removing one bud from shoots of the parent tree and inserting it under the bark of the stem of an established rootstock. In fruit growing the rootstocks themselves may be special types propagated by cuttings or layering, or may be seedlings which cannot be depended upon to grow good fruit.

SOME COMMON METHODS OF VEGETATIVE PROPAGATION

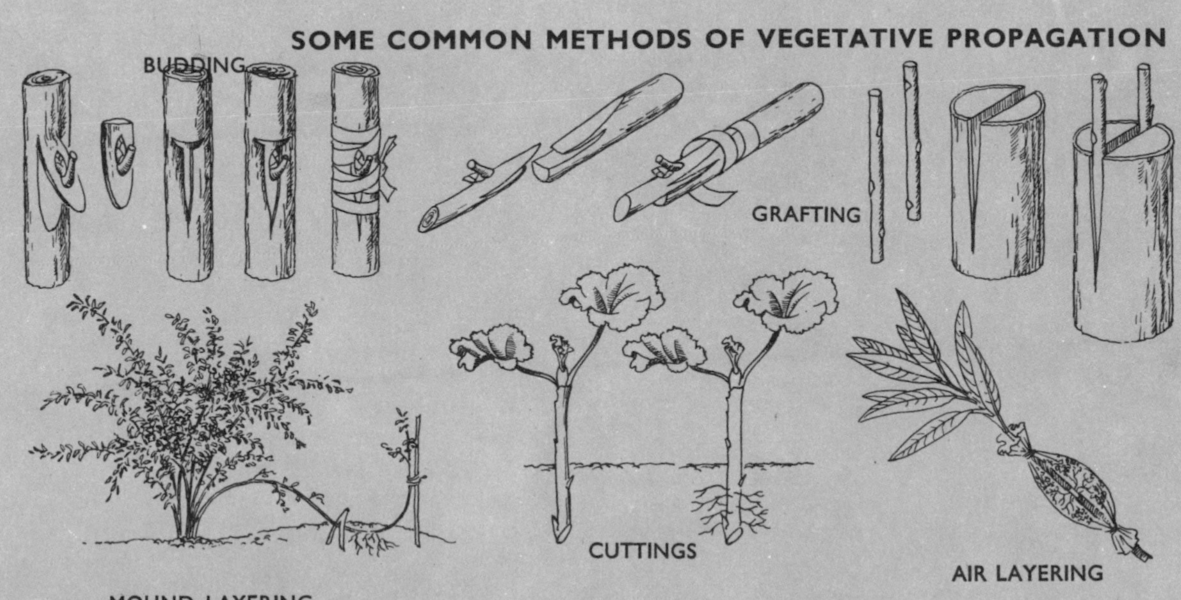

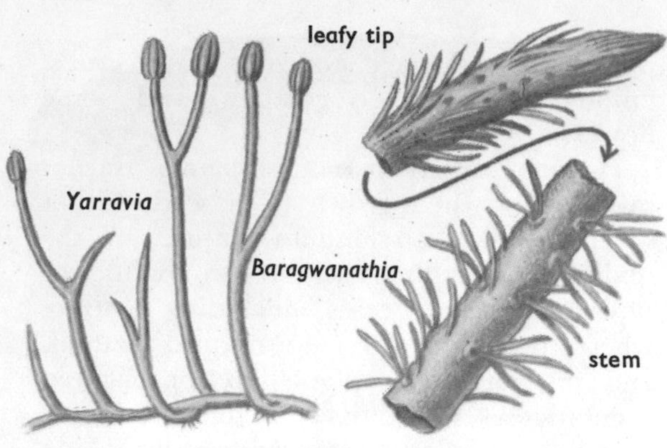

EARLY DEVONIAN PLANTS

PSILOPSIDS flourished during Devonian times, 300 to 400 million years ago. They were the first plants to conquer land. After Devonian times they declined greatly in importance, probably due to competition from more advanced land plants. Today only two genera represent this primitive plant group. These are *Psilotum*, found widely in the tropics, and *Tmesipteris*, found in the Philippines and also in New Zealand. (See DEVONIAN; NON-FLOWERING PLANTS; PSILOTUM.)

PSILOTUM or Whisk-broom Fern is not a fern but a very primitive vascular plant. It is found in tropical and sub-tropical areas in both Northern and Southern Hemispheres. It is related to the Club-mosses of Scottish mountains. These small plants have no roots, and their stems have no leaves. Part of the stem grows underground and serves for both anchorage and absorption.

Inside the stem is a simple vascular tissue. The first vascular plants are believed to have been rather similar to Psilotum. (See NON-FLOWERING PLANTS; PSILOPSIDS.)

WHISK-BROOM FERN
Psilotum nudum
6—18 in.

Psilotum **is a rootless, leafless plant, closely related to the extinct, primitive psilopsids.**

PUMICE is a white, grey, or yellowish volcanic glass so filled with gas bubbles that it will float indefinitely on water. The masses of glassy fibres that surround the gas holes are visible with a hand lens. Pumice is the froth on top of a lava flow formed by gases freed from magma when it appeared on the Earth's surface. Pumice may also be blown out of volcanoes during explosive eruptions. Pumice occurs as lumps, in layers, or as loose beds of powder. The rock is used locally in making concrete and provides excellent insulation against heat and sound. Lump pumice makes a good abrasive and is used for rubbing down metal or wood. Powdered pumice is graded for quality and size for use in cleaning, scouring, and polishing powders and in soaps. Recently large blocks of pumice have been used for sculptures. Pumice is produced in Italy, New Zealand, Japan, Canada and western United States.

PUMICE

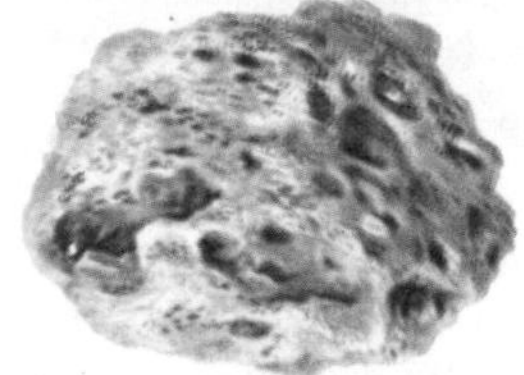

The chemical composition of pumice is the same as other igneous rocks, but because of its gas bubbles, it is much lighter.

PUMPKINS belong to the gourd family *(Cucurbitaceae)* which also contains cucumbers, watermelons, marrows, and melons. Pumpkins like most members of this family grow on a trailing plant which is capable of climbing by sensitive tendrils. They are usually allowed to mature before being picked. In contrast, marrows and cucumbers are ordinarily picked and eaten before the seeds or skin harden. Pumpkin pies sold commercially in America are usually made

from Winter Squash *(Cucurbita maxima)*. These may weigh as much as 75 pounds. All species of pumpkins, marrows and squashes are native to the tropical parts of the Western Hemisphere.

PYRITE, also called fool's gold, is an iron sulphide. It occurs as pale, bronze-yellow masses or as crystals. It is a brittle mineral with a green-black streak. Pyrite occurs in rocks of all kinds. It is found as concretions in sandstone, shale, slate, and coal. Pyrite is used in manufacturing sulphur dioxide and sulphur. It is common and worldwide in distribution.

Pyrite looks like the popular conception of gold ore. Genuine gold is rarely visible, is much softer, and has a yellow streak. Gold sometimes occurs in pyrite, but chemical tests must be made to determine its presence.

PYROXENES are a group of closely related rock-forming minerals. They are quite similar physically and chemically and are difficult to separate from the amphiboles. Pyroxenes crystallise at higher temperatures than amphiboles and therefore may form earlier in a cooling magma. If conditions are right, they may dissolve again later and recrystallise as amphiboles. Pyroxenes have two cleavages almost at right angles. Aegerite crystals are needle-like and green, black or brown. The mineral is found in sodium-rich igneous rocks that are low in silica, as in nepheline-syenite.

Pyrite, or 'fool's gold', is a compound of iron and sulphur with a brassy lustre.

crystal forms

PYRITE

Augite is found in four or eight-sided crystals that are black, dark green, or brown. It is found in igneous rocks of volcanic origin and also in metamorphic rocks. Spodumene is a white, pink, or green pyroxene mineral that occurs in pegmatites and granites. Diopside occurs in four or eight-sided prisms

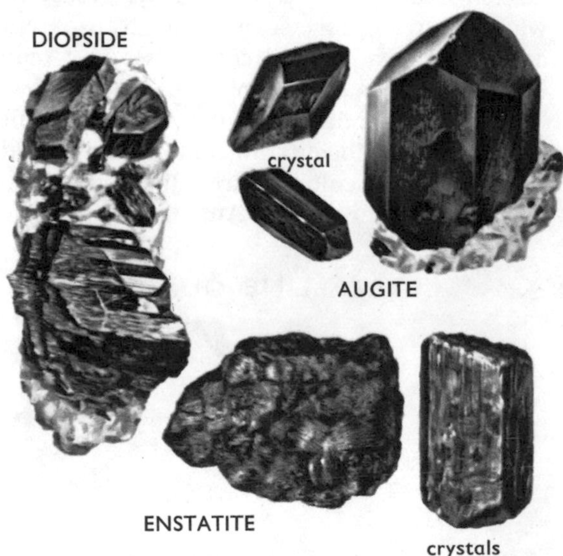

or as grains. It is white, grey, or pale green and is found generally in metamorphic rocks but also in calcium-rich igneous rocks. Enstatite grades from pale green to brown and yellow. It is found in leaf-like or compact masses in igneous rocks low in calcium and occurs also as a metamorphic mineral. Hypersthene is found in leaf-like masses, or grains, commonly in andesites. It is a black, dark brown, or green mineral. Jadeite is usually green and is found in metamorphic rocks. Good crystals are found in Norway, Sweden, Germany, U.S.S.R., Labrador, and the U.S.A., and may be used as gem stones.

QUARTZ, the most abundant mineral, forms in all kinds of rocks and veins and under varied conditions. Although there are many varieties of quartz, the mineral is easily identified. It is found in excellent crystals (up to several hundred pounds) and also occurs in masses and layers, as stalactites, or in globules like bunches of grapes. It has a shell-like fracture and a glassy, greasy or waxy lustre. Quartz can be as transparent as glass or opaque and colourless, or it may be black, white, or any colour of the rainbow.

Crystalline quartz, which is transparent or nearly so, occurs in many forms and colours. The colours are due partly to impurities in the quartz. Amethyst is a purple or lavender quartz. Good specimens are cut as gems. Among other varities are: cat's eye (grey, opalescent, and chatoyant – that is, showing a wavy or shifting band of light); citrine or false topaz (yellow); milky (white with a greasy lustre); rock crystal (colourless); rose (translucent to nearly transparent and pink); rutilated (needles of rutile in rock crystal); sapphire (blue); smoky (grey, grey-brown, or brown); star (shows a six-rayed star due to inclusions of fibres or tiny gas bubbles); tiger's eye (brown, red, green, or blue; fibrous and chatoyant, like cat's eye).

Cryptocrystalline quartz varieties have crystals too small to be seen with a microscope. They are translucent to opaque. They include the chalcedony group. Among them are agate (with banded or mixed colours), bloodstone or heliotrope (contains small spots of red jasper), carnelian (clear red or red-brown), chrysoprase (apple green), moss agate or mocha stone (moss-like inclusion), onyx (banded agate with straight layers usually black and white), plasma (bright green chalcedony), and sardonyx (red layers alternating with white or other colours). Other cryptocrystalline quartz varieties are

CRYSTALLINE QUARTZ

ROCK CRYSTAL ON DRUSY QUARTZ (crust of small crystals)

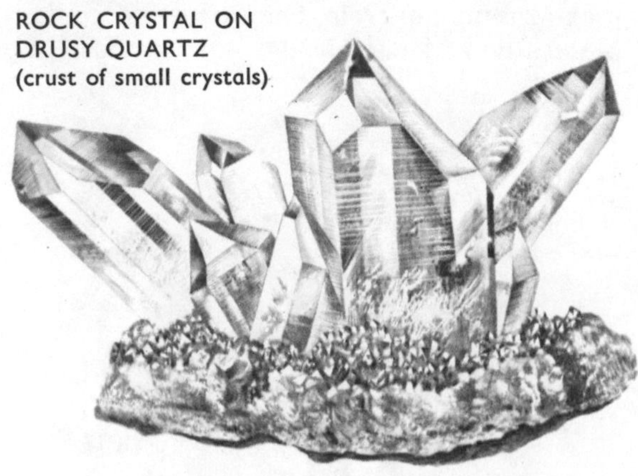

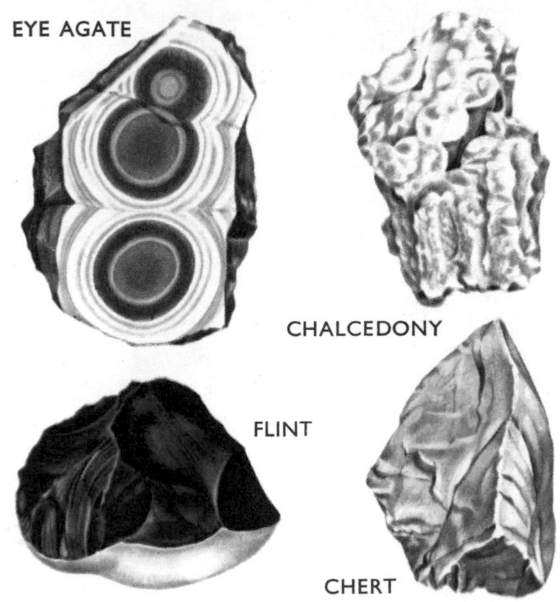

chert (opaque; white, grey, or brown), flint (translucent; grey, black, or dark brown), jasper (opaque; red, green, brown or yellow), prase (opaque; light green). Many forms also have unofficial local names.

Many rocks are composed largely of quartz. Most sandstones are almost totally of quartz grains cemented together by quartz. Quartzite is a metamorphosed sandstone. The building trades are the primary users of quartz today. Sandstone is a building stone, and quartz gravel and sand are used for concrete and plaster, glass brick and glass.

QUARTZITE is a metamorphosed sandstone so firmly cemented that it breaks smoothly across the grains rather than around them as in sandstone. Most of the sand grains are quartz, which is also the cementing material. Colours of quartzite are white, grey, pink, and red. Although it is the most durable rock known, quartzite has little use because it is difficult to shape unless favourable joint patterns have developed during the metamorphism. Hills and mountains in many parts of the world are formed of quartzite, as are many of the ledges, cliffs, and sharp peaks in the mountains of Scotland. A pink variety forms the cliffs to the back of Ullapool on the west coast.

QUATERNARY is a term used to describe the two most recent periods of time, namely the Pleistocene and the Recent and therefore the time during which we live today. The span represents about the last 2 million years of time.

The most distinctive feature of the Quaternary was the spread of continental ice sheets and glaciers in northern Europe and North America, in the Antarctic, and in such high mountain areas as the Alps and the Himalayas (see ICE AGES). In most areas there

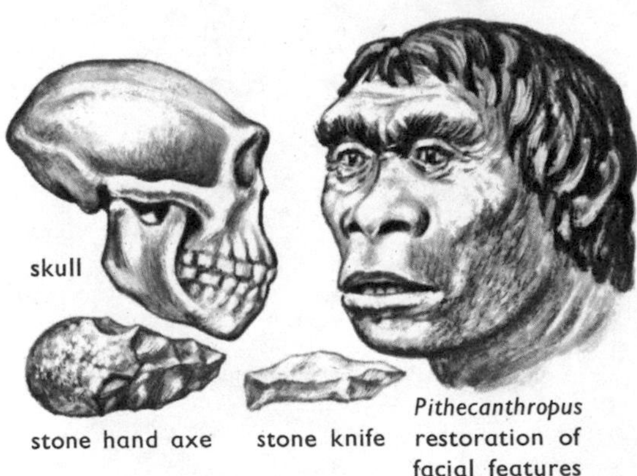

Primitive man appeared during the Pleistocene epoch of the Quaternary. Fossils of *Pithecanthropus*, the 'ape man', have been found in the Indo-Malayan region of southern Asia. Primitive tools have been found with the fossils, and because of these, *Pithecanthropus* is considered to have been more man-like than ape-like.

were apparently four distinct glacial episodes, each separated by a time of milder climate. Large quantities of water locked up in glaciers lowered the level of the seas. Glaciers scoured the Earth's surface, forming sharp mountain peaks and U-shaped valleys. Drift deposits from Pleistocene glaciers now cover much of Britain and northern Europe and North America. Courses of rivers were changed during the Quaternary, and rainfall increased in some areas.

Plants and animals were also affected by the glaciers. Many plants were destroyed as the glaciers advanced, but their descendants occupied the same regions again when the glaciers retreated. Arctic types of molluscs lived along the British coast. Numerous large mammals became extinct. Many modern mammals lived during Pleistocene times but their distribution was also controlled by the glaciers. Reindeer roamed in the tundra over parts of Britain and western Europe. Mammals, such as the Woolly Rhinoceros and the Woolly Mammoth developed heavy coats. But in warm interglacial periods lions, hippopotamuses, and hyenas, invaded the same areas.

The most important mammal that developed during the Pleistocene was Man. Chipped artifacts are found in Pleistocene deposits over most of Europe, and fossils of Man have also been found, although they are rare.

Glaciation, although it ended at slightly different times throughout the world, stopped generally 11,000 or 10,000 years ago. The epoch that followed — the Holocene or Recent — is marked chiefly by a different distribution of various animals and plants and by the rapid social evolution of Man.

The Woolly Mammoth (*Elephas primigenius*), 12 feet tall, was hunted by early Man.

Ruth Glacier on Mt. McKinley, Alaska, was once part of the vast ice sheet that covered much of the Northern Hemisphere in the glacial epochs of the Quaternary.

Steve McCutcheon

Pharmaceutical Society of Great Britain

Illustrated above are two types of cinchona bark from which the medicinal drug quinine is extracted.

QUINCE *(Cydonia oblonga)*, a close relative of the pear, is a small tree of Asiatic origin. It is widely naturalised in southern Europe. The two most common kinds cultivated for their fruit are the Portugal, and the Apple-shaped. These do well in southern England, but are best grown in moist soil. The fruit is too acid to be eaten raw, but when cooked it makes excellent fruit jelly and preserves. Quince is of minor commercial importance.

Selected types, especially Angers Quince, are propagated vegetatively (see PROPAGATION OF PLANTS) and are used as rootstocks on which pears are budded or grafted to produce dwarf, fruitful trees.

QUININE is a drug extracted from the dried bark of several species of *cinchona* trees. The trees are native to the Andes Mountains of South America but have been grown commercially in India, Jamaica, Java, and other parts of the world. Quinine was once the principal drug used in treating malaria, but synthetic drugs now available are less expensive and even more effective. While quinine kills the malaria parasites in the blood stream, it does not affect those in the tissues.

RADIO ASTRONOMY. Although radio waves from the Milky Way were discovered by Karl Jansky in 1932, radio measurements in astronomy were not common until after World War II. Now there are many radio observatories. Radio astronomy does not replace optical astronomy with its telescopes, spectroscopes, and cameras; it adds information that can not be obtained by optical instruments.

A radio telescope is a large antenna and connected to it is a radio receiver to collect radio waves rather than visible light. Some radio telescopes have shapes unlike optical telescopes; they are parabolic-shaped reflecting dishes made of sheet metal or wire mesh with a small collecting antenna at the focus. The largest 'dish' in operation – 250 feet in diameter – is at Jodrell Bank near Manchester. Other radio telescopes are large arrays of antennas, sometimes extending over large areas.

The radio astronomer records the strength of the noise his radio telescope receives to determine the radio 'brightness' of the object he is observing. Disturbances in the Sun's atmosphere produce great bursts of noise. Radio observations have also been used to measure the surface temperatures of the Moon and some of the planets.

Much of the observed radio radiation comes from broad regions of the sky, but there are also many 'point sources'. Some of these are remnants of old stellar explosions

Radio telescopes pick up even the faint emissions of radio waves from stars, galaxies and clouds of interstellar gas. Data gathered by these instruments has given us a better knowledge of the universe.

Keystone Press Agency Ltd

in the Milky Way, but others have been identified with distant galaxies. Of these, some are peculiar in form, while others may possibly be pairs of galaxies in collision — the most violent events in the universe. Some radio galaxies are such powerful radio emitters that they can be detected at greater distances than any other objects in the universe.

Barnaby's Picture Library

In some parts of tropical Asia the only river crossings are rattan bridges.

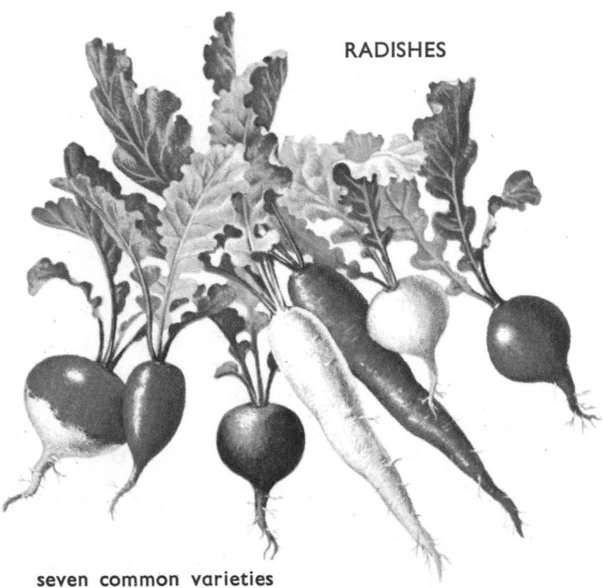

seven common varieties

RADISHES *(Raphanus sativus)* may be round or long; red, black, or white; and small to large. Some kinds grown in the Orient, weigh several pounds and are 2 or 3 feet long. Radishes grow rapidly, the most popular varieties producing their fleshy, edible roots within three to six weeks after he seeds are planted. They are eaten raw as a fresh vegetable and used in salads.

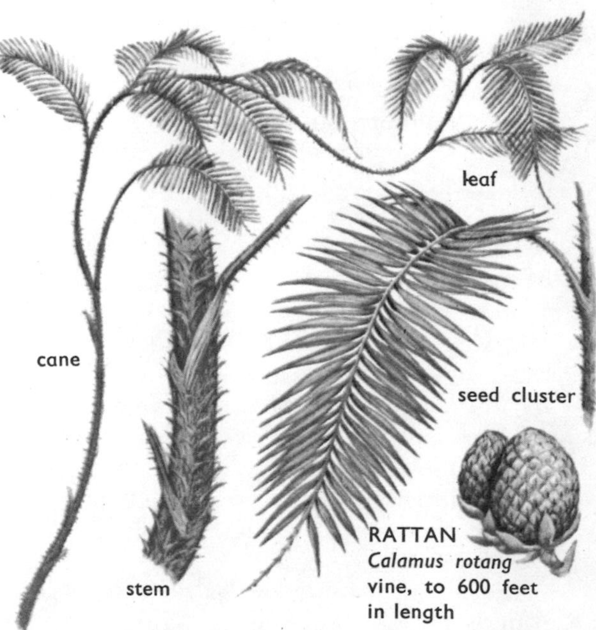

RATTAN *Calamus rotang* vine, to 600 feet in length

RATTANS are the long, slender stems of climbing palms (several species of the genus *Calamus*) native to tropical Asia. They produce numerous suckers from their base and climb in and out of forest trees for distances of 300 to 600 feet. The leaf tips of some species are as delicate as the tendrils of most climbing vines, but they are armed with short, steel-hard, curved spines with which they attach themselves to anything within reach. Large canes or stems are strong enough to be used as cables in making bridges or in tying the timbers of rafts together. Medium-sized stems are cut into strips; the pithy central portion is removed, and the hard flexible outer portion is used to make hats, bags, and chair bottoms. Smaller canes are used whole to make chairs, screens, baskets, and mats.

RED ALGAE contain, in addition to chlorophyll, a red pigment which gives them their name. Most kinds also have a blue pigment,

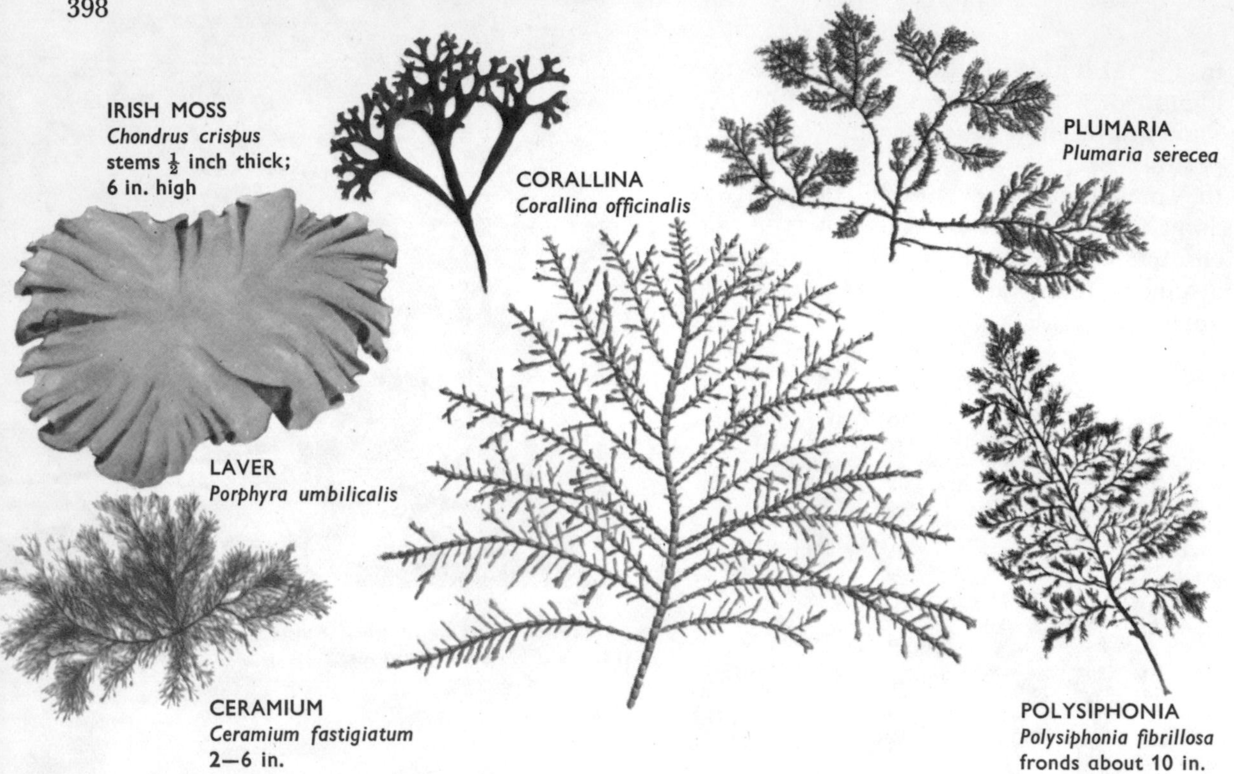

so their colour depends on which pigment is most abundant. Some are green and others are bluish-purple, although the majority are red. Nearly all of the red algae — about 4,000 species — grow in salt water. As red algae depend largely on blue and violet rays of sunlight for growth, they can grow both in shallow water and at a considerable depth — 100 to 200 feet down. Red algae are the most important group of algae used as food by Man. Agar, a gelatine used in biological research and in medicines, is manufactured from some species of the Orient. Irish Moss, Dulse, and Red Laver are among the kinds of red algae eaten in many regions of the world.

Many red algae grow as delicate plants. Among these is *Dasya*, a red, hairy branched species that grows along the Atlantic Coast of the U.S.A., down to the West Indies. *Gigartina* and *Gelidium* yield extracts. Laver (*Porphyra* spp.) grows in great rubbery pink sheets and is harvested for food, especially in Europe. (See ALGAE.)

In addition to these soft-bodied plants, a group of red algae called the corallines deposit lime or calcium carbonate. These plants feel stony and so are often mistaken for delicate corals. They are particularly common in coral reef areas of the tropics. *Lithothamnion* is important in forming and cementing together the coral reefs.

Red algae have complex life cycles. They produce several kinds of spores that float in the sea. In one type of reproduction, male cells fertilise the egg cell which remains attached to the parent plant. The fertilised egg then sprouts, produces a basket-like structure, and releases spores from the tip. Each of these spores eventually starts a new plant. (See CORAL REEFS.)

RHODODENDRONS (*Rhododendron* spp.) are flowering plants of more than 600 species, growing in all climates around the world. Some are low shrubs found above the timber line on mountain slopes; others are tall trees of boggy lowlands. Rhododendrons (ro-doe-DEN-druns) are most numerous in the Himalaya Mountains of southern Asia, but several kinds are natives of Europe. Wild rhododendrons growing in Britain produce a spectacular show of purple, red, pink or white flowers every spring.

Plant breeders have produced thousands of varieties by crossing the original wild kinds, many of which are also grown as ornamentals.

Gottscho-Schleisner

Rhododendrons are desirable shrubs for foliage alone, but are most famous for their spectacular blooms.

Azaleas also belong to the rhododendron group. Most cultivated varieties were produced by crossing species native to south-eastern Asia, especially India and China.

RHUBARB is one of the few plants in which the leaf stalks (petioles) are the part eaten. The leaves are mildly poisonous. Under favourable conditions, the succulent leaf stalks grow to a height of 3 feet. Rhubarb is often 'forced' in warmth to provide an early spring dessert. The most popular species grown commercially is *Rheum rhaponticum* and it does well only in cool climates.

RHUBARB
Rheum rhaponticum
to 3 ft.

RICE *(Oryza sativa)* is the main food for half the world's population. Many people of the Orient eat little else. About 95 per cent of the annual crop is grown in the Orient where the annual consumption ranges from 200 to 400 pounds a person. Rice has been grown in China for more than 4,000 years.

Many varieties of rice grow to a height of between 2–4 feet. Branched clusters of flowers mature into rice grains. Upland rice can be grown without irrigation, but is not as important as the more widely grown lowland rice, which needs a warm climate and abundant moisture for best growth.

Rice-growing in the Orient is still done with primitive methods, requiring much hand labour. Fields are flooded for 60 to 90 days as

Ernest A. Heiniger

Oriental methods of growing rice often involve hard labour for the whole family. These Japanese are terracing a hillside for rice fields or paddies.

RICE
Oryza sativa

polished grain

unpolished grain

Herbert Knapp

From India to Japan, the welfare of the people depends upon the success of the rice crop. Extensive systems of waterworks turn the countryside into vast lakes in the planting season.

the rice grows and are drained as soon as the rice begins to ripen. The crop is threshed by hand to separate the seeds from the heads. The rice is not polished for this removes the outer, more nutritious part of the grain. Rice is low in protein, therefore a rice diet should be supplemented by meat, fish or legumes.

A primitive method of threshing is to beat the plants against a frame, as this Japanese farmer is doing.

Fujihira-Monkmeyer

In the Orient, rice straw is used for hats, sandals and mats.

Wild Rice *(Zizania aquatica)*, an important food of the Chippewa (Ojibwa) and other North American Indians, grows wild in the wetlands of Minnesota and nearby lake regions. This cereal has never been cultivated. Wild Rice has somewhat longer, narrower grains than cultivated rice and is sold as a delicacy. It is not related to cultivated rice and has a very different flavour.

ROCKS are the natural materials that make up the Earth's crust. Rocks are usually thought of as solid masses such as granite or limestone, but they may also include such loose materials as soil, sand, clay, and gravel. Most rocks consist of one or more minerals. Coal and peat are formed of plant remains (see CARBONIFEROUS; COAL).

Based on their origin, scientists have set up three main classes of rocks: igneous, sedimentary, and metamorphic.

IGNEOUS ROCKS make up much of the foundation on which sedimentary rocks lie and from which sedimentary rocks originally came. Igneous rocks are formed from molten material beneath or on the Earth's surface. While still hot and liquid the material is known as magma. Radioactivity and the action of liquids cause hot spots where the rock is melted. Magma is formed from whatever materials are found at that location. Some magmas contain large amounts of silica and are thick and pasty like molten glass; others are rich in magnesium and iron and are more fluid. Highly fluid magmas can penetrate cracks and may move rapidly through them, spreading long distances. These magmas are exposed at the surface long after they have hardened. The action of wind, rain, gravity, ice, and streams wears away the rock closer to the surface.

Magmas gradually harden as they cool, and their gases escape. Large masses of magma deep beneath the surface may take

SOME EXTRUSIVE IGNEOUS ROCKS
(cooled at or near the surface)

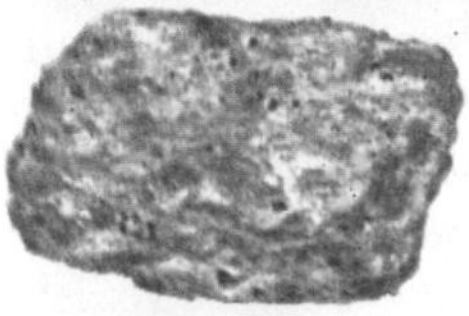

RHYOLITE

BASALT

OBSIDIAN

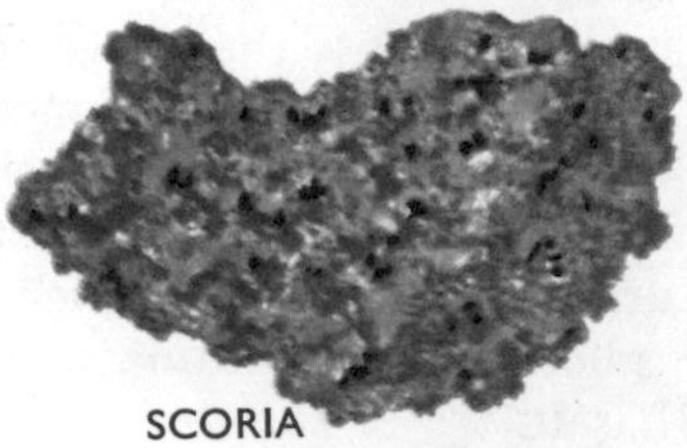

SCORIA

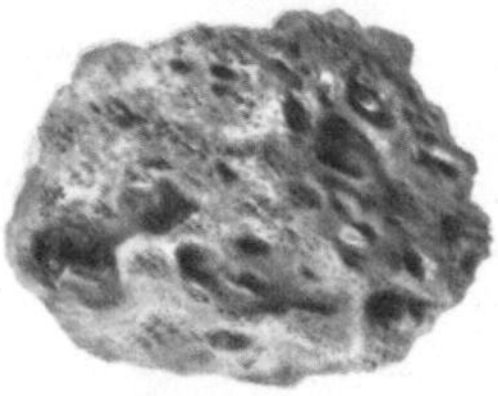

PUMICE

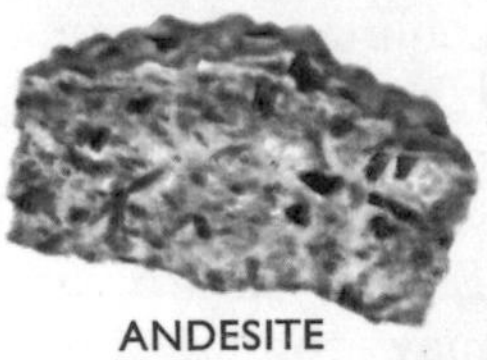

ANDESITE

SOME INTRUSIVE IGNEOUS ROCKS (cooled beneath the surface)

DIORITE

PEGMATITE

SYENITE

GRANITE PORPHYRY

GABBRO

PERIDOTITE

Magma and gases from the Earth's interior form igneous rocks as they cool. Magma spreading into older rocks in veins or large intrusions reacts with other rocks to form contact deposits, often in association with minerals.

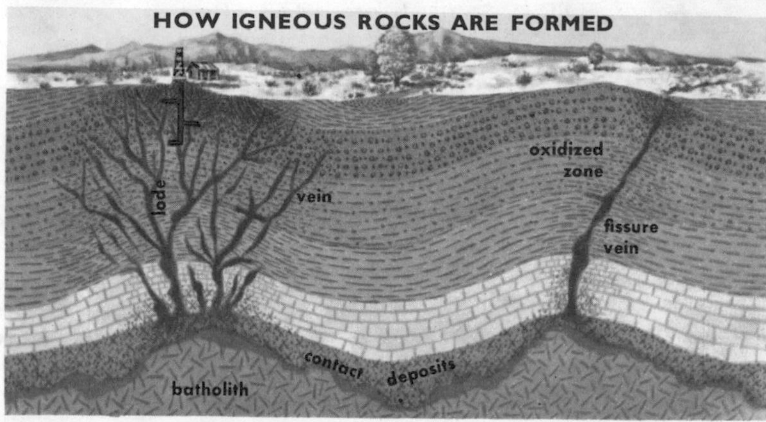

many thousands of years to cool. The longer the time for cooling and the more fluid the magma, the larger are the mineral crystals that form. Many magmas form rocks composed of crystals large enough to be seen with the naked eye. Those rocks in which the crystals are too small to be recognised without a lens are usually formed at or near the surface where cooling is faster. Glassy igneous rocks are those that have cooled too rapidly to form any crystals. Sometimes two sizes of crystals are formed and the rock is called a porphyry. The larger crystals (phenocrysts) are surrounded by much smaller crystals called the groundmass, often granite or basalt.

Rock formed underground by the slow cooling of magma is known as intrusive igneous rock. These may be large masses of paper-thin sheets. Large, irregular masses which cooled a mile or more beneath the Earth's surface are batholiths. A batholith may contain hundreds of cubic miles of coarsely crystalline igneous rock that has cooled over thousands of years. The batholith of Sierra Nevada, California, is 400 miles long and as much as 80 miles wide. The Leinster granite south-west of Dublin may be batholithic in origin as may be some of the granite masses of Devon and Cornwall. Since batholiths form at great depths, they are seen only where great uplifts and erosion have made them visible.

Laccoliths are lens-like or mushroom-shaped intrusions with a flat floor and arched roof. Laccoliths are smaller and occur closer to the surface than do batholiths. A lopolith is a similar formation reversed in shape — with a flat roof and down-warped floor. The older rock surrounding an igneous intrusion is referred to as 'country rock' and may be of any type. Its layers are usually warped to follow the lines of the intrusion.

Dykes and sills are sheet-like intrusions. Both are noted for uniform thickness over great distances — often tens of miles. Dykes — a few inches to several miles thick — cut across the structure of the country rock. Small dykes probably formed when magma filled and cooled in cracks and crevices; larger dykes result from huge wedges of magma that forced the older rocks apart. Sills are intrusions that run parallel to the surrounding rock, forming sheets between the layers of country rock. Irregular intrusions that swell, thin, twist, and turn are called veins. Dykes are common on the west coast of Scotland, on the Isles of Arran and Mull. The Great Whin Sill of northern England is famous and varies from a few inches to about 200 feet in thickness.

When magma comes to the surface, it is called lava, and rocks formed when lava cools are extrusive igneous rocks. Lava may come from fissures in the Earth's surface and spread over large areas. Lava plateaux,

Sills form parallel to sedimentary strata. An example is the Great Whin Sill of northern England.

Dykes, such as those exposed along the coast of the Isles of Arran and Mull in Scotland, are ridges of intrusive rock which cut through the sedimentary strata.

Batholiths (right) are large intrusions of igneous rocks.

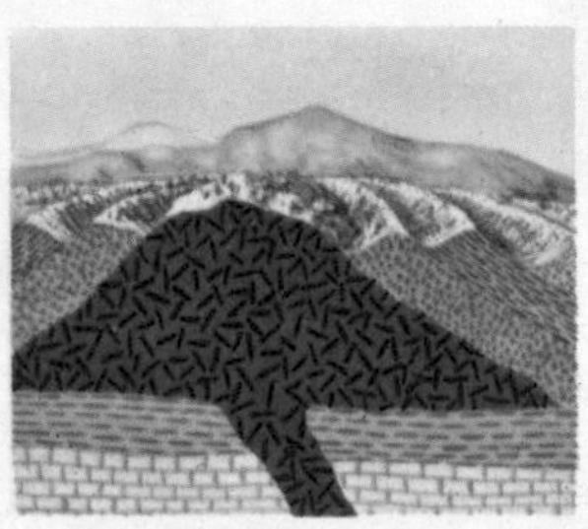

Laccoliths, common in western U.S.A., are domes of magma spread between layers of sedimentary rocks, lifting them as high as a thousand feet.

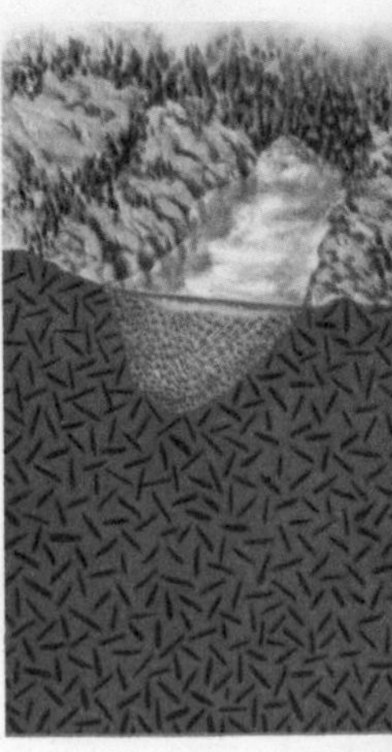

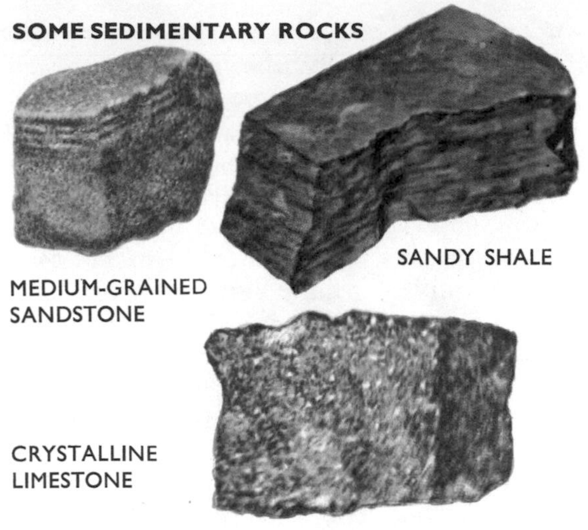

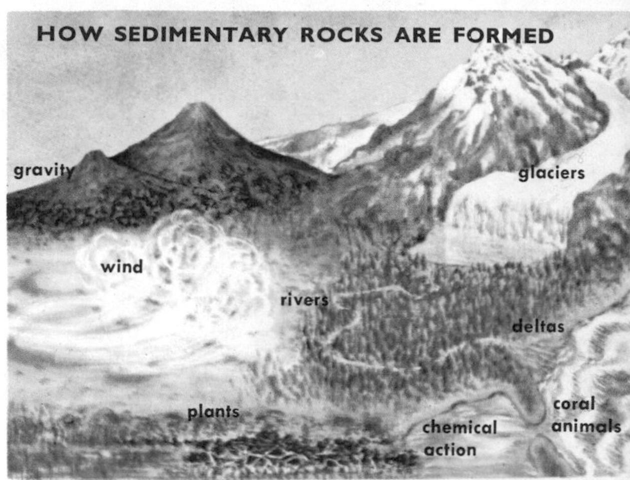

such as the Columbia Plateau of Washington, Oregon, and Idaho, may cover thousands of square miles. Lava from a vent may pile layer upon layer as shield volcanoes such as those that form the Hawaiian Islands. When volcanic eruptions are violent, the rocks are broken into pieces of varying size and hurled into the air. Lavas may be light or dark, glassy or grainy, solid or broken. Their appearance depends on their source, how fast and in what manner the material came to the surface and how rapidly it cooled. (See LAVA; VOLCANOES.)

SEDIMENTARY ROCKS are formed of materials that have been moved from their place of origin, usually by water, and deposited in a new location. Sedimentary rocks cover about 75 per cent of the Earth's surface. Most sediments are of marine origin, but some are deposited on the continents at the foot of mountains, in river valleys, and in lakes. They are formed from weathering of other previously formed rocks. Large rock masses are broken into boulders, pebbles, sand, or clay and are carried away by running water, ice, and wind. When these fragments stop moving, they settle in layers or strata. If they remain as loose mud or sand, they are known as sediments. Consolidated materials

SOME METAMORPHIC ROCKS

HORNFELS

GREY SLATE

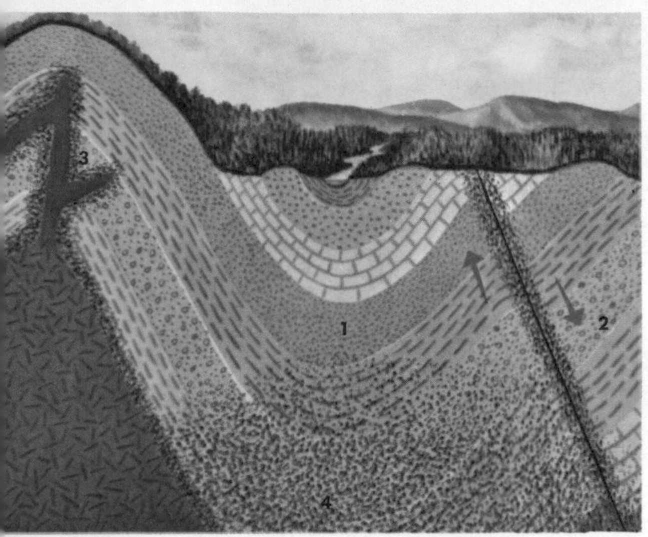

How Metamorphic Rocks Are Formed: (1) pressure and heat, due to depth; (2) crustal movements; (3) igneous activity; (4) percolating of mineral-bearing ground water, or penetration of rocks by gases and fluids from igneous rocks.

— those cemented by minerals like quartz, calcite, hematite, or limonite — are called sedimentary rocks. Conglomerate, sandstone, and shale are examples. Other sediments have been dissolved in running water and are deposited by evaporation, as are rock salt or gypsum. Others are deposited by chemical reactions, as are limestones.

Sometimes sedimentary rocks are pushed into folds or are broken across the layers by movements in the Earth's crust. If the fold is upward, it is an anticline. A downwarped fold is a syncline. Other movements cause joints (parallel fractures) and faults (breaks between blocks of rocks in which one is shifted in relation to the other). Anticlines are favourable traps for oil. Not all anticlines contain oil, of course, but if source beds (usually black shale) are nearby and there is a permeable, porous layer, oil may be stored in these natural reservoirs.

METAMORPHIC ROCKS are those that have been changed by heat, pressure, and liquids so that they are quite different from their parent rocks. All kinds of rocks — igneous, sedimentary, and even metamorphic rocks — can be changed. Small crystals may combine to form larger crystals, or various minerals may combine to form entirely new minerals. Generally the minerals are re-oriented to form bands perpendicular to the direction of the pressure applied. This results in foliation — the formation of leaf-like layers. Gneiss, a common metamorphic rock, always shows some banding or slight foliation. Often they are named after the parent rock, for example, granite gneiss. Schists are metamorphic rocks with such pronounced foliation that any rock readily splitting into slabs or sheets is said to show 'schistosity'. They are usually named after the principal minerals they contain. Minerals that form flat crystals, such as muscovite, biotite, chlorite, and talc, are prominent metamorphic minerals and are used in the names of the schists, as quartz schist and biotite schist. Other common metamorphic rocks are slate, marbles, quartzites, and some forms of granite. Slate is derived from shale, under great pressure. Marbles are recrystallised limestone, formed by heat and pressure. Quartzites were once sandstone. (See the Index for listings of various types of rocks described in separate entries.)

ROSES (*Rosa*) are the most popular flowers in the world. Historically, they have been favourites for more than 2,000 years. This means that roses have set a sort of endurance record in flower popularity — in spite of their thorny stems and branches — through much of temperate Europe, America, and Asia.

Roses admired centuries ago were quite different from those of today. They were smaller and had fewer colours, but the main difference is in the number of petals. Rose blossoms of long ago, as well as some of our modern ones, had only five petals. They were called single flower roses, and some of them were very beautiful.

Modern rose breeders have developed flowers with a large number of petals, making the flowers look bigger. These are called double or semi-double.

In rose blossoms, the extra petals were originally stamens. Compare the number of stamens in a double flower with the number in a single flower of the same kind. Chances are there will be many fewer stamens in a double flower. Semi-double flowers generally

Phot. M. Buzzini

have several layers of petals (instead of one) and a few stamens.

Roses are also popular because of their fragrance. Since ancient times, people have collected rose petals for perfume, rose water, and attar of roses.

Roses of about 200 species grow wild in every part of the world north of the equator except the tropics. Most wild kinds grow in moist places – even in swamps. Some do well in dry locations.

Some roses are climbers that cover fences and walls. Some can be grafted into so-called standard roses, and some grow into tall bushes. Others are dwarf-like. Many of the prettiest and longest-blooming kinds are tender and can be grown only in regions where the climate is mild. The rose is the national flower of England.

It takes about eight years to breed and reach a wide market with a new rose. Because of the mixed ancestry of modern roses the chance of producing one that is really outstanding is about 1:200,000.

RUBBER PLANTS yield a milky fluid called latex, which can be converted into rubber. Of more than a hundred kinds of latex producers, mostly trees and vines that grow in the tropics and sub-tropics, the most important is the Brazilian or Para Rubber tree *(Hevea brasiliensis)*, native to the tropical rain forests of the Amazon River basin in South America. From this tree, which is now grown on large rubber plantations in the Far East, comes most of the commercial natural rubber.

Long before Europeans explored the jungles of Central and South America, natives were using latex to waterproof their clothes and shoes. They even played with bouncing balls. They called the tree *cauchuc*, which meant 'weeping tree'. Joseph Priestley, the famous English chemist, discovered one of the earliest uses for latex in Europe – for erasers to rub out pencil marks. This gave the substance its name 'rubber'.

Crude rubber becomes sticky in hot weather and brittle in cold weather, and for these reasons rubber was not widely used until after 1839 when Charles Goodyear, an American inventor, discovered the process of vulcanisation. Goodyear heated raw rubber with sulphur, and the resulting rubber was stronger, more elastic, and unaffected by heat or cold.

For many years all of the world's rubber came from the trees that grow wild in the Amazon jungles. Crude and wasteful methods were used to collect the latex. In 1876, seeds of the Para Rubber tree were smuggled out of Brazil and planted in Kew Gardens, Surrey. The seedlings that sprouted were taken to Ceylon where they flourished, and from these came the great rubber plantations of Ceylon, Java, and Sumatra. Very

Ewing Krainin: Photo Researchers

Latex, flowing from cuts in the tree, is collected in cups.

little is obtained now from the native trees in the Amazon jungles.

Latex occurs in the twigs and leaves and also in a special tissue between the bark and the cambium layer in the trunk of the tree. As the latex-secreting tissue is not part of the tree's nutritional system, trees that are tapped correctly and carefully are not harmed.

To collect latex from a tree a series of diagonal cuts is made in the bark. The fluid flows freely from these cuts into a cup attached to the tree. Latex collected from wild trees is hardened by pouring the liquid over a wooden paddle which is slowly rotated over a smoky fire. A smoke-cured ball of rubber results. Plantation methods yield a higher quality and cleaner raw rubber. There the rubber is changed into a solid by adding an acid. It is rolled into sheets and cured in a smoke-house, then baled for shipment.

In wartime, scientists learned how to make synthetic rubber to take the place of the natural supply. Much of the rubber now used is made from butadiene and styrene, petroleum by-products.

Rubber has been obtained from many other plants, but none so far have been as productive as the Para Rubber tree. Guayule *(Parthenium argentatum)*, a desert shrub native to northern Mexico, was cultivated during World War II, when supplies of

Margaret Lang—Shostal

The sheets of crude rubber are first cured in a smoke-house and then dried on racks before shipment.

rubber from Asia were cut off. Russian Dandelions *(Taraxacum kok-saghyz)* not only give good yields but produce latex during the first year they are planted. The entire plant is harvested, and the latex squeezed from the roots. Thomas Edison produced rubber from Goldenrod (several species of *Solidago*), a common weed, but could not make the yields economically competitive.

S

SAGES (*Salvia* spp.) are a group of about 500 herbs and shrubs that grow throughout the world. Some are cultivated for their showy flower spikes, produced in summer, others for their aromatic leaves used as a seasoning. Garden Sage, a perennial native of southern Europe, is widely grown as a herb used in soups, dressings, and meats.

The popular, brilliant Scarlet Sage, a annual from Brazil, grows from 1 — 3 feet high. There are also lavender, pink, and white flowered forms. Another cultivated species is a blue sage from Mexico. All sage flowers are good honey producers, especially adapted for pollination by insects. (See FLOWERS.)

SALT. Common salt is sodium chloride ($NaCl$). Calcium, potassium, and magnesium are among the many other elements that commonly form salts.

Most salt is in the ocean where there is an average of about 2.35 per cent or about 3.5 ounces per gallon of water. Since salt is soluble in water, it is not abundant in soil where ground water circulates. Deposits of rock salt are found where water evaporated in the bays of ancient seas or in drainage basins.

No matter what the salt concentration is in the body fluids, it must be maintained within certain limits or animals die. This is generally accomplished by taking in salt with water or food and eliminating the excess. Higher animals eliminate salt by perspiration, tears, and urine. Some animals, such as marine turtles, lizards, snakes, gulls, petrels, and albatrosses, have a special gland around the eyes and nasal passages which extracts great quantities of salt. This allows them to drink sea water without harm. They convert

Most of the world's salt comes from mines. It was deposited on the floor of an ancient shallow sea as water evaporated.

Annan Photo Features

On this lake in Colombia, South America, workers rake up the salt from a natural salt lake and dry it in mounds.

the salt water into fresh water by getting rid of the excess salt through their salt glands.

Salt is a limiting factor in the distribution of both plants and animals. Most plants cannot live in salty soil, although many thousands of kinds do live in salt water. No animals live in the Dead Sea because of its high salt concentration, although many animals live in the inland Great Salt Lake, for example protozoans and brine shrimps.

Some animals can withstand considerable variation in salt concentration. Coral animals are very sensitive to changes in the salt content of the sea. Salmon and eels live part of their lives in sea water and part in fresh water. On the other hand, if water-dwelling animals are placed into distilled water which contains no salt, they die quickly because much of the salt from their fluids is lost into the water.

As a mineral, common salt is known as halite. Its use to season and to preserve foods is ancient. It is also important in industry.

Spiral evaporation pools (this one is in Lake Texoco, in Mexico) move the saltier water to centre pans, where the evaporation is completed and the salt harvested.

Compania Mexicana Aerofoto, S.A.

SANDALWOOD
to 25 ft.

SANDALWOOD, an oily, fragrant wood, comes from a small tropical evergreen tree *(Santalum album)* native to India. The wood is used for boxes, cabinet work, fans, and inlays. It is also used for carvings and is burned as incense in Buddhist religious ceremonies and at funeral rites. Distilled wood yields an oil used in perfumes.

Sandalwood leaves are thin and pointed. Clusters of small, straw-coloured to red flowers produce cherry-like fruits which turn black when ripe. The tree is a parasite, its roots attaching themselves by fleshy appendages to the roots of nearby plants. Most of the several hundred members of the sandalwood family grow in the tropics; some are found in temperate regions.

Fragrant, oily woods from trees in several other families are also known as sandalwood. Brazilwood or False Sandalwood *(Caesalpina echinata)* grows in tropical South America.

SANDSTONE is a sedimentary rock covering about 20 per cent of the Earth's land surface. It is made of consolidated sand that accumulated on beaches, in shallow waters, as sand dunes, or alluvial fans at the mouths of streams. Sand grains consist of rock and mineral particles. Most sand grains are quartz, a mineral which resists physical and chemical weathering. Other minerals present in varying amounts are feldspars, calcite, kaolinite, mica, and a small quantity of such heavy minerals as magnetite and garnet. The heavy minerals are often important clues to the origin of sandstones. Sands are commonly cemented with quartz, calcite, hematite, and limonite. Both the sand grains and the cements contribute to the wide variety of colours found in sandstones. Pure quartz or calcite sandstone may

In Monument Valley at the Arizona-Utah border, water and wind erosion has carved the sandstone into fantastic shaped cliffs and towers.

be white. Hematite (iron oxide) cements cause pink, red, and purple hues. Buff, yellow, and brown coloured sandstones are caused by limonite. Green usually indicates the presence of chlorite, but glauconite may provide the colour in greensand.

Sandstones form in layers of differing composition. Variations in the weather and differences in the impurities deposited with the sand caused variations in the appearance and thickness of the beds or layers. Sandstones may appear to be uniform in 10 or 20-foot thicknesses, but close examination shows that no beds are uniform for much more than 2 feet. Many sandstones are cross-bedded — that is, a layer of tilted beds between horizontal layers. A change in water currents caused this cross-bedding by altering the direction or steepness of a layer's slope as it was deposited. The tops of cross-bedded layers are usually truncated (cut off), while the bottoms merge into underlying layers. Wind and water also form ripple marks in sand. This often helps to determine the disposition of the beds.

Arkose is a variety of sandstone that contains more than 25 per cent feldspar. Greywacke is a grey sandstone that contains feldspar and enough dark minerals (hornblende, augite, biotite, and magnetite) to

David Muench

MEDIUM-GRAINED SANDSTONE

SANDSTONE, cemented by iron oxide

ARKOSE, showing feldspar grains

SANDSTONE, showing ripple marks

SANDSTONE with iron concretions

SARGASSUM OR GULF WEED *Sargassum* sp.

give it a grey colour. Grit is a coarse sandstone with angular quartz grains. Grit is used for millstones and small grindstones.

The shape and size of the sand grains and the amount of cement in sandstones determine its porosity (space between the grains) and its permeability (ease with which fluids can flow through the rock). Sandstones made of well-rounded grains of uniform size are more loosely packed and have more pore space than those composed of angular grains of many different sizes. Due to their high porosity (up to 30 per cent) and permeability, many sandstones are important sources for underground water. Many artesian well areas in Europe, Australia, and the United States originate in sandstones. Porous sandstones are also good reservoirs for petroleum, but the petroleum cannot be produced easily if the rock is not permeable. Sandstones are used as building stones and as flagstones. They are quarried for use locally but are rarely shipped great distances. Pure sandstones are used in the manufacture of glass. (See ROCKS.)

SARGASSUM or Gulf Weed. Many miles of this weed with its round berry-like floats are found in the Sargasso Sea off Bermuda, and great mounds of the weed are washed on to beaches. Most sargassum, which is a collective name for more than 150 species of brown algae, grow attached to the bottom of shallow tropical seas, and the little floats hold the plants up to the surface where they get additional sunlight. When the sea becomes rough, the plants are torn free and are carried by the currents. Some species spend their entire life cycle floating at the surface.

SATELLITE is the astronomer's word for a moon. Only Mercury, Venus, and Pluto, in our planetary system, are without satellites. Mars has two satellites, Jupiter twelve, Saturn ten, Uranus five, and Neptune two. These satellites revolve around their planets just as our satellite, the Moon, goes around the Earth. The outer planets could easily have other small satellites that have escaped notice because they are so faint and far away from us.

Satellites vary in size from the little 10-mile chunks of rock that circle Mars up to

Jupiter has twelve satellites, or moons. Four of the largest can be seen with binoculars. They move at varying distances and speeds from their mother planet and in constantly shifting relationships.

Jupiter's two largest satellites, each of which is larger than the planet Mercury. Four other satellites are about as large as or larger than our Moon, but our Moon is the only satellite that remotely resembles its parent planet in size. Orbits of satellites also differ widely. Phobos goes around Mars in less than eight hours and to an observer on Mars it would appear to cross the sky from west to east. At the other extreme, the outermost satellite of Jupiter has an orbital period of more than two years. Four satellites of Jupiter, one of Saturn, and one of Neptune are unusual in that their motion is opposite in direction to everything else in the solar system (see SOLAR SYSTEM).

Satellites are barren. Only Saturn's Titan has an atmosphere. Many satellites of Jupiter and Saturn seem to be ice-covered, but the rest are bare rock. (See ARTIFICIAL SATELLITES.)

SATURN, the second largest planet, has a diameter of 75,000 miles or nine Earth diameters. Saturn's mass of 95 times the Earth's is surprisingly little considering its large volume. As its average density is less than that of water, Saturn must be made of

Saturn's rings are probably fragments of ice, held in place by the balance between the centrifugal force of rotation and the restraining pull of the planet's gravitational field.

Tilting of the planet's axis gives us a changing view of the flat, thin rings that circle Saturn's equator.

very light material — probably hydrogen and helium compressed to a solid by the tremendous pressures inside the planet. We never see the surface of Saturn because of its dense, cloudy atmosphere probably composed of hydrogen and helium, plus some of the poisonous methane and ammonia gases.

Saturn is the sixth planet in distance from the Sun. Its average distance from the Sun is 886 million miles or $9\frac{1}{2}$ times the Earth's distance, and it takes $29\frac{1}{2}$ years to circle the Sun. Saturn receives so little sunlight that its temperature is about minus 157 degrees centigrade (250 degrees Fahrenheit below zero). Despite its great distance, Saturn is a conspicuous object in our sky.

The unique feature of Saturn is its system of rings, which form a nearly continuous disc in the plane of Saturn's equator. They begin about 9,000 miles from Saturn's surface and have more than twice the planet's diameter. The ring system is extremely thin — about 10 miles thick — and seems to consist of three parts. The middle ring is brightest and widest and is separated from the outer ring by a dark gap about 2,000 miles wide. This dark gap is known as the Cassini division, discovered in 1675 by an Italo-French astronomer. A much less distinct gap separates the middle ring from the inner one. The inner ring is very faint and hard to see. It does not show up on most photographs.

We see Saturn's rings better some years than others. The planet's equator and the whole ring system are inclined to its orbit by 27 degrees. So at two points in Saturn's $29\frac{1}{2}$-year orbit we are 27 degrees above or below the plane of the rings and see them very well. When we look along the plane of the rings, we can hardly see them at all.

Saturn's rings consist of a swarm of small solid bodies, probably bits of ice. No large body can exist so close to Saturn, because of the planet's strong tidal forces. We do not know whether the rings are a broken-up satellite or just material that was too close to Saturn to be gathered into a single satellite. Saturn's ten satellites are well beyond the edge of the rings, but the innermost satellite affects the rings gravitationally. Its disturbances are responsible for the gaps in the rings. (See PLANETS.)

Central Office of Information

The seas around the British Isles can be very dangerous and lifeboats are often called upon for help.

SAXIFRAGES (*Saxifraga* spp.) grow wild in temperate or cool regions throughout the world. About 20 kinds grow in Great Britain, mainly in woodlands or in mountainous areas. Some are alpine plants found on high rocky peaks. Many of the hundreds of dainty-flowered species are well-suited for rock gardens. In fact, saxifrage means 'rock breaker'.

One showy saxifrage is grown as an ornamental. Beautiful pink flowers appear above its cluster of large leaves each spring.

Hydrangeas are members of the same family, as are currants and gooseberries (see BERRIES).

SEAS cover about 70 per cent of the Earth's surface. They vary from shallow waters of the Arctic Ocean to great depths in the Pacific where man has descended in the bathyscaphe to depths of seven miles.

Less than a century ago the floor of the sea was believed to be a vast, smooth plain, barren of life and bathed in total darkness. From deep-sea soundings we know now that in some places the ocean floor is more rugged than our continents, with great canyons and towering mountain ranges with peaks higher than Mount Everest. One of the largest ranges is the Mid-Atlantic Ridge. We know, too, that life swarms in oceans from the surface to the greatest depths sampled by man.

Waters of the seas are never still, even on the calmest day. In the Southern Ocean (also called Antarctic Ocean) below Cape Horn, great ocean rollers sweep round the world uninterrupted by land. In the North Pacific and the North Atlantic, great seas whipped by winter winds batter the coastlines of Britain, Canada, Washington, and Oregon, sometimes destroying shipping in their path, and damaging the dykes. In summer these same seas are nearly still.

The salt content of the sea has changed little in millions of years. In the open ocean it is nearly constant at 35 parts of salt by weight to 1,000 parts of water. Near the poles where ice melts during the summer, the surface water may be less salty — even brackish. In the Red Sea, where the water is surrounded by land, the salinity may rise to 42 parts per thousand, but in most areas of the sea, except in bays, near river mouths and similar places, the salinity changes little except seasonally.

The temperature of seas varies from about — 2 degrees centigrade (28 degrees Fahrenheit) at the bottom and near polar ice floes to about 30 degrees centigrade (86 degrees Fahrenheit) in the tropics. In most temperate and tropical oceans a layer of warm water

Laurence Lowry/A. Devaney

Lighthouses are designed to withstand waves that may bury them in water.

overlays the cold waters of the ocean depths. This layer is comparatively shallow near the equator where it is only 300 feet deep. This upper layer, where sunlight penetrates, teems with life and also strongly affects the climates of many countries. Sea water holds heat from the sun far longer than the atmosphere does, and a loss of even a small amount of heat from the surface layers of the sea will raise the temperature of the mass of air above by as much as a thousand times. This explains why the coast of Europe has comparatively mild winters, for the air reaching the continent has passed over the warm waters of the Gulf Stream.

Sea water contains nearly every known element in solution. The gold and silver it contains would make every person on Earth wealthy — if it were possible to extract these metals cheaply. Oxygen for respiration is present everywhere in the open ocean. Phosphates and nitrates, the fertilisers of the sea, are scarce in some areas, while in others storms and upwellings bring them up in great enough quantity to cause 'blooms' of plankton. These maintain the ocean fisheries at high levels. Pressure in the sea increases by one pound per square inch for every 2 feet in depth. Pressures at the bottom of the sea are enormous by surface standards, but the bodies of animals living at these depths are modified so that they are unaffected.

LIFE IN THE SEA. The seas are considered to be the ancient home of most life. Sea water is very similar in composition to the blood of marine animals. Indeed, many small forms of life do not have an internal blood system but depend on constant bathing in sea water to furnish oxygen for their cells and to carry away wastes. Sea water has about the same density as the organisms that live in it and therefore supports swimming and drifting life that lack skeletons. Also, sea water is filled with an abundance of food. Minute drifting plants are the meadows of the sea for small animals that filter their food from the water.

Life is more concentrated in the upper layers of the sea where sunlight penetrates and plants can grow. Sunlight penetrates with sufficient illumination for plant growth to depths of only a few hundred feet.

The sea is home for the smallest and largest of animals. Single celled animals, often microscopic in size, abound. The Giant Squid, largest of the invertebrates, and the Blue Whale, largest of the mammals, have the sea as their habitat.

Phot. Jacques Bauguet

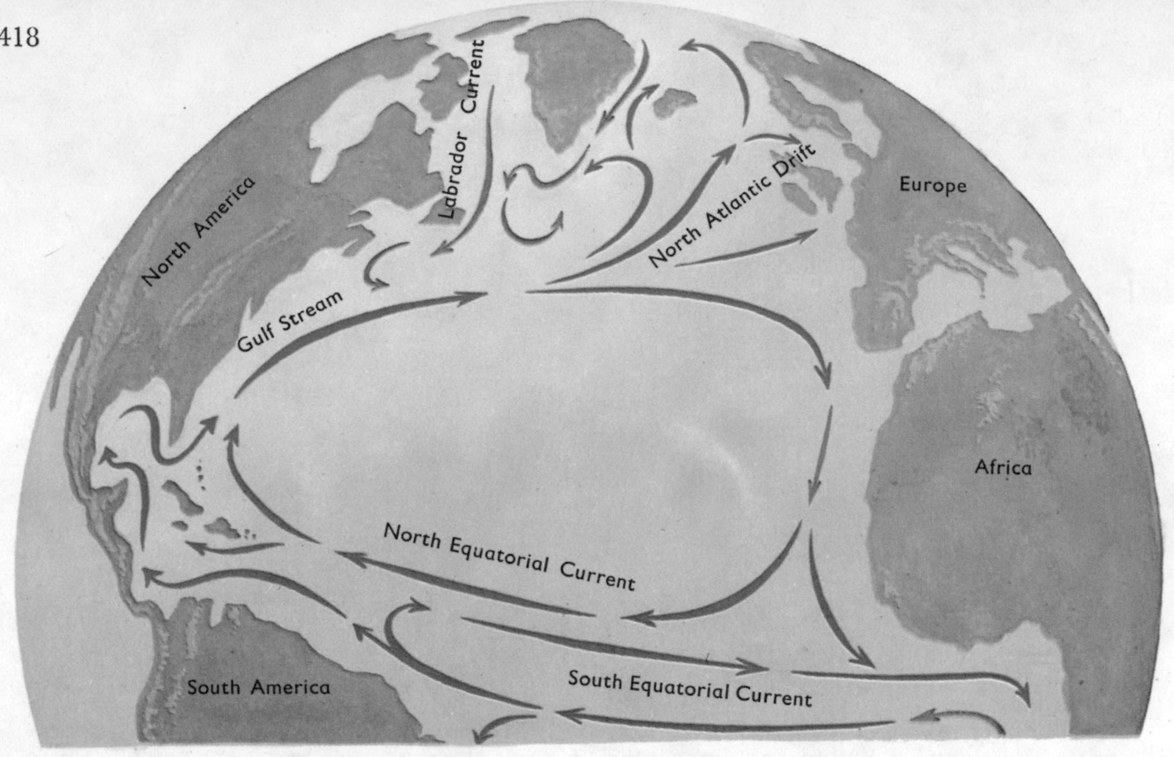

All the currents of the North Atlantic are part of a tremendous system of recirculation. The rotation of the Earth modifies the prevailing winds, and the trade-winds move the waters westward just north of the equator.

CURRENTS in the sea are caused by strong winds such as the south-east and north-east trade-winds, by differences in water density, and by the effect of tides and local winds. Currents along the shore are primarily set in motion by local winds and the tides. In the open ocean some currents are so great they become actual rivers within the sea. The North Atlantic circulation, for example, originates in the Atlantic between Africa and Brazil where the north-east trade-winds drive the water westwards. Part of it enters the Caribbean Sea and then the Gulf of Mexico, and since the water level is slightly higher than in the Atlantic, the water flows swiftly out through the Florida Straits at about 4 miles per hour. North of the Bahamas, the current slows and spreads out. About opposite New York it turns eastwards as the Gulf Stream. West of Ireland the current divides into a northerly Norwegian Current which bathes the coasts of Britain and Scandinavia and then flows into the Arctic Ocean. The main branch, the Canaries Current, flows southwards into the trade-wind region to complete the circle.

The Kuroshio, a similar current, occurs off Japan. Other great ocean currents are the Brazil Current off Brazil, Humboldt or Peru Current off the west coast of South America, Algulhas Current off South Africa, and California Current off western North America.

Currents are important means of transportation for marine life. In the Northern Hemisphere, the water currents tend to move towards the right while in the Southern Hemisphere they tend to turn to the left. This is due to the rotation of the Earth.

Winds push the water forward. They give each wave a rolling motion, causing it to break on the beach.

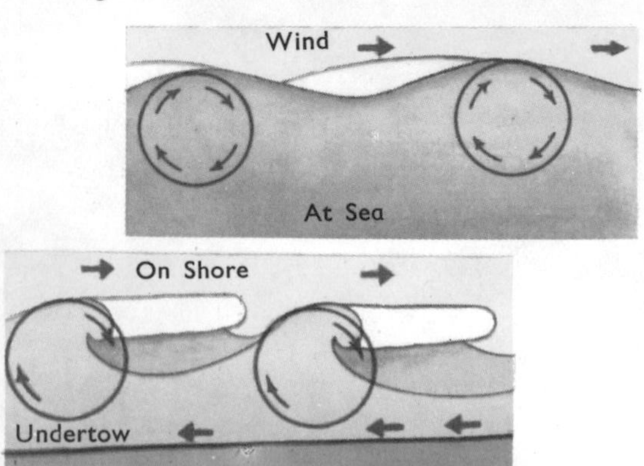

TIDES are noted on shore as a vertical rise or fall in the level of the sea. They are caused by the Sun and Moon, which pull the seas towards them. Because the Moon is much nearer the Earth, its pull is greater than the Sun's.

When the Sun and the Moon are in a straight line with the Earth, their pull is greatest and spring tides occur. These tides have nothing to do with the time of the year. The rise and fall in the sea is greatest then. When the Sun and the Moon pull at right angles, they tend to counteract their pull. Tides are then at their lowest, and are called neap tides.

Since two tidal waves occur, one on each side of the Earth, and the Earth rotates every 24 hours, there are in most places two high tides and two low tides every 24 hours. In some areas, such as parts of the Gulf of Mexico, there is only one high and one low in each daily cycle. The height or range of tide depends on the latitude and the form of the land. In tropical oceanic islands, as at Key West, Florida, the tidal range is only about 1 foot, but on the French channel coast there may be a 30-foot difference between high and low tides. The greatest known range is 54 feet, which occurs in Minots Basin, on the coast of Nova Scotia.

WAVES are caused by the action of the wind on the surface of the sea. Only ripples form when the winds are gentle, but as the wind increases in force the ripples become wavelets, then full waves, and finally great breakers that roar ashore along coasts.

The height and length of a wave is determined by three things: the force of the wind, the length of time it has been blowing, and the distance the wave has travelled. Some of the largest waves are caused by storm centres hundreds of miles away.

Large waves crash on to the shore with a force equalling many hundreds of tons. They can injure marine life and tear up breakwaters or scour the land. Ocean waves sometimes reach a height of 45 feet. An ocean wave grows in steepness as it comes ashore, the shallow water forcing it up and slowing it down until the wave peaks up and falls forward as a breaker. Long waves called tsunamis are caused by submarine earthquakes. Fortunately they are rare, for they move at speeds of hundreds of miles an hour and can be up to 200 feet high. Tsunamis (so-called tidal waves) that swept the shores of Hawaii and Japan in 1960 originated in earthquakes thousands of miles away in Chile.

Rock pool

SEASHORE LIFE. Because of the many kinds and forms of material, such as rocks, sand, mud, crevices, holes, and rubble, the seashore offers a far greater variety of habitats for animals and plants than does the open ocean. Many kinds of life that flourish along coasts cannot live far out at sea. The richness of life along seashores makes them the favourite collecting places for most students of biology.

Life on the seashore is subject to many drastic changes during a tidal cycle. When the tide is high, shore life is covered by water and often pounded by breakers. When the tide is out, the life is exposed to drying winds, to the sun, and to flooding with fresh water during rain storms. Plants and animals that live along the seashore must become adjusted to such changes. According to the need for sea water and ability to live exposed to the air, shore life is separated into zones from sea depths exposed only on extreme low spring tides to above the high tide mark. Life in the upper zone is dampened only occasionally by waves or by the fine spray and mist that nearly always occur along the beach.

Pounding seas on rocky shores, exposure to the air, shifting sand along exposed beaches, and mud and sand carried by the water have caused many changes in form and way of life of seashore plants and animals.

Keystone Press

Where conditions will allow, surf-riding is an immensely popular sport.

Marine biologists have made an interesting observation about rocky shores in many parts of the world. At low tide the shore is often divided into distinct bands of colour. These zones can be used as a measure of shore-life distribution up and down the beach and are a clue to how well animals and plants are adapted to exposure to the air.

ROCKY SHORES. Rocks offer a firm, unchanging surface to which animals and plants can cling. Numerous holes, cracks, and crevices become hiding places in which to avoid enemies and to be protected from waves. Most rocks are found on exposed shores and food is abundant for animals living there.

During storms, large waves may tear the animals and plants loose from the rocks. Algae cling to rocks with their 'holdfasts', and the dome-shaped shells of barnacles and snails help to protect them from the force of the waves.

Even life in tidal pools experiences many changes. On a hot summer day the Sun evaporates the water until it turns to brine. A thin crust of salt may form across the pool. Or during heavy rains, the water may turn fresh.

SANDY SHORES. Except for broken and dead shells, sandy shores show little evidence of life. However, an experienced observer can nevertheless find an abundance of living things along a sandy shore, though less than on rocky shores. The sand offers no hard surface to which living things can cling. During storms, the sand is often carried great distances by the waves. Algae cannot grow on sandy shores except on dead shells or pieces of rock.

Exposure to sun and air affects sandy shore dwellers just as it does rock dwellers, but it is overcome in different ways. In shallow, sandy bays and around inlets, eelgrass and turtlegrass may form great marine meadows, fastening to the bottom with their extensive root systems. These great green pastures offer refuge to a large variety of animals.

MUDDY SHORES are characteristic of protected bays and lagoons. They contain large amounts of decaying plant and animal remains mixed with fine particles of silt and clay. Walk across a mudbank at low tide and bubbles, accompanied by the odour of rotten eggs, rise from the mud. This is caused by sulphide gases released from decaying matter. Just below the surface there is little oxygen; only those bacteria that can live without oxygen can survive.

Mudflats are economically valuable. They support vast populations of edible clams, and are feeding grounds for many species of game and commercial fishes when the tide is in.

In regions where mud and sand meet, living things are most abundant in the sea. Where sand and mud meet along the continental shelf an abundance of fish is often found.

FOOD CHAIN IN THE SEA. All animal life in the sea depends either directly or indirectly on plants for food. Only plants can assimilate the nutrient salts (mainly nitrates and phosphates, but many others in small amounts) and in the presence of sunlight convert these into living tissue.

Positions of the Sun at sunrise, noon, and sunset in middle northern latitudes at the mid-point of each season.

Studies of shallow, tropical grass flats have shown that these marine meadows produce as much food per acre as does an acre of cultivated sugar cane. It is believed that the amount of food manufactured in the open sea by tiny plants called phytoplankton is about the same as in average grasslands on shore.

Seaweeds growing attached to shore rocks or hard areas beneath the surface of the sea are only a fraction of the plants of the sea. They are limited to the narrow band of shoreline and cannot grow below the zone of light penetration. Most plants growing in the sea are so small they cannot be seen with the naked eye. They are single-celled algae, drifting in the upper layers of the world's oceans. This layer may be several hundred feet thick in tropical seas; in polar seas, only a few feet thick. In this narrow zone, phytoplankton manufacture food by photosynthesis. Only very small animals can feed directly on these small plants, filtering them from the sea through some sort of network or screen. These small plant eaters, mostly copepods and other small crustaceans, are in turn eaten by both large and small carnivores. Arrow-worms, often not much more than an inch long themselves, feed heavily on copepods and other types of zooplankton.

Large animals also feed on these plant-eating copepods. Practically the only food of the Atlantic Herring is a small copepod that flourishes in tremendous numbers in northern seas. The largest of these filter feeders is the Blue Whale, which attains a length of more than 100 feet. The whale barges through the sea with its mouth wide open, scooping up vast quantities of water at a time. Then it closes its jaws and squirts the water out through the baleen, which forms a feathery, bony strainer in its jaws. It eats the plankton left behind. The Basking Shark, one of the largest of living fishes, also feeds in this manner. Food chains may be involved and long, however, with many animals from small to large eating each other.

When the animals die, they decompose. Bacteria convert their flesh into nitrates and phosphates, and the cycle is complete.

SEASONS. We are not absolutely sure how the weather will change from day to day, but in the temperate zones we can be sure that part of the year will be hot and part of it cold. In this region we divide the year into four seasons. In spring it gets warmer; in summer, hot. In autumn it gets cooler; in winter, cold.

The seasons change gradually. Spring comes earlier in southern areas than farther north. Also, seasons are different at different latitudes on the Earth. Near the equator

Because of the tilt of the Earth's axis the length of day varies with the season.

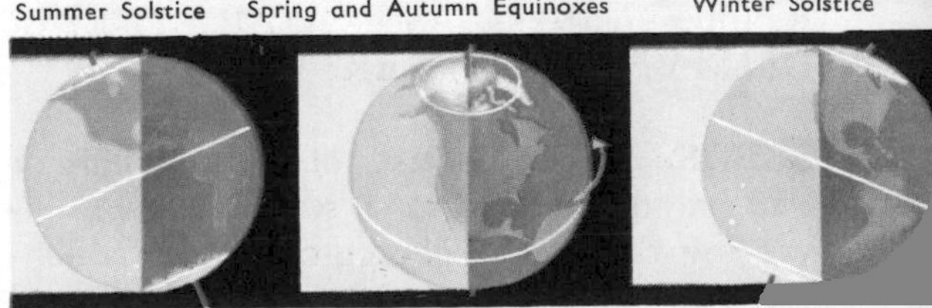

there is no summer or winter, though there may be a wet and a dry season. In the southern parts of the Southern Hemisphere, the seasons are the opposite of those in the Northern Hemisphere. It is hot in January, and cold in July.

Seasons are caused by the Earth's axis being inclined at about 23½ degrees, and as the Earth orbits the Sun, its axis always points in the same direction. In June the North Pole is leaning towards the Sun, so in the Northern Hemisphere the Sun is at this time high in the sky and its rays are more concentrated on the Earth's surface. Days are much longer than nights. In December the North Pole is leaning away from the Sun, and the Northern Hemisphere receives less sunlight. The days are short, and the Sun is low in the sky so that the sunlight is spread thinly over the Earth's surface. The seasons in the Southern Hemisphere are just the opposite.

In the Northern Hemisphere the Sun is highest in the sky on June 22. That day, called the summer solstice, is the longest in the year; its night is the shortest. The Sun is lowest in the sky on December 22, the winter solstice. This is the shortest day of the year, and its night is longest. Day and night are each 12 hours long on March 21, the vernal equinox, and on September 23, the autumnal equinox.

The Northern Hemisphere receives the most sunlight on June 22, but this is not the hottest time of the year. So much sunlight is received then that the Earth continues to get hotter for another month. July is hotter than June. For the same reason December 22 is not the coldest day of the year. The coldest time comes about the end of January.

If the Earth's surface was of uniform composition, season and weather would be interchangeable terms. As it is, the different rates of heating of air over land and water masses create local conditions which are responsible for the often unpredictable weather patterns. (See ATMOSPHERE; CLIMATE; WEATHER; WINDS.)

SEEDS. A seed consists of a tiny plant or embryo derived from a sexual process involving the fusion of egg-cells and pollen-cells, and is surrounded by a supply of food to nourish it until it is large enough to make its own. These parts are covered by a hard coat which bursts when the seed germinates.

Seeds germinate when moisture and temperature conditions are suitable and if the seed has passed through its period of natural dormancy. In temperate regions many seeds produced in the autumn do not sprout until spring. If conditions are suitable, however, they may germinate sooner. Seeds may also remain dormant for several seasons if kept dry.

As soon as a seed sprouts the embryo plant begins to develop roots and leaves. Until it turns green, however, it is nourished by food

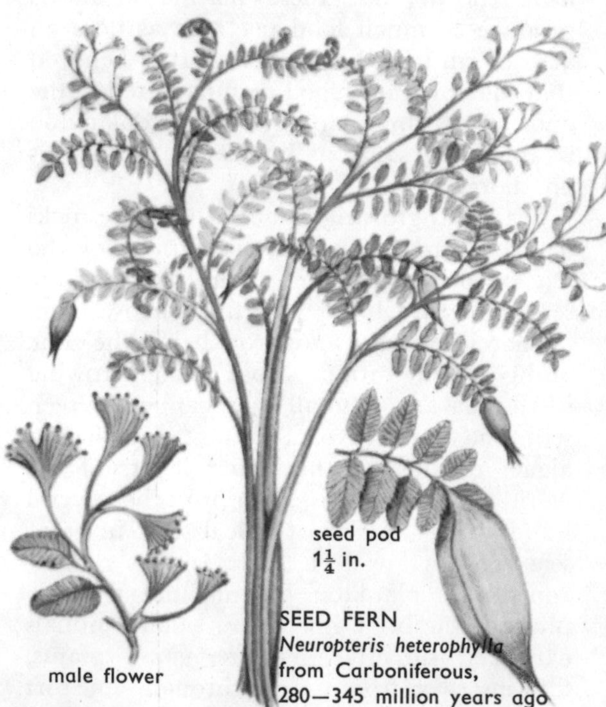

SEED FERN
Neuropteris heterophylla
from Carboniferous,
280—345 million years ago

stored in the seed leaves (cotyledons) or a special adjoining tissue (endosperm). Some cotyledons remain below the ground; others are pushed above the ground where they turn green and become the new plant's first leaves.

Seeds are distributed by various methods. One of the most common means of seed dispersal is the wind. Seeds of aerial orchids, for example, are very tiny and easily blown by the wind from one aerial perch to another. Seeds of dandelions, thistles, and milkweeds have hairy plumes and drift with the slightest

Union Pacific Railroad

One Giant Sequoia can contain 600,000 board feet of timber, enough to build 300 three-bedroom houses.

breeze. Poppy seeds, which are small and hard, stay in the dried seed container, with holes in its top like a salt shaker, and when the wind shakes the plant the seeds are thrown some distance.

Other seeds, such as those of cleavers, have hooks or barbs and cling to hair, fur, or clothing. They may be carried long distances before being dropped. Or seeds that drop in the mud may be picked up on the feet of birds or other animals and transported to spots far removed from the parent plant. One experimenter grew more than 500 plants from about seven ounces of mud scraped from the feet of a flock of wading birds. Still other seeds are eaten by birds or other animals along with the fleshy fruits that surround them. The seeds pass unharmed through their digestive tracts and are dropped in spots away from the parent plants.

Waterlily seeds float in the water until they catch in the mud and germinate. Other seed pods, such as those of geraniums, explode

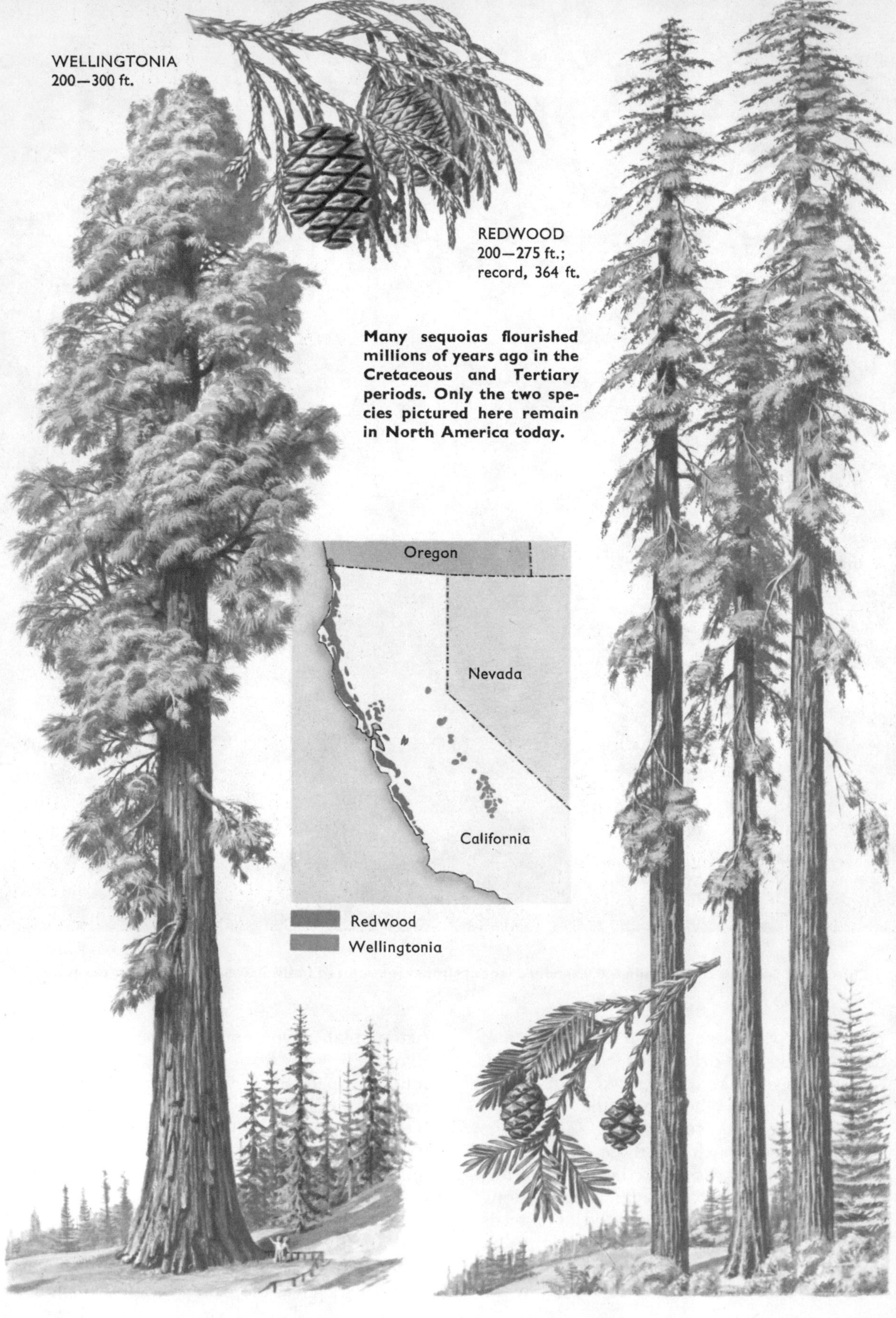
WELLINGTONIA
200—300 ft.
REDWOOD
200—275 ft.;
record, 364 ft.
Many sequoias flourished millions of years ago in the Cretaceous and Tertiary periods. Only the two species pictured here remain in North America today.
Oregon
Nevada
California
Redwood
Wellingtonia

when ripe and scatter seeds over a wide area.

Floating coconuts are sometimes carried long distances by ocean currents. The winged seeds of sycamore and ash are whirled away from the parent tree by the wind. Witch-hazel seeds are thrown several feet from the tree when the ripened seed pods split and eject them. (See DISPERSAL.)

SEQUOIAS are famous for their tremendous size and age. Their name honours a Cherokee Indian who developed an alphabet in the language of his people. Fossils of some of the 40 species that grew in many parts of the Northern Hemisphere about a million years ago can be seen today in the petrified forests in the western United States. Only two kinds of sequoias now exist in North America. These are the Wellingtonia *(Sequoiadendron giganteum)* and the more widespread Redwood *(Sequoia sempervirens)*.

The Wellingtonia is found only in groves at altitudes of 4,000 to 8,000 feet on the western slopes of the Sierra Nevada in central and southern California. The Redwood grows only in the 'fog belt' along the south-western Oregon and northern California coasts where the climate is moist and mild. Both are evergreen trees. Leaves of the Redwood are flat and needle-like with pointed tips; the smaller leaves of the Wellingtonia are pointed scales which overlap at their bases. Both trees have woody, oval cones. Cones of the Wellingtonia are thicker and twice as long (2—3 inches) as those of the Redwood.

The Wellingtonia is larger than the Redwood in overall size and reaches a greater age, but the Redwood is the taller of the two. The largest Wellingtonia is the General Sherman tree in Sequoia National Park. Nearly 4,000 years old, it is more than 30 feet in diameter at its base and 272 feet high; its estimated weight is over 6,000 tons. Largest living Redwood is the Founder's Tree near Dyerville, California; it is 364 feet high and 15 feet in diameter. Both species have been planted as ornamentals in Britain.

Several other members of the sequoia family grow in China, Formosa, North Borneo, and Tasmania. Metasequoia, once thought to be extinct, was discovered growing in China in 1948.

SHALE is formed of mud, clay, or silt consolidated into a firm, fine-grained sedimentary rock. Because shales are deposited as soft muds, they sometimes show impressions of raindrops or the footprints or trails of animals. Shales cover about half of the Earth's land surface. Unlike clay, most shales will not soften when soaked in water. They are commonly brittle or flake easily; those containing quartz are quite hard. As the number and size of quartz grains increase, shales grade into sandstones. In most shales

the particles are so small they cannot be seen even with a lens. X-ray analysis reveals that shales are composed of several clay minerals: muscovite, chlorite, calcite, and limonite. Flaky mica particles usually lie flat. The many thin layers or beds of shales tend to split parallel to their bedding. A few shales are white. They are usually grey, black, red, brown, or green. Rounded calcite and limonite concretions are often found in shales.

Shales are used in the manufacture of pottery, bricks, tiles and sewer pipes. They are also used in the manufacture of refractory bricks especially if the alumina content is high.

Shales that contain petroleum are known as oil shales. Oil is distilled from oil shales in Europe, China, Australia, and Africa. There are immense reserves of oil shales in western United States, where at present it is still more economical to draw oil from wells.

Silurian oceans teemed with invertebrates, the largest of which was the Giant Sea Scorpion pictured above

SILURIAN. This period of the Palaeozoic began about 440 million years ago and lasted about 45 million years. Its name comes from *Silures*, a Celtic tribe that lived in Wales where these rocks were first described. Silurian animals resembled those of the Ordovician although they were of different families and genera. Silurian marine invertebrates included corals, brachiopods or lamp shells, sea lilies, trilobites, and ostracods, all of which were common in sandstone and limestone deposits. Graptolites are found in black shales. Some sea scorpions that lived in estuaries reached a length of 9 feet. Primitive fishes also existed in the Silurian period, and the oldest known land plants appeared. (See PSILOPSIDS.)

On the land, forms of life similar to modern scorpions and millipedes appear to have been the only representatives of the animal kingdom. Present evidence is too scanty to determine if either of these were truly air-breathing, but it can be assumed that they were somewhere in the process of evolution in that direction. These early creatures were no larger than their present-day descendants.

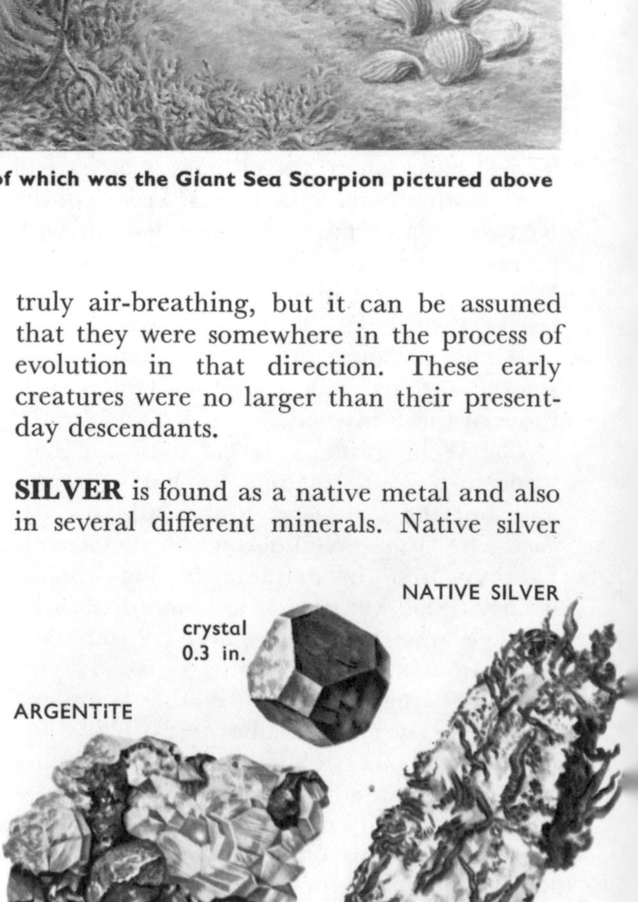

SILVER is found as a native metal and also in several different minerals. Native silver

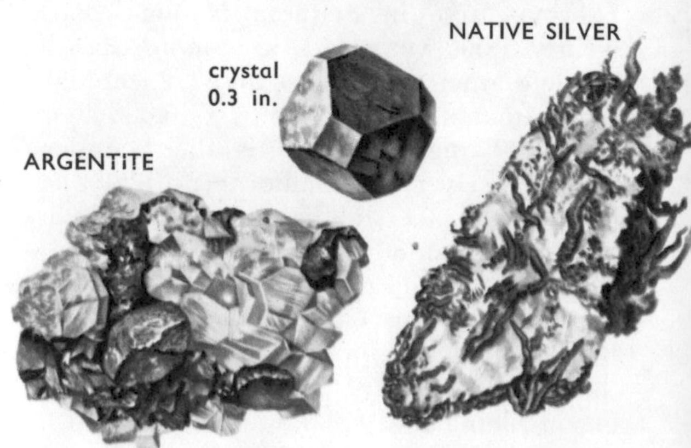

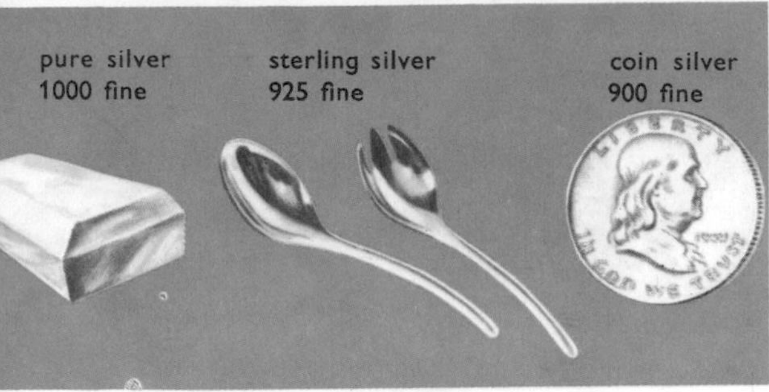

occurs in irregular masses up to 750 pounds in weight. It is found also as scales and wire. Less commonly it is found as crystals. The metal is silver-white but tarnishes black quickly. It is easily shaped by pounding or can be pulled into wire. It is soft enough to be cut with a knife. Silver is widely distributed in hydrothermal veins spread through other rocks, or as a secondary mineral. In some areas it has settled from flowing water as placer deposits.

Argentite is a silver mineral, a compound of silver and sulphur. It occurs in compact coatings or masses that are metallic lead-grey in colour but tarnish to black quickly.

Silver has long been a favourite metal of craftsmen, for it is easily worked. These belts, bow-guards, and hatbands were made by Navaho Indians, who learned their art from the Spanish silversmiths.

Indian Arts Fund

Cerargyrite is a secondary mineral found as waxy-grey masses that become black on exposure to light. Pyrargyrite occurs as compact masses or crusts. It has a bright lustre and is dark red or black with a purple-red streak. Proustite, found as compact masses and crusts, is translucent to transparent and scarlet in colour and streak.

Since before written history man has used silver for utensils and ornaments. Today most silver is used for coins and to back up paper currency.

Large amounts are used also in photography. Many silver compounds decompose on exposure to light, then a developer is used to reduce the decomposed compound to silver again. The remaining sensitive silver compound is dissolved away by a fixer, and the result is the negative from which pictures (positives) can be made. Sterling silver (7.5 per cent copper) is harder than pure silver and is used for jewellery, insignias, novelties, and cutlery. Silver plate is pure silver on a base metal. Silver solders and brazing alloys are used in joining pipes and for electrical connections. Silver salts are used as astringents, caustics, and antiseptics. Silver metal with mercury is used in dental fillings.

Silver minerals are widely distributed, but the largest deposits are in the Western Hemisphere — in Bolivia, Honduras, Mexico, Canada, and the western United States. Mines are also located in Norway, Germany, the U.S.S.R., Japan, Philippines, and Australia.

SISAL is a hard fibre extracted from the long, narrow, pointed leaves of the Agave or Sisal Plant *(Agave sisalana)*, a native of Mexico and Central America. The leaves grow to a length of 40 to 50 inches and are ready to be harvested for the first time two to six years after planting. More leaves grow, and the harvesting is continued for six to ten years until the plant flowers and dies.

Scraping wheels are used to remove the pulp from the leaves. The fibres are then washed, dried, baled, and graded. Sisal fibres are primarily manufactured into binding twine and other types of cordage. Most of the sisal marketed in the world is grown in Mexico, Haiti, East Africa, East Indies and the Philippines.

Sisal leaves are harvested by hand, and only lower leaves are removed. The tips are hard and sharp.

W. R. Donogho-Shostal

SLATE is such a fine-textured metamorphic rock that its minerals can only be seen with a microscope. Common minerals in slate include quartz, biotite, chlorite, graphite, hornblende, and kyanite. The usual colours are black, grey, red, or green. Slate breaks readily into thin sheets. Slate was formed from shale by heat and pressure as these rocks were tilted, folded, and squeezed during mountain building. Their minerals are re-oriented or re-combined to form new minerals. Their small crystals have their greatest length perpendicular to the folding. This gives them their slaty cleavage, called foliation. The same sort of cleavage is found in schists. Slate usually cuts across the bedding of the original shale. Continued pressure and heat change slate to phyllite (a slate with minerals large enough to give the rock a shiny lustre) and finally to schist. In addition to its slaty cleavage, slate usually has closely spaced cross joints along which it breaks into blocks, too small to be of use.

Slate is soft and therefore it can be cut easily, yet it has good strength and durability. Most slate is used for roofing. Shingles are hand split from sawn blocks. Exceptionally

Because slate is found near the surface, it is quarried from open pits like this one near Caernarvon, North Wales.

Central Press

large blocks of slate were used for blackboards. Other uses of slate include electrical panels, steps, floor tiles, table tops, vats, and wall veneer. About three-quarters of the slate is wasted in quarrying and processing. Costs are therefore high, but slate competes favourably with substitutes because it is so durable. The ground-up waste is often used as a coating on roofing paper and asbestos shingles. Recently, waste slate has been ground to a slate flour, then pressed into sheets of synthetic or 'recomposed' slate for blackboards and instrument panels. Slate flour is used also as a filler in paints. Some waste is substituted for shale in the manufacture of Portland cement. Slate is found in shield areas and mountain regions. Because slate is found on or near the surface, it is quarried from open pits rather than mined. The slate quarries of North Wales are well known.

John Strohm

Customs of Indian families in rural Guatemala have changed little since the days of their Mayan ancestry.

SNAPDRAGONS (*Antirrhinum* spp.) once grew wild in the Mediterranean region. Many cultivated varieties are now grown in gardens throughout the world. Their flowers range in colour from white or yellow to orange, brown and red. There are also tall (3 feet), medium (2 to 2½ feet), and dwarf (1 to 1½ feet) types. Snapdragons are easy to grow and in mild climates live from one year to the next, but plants older than one year are particularly susceptible to Antirrhinum Rust. Rust-resistant strains are now available.

When a bee alights on the lower lip-like petal of a snapdragon flower its weight forces the petal down and beneath the opening is the inside of the blossom. Shortly the bee, laden with pollen, pushes its way out and flies to another flower.

Snapdragon flowers resemble a dragon's head. The seed capsules look like tiny skulls.

The tall, graceful flower stalks, densely covered with velvety blooms, are favourite cut flowers for bouquets.

SOCIAL BEHAVIOUR OF MAN. Of all animals, Man has developed the most complex social organisation. Often his behaviour patterns are so elaborate that their relationship to his basic needs, which are the same as those of all other animals, is completely obscured. Man has improved on the environment provided by nature, and this complex man-made environment is called culture. Culture determines the way a man lives his daily life — the kinds of food he likes, the style of clothes he wears, the entertainment he prefers, and the education and type of work available to him. It includes the tools, ideals, rules, customs, and knowledge by which he guides his life and also the language that he learns to speak. All peoples, from primitive tribes to progressive nations, have complex cultures through which most of their members lead satisfying and orderly lives. Culture is learned by being part of a society that transmits its knowledge, language, and standards to its members.

FAMILY AND KINSHIP. Man lives in family groups, as do many other animals. Customarily, the family group consists of the parents with their children. Outsiders normally enter the group only through marriage. In some cultures, the woman marries into her husband's family, joins his tribe and either lives with his relatives, or, as in Western civilisation, takes his name. In others, the man may leave his home to live with his wife's relatives.

Members of a family usually share the same home and contribute to feeding and clothing all who belong. The young receive from their family the basic training in the way of life that forms the culture of their society.

In many parts of the world, greater importance is given another kind of family — the family of blood relatives. In some cultures, the father does not support his own children. Rather, he supports his sister's children, who are his blood kin. His children, in turn, are supported by his wife's brother. While these people recognise the family group of husband and wife, it is the family of direct bloodline descent that owns the land and governs the raising of the young.

Among many peoples, the idea of blood relationship or kinship is elaborated into the clan, which is a group composed of all those families who claim a common ancestor. Marriage between members of the same clan is usually prohibited. Frequently clans hold property in common and are united by strong bonds of loyalty. Often, among primitive peoples, a supernatural being resembling a familiar animal, plant, or other natural object is accepted as the original clan ancestor and becomes the totem of the clan. Totems are always respected, and clan members may be prohibited from injuring, killing or eating any living representatives of the totem, under the penalty of severe punishment.

Metropolitan Museum, Rogers Fund, 1919

Egyptians believed the Cow Goddess Hathor (above) watched over beautiful women. Horus the Hawk God protected the reigning pharaoh in life and battle. (XVIII and XXX dynasties.)

MARRIAGE. In all societies of man, there are rules that determine how men and women may live together and raise their children. In Western civilisation, it has become the general custom for those of marriageable age to find their mates. Formerly, choices were limited. Royalty could marry only into royalty. Even among commoners there were strict social strata within which marriage was permissible. The custom of 'giving the bride' is a relic of the days when parents did give their daughter away.

In many non-Western societies today, marriage is thought to be principally the

Canadian National Railways

Totem poles of the North-west Coast Indians trace the family myths of the chief for whom the pole was carved. Each figure represents an animal totem.

business of the two families who are joined by the alliance. Such matters as family, position, and wealth are considered more important than the individual choice of the boy and girl, who often do not see each other before their marriage. In these societies, a marriage arranged in this manner is just as normal as is courtship in Western civilisations.

In every society there are rules about who may be married to whom. Marriages between close relatives, such as brother and sister, are forbidden universally. In India, one may marry someone of his own caste but may not marry anyone born in his own village.

Most peoples of Europe and America insist that a marriage be between one man and one women. This type of marriage is called monogamy. Many non-Western cultures permit plural marriages. Usually these allow one man to have several wives (polygyny), but in a few societies a woman may have more than one husband (polyandry). Both types of plural marriages are referred to as polygamy. In still fewer societies group marriages occur, with several husbands and several wives making up the marriage unit. Group or plural marriages are usually controlled by the economic conditions in the society. In polygyny, a man is allowed to have only as many wives as he can support, or in the opposite situation a woman may be permitted more than one husband only if one husband is not able to support her. In practically all societies marriages may be broken through the process of divorce.

MYTHS. Every human society possesses stories about its origin and past. Often these stories attempt to explain how things came into being: the Earth, the gods, the sky, animals, and Man himself. When such stories are not based on historical fact, they are called myths. Folk tales are stories passed along by a people from generation to generation. They are the 'literature' of people who do not have writing. Myths are stories which go back to an imaginary or mythological time and deal with gods and other supernatural beings and events. Mythology is closely linked with religion, yet its stories may have been invented to provide entertainment.

Myths provide explanations of the seeming miracles of Man's existence and the wonders of the natural world. They give a people pride in the great and heroic deeds of their ancestors and inspire their descendants to do similar deeds of greatness.

MAGIC is Man's way of trying to influence supernatural forces to work for him. Few if any peoples have lived without belief in supernatural powers, and practically all have had ceremonies designed to enlist the help of these powers to aid them in gaining their desires. Ways of working magic vary from repeating a few special words to going through a long series of actions or rituals. Both words and actions must be carried out exactly as custom demands or the magical spell is believed to have no value.

It seems likely that some of the cave paintings of animals done by Old Stone Age men were intended to give a magical control over the animals portrayed, perhaps to make them more plentiful. In many early civilisations, kings were believed to have the supernatural power to make seeds and fields fertile. Magical rituals may also be practised at certain seasons of the year. Most primitive societies, for example, have ceremonies in late December, when the days are shortest, to make certain that the weakened sun will recover its lost strength and shine strong again.

In many societies demons of disease are driven from their victim by means of charms and dances. Magic strings are tied around an ill person's wrists, neck, or body to ward off aches and pains. In one society an arrow that wounds a man is carefully cleaned and wrapped in damp leaves to make the wound heal more rapidly.

When magic is used to do evil to another person, it is called black magic or sorcery. One common type of black magic is for the

Morris dancing is one of the oldest and best-known English village ceremonies. It is usually performed at Whitsuntide and celebrates the conquest of spring over winter.

Picturepoint Ltd

sorcerer to make an image of the victim. This charmed or cursed image is then mutilated. The victim is supposed to feel the pains of the torture, and if the sorcerer wills it, may die. There are many recorded cases of persons dying as the result of sorcery; believing he is doomed, the victim loses his will to live.

As Man gains greater control over nature through science and machines, he feels less and less need for magic. Science is magic's greatest enemy. Magical practices live on, however, especially in matters where chance, fate, or luck are present. People of all civilised countries still practise magic to some extent.

Belief in the terrible power of black magic is not limited to primitive early Man. In Salem, Massachusetts, people believed so strongly in the power of black magic that hundreds of persons were arrested as witches in 1692. Nineteen of them were hanged and one was tortured to death. Such devices as fortune-telling cards, ouija-boards, and books interpreting dreams are still current in the most advanced countries of the world.

Many forms of magic are recognised today as superstitions. Touching wood to ward off evil is traceable to the magic of the Druids, tree-worshippers of ancient Britain. Crossing one's fingers, fear of the number 13, refusing to cross the path of a black cat, avoiding stepping upon cracks in pavements, and many other common superstitions are relics of magical systems. Today, however, magical practice in its extreme of life-and-death importance is confined largely to undeveloped countries.

Navaho Indians still make sand paintings as part of healing ceremonies for members of the tribe.

Museum of Navaho Ceremonial Art — New Mexico

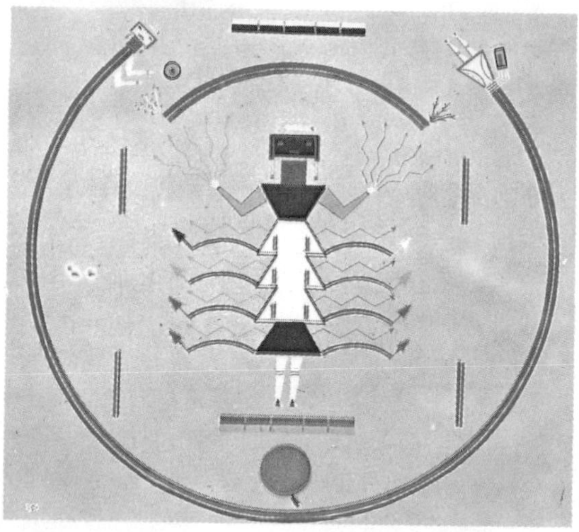

J. Allan Cash

A witch-doctor, or medicine man, explains some of his wares to a potential customer.

CEREMONIES. All societies of Man insist that certain actions be carried out in accordance with traditional procedures. Ceremony puts order and solemnity into a situation so that people remember the event and its significance. By joining together in ceremony, group members are more strongly linked in loyalty.

When ceremonies deal with matters of great solemnity, especially those having magical or religious meaning, they are often called rites, or rituals. Many societies, including our own have always surrounded important events with ritual — for example, the ploughing of fields, setting out on a journey, launching a ship, planting and harvesting crops, naming a baby, marrying, and entering adolescence, old age and death.

Societies vary greatly in the amount of emphasis placed on the different milestones in the course of life. In some, puberty is accompanied by great celebration, as the child is now ready for its role as an adult. The same society may regard marriage as a contract between two people but one of no interest to the society as a whole. In others, puberty is unmentionable, and marriage is a most important social event.

RELIGION. Every society of Man, in all ages, has had some form of worship, including ritual, prayer, or sacrifice, and occasionally all three. These acts represent Man's attempt to communicate with the forces of creation. The many religions in the world are evidence of the great variety of religious theory.

Religion is often one of the most important cultural influences in a society. The concept of the Golden Rule, which is shared by many religions, is a powerful influence on the conduct of members of societies. The doctrine of the Day of Judgement, with its promise of retribution for evil and reward for good, is of unquestionable importance as a civilising influence. Religion is a great power in controlling the moral behaviour of people in all societies, from the simplest tribal level to the most highly complex civilisation.

Faithful Moslems face Mecca, where their religion was founded, and pray at dawn, noon, and sunset. This is a mosque in Morocco, on the North African coast.

Paul Hufner — Shostal

The largest of the major faiths is Christianity, based on the teachings of Jesus of Nazareth. The more than 840 million followers of Christianity are divided among the Eastern branch, led by the Eastern Orthodox Church, and the Western branch, formed of the Roman Catholic Church and the many Protestant sects that appeared during the sixteenth century. The Eastern Church is strongest in the Middle East and was the state church of Czarist Russia. Europe is the traditional stronghold of the Roman Catholic Church, which was spread with the wave of European migration to Spanish, Portuguese, and French settlements in the New World. The many Protestant churches have assumed primacy in Britain, Scandinavia, and other regions of northern Europe or in the lands colonised by them.

Over 400 million people are followers of the religion founded by Mohammed. Believers are called Moslems, Muslims, Islamites, or Mohammedans. The prophet Mohammed lived in Arabia between A.D. 570 and A.D. 632. He wished to see the world return to the religion taught by Abraham of the Old Testament. From Judaism he also took his ideas of a single God and of life after death.

Judaism developed from a code of ethics of a wandering desert tribe. It became the religion of the Semitic people who settled in the Land of Canaan, now Israel, some 2,000 years before the birth of Christ. Both the people and their faith flourished until 586 B.C., when the Babylonian Empire engulfed the smaller nation and dispersed its peoples. Since that time, members of the faith have spread their worship to all the corners of the Earth.

Hinduism, which also had its beginnings more than 2,000 years before Christ, is the

Religious experiences and doctrines of the world's major faiths are inscribed in holy books. These volumes form the foundations for the teachings of the religious leaders of their respective faiths.

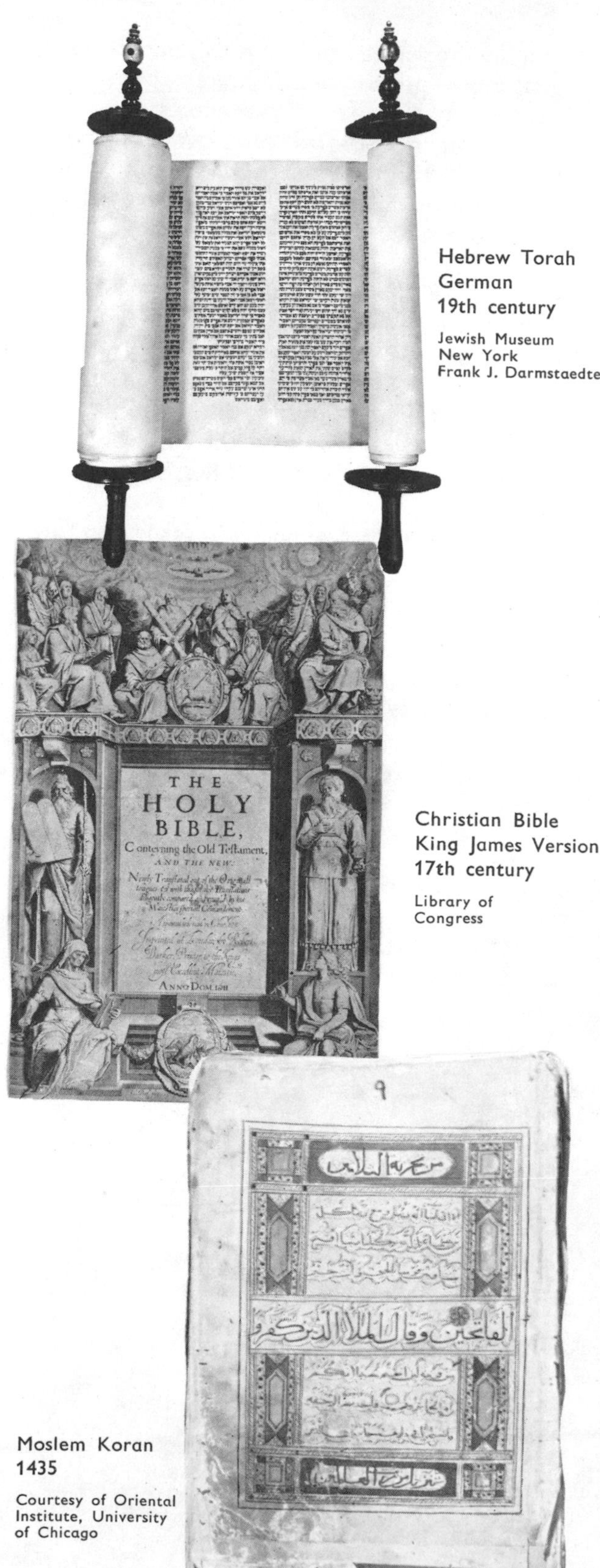

Hebrew Torah
German
19th century

Jewish Museum
New York
Frank J. Darmstaedter

Christian Bible
King James Version
17th century

Library of
Congress

Moslem Koran
1435

Courtesy of Oriental Institute, University of Chicago

religion of 300 to 400 million persons. Most of them live in India, where about 85 per cent of the population is Hindu. It is difficult to separate Hinduism as a religion from the total way of life found in India.

Over 150 million people call themselves Buddhist in religion. Buddhism is followed widely through south-east Asia, Ceylon, and Tibet, and is important in China, Korea, and Japan. Some people view Buddhism more as a philosophy of life than as a religion. Buddhism was founded by Siddhartha Gautama, a prince who lived in northern India more than 500 years before Christ. Gautama, who came to be called the Buddha, is not worshipped as a god, but rather as a great teacher who offered enlightenment. The word Buddha means 'the Enlightened One', signifying knowledge rather than divinity.

GAMES AND SPORTS. From earliest times, men have found some activities, contests, and skills enjoyable. Games include contests involving luck, skill, or strength, though many games are not contests but require playing out parts like actors on a stage. Still others, like dancing round the Maypole, are fun because they involve singing and dancing with other people, although the Maypole dance was once a fertility rite of importance in some societies. Sometimes games are for more than simple enjoyment. Frequently they have been ways of training young men to be warriors. This is especially true of games we call 'sports'. The Olympic Games, which date from 776 B.C., were a festival in honour of Zeus, the chief god of the Greek pantheon.

Sports have often been part of the play pattern of boys, including many sports that were dangerous. Indian boys practised spear throwing and archery. They raced ponies, swam, and wrestled. Feats of strength and bravery were prized and individuals were rewarded with ceremony. Iroquois Indians played lacrosse, with broken bones or bleeding heads a usual occurrence. Greek boxers fought with a piece of leather studded with

National Museum, Rome

The Ancient Greeks idealised sports. This statue of a discus thrower was cast in bronze about 450 B.C.

metal wrapped around each fist, and Roman gladiators (professional fighters) used spears, daggers, and swords. From sports organised to demonstrate fighting strength or skill there developed eventually competitive sports as we know them today, played for fun and for physical development.

ETIQUETTE. Every society has rules that govern the proper ways of behaviour of the individual in every situation. These rules of 'good manners' vary from one society to another and may differ considerably between social levels within the same society. In some countries in earlier times, any

The game of lacrosse, as played by the Indians who originated it, had as many players as the competing tribes could provide. It was fiercely competitive, and rules against harming one's opponents were unknown. The Indians used it as a substitute for warfare on some occasions, and considered it good training for actual combat. This painting shows a game played by Choctaws in the 1840s.

Smithsonian Institution — U.S. Nat'l Museum

Milwaukee Journal Photo

Polo is a fast game that requires a high degree of training and skill on the part of both man and pony.

commoner who failed to use the proper form of address to a superior was killed immediately. In most Western countries, spitting in a man's face is an invitation to combat, but in an African tribe, the Chagga, spitting in the face is a form of greeting which denotes brotherhood. To a European, a wave of either hand is a friendly salute; to a Moslem, a gesture with the left hand is extremely insulting.

Etiquette in eating is recognised even among peoples who have no eating utensils. Many primitive peoples have rules that determine in which sequence diners must be served. In several societies a husband and wife never eat in each other's presence, nor do they use the same eating vessels. American Plains Indians considered it good taste for a dinner guest to ask for a container so that he might take home any of his uneaten food. Most South Asians today prefer to eat with their fingers and have definite rules how this should be done. A Bolivian Indian licks honey from an implement like a shaving brush and then passes it on to his neighbour. In the East African kingdom of Uganda, hand washing before and after meals is made into a ceremony. Great care is taken not to touch another person's food.

Etiquette in our own Western civilisation has had a fascinating history. The handkerchief for nose blowing is a fairly recent introduction. At the end of the Middle Ages, children of refined families were told not to blow their noses with the hand which they used for eating. By 1530, the use of handkerchiefs was considered polite. In the Middle Ages it was customary for a group of people to eat out of a common bowl, and only people of wealth used spoons. Individual plates did not come into use until the sixteenth and seventeenth centuries. Until about 1550 it was usual in Europe for all guests to drink from a common glass.

EDUCATION. The process by which the vast mass of cultural material is passed from one generation to the next is called education. Education goes on wherever people play, work, or live together. It is a characteristic

Japanese etiquette prescribes in detail each step in the tea ceremony; these girls are entering the tea house.

activity of man and is as important to primitive peoples as it is to those living in the most advanced societies. Education begins with birth and continues until death but is most important in childhood. It is the means by which the young are taught the ways developed by their ancestors to cope with the problems of living in their own particular environment.

In primitive societies, education is usually in the practical arts of hunting, fishing, agriculture, homemaking, and the techniques of teaching are watching and helping. In advanced societies in which there is written language, schools are organised for teaching the youth. Education in today's world concerns such subjects as writing, literature, mathematics, and science, all of which are important to living in modern societies. These subjects are of little practical value in the world of primitive man.

LAW. All societies of Man have rules and customs to guide and control their members' behaviour under all possible circumstances. Custom and rules become laws when they are enforced regularly by society through persons given the authority to do so. In modern societies and to some extent in primitive societies, the government, or state, holds this power. The first written system of law of which we have knowledge was the Code of Hammurabi, written in ancient Sumeria about 4,000 years ago. Records of that empire show that there were courts to try cases to determine whether penalties should be enacted for offences against the law of the land.

Some of our modern laws have roots in custom, others in rules passed by legislatures. Generally we recognise two great branches of the law. One of these is 'criminal law', or laws dealing with actions which are believed to harm society as a whole. Offenders are called criminals, and their acts are crimes. The other is 'civil law', or laws having to do with private matters between citizens, such as land or money. In these cases society itself is not endangered but the court is asked by the plaintiff (the one who complains) for assistance in righting a wrong done to him as an individual.

GOVERNMENT is a system of social organisation developed by man to bring about order and to safeguard the welfare of the members of a society. In its original form, anthropologists believe, the strongest male

Powerful chiefs of North-west Coast tribes often killed slaves with clubs like this one to demonstrate their power and wealth, and to shame rival chiefs.

In The Brooklyn Museum Collection

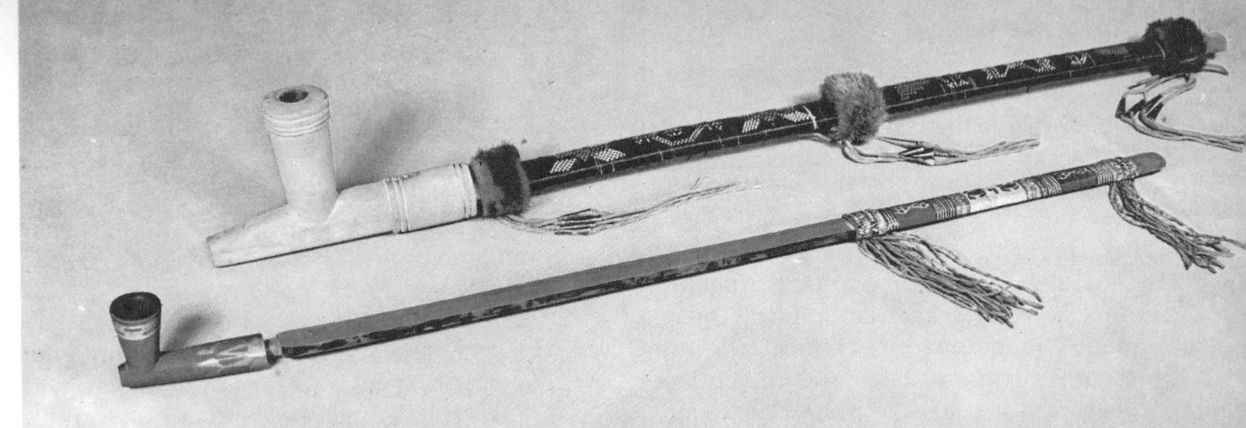

Museum of the American Indian/Heye Foundation

'Peace Pipes' were often smoked ceremonially by Plains Indians and were used in welcoming friendly travellers.

in the family group assumed the leadership of the band of related members. When the family unit became the tribe, various methods of selecting a chief were developed, from election or inheritance to the use of magic to determine the will of the gods. When certain tribes gained the strength to control other tribes, the institution of kingship appeared. The last two hundred years have seen the gradual disappearance of the monarchies and the rise of both democracies, in which the rulers and policies are selected by the voters, and dictatorships, in which intrigue and assassination are the stepping-stones to power.

Modern governments may be classified under four broad headings: (1) totalitarian-capitalistic, (2) totalitarian-socialistic, (3) democratic-socialistic, and (4) democratic-capitalistic. To say that a country is totalitarian is to say that it is governed by a dictatorship which holds power by strength rather than by free elections. Democracy means that the people, through regular expression of their will, determine their national policies and their leaders. Britain is a democratic-socialistic country, in which the people closely control their leaders and policies. Socialistic countries, whether totalitarian or democratic, believe that many services should be provided to all citizens regardless of their ability to pay.

Soviet Russia is totalitarian-socialistic. Here, the governing bodies are not determined by free elections, and the government, not individuals, owns the factories and other productive machinery.

Nations like the United States are democratic-capitalistic. Their citizens determine leadership in the government, but the policies and leaders in business and industry are determined by the persons who own the particular business or industry. Individuals purchase most services and goods in accordance with their ability to pay for them.

Totalitarian-capitalistic countries are those in which dictators maintain a system of business for profit within the nations they rule. This kind of system is found in countries like Spain, Portugal, and several nations of South America and the Far East.

SLAVERY. When an individual is legally owned by another and is denied the right to act as a free individual, he is termed a slave, and the system under which he exists is called slavery. This institution is found

Before man learned to work iron, cutting tools were made of bronze. These were from the Near East.

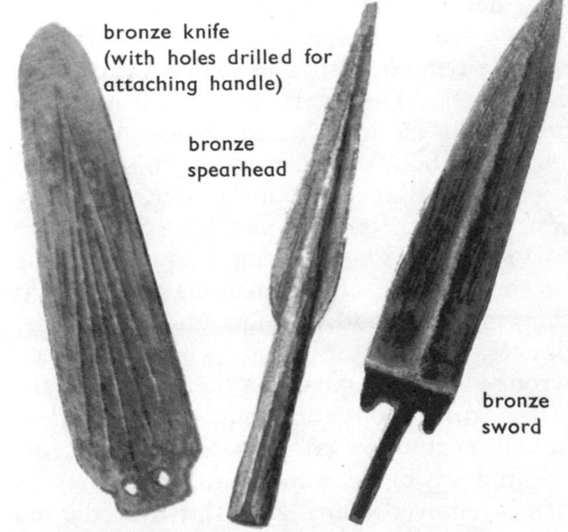

among both civilised and primitive peoples, but it has been most frequently and most extensively practised by the civilised. The simplest hunting and fishing societies rarely had slaves; when they did, only members of other tribes were enslaved, as a rule. More advanced pastoral and agricultural peoples frequently made slaves of prisoners captured from other tribes. This was a common practice in much of Africa, and also among Indians of the Pacific North-west and in Central and South America.

Practically all of the civilised peoples of the ancient world had slaves. Probably at first these were prisoners captured in war, but later slave trades developed based upon raids for the purpose of taking slaves. During the Middle Ages in Europe there appeared a sort of limited slavery, known as serfdom. Not long after serfdom disappeared, slavery came again into style. In the nineteenth century, all the major nations of the world turned against slavery, and it has disappeared from all but a few regions of the world.

WAR. All civilisations and most primitive societies have used violent methods in forcing enemies to yield to their will. War is organised violence of one group against another, and total war, affecting all aspects of community life, is a product of civilisation. Savages may on occasion steal from another tribe or may even murder, but organised armies attacking an enemy repeatedly would make sense to few primitive peoples. Primitive types of war include raids on neighbouring bands to steal horses or sometimes women.

One common type of primitive warfare is really a regulated, though somewhat dangerous contest. The Murngin tribe of Australia held such affairs, as did many American Indian tribes. When a Murngin man had been hurt or killed by an outsider, a message was sent to the enemy people inviting them to a *makarata*. The *makarata* is a peacemaking ceremony in which violence plays a part. At this meeting both groups do ceremonial dances. Finally the group which has been wronged throws spears at the enemy as the latter run about dodging. Except when aimed at the actual persons who did the original wrong, the spears have their stone heads removed. During all this time the old men of the group being punished warn their men against losing their tempers and fighting back. When one of the actual killers has been wounded, the 'war' is over and a state of goodwill is restored.

Primitives rarely use violence against others to gain territory, as their wars usually have little to do with economics. More often they are to avenge wrongs done them. Very frequently war parties are more like groups of competing athletes, and the war like a dangerous sport in which young men can prove themselves brave and skilful.

Among the civilised peoples of antiquity, some considered warfare to be ennobling and desirable, while others gave it no recognised place. The Mayans were a peace-loving people, as were the people of ancient India. On the other hand, the Aztecs were warlike, requiring many prisoners as blood sacrifices in religious rituals. One need only read the Old Testament to recognise how warlike were the early civilised peoples of the Middle East. With the Greeks and Romans, warfare continued to be a highly acceptable profession, and the soldier was respected and honoured. In the modern world there has been much development of industrial techniques in the effectiveness of the methods of human slaughter, and property destruction.

In spite of the bloodthirstiness of most early civilisations, modern societies are vastly more skilled in killing than any before them. The present century is already the bloodiest in all human history, and it is not yet three-quarters over. After World War I (1914—1918) the League of Nations was created with the purpose of preventing future wars. After World War II (1939 to 1945) the United Nations organisation was created with a similar purpose.

SOLAR SYSTEM. Earth is one of nine planets surrounding the Sun, which is an average sort of star. Other stars are so far away that the Sun dominates the region around it; in this region are the planets and other bodies that make up our solar system.

The central body of the solar system is the Sun. It is the largest body — far larger than all the others put together — and it is the only body that generates its own light and heat. (See SUN.) The bodies of several types

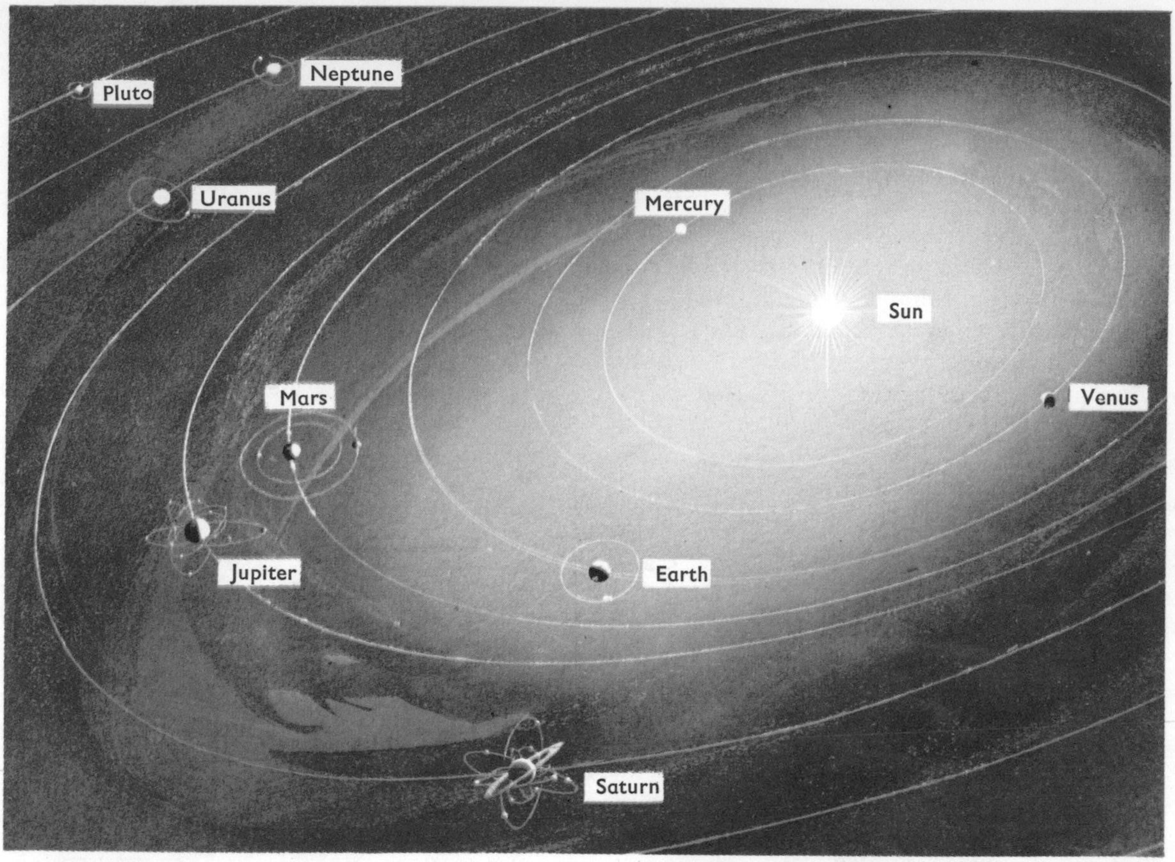

Our solar system includes nine planets revolving in their orbits about the Sun, many with moons or satelites. Asteroids, smaller bodies that are possibly parts of a vanished planet, comets and meteors complete the picture.

that go around the Sun are held in their orbits by the Sun's powerful gravitational pull. The largest of these are the nine planets, which range in size from less than half the Earth's diameter up to more than ten times the Earth's diameter. The planets also differ widely in distance from the Sun. Mercury, the closest planet, is less than half of the Earth's distance from the Sun, while Pluto, the most distant, is forty times the distance of the Earth from the Sun. (See PLANETS.)

The planets are so far apart that most of the solar system is empty space. In a scale model, if the Sun were a marble, the Earth would be a grain of sand a yard away. The other planets would be spread through a region 80 yards in diameter. Yet the surrounding space is even emptier. On this scale the nearest other star would be 150 miles away.

Asteroids are another class of bodies circling the Sun. There are many thousands of these, each following its own orbit. Most of them remain between the orbits of Mars

Our solar system is composed of a star (our Sun) and all heavenly bodies which occur within the orbit of Pluto, the outermost planet. According to one theory, clouds of gases once surrounded the Sun. As these condensed, they formed the planets and their satellites.

and Jupiter, the fourth and fifth planets. The largest asteroid has less than one tenth the diameter of the Earth, and most are only a few miles in diameter. (See ASTEROIDS.)

Comets also follow orbits around the Sun, but most of them inhabit the distant outer reaches of the solar system, hundreds of times farther than the planets. Those that on occasion hang so spectacularly in our sky are ones with elongated orbits that bring them deep into the inner parts of our solar system. Their tails stretch for millions of miles but are composed mainly of thin gases, and very little solid matter. (See COMET.)

The planets move in orbits that are nearly circular and nearly in the same plane. Most asteroids have more elongated and more inclined orbits, while comets have highly elongated orbits inclined at all angles. The orbits of bodies change very little, because, except for the Sun, the other members of the solar system have very little influence on each other. On rare occasions, however, a small body passes close to one of the planets and experiences a sudden, large change in its orbit. (See ORBIT.)

Just as the Sun has planets going around it, most of the planets have satellites going around them. Satellites are solid bodies that range from the size of Mercury, the smallest planet, down to chunks of rock 10 miles in diameter. Thirty-two satellites are known. Jupiter has twelve, the largest number. Each satellite, or moon, follows an orbit about its parent planet and remains fairly close to it. (See SATELLITES.)

These bodies, along with a scattering of gas and dust, make up the solar system, which is held together by gravitation and has existed in nearly its present state for between 4,000 and 5,000 million years, according to present evidence. (See EARTH; FOSSILS; GEOLOGY.)

Astronomers have spent much thought about the origin of the solar system. One theory has suggested that the Sun was once as large as the whole solar system. As it contracted, it spun faster and threw off rings of material. Each of these rings condensed into one of the planets. But we know now that a rotating mass of gas could not have produced the present arrangement of planets in this way. Another theory suggested that another star once passed so close to the Sun that its gravitational force pulled great masses of material out of the Sun. These condensed into the planets. Unfortunately this theory has to be abandoned too, for modern analysis shows that such a process could not lead to the present arrangement of widely spread planets.

Modern astronomers incline to the view that the planets were formed at the same time as the Sun, as a cloud of interstellar gas and dust condensed and contracted. Instead of a single condensation, many bodies were formed. The largest became the Sun, and the smaller condensations became planets. As the cloud contracted, it spun faster, and the planets acquired their present orbits. If this view is correct, solar systems must be very common, and planets similar to the Earth must exist elsewhere, going around other stars just as the Earth goes around the Sun.

FALSE SOLOMON'S-SEAL *Smilacina racemosa* (U.S.A.)

SOLOMON'S-SEAL *Polygonatum*

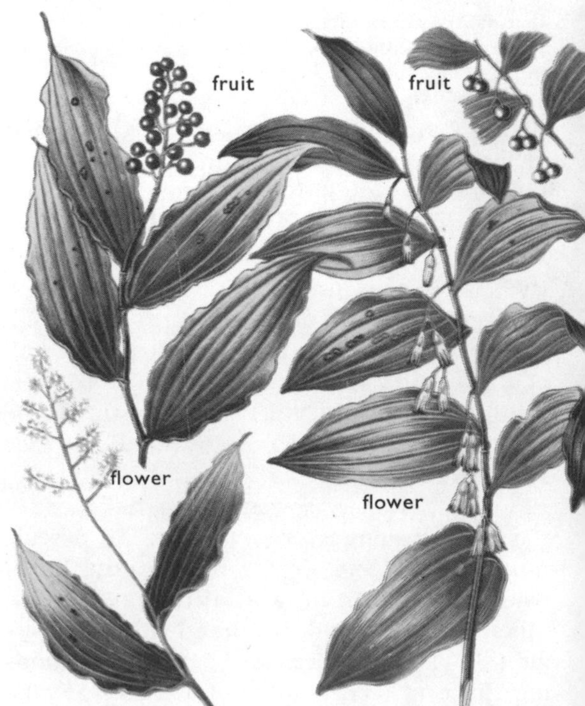

SOLOMON'S-SEALS (*Polygonatum* spp.) are plants of the woodland floor. They are named for circular protuberances on the thick storage roots, said to resemble the seal on

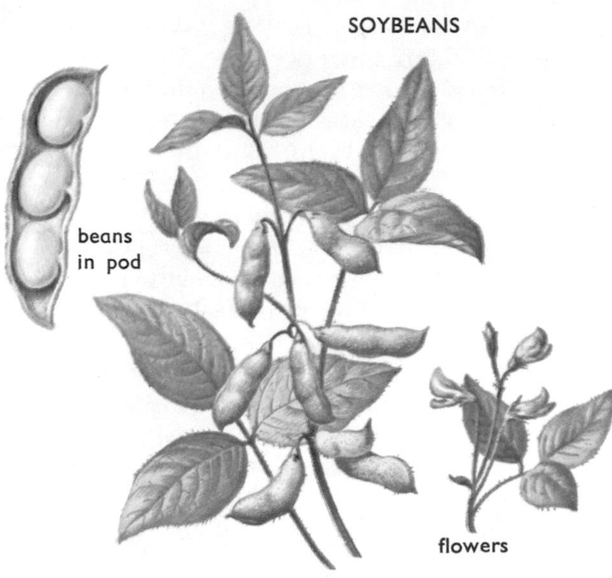

Soybeans add nitrogen to the soil, and the plants may be ploughed under as green manure.

King Solomon's ring. Several species grow in the British Isles where they prefer damp woods. These, and other species from abroad are cultivated in our gardens.

The flowers of most species of Solomon's-Seal are white, tipped with green and are bel-shaped. They hang from the axils of the leaves along the long, gracefully drooping stalk. The berries are rounded and are purple or red and the leaves often turn yellow in autumn giving a late patch of colour.

SOYBEANS *(Glycine max)* have for centuries served as an important supplement to the basic rice diet of people in the Far East. Soybeans were not introduced to Europe or America until the 1700s, and only in the past 50 years has their use been explored. Research by government agencies and private industry has revealed many values.

Soybeans contain approximately 20 per cent oil and from 30 to 45 per cent protein. Although soybeans are still of minor importance as a vegetable in the United States, many products are now derived from them. Soybean oil, extracted from the beans either by crushing them or by the use of chemicals, is now one of the major vegetable oils in that country. It is used in manufacturing margarine and as a salad and cooking oil.

It is used industrially in varnishes, candles, soap, linoleum, insecticides and many other items. Livestock feed, soy flour, fertiliser, plastics, and adhesives make use of the press cake that is left after the oil is squeezed from the beans.

SPACE TRAVEL. With the successful launching of artificial satellites, we stand on the threshold of a new era of exploration. Before many years have passed, rockets will regularly carry men to the Moon and to near planets of the solar system. Space travel will be difficult, hazardous and expensive.

The first problem is getting away from the powerful gravitational field of the Earth. A rocket shot into the air with a low speed will rise a short distance and then fall back. If it starts with a higher speed, it will rise higher before turning back. The speed just sufficient to leave the Earth is called the escape velocity. From the Earth's surface it is necessary to travel 7 miles per second,

Astronauts Eugene A. Cernan and Thomas P. Stafford about to set off on another voyage of space exploration.

or 25,000 miles per hour, to escape the gravitational field of the Earth.

Reaching this very high speed cannot be done suddenly. The very rapid acceleration would destroy the contents of the rocket, and air friction would burn up the remains. A rocket must speed up gradually and reach its final speed only after it is outside the major part of the Earth's atmosphere.

A rocket engine develops its power by burning fuel and driving the exhaust out of the back at high speed. As the exhaust gases are pushed backwards, the recoil pushes the rocket forward. The rocket must start with all the propellant it will need, and most of the initial fuel is wasted speeding up the rocket while it is heavily loaded. Present-day space rockets waste more than 99 per cent of their fuel in this process. But rocket engineers hope to develop a new type of engine, called an ion engine, that will be much more efficient.

How far a rocket goes depends very critically on its speed. It is as if the Earth were at the bottom of a deep, round trough, with sides that are very steep near the centre, and much less steep at the edges.

A rocket launched with more than the escape velocity slows down as it rises, but eventually finds itself travelling away from the Earth with a small, steady speed. As seen from the Sun, it has the Earth's orbital speed of 66,000 miles per hour, with its own small speed added in whatever direction the rocket was launched. The rocket will now follow its own orbit around the Sun (see ORBIT). This orbit will differ from the Earth's orbit because of the rocket's velocity relative to the Earth. If the rocket is launched in the direction of the Earth's orbital motion, it will follow a larger orbit and swing farther from the Sun. If it is launched in the backward direction, it will have a smaller orbit and move closer to the Sun.

To get to Mars a rocket needs to travel away from the Earth with a speed of 6,600 miles per hour. Nearly the same speed in the other direction will take the rocket to Venus. In terms of initial speed this is not so hard, for the 25,000 mile-per-hour velocity for bare escape rises only to 26,000 miles per hour initial speed to reach Mars or Venus.

Space travel is not likely to be comfortable. Aside from the crushing accelerations at the beginning and end of the trip, there will be discomforts and dangers en route. Passengers will be weightless — and perhaps 'space sick' — unless the ship is spun to produce an artificial gravity. Shielding against cosmic rays and meteors will have to be provided, and some ships nevertheless may be destroyed by large meteors. A space ship must carry

The Earth is in orbit about the Sun, and the Moon about the Earth. Space flights must be planned and the space vehicle aimed at the spot where it will meet its target. The path and velocity of the Earth, the target and the vehicle must all be considered.

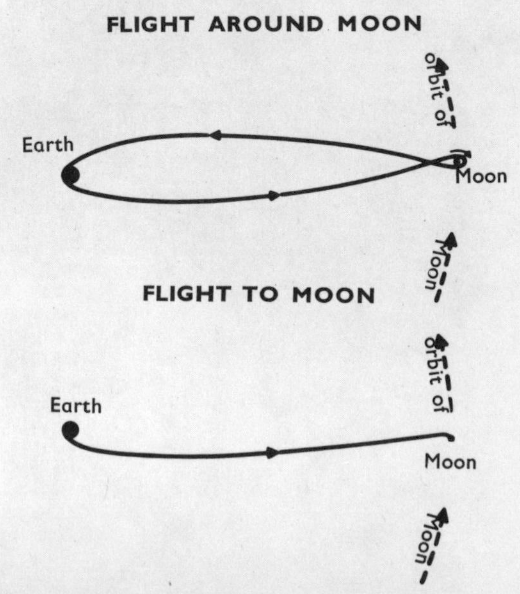

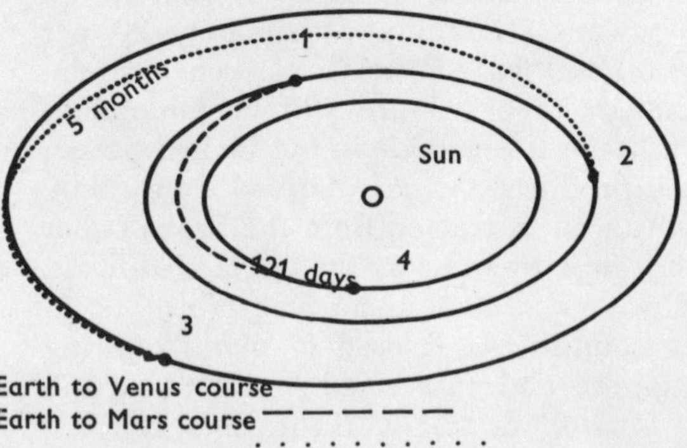

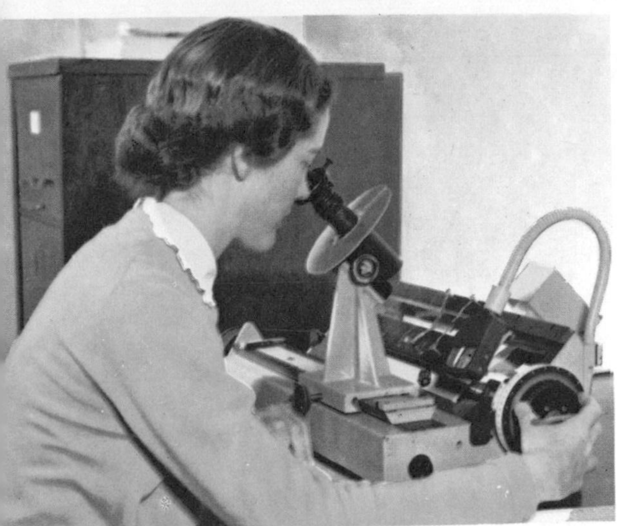

Mt. Wilson and Palomar Observatories

By studying a star's photographed spectrum under a special microscope, astronomers learn a great deal about the star's speed, temperature, and composition.

enough air and food for a voyage of months or years. Nor will the conditions be much better at the destination. There is no other body in the solar system on which the human being can live outside an airtight building or space suit. Growing food will also be a serious problem, and in most places heating or cooling plants will be needed too.

Visits to other planets will be for the purpose of scientific exploration. Colonising seems hopelessly expensive, and so does mining, because of the cost of transporting the material back to Earth.

Beyond the solar system lie the stars, almost infinitely far away. A rocket launched at 40,000 miles per hour would leave the solar system at 15,000 miles per hour, but at that speed it would take 200,000 years to reach the nearest star. Obviously much higher speeds and a more efficient fuel would be needed to reach a star.

SPECTRUM. In studying heavenly bodies, all that the astronomer has to work with is their light. He can draw many conclusions from position and brightness, but the richest information comes from analysing starlight in detail. Ordinary light is a mixture of many colours, as you can see by passing it through a prism to separate the colours. Astronomers do this with a device called a spectrograph, which spreads the light out evenly according to colour. The result is a photograph showing a long band of light in which each point corresponds to a different colour, and the brightness at that point tells how much light there was of that colour. The spread-out band of light is called a spectrum, and a position in the spectrum — that is, a precise colour — is produced by a light of very definite wave length.

The spectrum of a star, such as the Sun, is not an unbroken band of light; instead it is crossed by many dark lines (Fraunhofer lines). These lines indicate missing wave lengths; light of those colours has been removed by gases through which the light has passed. It is the dark lines, or absorption

The more distant stars which move away from us faster show a greater red shift in their spectra.

Mt. Wilson and Palomar Observatories

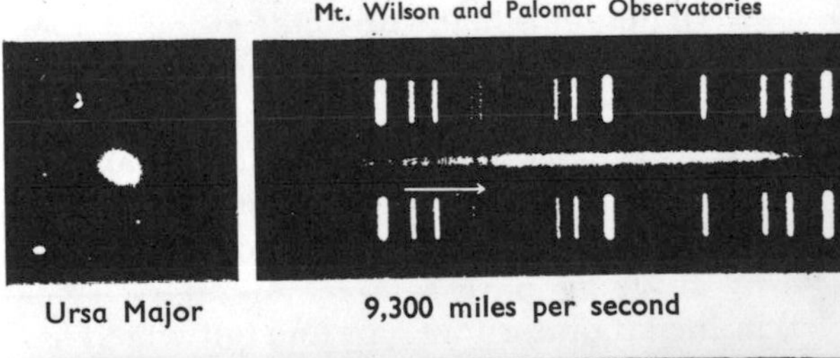

Ursa Major — 9,300 miles per second

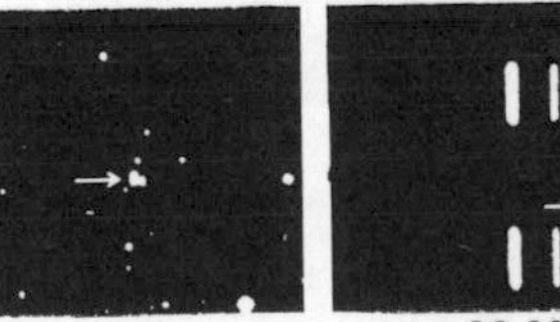

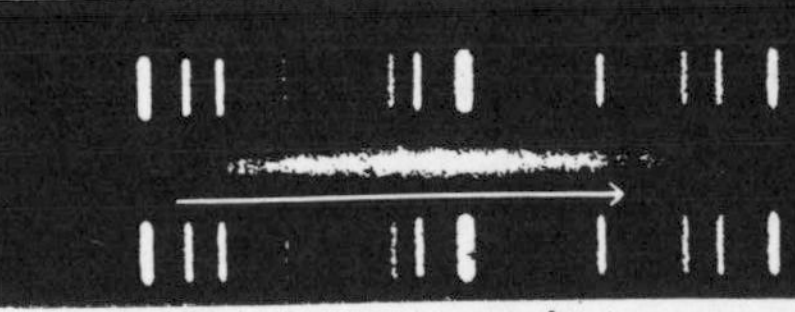

Hydra — 38,000 miles per second

The dark lines in the absorption spectrum of the Sun reveal the presence of chemical elements, each of which has its own distinct pattern.

Mt. Wilson and Palomar Observatories

In making a spectrograph, the telescope can be focused so that the light from only one star enters.

lines, that contain a wealth of astronomical information. They tell us about the atoms within the atmosphere of the star.

All matter is made up of the atoms of about 100 different chemical elements, and the atoms of a particular element behave according to just the same rules in the atmosphere of a distant star as they do on Earth. Each element has its own set of spectral lines, and by studying pure samples of each element in the laboratory we can find out which lines belong to which elements. Then by measuring carefully the wave lengths in the spectrum of a star we can say which lines are produced by hydrogen in the star's atmosphere, which by iron, and so on. Since each element produces many lines, most stellar spectra are quite complicated; nevertheless most of the lines in them have been identified. In the Sun about 70 elements have been found by means of their spectral lines.

By studying spectral lines we can tell what stars are made of (see STARS). But determining the actual percentages of the elements in their makeup is very difficult because the strength of a line depends not only on how much of that element is present but also on the temperature and pressure to which it is subjected. Indeed, the compositions of the various stars turn out to be very similar in spite of the big differences in the appearance of their spectra.

The biggest difference in stellar spectra is caused by temperature. An atom absorbs some of its lines better at high temperature and some better at low temperature; so the spectra of hot and cold stars look very different even though they are made of the same material. A hot star has only a few strong lines in its spectrum. These are produced by hydrogen and other elements that we know as gases. A cool star, on the other hand, has a very large number of lines produced by the heavier metallic elements.

Astronomers classify stars according to their spectra into seven main groups from hot to cool. These spectral classes are important in studies of the characteristics of groups of stars and the evolution of individual stars. It is also possible from fine details in the spectrum to tell whether a star is large and bright or small and faint.

Stellar spectra have other applications, too. Motion towards or away from us causes a slight shift in the spectral lines, and these shifts tell us much about the motions of the stars. Spectra of gaseous nebulae reveal their nature and composition, and spectra of the planets tell us what gases make up their atmospheres.

SPICES have been used by Man since earliest times to improve the flavour of his food and as preservatives. Most of them originated in the Asiatic tropics and were known to the ancient Chinese and Japanese. The Arabs were the first to control the spice trade, bringing the spices to Europe by caravans. In their search for sea routes to the spices of Asia and the East Indies, Spanish and Portuguese explorers discovered the New World. Even today most spices are grown in Asia. Many owe their flavour to the essential oil they contain. Most spices are dried and ground, but nearly all can be used before curing.

Ginger *(Zingiber officinale)* was one of the

first spices of the Orient known in Europe and is still the most important spice obtained from roots. Dried or cured ginger is prepared by cleaning, peeling, and drying the roots. Candied ginger is made from young roots that have been boiled in water until tender and then boiled again in a sugar solution. Ginger is used in bakery products, curries, drinks, and medicines.

Mustard seeds, the source of mustard used in condiments and medicines, are obtained from both black and white mustard plants, (*Brassica nigra* and *alba*). White mustard plants produce bristly pods that contain small yellow seeds. The familiar mustard spread is a combination of ground seeds of black and white mustard together with salt, vinegar, and other flavouring ingredients. Leaves of mustard plants are sometimes cooked as 'greens'. Mustard is grown today in most of the temperate regions of the world.

Nutmeg and mace are both obtained from the fruit of a tree *(Myristica fragrans)* native to the East Indies but now grown in the West Indies. The golden-yellow fruits look like plums but split open when ripe, exposing a large brown seed which is partly enclosed in a red, leathery, finger-like membrane. Nutmeg comes from the kernel of the seed and mace from the red membrane. Oil of nutmeg is used in perfumes and in toothpastes.

Caraway *(Carum carvi)*, native to Europe and western Asia, is used as a flavouring in cakes and other bakery products, sausages, and cheese.

Cloves are the dried flower-buds of *Syzygium aromaticum*, a tree of some 40 feet in height native to the Moluccas or Spice Islands in the Pacific. They are used as a flavouring.

Peppermint and spearmint are obtained from two small aromatic herbs (*Mentha piperita* and *spicata*) that grow in temperate regions. The leaves of both are used for flavouring, but more important are the flavouring oils of the leaves used in sweets, chewing gum, toothpaste, and in various medicines. (See CLOVES; DILL; HOPS; PARSLEY; PEPPER; VANILLA.)

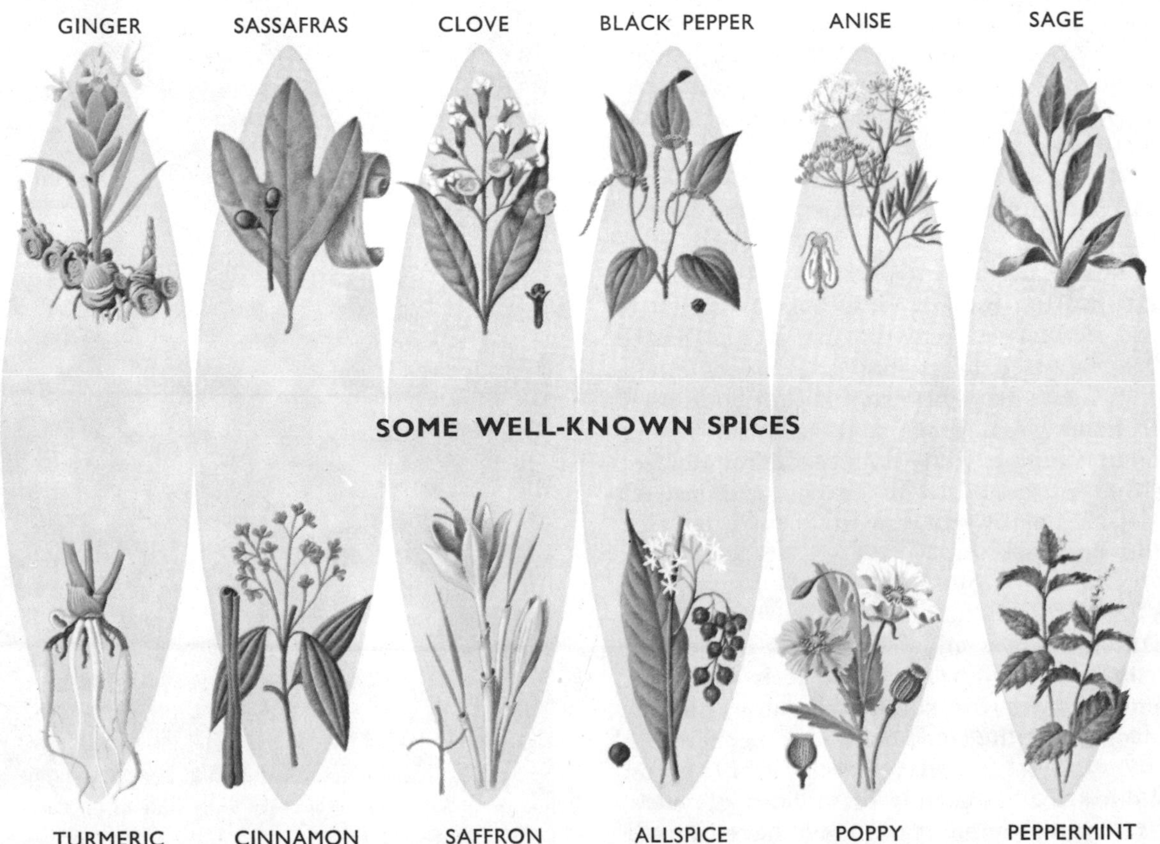

SOME WELL-KNOWN SPICES

Fresh, crisp leaves of spinach have been grown for markets in the Western world for over 500 years.

SPINACH *(Spinacia oleracea)*, a native of south-western Asia, is a green vegetable sold fresh, canned, or frozen. Spinach is well known as a source of vitamin A and for its mineral content, mainly iron.

STARCH, the chief food reserve of plants, is distributed throughout the tissues of a plant and concentrated in such storage organs as bulbs, corms, tubers and seeds. Sugar produced by photosynthesis is frequently changed into starch in the leaves. Since starch will not dissolve in water, it must be converted to sugar again before it moves from the leaves to storage organs.

The major commercial sources of starch are cereals and tubers.

Maize is the most important source of starch in many parts of the world. In the Philippines, East Indies and the Caribbean, manioc roots produce cassava starch. Some is converted into tapioca. Cassava starch is also used for sizing textiles and making paste. Dextrin, used in making glue, is obtained from maize or potato starch. Cornflour, used in making puddings and as a thickening agent, is a fine, white flour made from maize. Other sources of starch for food or industrial use are arrowroot, potatoes, wheat, rice and sago palms.

STARS. Each star is a large brilliant body like our Sun, a middle-aged star of medium size. A star shines because it is very hot, and it goes on shining because nuclear reactions at the star's centre keep generating energy. Most stars have enough fuel to go on shining for thousands of millions of years, but even among stars some have shorter lives than others. All around us are young stars and old stars, some newly born and some just dying.

SIZES OF STARS. Stars look like tiny points of light in the sky, but nearly all the stars are much larger than the entire Earth. Our Sun has a diameter of 864,000 miles, more than a hundred times the diameter of the Earth.

By size we usually mean diameter, but size can mean other things, too. For example, the *mass* of a star is another kind of size. For the objects that we deal with every day, mass is very much like weight. If we could

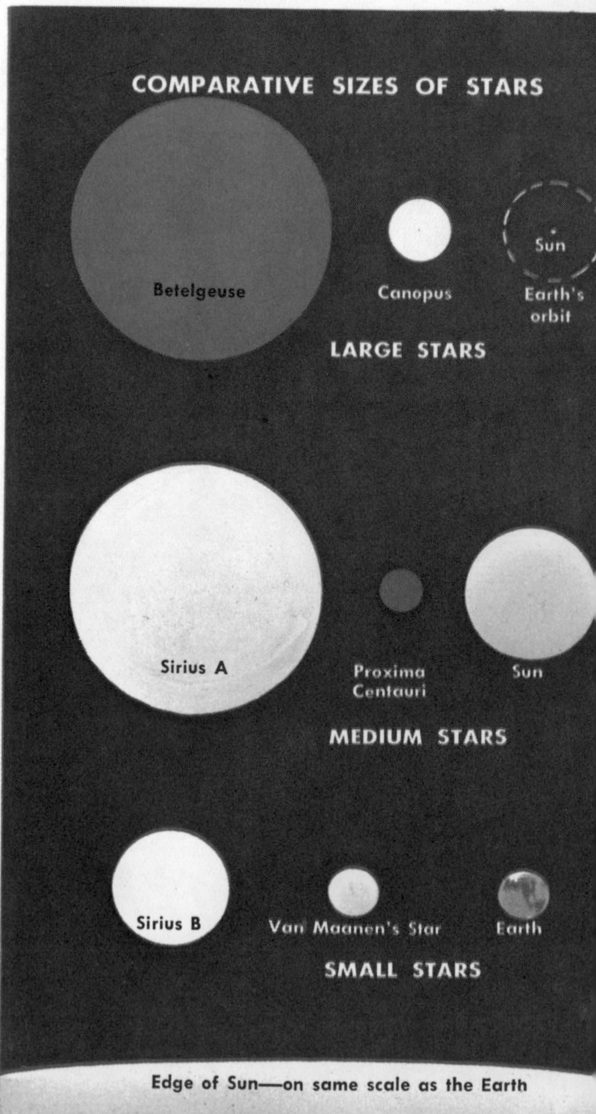

weigh a star, the total weight would be its mass. Some stars are very massive. The Sun, for instance, has enough mass to equal more than 300,000 Earths.

Some stars are much larger than the Sun; others are much smaller. The largest stars are the very bright red super-giants. The star Betelgeuse is so large that if it were put in place of the Sun it would swallow up the whole orbit of the Earth. But even though it has such a large diameter and occupies more than a million times the volume of the Sun, Betelgeuse does not have such a large mass. It has in it only twenty times as much material as the Sun, and most of its material is such thinly spread gas that it would be hard to tell a sample of it from a vacuum.

Not all bright stars are so large. Bright blue stars, like Sirius, have only twice the diameter of the Sun but have about twice as much mass.

Faint stars are smaller than bright stars. Of course this means stars that are really faint rather than stars that look faint merely because they are far away. A typical sort of faint star is a red dwarf, like Proxima Centauri, the closest star to the Sun in space. Proxima has a quarter of the Sun's diameter and one-tenth as much mass.

The smallest of all stars are the white dwarfs, like the faint companion that goes around Sirius. These stars have diameters hardly larger than the Earth but have nearly as much mass as the Sun. To have so much material in such a small space, the white dwarfs must be tremendously compressed. In fact, a cubic inch of white-dwarf material would weigh a ton on the Earth.

We know a great deal about the size of stars, yet we cannot tell how big a star is just by looking at it through a telescope. Stars are so very far away that even in the most powerful optical telescopes available they are simply points of light.

Astronomers have to calculate the sizes of stars from other kinds of observations. One opportunity comes when the two parts of a double star eclipse each other. Another sort of calculation depends on knowing just how the stars radiate light. In any case, measuring the sizes of stars helps us to understand what the stars are and why they shine.

DISTANCES OF STARS. The stars and the planets are at very different distances from us. The planets are relatively close, while the stars are very much farther away. If we imagine the Sun to be the size of a marble, then the Earth is a grain of sand a yard away, and the other planets are all within about 100 feet. On this scale the nearest other star is 150 miles away.

When we look at a star we see only a point of light, with no indication of how far away it is. Finding out the distances of the stars is one of the most difficult problems in astronomy. Many different methods areu sed, and all of them require careful measurements and mathematical calculations.

A surveyor finds the distance to an object by measuring the angle to the object as seen from the ends of a base line of known length. Similarly astronomers determine the distances to the stars. The base line in astronomy is the diameter of the Earth's orbit.

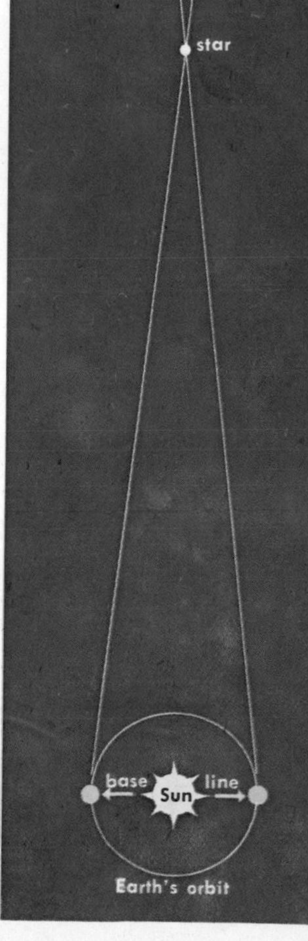

The distances of the nearest stars are measured by means of their parallaxes. By parallax is meant the change in the direction of an object as the observer moves around. If you hold up a finger and look at it while moving your head from side to side, the finger seems to move back and forth. In just the same way, as the Earth goes around the Sun every year the nearby stars seem to move back and forth against the background of more distant stars. The amount by which a star appears to move back and forth every year is called its parallax. The closer a star is, the larger is its parallax, so that the largest parallax belongs to the nearest star Proxima Centauri, whose parallax is the same as the apparent size of a halfpenny 3 miles away. No wonder parallaxes are so hard to measure!

Because the stars are so far away, astronomers use a unit of length called a parsec. This is about 200,000 times the distance from the Earth to the Sun, so that a parsec is just under 20 trillion miles. The parsec is chosen as a unit because it is the distance at which the parallax of a star is exactly one second of arc or 1/36000 of a degree.

Although astronomers measure distances in parsecs, some books on astronomy use another unit of distance, called the light year. A light year is the distance that light travels in a year. The speed of light is 186,000 miles per second, so in a year a ray of light travels about a third of a parsec. More precisely, one parsec equals 3.26 light years. Ten parsecs is the standard distance used in comparing the luminosities of stars.

Measured in parsecs, the distances of the stars become comfortable numbers. The nearest other star to the Sun is just over a parsec away, and neighbouring stars are a parsec or two apart. Within 5 parsecs of us 50 stars are known, and within 20 parsecs nearly 1,000 have been found. Most of them are very faint, however. Many more stars are easily visible — 6,000 can be seen without a telescope — but most are much farther away. Only a few of the stars are near neighbours of ours, and it is hard to pick them out of the background of countless more distant stars. Among the stars of first magnitude, Alpha, Centauri, Sirius, Procyon, Vega, and Altair are only a few parsecs away. Some of the brightest stars, such as Rigel and Deneb, are hundreds of parsecs from us.

A few thousand stars have had their distances found using parallax measurements. But most of the stars are such distances away that their parallaxes are too small to measure. Other methods must then be used to find their distances. One method uses the motions of the stars. As the stars move about, each with its own speed and direction, the nearby stars appear to move by us more rapidly than the distant ones. Their motions are very small, but they can be measured; and the motions of stars help astronomers to judge their distances.

Parallaxes are used for measuring distances up to 40 parsecs, and stellar motions help up to a few hundred parsecs. But the large distances in the universe are all measured by means of the brightnesses of the stars. To understand this we must distinguish between a star's brightness, or how bright it looks to us, and its luminosity, which is how bright it really is. The same star moved farther away would look fainter, while if it were closer to us it would look brighter. If we know how bright a star really is, we can calculate how bright it should look at any given distance. Seeing how bright it does look, we can then tell its distance. But in order to use a star's brightness to measure its distance, we must first know its luminosity.

The luminosities of several types of stars are known, and the distances of these stars, can thus be measured. Often such a star is a member of a large group, so that measuring the distance of the one star it tells us the distance of the whole group. In this way the distances of star clusters and galaxies have been measured. The most valuable stars for measuring large distances have been the cepheid variables. (See CEPHEIDS.)

Most of the stars that we see in the sky at night are within 100 or 200 parsecs of us, but this is just a tiny part of the whole stellar system that we live in. This system, the Milky Way, is in the shape of a great disc, 30,000 parsecs in diameter and from 500 to 2,000

Fox Photos

A fine view of the Jodrell Bank steerable radio telescope used by modern astronomers to probe the secrets of the depths of space.

parsecs thick. The centre of the Milky Way is 10,000 parsecs away from us. Our Milky Way is a galaxy — just one galaxy among many. Large empty distances separate the galaxies, and there are only a few within a million parsecs of us. Galaxies are scattered everywhere as far as we can see into the distance. Distant ones are just smudges on a photograph. We cannot see their individual stars but instead judge their distances from the brightness of the whole galaxy. The most distant galaxies, seen on photographs taken with the 200-inch telescope, are over 2,000 million parsecs away from the Earth. The light that we see today left those galaxies before the Earth was formed and has travelled for 6,000 million years to reach us. (See UNIVERSE.)

MOTIONS OF STARS. The stars are sometimes referred to as the 'fixed' stars to distinguish them from the planets, which move about among the constellations. But the stars are not truly fixed in position. Some of the brighter stars, such as Sirius and Arcturus, have moved quite noticeably since first recorded on ancient Greek star maps. By means of careful measurements, comparing positions on current photographs with positions on photographs taken 50 or 60 years ago, we can measure the motions of many thousands of stars. These motions of the stars across our line of sight are called proper motions. A star's proper motion indicates how fast it is travelling past us but also depends on how far away the star is from us.

Arcturus is now at about its closest point to our solar system. Soon it will begin to move away.

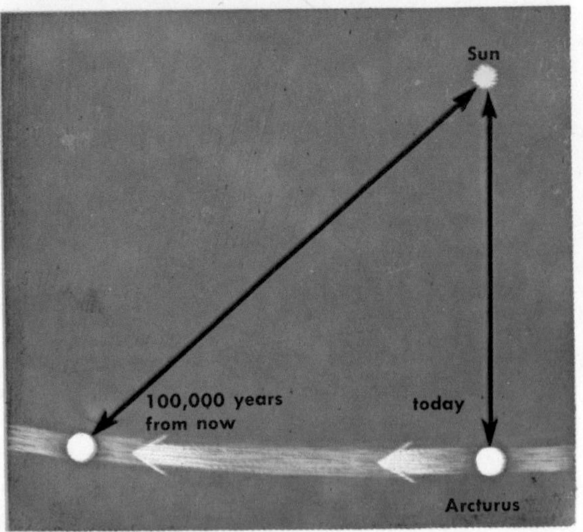

This dependence of a star's proper motion on its distance as well as on its true velocity has been put to use in two ways by modern astronomers. First, the proper motions of a large number of stars may be used to find their average distance. Second, a search for stars with large proper motions has served to pick out the Sun's closest neighbours, the nearby stars, from among the tremendous numbers of equally faint stars.

If a star is moving towards or away from us, the dark lines in its spectrum are shifted in wave length, and the amount of the shift tells how fast the star is moving along the line of sight. This part of a star's motion is called its radial velocity.

Combining a star's proper motion, suitably adjusted for distance, and its radial velocity, we can find its actual velocity through space. The stars around us have completely haphazard motions, with speeds of around 10 or 20 miles per second. The Sun is also moving, carrying the whole solar system with it. With respect to the average of all the stars around us, we are moving at 12 miles a second towards a direction not far from the star Vega. Since there are no forces of appreciable size acting, each star moves along for millions of years in the same straight line with unchanged speed. The speeds may seem large, but the distances between the stars are so great that it takes a hundred thousand years for even our near neighbours to move on and be replaced by other stars. Furthermore, the stars are so tiny compared with the distances separating them that they almost never collide with each other. Among the 100,000 million stars in the whole of the Milky Way, it is calculated that there is an average of only one collision every million years.

DOUBLE AND MULTIPLE STARS. The stars nearly all look like single points of light, but a few occur in pairs. Mizar and Alcor, in the handle of the Plough, are a conspicuous pair, and Epsilon Lyrae can be seen to be multiple by people with sharp eyes. But when we use a telescope, many more stars turn out to be double. Others are triple;

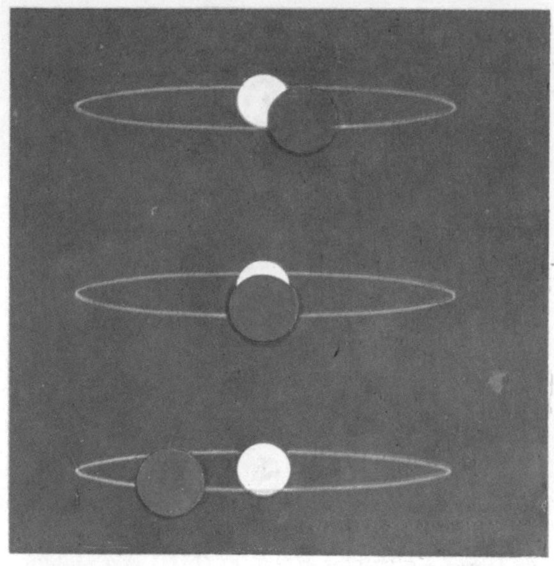

One of the stars of the binary Algol is very dim. It obscures its brighter twin every $2\frac{2}{3}$ days.

and some, like Epsilon Lyrae, are quadruple. The most complicated multiple systems that we know have six stars, not all of which can be seen separately. Castor, in the constellation Gemini, is a sextuple star.

Astronomers call double and multiple stars, binaries, and classify them according to how they are observed. In our immediate neighbourhood in space — the only region for which we have a complete survey — a third of the stars are binary. Stars that can be seen to be double in a telescope are called visual binaries. Some are easy to see in a small telescope — for instance Castor (Alpha Geminorum), Alpha Centauri, and Mizar. (Mizar and Alcor form a wide pair, but Mizar itself is a double.) But many visual binaries are very close pairs and look single except in a large telescope under good observing conditions. Sometimes the difficulty is that the second star is much fainter. Sirius, for instance, has a companion that is 10,000 times fainter. The companion can be seen only in a large telescope.

In some visual binaries the two stars can be seen to move around each other as the years pass. From the size of the orbit and the period of revolution astronomers can determine the masses of the two stars. The two components of Alpha Centauri go around each other in 79 years, while in Castor the orbital period of the components is 300 years.

In some binaries the two stars are so close together that even in the most powerful telescopes they look like a single point of light. But the fact that the star is double may show up in some other way. Spectroscopic binaries are discovered when an astronomer photographs the spectrum of a star and finds that the light actually comes from two stars, one moving towards us and one away from us. If the two stars are observed often enough, they are found to be going around each other in an orbit, with each one alternately moving towards and away from us. Even though there appears to be only a single point of light, the spectrum shows that the star is double.

In other binaries the orbit is lined up with us in such a way that one star passes in front of the other and eclipses it. Such a star is called an eclipsing binary. It is purely by

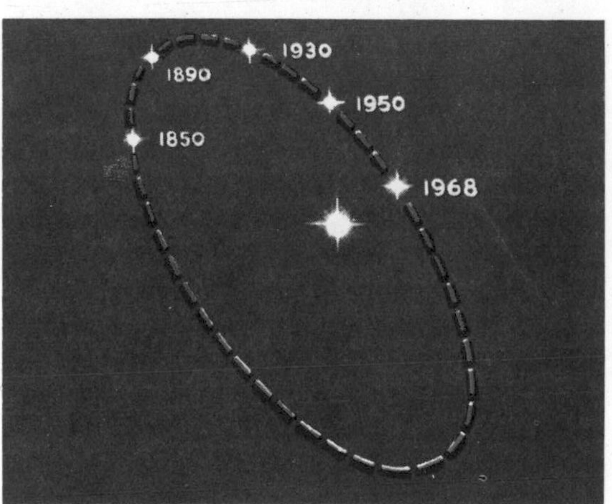

One of the brightest binaries is the star Castor. Its two brightest stars take 300 years to orbit about one another.

chance that the orbit is turned this way, but out of all the binaries in the sky, some are bound to be lined up just right. When one of the stars eclipses the other, it cuts off the light of the other star, and the combined light of the pair becomes dimmer. We see only a single point of light; but when it dims for a little while and then recovers, we know that an eclipse has taken place and the star must be double. The most famous eclipsing binary is Algol or Beta Persei. Once every two days and twenty-one hours it drops to

Yerkes Observatory Photograph

The Pleiades, in the constellation Taurus, is a galactic or open star cluster, with hazy, cloud-like areas.

Mt. Wilson and Palomar Observatories

The Great Cluster of Hercules (M13) is a globular cluster of more than 50,000 bright stars.

a third of its usual brightness. After ten hours it is back to normal and remains unchanged until the next eclipse, nearly three days later.

Astronomers follow eclipsing binaries with great interest. From their measurements of brightness they plot a light curve, which shows the brightness of the star at each moment during the eclipse. Careful analysis of the light curve allows them to calculate the masses and the diameters of the two stars. Other details of the light curve often show how the brightness changes over the surfaces of the stars, and sometimes they make it possible to tell how dense the material is deep down near the centres of the stars. Except for eclipsing stars, some of these facts cannot be found out for any star except the Sun, and even the density of the interior of the Sun cannot be observed directly.

STAR CLUSTERS. Some stars are members of large groups called star clusters. In a star cluster the individual stars mill about haphazardly, while in a multiple star each member has a regular orbit.

Star clusters are of special interest to astronomers because they are born as clusters, and all the stars have the same age. By comparing stars in different clusters, astronomers have determined which clusters are old and which are young. They have even determined how the individual stars change with time.

Clusters are of two types: galactic and globular. Galactic or open clusters inhabit the thin disc of the Milky Way. Several hundred are known, but a much larger number undoubtedly exist at greater distances from us, hidden behind the dust clouds of the Milky Way. A typical galactic cluster has a few hundred stars. Globular clusters are scattered through the halo of the Milky Way. About a hundred are known. A globular cluster contains hundreds of thousands of stars. In photographs the stars look closely packed together, but actually they are no more crowded than marbles a mile apart.

A star cluster does not last forever. Eventually the stars go their separate ways and can no longer be recognised as coming from the same origin. Globular clusters last for long periods of time, but most galactic clusters break up after less than a thousand million years. This may sound like a long time; but many stars, like the Sun, are much older. Most galactic clusters that we observe are young because they do not last long enough to grow old. Only a few rich galactic clusters have remained intact into their old age.

A star cluster has two sorts of stress — from outside and from inside. The difficulties that arise from outside are caused by the gravitational forces of other large bodies, such as the central bulge of the Milky Way. Such a force is stronger on the near side of the cluster than on the far side, and the result is a stretching force that will pull the cluster apart unless the cluster is compact enough to resist. A dense cluster, on the other hand, has internal stresses. Occasionally two stars in the cluster pass close to each other, swing round each other, and go off in new directions. As a result of encounters of this sort, some stars speed up enough to escape from the cluster. These stars are never replaced. As one star after another escapes, the cluster slowly dwindles. Thus the loose clusters are pulled apart and the dense clusters throw out their own member stars.

VARIABLE STARS. Stars vary in brightness for a number of reasons. Some stars are double, and as the two move around each other they alternately eclipse each other. The two stars are so close to each other that we see them as a single point of light, which becomes temporarily fainter during the eclipse (see page 453).

Most variable stars are single and change in brightness because of something inside them. Some, for instance, pulsate. They alternately swell and shrink, and consequently we see them change in brightness. Best known of the pulsating stars are the cepheids, which have helped astronomers in measuring most of the larger distances of the universe. (See CEPHEIDS.) Among the other sorts of pulsating stars are the long-period variables that vary in brightness by 100 times in a period of about a year. Long-period variables do not flicker or pulsate; their change in brightness is steady and rhythmic. U Orionus, a long-period variable, is about 100 times brighter than the Sun. Another sort of variable star increases tremendously in brightness because of an explosion. One type, called a nova, merely blows off its skin and then subsides to its original faintness. A supernova is a star that explodes, as did the nova Cassiopeia that appeared in 1572 and had disappeared two years later.

BIRTH OF STARS. Each star has an age, and each star was born at some time in the past. The oldest that we know are 10,000 or 20,000 million years old but the youngest are less than a million years old. Perhaps a million years does not seem like a short time, but it is a thousand times shorter than 1,000 million years.

In 1572, there appeared in Cassiopeia a nova so bright that it was visible in daylight. By 1574, this spectacular nova, or exploding star, had disappeared.

It is easy to tell that some stars are young. For instance, the very bright stars called super-giants are radiating light and heat into space so fast that we know they cannot last more than a few million years. Even stars cannot keep shining without some kind of fuel. Their fuel is nuclear and can supply energy for a long time, but even nuclear fuel is eventually used up. The super-giants are using their fuel so fast that we know they will never live to be old; therefore, any star with a high luminosity, or super-giant, is a young star. The first-magnitude stars Deneb, Rigel, Betelgeuse, and Antares are super-giants.

Many stars are born in groups. They soon go their separate ways, but the very youngest groups have not yet had time to disperse. These groups are called associations. Most of the stars in the constellation Orion belong to such an association.

Stars are probably born where the youngest stars are, in the regions where there is a great deal of gas and dust in the space between the stars. Astronomers therefore believe that clouds of interstellar gas and dust condense into new stars. The interstellar material is scattered through space in a very irregular fashion, and some regions are much denser than others. Many clouds of gas and dust dissipate or spread out again, but it is possible for the very densest clouds to begin to contract and become even denser. Some astronomers believe that this first contraction is caused by the pressure of starlight. The light of the stars exerts only a very weak force, but after a million years, even a weak force can have a great effect. After the contraction is started, gravitation does the rest. Every part of the cloud attracts every other part, and the more the cloud contracts, the stronger the attraction becomes. As the material falls towards the centre of the cloud it releases energy. The energy released in the cloud becomes heat. When the centre of the cloud reaches a high enough temperature to set nuclear reactions going, the cloud has become a new star.

EVOLUTION OF STARS. The light of a star is energy that is lost to it; and if that energy were not replaced, the star would soon cool off and stop shining. To keep shining the star must burn fuel continually. It starts its life with a certain amount of fuel and can continue shining only as long as that fuel lasts. Fortunately the fuel is of a very efficient nuclear type, and the star begins life with a very large stock of it so that stars do have very long lifetimes.

The stars are made mostly of hydrogen. This is their fuel, and the burning process is nuclear fusion. At the centre of a star, where the temperature is millions of degrees, hydrogen is converted slowly to helium, and this conversion supplies the energy that keeps the star shining.

Since the fuel that is burned keeps up a star's light the brightness of the star shows how fast it is burning up fuel. We know how much fuel a star has, so we know how long it will last. Faint stars are burning their fuel slowly and will last many thousands of millions of years, but the brightest stars are using fuel so rapidly that they can last only a million years or so. The Sun, the Earth, and the rest of the solar system are about 5,000 million years old and so a star that has a life of only a million years really is a brief visitor to the astronomical scene.

Stars are being born all the time, as condensing clouds of interstellar dust and gas. The clouds contract and heat up, until each cloud centre is hot enough to start nuclear reactions. Each star then settles down to a steady brightness, temperature and size. This steady phase lasts for most of the star's life and ends only when the star has used up all the nuclear fuel at its centre.

Then the star changes again. For all of its life it has kept up its energy supply by converting hydrogen into helium around its centre where the temperature is highest. Now the star has a small central region in which nothing is left but helium. But the surrounding cooler layers still have hydrogen, and the temperature of the star rises to use it. Thus the hydrogen fusion reaction slowly eats its way outwards through the star, leaving inside it a growing central core oı helium. As the location of the nuclear fire changes, the star's whole structure changes, too. It grows larger and brighter, and its surface cools. Some types of stars brighten

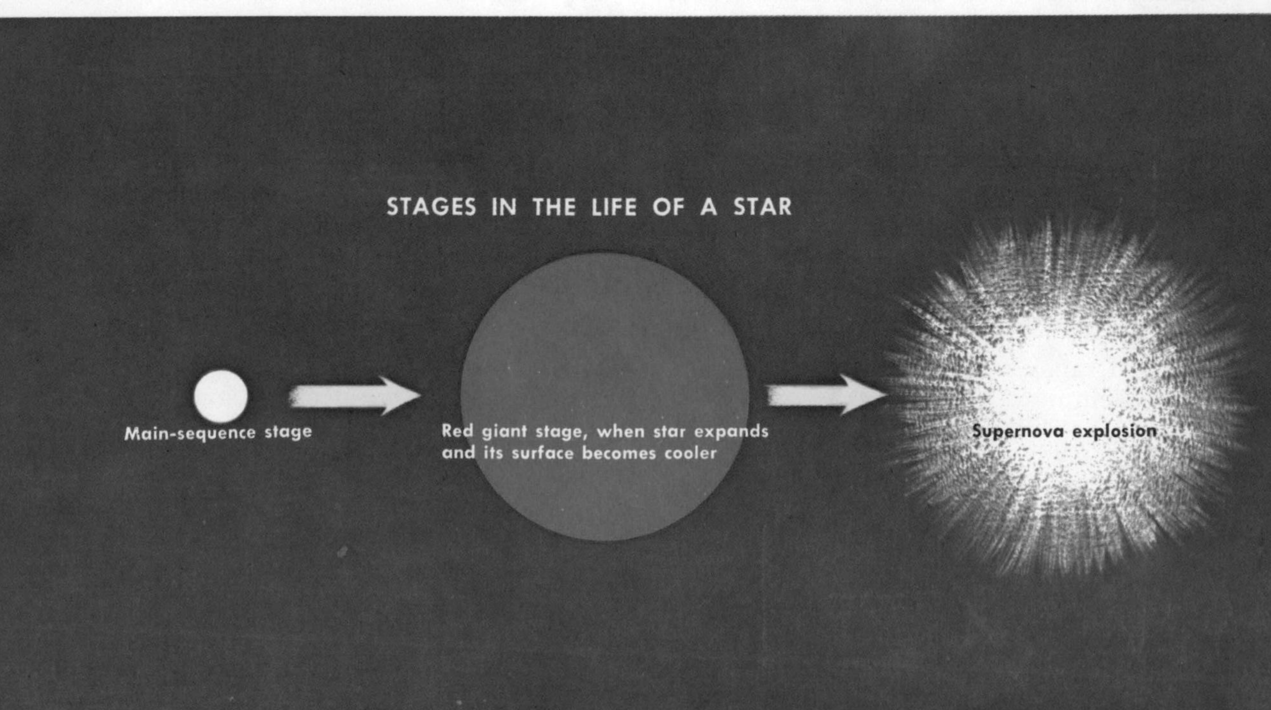

a great deal, and this is most unfortunate for them, since then they must burn fuel even faster and the end comes even sooner.

The hydrogen burning does not proceed very far out through the star because something new happens at the centre. The temperature at the centre of the star continues to rise as the helium core grows. Eventually the core becomes so hot that the helium atoms start to fuse with each other and form carbon atoms. Helium, which was the burned-out ash of the hydrogen fusion reaction, has suddenly become a fuel! The appearance of a new source of energy changes the star's structure again, and its evolution goes in a different direction. We do not know the details of these late stages of a star's evolution except that they do not last very long.

The end is now near. Stars of some types begin to scatter their material away into the space around them. But for others the end is more spectacular. As the star's central temperature rises, a new nuclear reaction begins. The energy that it generates raises the temperature higher, and the reaction goes even faster. The nuclear reaction runs wild, and the star blows up in one sudden blast. This is probably the cause of what is called a supernova — a star that suddenly flares up to be brighter than any steadily shining star and then subsides to almost nothing, as happened in the nova Cassiopeia that appeared in 1572 (see page 455).

White dwarf stage, the small remnant, cooling slowly

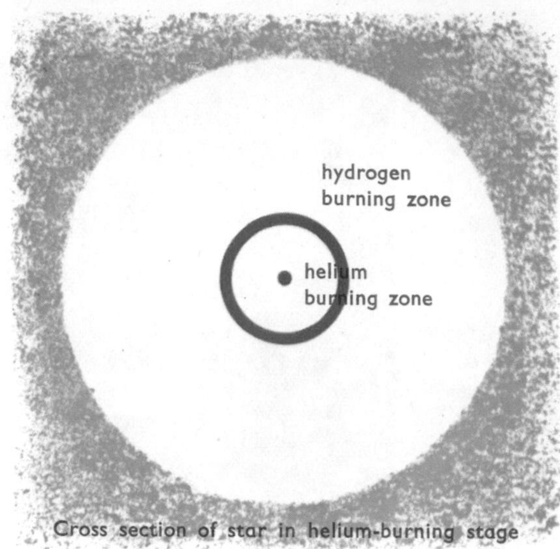

Cross section of star in helium-burning stage

The material thrown out of the star spreads through interstellar space and is available for making new stars. The cycle begins again but with one important change: the nuclear reactions inside a star build hydrogen into helium, helium into carbon, and so on — always building nuclei of heavier elements. The abundances of the different chemical elements in the universe are probably a result of this repeated process of stellar cookery. The atoms that make up the Earth and the objects on it (even our bodies) were once heated to millions of degrees at a star's centre and owe their nature to that experience.

STRUCTURE OF STARS. A star is a large sphere of hot gas, held together by its own gravitation. It shines because it is so hot, just as a hot coal glows. Light and heat are lost from a star's surface so rapidly that it would soon cool off if energy did not flow continually from the interior of the star. The source of energy at the star's centre is in nuclear reactions in which hydrogen is converted to helium. This releases a very large amount of energy from a very small amount of fuel, as in the hydrogen bomb. These reactions require a very high temperature to make them go, and only at the very centre of a star is the temperature high enough. The 10,000 degrees surface temperature of the stars seems high to us, but at the centre of a star the temperature is millions of degrees.

All stars have the same general structure,

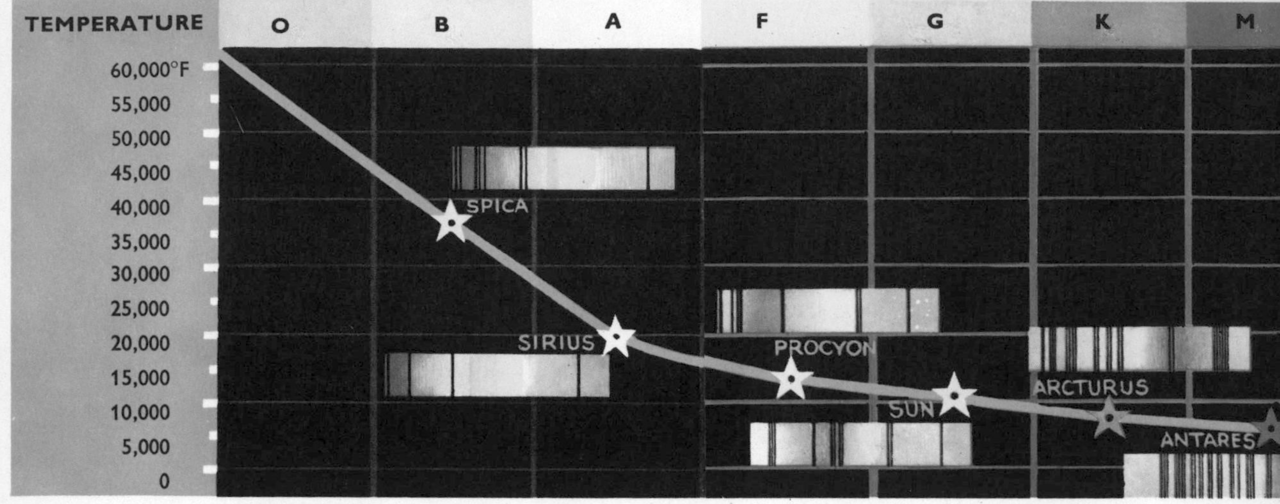

Star classification is based on its spectrum, as shown in the diagram above and in the chart on the right.

STAR CLASSIFICATION

Star class	Approx. Temp. (degrees F.)	Colour	Spectral character	Examples
O	over 55,000	Blue-white	Gases strongly ionized	Iota Orionis (in sword)
B	36,000	Blue-white	Strong neutral helium	Rigel Spica
A	20,000	White	Hydrogen predominant	Sirius Vega
F	13,500	Yellowish white	Hydrogen decreasing; metals increasing	Canopus Procyon
G	11,000	Yellow	Metals prominent	Sun Capella
K	7,500	Orange	Metals surpass hydrogen	Arcturus Aldebaran
M	5,500	Red	Titanium oxide present — violet light weak	Betelgeuse Antares

but they differ greatly in size, brightness, colour, and many other properties. Astronomers generally classify them according to two properties that are easy to determine by observation: the spectrum and the luminosity or true brightness. The spectral class of a star is an indication of how hot its surface is; it also varies closely with the star's colour. The luminosity of stars can be expressed as so many times brighter or fainter than the Sun, but astronomers more commonly express it as the magnitude that a star would appear to have if it were ten parsecs away from us. This is called absolute magnitude. Imagining all stars at the same distance corrects for the fact that some of them look faint merely because they are far away. In detailed classifications, astronomers divide each of the seven basic classes, shown in the chart above, into ten sub-classes.

To compare the properties of different stars, astronomers plot them on an HR diagram, named after the astronomers Hertzsprung and Russell who first used it. Spectral types are marked along one edge of the diagram and absolute magnitudes along the other, so that each star is represented by a dot opposite its correct spectral type and absolute magnitude. When we plot such a diagram, the points representing the stars do not scatter uniformly over the diagram but instead show a strong preference for certain regions. Most stars fall on a line called the main sequence, which runs diagonally down through the diagram; but other regions are filled, too. Stars on the lower half of the main sequence are called dwarfs, and brighter stars at the same spectral type are referred to as giants or supergiants, as illustrated on page 456. Stars in these various classes are in different stages of evolution.

Depending on their ages, different groups of stars have different HR diagrams. Stars on the upper main sequence have short lives, so they are missing in all but the youngest groups. In fact, astronomers can tell the age of a group of stars simply by plotting their HR diagram and seeing how much of the top of the main sequence is left. In this way we find that stars are born in the spiral arms of our Milky Way and gradually diffuse through the rest of the system.

In the Sun's neighbourhood we have a mixture of young stars and old ones. Some are only a few million years old; others are 10,000 million years old or even older. The Sun itself is a middle-aged main-sequence star. The most common stars around us are lower-sequence stars, called red dwarfs. White dwarfs are also very common. Stars of both types are so faint that they are hard to find, but they make up the majority of stars of the universe.

Finally, in some regions of space there are groups of stars, such as the globular clusters, that have quite different HR diagrams. These we cannot explain by age alone; the stars there must have a different chemical composition from the stars around us.

COLOUR OF STARS. Stars differ not only in brightness but also in colour. Some of the bright stars have quite noticeable colours. In the constellation Orion, for instance, Rigel is blue and Betelgeuse is red. In the summer sky, the bluish white of Vega contrasts with the orange of Arcturus and the red of Antares. The faint stars have colours, too, but they are not so easily seen because the human eye does not register colours of faint objects. With a telescope many of the fainter stars look bright enough for their colours to be striking. Some double stars are especially pretty. Albireo, or Beta Cygni, consists of a blue star and an orange one, side by side. By contrast with the orange, the blue looks green to some people. Photographs are one of the best means of determining the colours of stars.

The reason for the difference in the colours of the stars is that some stars are hotter than others. Nearly all stars are so hot that the various substances in them are completely vapourised.

To find out how hot a star is, we measure its colour. A blue star like Spica has a temperature of about 33,000 degrees centigrade (60,000 degrees Fahrenheit), while the temperature of a cool red star like Antares is about 3,300 degrees centigrade (6,000 degrees Fahrenheit).

The Sun is a yellow star, with a temperature of about 7,000 degrees centigrade (11,000 degrees Fahrenheit). (See chart on page 458).

These are the temperatures at the surfaces of the stars. We cannot see inside the stars, but we know that the temperatures are much higher there. Most of the interior of a star is hotter than a million degrees, and the

This photograph of a portion of the Milky Way shows myriads of stars, dark patches of gas and dust that obscure other stars, and bright nebulae that reflect light from nearby stars.

Yerkes Observatory Photograph

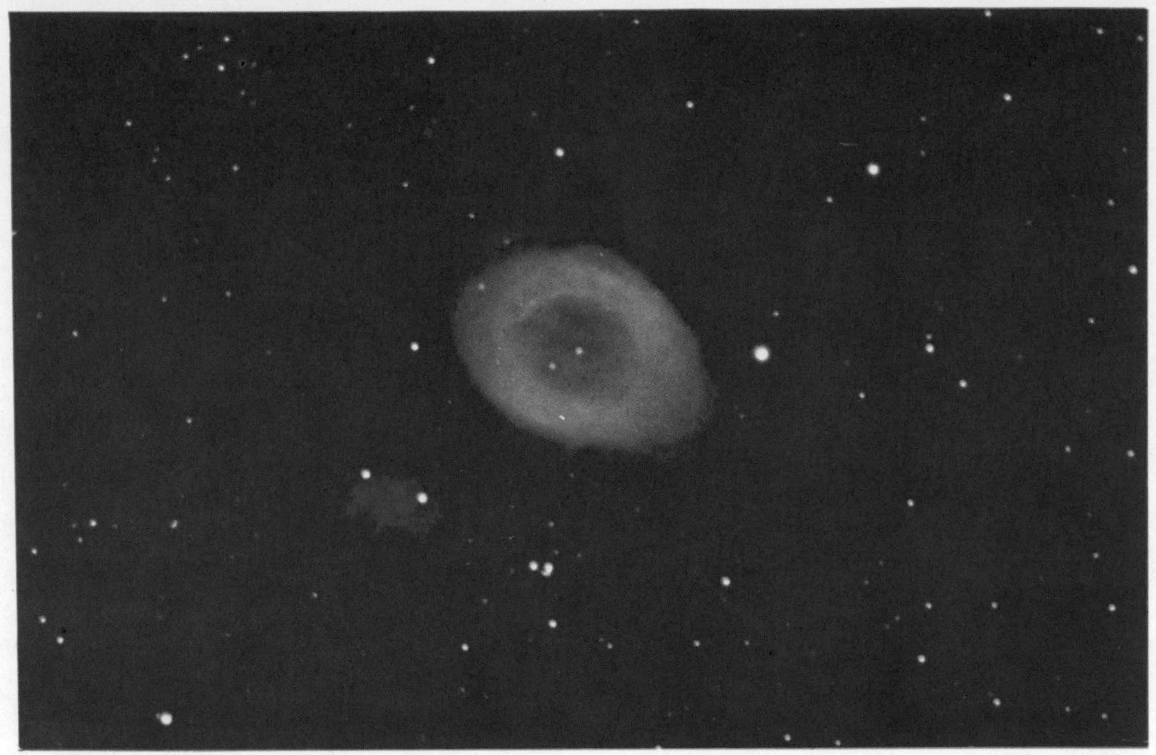

Mt. Wilson and Palomar Observatories

The famous Ring Planetary Nebula in Lyra is a gaseous envelope surrounding a very hot blue star in the centre. The nebula glows because of the intense short-wave radiation from the central star.

temperatures at the centres of the stars are many millions of degrees. At the centre of the Sun the temperature is over 14 million degrees centigrade (25 million degrees Fahrenheit).

COMPOSITION OF STARS. The stars are remote and very different from the Earth, but they are made of the same sort of material. When we pass starlight through a prism and photograph its spectrum, we see dark lines that are the same as those produced by familiar chemical elements here on the Earth (see SPECTRUM). It is thus easy to see what the stars are made of, but it is much harder to tell how much of each chemical element is present. Most of the differences between stellar spectra are caused by temperature differences rather than differences in chemical composition. For this reason the composition of a star can be determined only from a detailed study of its spectrum and an analysis of the star's atmosphere.

In the Sun and in most of the other stars around us, about three quarters of the material is hydrogen. Most of the remainder is helium, leaving only 2 per cent for all the rest of the elements. So carbon, oxygen, silicon, iron, and all the other chemical elements that make up most of the Earth, compose only a small fraction of the material of the stars. Since the stars contain most of the material of the universe, it is the Earth that is unusual. (See EARTH; PLANETS.)

The material of the stars is also in a different form than is the material on Earth. The Earth is a relatively cold body and the atoms that make it up are grouped together into molecules of the thousands of different compounds that make the material around us so complex and varied. But a star is so hot that nearly all molecules are broken into their separate atoms, and all are mixed together into a single hot gas. In a star, simplicity, not variety, in the form of the material content is the rule.

The stars around us are very similar in composition, and this is just what we should expect if all these stars were made out of a common stock of interstellar gas and dust. But occasionally we find a star whose chemical composition is different. Such stars usually have high speeds, indicating that they come from distant parts of the Milky

Yerkes Observatory Photograph

The multitude of stars in the Beehive Cluster (M44) are barely visible to the naked eye. Telescopes reveal the cluster to contain such a large number of stars that naming them is impossible. Each is identified by a number.

Way. Astronomers call these stars Population Type II, and they inhabit the outer halo of the Milky Way. In the central disc of the Milky Way, where we live, nearly all stars are Type I, like the Sun (see MILKY WAY).

The Type II stars are made almost completely of a mixture of hydrogen and helium. All the rest of the chemical elements, which astronomers call the heavy elements, make up only a fraction of one per cent of the material of a Type II star. The other striking thing about Population II is that its stars are all old, whereas Type I stars run through the complete range from newborn to old. Many astronomers believe that the Type II stars date from an earlier stage in the development of the Milky Way, before the present supply of heavy elements had been made. According to this view the proportion of heavy elements has gradually been increasing and the producers are the stars. The nuclear reactions that generate a star's energy also change the composition of the material. In the late stages of a star's development, heavier and heavier elements are built up, and when the star dies this material is strewn about in interstellar space. In the end it gathers together to form new stars, which are richer in heavy elements than were their predecessors.

STAR NAMES. Ever since ancient times the brighter stars have been given names. Some of the star names that we use today are Latin and Greek, but most are Arabic. When too many stars have special names, it becomes difficult to remember them all. Therefore astronomers have developed other systems of naming stars. The scheme most commonly employed for the brighter stars uses the name of the constellation the star belongs to and assigns a different Greek letter to each star. In most constellations the brightest star is called Alpha, the second Beta, and so on. For instance, the brightest star Sirius is Alpha Canis Majoris, while Albireo is Beta Cygni.

The Greek alphabet has only 24 letters, however, so not many stars can be named in this fashion. For fainter stars astronomers commonly use the star's number in some large catalogue; for example, HR 5183 or BD + 42° 2807. All stars down to tenth magnitude have been catalogued —

nearly a million of them. For fainter stars the best that an astronomer can do is to show a picture of the region with the right star marked.

The catalogue method is also used for the naming of non-stellar objects — star clusters, nebulae, and galaxies. The brightest ones are known by their numbers in the catalogue of the eighteenth-century astronomer Messier. Thus the Great Galaxy in Andromeda is M 31. A much larger number of objects are contained in the volume called the New General Catalogue. For instance, M 31 is NGC 224, while the great globular cluster in Hercules is M 13, or NGC 6205.

MAGNITUDE OF STARS. The comparative brightness of stars as we see them is called magnitude. The Greeks referred to the brightest stars as first magnitude, and so on. Stars that were barely visible to the naked eye were called sixth magnitude. Modern astronomers use the same system but with a higher precision of measurement. Also, the scale has been extended to include brighter stars, which are assigned zero or even negative magnitudes, and to fainter stars, which have magnitudes higher than 6. The brightest star, Sirius, has a magnitude of −1.4, but the planet Venus may become as bright as magnitude −4.4 at times. At the other extreme, the faintest stars that can be photographed with the 200-inch telescope are of twenty-third magnitude.

Stars of each magnitude are $2\frac{1}{2}$ times as bright as those of the next fainter magnitude. Thus a first-magnitude star is $2\frac{1}{2}$ times as bright as a second-magnitude star, $6\frac{1}{4}$ times as bright as a third-magnitude star, 16 times as bright as a fourth-magnitude star, and so on.

There are 21 stars in the sky whose magnitudes are brighter than 1.5. They are referred to as the first-magnitude stars, though many are actually brighter than first magnitude.

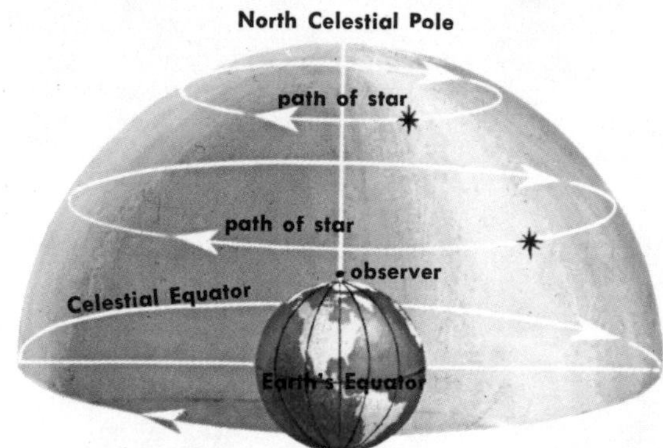

When the observer is at the North Pole, the Celestial Equator is at the southern horizon and the North Celestial Pole is straight overhead. Stars north of the Celestial Equator never appear to rise or set; those in the south celestial hemisphere are never seen.

When an observer is at the equator, with the celestial poles at the horizons, all stars appear to rise and set. Each star is visible above the horizon for twelve hours.

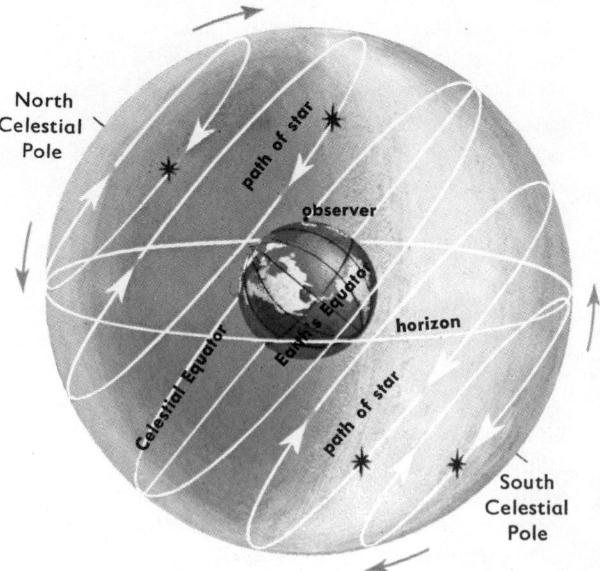

To an observer located at a midpoint between the pole and the equator, the stars traverse the heavens obliquely along the diurnal circles of the celestial sphere. In the Northern Hemisphere, the stars of the north polar region never set; they are called circumpolar stars. Those near the South Celestial Pole are never seen. Stars within 50 degrees on either side of the Celestial Equator rise and set.

THE BRIGHTEST STARS

Name	Constellation	Magnitude
Sirius	Canis Major	−1.4
Canopus	Carina	−0.7
Alpha Centauri	Centaurus	−0.3
Arcturus	Boötes	−0.1
Vega	Lyra	0.0
Capella	Auriga	+0.1
Rigel	Orion	+0.2
Procyon	Canis Minor	+0.4
Achernar	Eridanus	+0.5
Beta Centauri	Centaurus	+0.7
Betelgeuse	Orion	+0.7
Altair	Aquila	+0.8
Aldebaran	Taurus	+0.8
Alpha Crucis	Crux	+0.9
Antares	Scorpio	+1.0
Spica	Virgo	+1.0
Fomalhaut	Piscis Austrinus	+1.2
Pollux	Gemini	+1.2
Deneb	Cygnus	+1.3
Beta Crucis	Crux	+1.3
Regulus	Leo	+1.4

RISING AND SETTING OF STARS. One of the most popular and universal concepts of astronomy held that the Earth was the centre of the universe and the stars were movable lights in the dome of the sky. As men made careful observations and learned the use of the telescope and other instruments, this belief was replaced by what is considered to be one of the greatest triumphs of the mind — the concept of the celestial sphere. Though outdated, this important concept is still useful in observing the stars and for measuring their apparent motions.

Directly above the observer is a point on the imaginary celestial sphere known as the *zenith*; directly beneath him, and exactly opposite the zenith, is the *nadir*. Halfway between those two points is the observer's horizon. The Earth's poles and the equator have their celestial counterparts above us on the celestial sphere. (See CELESTIAL SPHERE.)

As the Earth rotates on its axis every day, it makes the stars appear to rise in the east, move across the sky, and set in the west. If we watch the stars carefully, however, we find that they do not all follow the same sort of path. The heavens appear to turn about a point called the celestial pole. For observers in mid-northern latitudes, the pole is about halfway up from the northern horizon to the zenith. Every star follows a daily path, or diurnal circle, around this point. Stars close to the celestial north pole have diurnal circles completely above the horizon; they never set and so are called circumpolar stars. Beyond a certain distance from the pole (equal to the observer's latitude), stars rise and set. The farther south a star is, the shorter the time it spends above the horizon. Finally, stars that are close to the south celestial pole circle are completely below the horizon and never appear at all in middle northern latitudes.

The sizes of the circumpolar regions, and the slope of the diurnal circles, depend on the observer's latitude on Earth. At the North Pole, all diurnal circles are parallel to the horizon. The entire northern half of the celestial sphere is circumpolar, and the southern half never appears at all. As one travels towards the equator, the circumpolar region shrinks, and there is a growing equatorial region of the sky in which all stars rise and set. For an observer on the Earth's equator, both celestial poles are on the horizon. All diurnal circles come straight up from the horizon, and all stars rise and set. An observer in the Earth's Southern Hemisphere sees a circumpolar region around the south celestial pole, while in the extreme north is a region of the sky that he never sees.

Besides the daily change of the constellations, there is a change throughout the year, because of the Earth's motion around the Sun. Each night the stars rise and set four minutes earlier, so that after a month they are rising and setting two hours earlier. Thus in each season we have a new set of constellations, until at the end of a whole year we are back to where we originally started. (See CONSTELLATIONS.)

STOCKS (*Matthiola* spp.) are a group of fragrant ornamentals that grow in southern Europe and the Mediterranean region. They belong to the mustard family along with candytufts and Sweet Alyssum. One species has been cultivated, and many varieties have been produced.

Stocks are easy to grow, bloom freely, and furnish cut flowers for fairly long periods. One kind is known as Cut-and-come-again because of its ability to continue flowering. The popular night-blooming forms are highly scented.

STRAWFLOWERS (*Helichrysum* spp.) stay fresh and bright without water. They are commonly used for winter bouquets. Some people call them 'everlasting flowers'. These daisy-like natives of Africa and Australia are less popular today, possibly because plastic flowers are being used so much for decoration.

Strawflower blossoms are really not blossoms, but the scaly bases of flower heads. In most members of the daisy family, these basal scales are green, but in strawflowers they are tinted various shades of red, pink, yellow, and orange. They really do look like flower petals. The tiny, true flowers are in the flat area enclosed by the coloured scales.

STREAMS. Where the waters of a stream flow very rapidly, especially near the stream's origin, loose sand and soil are washed from between stones. Plants cannot get rooted. Mosses and algae that grow on rocks are the only plants able to survive.

Churned waters of a fast stream contain more oxygen than do the waters of a slow stream. Fast waters are also more likely to be pure. The temperature of the water in a fast-flowing stream is constantly low since it is not exposed to the air long enough in any one place to be warmed.

Farther downstream from its source, the stream's current becomes slow. Side pools appear and rooted plants grow in the pebbles and silt deposited on the bottom. Then more silt is collected around their roots. Quiet waters contain less oxygen, and the water temperature is closer to the temperature of the air. Plants that grow in quiet waters do not need woody stems. They are light and porous and easily buoyed by the water. Most of these plants lack roots or use their roots only for anchorage. Nutrients and minerals dissolved in the water are obtained through their porous stems. Underwater leaves are usually long filaments; those above water are frequently broad, floating pads. Stems with flowers project into the air so that pollination can occur. Many plants grow in such abundance that they furnish excellent food for ducks and other water birds. Canadian Water Weed *(Elodea canadensis)*, Water Hyacinths *(Eichhornia)*, and Pondweed *(Potamogeton)* can grow so thickly that they check the flow of streams. Much of the water's surface may be covered with waterlilies.

A third distinct habitat occurs where rivers join oceans. There salt water mixes with the fresh and makes a brackish-water environment. Widgeon Grass *(Ruppia)* forms waving masses beneath the surface and long ribbon-

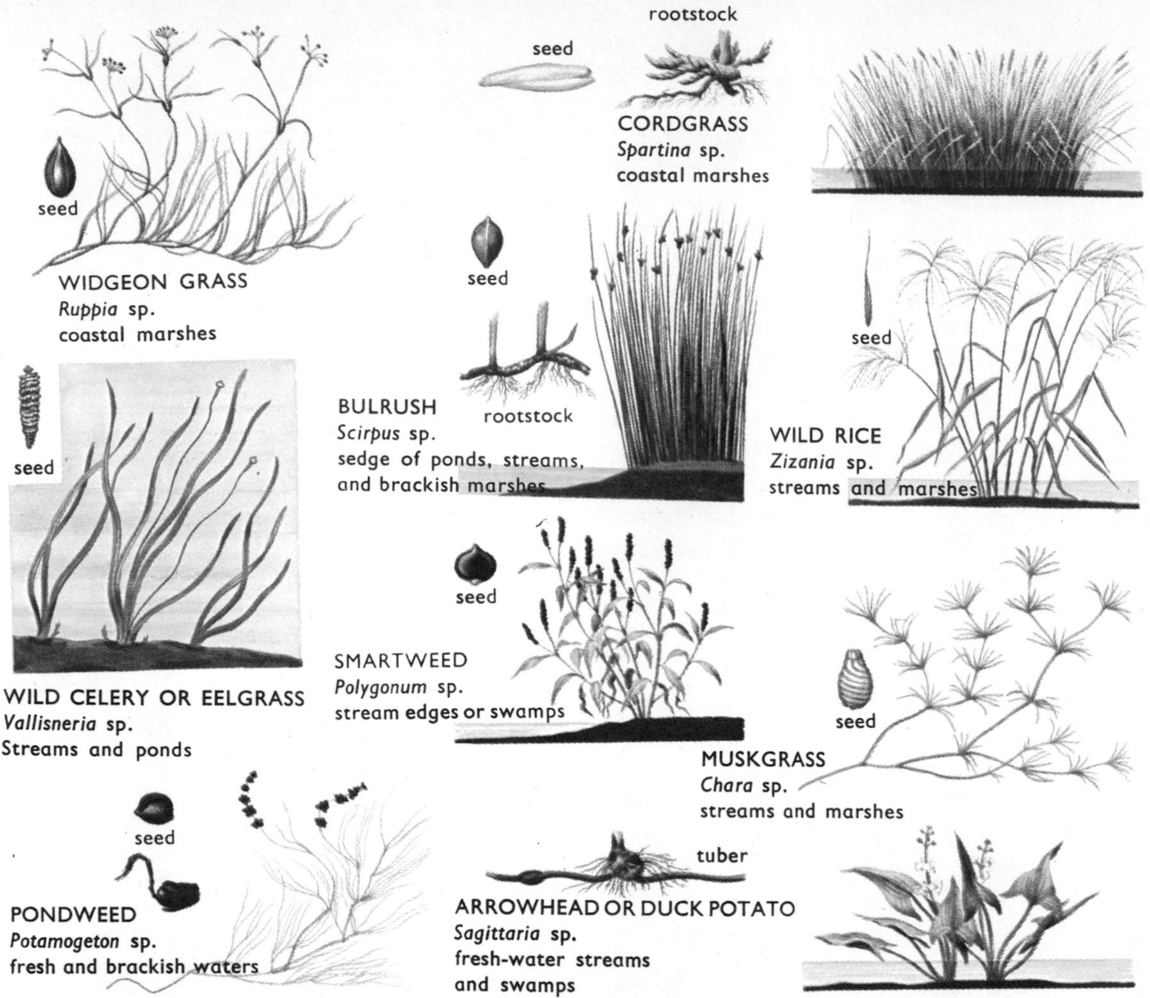

SOME WATERFOWL FOODS OF STREAMS AND MARSHES

like leaves of Eelgrass *(Zostera)* grow abundantly from creeping rootstocks.

STRONTIANITE *(Strontium carbonate)* is a mineral found as crystals in needle-like clumps or in compact, granular masses. It is white, has two good cleavages, and bubbles vigorously in cold acid. It occurs with lead ores in low temperature veins.

Strontium nitrate, made from strontianite and celestite, is used in fireworks, flares, and tracer bullets because of its bright red flame. Strontium compounds are used in medicines and in the recovery of sugar in sugar beet refining. Strontium is used in electronic tubes to absorb gases. Scotland and Mexico are the largest producers, although some comes from Germany, Austria, Canada, and the U.S.A.

SUCCESSION is a gradual change in a community of plants.

A good example is the change of a pond into a dry land community. Water plants, plankton, and other living things die and accumulate at the bottom. Silt is washed in from surrounding land. Gradually the open water is reduced to a swamp. Sedges and rushes grow along the margin and add still more solid material. They themselves are replaced by shrubs. As the soil continues to build up and becomes drier, small trees invade the area and crowd out many of the shrubs. In this way, woodlands finally give way to forests.

Any land laid bare by burning, cutting, or other means goes through definite succession stages. In a forested region, exposed land is pioneered by weeds. Then shrubs grow and finally trees. Often whole forests of some types of trees grow and disappear before the climax forest stage is reached. For example, a beech-maple climax forest may be preceded by forests of pines and oaks. Similarly, the climax vegetation of grasslands consists of particular species of grasses. Other types may dominate before the vegetation reaches the climax stage and is stabilised.

Succession occurs even in communities of microscopic plants and animals. In cultures, bacteria are dominant first. Then ciliated protozoans become quite numerous. They decline and are followed by a build-up of *Paramecia*. *Amoeba* dominate the culture next, followed by stalked ciliates called *Vorticella*.

It may require a few years for a fallen tree to decompose or a few hundred years for a pond to become dry land. Succession has occurred since the beginning of life on Earth. (See LIFE'S ORIGIN AND DEVELOPMENT.)

SUGARS are manufactured by plants from carbon dioxide and water in the presence of sunlight and chlorophyll. This process is called photosynthesis. Plants utilise these sugars, or foods converted from them, in their growth and development. Man and other animals are also dependent on plant sugars.

Sediments and dead plants fill a pond in this succession from aquatic to a dry-land environment.

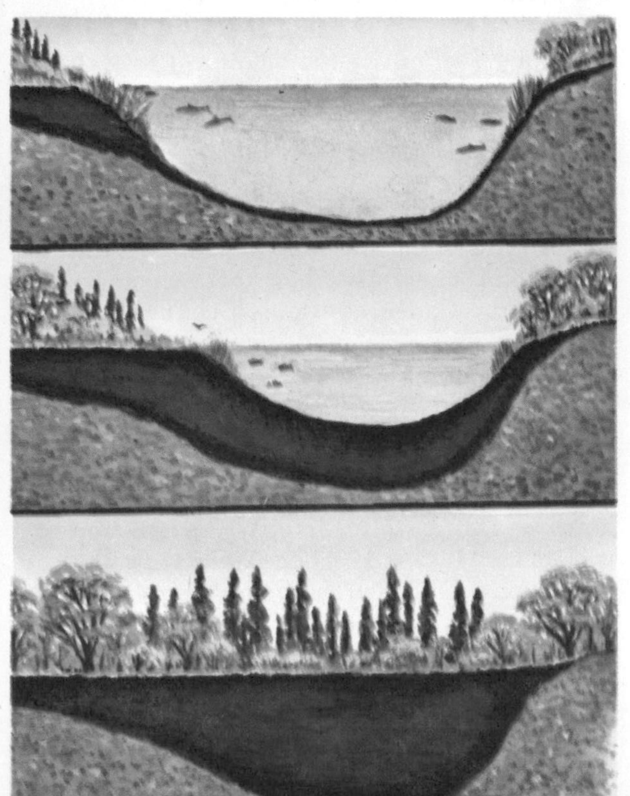

SUGAR CANE
Saccharum officinarum
to 12 ft.

Sugar cane is one of the most important cash crops of tropical agriculture. This scene, on Taiwan Island, shows fields of cane, bamboo windbreaks, rich well-watered soil, and a group of peasants harvesting the crop.

Two important commercial sources of sugar are Sugar Cane and Sugar Beets. Sugar is also obtained from such other plants as maple trees, sorghums and palms.

Sugar Cane (several species of *Saccharum*) is a member of the grass family that was originally native to south-eastern Asia. Egyptians were probably the first to produce this 'sweet salt', but it took a period of some 3,000 years for the cultivation of Sugar Cane to spread to the tropical areas of the world. For many years after it reached Europe, sugar was used only medicinally. Sugar did not become important in European diets until tea and coffee became popular during the 1700s. Spanish and Portuguese explorers introduced Sugar Cane into the West Indies and South America. It was first grown in Louisiana in the United States of America in 1751 and in Hawaii in 1835.

On Sugar Cane plantations pieces of cane are planted in furrows. New roots and tops grow from their joints (nodes). The cane is ready to harvest in about a year and a half, growing 8 — 10 feet tall and 1 inch to 2 inches in diameter. Sugar Cane grows best in hot, wet climates. Often irrigation is needed to give growing plants enough water.

In some areas the cane is harvested mechanically, but most cane is cut by machete. It is common to set the field on fire to destroy leaves and rubbish and make it easier to cut the stalks, which are hauled to a processing plant. Trains or lorries move loads of cane from field to factory. In Hawaii, the cut stalks are floated to factories in sluices. New cane will sprout from stubs or roots that are left in the fields, but since the yield is less after each cutting, fields of cane are replanted every two to four years.

Hamilton-Wright Organisation, Inc.

Courtesy United Fruit Co.

Machetes are used to cut Sugar Cane in Cuba, Mexico, and other Central American countries.

At the factory, the cane is cut into short pieces and crushed between rollers. Each series of rollers is set closer together so that as much juice as possible is squeezed from the stalks. The stalks yield about 15 per cent sugar and 78 per cent water. The remainder is fibre. The pressed stalks, known as bagasse, are used as fuel or in making paper or wallboard. The extracted juice is treated with lime to prevent fermentation and then filtered and evaporated under vacuum, until it begins to crystallise in a heavy liquid. Finally, giant centrifuges spin off the molasses and leave the raw sugar in the basket of the centrifuge. Molasses is used as a syrup or is mixed in cattle feed. It is also manufactured into vinegar, ethyl alcohol, or rum. The crude or raw sugar is shipped to a refinery where it is treated to remove impurities and colour. India, Cuba, Brazil, the Philippines, Java, Puerto Rico and Hawaii are major growers of Sugar Cane.

Sugar Beets, a variety of the Common Beet (*Beta vulgaris*), are grown in temperate zones throughout the world. They are a major crop in many counties in England, as well as in several western states in the United States of America. Sugar Beet is also grown extensively in Russia, France, Germany, Japan and China. Seeds are planted in early spring, and the crop is ready for harvest in mid-autumn. The beets, by this time, can weigh anything from one to five pounds.

Modern sugar beet refineries include conveyor systems to carry the beets to the extraction plant.

Courtesy Sugar Information, Inc.

In processing factories the beets are washed and sliced into thin chips or shreds. Hot water circulated through the shredded beet extracts about 97 per cent of the sugar. Finally, the beets are pressed to remove the remaining sugar and water. The solids (press-cake) are used as fertiliser and live-stock feed. The extracted sugar solution is concentrated by evaporating the liquid, and the crystallised sugar is then refined to remove the impurities.

Early colonists in North America learned from the Indians how to collect sap from maple trees and convert it into syrup and sugar. Sap is extracted from several kinds of maples that grow in north-eastern United States. The Sugar Maple *(Acer saccharum)* yields the most. In early spring, when the sap begins to flow, holes are drilled into the sapwood and drains inserted so that the sap flows into containers attached to the tree. The sap is boiled down to a thick syrup in large kettles and then poured into moulds to

Freshly mined sulphur is a soft solid that turns to dust on exposure to the air and drying.

Freeport Sulphur Co.

crystallise or is evaporated in shallow pans to make maple syrup or sugar. Sap flows for about a month, each tree producing enough to make approximately three pounds of sugar. Maple sugar and syrup are expensive but are very much prized for their delicious flavour.

Palm sugar is collected from several species of palm trees which are tapped to get their sap in much the same manner as are maple trees. As much as a gallon of sap a day may be collected from each palm tree for several months. The sap, referred to as 'toddy' is boiled down to form a sugar called 'jaggery'. The toddy can be fermented and consumed as a drink. Palm sugar is produced commercially in India, Ceylon, and Indonesia.

The sweet juice from the stem of a sorghum *(Sorghum vulgare)* has been used as a source of sugar in China for centuries. Sorghum is grown in mid-western and southern United States for sorghum syrup rather than sugar.

SULPHUR is an element that occurs as bright yellow crystals or as resinous granular or powdery masses and crusts. It burns with a blue flame that gives off a suffocating odour. Sulphur crystals develop around volcanic vents, but most sulphur is formed by the breaking down of such sulphates as gypsum and anhydrite. It is found in great masses or is spread through sedimentary rocks, such as along the coasts of Texas and Louisiana. Sulphur also occurs as a decomposition product of sulphides in coal beds and may be precipitated in hot springs by the action of bacteria.

Sulphur is used in many industries as pure sulphur or as sulphur compounds. These are produced from pyrite, gypsum, anhydrite, and in the smelting of sulphide ores. Sulphur is mined in the United States by drilling a well into the sulphur formation and lowering into the well four pipes, one within the other. Super-heated water is pumped down the outer two pipes, and air is pumped down the inner pipe. Melted sulphur, air, and water are forced up the remaining pipe.

Sulphur is used for vulcanising rubber and for fungicides. Carbon disulphide is a powerful fumigant. Sulphuric acid is necessary in many industries, as in the manufacture of fertilisers, insecticides, paints, paper, rayon and cellulose plastics, alcohol, explosives, detergents, storage batteries, and others. It is also used in purifying petroleum products, in cleaning iron and steel, and in producing lead.

SUMACHS *(Rhus)*, members of the cashew family, are shrubs or small trees (occasionally 25 to 30 feet high). Most kinds have thick, pithy twigs and large pinnately compound leaves arranged alternately. In autumn the leaves turn red.

In Great Britain some sumachs are grown in cultivation for their autumn foliage. They include Sumach *(Rhus crotinoides)*, the Smoke Tree *(Rhus cotinus)* and Stag's Horn Sumach *(Rhus typhina)*. Most sumachs bear dense clusters of small red fruits. Berries of Stag's Horn Sumach can be used to make

STAG'S HORN SUMACH
Rhus typhina
20—30 ft.

SMOOTH SUMACH
Rhus glabra
15—25 ft.

a sour lemonade-like drink. The leaves are an important source of tannin in the United States. (See CASHEWS; NUTS.)

Other members of the cashew family, such as the Varnish-tree *(Melanorrhoea usitata)* of the Orient, are sources of various waxes and lacquers. Some species are valuable for their timber, and the hard wood of the Quebracho-tree *(Schinopsis)* of South America is rich in tannin. The Pepper tree *(Schinus)*, which is native to South America, is a member of this family, as are cashews and the mangoes. (See MANGOES.)

SUN. The central body of our solar system is the Sun, which is the source of all the light and heat that the planets receive. The Sun is a typical star (see STARS). This great globe of hot gas, 864,000 miles in diameter, is much larger than all the planets, satellites, and asteroids put together.

The Sun is so hot that all its substances are vapourised. It shines so brilliantly because of its high temperature — about 7,000 degrees centigrade (11,000 degrees Fahrenheit) at its surface. The interior is even hotter — about 14 million degrees centigrade (25 million degrees Fahrenheit) at the centre. It is in the centre of the Sun that hydrogen nuclei are changed into helium, providing enough energy to keep the sun shining for thousands of millions of years in the past and thousands of millions of years in the future.

The surface of the Sun is so intensely bright that we normally do not see the Sun's faint outer parts. But a total eclipse of the Sun completely hides the Sun's face so that we can see the faint glow of the corona, the Sun's intensely hot outer atmosphere. Even the Sun's face is of great interest. When we dim it and magnify it suitably — for instance, by using a telescope to project an image of the sun on a screen — its surface no longer looks evenly bright. We can see granulation — a speckling of the surface — as hotter and cooler currents of gas rise and fall in the vast turbulence of the flaming gases.

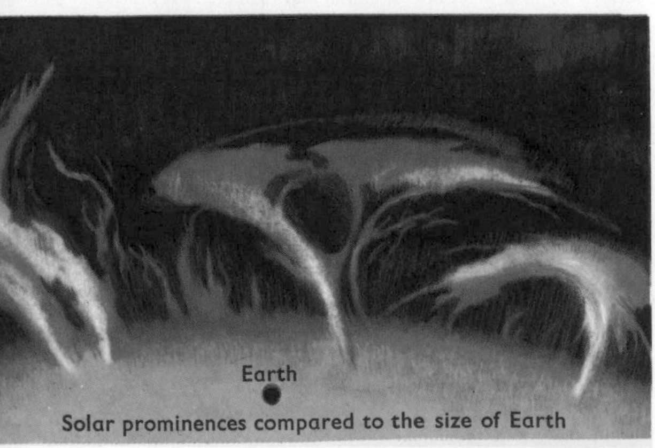

Solar prominences are short-lived, gigantic tongues of incandescent gases that often shoot up 100,000 miles from the Sun's surface. They are clearly visible during a solar eclipse, when the Moon covers the Sun's disc.

The dark core (umbra) and outer grey band (penumbra) of sunspots are white-hot gases. They appear dark in contrast to hotter gases of the photosphere.

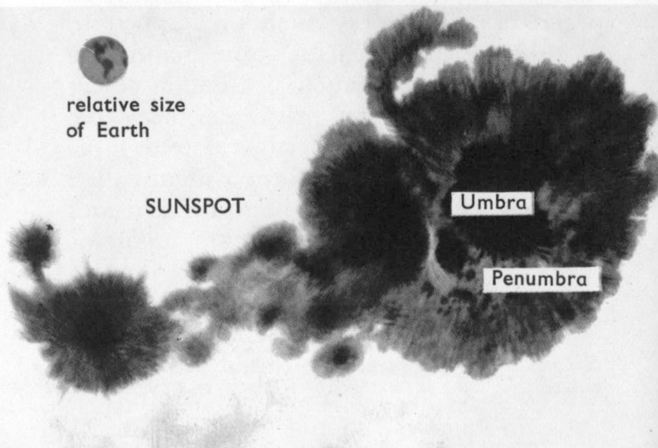

Hamlyn Group Library

Throughout the history of mankind, the Sun, representing the source of our life, has been an object of veneration and worship. Shown above is a carving of a Mayan Sun God.

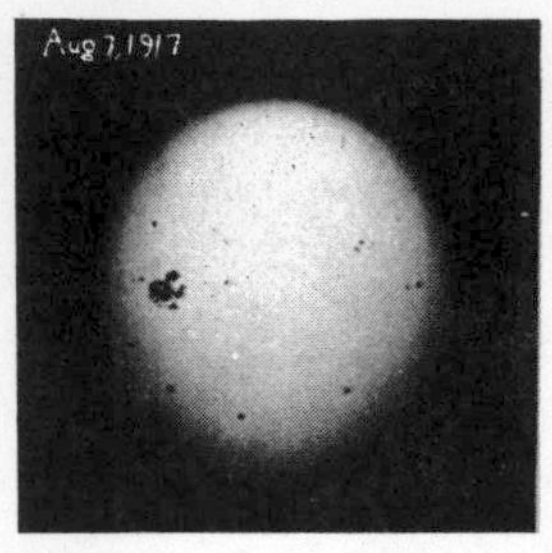

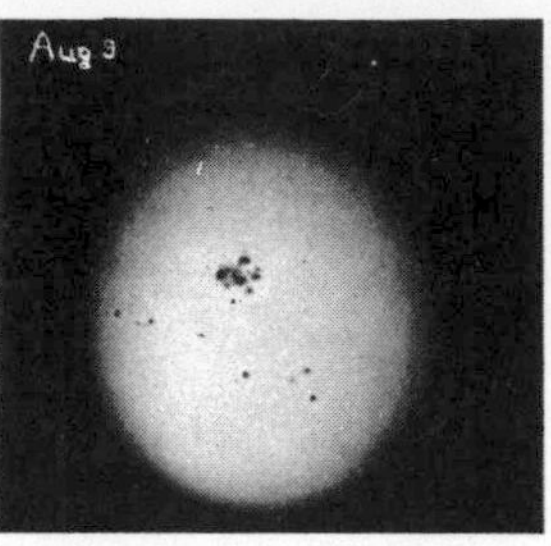

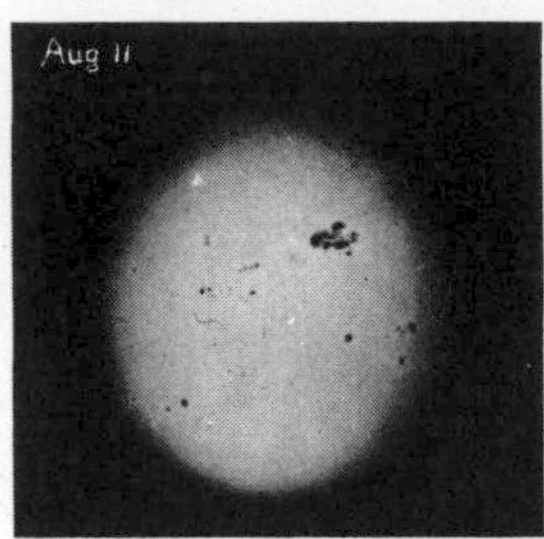

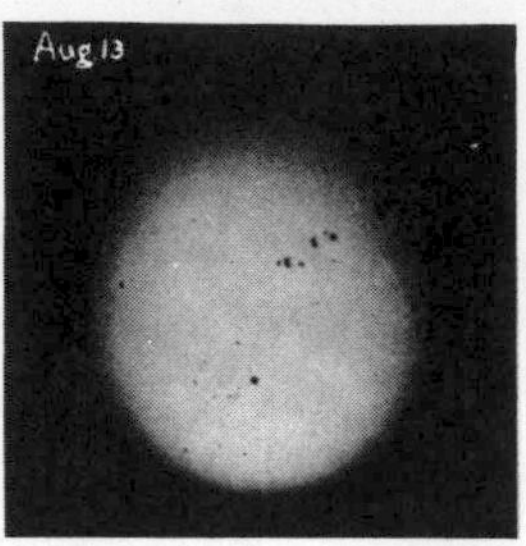

Yerkes Observatory Photograph

Photographs show gradual movement of sunspots across Sun's disc, proving that the Sun rotates.

Most striking of all are the sunspots. These look like black spots on the Sun's surface, some of them larger than the Earth itself. They are not black really but are simply cooler than the rest of the Sun's surface and therefore look dark by contrast. No one knows what causes sunspots, but the cause is probably connected with the intense magnetic fields that are found in them. Spots come and go, but most can be followed for many days as the Sun's monthly rotation takes place.

Some years there are many more sunspots than in others, and the Sun's spottedness varies fairly regularly in an 11-year cycle. The last sunspot maximum came in 1958 and was an extremely intense one. Along with the sun spots come other forms of solar activity: great bursts of radio noise and flares of ultra-violet light and X-rays. The flares have a quite noticeable effect on the Earth; the upper atmosphere changes its electrical properties, and long-distance radio communication fades out. Solar activity is also responsible for the irregularities of magnetic compasses and for auroras (see AURORA).

ENERGY FROM THE SUN. All of the currently used sources of energy on Earth are

Berniere's great burning glass, an early attempt to use solar energy, had controls and wheels that permitted it to be moved with the Sun. Dark glasses protected the operator's eyes during chemical experiments.

E. F. Smith Mem. Collection, University of Pennsylvania

derived either directly or indirectly from the Sun. Coal and oil represent sunlight stored in the bodies of plants and animals in past ages that, on death, became part of the rocks of the Earth. Basic foods are produced when sunlight brings about photosynthesis in plants. Even hydro-electric power depends on solar energy. The cycle commences when the Sun evaporates water from the land and lifts it as a vapour into the clouds. Later it is released from the clouds as precipitation and forms the rivers and lakes that supply the water power that is harnessed by turbines to run electric generators.

Russ Kine

Sunlight is caught by the collecting mirror (right) then concentrated (left) on the equipment in the test chamber in this solar furnace built by the U.S. Army.

Every daylight hour the Earth's surface receives solar energy equalling the amount of power contained in more than 20,000 million tons of coal. Only a fraction of this total — about one two thousand millionth is converted into energy that can be utilised. Approximately 90 per cent of all the photosynthesis that occurs on Earth takes place in oceans, where even less of the foods are available to man. Scientists calculate that utilisable food from the sea could be increased from the present 80,000 million pounds annually to more than 500,000 million

The Sun's surface, or photosphere, is marked with dark blemishes called sunspots. Great streamers of glowing gas (solar prominences) shoot up from the surface. These may pass through the enveloping chromosphere to penetrate the outer, halo-like corona.

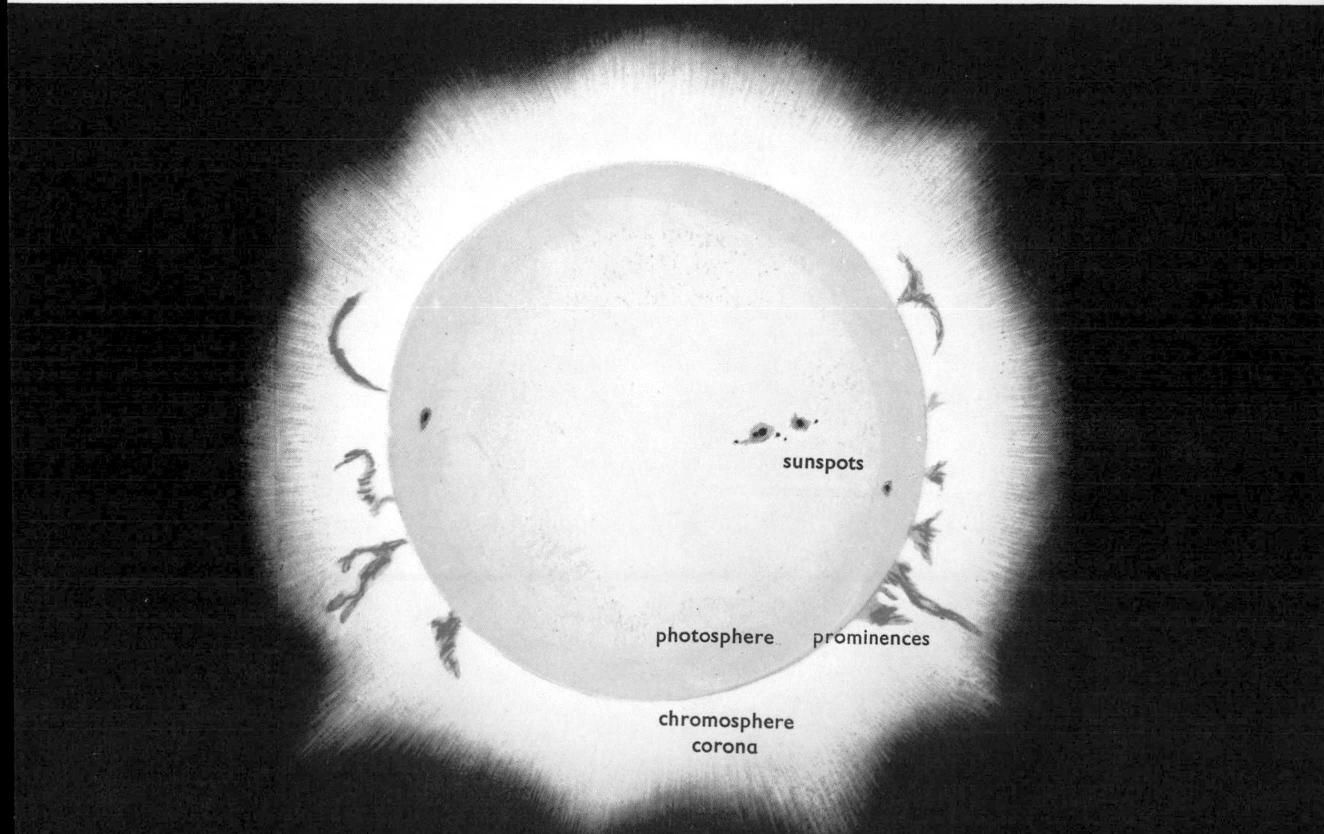

pounds without disturbing the production. This could be done simply by making more efficient use of already harvested fish. Better use of this protein food resource, made available from the energy of the Sun creating lush

Courtesy Bell Telephone Co.

A solar battery developed by Bell Telephone Laboratories will generate 10 watts in direct sunlight.

The water for the central heating system of this house in Lexington, Massachusetts, U.S.A. is heated in a 640 sq. ft. collector tilted at 60°.

Durrance/Rapho-Guillumette

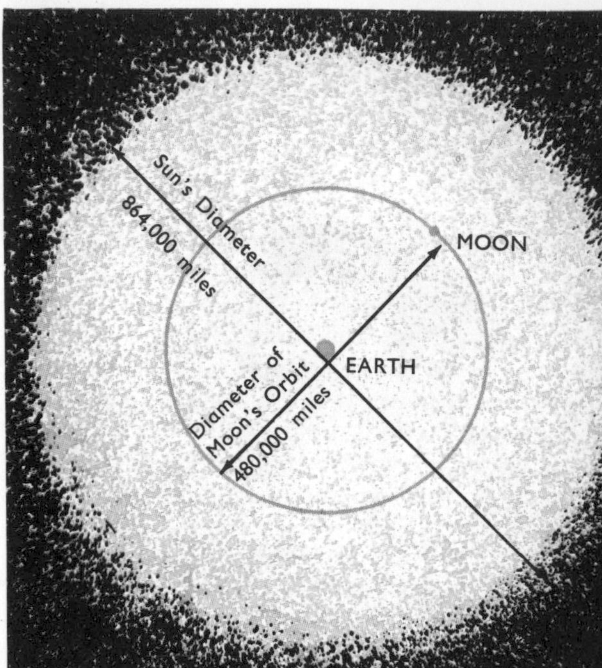

The Sun is larger than the entire Earth-Moon system.

pastures of plankton in the sea, would aid greatly in checking the increasing problem of world hunger and malnutrition.

For many centuries Man has recognised the great power of the Sun and has tried to harness its energy for more effective use. One of the most ancient methods is by means of the solar furnace, which works on the principle of concentrating the Sun's rays at one focal point, much as a magnifying glass does. Even a small lens can concentrate enough rays to burn holes in paper, cloth, or wood.

The exact method of focusing the rays has been refined considerably over the years to increase the efficiency of the furnaces. Some solar furnaces have two sets of mirrors. One collects the Sun's rays and reflects them to the second mirror, which then focuses them on a boiler to produce steam for driving generators. Other furnaces have the mirrors mounted on a moving assembly so that the mirrors always face the Sun.

A more common use of solar power is in heating water. Solar water heaters are made quite simply by placing blackened copper water pipes inside a black box which has a pane of glass on top. The Sun's rays penetrate the glass and heat the pipes and the water inside them. The glass prevents some of the heat from escaping. Many homes in warm, sunny regions, including southern United States and Japan, have these solar heaters installed on the roof.

Small solar heaters have been developed for domestic use, as for cooking. Larger installations have not become common. Not only are they expensive to build, but they have one large drawback: during the hours of darkness, or on cloudy days, the solar energy plant is out of operation. This disadvantage can be partly overcome by collecting and storing the heat in tanks of water that can be drawn on when the Sun is not shining.

A recent development of a type of photoelectric cell, the silicon solar battery, has been used successfully to power small portable radios, and even to run a rural telephone system. A series of silicon discs treated with boron are linked together, and each disc generates about half a volt of current when exposed to sunlight. Again, the system only works when the Sun is shining. This is of course an obvious disadvantage.

As the world's power sources dwindle under the increasing demands that are made on them, more efficient ways to use solar energy will undoubtedly be developed.

SWAMPS, MARSHES AND BOGS are wet flatlands that commonly develop in filled-in lakes, glacial pits and potholes, or in poorly drained coastal or flood plains.

Bogs lack a solid foundation. They are formed differently from swamps and marshes. If a lake or pond disappears gradually as silt is deposited on the bottom, it will become either a swamp, in which trees grow, or a marsh, which is a watery grassland. If the lake or pond fills in from the top down, due to growth of surface vegetation that traps the soil and leaves a layer of water underneath, it becomes a bog. The surface may appear solid but will not support weight. *Sphagnum* moss is a characteristic of bogs. Peat, decayed *Sphagnum*, builds at a rate of about 1 foot every 100 years. *Sphagnum* and other bog plants secrete acids so that few animals can live in the bog waters. Many peat bogs are to be found in Ireland.

The largest swamps in the United States of America are the Everglades in Florida along the Florida-Georgia boundary, and Dismal Swamp in North Carolina and Virginia. Swamps are also numerous along the Atlantic and Gulf coastal plains of the U.S.A.; they make up about two thirds of all the poorly drained land.

Cypress swamps are typical of south-eastern United States, though they occur up the Mississippi Valley as far as southern Illinois.

Bob Taylor, FPG

The arctic tundra consists largely of low-lying swamps in summer that become frozen deserts in winter. Then the plants and insects die and the birds migrate to warmer climates.

SWEET PEAS *(Lathyrus odoratus)*, annual legumes, reputedly native to Ceylon, were introduced into Britain from Sicily. The original flower was purple, highly perfumed, and had plain petals. In 1899 a sport or mutation with large frilly flowers, the 'Spencer' type, was found and raised and from this type all modern Sweet Peas have been raised, in colours of cream, pink, red, and lavender.

In Britain the many varieties flower best in the summer months. Breeders in the United States have raised a number of distinct forms, including early or 'winter' flowering, dwarf, and many-flowered (multiflora) types.

They are decorative plants in their own right in the garden, or can be used for cut flower production.

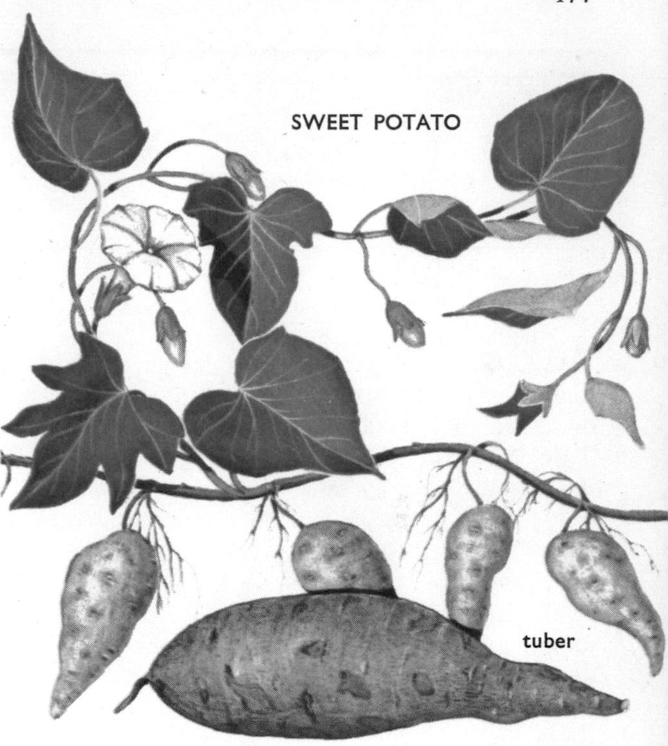

SWEET POTATO

SWEET PEAS

SWEET POTATO *(Ipomoea batatas)*, believed to be native to tropical America, is a trailing vine with heart-shaped leaves. It produces on its roots enlarged areas known as tubers. (Tuber in the case of the White Potato refers to enlargements of the underground stems.) Sweet Potatoes grow best in hot climates and are widely grown in southern United States, Africa, tropical America, China, India, and Japan. Most of Europe is too cold for growing Sweet Potatoes.

Sweet Potatoes are grown from shoots of seed potatoes or from vine cuttings. Harvested tubers are dried for a few days before being stored. Sweet Potatoes are a good source of vitamins, iron, calcium, and carbohydrates. They can be eaten baked, or boiled or made into pies. Much of the crop is used as livestock feed, and some is manufactured into flour, alcohol, and starch.

SYENITE is a light-coloured, usually coarse-grained igneous rock. It resembles granite but contains little or no quartz. Common colours of syenite are pink, yellow, and grey. Its major mineral is orthoclase, although corundum is often prominent in syenite containing nepheline. Syenite is rarer than granite but is a better building stone. Deposits of this rock occur in Sutherland.

Syenite is an igneous rock, similar to granite but lacking quartz.

SYENITE

Phot. Roger Perrin

T

TALC occurs in white or apple-green leaf-like or granular masses that have a slippery or soapy feel. Its cleavage flakes are flexible. Talc is formed by the metamorphism of magnesium-rich rocks by hot vapours. Talc is the softest mineral, rated as number 1 on Mohs' scale. It can be easily scratched with the fingernail. (See MINERALS.)

Soapstone is a rock rich in talc. Because of its chemical and electrical resistance it is used for laboratory table tops, tanks, switchboards, and in buildings. Pleasingly coloured soapstone is carved into vases, lamp stands, ash trays, or similar objects. A small amount is used to make steel-marking pencils. The mark they make does not burn off when the steel is heated. Ground talc is used for ceramics and as a filler in paints, rubber, insecticides, roofing, textiles, paper, and asphalt tiles. It is also used to polish wood and such food products as rice, beans, and peanuts. Talcum powder is made from finely ground, sifted, and perfumed talc. Talc occurs in Europe, Australia, and the U.S.A.

Talc has many uses. The best grades are cleaned, ground, sifted, coloured, and perfumed to make talcum powders.

TEA is an evergreen shrub or small tree *(Thea sinensis)* native to south-east Asia. In the wild it may grow to a height of 20 or 30 feet but under cultivation is usually pruned to a height of 3 or 4 feet to make it easier to harvest the leaves. About 1600 the Dutch brought tea to Europe, and within 50 years tea drinking became popular in England. The custom then spread to America. By 1773 the English East India Company dominated the tea trade, and the British passed the Tea Act to maintain their monopoly. Americans protested against the tax by dumping tea cargoes into Boston Harbour. The most famous of these dumpings became known as the Boston Tea Party. The famed clipper ships were designed primarily as speedy carriers of tea from the East. Large bonuses were earned by the fastest ships.

Tea is grown in many tropical and subtropical areas of the world. China leads in world production but not in the exportation, since much is consumed locally. In China and Japan most tea is grown in small home plots, while in India and Ceylon it is grown on plantations. India leads in the exportation of tea. Ceylon began to cultivate tea when all its coffee plantations were attacked by a fungus disease; it is now second in world production. Like coffee, most tea is grown under the shade of other trees, and tea grown at high elevations has a better flavour than tea produced at low altitudes.

Tea is usually harvested by women and children. They break or cut off the terminal shoots and put them in large baskets slung over their backs. One picker can gather from 50 to 80 pounds of tea leaves in a day. The leaves are weighed and then taken to a factory for drying and processing.

Tea leaves may be processed to produce either green or black tea. For black tea, the leaves are spread out on racks for

Ed Drews, Photo Researchers

Tea leaves cannot be harvested mechanically, as different grades of tea are made from leaves that grow on different levels of the same tea plant. These women pickers are at work on a hillside plantation in Ceylon.

about 24 hours in withering or drying sheds. Then they are crushed and twisted by machinery to break the leaf cells and release the juices. The leaves are then fermented for a few hours in a warm, humid room, a process that darkens the leaves and develops the fragrant odour of tea. Finally the leaves are placed in a dryer to stop the fermentation and reduce their moisture content. After being sifted through screens, the tea is graded and packaged for market. Black tea is produced mostly in India, Indonesia, Ceylon, and Brazil, and exported to Europe and the Americas.

In Japan, lack of arable land has led the tea grower to shape and trim his trees to obtain maximum yield.

David Forbert — Shostal

Green tea, produced chiefly in China and Japan, is dried without allowing it first to ferment, and much of it is rolled by hand rather than by machine. Oolong tea is intermediate between green and black tea, since it is partially fermented before drying. Jasmine tea is also partially fermented and owes its name to the fact that the leaves are left in contact with jasmine flowers to absorb their odour.

Maté or Paraguayan Tea is made in South America from the leaves of *Ilex paraguensis*.

In the United Kingdom people consume approximately 11 pounds per person every year.

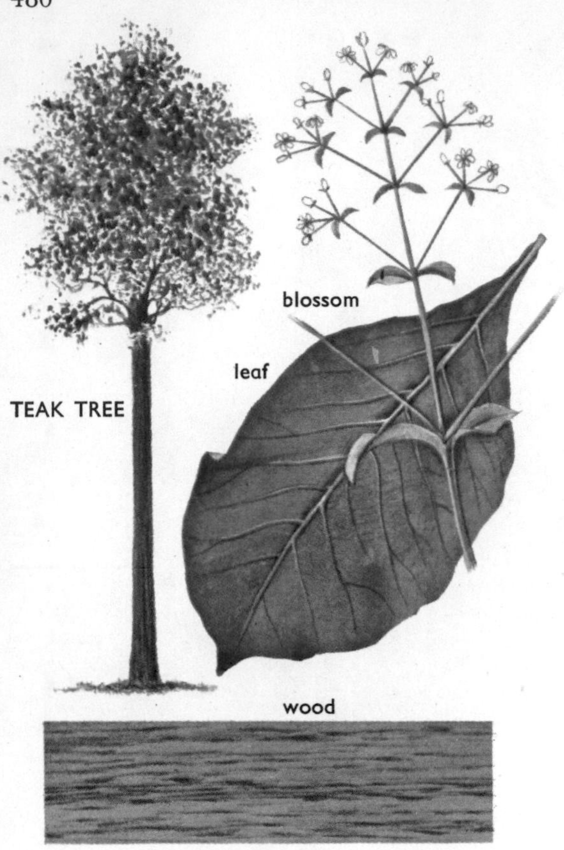

TEAK *(Tectona grandis)*, one of the world's most valuable woods, comes from a large deciduous tropical tree native to India, Burma, and other countries of south-eastern Asia. The tree grows 80 to 150 feet high and may measure 4 feet in diameter. Its straight trunk, usually buttressed at the base, is often free of branches as much as 80 feet from the ground. Branchlets of its wide-spreading crown are square and contain four pith chambers. The tree's large (12 to 24 inches), rough leaves resemble tobacco leaves. They are shed during the dry season, then reappear in the rainy season. Small white flowers are borne in large clusters at the tips of the branches, and form brown seeds less than an inch in diameter.

Teak wood is tawny, yellow to brown. It resembles walnut wood but is oily. Teak is noted for durability and beauty and is used for marine decking, furniture, panelling and veneer.

A few other richly coloured woods are also called teak. Among these are Irobo, or African Teak, of the spurge family, and Rhodesian Teak, of the pea family.

TELESCOPE. The bodies of the heavens are all very far away and therefore appear small and faint. The principal instrument of astronomy, the telescope, tries to remedy both of these difficulties. For objects like planets, magnification allows us to see more detail. But for stars, which are so far away that they can never be seen as anything but points of light, magnification is useful only in separating neighbouring stars from each other. For stars, the important item in a telescope is light-gathering power, by which a telescope makes a star look brighter.

Telescopes are of two types, refracting and reflecting. In a refractor a large lens brings the light to a focus and forms an image of the objcct at which the telescope is pointed. Usually a double lens is used, because a single lens does not bring light of all colours to the same focus. Behind the focus is an eyepiece with which the observer looks at the image. A reflecting telescope uses a large concave mirror that sends the light back up the tube of the telescope to the focal point. To bring the image outside the tube, two arrangements are commonly used. In a Newtonian reflector a flat mirror reflects the

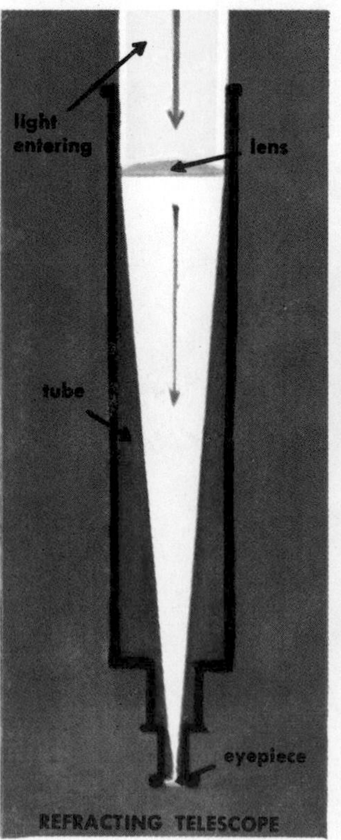

REFRACTING TELESCOPE

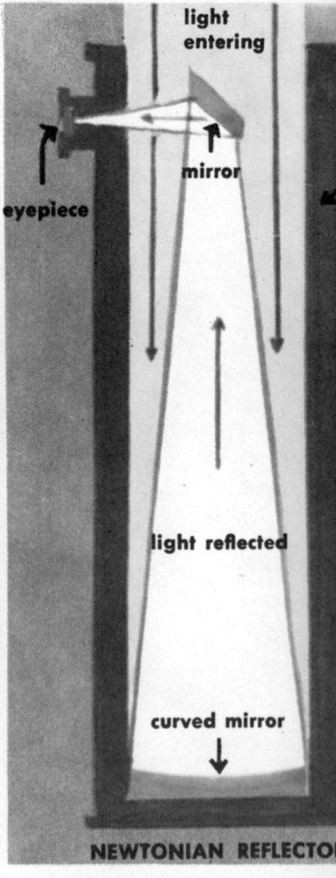

NEWTONIAN REFLECTO

light out to the side, while a Cassegrain reflector has a convex mirror that sends the light back down the tube and through a hole in the main mirror.

Astronomers rarely look through telescopes. They prefer to use their telescopes to take photographs, which are more permanent and take in a wider area of sky. Many telescopes are especially designed for photography. Among these are the Schmidt cameras, which use a mirror combined with a weak lens called a correcting plate. A Schmidt camera can take a sharp photograph of an especially wide area of sky.

The largest telescopes today are all reflectors, because a large mirror is easier to make than a lens. The major observatories tend to be far from the lights of cities, in places where the air is clean and steady. Moisture in the air also causes distortion of light waves, so observatories are commonly located in dry climates and at heights that set them above the low, moist air layers. (See OBSERVATORY.)

Wilson and MacPherson Hole

An astronomer is going up in the lift to the observer's cage of the 200-inch Hale reflector telescope on Mt. Palomar, California.

THISTLES (including both *Cirsium* spp. and *Curduus* spp.) have beautiful, fluffy, purplish or reddish blossoms. Of several hundred species twelve are native to the British Isles. With one exception they are perennials, and are found in grasslands where they are regarded as troublesome weeds. The sharp spines on leaves, stems, and flower-heads make them inedible by cattle and sheep, and difficult to remove by hand. Their hairy-plumed seeds are dispersed widely by the wind.

TIME. One of the jobs of astronomy, ever since ancient days, has been to tell time. The heavens are an accurate, permanent clock, and observations of them can be used to keep track of the time. Our standard for measuring time is the Earth. Its rotation on its axis measures our day, while its revolution around the Sun gives us the year.

The Earth's rotation is an excellent timekeeper, because almost nothing can disturb its constant rate. As the Earth turns, the stars cross the sky, and the time at which a star crosses the central line of a telescope's field can be marked very accurately. Time measured directly from the stars is called

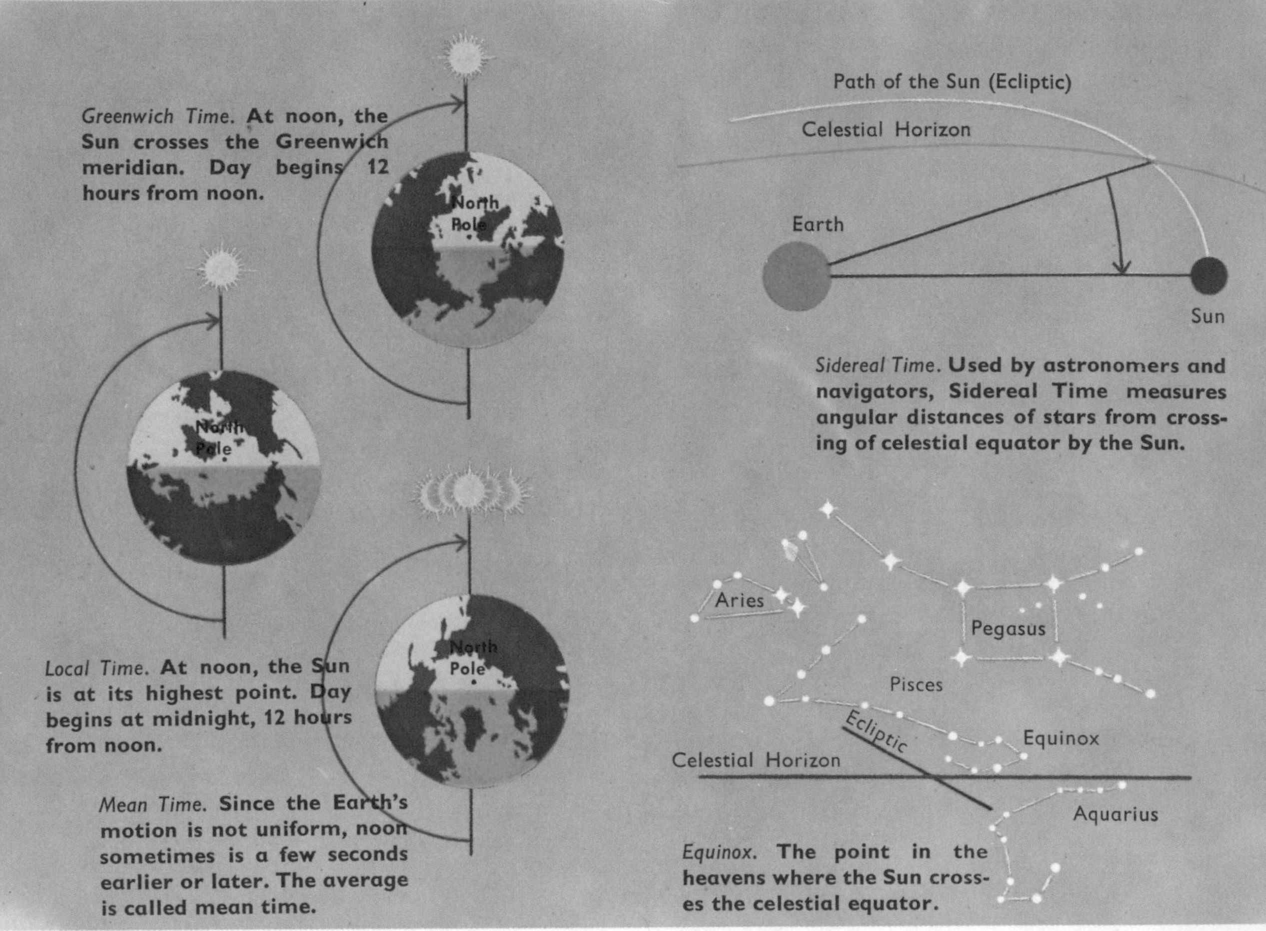

Greenwich Time. **At noon, the Sun crosses the Greenwich meridian. Day begins 12 hours from noon.**

Local Time. **At noon, the Sun is at its highest point. Day begins at midnight, 12 hours from noon.**

Mean Time. **Since the Earth's motion is not uniform, noon sometimes is a few seconds earlier or later. The average is called mean time.**

Sidereal Time. **Used by astronomers and navigators, Sidereal Time measures angular distances of stars from crossing of celestial equator by the Sun.**

Equinox. **The point in the heavens where the Sun crosses the celestial equator.**

Sidereal Time. It is determined from day to day by observatories in several countries. But for practical purposes we want our clocks to agree with the Sun rather than with the stars so that noon will always come at the same time of day by our clocks. For this reason our clocks are set to keep mean Solar Time, which differs from Sidereal Time because of the Earth's annual motion around the Sun. Astronomers observe Sidereal Time and convert it to mean Solar Time, which is broadcast by short-wave radio. For the most reliable standard, astronomers use the motions of the planets in their orbits. This requires extremely complicated and exacting calculations.

Time differs at different points on the Earth, because the Local Time depends on the observer's longitude. At latitude 40 degrees, moving only 13 miles east or west changes the Local Time by a whole minute. It would be hopelessly confusing if everyone's clock kept Local Time, so the world is divided into 24 standard time zones. Within a time zone everyone keeps the same time, which is the Local Time of a longitude that is divisible by 15 degrees — for instance 75 degrees, 90 degrees, etc. Finally, in order to have a fixed time that is independent of the observer's location, astronomers quote their observations in Universal Time, which is the standard time of the zone at zero longitude, running through the Greenwich Observatory, London. It is also called Greenwich Mean Time.

TIN comes principally from one ore, cassiterite. Cassiterite is formed as brown or black grains, pyramids, or granular masses. It has a brilliant lustre and a white or pale streak.

Stannine or stannite is another source of

tin. It is usually found with cassiterite, copper pyrites, or galena. Both of these minerals have been found in Cornwall.

Tin plate has been used for almost 2,000 years, and today the United States produces and uses more tin plate than the rest of the world. Most of it is used for tin cans. Tin plate consists of an almost microscopic film of tin on soft steel. This is done by dipping the steel in molten tin or by electrolytic methods. Solder, an alloy of tin and lead, uses 25 per cent of the tin produced each year. Babbitt, an alloy of tin, antimony, and copper, is used for wheel bearings. (Cadmium alloys which will withstand higher temperatures are replacing babbitt, however.) Bronze is an alloy of copper, zinc, and tin; type-metal, of lead, tin, and antimony. The metal from which bells are made is an alloy of tin (20 to 30 per cent) with copper. Tin chloride added to silk increases the weight of the silk and makes it rustle.

Tin ore comes from Malaya, Indonesia, Thailand, the Congo, Nigeria, and Bolivia. Since such a large user of tin as the United States depends on foreign tin, substitutes are experimented with continually. Glass and plastic is being used for food containers. Aluminium is replacing sheet tin plate in the building trade, and a number of substances are being tried to replace the tin used in cans.

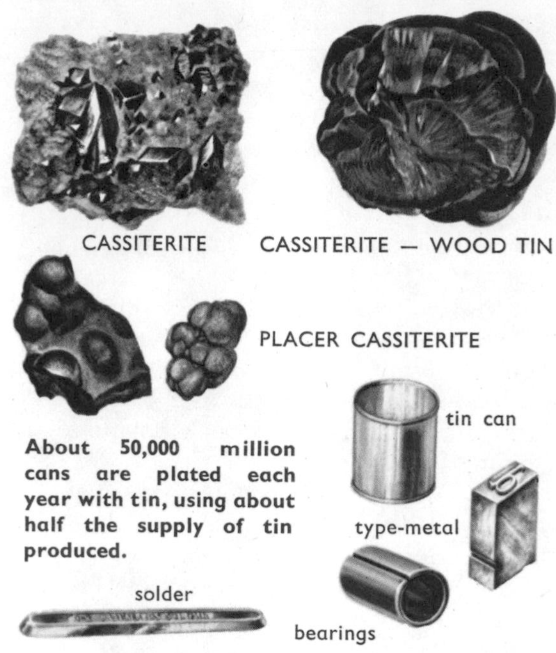

About 50,000 million cans are plated each year with tin, using about half the supply of tin produced.

The chart shows time in zones throughout the world when it is noon at Greenwich, London. Greenwich time is the Universal Time of astronomers and navigators. It is also called Greenwich Mean Time.

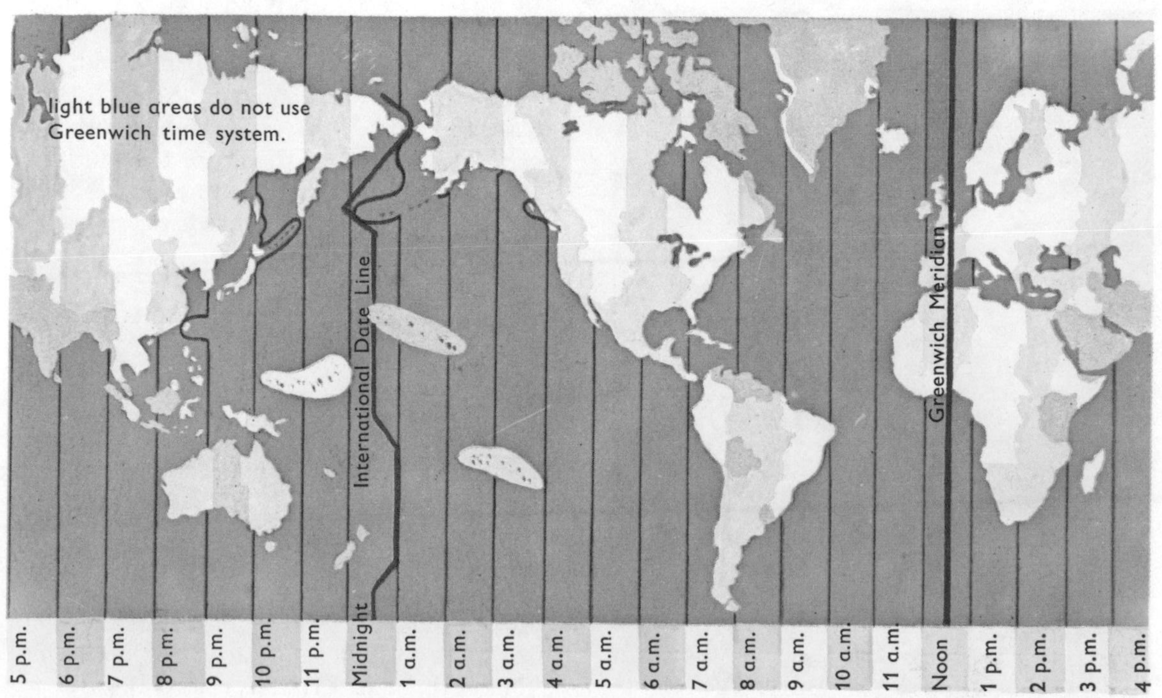

TOBACCO *(Nicotiana tabacum)*. Long before Columbus discovered America, the Indians smoked tobacco during ceremonials. Early explorers took tobacco to Europe where it was grown first as an ornamental. Gradually its use in smoking spread through Europe and to the Orient.

The United States, China, India and Rhodesia are the principal tobacco growing countries. Lesser amounts are grown in Russia, Brazil, Turkey, Japan, and other countries. Some of the most expensive cigars are made of tobacco grown in Cuba, but Turkish or Oriental tobacco is favoured in cigarette blends.

Tobacco seeds are so small that it requires as many as 400,000 to weigh an ounce, each plant producing about a million seeds. The seeds are first planted in seed beds where the soil has been sterilised. When the young plants have reached a height of 4 — 6 inches, they are transplanted to fields. In some areas the fields are covered with lath or cheesecloth shades. Topping — the removal of the tip of the plants to keep them from flowering — directs the plant food into the leaves and encourages their lush growth.

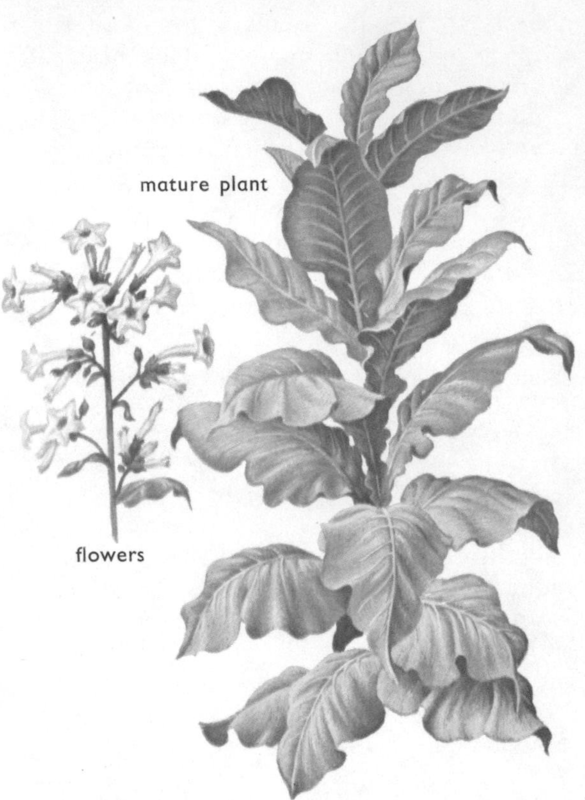

Tobacco plants grow to a height of 5 feet. Their bell-shaped flowers are formed of five united petals.

Tobacco is cured carefully to produce a desired aroma.

USDA

Tobacco is harvested either by cutting off the complete plant or by picking individual leaves by hand as they mature. In either case, the harvested leaves are hung in curing sheds until much of their moisture and green colour is gone. Sometimes the curing is done by artificial heat. The cured leaves are then sorted and marketed.

As early as 1690, extracts of tobacco were recommended for spraying plants to protect them from insects. The nicotine in tobacco is a contact poison, lethal to insect pests and parasites. Insecticides and fertilisers are produced from the stem and leaf wastes rejected during the manufacture of other tobacco products.

TOMATOES *(Lycopersicon esculentum)* are native to the Americas and were eaten by the Indians of Mexico and Central America in prehistoric time. Early explorers introduced them to Europe, where Italians were the first to appreciate their fine flavour. Settlers in North America considered tomatoes poisonous and grew them only as ornamentals until about 150 years ago. Since then they have become widely grown throughout the sub-tropical and temperate regions. The plants are not hardy and in northern Europe, especially in Britain and Holland, they are mainly grown under glass. In southern Europe and in America, where summers are hotter, they are usually grown in the open ground.

The fruit have a high vitamin A content. They may be pear-shaped or round, yellow or red. They vary in size from no larger than cherries to almost as big as grapefruit.

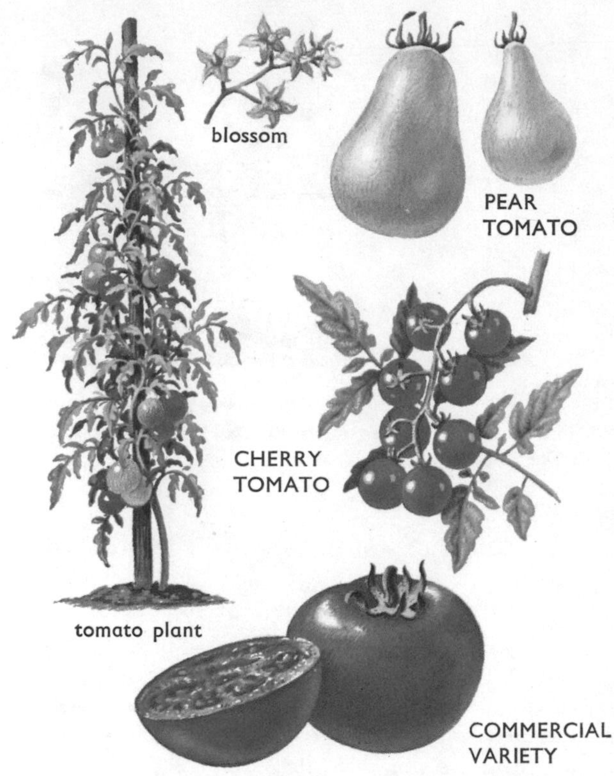

Tomatoes belong to the same family as tobacco and potatoes. They come in a variety of shapes and sizes.

TOOLS. Although Man is not the only tool-using animal, he is the only one that uses tools regularly and is also the only animal that uses one tool to make another, more complicated tool with a wider range of utility.

The first of Man's tools were probably stones, sticks, or bones, fashioned by nature and not by Man himself. The sticks and the bones turned into dust long ago, but some of the crude stone tools of early Man have been found. Some ancient tools have been dated at an age of over a million years. They are called eoliths, or dawn stones.

About a million years ago, new types of stone tools appeared. These show clearly that their makers understood how to quarry rocks, and to shape them into points or cutting edges, and how to put handles on them for use as axes and clubs. With his development of stone implements, Man entered the Stone Age. With sharp tools of stone that could kill animals for meat and warm skins, and that could chop wood for fires, Man was able for the first time to survive in cold climates.

While almost any hard stone can be used as an implement, some kinds of rock split naturally into thin pieces with sharp edges. Flint, in particular, has this characteristic, and it was the mainstay of the Stone Age. In some parts of the world, the Stone Ages have continued up to the present. When Columbus discovered the New World, the American Indians were living in a Stone Age culture. Some primitive peoples today live as Man did in Europe more than 20,000 years ago.

The earliest stone tools were probably blunt hand-axes. Thin flakes of rock that could be tied to sticks became spear points. Other sharp pieces, held in the hand, were the first knives. Later, Man became more skilful in chipping and shaping stones to make more efficient tools. Throwing spears and bows and arrows were among the important inventions of Stone Age Man. These weapons increased man's range for killing game and made it possible for him to hunt larger animals.

The Stone Age has been divided into three periods: Old, Middle, and New. These refer to cultural levels, which did not occur in all regions simultaneously. They are told apart by the degree of skill used in the shaping of the tools then in use. In the Old Stone Age, tools were extremely rough and heavy. In the Middle Stone Age, they were much lighter, sharper, and undoubtedly more useful. Many of the stone implements of the

Royal Lowy — American Indian Archives

The fishing net is a simple tool used by Man since the dawn of history.

New Stone Age were smoothed and polished, showing a great concern for craftsmanship. The outstanding achievements of Man in the New Stone Age were not in stone but were the invention of agriculture, and the domestication of animals, and the use of the wheel. Pottery was most probably an earlier invention, in the Middle Stone Age, as was weaving. (See AGRICULTURE; CRAFTS AND ARTS OF EARLY MAN.)

Stone Age Man had used metals, but only as he used rocks — to pound with or as scrapers. They did not become important in his cultural advance until he learned how to melt the metals and to cast them in moulds to make the shapes he desired.

The New Stone Age waned with the discovery of the art of smelting copper. Though quite soft as compared to iron, copper could be given a sharper edge than stone, and an edge that would not chip away. Copper could also be worked and shaped more easily than flint. The beginning of the Copper Age has been set at about 4500 B.C., and it lasted until it became common to add tin to copper to produce bronze, about 3000 B.C. The earliest written records date from the Copper Age. The Bronze Age is considered to have ended about 1200 B.C. as iron was then in use.

The first mention of iron was about 1500

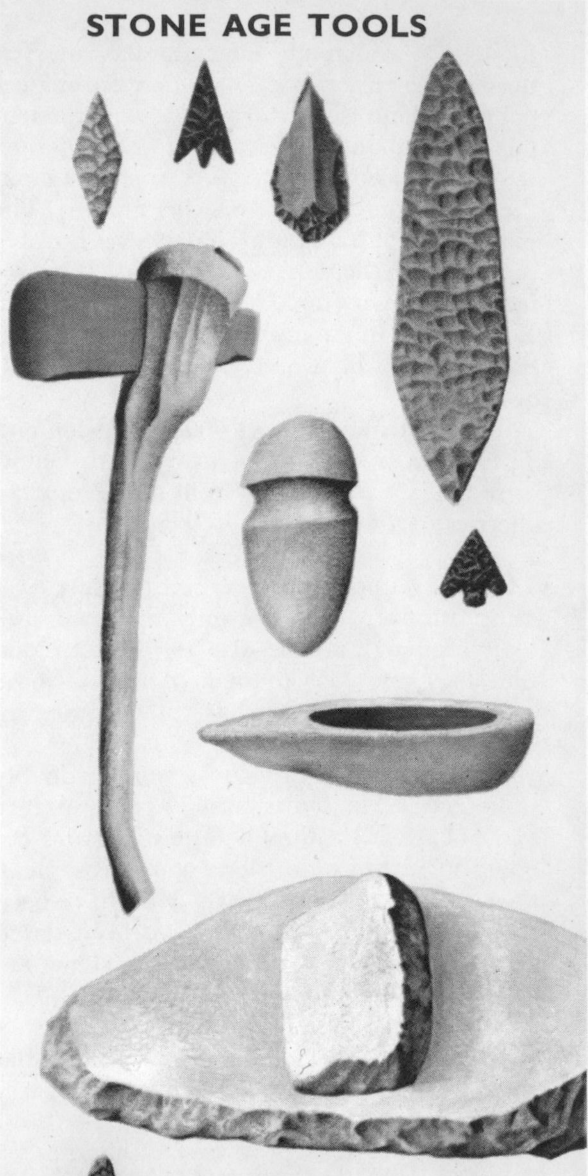

STONE AGE TOOLS

As man progressed in the use of stone tools, he gained greater control over his environment. The crude hand axes (lower) were supplanted by the finely chipped knives, arrow points, and axes (top). The flat stone in the centre is a grinding board.

B.C. The Hittites proved the superiority of the new metal in weapons by defeating the Egyptians, who still had bronze weapons. The use of iron spread rapidly through the Mediterranean Basin, and provided a foundation for the rise of Greece and Rome. Iron was far more difficult to work than were such soft metals as copper and tin. Cast iron is brittle, lumpy, and often filled with air holes. These drawbacks were overcome when the arts of forging and tempering were learned.

Simple machines known to the ancient world were six in number. These were the wedge, lever, wheel and axle, pulley, screw, and inclined plane. All of the complex mechanical creations that Man has made are elaborations and combinations of these six basic machines.

All of the simple machines were made of wood, but metal outlasts and out-performs wood.

TOPAZ, an aluminium silicate with fluorine and water, occurs as white, yellow, brown, or blue crystals or in cleavable masses. Transparent topaz is an important gem

stone, and yellow is the most highly prized colour. Pink and blue are also common topaz colours. Topaz is found in the U.S.S.R., Czechoslovakia, Ceylon, Australia, Brazil, and from Maine to Georgia in the Appalachians of the U.S.A.

TREES. A tree is a woody plant, and so are shrubs and vines. A tree is at least 10 feet high, usually has a single trunk several inches in diameter, and has a well-developed crown of leaves. Shrubs, generally smaller, grow from a clump of stems rather than from a single trunk. Vines do not have a crown of branches and foliage, and their stems are too weak to support them.

Trees live longer than any other living things. Maples may live for 500 years; oaks more than 1,000 years. The estimated age of many Wellingtonias and of several venerable

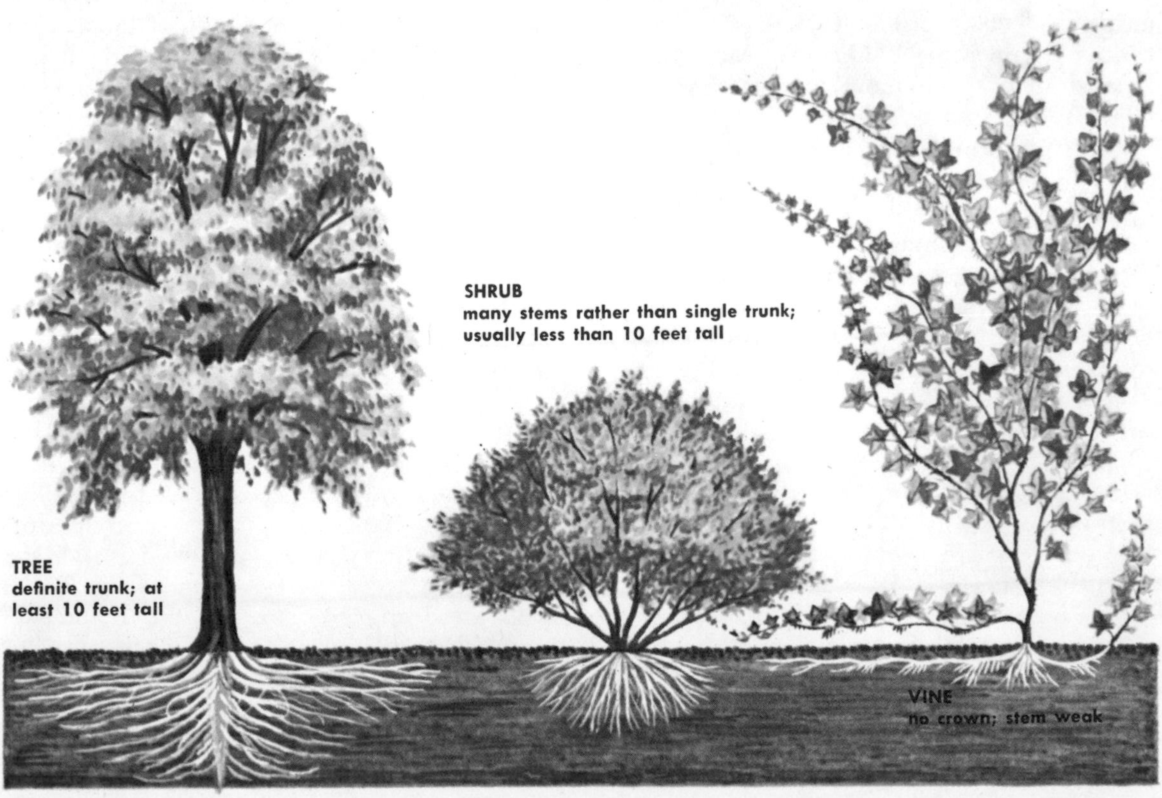

TREE
definite trunk; at
least 10 feet tall

SHRUB
many stems rather than single trunk;
usually less than 10 feet tall

VINE
no crown; stem weak

Man has always valued trees, for decorative purposes as well as for usefulness. A variety of trees can add elegance to a fine park.

junipers is 3,000 to 4,000 years. A huge Montezuma Cypress near Oaxaca, Mexico, is thought to be even more ancient than the oldest Wellingtonia. A gnarled Bristlecone Pine in California is listed at 4,600 years of age.

The largest and bulkiest of all living things are the Wellingtonias. Several are over 30 feet in diameter; one is more than 300 feet high, others over 250 feet. A Redwood that stands 364 feet high is the world's tallest tree. One that was 380 feet high was cut several years ago, and many living Redwoods are more than 300 feet high.

The highest hardwood is a eucalyptus tree over 300 feet growing near Melbourne, Australia.

Some trees are not tall but have broad crowns. A single banyan, a species of fig, drops so many aerial roots that it becomes a grove with a single broad crown as much as 1,500 feet in circumference.

About 50 different kinds of trees are mentioned in the Bible. Ancient Hebrews often conducted services in groves of trees. The Bo Tree, a species of fig, is sacred to Buddhists, for Buddha is said to have meditated under its branches. The Maoris of New Zealand thought their gods lived in giant kauri 'pines'. Druids of ancient Britain held their religious ceremonies in oak groves, and early Greeks often worshipped their gods in the forest. The peoples of many lands have believed that a spirit inhabits each tree.

PARTS OF A TREE. A tree consists of three distinct units — roots, trunk, and crown.

Roots anchor the tree in the soil. Some trees have one main root, called a taproot, which pushes deep into the ground. Smaller branch roots grow from the side of this main root. Other trees have many roots of nearly equal size that spread into the soil. This is called a fibrous root system. Fewer still have roots above the ground. Called prop roots, these may be leg-like, branching from the main trunk as in mangroves, or they may grow downwards from the branches and take root in the ground like propping poles, as in the banyan. Roots of the Parasitic Fig wrap around their host grotesquely. Those of cypress trees stick out of the water as 'knees' through which the trees take in air for the roots below. When not crowded, a tree's roots sprawl over four or five times as much space as the leafy crown.

The very tip of each growing root is covered by a protective cap of cells which pushes the root into the soil. Behind this cap are numerous tiny, white root hairs, too small to be seen with the naked eye. These extensions of the root cells grow between the soil particles, and through their thin walls the root absorbs water and dissolved minerals.

Above the roots is the woody trunk, the main support for the leafy crown. In the centre of the trunk is the heartwood, which consists of dead plant cells packed with gums and resins. Heartwood makes the best timber. The lighter coloured area just outside the heartwood is called sapwood. Some of its cells are dead, but those nearest the outside are living cells produced by the growing section of the trunk, called the cambium layer. This is a single layer of cells which produces the two most important elements of the trunk. Cells that grow from the inside of the cambium form the xylem (ZIGH-lem), the outermost cells of the sapwood. These cells carry the water and dissolved minerals from the roots to the leaves. Cells produced by the outside of the cambium form the phloem (FLO-em), or inner bark. These cells form the channels which carry food manufactured in the leaves down to the roots and to other parts of the tree. Outside the phloem is the corky bark.

A tree's bark is often distinctive in appearance. The beech's bark is smooth and grey. The oak's bark is rough. A plane's bark scales off in irregular patches so that the tree's trunk becomes a mottled greenish-white and tan.

A tree will die if a notch is cut around its trunk deep enough to pass through the phloem, cambium, and xylem. This thin area is vital to the tree. Even a piece of wire drawn tightly around a tree may injure it seriously for if it cuts through only the phloem, it will rob the roots of nourishing foods from the leaves above. Yet decay may consume all of the heartwood and nearly all of the sapwood, almost completely hollowing the trunk of the tree, without killing it.

A tree's age can be determined by counting the number of annual rings in its trunk. This is easy to do when a tree is cut down. Light areas in the wood are formed of large thin-walled cells that develop in the spring when the tree is growing rapidly and needs large amounts of water and minerals. Dark rings consist of thick-walled cells that form in late summer when the tree's growth is slowed. Each pair of rings represents one year.

Foresters can tell the age of a tree without cutting it down. They use a special instrument called an increment borer. This operates like a brace and bit, but the bit — the portion that bores into the tree — is hollow. The forester counts the annual rings on the pencil-like core of wood taken from the hollow bit.

A tree in a dense forest grows tall and slender. It competes with surrounding trees for water and minerals in the soil, for light, and for space to spread its crown. Thinning a crowded forest reduces this competition, and trunks of trees that are left standing increase in size.

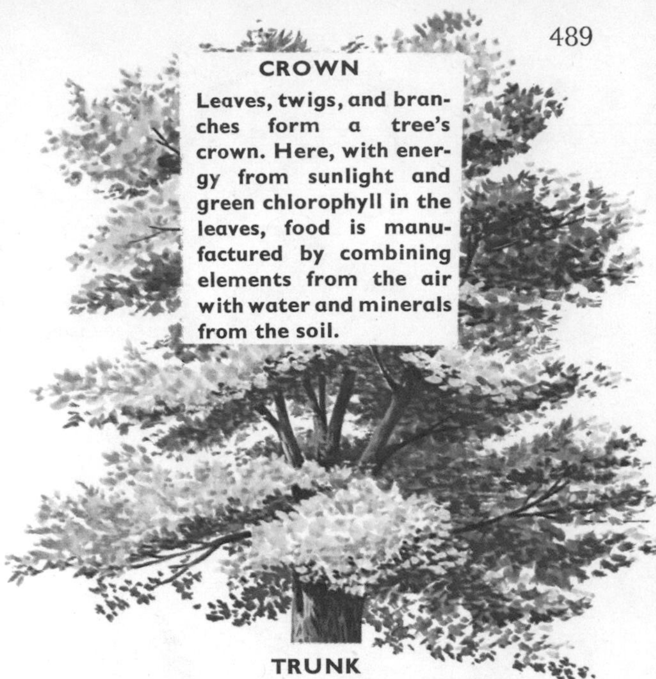

CROWN

Leaves, twigs, and branches form a tree's crown. Here, with energy from sunlight and green chlorophyll in the leaves, food is manufactured by combining elements from the air with water and minerals from the soil.

TRUNK

A tree's trunk supports its widespread crown. It also channels water and nutrients from the soil to the leaves and either stores food or transports it to the roots. Wood consists of dead cells in a tree's trunk.

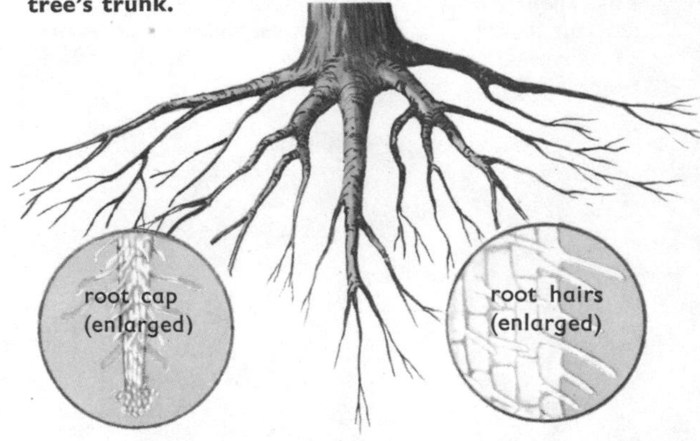

ROOTS

Roots project downwards and away from the base of the trunk and hold the tree in an upright position. The roots divide again and again, ending in tiny root hairs that absorb water and nutrient materials from the soil. Each root hair is tipped with a cap, a layer of tough cells that protects the softer growing cells behind it as the root grows. Some plants have one main root, while others have many roots of nearly the same size.

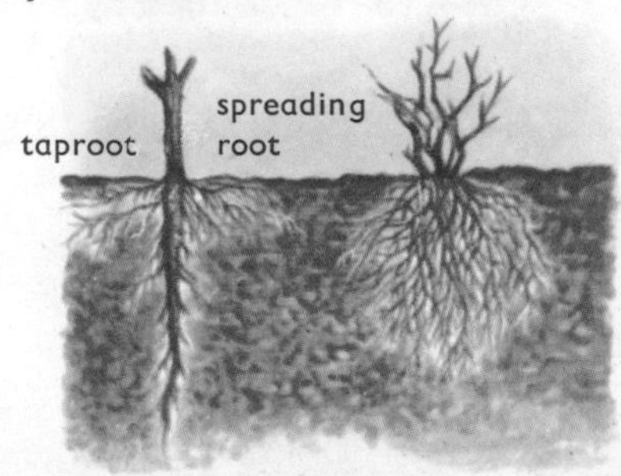

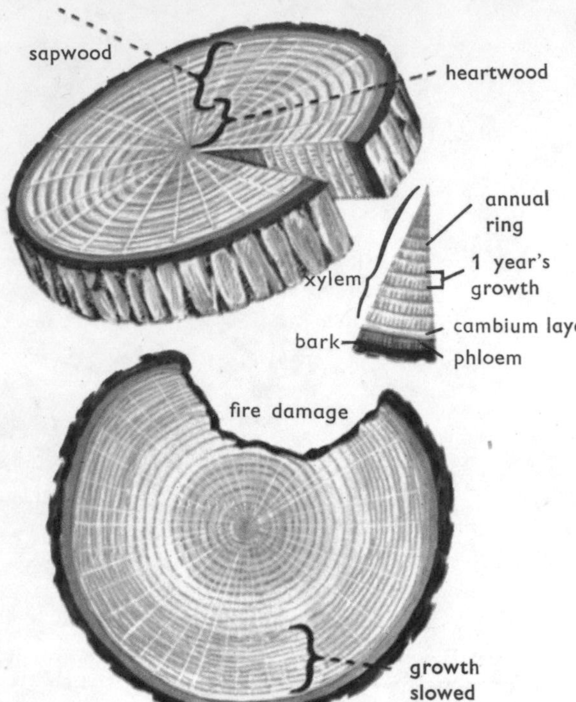

This tree was damaged by fire, which opened the way for insect pests and diseases. Note the closeness of its annual rings after the damage, showing that its rate of growth was slowed greatly.

Annual rings in this tree's trunk show a more rapid growth after the trees around it were cut, reducing the competition for space, water, and nutrients.

Many kinds of trees can be identified by their bark.

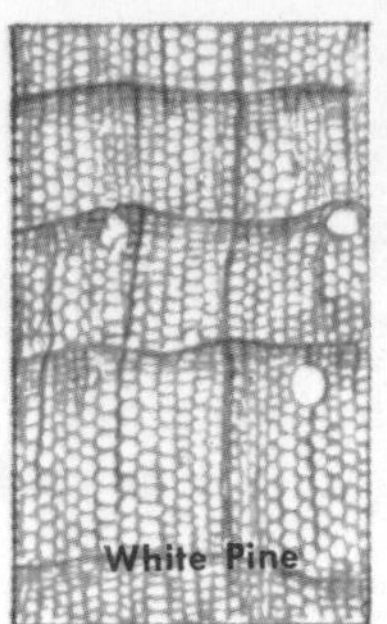

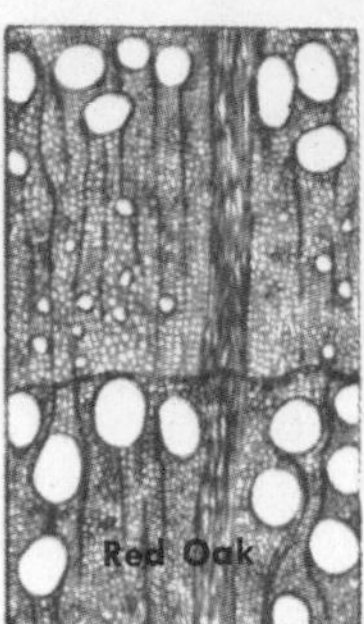

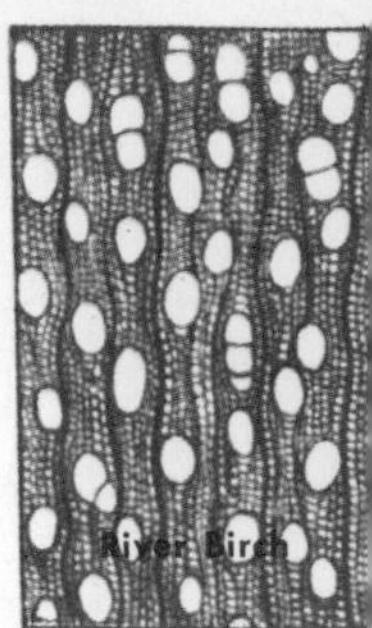

Thin sections examined under a microscope show cells and canals that give wood its characteristic grain.

Trees of the tropics grow the year around. They do not produce annual rings. In some warm climates, trees form rings which indicate the wet and dry seasons, but generally it is difficult to tell the age of a tree which grows in a region with no definite seasons.

Each kind of tree produces a different type of wood. Thin sections of wood under a microscope show the differences in arrangement of the wood cells and canals. Coarse-grained wood has widely separated annual rings. Rings in fine-grained wood are close together.

LEAVES manufacture food by a complex chemical process called photosynthesis. Dissolved minerals and water absorbed by the roots pass up the trunk to the leaf cells where they combine with carbon from carbon dioxide in the air to form sugar. Trees convert most of this sugar into cellulose, the substance of which wood is formed.

Photosynthesis takes place only in the presence of light and chlorophyll, the green pigment in leaves. The process stops at night.

On the under surface of leaves are numerous small slit-like openings called stomata. Their size is regulated by guard cells, one on each side of the opening. Leaves get rid of excess moisture through these openings. In dry weather the stomata are closed. In rainy weather or when the tree can absorb large amounts of water from the soil, the stomata are open. At such times a normal sized elm is estimated to discharge more than 200 gallons of water a day through its leaves.

Stomata also take in the carbon dioxide

used by the leaves in photosynthesis, and they give off oxygen, a waste product of photosynthesis. At night, when leaves are not manufacturing food, stomata give off carbon dioxide, a waste product of respiration. This continuing energy-releasing process, also essential in maintaining animal life, occurs in leaves and all other living plant tissues.

Leaves are arranged on the branches of a tree so that they are exposed to the maximum amount of light. Sometimes branches or stems bend in growth as the leaves stretch towards the light. Shaded leaves of a tree tend to be larger than those exposed to direct sunlight, and leaves on trees which have an adequate supply of water are generally larger than leaves on the same kind of tree growing where the supply of water is not great.

Trees are frequently identified by the shape of their leaves and their position on the twigs. Leaves of pine trees are so slender they are called needles. Simple leaves consist of a single blade attached to the twig by a stem called a petiole. Those kinds that have no petioles are called sessile leaves. Compound leaves have a number of blades, called leaflets. Some compound leaves have leaflets arranged on each side of a central stem. These are pinnately compound leaves. Those of the mimosa are twice pinnately compound. Compound leaves with leaflets attached to one central point, as in the horsechestnut, are palmately compound.

Some leaves are arranged alternately on a branch — a leaf on one side of the stem, then on the other. Others are oppositely arranged. Still others are whorled — that is, with three or more arising from the same place on the stem. Some leaves are smooth-edged; others toothed or lobed.

Green chlorophyll in leaves is not replaced in autumn as rapidly as it is used; thus leaves change colour in autumn. Bright yellow and orange pigments show through as the green fades. Pigments produced in the manufacture of food make some leaves red or purple. Finally the leaves wither and die. As their bright pigments fade, leaves become brown. Only the abundance of tannin in their

A plant manufactures food in its green leaves.

leaf of a Tulip tree

Tall 'palisade' cells on the upper surface of the leaf absorb sunlight, the energy used in the manufacturing of food.

palisade cells

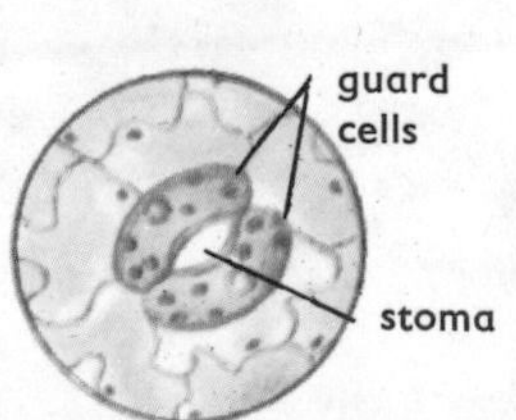

Guard cells surround and regulate the size of openings (stomata) on the underside of a leaf. They control the amount of water to be discharged and regulate the amount of air.

PHOTOSYNTHESIS
(stores energy as food)

RESPIRATION
(releases energy in stored foods)

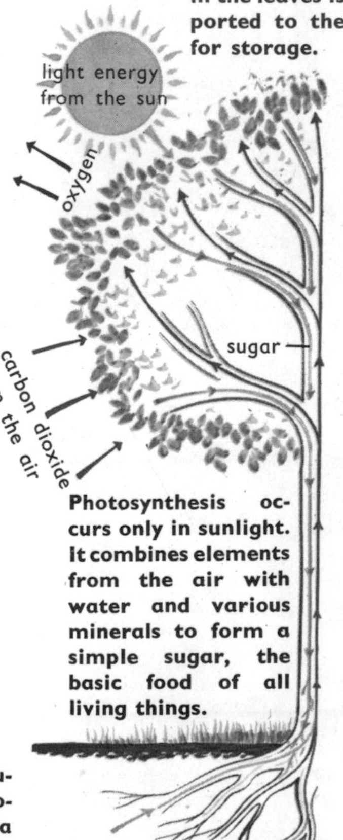
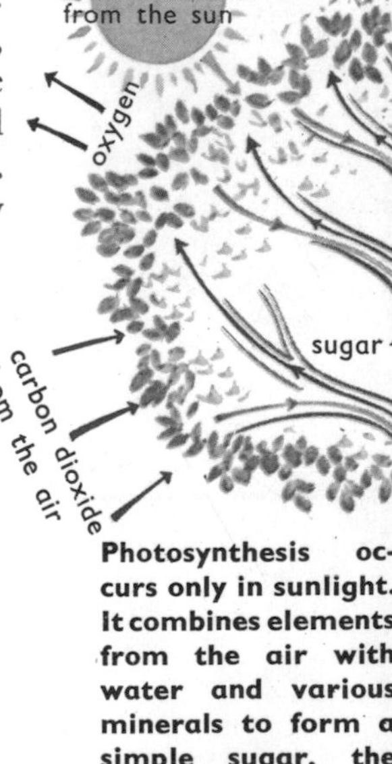

Photosynthesis occurs only in sunlight. It combines elements from the air with water and various minerals to form a simple sugar, the basic food of all living things.

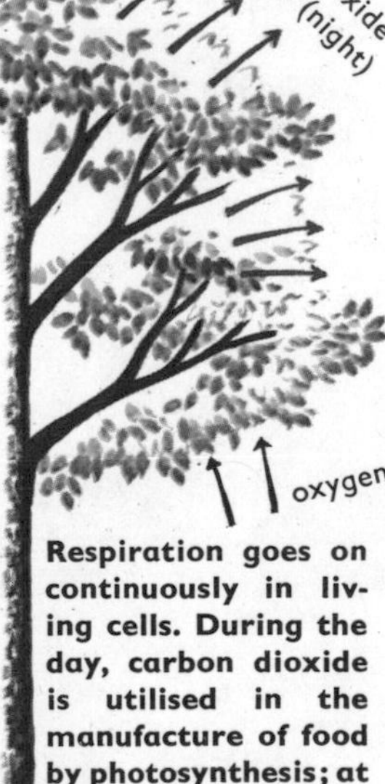

Respiration goes on continuously in living cells. During the day, carbon dioxide is utilised in the manufacture of food by photosynthesis; at night it is released in the air.

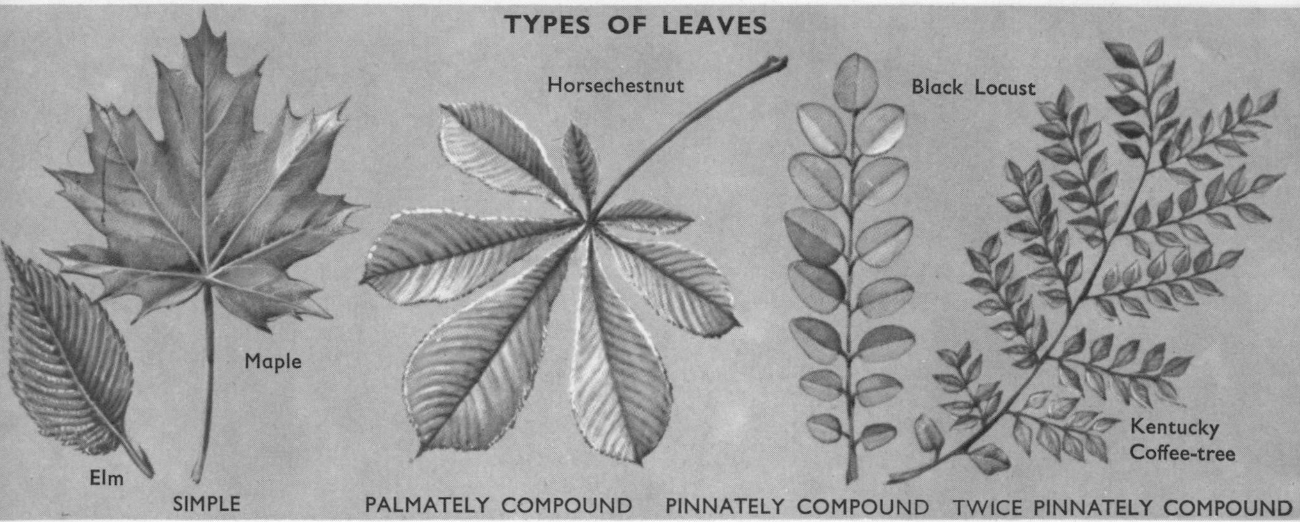

tissues remains. Finally they drop to the ground.

Trees prepare to lose their leaves many weeks before the shedding occurs. In midsummer a layer of loose cells begins to grow across the base of the leaf stem where it attaches to the twig. Only the cellular channels through which the leaf receives minerals and water from the roots, and along which manufactured food travels, remain open. Soon a second layer of corky cells forms beneath the first one.

Wind, rain, and sometimes the formation of ice crystals between these two cell layers finally break the leaf from the stem. The lower layer of corky cells formed earlier becomes the leaf scar on the twig. These scars are so distinctive in size and shape that they can be used to identify trees.

Evergreen trees lose their leaves, too, but only a few at a time. Thus they remain green the year around. Some evergreens keep their leaves for long periods of time. Bristlecone Pines keep their needles for seventeen years.

FLOWERS of some kinds of trees are large and showy. Others are so small or colourless they are not ordinarily seen. But all trees, except pines and related species, have flowers of some sort. Flowers are a tree's reproductive organs. They form the fruit containing the seeds that develop into new trees.

Some flowers occur singly, as in magnolias. Others are in clusters. The greenish flower

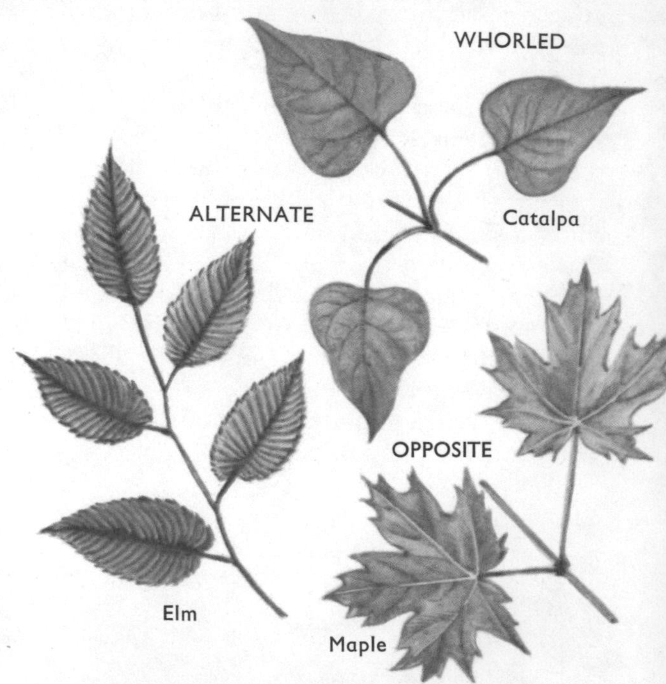

LEAF ARRANGEMENTS ON BRANCH

A tree's foliage changes with the season.

clusters of Dwarf Cornel form a neat head which is surrounded by white, modified leaves, called bracts, that look like petals. Willow flowers, called catkins, are in upright clusters, while the catkins of walnuts and birches droop.

The essential parts of a flower are its stamens and pistils. Each stamen consists of a slender elongated stalk — the filament — terminated by an enlarged anther which contains the pollen grains. The pistil, located in the centre, is commonly flask-shaped; its swollen base is the ovary. Its neck is the style, and the expanded top, which receives the pollen, is called the stigma. Some trees have both stamens and pistils in the same blossom. Others, such as birches, walnuts, and oaks, have two kinds of flowers on the same tree; one type of flower bears only the stamens, the other pistils. Still others — willows are examples — have male flowers (with stamens) on one tree, and female flowers (with pistils) on another. A complete flower contains four kinds of floral organs — sepals, petals, stamens, and pistils. Incomplete flowers lack one or more of these organs. The types of flowers, their colour and form, are used as a most important characteristic in identifying plants.

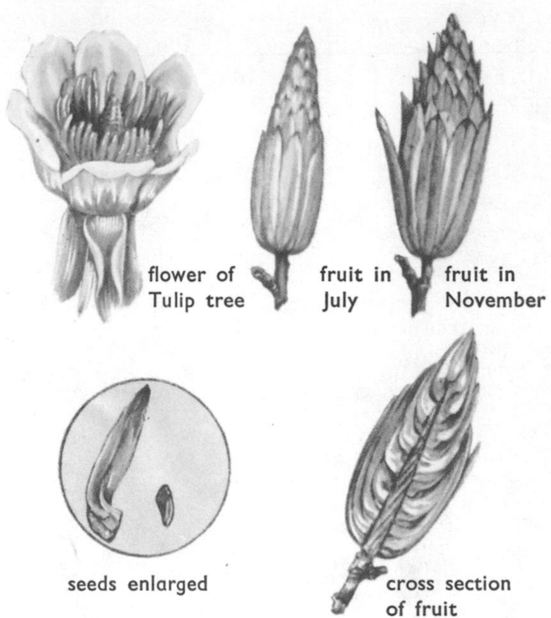

The ripened fruit splits open to release the seeds.

TWIGS AND BUDS. Twigs also have special features. Sassafras twigs, for example, have an easily recognised flavour. Elder twigs have a pith centre. Twigs of the broom are five-angled; those of the Purple Willow are purplish at first, later olive or yellowish-

PARTS OF A TYPICAL FLOWER

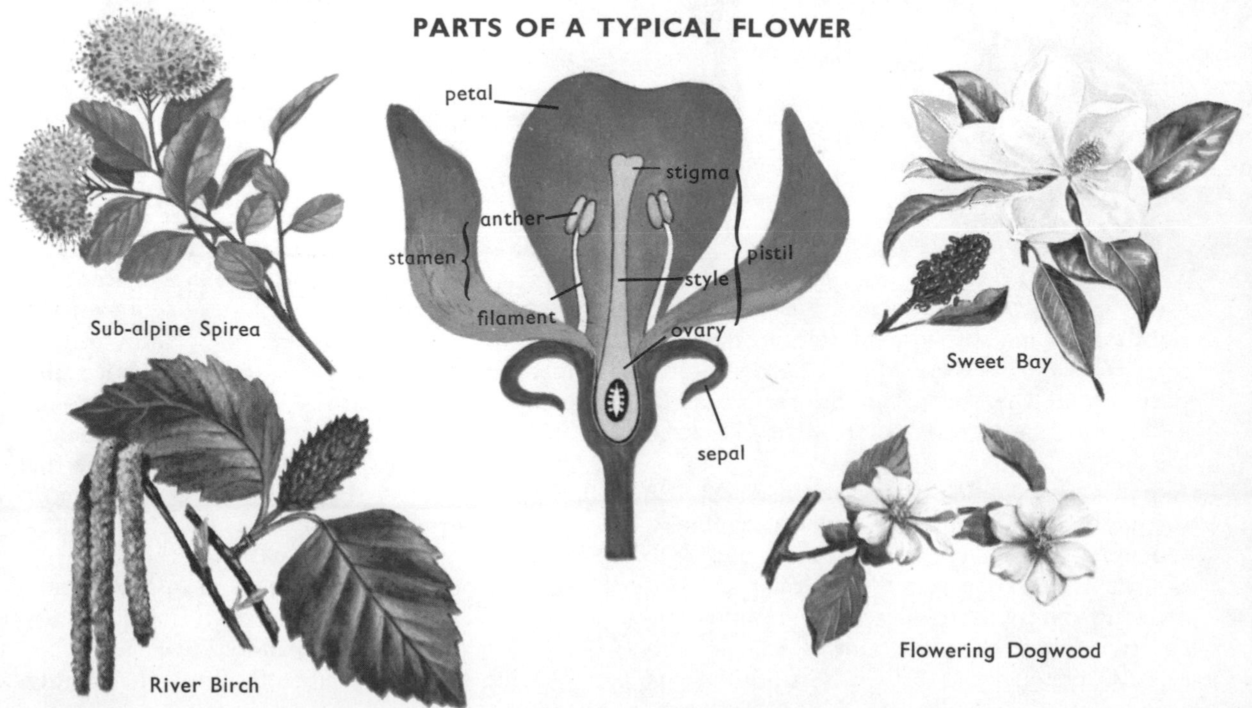

grey. A milky sap flows from the fig's twigs when they are damaged.

The size and shape of the scars left after a leaf is shed from a twig also varies with different groups of trees. The leaf scars of the horsechestnut are large and shield-shaped; those of the catalpa are round. Leaf scars of sycamores are narrow and either U or V-shaped. Like the leaves, the leaf scars may be either alternate, opposite, or whorled in their arrangements on the twig.

Tiny dots on the surface of the leaf scar mark the ends of channels called vascular

PARTS OF TWIGS

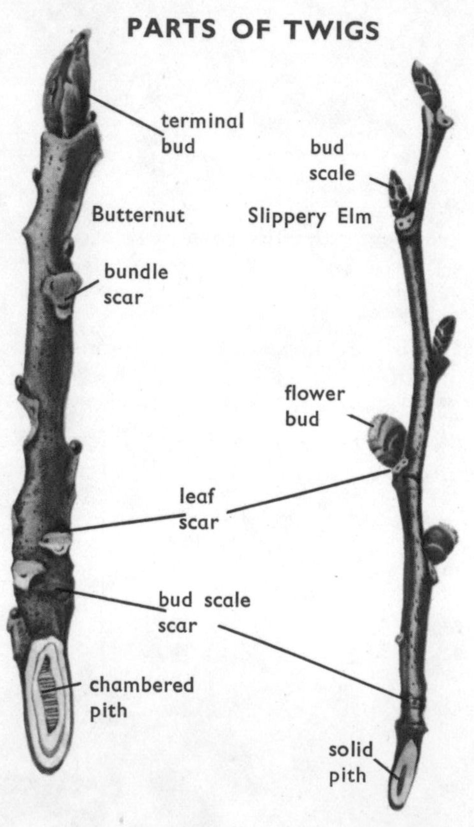

bundles, which carry food solutions to the leaf. These tiny scars appear in distinctive patterns on the surface of the leaf scar. In ashes, for example, they are in a C-shaped line.

Just above the leaf scars are the buds, also distinctive in size, shape, and arrangement. On some twigs there is a terminal bud with a scar at its base where the twig stopped growing the previous season. Some buds hug the twig closely, as do buds of certain willows. Others project outwards from the twig, as do the long spindle-shaped buds of beeches. Most buds are covered with scales which protect them during cold winter months. Buds of willows and magnolias have only one scale, while those of oaks, birches, and beeches have numerous overlapping scales. Still others are naked, covered only by a pair of thick and waterproof leaves that are the first to unfold the next season.

WHERE TREES GROW. Differences in the temperature north and south of the equator determine the broad and varied forest zones throughout the world. Entirely different trees may grow in forest zones with similar temperatures, however. Trees of the forests in the Northern Hemisphere, for example, are not the same as those in the Southern Hemisphere regions with the same temperature. There are also differences in trees between the Eastern and Western Hemispheres. No trees grow in the Arctic and the Antarctic or above the timber line on the slopes of mountains.

Each of the world's primary forest zones is divided into smaller regions containing its distinctive types of trees. These areas are determined largely by the amount of moisture and by the nature of the soil. Forests are generally most luxuriant where there is an abundance of moisture. Where rainfall is limited, trees are wider spaced, and there are fewer kinds. Where there is no moisture at all, as in arid deserts, there are no trees.

Trees adapted to extreme cold, high winds, and deep snows occur at the tree line on mountains. In the Alps, the Silver Fir, larch, and the pine are trees of this sort. A change in altitude of 1,000 feet causes a difference in climate equal to a change in latitude of about 300 miles. Thus, a series of 'life zones', each with its distinctive plant and animal life, occur on mountain slopes. Above the tree line is a rigorous land of barren rocks and either glaciers or perpetual snowfields. Perennial herbs, mosses, and lichens are the only plants. At the tree line are the most hardy trees, dwarfed and twisted by the wind, rain, and snow. Below this are the sub-alpine meadows, where clumps of conifers and brightly-coloured wild flowers grow. Farther down the mountain are the cone-bearing trees adapted to the more temperate

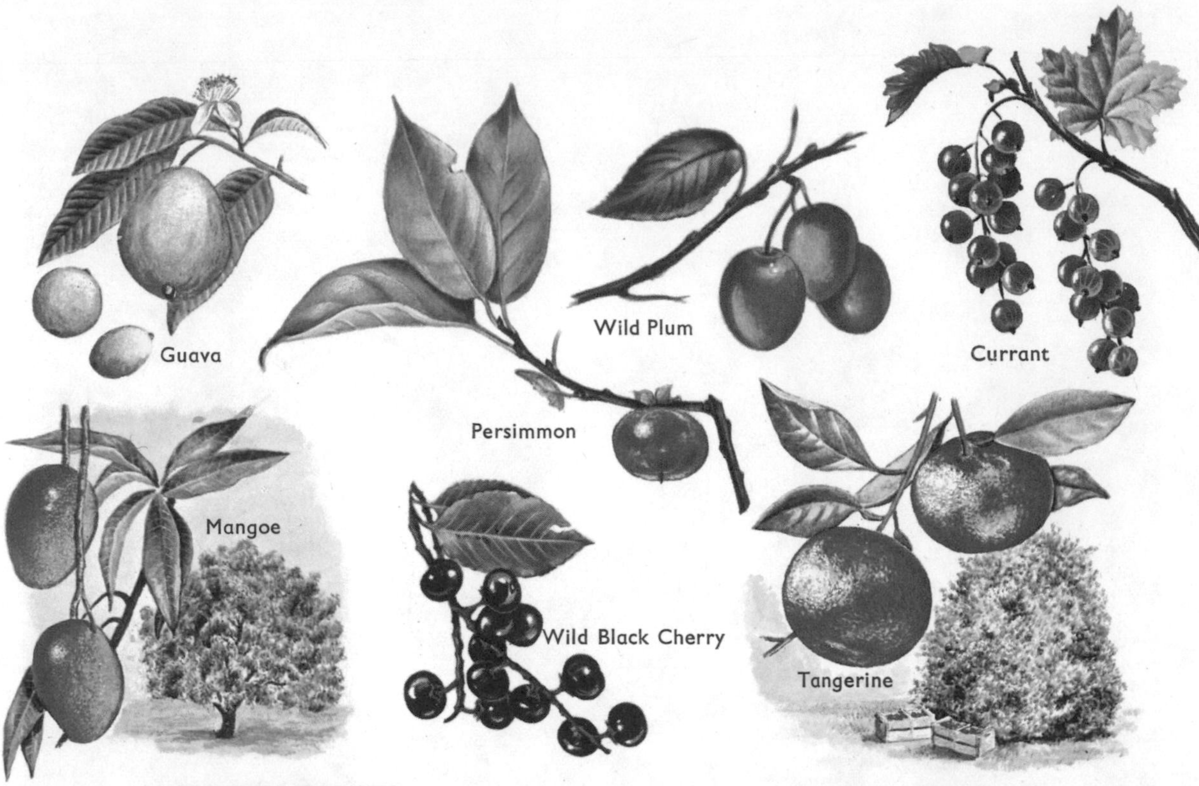

Guava
Persimmon
Wild Plum
Currant
Mangoe
Wild Black Cherry
Tangerine

FLESHY FRUITS

Pulpy walls surrounding some seeds are eaten by Man and other animals. The seeds are dropped as the fruit is eaten or pass through the animal's body undigested. In this manner the seeds are widely distributed.

DRY FRUITS

The wall surrounding some seeds is hard or woody, as in nuts. The pods of legumes split open and release their seeds when ripe. Papery thin wings or plumes attached to other seeds are easily blown by the wind.

Mountain Maple
Pinyon Pine
Mockernut Hickory
Black Locust
Bitternut
Pecan
Oak
Western Plane

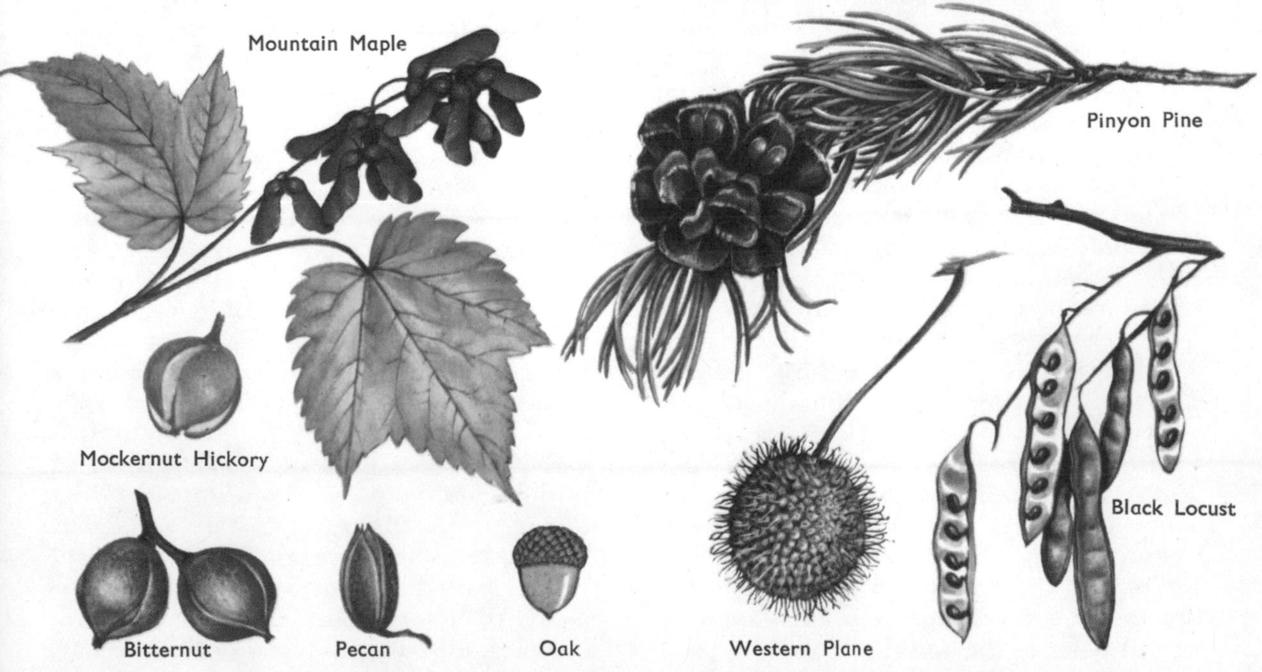

Courtesy of Weyerhaeuser Company

Thinned forests soon grow back. Young trees in the foreground are new growth timber in an area felled a few seasons ago. The bare patch at the foot of the ridge is the site of a recent felling operation.

climates. Then a mixture of conifers and hardwoods appear, and finally the pure hardwood forests. Complete ranges of this sort occur on certain mountains in and close to the tropics.

Some trees grow only in deep, rich soils; others can exist in thin, rocky soils. Many conifers thrive in acid soils, and other trees grow only where certain bacteria or fungi exist. Some kinds grow in dense stands and reproduce best in shaded locations; others require sunlight and grow widely spaced.

Tropical rain forests are rank, humid, dimly lighted areas. They contain a great variety of trees, vines, and other plants. Forests of this sort are found in the lowlands of the West Indies, Central America, the Amazon basin of northern South America, Central Africa, south-east Asia, the East Indies, and the northern fringe of Australia. Brackish, coastal mangrove swamps found in several parts of the world are also a type of tropical forest. Many tropical regions have little rainfall, however. In these areas the trees are scattered in the dry grasslands or are clustered around the water holes.

One of the world's largest coniferous forests grows along the Pacific Coast from south-eastern Alaska to northern California. Moisture-laden winds that sweep in from the Pacific are blocked by the coastal mountain ranges, and so an abundance of rain falls all along the coastal lowlands. The forests are luxuriant, although many of the original stands have been cut for timber.

East of this coastal mountain barrier the coniferous forests grow in drier soils. In a vast inland area of western North America, from Canada to Mexico and from the Great Plains to the drier regions of the Pacific Coast states, the Ponderosa Pine is dominant. To the east this forest belt merges with the nearly treeless grassland of the Great Plains.

Soil and moisture conditions determine

also the nature of the hardwood forests. Many willows, for example, grow best in moist soils and are most common along streams. Beach trees, with their shallow, widespreading root systems, also thrive where surface soil is fairly moist. Most oaks have deep root systems and grow best in deep well-drained soils. Trees of dry regions need extensive roots to collect moisture.

Cone-bearing trees can grow in colder regions than can most hardwoods. The two kinds are mixed in intermediate climates, where winters are cold and summers hot.

Spruces, larches, true firs, certain pines, and some birches and poplars make up the world's most northern forests. The Scots Pine grows on poor, dry, sandy soils. Black Spruce and Balsam Fir often grow in northern swamps or bogs of Canada. Black and White Spruces and the Eastern Larch mark the northern edge of the North American forest. Farther north is the treeless tundra.

Smaller groups of trees that do not conform to the regional picture are the result of special circumstances. The wild olives of the Saharan mountains, which are related to the European Olive, are relics of an earlier, moister age. The arbutus of Ireland is all that remains in Britain of a distribution that formerly was more widespread. It is still found in the Mediterranean region and Brittany.

HOW WE USE FORESTS. Long ago Man found his food and shelter in the forests. Today we are equally dependent upon trees — perhaps even more so. A complete list of useful products derived from our forests would contain many thousands of items important in our life.

Each year more than 50,000 million cubic feet of wood is cut in forests throughout the world. About 44 per cent is used for fuel. Timber and veneer, used for building, furniture, and similar purposes, are manufactured from 34 per cent. About 15 per cent is converted into wood pulp for books, magazines, newspapers, cartons, and other paper products. The remainder is used for poles, posts, pilings, and miscellaneous items.

Wood is most valuable for fuel in the least developed regions of the world. The majority of the world's people live in the largest tree growing areas — the temperate forest regions of the Northern Hemisphere. In heavily industrialised regions most of the trees cut are processed to make different products. In North America, 53 per cent of the wood cut is used for timber and veneer; 28 per cent for wood pulp; 15 per cent for fuel; and 4 per cent for posts, poles, and pilings. In Africa, 90 per cent of the timber cut is used for fuel; only 8 per cent for timber; 1 per cent for wood pulp; and 1 per cent for miscellaneous items. More than half the wood

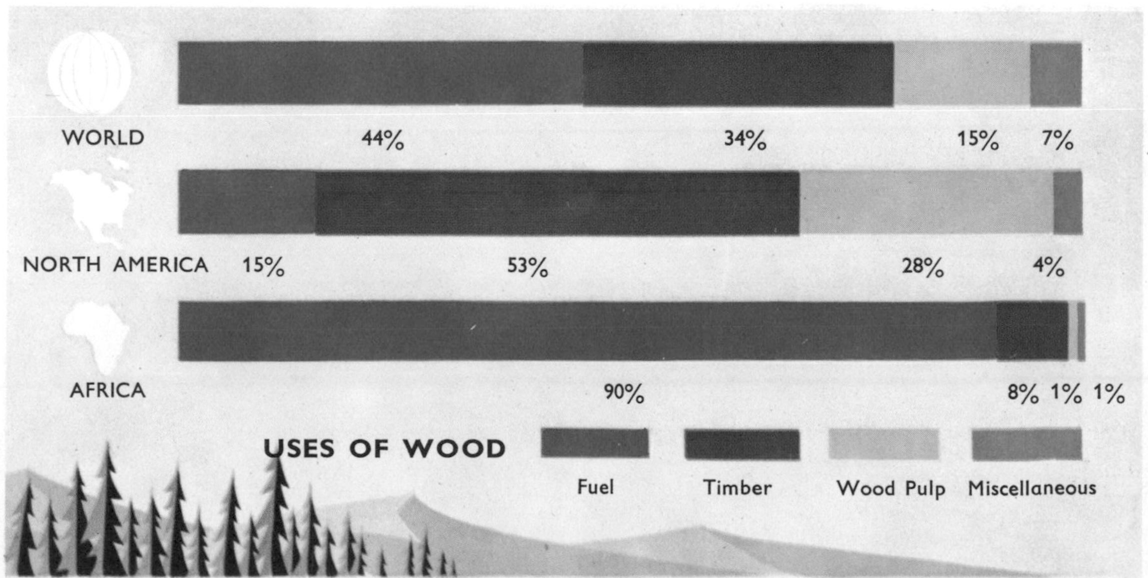

cut in Europe and the Soviet Union is used for various industrial purposes. In Asia, 67 per cent of the wood cut is used for fuel; in Central and South America, the figure is also 67 per cent.

Tropical forests are not heavily utilised. Few people live in the tropics and the forests are too remote from centres of population for shipping the timber or timber products to market. Also, tropical forests are made up of a mixture of many kinds of trees while in temperate forests there are fewer kinds but in nearly pure stands. Trees are cut and used locally in the tropics, however.

Trees are a crop, grown and periodically harvested just as farmers grow and harvest maize or wheat. The principal difference is that farm crops are harvested one or more times each year, while forest tree crops can be harvested only after a period of years.

Modern forestry practices keep our forest lands productive. Trees that are harvested are replaced with seedlings. Idle forest land is lost growing time in the production of valuable timber.

Different trees thrive best in different conditions of temperature, soil, and moisture. Species must be carefully chosen to give the best economic return for these conditions. Douglas-fir forests are harvested by clean-cutting the trees in strips or blocks. In contrast, young Ponderosa Pines grow well in shade. In harvesting such forests only larger trees are cut so that shade remains for the young trees.

Forests are sometimes harvested so that nature supplies the seed for the new crop of trees. It may require several years to get a new forest started by this method. Foresters often replace trees nowadays by artificial means. Blocks or strips that have been clean-cut are seeded by helicopters or planted with

With modern power-driven saws, lumbermen can cut more wood than with hand saws and axes.

Courtesy of Weyerhaeuser Company

A sawyer cuts the log into planks. These first cuts determine how the log will be processed.

Changes in vegetation zones in the Alps with increasing altitude. The tree line is between the green of the sub-alpine meadow and the brown of the alpine zone proper.

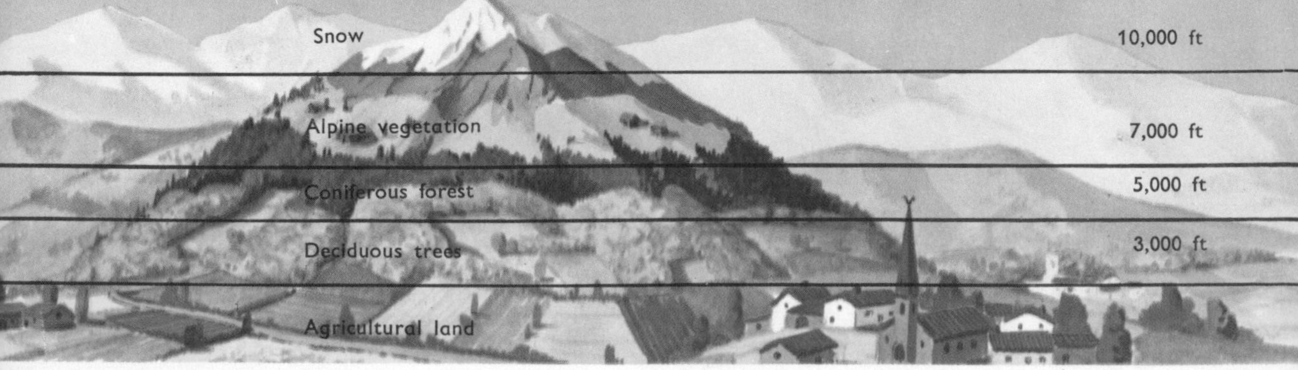

Courtesy of Weyerhaeuser Company

young trees from nurseries. In this way a new forest is started much faster than by natural seeding. Because every year wood is becoming more valuable and serves wider needs, this is often a less expensive method.

Often a stand of trees is thinned to give the remaining trees more space in which to grow. This also improves the health of the remaining trees, reducing damage done by destructive diseases and insects which are more common in crowded, slow-growing forests. Trimming the lower branches also helps to encourage good growth.

Felling operations vary according to the size, number, and kind of trees being harvested. Some operations involve a few men with horses or light equipment; others are industries, employing skilled men and special heavy machinery.

Much skill is required to fell a tree without damaging it. First the fallen tree is trimmed of its branches. Then it is cut into logs of desired length.

On arrival at the saw-mill the logs are firmly secured on to the saw's carriage. The carriage passes swiftly back and forth, slicing the log into rough planks. The thickness of the planks is determined by the sawyer who operates the saw's mechanical controls. Sometimes 'gang saws' are used to cut many rough planks at one time.

The rough boards, carried to other machines by rollers or endless belts, are then edged, cut into desired lengths, and trimmed

The modern printing industry uses most of the wood pulp produced by the conifer forests of the North. Huge printing presses, such as this one, print full-colour books or magazines in a single press run.

to get rid of defects. This timber is carefully dried in 'kilns' and then planed or smoothed.

In plywood mills a log is turned against a sharp blade so that a thin section of wood is sliced off. These thin sections are glued together with the grain of one at right angles to that of the next. This greatly increases the strength of the resulting sheets.

Saw-mill waste products are the raw materials for other products. Paper, fibre-board and hardboard are made from sawdust, chips, and trimmings. Many parts of a tree formerly wasted are now turned into such useful items.

Forests are also important in supplying the water for homes and industries, and for the development of hydro-electric power. They will retard excessive run-off from rain and melting snows, thus reducing the danger of floods in lowlands. They hold soil on steep slopes, preventing landslides and soil erosion. Wild animals seek food and shelter in the forests, and fish live in forest streams and lakes. Millions of people enjoy picnicking, hiking, hunting, camping, and various other types of outdoor recreations in forests and woodlands.

CARING FOR OUR FORESTS. Foresters wage a constant battle against forest enemies. The worst of these are fires, insect pests and diseases. Lesser damage is caused by floods, dry weather, avalanches, and wild or domestic animals. Poor use of forest lands,

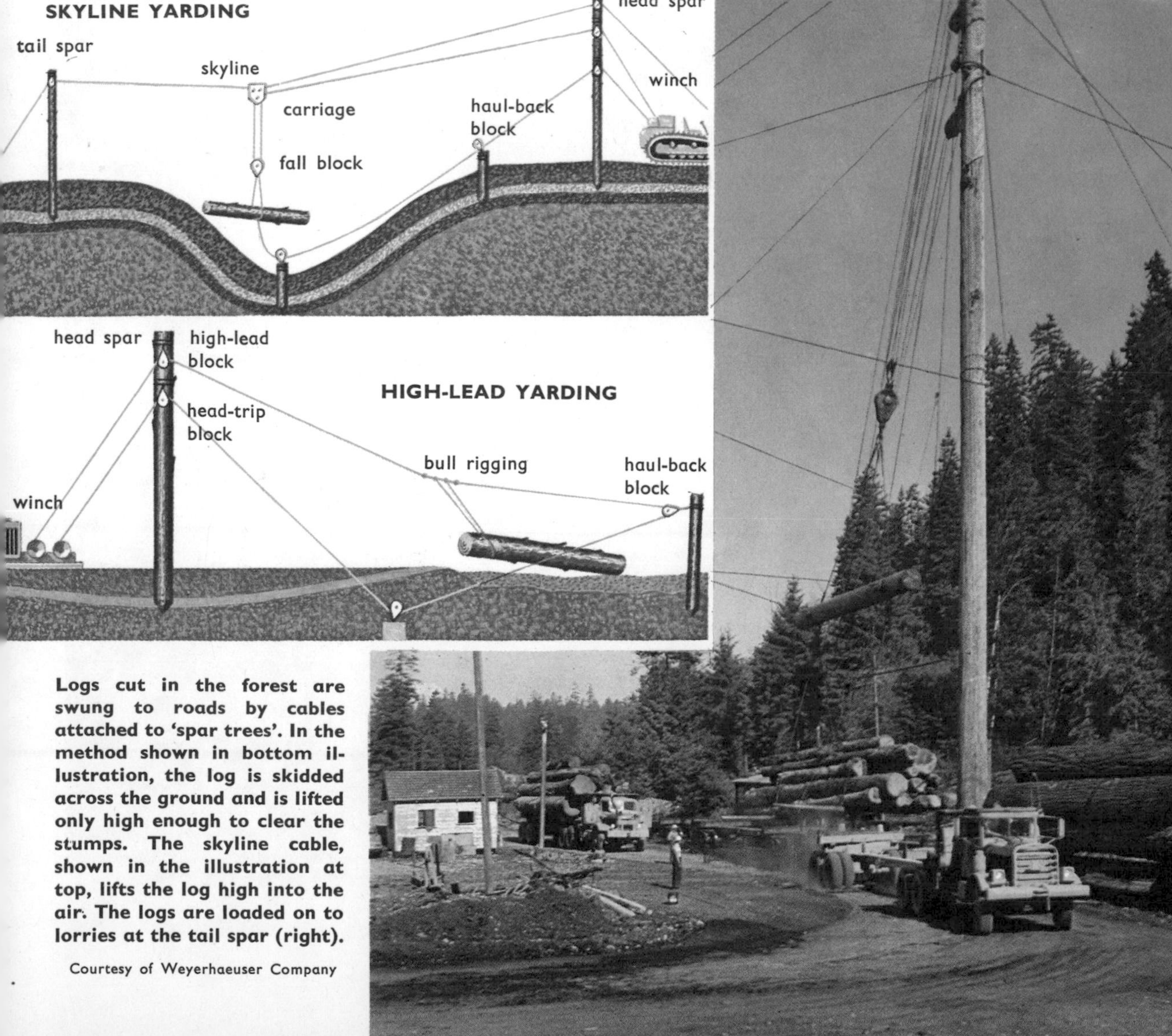

Logs cut in the forest are swung to roads by cables attached to 'spar trees'. In the method shown in bottom illustration, the log is skidded across the ground and is lifted only high enough to clear the stumps. The skyline cable, shown in the illustration at top, lifts the log high into the air. The logs are loaded on to lorries at the tail spar (right).

Courtesy of Weyerhaeuser Company

Courtesy of Weyerhaeuser Company

Logs are stored temporarily in ponds near the mill. They are sorted before being pulled out for sawing.

such as improper harvesting of trees, also causes considerable damage.

Once it was believed that the world's forests were so vast they could never be destroyed. Now we know this is not true. As our population grows, demands for wood, water, and recreation will continue to increase. Making certain our forests are productive now and in the future is important to human welfare.

Insect pests and tree diseases actually do more damage to forests than do fires. Grubs of bark beetles bore into a tree's vital cambium layer. When these pests are numerous, many trees are girdled and killed in a short time. Caterpillars of some kinds of moths and butterflies eat the leaves from trees, starving the trees by preventing them from manufacturing food. Other kinds of insects suck the fluids from a tree's stems or leaves, and some attack only the flowers or seeds. No tree is immune to insect attack at any stage of its life. Foresters control outbreaks of destructive insects by good forest management. Healthy, vigorous trees are susceptible

Most timber is grown and processed far from the place where it will be used. Finished boards and timbers are transported by ship, train, and lorry.

Courtesy of Weyerhaeuser Company

less to insect attacks, but when insects become abnormally abundant, spraying with insecticides is often necessary.

Insects can also be beneficial. Some kinds destroy pest insects. Others hurry the decay of fallen or damaged trees, converting them to rich and usable humus on the forest floor.

Fungi kill by growing among the tree's cells and feeding on its tissues. Most trees have a natural resistance to the diseases in their own area, and only the weak specimens are affected. But diseases from foreign lands can cause sweeping damage. White pine blister rust, introduced to North America from Europe, has destroyed great numbers of certain pines. The Dutch elm disease, also from Europe and spread by a bark beetle, has killed thousands of American Elms in the United States.

Lesser damage, though sometimes serious locally, is caused by mammals that eat bark, young trees, or the leaves of trees. Deer, rabbits, and mice are among these offenders.

TYPES OF TREES. Trees belong to one of two major groups of plants — either gymnosperms or angiosperms.

Gymnosperms, which means 'naked seeds', are the most ancient group of seed-bearing plants. Their seeds, usually borne on the scale of a cone, are not protected within the fruit as are the seeds of angiosperms. Fossil gymnosperms found in rock formations reveal that they appeared about 300 million years ago. Included in this group are the sequoias, pines, spruces, firs, yews, cedars, and other trees with scaly or needle-like leaves. Primitive, palm-like tropical cycads, once the dominant plants on Earth, and the unusual ginkgo tree are also gymnosperms.

Evergreens, softwoods, or conifers are other names often used to refer to gymnosperms. Some members of the group do not fit these names, however. Larches lose their foliage completely each autumn, hence they are not evergreen. Certain pines that grow in the southern United States have harder wood than some of the so-called hardwoods of the angiosperm group. And some gymnosperms, such as the yews, do not have cones.

Trees of the angiosperm group produce seeds which are protected by a fleshy, woody,

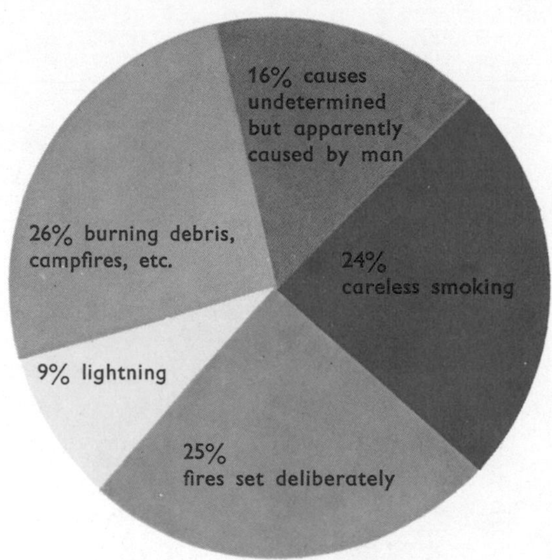

Man is responsible for most forest fires, and the majority of the fires are started through carelessness. Better detection methods, rapid communication, and improved fire-fighting techniques have reduced forest fires.

***Gymnosperms*, which include the conifers, are the simplest of the seed plants. Their seeds are 'naked' — that is, not surrounded by a protective wall. *Angiosperms*, or higher seed plants, have seeds enclosed in a fruit. There are two groups: Monocotyledons, with only one leaf or cotyledon in their seed embryo; and Dicotyledons, with two leaves in their seed embryo.**

or leathery covering. Included in this group are most of the familiar fruit trees, and also willows, poplars, walnuts, oaks, chestnuts, elms, maples, and many others. Often they are called deciduous (which means that they drop their leaves in winter), hardwood, or broad-leaved trees, but there are exceptions to these generalised names, too. Many kinds of oaks, hollies, and most trees that grow in warm climates keep their leaves the year around, hence they are evergreen. Some angiosperms have soft wood; balsa wood, for example, is one of the lightest and softest woods known. Also, willows and other angiosperms have very narrow leaves, while cycads and the ginkgo of the gymnosperm group have broad, flattened leaves.

Angiosperms are further divided into two broad groups called monocots and dicots. Monocots have only one embryonic leaf or cotyledon in their seeds. Dicots produce two, as the name suggests.

Palm trees are monocots. They are more closely related to grasses (which includes the woody bamboos), bananas, and lilies than to other large trees. Veins in a monocot's leaves run nearly parallel, and their trunks are not clearly divided into heartwood, sapwood, cambium, and bark. Willows, poplars, walnuts, oaks, chestnuts, maples, and magnolias are among the trees of the dicot group. Woody shrubs and vines and most herbaceous plants are dicots, too.

Common names for trees vary from region to region and often are not really accurate. The Douglas-fir, for example, is sometimes called the Douglas Spruce, and its timber was for years marketed under the trade name of Oregon Pine. Yet the Douglas-fir is neither a spruce nor a pine. Neither is it a true fir. Cedar is an even more confusing common name, for it is used for a great many kinds of cone-bearing evergreens.

Botanists — and zoologists, too — have an

PLATEOSAURUS

Among the early dinosaurs of the Triassic Period, some 200 million years ago, were *Saltoposuchus* and *Procompsognathus*, swift creatures about the size of present-day turkeys. The giant dinosaur of the day was *Plateosaurus*, a 20-foot vegetarian. It belongs to group that gave rise to the dinosaur giants of later periods. Equally as large was the carnivorous, *Phytosaur*, a crocodile-like offshoot from the thecodont reptiles. Cycads and primitive conifers grew on the upland areas, while ferns and rushes prospered in the lower, moist regions.

organised system for naming plants and animals. Scientific names are in Latin, since the language is not spoken by anyone today and its words will not change in meaning. Each plant's scientific name consists of two parts — its genus and its species. The Evergreen Oak, for example, is also known by such common names as Holm Oak and Ilex. *Quercus ilex*, its scientific name, identifies it for botanists the world over.

TRIASSIC, the oldest period of the Mesozoic era, began about 225 million years ago and lasted about 30 million years. Both plants and animals of the Triassic were quite different from those of the preceding Permian era.

Cycads, cycadeoids, and conifers were abundant on land, while animals included the mammal-like reptiles and insects, scorpions, fresh-water crustaceans, and lung-fish. Amphibians continued to be widespread and common, while reptiles became more numerous and varied.

Semi-arid climates were widespread in North America and Europe. (See LIFE'S ORIGIN AND DEVELOPMENT; MESOZOIC.)

TROPICAL FRUITS of many kinds have become popular throughout the world. Others, though not well known in temperate climates, are highly important in the regions where they are grown.

Akees *(Blighia sapida)* are native to Africa, but are grown on a limited scale in the West Indies and tropical America. The tree produces beautiful yellowish-red fruit that split open when ripe. Inside are shiny black seeds surrounded by whitish flesh. The fruit should not be eaten before it splits open naturally, or 'yawns', as both the unripe flesh and seeds are highly poisonous.

Among the better known annonas are the Cherimoya, the Sugar-apple, Bullock's Heart, or Custard-apple, and the Sour Sop. Cherimoyas *(Annona cherimola)* are yellowish-green, oval to conical fruit that range up to two pounds in weight. Their custard-like flesh has a pineapple-banana flavour. Sugar-apples or Sweet Sops *(Annona squamosa)* are smaller, and the individual ovaries are not as closely fused as in Cherimoyas. Their flesh is sweeter. Larger than either Cherimoyas or Sugar-apples, Sour Sops *(Annona muricata)* may weigh several pounds. Their spiny skins are deep green, their white, cottony flesh very juicy. They are used as fresh fruit and in drinks.

Barbados Cherries *(Malpighia punicifolia)* are spreading evergreen shrubs that produce crimson-coloured fruit about an inch in diameter. The ripe fruit contains approximately forty times more vitamin C than an equivalent weight of orange juice.

Loquats *(Eriobotrya japonica)* are spherical or elliptical and about an inch and a half in length. Their skins are similar to a peach in colour, and their flesh is very sweet and juicy. Loquats are eaten fresh or they can be preserved.

Mangosteens *(Garcinia mangostana)* are the most highly praised of all tropical fruits. They are native to tropical regions of Asia

PITANGA (or SURINAM CHERRY)
Eugenia uniflora

MANGOSTEEN
Garcinia mangostana

SAPODILLA
Achras zapota

MAMEY SAPOTE
Calocarpum sapota

LOQUAT
Eriobotrya japonica

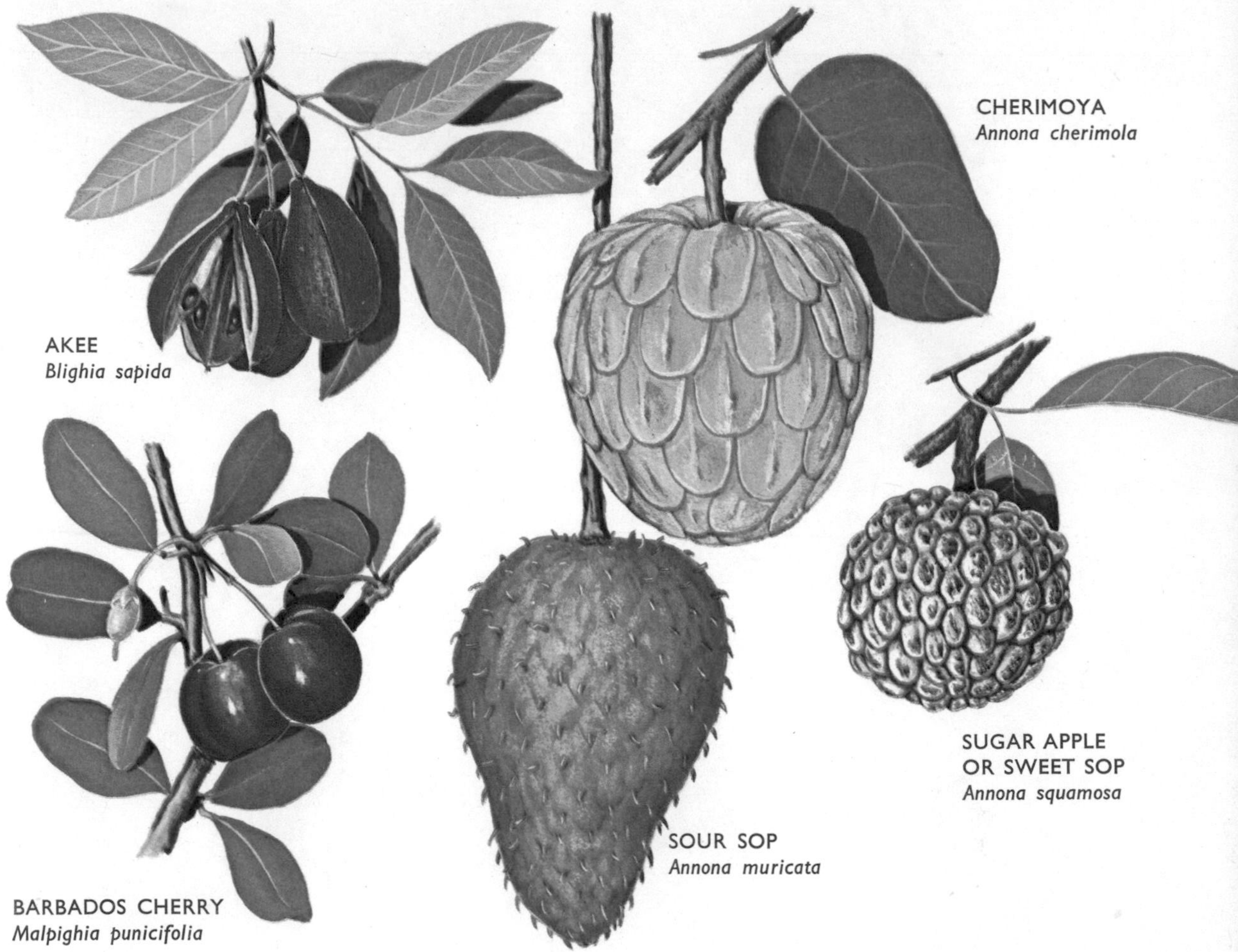

and the East Indies, but are also grown, though not as extensively, in the American tropics.

Sapodillas *(Achras zapota)* are produced on the trees from which chicle, used in chewing gum, is obtained. Slightly smaller than apples, they have a greyish-brown skin and sweet, yellowish-brown, granular flesh. Sapodillas are usually eaten fresh, but are also delicious when baked with butter and sugar.

Several kinds of fruits are called sapotes. Among these are Mamey Sapote *(Calocarpum sapota)*, Black Sapote *(Diospyros ebenaster)*, and Green Sapote *(Calocarpum viride)*.

Surinam Cherries or Pitangas *(Eugenia uniflora)*, which are eaten fresh or are made into jams or jellies, are small, reddish-orange fruit with rather deep ribs. They look like tiny pumpkins.

TROPICAL RAIN FORESTS extend 5 to 10 degrees on either side of the equator. They have uniformly high temperatures and heavy rainfall (up to 120 inches, with an average of about 90 inches per year) and no dry season. Tropical rain forests occur in the Amazon basin of South America, in the Congo of West Africa, and in Malaya and Indonesia. These are the world's natural hothouses.

Layering of vegetation is a characteristic of rain forests. The uppermost layer consists of very tall trees, forming a completely closed canopy. Below these are one or two layers of shorter trees and shrubs. Beneath the trees is a ground cover of ferns and herbs.

Roots of the tall trees, such as mahogany and ebony, are usually shallow. Many of these trees would topple if it were not for the huge supporting buttresses or pillars that

PERIGORD'S TRUFFLE
Tuber melanosporum
3 — 4 in.

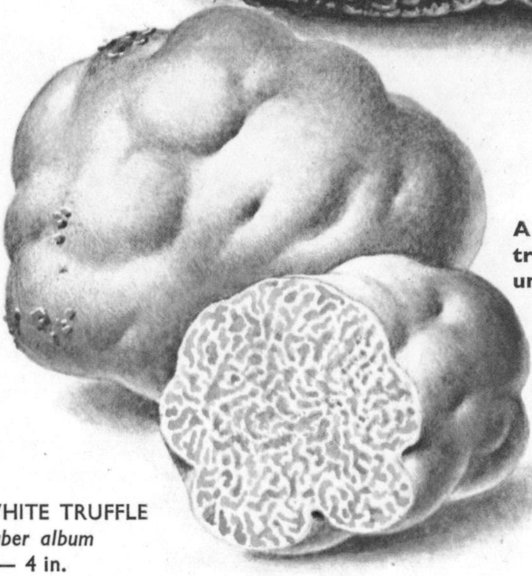

A truffle hunter and his trained pig search for the underground delicacies.

WHITE TRUFFLE
Tuber album
3 — 4 in.

Hans von Meiss — Photo Researchers

grow from their sides. The tall trees do not send out branches until they emerge above the lower ones. The long unbranched trunk makes many tall rain-forest trees ideal for timber. No one knows the age of rain-forest trees because they do not show annual rings by which years can be counted. Giant liana vines, sometimes 2 feet thick and 500 feet long, climb and twine about the tall trees. Lianas are the highways through the forest for many climbing animals. Many air plants (epiphytes), such as a great variety of orchids and members of the pineapple family, add to the colourful display of rain-forest flowers. Ferns, rhododendrons, bananas, plantain, and castor beans make up the lower stratum.

'Jungle' refers to the dense growth at the

The edge of a tropical rain forest is a jungle, an impenetrable tangle of bushes, trees, and vines.

forest edge and along streams where light penetrates. The interior of an upland rain forest is easy to move through since not enough light can penetrate the overhead canopy to make dense plant growth possible on the forest floor. (See FORESTS.)

TRUFFLES are a delicacy and probably the most expensive of all edible fungi. They grow entirely underground.

For at least 500 years the Italians have trained pigs to dig truffles for them. However, dogs are trained to scent out and dig for truffles in England and parts of France. Small dogs are used, although Basset Hounds used to be used quite a lot, especially in France.

In France and central Europe the truffle industry is very important.

Truffles usually grow 3 or 4 inches below the surface, although they may occur deeper. Normally, they weigh only a few ounces, but may reach two pounds or more.

The most important of several genera of truffles are *Tuber* and *Terfezia.* 36 species of *Terfezia* are now known, most of them growing in the region around the Mediterranean and Asia Minor. They are sold in the markets of Damascus, Baghdad, Smyrna, and all parts of Greece and North Africa.

About 50 species of *Tuber* occur in Europe and the United States. Those best known for eating (canned or fresh) come mostly from France and Italy. The Summer Truffle *(Tuber aestivum)* is nearly round and a glistening bluish-black when fresh; it becomes brownish-black when dry. Perigord's Truffle *(Tuber melanosporum)* is much desired and has a more distinct aroma than the Summer Truffle, which it resembles in colour and shape. The spores of the two differ, however, both in shape and markings.

Truffles are related to cup fungi and morels. They are sometimes confused with common underground fungi of the puffball group. Truffles are usually baked or are combined with other foods in casseroles.

TULIPS (*Tulipa* spp.) A tulip flower turned upside down looks like a turban, which is what the word tulip means in Persian. Most of the 100 species which are known grow wild in the Middle East.

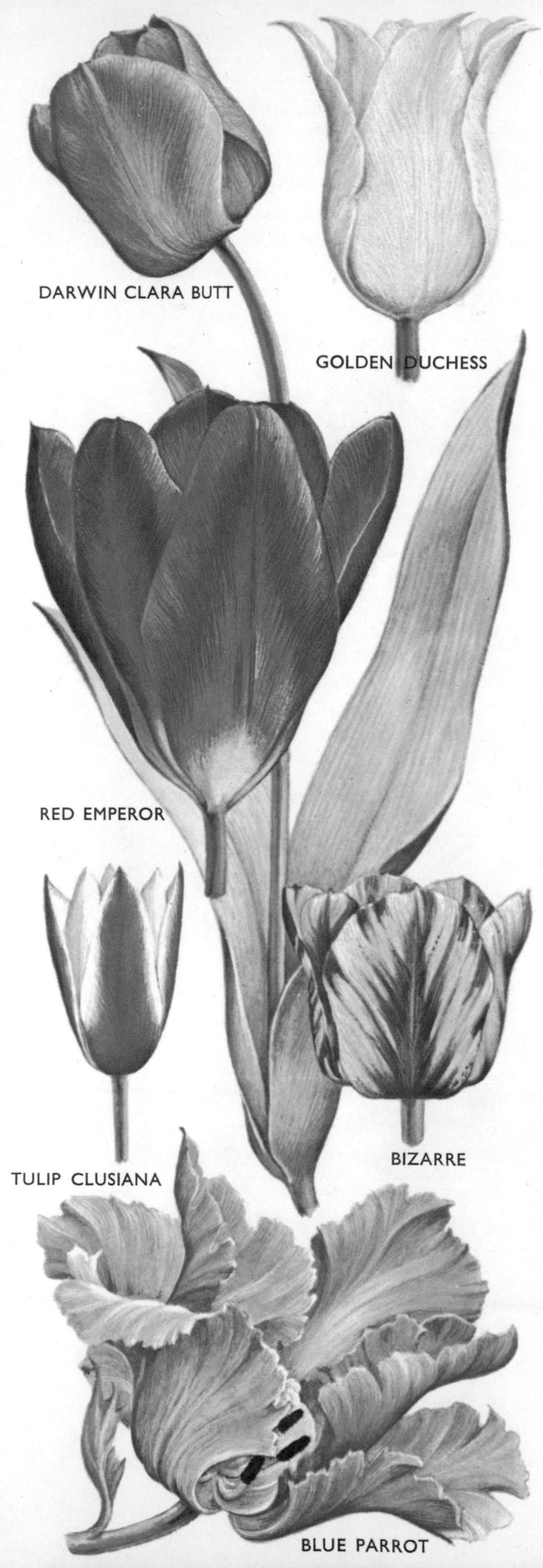

Tulips were brought into Europe from Turkey about 400 years ago. They have been improved by breeding and selection, mainly in Holland and England. Some bloom early; others late. There are single flowers and doubles; flowers with pointed or rounded petals; and others with fancy scallops and frills. There are many colours and shades.

Holland is the world centre of tulip bulb raising.

TULIP TREES *(Liriodendron tulipifera)* are attractive hardwood trees found in north-eastern United States and southern Canada. They are also planted as ornamentals. Tulip trees grow tall and straight, often 100 feet high and 3 — 5 feet in diameter.

Tulip tree leaves have tulip-shaped outlines, but the tree is named for its cup-shaped flowers. The flowers have greenish-yellow petals which are orange at the base. They appear in the spring after the leaves have developed. Winged seeds develop in upright, cone-like clusters that dry and fall apart when mature.

TULIP TREE

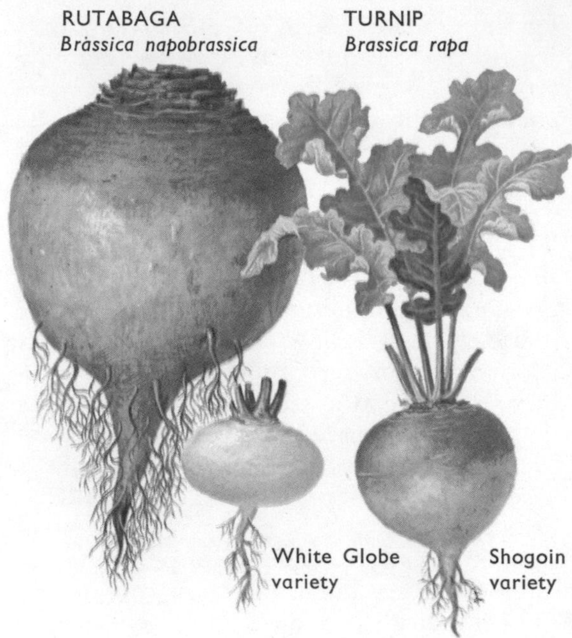

TURNIP *(Brassica rapa)* and Swede *(Brassica campestris)*. These plants are biennials which during the first year form a rosette of leaves on the ground and a swollen root containing food material. This has been greatly increased in size by plant breeding. Turnip roots are spherical with white flesh, while swedes are longer rather than broad, with yellow flesh.

Both crops need fertile, deep soil, and the additional manuring and cultivation they required led to their widespread adoption by farmers as 'soil improving' crops, which were grown at regular intervals in the crop rotation, and provided winter feed for cattle and sheep.

A few are grown as vegetables for human consumption.

TURPENTINES are mixtures of resins and essential or volatile oils obtained chiefly from pine trees. Crude turpentines were originally used to caulk wooden ships and to waterproof ropes. For this reason the name 'naval stores' became applied to the turpentine industry. Several species of pines, including the Longleaf Pine *(Pinus palustris)* and Slash Pine *(Pinus cariboea)* have been used as sources of turpentine. The naval stores industry has been highly developed in France and the U.S.A.

Crude turpentine occurs in numerous ducts or resin canals in pine trees. When a tree is injured, the turpentine gum or pitch oozes from the wound. An early method of turpentining involved cutting a cavity or 'box' at the base of the tree. Turpentine collected in this cavity. These deep cuts never healed, and so the trees were less valuable for timber and were subject to decay.

Newer methods are less harmful and yields of turpentine are higher. Instead of cutting a deep V in the wood, a slanting slash is made in the bark. A tin gutter guides the gum into a cup. Normally the flow stops

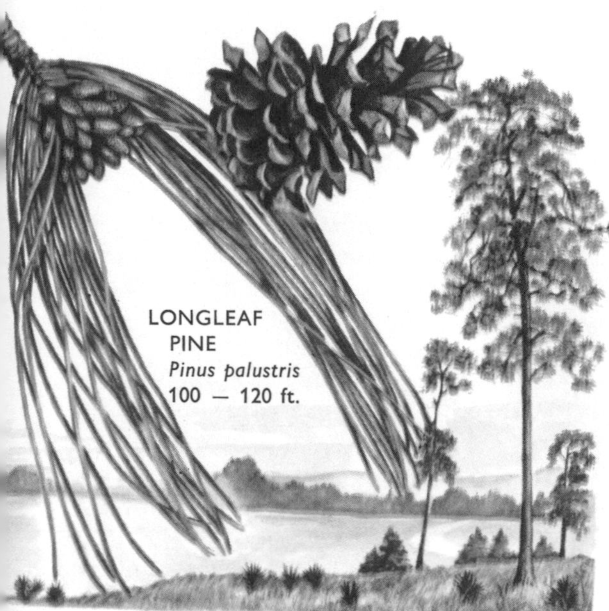

The Longleaf Pine is one of several pine trees that are important sources of turpentine in the United States.

within three days, and new chipping is required weekly. If the slash is sprayed with an acid or weed killer, the gum does not harden and clog the canals but may continue to flow for several weeks. Slashed trees are not deeply scarred and can still be sold as timber.

Crude turpentine or pitch is distilled to separate the turpentine oil (spirits of turpentine) from the heavy residue known as rosin. Turpentine stills may consist only of kettles placed over an open fire or may be elaborate steam distillation equipment.

Picturepoint Ltd

After the pine bark has been slashed, crude turpentine will continue to flow for days.

Rosin is used in waxes, varnishes, sizing of paper, oilcloth, linoleum, roofing materials, drugs, printers' ink, and soap. Oil or spirits of turpentine is used mostly as a solvent and thinner in paint and varnish. It is also used as a solvent for rubber and in the manufacture of various chemicals and medicines.

TURQUOISE occurs in blue or green smooth stalactites or in round crusts or veins. It has a shell-like fracture. Turquoise is a secondary mineral formed by the action of water on volcanic rocks; it is a hydrated copper aluminium phosphate. In south-western United States turquoise was highly prized by the Indians for bartering. Today much blue glass that simulates turquoise is being used, and it is difficult to detect from genuine turquoise. Gem varieties of turquoise come from Iran, the U.S.S.R., Turkestan, Germany, France, New Mexico, and Arizona.

Turquoise was mined by American Indians of the south-west before the arrival of the white man.

TURQUOISE

U - V

UNIVERSE. The bodies that make up the heavens differ so widely in size that we need to look at them on very different scales. The solar system is much larger than the Earth; the stars are separated by distances many times larger than the solar system; and the Milky Way, one of hundreds of millions of galaxies, is many times larger still. Studying other galaxies requires an even broader point of view, and the broadest view of all is to consider the whole universe. The study of the structure of the whole universe is called cosmology. Cosmology does not concern itself with the details of the galaxies — how big they are and what sort of stars they contain. It considers them as points and bothers only with their average motion and average mass. Cosmology looks at the universe as a single large piece of machinery.

Both in space and in time, cosmology works on a larger scale than anything else in our experience. As a result, new ideas occur that are beyond anything in everyday experience. One of these new ideas is the expansion of the universe. When astronomers observe distant galaxies, they find that their spectral lines are all shifted towards the red end of the spectrum. This red shift means that the galaxies are moving away from us; the larger the shift, the faster the motion. The red shift is small for nearby galaxies but it grows larger and larger with increasing distance. Distant galaxies are rushing away from us at speeds of more than 80,000 miles per second — nearly half the speed of light.

In every direction around us the galaxies are rushing away. It would be asking too much to believe that our galaxy is right at the centre of this universe. The solution to this paradox comes when we ask how these motions would look to someone in one of the other galaxies. The answer is that the universe would look the same to him — all the other galaxies rushing away, with a speed that

RELATION BETWEEN RED SHIFT AND DISTANCE OF GALAXY

Mt. Wilson and Palomar Observatories

H+K

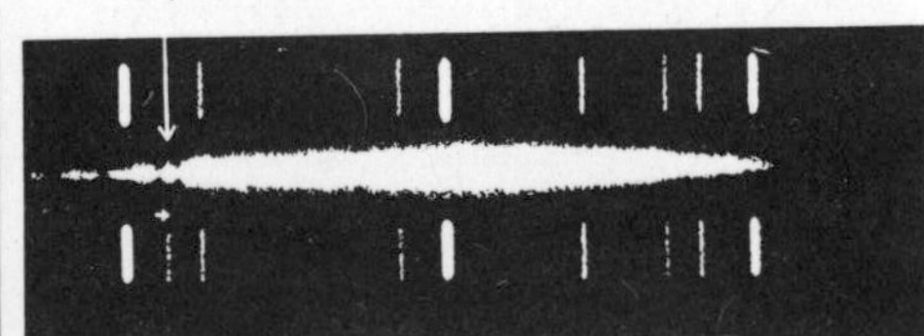

Nebula in Virgo — 23,000,000 Parsecs
750 Miles Per Second

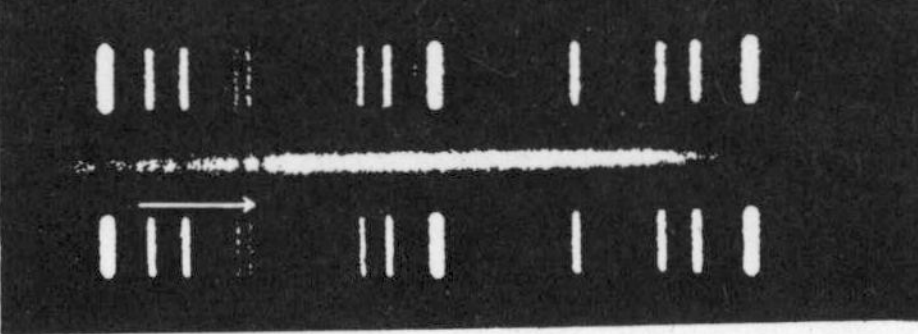

Nebula in Ursa Major — 30,700,000 Parsecs
9,300 Miles Per Second

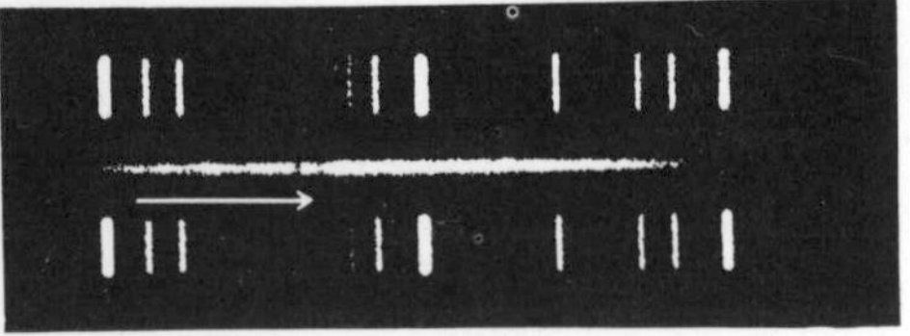

Nebula in Corona Borealis — 40,000,000 Parsecs
13,400 Miles Per Second

Many astronomers believe that our universe is expanding in all directions. Evidence for this comes from photographing light from many galaxies at varying distances. The further the galaxy the redder the light from it — an effect that could be produced by the more distant galaxies receding at tremendous speeds. Photographs on the right show some of these galaxies, their distances and the speed at which they seem to be moving away from our galaxy.

Picturepoint Ltd

Prospecting for uranium with a geiger counter. Uranium is in great demand because of its use in atomic power plants.

increases with distance. *Everything* is moving away from everything else; this motion is called the expansion of the universe.

It is hard to imagine a universe that is expanding. A small body that expands is easy to visualise; it simply spreads out to fill more and more of the space around it. But the universe is everything, so there is no additional space around it. How then can it expand? The answer is that it is perfectly possible for the universe to expand; our mistake is trying to *visualise* the expansion. An analogy may make this clearer. Imagine a group of flat creatures who live on the surface of a balloon; and imagine them completely confined to the surface, so that they know nothing but the two dimensions of the surface and cannot imagine height above or below the surface. Now if the balloon is gradually blown up, their 'universe' will expand. With their two-dimensional senses, they also will be unable to visualise what an expanding universe means.

The flat creatures would also find it difficult to understand if we told them that their surface was curved, and was not infinite in size. Yet with our ability to visualise a third dimension we can see that the surface of their balloon is curved and finite. And again, we in our universe have the same inability to visualise a curved space; yet it is quite possible that our universe is curved — and perhaps finite, too.

URANIUM is produced from the mineral uranite (uranium oxide), which is found as black grains or as velvety, grape-like crusts (pitchblende) that have uneven fracture. Its streak is a shining brown or green. Uraninite occurs in igneous rocks or hydrothermal veins. It is very soluble and so is quickly carried away and deposited as a secondary mineral in sedimentary rocks, particularly those containing organic matter. Carnotite, one of the secondary minerals, is found as powdery, canary-yellow coatings on rocks or as filling in the pores of sandstones. It is never found with sulphides. Autunite, another secondary uranium mineral, occurs as lemon-yellow scales or thin tabular crystals. It has one perfect cleavage and fluoresces a bright yellow-green. Though autunite

is common, it occurs in small amounts.

Small amounts of radium can be extracted from uranium, but the cost is high — about £4,000 per gram. Cobalt-60 is used in radiotherapy instead, as it is equally good and is reasonable in cost. Some uranium is used in ceramics to produce brown, yellow, orange, and dark green colours in pottery and for opalescent glass. A special steel for high-speed tools contains uranium. Most uranium is used now for atomic bombs, though it has many uses in peace-time industry and for scientific research. A pound of uranium 235 releases about 2,500,000 times the amount of energy generated by burning a pound of coal. Atomic power plants are producing electricity and supplying power for submarines and surface vessels. Atomic power plants for aircraft may be produced in the future. The only draw back is the great weight and bulk of the shielding devices necessary.

Only a fractional part of uranium is uranium 235 (1 part in 140); the remainder is uranium 238. Concentrating uranium 235 is costly. Most of the uranium 238 obtained in the process is used to produce plutonium.

The more than a hundred uranium ores require chemical and optical tests for identification. Refining of the ore is a difficult and expensive process. The crushed rock must be treated to remove impurities, and

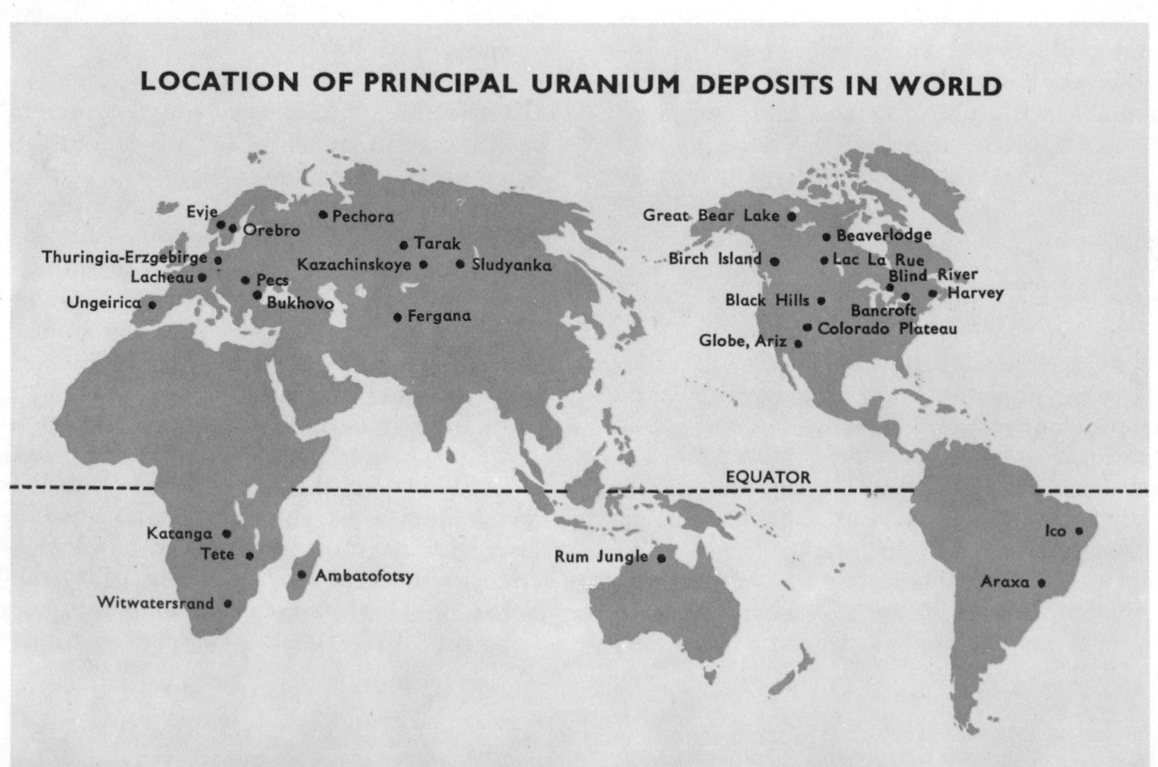

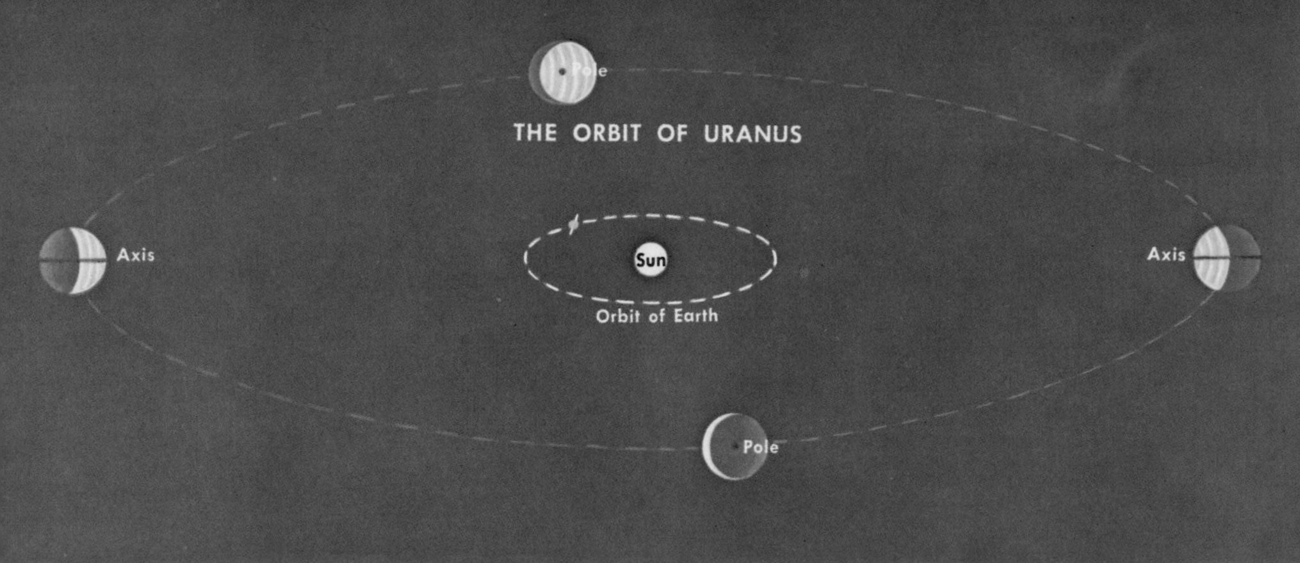

the ore is concentrated as a uranium oxide. In a second operation the oxide is refined into a powder of pure uranium or into a compound known as uranium hexafluoride, which must be vapourised to obtain pure uranium. This is the final product, ready for use in atomic reactors.

The leading producing areas of uranium minerals are Poland, Czechoslovakia, the Congo region of Africa, Brazil, Canada, and western United States — Utah, Arizona, New Mexico, and Wyoming.

URANUS, the seventh planet, circles the Sun in an 84-year period. As it is 1,783 million miles from the Sun or 19 times the Earth's distance from the Sun, Uranus is barely visible to the naked eye and was actually unknown until its accidental discovery by Sir William Herschel in 1781. Even through a telescope little can be seen of Uranus, and a high magnification is required to tell it from a star.

Physically, Uranus is very similar to Neptune. Its diameter is 29,300 miles or nearly four times the diameter of the Earth, and it has 15 Earth masses. Like the other large planets, Uranus has a low density and is probably made mostly of solid hydrogen and helium. Its atmosphere is also mainly hydrogen and helium gases, mixed with some methane. Uranus is so far from the Sun that it receives only 1/400 as much sunlight as we do, and the temperature of its surface is about −184 degrees centigrade (−300 degrees Fahrenheit). Uranus rotates on its axis in $10\frac{3}{4}$ hours and has five satellites with orbits in the plane of its equator. This plane is almost perpendicular to the plane of its orbit, so a large part of Uranus has 42 years of sunlight and 42 years of darkness as the planet travels around the Sun.

The five satellites are quite small; the largest, Titania, is about 2,000 miles in diameter.

VACCINES are killed or weakened suspensions of disease organisms inoculated into the body to prevent disease. The first vaccine was developed by Edward Jenner in 1796 to immunise people against smallpox, which was until that time one of the world's most dreaded diseases. Jenner noticed that dairy workers who had had cowpox, a less severe disease, were not as likely to contract smallpox. He advocated the inoculation of cowpox virus as a protection against smallpox. Today most people in civilised countries are vaccinated with cowpox virus. As a result epidemics of smallpox have been eliminated in most places.

Those who live or travel in areas where drinking water might be infected with typhoid bacteria are advised to be vaccinated. The typhoid bacteria are killed by heating them or by treating them with formaldehyde or phenol. Then they are suspended in salt solution which is injected into the body.

Some vaccines are very effective; others are not. For example, vaccines against the common cold have not been successful, but vaccination against yellow fever is highly

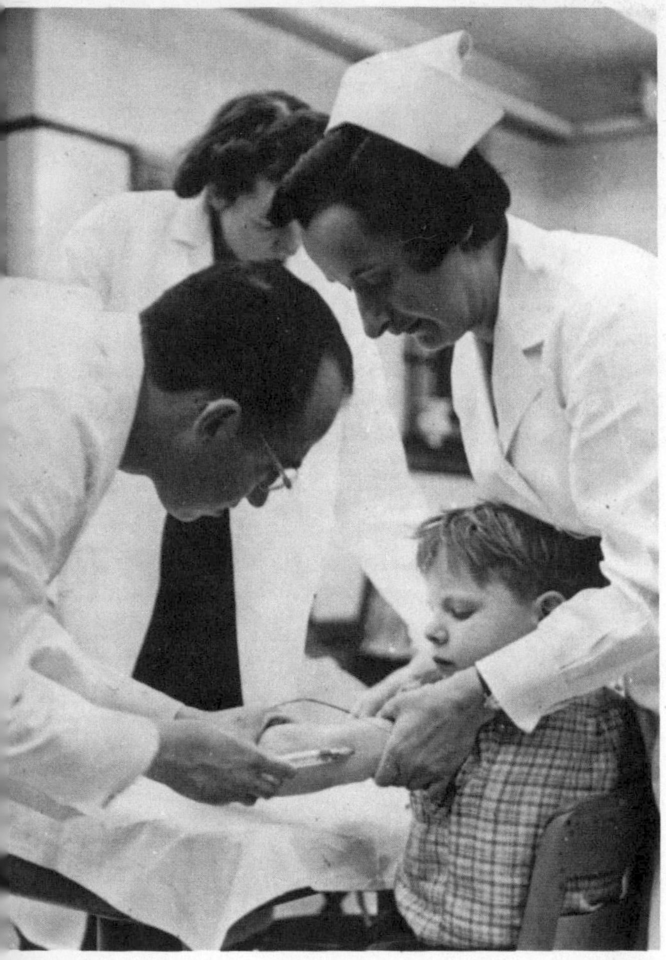

U.S.I.S.

The photograph shows Dr. Tonas Salk administering his polio vaccine, which has largely controlled this dreaded disease.

successful. Vaccines against bubonic plague, some types of influenza, and cholera are sometimes effective and sometimes not. The Salk vaccine has proved successful against polio. (See BACTERIA; VIRUS.)

VANILLA. Indians of tropical America were using vanilla as a flavouring for chocolate before the arrival of Spanish explorers. They had learned to ferment (cure) the seed pods of a climbing orchid *(Vanilla planifolia)* and extract the aromatic essence. The Spaniards took some of the dried pods to Europe where the popularity of the flavour spread rapidly.

Although the greenish-yellow flowers of this orchid are fragrant, the fleshy fruit pods that develop from the flowers have no aroma until dried and cured. The slender, 6 — 9 inch pods, called vanilla beans, contain an oily pulp and numerous tiny seeds. They are picked green, but have a chocolate-coloured, wrinkled look when cured. Only about 2 per cent of each vanilla pod is vanillin, the aromatic oil used in flavouring. It is extracted from the pods with alcohol.

Vanilla extract is used as a flavouring in sweets, ice-cream, chocolate, drinks, and tobacco. In recent years, synthetic vanilla flavouring has largely replaced the natural vanilla extracted from orchid pods.

VENUS is the second closest planet to the Sun — 67 million miles or about 7/10 as far from the Sun as we are. In size, Venus is just a bit smaller than the Earth. It travels around its nearly circular orbit in 225 days. After the Sun and Moon, Venus is the brightest object in our sky, partly because it

VANILLA ORCHID
Vanilla planifolia

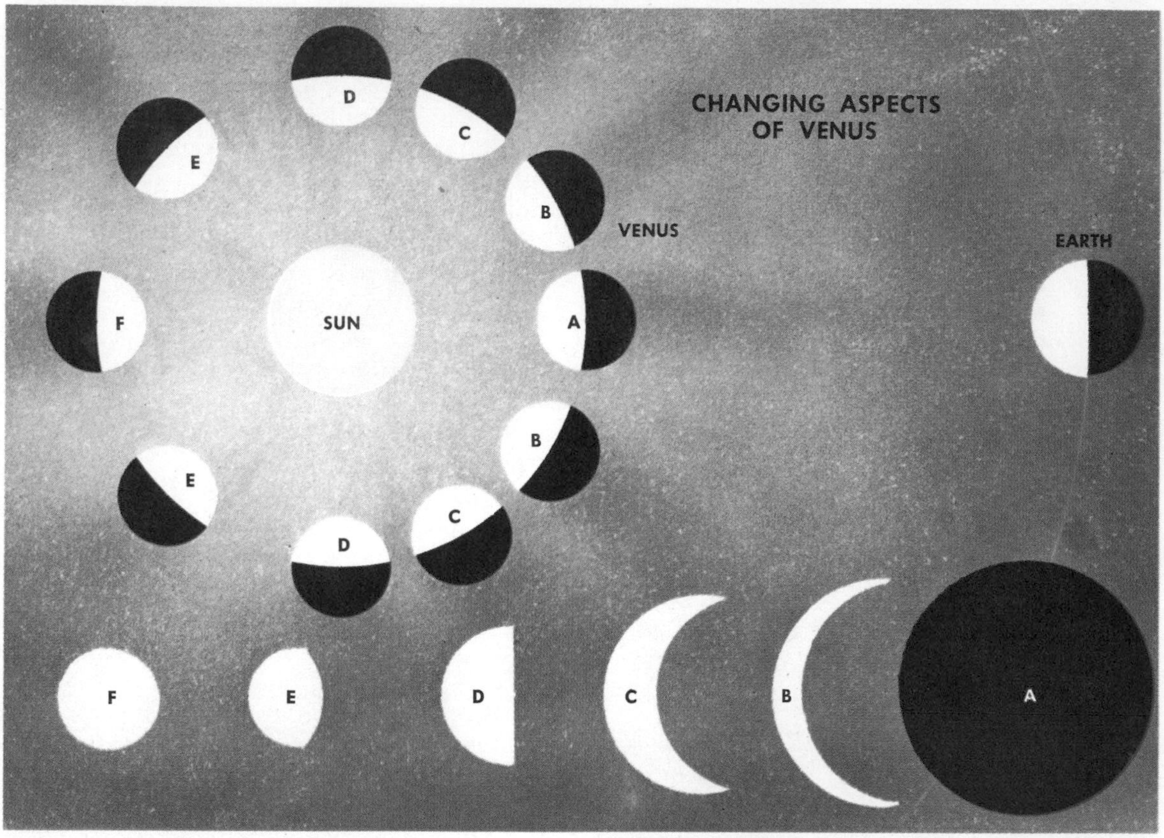

As Venus orbits the Sun, it presents a series of different aspects to the Earth. These range from full-face illumination to complete shadow, and travel through all of the phases that our Moon also shows. The letters on the various stages of the planet shown around the Sun correspond to the visible stages with the same letter, on the bottom of the illustration, as seen from the Earth.

is never very far away from us. Venus can come within 25 million miles of the Earth, closer than any other planet. At that time it is not easy to see because it is almost directly between us and the Sun. A few weeks earlier or later it can be seen in broad daylight. We see it either in the west after sunset or else in the east before dawn. As the months pass, Venus appears to swing back and forth from one side of the Sun to the other. The full cycle, or synodic period, takes 19½ months. On very rare occasions Venus passes directly in front of the Sun and can be seen through a telescope as a black dot crossing the Sun's face.

Through a small telescope Venus looks like the Moon and shows all the different phases at various points in its orbit. Not much more can be seen with a higher magnification because the atmosphere of Venus is completely cloudy. We never see

Venus, also called the evening or morning star, shown in crescent phase, is about 26 million miles from Earth.

VENUS	
Volume	9/10 of Earth
Average distance from Sun	67,000,000 miles
Equatorial diameter	7688 miles
Period of rotation (day)	30 days
Period of revolution (year)	224.7 days
Orbital speed	21.8 miles per second
Surface gravity	0.87 of Earth
Escape velocity	6.4 miles per second
Number of moons	none
Density (water=1)	5.0
Mean day temperature	over 260°C.
Mass (Earth=1)	0.82
Nearest approach to Earth	25,000,000 miles

the planet's surface. Radio waves pass through the clouds, however, and the radio radiation from the surface shows that Venus is hot — about 315 degrees centigrade (600 degrees Fahrenheit). Its atmosphere contains water vapour and carbon dioxide, and probably nitrogen.

VIOLETS (*Viola* spp.) have blossoms so characteristic — two petals arched upwards, three below, and a yellow centre — that almost everyone recognises them. Not all of the more than 800 species are blue. Some are purple (even reddish-purple), many others are yellow or white, and some have two colours in the same flower. Most of the showy violet blossoms are sterile, producing no seeds. Late in the season many violets develop seeds from inconspicuous flower buds that do not open. Violets are partial to moist places and open woods, but some grow along roadsides or in open fields.

Yellow-flowered violets are generally taller and have heart-shaped leaves on branching stems. Leaves of one white violet are long and narrow (lance-shaped), while those of blue and purple kinds vary in shape.

Many kinds of violets are cultivated for garden and commercial use. Some are double-flowered, and some especially fragrant. A perfume is obtained from the English Violet. The pansy, a common garden flower developed from the violet, is a native of Europe.

VIRUS. This is the name given to a group of infectious agents, all very much smaller than bacteria, which cause disease in plants and animals. They are living organisms in so far as each carries distinct inherited characters and can reproduce its own kind; and a given type can give rise to new and distinct strains by means of 'mutations'. Yet the complex

SWEET VIOLET
Viola odorata

MARSH VIOLET
Viola palustris

HORNED VIOLET
Viola cornuta

MOUNTAIN PANSY
Viola lutea

WILD PANSY
Viola tricolor

Ford Almanac 1962

Ford Almanac 1962

New techniqes make it possible for pigs to be born (left) and raised for a week or more (right under sterile conditions. This breaks the chain of infectious diseases passed on from the mother to the litter.

cellular organisation we find in other living organisms does not exist in viruses.

Viruses are completely parasitic and can only multiply *inside* living cells of other organisms. When a virus particle infects a susceptible cell it enters the nucleus which contains the control mechanism for the cell, and thus causes the cell to produce more virus particles like the first. Virus particles are almost entirely made up of D.N.A. (deoxyribonucleic acid) the most important constituent of nucleoprotein.

Few viruses can be seen under the highest magnification of a light microscope, so they are studied with the electron microscope. Some viruses are spherical, others rod-shaped and others tadpole-shaped.

Polio, the common cold, influenza, smallpox, measles, mumps, rabies, herpes and yellow fever are among the diseases which attack humans. Sugar Beet Virus Yellows, Tomato Mosaic, and Potato Leaf Roll are pernicious virus diseases of crops. Bacteria are attacked by viruses but not fungi.

In animals virus infections can be destroyed by the production of antiobodies; thus vaccines, which stimulate their production, have been successful in the prevention of outbreaks of smallpox, polio and yellow fever. Antibiotics have little effect on them.

Plants, once virus infected, remain so for the rest of their lives, but the disease rarely enters the seed. Insects, especially aphids, carry many virus diseases among crop plants. With fruit and other plants which are propagated vegetatively (see PROPAGATION OF PLANTS) special methods are used to obtain virus free stock plants, and to multiply them in isolated places so they do not become re-infected.

VOLCANOES. The Earth's crust is believed to be from 10 to 30 miles deep. It overlies the mantle, a layer of rock a thousand miles thick surrounding the Earth's core. Because of the tremendous weight of the miles of rock above, the mantle is very dense and hot. The pressure probably keeps it from liquefying. Whenever a weak spot occurs in the crust, the super-heated rock below expands

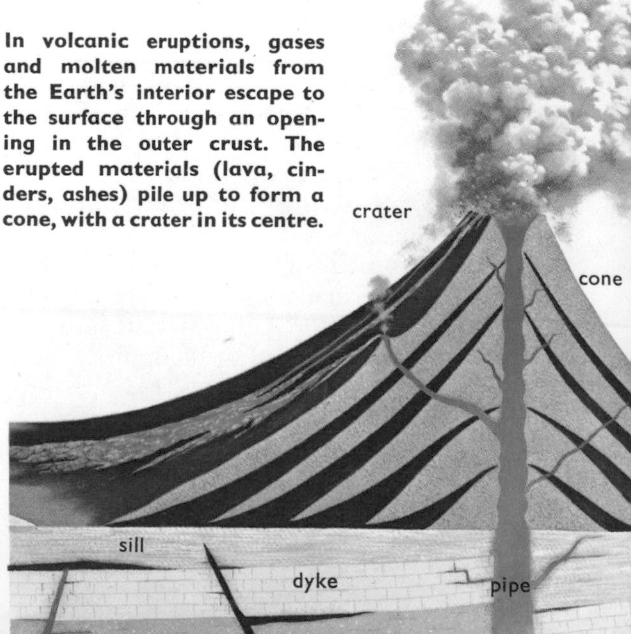

In volcanic eruptions, gases and molten materials from the Earth's interior escape to the surface through an opening in the outer crust. The erupted materials (lava, cinders, ashes) pile up to form a cone, with a crater in its centre.

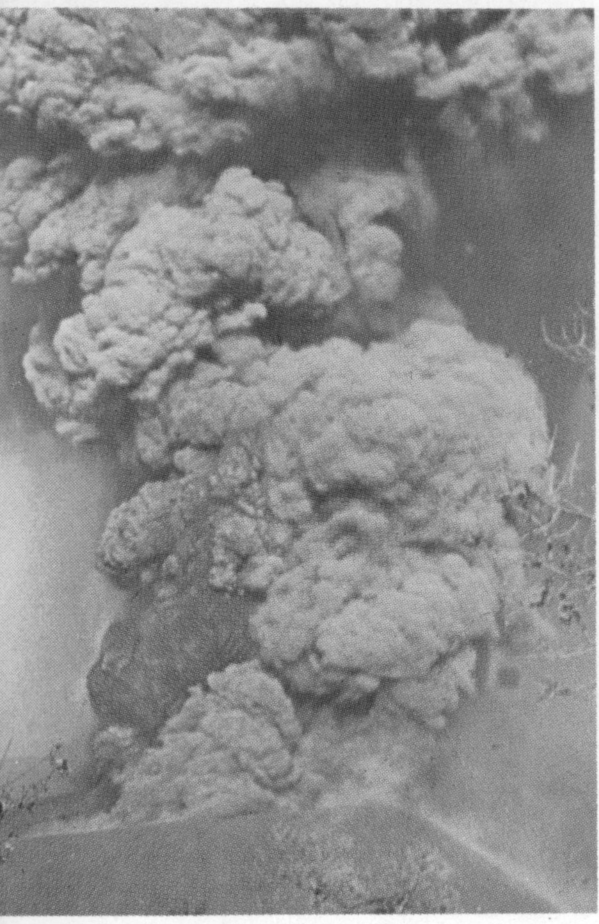

F. H. Pough, American Museum of Natural History

Volcanic eruptions can last for years. Paricutin, in Mexico, born in 1943, became quiet in 1952. Its cone rose 1600 feet in once fertile farm land. Lava, 300 feet deep in places, was spread over 100 square miles.

and becomes a liquid, with a temperature of more than 1,100 degrees centigrade (2,000 degrees Fahrenheit). The liquefied rock bursts through the crust as a gushing molten mass, called lava. These eruptions are called volcanoes. They usually build cones with a central crater from which the lava escapes.

Most of the presently active volcanoes are located in two belts of volcanic activity. One surrounds the Pacific Ocean, from Alaska to Cape Horn and the Antarctic and through the South Pacific to the Philippines and Japan; the other and smaller belt runs eastwards from the West Indies through the Mediterranean region and on into the Far East.

Some volcanoes are active continuously. Sailors still steer by the flames of Stromboli off the coast of Sicily as did the Phoenicians. Most volcanoes have a shorter life. They erupt, building up cones of cinders and ash; then they become inactive, as the magma they still contain hardens. Erosion removes the outer layers, leaving the hardened inner core as sharp peaks that stand high above the surrounding land.

Among the more famous volcanoes are Vesuvius, near Naples in Italy, that destroyed and buried the Roman city of Pompeii in A. D. 79. Less famous was Mount Pelee, in the West Indies, whose eruption in 1902 killed 30,000 people in the city of St. Pierre, Martinique. At least 36,000 people died because of the volcanic explosion that turned Mount Krakatoa, in the East Indies, into dust in 1883. The deaths were due not to the blast itself but to the huge tides that the

Bob Ebert/Photo Library

violent volcanic explosion caused in the sea.

Not all volcanoes are spectacular. Some, such as the ones that typify the Hawaiian volcanic region, pour forth great quantities of pasty magma. This laps over the broad crater and runs down the volcano's side, usually ending in the sea. This type of volcano, called a shield volcano, is broad at the base and rises slowly to a rounded crater. It is quite different in structure from the cone volcanoes, such as Vesuvius, that rise steeply to a thin and tapered crater.

Although volcanoes themselves are a menace to the life and property of those who dwell near them, volcanic soil is exceptionally rich in the minerals needed by plants. Regions of former volcanic activity are among the most productive of all agricultural lands. (See EARTH; GEOLOGY; LAVA; MINERALS; ROCKS.)

Jerome Wyckoff

Devil's Tower, in Wyoming, is a cooled lava plug. The volcanic cone that surrounded it has eroded away.

Kilauea Crater, in Hawaii, glows with reds and yellows of molten lava seeping up from beneath the Earth's crust. The black cake on the red lava is cinders and ashes that have cooled and hardened.

WALLFLOWER
Cheiranthus cheiri

WALLFLOWERS are derived from *Cheiranthus cheiri* a species native to the British Isles, which commonly grows in dry places and on old walls. It has long been cultivated in English gardens.

The Wallflower is a woody perennial, but it does not last many years and needs renewing frequently by growing from seed. It grows up to 18 inches in height and produces yellow, reddish, or orange flowers.

WALNUT trees (*Juglans* spp.) are cultivated as a timber tree and for their edible seeds. Some walnuts are round, others oblong, but all have thick, rough shells and are enclosed in green, leathery husks that turn dark brown or black when ripe. Their large, deciduous leaves are pinnately compound and arranged alternately on the branches. In spring, tassel-like catkins of pollen-bearing flowers hang from near the ends of the branches.

WHITE WALNUT
30—50 ft.

The Black Walnut *(Juglans nigra)*, one of the most valuable hardwoods introduced from North America, has dark, lustrous wood, which is prized for furniture and quality cabinet work. A large tree (100 feet high; 3 feet in diameter) with a wide-spreading, rounded crown, the Black Walnut's leaves may measure a foot in length and have 15 to 23 toothed leaflets. The brown to black bark of large trees is ridged.

Butternut or White Walnut *(Juglans cinerea)*, also introduced from North America, has smaller leaves with fewer leaflets (11 to 17). Its nuts are oblong rather than round, and the surface of their husks is sticky. The Butternut is a smaller tree and both its bark and wood are lighter in colour.

English walnuts, the familiar round, relatively thin-shelled nuts commonly sold in shops, are grown commercially. The English Walnut tree *(Juglans regia)* is native to southern Europe and Asia. (See NUTS.)

WATER. All plants and animals depend on water. Water is the base and the framework of any food chain, for without it no plant or animal could live.

The external environment of plants and animals is either water or air, but internally there is always water. Water in plants and animals enables the transportation of food, oxygen, carbon dioxide, salts, wastes and heat. Although plants and animals moved from a water habitat to land long ago in the geologic past they still remain chained to water as their internal medium.

Water covers nearly three-quarters of the Earth's surface. It dissolves many substances but does not react with them chemically; water transports salts and gases without change. Water occurs as a gas, vapour (water particles suspended in air), as a solid (ice), and as a liquid. Unlike air, water absorbs and gives off heat slowly. Consequently water-dwelling plants and animals experience relatively slow changes in temperature. Land dwellers are frequently faced with rapid changes in temperature.

Distribution of water over land areas is quite uneven. Deserts are at one extreme, tropical rain forests at the other. Plants and animals that live in deserts must necessarily conserve water within their structure. (See CACTI; DESERTS; TROPICAL RAIN FORESTS.)

In temperate regions, man has affected the water resources greatly by his use of the land for agriculture and to supply the needs of large cities.

WATERLILIES (*Nymphaea*, *Castalia*, and *Victoria)* reign in pools and water gardens the world over. They have little competition, for most aquatic plants lack attractive flowers.

Waterlily leaves, or pads, rise to the surface from their heavy stems, which grow flat in the mud. Food is stored in the root-

One of the significant features of the Earth is its abundance of water, on which all life depends. Rivers, lakes, seas, and oceans cover nearly three-quarters of the Earth's surface.

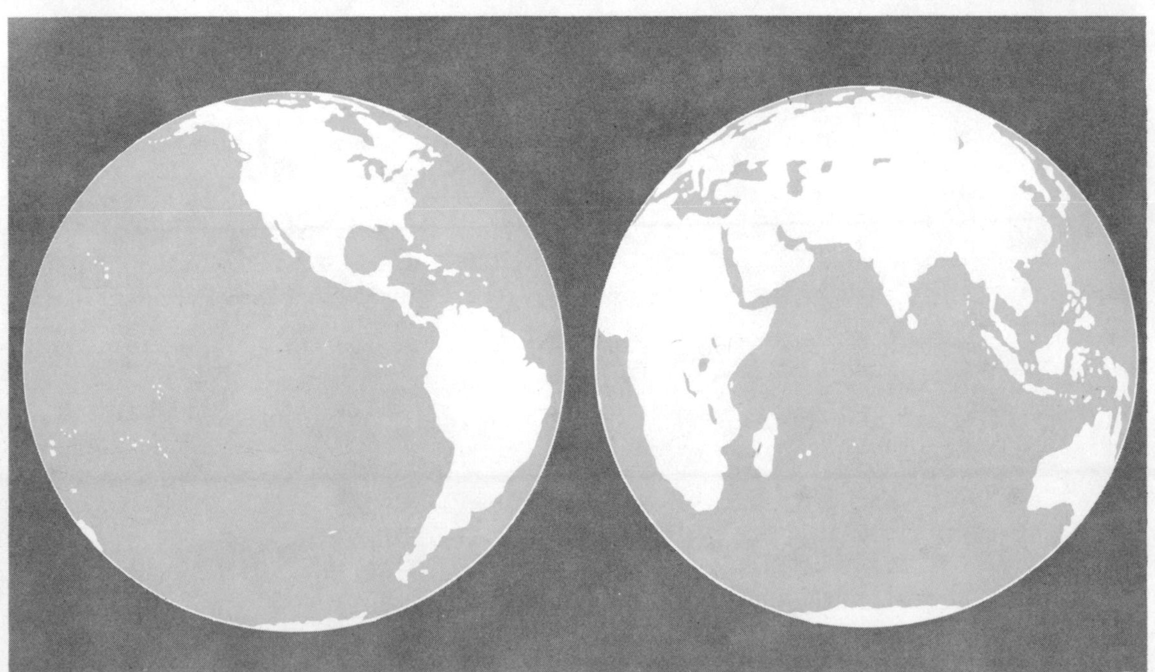

YELLOW WATERLILY
Nuphar lutea

like stems for new growth the following year. The starchy stems are good to eat, as are the seeds.

Waterlily plants are found only in rather calm water, usually in shallow depths of 3 — 6 feet. They are easily torn loose by the rough waves of large lakes unless they are in a sheltered cove or bay.

Most waterlily flowers are white or yellow, and some are quite fragrant. Pink-flowered ones are not rare, however, and along the Gulf Coast of the United States there are blue and lavender waterlilies.

Many of the brilliant red, pink, and blue cultivated waterlilies are imports from tropical areas and are unable to endure the cold weather of northern winters. They die, and must be replanted in pools each year. These cultivated kinds usually differ from the native species in having their flowers raised a few inches above the water surface.

The Royal Waterlily of the Amazon has gigantic, floating leaves, as much as 6 feet in diameter and with turned-up margins. Large birds can easily walk on these leaves.

The sacred lotus of the ancient Egyptians was not a true lotus but a member of the waterlily family.

WATERMELONS *(Citrullus vulgaris)* have been grown in Mediterranean regions since prehistoric times. About 100 years ago Scotland's noted explorer-missionary, David Livingstone, found extensive patches of wild watermelons growing in the heart of central Africa, confirming the belief that they originated there. Both bitter and sweet watermelons grow side by side in the wild state. Watermelon is a very appropriate name, for their water content exceeds 90 per cent. In desert areas of Africa, the juice of watermelons is used to quench thirst during dry periods.

Watermelons vary in weight from five to

SOME VARIETIES OF WATERMELONS

Phot. Ciccione-Rapho

more than fifty pounds. Some varieties are round, others oblong. Their hard but fragile rinds may be light or dark green and are often striped. They are eaten raw and in salads. Red, pink, yellow, and white-fleshed varieties are common. Citrons are white, hard-fleshed melons used for pickling and in preserves and jellies.

Watermelons are cultivated in a wide belt from the Mediterranean area eastwards to China, and in the southern United States.

WAXES of commercial importance can be obtained from several kinds of palms and also from other plants. Waxes generally occur on leaves, stems, or fruit, and protect the plants from drying out or from insect attacks. Candelilla wax is discharged at certain times of the year, commonly during the winter months, from pores in the stems of a small desert shrub *(Euphorbia antisyphilitica)* that grows in Texas and Mexico. Cauassú wax is produced on the leaves of a tall herb *(Calatheal utea)* that grows in the Amazon region. Cauassú and candelilla waxes are used in soaps, candles, varnishes and many other products. Myrtle wax, which collects on the surface of the fruit of Bayberry *(Myrica pensylvanica)* and Candleberry *(Myrica cerifera)* was used in the manufacture of aromatic candles and soaps.

Much labour is required in collecting waxes from plants. Efforts are being made to produce these waxes artificially to supplement the world's natural supplies.

WEATHER. Day-by-day changes in temperature, wind velocity and direction, humidity, and barometric pressure are the elements that make up weather. The average of these conditions through the seasons and the years constitutes the climate of a region.

Both climate and weather result from differences in the warming of the Earth's atmosphere from place to place. In equatorial regions, where the Sun's rays strike the Earth most directly, the air is warmed more than in polar regions, where the Sun's rays strike the Earth at an angle. Heated air over the equatorial region rises, while the cooler, heavier air moves in from each side. The warmed air flows towards the polar regions, where it descends after being cooled. The

ABSORPTION OF SUNLIGHT BY DIFFERENT SURFACES

Sunlight absorbed by land and water is converted into heat (above). Unequal heating produces local winds (below), depending on the terrain and other factors.

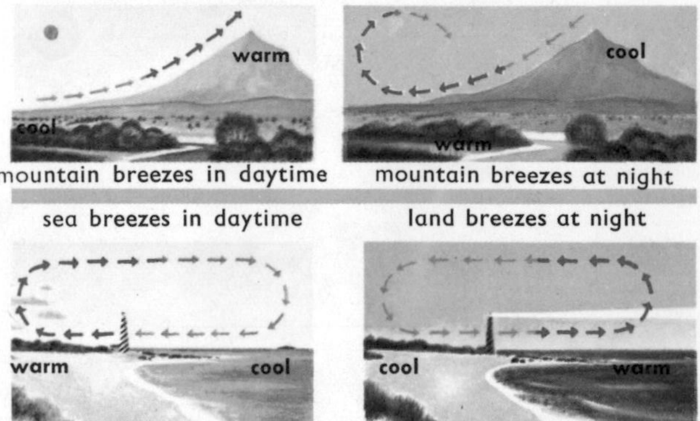

Earth's rotation causes these air movements or prevailing winds to follow a curved path. In the Northern Hemisphere, winds are deflected to the right or clockwise; in the Southern Hemisphere, to the left. (See WINDS.)

Local winds are also created by the heating effects of the Sun's rays. Over bare or rocky areas, air heats faster than over heavily forested areas that absorb more of the warmth. The heated air rises in vertical columns, called thermals, and cooler air from surrounding areas moves in to take its place. As the warmed air penetrates the cooler regions of higher altitudes, the moisture it contains is condensed in the form of clouds. Sometimes clouds are blown by prevailing winds to points far distant from their place of origin.

Water is carried in the atmosphere in three forms: as a vapour, which is measured as relative humidity; as a liquid, in the form of water droplets in the lower clouds; and as a solid, in the form of snow and hail or the ice crystals that form the highest clouds.

Vapour accumulates in the air as water is evaporated by the heat of sunlight from bodies of water and from earth. Evaporation continues until the air holds all the water vapour it possibly can at that temperature. This is its saturation point. If the temperature rises, the air can hold more moisture, and evaporation then continues. If the temperature drops, the air can hold less moisture, and the water vapour condenses. If warmed air remains at the surface level and is cooled by a rapid drop in temperature, such as usually occurs at sunset, the condensation becomes dew (when it forms on objects) or fog (when it floats above the ground). If the warmed air rises and its vapour condenses above the Earth, clouds are formed. Clouds are also formed when warm air blows over colder land masses or water, when it travels over a colder air mass, when it moves up a slope, and when rain, snow, or hail from clouds above fall through warmer layers of air below.

Each type of cloud formation is named. Each forms in a characteristic way and occurs in a particular altitude range. The various cloud formations are associated with different kinds of weather, and so a knowledge of clouds is important both to professional and to amateur weather forecasters.

Air, though it appears to be light and insubstantial, has a measurable weight. An inch-square column of air extending from sea level to the upper limits of the atmosphere weighs 14.7 pounds. This is an average weight or pressure that may vary considerably with weather conditions. In a rising column of air, the pressure is lower than in a descending column. Also, the pressure is less at high altitudes than at sea level, even in otherwise similar weather conditions.

In areas of high pressure, usually called *highs*, air tends to be cool. Winds blow outwards from the high but are deflected (to the right in the Northern Hemisphere) by the Earth's rotation. Their motion is termed anti-cyclonic. A high-pressure area may be several hundred miles in diameter and usually indicates fair weather.

These large high pressure areas where, at any level, the conditions of temperature and moisture are stable are called air masses. Major air masses exist over each of the poles. Others form, are modified, and move in well-known paths, taking on characteristics that depend on the surface over which they flow. Air masses may be continental or maritime, polar, or tropical, hot or cold. The vast areas of continents and oceans influence world-wide weather patterns. Over the interior of Canada and Siberia, cold dry (continental polar) air accumulates, while over the North Atlantic and North Pacific, cold moist (maritime polar) air gathers. Mexico and the land masses of South Asia and North Africa give rise to warm, dry air (continental tropical), while the oceans north of the equator spawn warm, moist air (maritime tropical). Still other air masses form over the arctic and equatorial regions. Similar masses of air form in the Southern Hemisphere.

If these air masses never moved, weather would be strictly local in occurrence. But the prevailing winds and the existence of low pressure areas nearby cause each of these air masses to move from its point of origin. The meeting of these various moving masses of air of different temperatures, humidities,

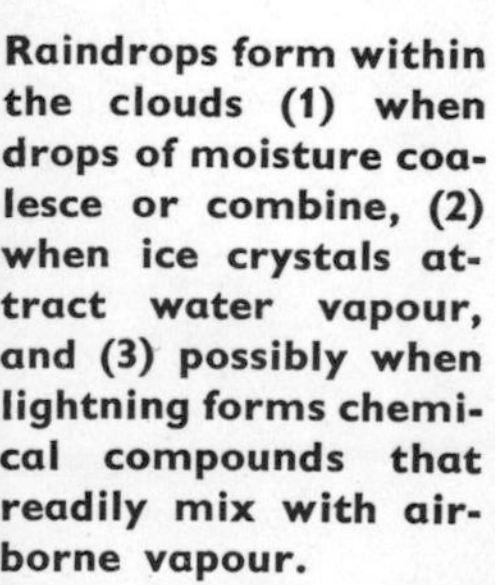

Raindrops form within the clouds (1) when drops of moisture coalesce or combine, (2) when ice crystals attract water vapour, and (3) possibly when lightning forms chemical compounds that readily mix with airborne vapour.

CIRRUS

CIRROCUMULUS

CIRROSTRATUS

HIGH CLOUDS are usually thin clouds formed of ice crystals. They are found at an altitude of 20,000 feet or higher.

ALTOSTRATUS

ALTOCUMULUS

MID-LEVEL CLOUDS, higher than 10,000 feet, occur as dense veils of clouds or puffy patches.

STRATUS

NIMBOSTRATUS

STRATOCUMULUS

LOW CLOUDS occur from the ground to heights of about 6,500 feet. There are three principal types.

TYPES OF CLOUDS: The two basic types of clouds are classified according to the way they are formed. Cumulus clouds form puffy or rounded masses as air currents rise to saturation level. Stratus clouds are flat or sheet-like. They form without vertical movement when air reaches its saturation point in contact with colder air or land. These types are further modified by the altitude of formation, producing clouds of high, middle, and low level. Great variation in clouds occur; the pictures above show some typical formations.

CUMULUS

Another group of clouds is the cumulus type that may grow to towering heights. Fair weather cumulus clouds (left) often form on warm afternoons. If development continues they may become cumulonimbus thunderheads (right) rising to 60,000 feet or more with a typical anvil top. Here thunderstorms occur, with lightning and with heavy showers. Sometimes tornadoes develop under these conditions.

CUMULONIMBUS

Air loses heat as it moves up a slope. If it is cooled below its saturation point, clouds form.

The Earth cools rapidly at night. Warmer air is chilled and may form clouds or fog.

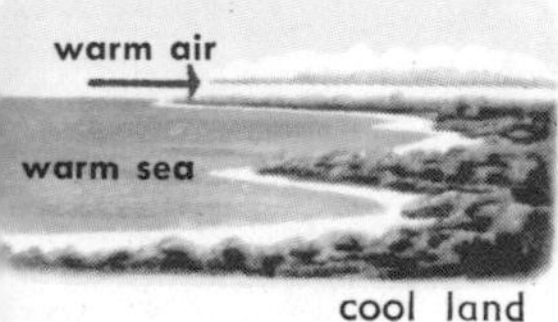

As warm air moves over a cooler surface, its moisture condenses as clouds or rain.

When warm and cool air meet, the warm air is cooled by lifting or by contact and forms clouds.

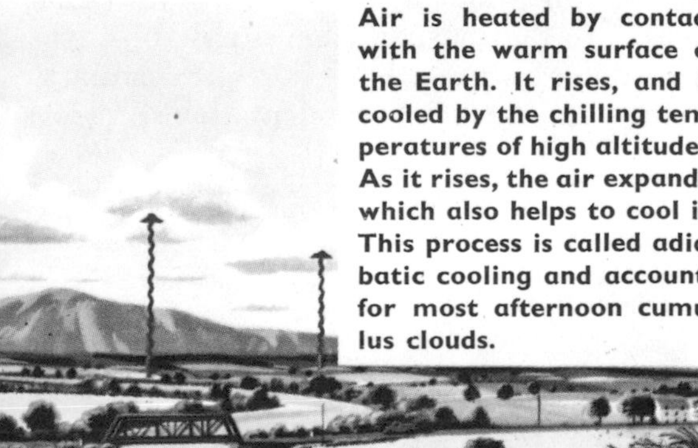

Air is heated by contact with the warm surface of the Earth. It rises, and is cooled by the chilling temperatures of high altitudes. As it rises, the air expands, which also helps to cool it. This process is called adiabatic cooling and accounts for most afternoon cumulus clouds.

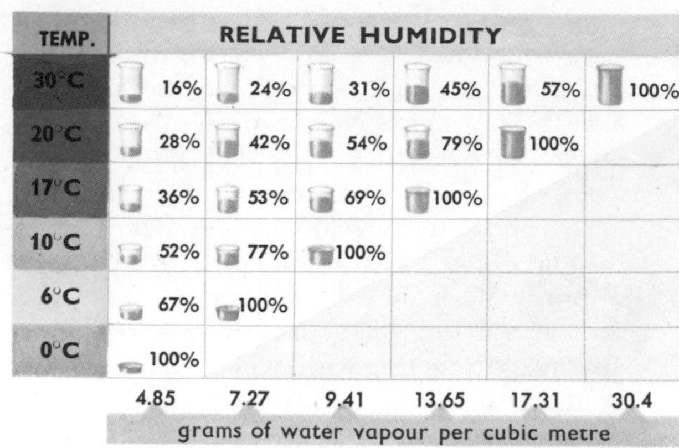

TEMP.	RELATIVE HUMIDITY					
30°C	16%	24%	31%	45%	57%	100%
20°C	28%	42%	54%	79%	100%	
17°C	36%	53%	69%	100%		
10°C	52%	77%	100%			
6°C	67%	100%				
0°C	100%					
grams of water vapour per cubic metre	4.85	7.27	9.41	13.65	17.31	30.4

Water vapour present in the air can be measured as relative humidity. When temperature drops, air can hold less water. The surplus condenses as droplets to form clouds and perhaps rain or snow.

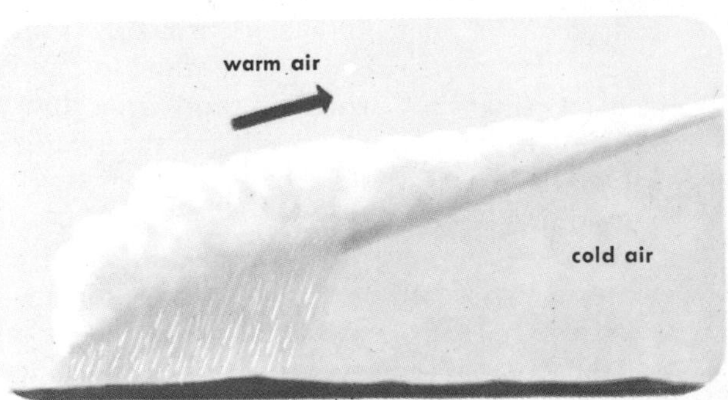

Warm air pushed over a mass of cooler air cools, losing moisture and forming clouds as it gains altitude.

Falling rain or snow may cool the layers of warm air below, forming clouds within that lower layer.

SOME OF THE WAYS THAT CLOUDS ARE FORMED

and speeds creates much of the variations in the weather that we experience. Because of their distinctive characteristics, air masses do not usually blend or mingle when they meet. A sharp boundary or front forms where the two masses are in contact and, because the air masses move, fronts are usually in motion also. Along this zone of interaction, people experience 'frontal weather' — unsettled, changing, and stormy.

The fronts that form when air masses meet are thin wedges of air each of different temperature and humidity which push against the adjoining air mass. When a cold wedge pushes warm air back, a cold front has formed. When a cold wedge retreats and warm air pushes up over it, we have a warm front. The major Northern Hemisphere air mass lies over the North Pole, and as the cold air pushes out from it, different patterns of fronts develop in summer and in winter. The fronts advance more slowly in summer than in winter. In either case the stormy weather of the front is heralded by a falling barometer, with winds shifting from south to west and with squally rains. As the front passes, winds steady from the west or north-west and the barometer rises.

A warm front forms as warm air advances, pushing over a cold air mass. The advance is slower than a cold front and is marked by changes of clouds from cirrus to stratus. The barometer drops and rains may be slow and steady under grey skies till the front passes. In some cases a fast-moving cold front overtakes a warm front, and an occluded front is formed. The result for the people who live in the area is bad weather twice compounded.

At some seasons of the year the Earth's rotation causes the warm air masses, formed over tropical oceans, to spin in the direction of the prevailing winds. Their whirling velocity becomes greater as more warm surface winds blow into the system. Air in the centre is forced up, and its moisture condenses. Heat is released in the condensation process, warming the air still more and causing it to rise more swiftly. The winds below increase in force, and the whirling air mass grows into a storm and finally into a hurricane. The tremendous power in a hurricane is due to the inexhaustible supply of warm, moist air surrounding it. The continual release of heat by condensation provides

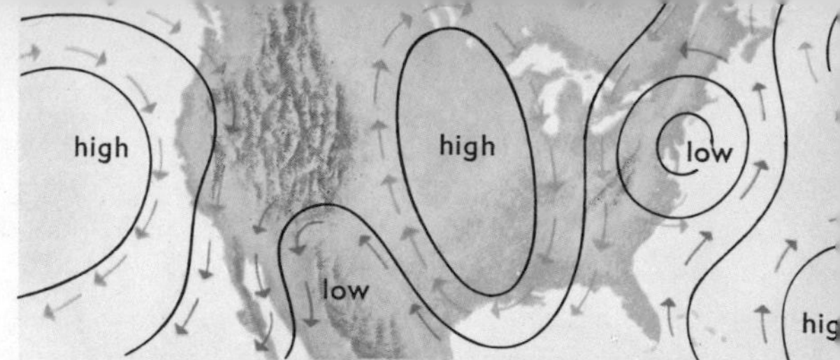

Winds circle clockwise around highs, which usually move from west to east across North America. Blue arrows indicate cool air; red, warm.

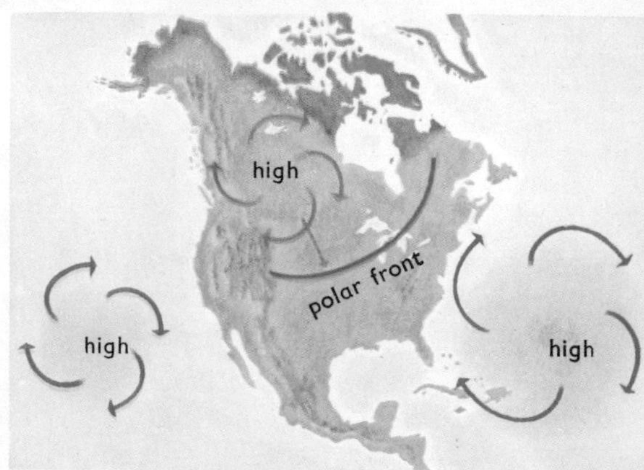

The polar high or polar air mass pushes south against warm, moist air. Where these two air masses meet, the polar front is formed.

Continental polar air is cold and clear.

Maritime polar air is moist at low levels.

Maritime polar air loses moisture in mountains.

Maritime tropical air is warm and moist.

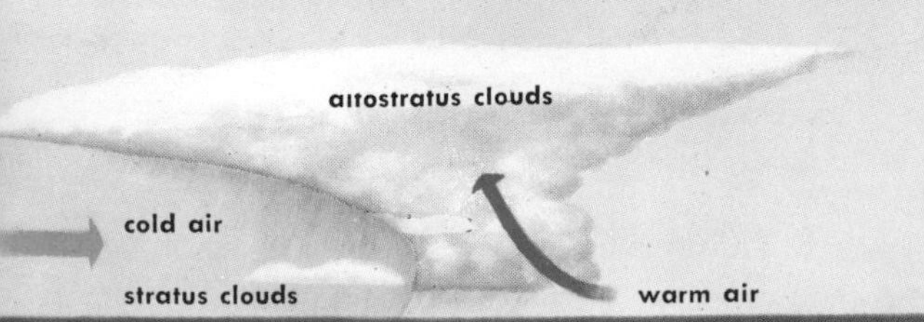

The blunt nose of a cold front lifts warm air rapidly, brings sudden rains, thunderstorms, and squalls.

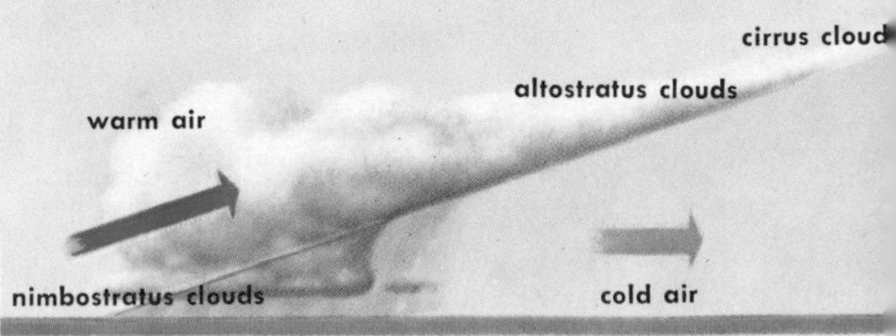

In a warm front, warm air is pushed slowly up over a wedge of cold air, often producing a slow rain.

more and more energy. At the surface, hurricane winds may blow 75 to over 200 mph. Hurricanes die when prevailing winds carry them across land masses, cutting them off from their supply of warm, moist winds, or when they are blown into cooler regions of the oceans where the drier air cannot supply them with the moisture they need to replenish themselves and to continue the power-releasing action.

Climate and weather determine the distribution and variety of plant life, and plants control the distribution of animals. In severe climates, as on the heights of mountains, in polar regions, or in barren deserts, trees and grasses cannot grow. Many desert plants survive seasons of unrelieved dryness as seeds. The tiny embryo plants are encased in a thick covering which is softened to let the plant spring to life when a passing shower moistens the ground. In cold climates, too, plants become dormant until warm weather thaws the ground and water flows again. Still other plants are adapted to a life in water and will not survive on land.

These broad adaptations are to the climate of the regions, which is reasonably the same from year to year. Weather, which changes from day to day, also affects both plants and animals. If weather conditions bring a prolonged rainy or dry period, either of which is not characteristic of the region, plants may rot from too much water or die from the lack of it. Similarly, an unseasonably warm spell in late winter or early spring may cause buds of trees to burst or the eggs of insects to hatch prematurely. The return to normal freezing weather will damage the plants or kill the newly-hatched insects.

Countless microclimates exist in each region. These smaller areas differ from the general average due to special circumstances. As an example, the south side of a hill in the Northern Hemisphere receives more sunlight and is warmer than the north side. A tree or other plant that flourishes on the south side may not be able to grow in the slightly cooler weather on the northern slope, which may be able to support plants characteristic of more northern regions.

Some species of animals are smaller in the warmer areas of their range. In colder climates, however, the exposed parts, such

The centre of a hurricane, called its 'eye', is a zone of quiet surrounded by rapidly circulating wind.

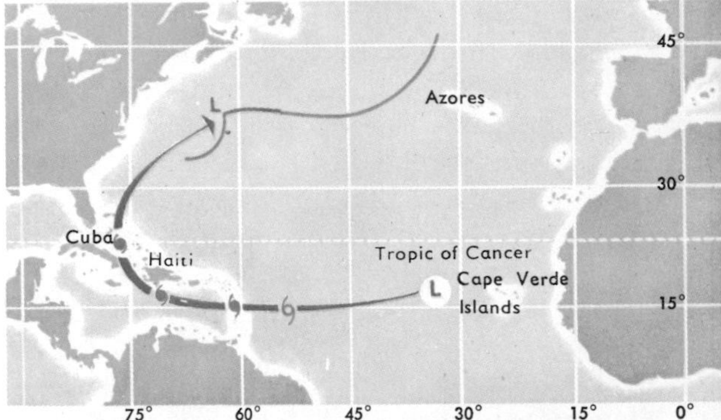

A typical Atlantic hurricane begins as a tropical low near the coast of Africa, develops force as it travels over the warm water and approaches land. It ends as a wave of bad weather over the North Atlantic.

HOW A HURRICANE FORMS

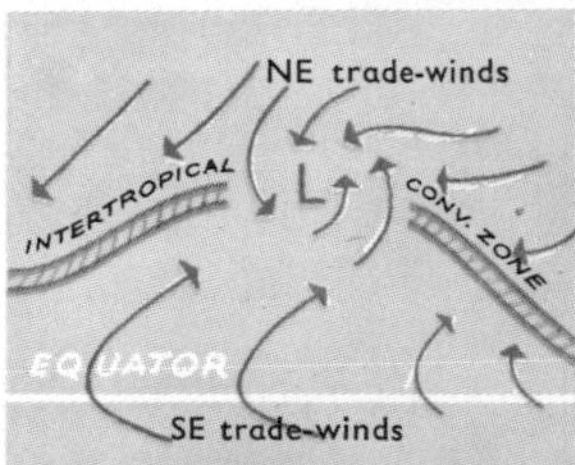

Hurricanes begin where opposing tropical winds meet.

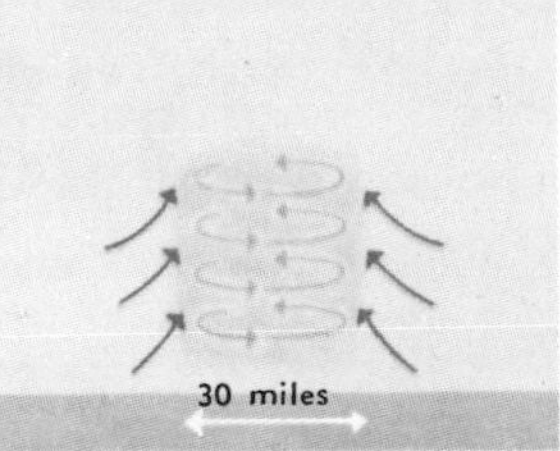

The whirling air in the centre is forced upwards.

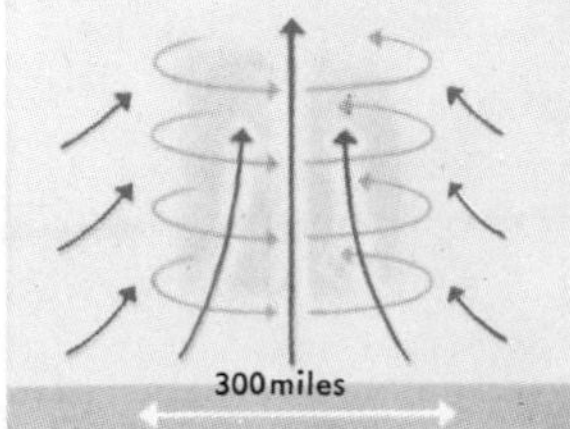

As the moist air rises, it is heated and rises faster.

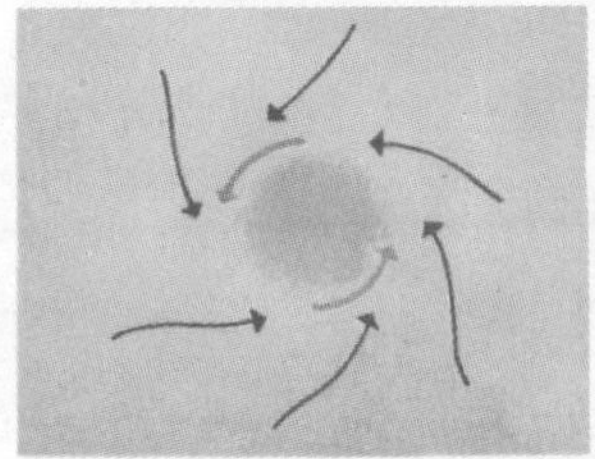
Winds blow in towards the whirling mass.

as tails, bills, ears, and other extremities, are smaller than on animals of the same species in warmer climates. These local variations within a species are called races.

The average number of young in a litter of mammals is larger in a cool climate than for the same species in a warm climate. The same is generally true of birds: those of cool climates lay more eggs than do members of the same species in warm climates. In colour, animals of warm regions are usually darker than those of the same species living in colder regions. Birds of cold regions tend to have longer wings and are more likely migratory.

Plants and animals in a sense are imprisoned by the climate and weather of their environment, for their adaptations restrict them to an existence in those conditions. They can extend their range successfully only into places that have a similar or more suitable weather and climate. (See ATMOSPHERE; CLIMATE; SEASONS; and WINDS.)

WHEAT is the most important food crop in temperate countries, but has been grown in the sub-tropics to near the Arctic.

It is probably the oldest domesticated cereal, and the known types are derived from the genus *Triticum*. They can be classified into 7, 14 and 21-chromosome types, depending on the number of chromosomes present in the cell nuclei. (Chromosomes are very small, rod-shaped bodies that contain genes — hereditary units.) Wild einkorn wheat has 7 chromosomes; 14-chromosome wheats, which include emmer and macaroni wheats were derived from hybrids between 7-chromosome wheats and wild grasses; while 21-chromosome wheats were derived from hybrids between 14 and 7-chromosome wheats. All these kinds existed by 4,500 years ago and probably developed in the plains of south-west Asia, but were not introduced into North America until about 1520 by the Spanish.

Today there are many varieties available in every region of the world, and these have been selected for adaptation to climate; disease resistance; milling and baking quality of the flour; and yield and stiffness of straw.

Wheat is an annual grass. The seed head or spike is typical of grasses. Wheat grains consist of an outer husk or bran, an inner endosperm, and an embryo or 'germ'. The endosperm consists of starch (from which flour is made) embedded in a sticky protein called gluten. Spring wheat is usually planted in March and harvested the following autumn. Winter wheat, grown where winters are mild, is planted in autumn and harvested the following July. Flour from both is used in baking bread.

Wheat seed is still broadcast by hand in a few areas, although the sowing is done by machines on all modern farms. On a small scale harvested wheat is threshed to separate the grain from the spike and then winnowed to separate the grain from the hulls, but in almost all wheat-growing areas combine-harvesters are extensively used. This machine cuts, threshes, grades, and bags the grain and also binds the straw. Wheat is often stored in grain elevators before it is milled.

Early man ground the grain between stones. The mortar and pestle was the first major technological improvement followed by the millstone, which was used until approximately 70 years ago when the roller process was introduced. In the roller process, the grains are moistened and then run through a series of rollers to crush them. The

outer part of the grains and the embryo or 'germ' are removed, and then the remaining portion is pulverised between the rollers to make flour. Most people today demand a refined type of flour from which the outer portion of the grain and embryo have been removed in processing. These most nutritious parts are used chiefly as feed for Man's livestock. Wheat germ is now sold in most grocery stores as a dietary supplement of great nutritional value.

Wholemeal flour is made from the whole wheat grain. Flours made from so-called hard wheats, which have a high protein content, are used as bread flour. Durum is a hard wheat used for making spaghetti and macaroni. In addition to use in flour for bakery products, macaroni, spaghetti, and noodles, wheat is also consumed as breakfast cereals and is fermented into alcohol. Wheat straw is used in weaving and thatching. (See GRASSES.)

WILLOWS are most common in the cool regions of the Northern Hemisphere. A few of the more than 300 species in the family grow in the tropics, and a dwarf willow, only a few inches high, is found in the Arctic or above the timber line on high mountains. Some willows are of tree size, while others are shrubs.

All willows need an abundance of moisture, so they usually grow along streams,

BLACK WILLOW
Salix nigra
30—60 ft.

around lakes or ponds, or in boggy soils. They help hold the soil and prevent erosion. Willow twigs, generally yellowish, bend without breaking. Called osiers, they are used to weave baskets and wicker furniture. Many kinds are planted as ornamentals. Their roots draw large amounts of moisture from the soil and often become troublesome.

All willow leaves, which are simple and alternate, are quite lengthy and have short petioles. Pollen-bearing and fruit producing flowers are on separate trees and usually in dense catkins. Buds, one of the most distinctive features of willows, are flat against the stem and are covered by a single, cap-like scale.

The Weeping Willow *(Salix babylonica)*, a large tree native to eastern Asia, is planted throughout the world as an ornamental. It has lance-shaped leaves and a broad, rounded crown of drooping branches. The Crack Willow *(Salix fragilis)*, native of Europe and western Asia, has similar leaves, but its slender twigs break off easily, often taking root in moist soil.

The Cricket-Bat Willow *(Salix alba var coerulea)*, a native of Britain, the fastest growing of our native willows, is the only tree suitable for good quality cricket bats.

WINDS are air in motion. They are produced by unequal heating of the Earth. Near the Earth's surface, winds affect rainfall, soil, erosion and the type of vegetation.

Formerly fertile and productive lands of many countries, especially in arid or semi-arid regions, have been stripped of their topsoil by winds. Many tall, weak-stemmed or shallow-rooted plants cannot survive long in regions of strong winds. Water loss from soil and plants by evaporation is much greater in windy regions. Winds also increase the rate of evaporation from flooded areas. Wind, of course, also disperses pollen and seeds.

Waves, caused by winds, are important in lakes, ponds, and oceans. They stir surface waters so that oxygen from the air can be absorbed more rapidly and waste gases be given off. They are also important in distribution of heat. In the spring, fish are more likely to be found near a shore towards which wind is blowing. This is because the warmer

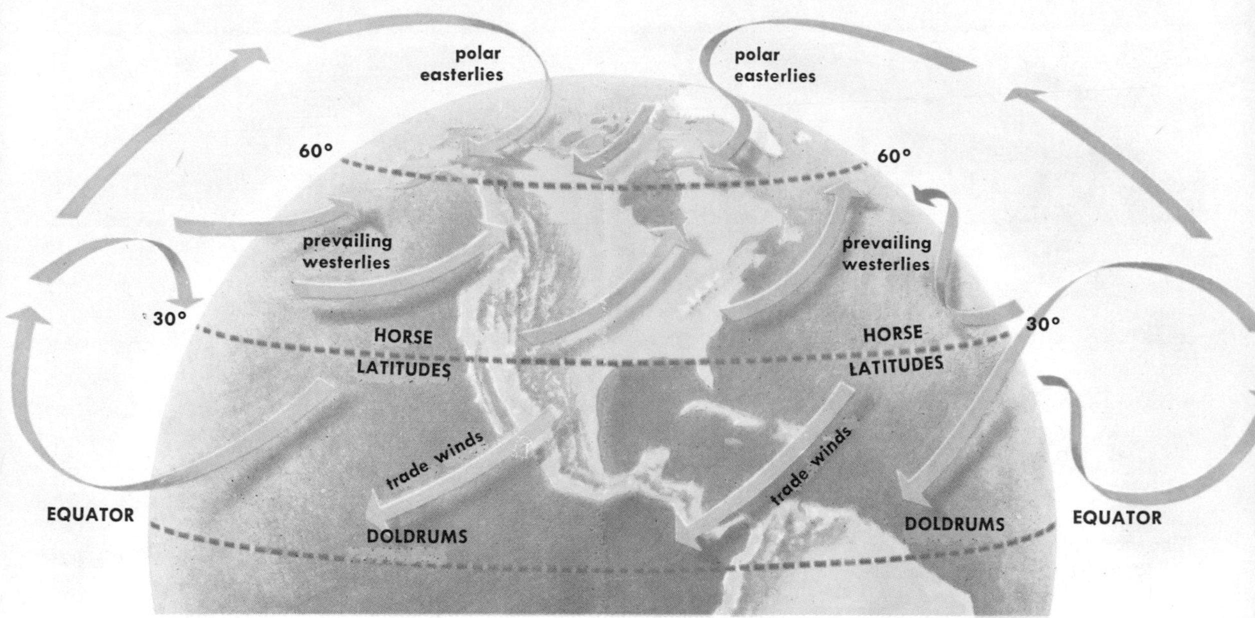

Warm air rises over the equatorial belt, drops back again at about 30° latitude. A portion of this air con tinues at high altitudes to the polar regions, where it cools and sinks to the surface forming cold winds which then move towards the equator.

surface layer of water is blown towards this shore.

Wind causes air currents high above the Earth. They induce clouds to move. Rain clouds formed over oceans may deposit their rain over land areas. Variations in moisture, temperature, and pressure — all are closely related to the varied movements of air or wind. (See WEATHER.)

WOODSORRELS (*Oxalis* spp.) belong to a family of about 800 species most abundant in the tropics. About 10 kinds grow wild in Britain, most of them about 6 inches in height. A few are cultivated for use as low edgings in flower gardens. All sorrels have leaves in three's, like clovers. The leaves are notched at their tips, and the two halves are folded together at night. In dull weather, the flowers also close. Leaves and stems contain oxalic acid that gives them a sharp taste.

Most common in Britain is the species *Oxalis acetosella*. This plant is widespread in woods, hedgerows and other shady places. The flower petals are usually white with lilac coloured veins and the leaves are a delicate, pale green.

There are also numerous species to be found in North America. The most common is the woodsorrel *Oxalis stricta*, with yellow flowers. The violet woodsorrel, *Oxalis violacea*, is a native of the eastern United States.

X-Y-Z

X-RAYS are a form of radiation similar to light, heat and radio waves. They are invisible and travel in straight lines at the speed of light, that is, at 186,000 miles a second. They can penetrate considerable thicknesses of material, for example, up to 11 inches of steel. This means, of course, that X-rays can easily penetrate human bodies.

Although X-rays are invisible, if they are directed at a screen coated with a special substance the screen will glow. If an article, a hand for example, is placed in front of the

Whether it is in the heart of a great city or in the depths of the bush, X-rays play an important part in man's fight against disease

W. H. O

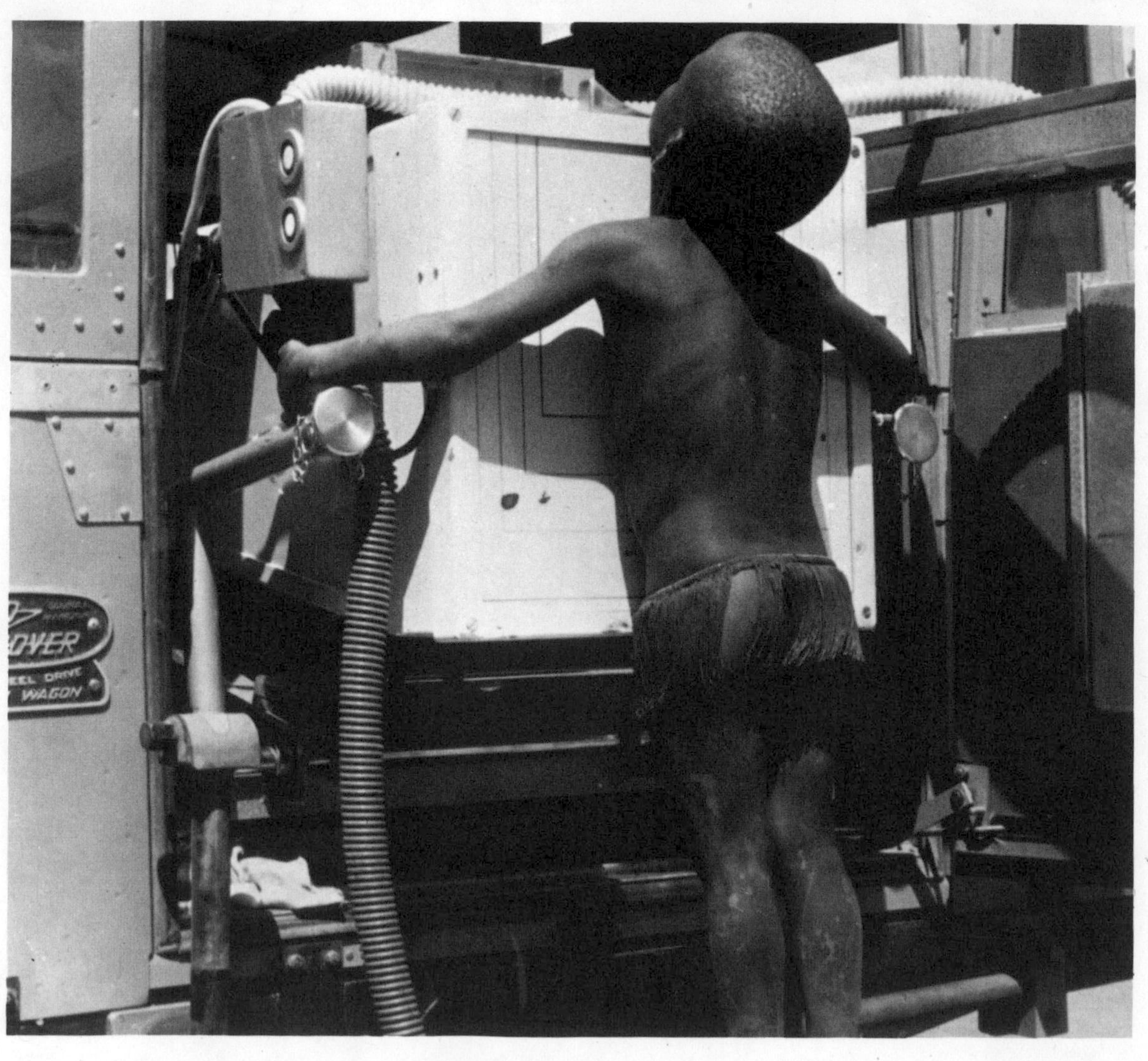

screen, a bright shadow of the hand will be cast on the screen, with the bones casting a deeper shadow than the flesh so that they stand out clearly. The picture thus shows not only the outline of the hand but the internal structure.

A thick, dense object, for example, a brick, placed in front of the screen, will cast a simple dark shadow. If the brick is left in position for several minutes, weak waves will penetrate it and reach the screen. These rays can be recorded on a photograph known as a radiograph.

Radiographs are used by doctors to examine broken bones and to trace articles, such as coins, that may have been swallowed. Engineers use the unique penetrating powers of X-rays to examine metals to ensure that they are free from cracks or other flaws. X-rays are widely used in aviation as they permit the internal structure of the wings and fuselage of aircraft to be examined without dismantling.

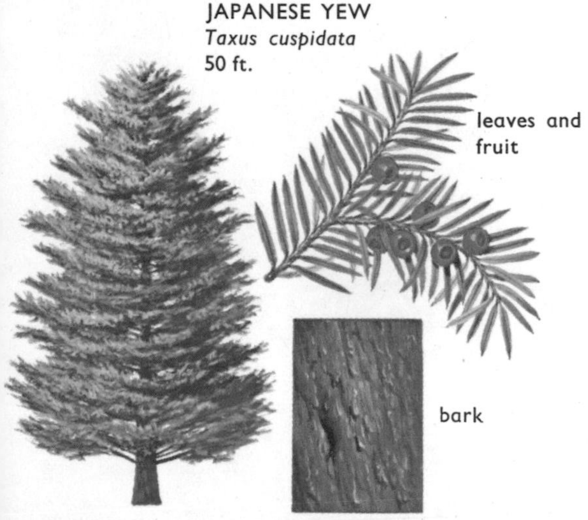

YEW *(Taxus baccata)* is an evergreen tree or shrub with needle-like foliage. The needles, which grow flat along the branches, resemble those of Silver Fir, but are light green on the underside and lack the two silvery bands. Yews do not bear cones. Their small hard seeds are partly enclosed in a bright red, jelly-like cup called an aril. These are produced singly on the branches. Most kinds usually have the pollen-bearing and seed-producing flowers on separate trees. They are commonly found growing in church-yards.

YUCCAS, natives of North and South America, are distinct in appearance from any other group of shrubs. The long, narrow, pointed leaves form a cluster around the base of the tall flower spike, which may reach a height of 5 feet. Although most species of Yucca are very tall there is a dwarf variety.

You may often notice species of Yucca growing in the gardens of town houses. This is because the plant is very resistant to the effects of smoke and grime, which might easily harm less hardy plants. Yucca is a member of the lily family.

ZEOLITES are a large group of silicate minerals found in cavities in igneous rocks. They were carried there by hot water. All zeolites are soft, pale, and contain water.

If heated in a blowpipe they boil, hence their name, from the Greek, *zein*, to boil, and *lithos*, stone. They occur on a worldwide scale and especially in Scotland, Ireland, Scandinavia, France, India and the U. S. A.

There are about 25 minerals in the zeolite group. If heated gently, water can be driven off through channels in their very wide-spaced crystalline network without harming

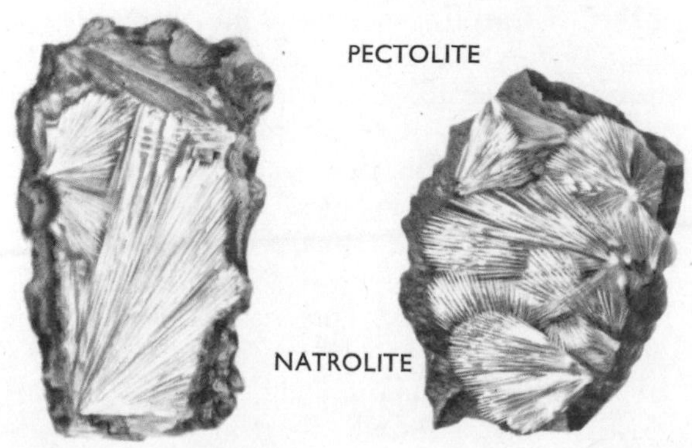

their structure. Analcime, one of the common zeolites, occurs as well-formed white crystals; chabazite, as white or pink rhombohedral crystals; heulandite, as flat, white crystals with perfect cleavage; natrolite, as radiating clusters of needle-like square crystals that are colourless to white; and stilbite, as white or pale-yellow, sheaf-like groups of crystals. Other members of the group are scolecite, thomsonite, apophyllite and phillipsite. Artificial and natural sodium zeolites are used in water softeners because their open crystal structure permits fluids to flow through, and the sodium of the zeolite is replaced by the calcium of the hard water. The calcium can be washed from the zeolite by putting the zeolite in a sodium chloride brine which reforms the sodium zeolite for further use.

BLENDE

crystal
0.2 in.

ZINCITE, WILLEMITE, AND FRANKLINITE

FRANKLINITE
in calcite

ZINC is produced from four minerals — sphalerite, smithsonite, zincite, and franklinite. Sphalerite (zinc sulphide), also called blende, is the most common. It occurs in brown, cleavable masses or frequently in small brown-red crystals. It has six perfect cleavages, a pale streak, and a resinous lustre. Sphalerite forms in hydro-thermal veins. Smithsonite (zinc carbonate) occurs as grey, white, brown, or green stalactites or honeycomb masses (dry bone). Zincite (zinc oxide) is found as red or orange, leaf-like or granular masses or as scattered grains that are cleavable. It has an orange-yellow streak. Zincite is commonly associated with franklinite and willemite (zinc silicate) in zinc deposits of New Jersey. Franklinite (zinc-iron oxide) occurs as black, well-formed eight-sided crystals or as compact masses. It has a red-brown streak and is slightly magnetic.

Zinc is used principally for galvanising, the most economical method of protecting iron against corrosion. Galvanised iron is used for roofing, nails, wire, pans, pipes, and exposed structural steel. Zinc die castings are used for carburettors, radiator grills, door handles, zip parts, electrical apparatus, business machines, building hardware, and toys. Brass is composed of zinc and copper, and bronze also contains some zinc. Sheet and rolled zinc is often alloyed with other metals and made into jar lids, cases for dry batteries, weather stripping, and pipelines. It is preferred to copper in building construction because it does not stain walls. Rubber paints, ceramics, drugs, textiles, floor coverings, fire hose, and conveyor belts are among the many products that contain

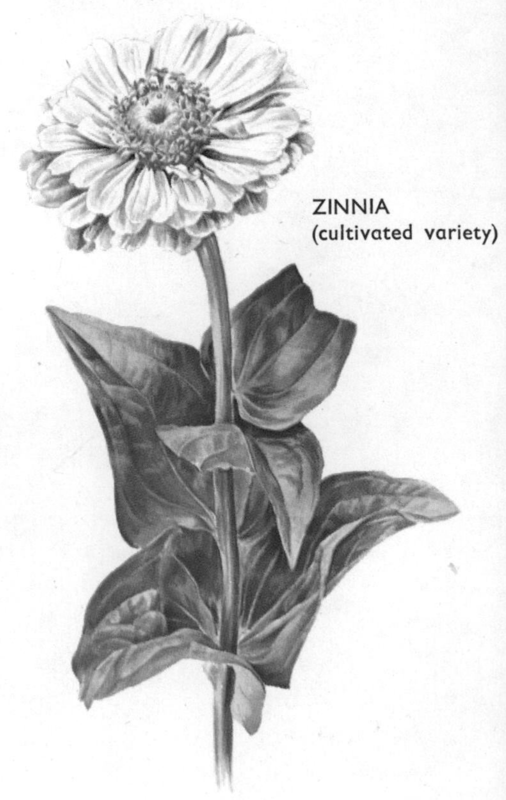

ZINNIA
(cultivated variety)

Reflection of sunlight from the shiny surfaces of tiny meteor particles causes the phenomenon known as zodiacal light. It is very faint and can only be seen on clear, moonless nights.

zinc oxide. Other zinc compounds are used for coated fabrics, paper filler, printing ink, varnishes, wood preservatives, soldering flux, and in oil refining. Rayon, fertilisers, insecticides, and dyes contain zinc sulphates, and a small quantity of zinc powder is used in the recovery of gold and silver from lead.

ZINNIAS (*Zinnia* spp.) are standard garden favourites, although some people do not like them because of the stiffness of the plants.

Great improvements have been made in zinnias in recent years. There are giant ones with huge double flowers, like dahlias; at the other extreme are tiny pompons: Tom Thumb, and Mexican zinnias. Other kinds have beautifully crinkled or quilled petals. All zinnias come in a variety of shades and combinations, and all types are long blooming and provide excellent cut flowers.

ZIRCON is a brown or grey mineral, a silicate of the metal zirconium. Its short, square crystals are found in igneous and metamorphic rocks. Transparent zircon crystals are used as gems. Other zircon gem stones are blue, yellow, grey, green, and red. Zircon is used also in polishing powders.

ZODIACAL LIGHT. On clear, moonless evenings, when the sky has become completely dark, you can sometimes see a faint glow standing up from the horizon in the west. It runs along the zodiac, the band of constellations through which the Sun, Moon, and planets appear to travel, and it is called the zodiacal light. This glow is sunlight, reflected from dust particles scattered through the solar system. It is brightest near the Sun, so we see it after sunset or before dawn when the Sun is just far enough below the horizon to leave the sky completely dark. Also, in the very darkest midnight sky, a very faint glow can sometimes be seen in the direction exactly opposite the Sun. It is called the Counterglow, or Gegenschein, and is also caused by small particles in interplanetary space.

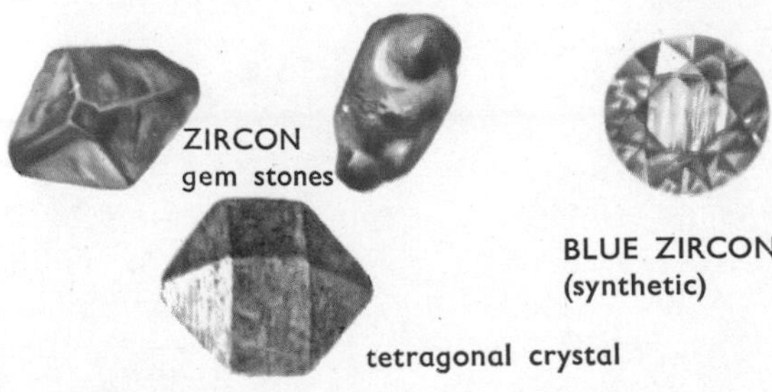

INDEX

D

E

F

G

H

I

J

K

L

M

N

O

P

Q

R

S

T

U

V

W

X

Y

Z